NEW CENTURY BIBLE

General Editors

RONALD E. CLEMENTS
M.A., B.D., PH.D. (Old Testament)

MATTHEW BLACK
D.D., D.LITT., F.B.A. (New Testament)

The Book of Psalms

Volume I

NEW CENTURY BIBLE

Based on the Revised Standard Version

The Book of Psalms

A. A. ANDERSON

M.A., B.D.

Senior Lecturer in Old Testament Studies in the University of Manchester

VOLUME I

INTRODUCTION AND

PSALMS 1–72

OLIPHANTS

OLIPHANTS

MARSHALL, MORGAN & SCOTT
BLUNDELL HOUSE
GOODWOOD ROAD
LONDON SE14 6BL

Volume 1 ISBN 0 551 00267 0
Volume 2 ISBN 0 551 00268 9

Made and printed in Great Britain by
Purnell & Sons Ltd., Paulton, Somerset, England

Dedicated

to

FREDERICK FYVIE BRUCE

Rylands Professor of
Biblical Criticism and
Exegesis in the
University of Manchester

CONTENTS

Volume 1

Volume 2

PREFACE

This commentary is essentially a humble tribute to generations of scholars whose work and thoughts have guided me through the Psalter, and who have greatly contributed to this volume. I am particularly indebted to Sir Godfrey Driver, whose masterly lectures on the Psalms were a constant inspiration; to Prof. F. F. Bruce, whose help, both direct and indirect, made this work possible; and to the late Rev. Prof. H. H. Rowley, who made a number of valuable suggestions.

I also wish to thank the Rev. Dr. R. E. Clements for his gracious assistance on many points, as well as Mr. A. H. W. Curtis who read the original manuscript and improved its style and language, and drew my attention to a number of Ugaritic parallels. To Miss Margaret Hogg I am indebted for her help in typing the manuscript.

Last, but not least, I am deeply grateful to my wife, without whose understanding and sacrifice this work would not have been completed. Similarly, I owe much to my children, Elaine, Ian, and Lindsay, who helped according to their abilities, often more than they realized.

The manuscript was completed in May, 1968, but thanks to the kindness of the present publishers I have had the opportunity to take some account of more recent publications, including the *New English Bible*. The additions serve primarily an illustrative purpose.

A.A.A.

ABBREVIATIONS

BIBLICAL OLD TESTAMENT (*OT*)

Gen.	Jg.	1 Chr.	Ps.	Lam.	Ob.	Hag.
Exod.	Ru.	2 Chr.	Prov.	Ezek.	Jon.	Zech.
Lev.	1 Sam.	Ezr.	Ec.	Dan.	Mic.	Mal.
Num.	2 Sam.	Neh.	Ca.	Hos.	Nah.	
Dt.	1 Kg.	Est.	Isa.	Jl	Hab.	
Jos.	2 Kg.	Job	Jer.	Am.	Zeph.	

APOCRYPHA (*Apoc.*)

1 Esd.	Tob.	Ad. Est.	Sir.	S 3 Ch.	Bel	1 Mac.
2 Esd.	Jdt.	Wis.	Bar.	Sus.	Man.	2 Mac.
			Ep. Jer.			

NEW TESTAMENT (*NT*)

Mt.	Ac.	Gal.	1 Th.	Tit.	1 Pet.	3 Jn
Mk	Rom.	Eph.	2 Th.	Phm.	2 Pet.	Jude
Lk.	1 C.	Phil.	1 Tim.	Heb.	1 Jn	Rev.
Jn	2 C.	Col.	2 Tim.	Jas	2 Jn	

TEXTS AND VERSIONS

Aq	Version of Aquila
AV	Authorized Version
AVm	Authorized Version margin
BH	*Biblia Hebraica* (4th edn)
LXX	Septuagint (LXX^A Codex Alexandrinus; LXX^B Codex Vaticanus)
M.T.	Massoretic Text
NEB	*The New English Bible*
PBV	The version of the Psalms in the *Book of Common Prayer*
PLE	*The Psalms in Latin and English* (Eng. tr. by R. Knox, 1964)
PNT	*The Psalms: a New Translation* (Fontana Books, 1963)
RP	The Revised Psalter (1964)
RSV	Revised Standard Version
RSVm	Revised Standard Version margin
RV	Revised Version
RVm	Revised Version margin
S	Syriac Version (S Syrohexaplar)
Sym	Version of Symmachus

T	Targum
Theod	Version of Theodotion
V	Vulgate

DEAD SEA SCROLLS

1QM	War of the Sons of Light against the Sons of Darkness
1QpHab	Habakkuk Commentary
1QS	Rule of the Community (Manual of Discipline)
1QSa	(=1Q28a) Rule of the Community (Appendix)
1QSb	(=1Q28b) Collection of Benedictions
4Q	Manuscripts from Qumran Cave 4
11QPs[a]	The Psalms Scroll of Qumran Cave 11
CD	Fragments of a Zadokite Work (Damascus Document)

(*The same convention is followed in designating other scrolls. The numeral preceding the letter Q refers to the cave in which the scroll was found, and the succeeding symbols specify the contents of the scroll and the section under discussion. The details of any given scroll may be discovered in the published volume(s) devoted to the materials from the cave concerned.*)

GENERAL

AB	*The Anchor Bible*
AHPL	G. Widengren, *The Accadian and Hebrew Psalms of Lamentation as Religious Documents* (1937)
AI	R. de Vaux, *Ancient Israel: its Life and Institutions*, Eng. tr. by J. McHugh (1961)
ANEP	*The Ancient Near East in Pictures Relating to the Old Testament*, ed. by J. B. Pritchard (1954)
ANET	*Ancient Near Eastern Texts Relating to the Old Testament*, ed. by J. B. Pritchard (1950)
AOTS	*Archaeology and Old Testament Study*, ed. by D. Winton Thomas (1967)
APOT	*The Apocrypha and Pseudepigrapha of the Old Testament*, ed. by R. H. Charles *et al.* II (1913)
ASTI	*Annual of the Swedish Theological Institute*
AWBL	Y. Yadin, *The Art of Warfare in Biblical Lands* (1963)
BA	*Biblical Archaeologist*
BASOR	*Bulletin of the American Schools of Oriental Research*
BCP	F. Delitzsch, *Biblical Commentary on the Psalms*, Eng. tr. by F. Bolton (1871), 3 vols.
BDB	F. Brown, S. R. Driver, and C. A. Briggs, *A Hebrew Lexicon of the Old Testament* (1907)
BJRL	*Bulletin of the John Rylands Library*
BK	*Biblischer Kommentar: Altes Testament*, ed. by M. Noth

BP	E. J. Kissane, *The Book of Psalms* (1964)
BPCB	A. F. Kirkpatrick, *The Book of Psalms* (*Camb. B.*) (1902)
BPPI	T. K. Cheyne, *The Book of Psalms* (1888)
BPss	J. J. S. Perowne, *The Book of Psalms* 7th edn (1890)
BZ	*Biblische Zeitschrift*
BZAW	*Beihefte zur Zeitschrift für die alttestamentliche Wissenschaft*
Camb. B.	*Cambridge Bible*
CBQ	*Catholic Biblical Quarterly*
CECBP	C. A. Briggs and E. G. Briggs, *The Book of Psalms* (*ICC*) (1907), 2 vols.
Cent. B.	*Century Bible*
Cent. BP.	W. T. Davison and T. W. Davies, *The Psalms* (*Cent. B.*), n.d., 2 vols.
CH	The Code of Hammurabi
CJ	E. Dhorme, *A Commentary on the Book of Job*, Eng. tr. by H. Knight (1967)
CJT	*Canadian Journal of Theology*
CML	G. R. Driver, *Canaanite Myths and Legends* (1956)
CPAI	A. R. Johnson, *The Cultic Prophet in Ancient Israel*, 2nd edn (1962)
CPBP	J. H. Patton, *Canaanite Parallels in the Book of Psalms* (1944)
DB	*Dictionary of the Bible*, ed. J. Hastings, 2nd edn by F. C. Grant and H. H. Rowley (1963)
DLBT	W. Corswant, *A Dictionary of Life in Bible Times*, Eng. tr. by A. Heathcote (1960)
DOTT	*Documents from Old Testament Times*, ed. by D. Winton Thomas (1958)
DP	F. Wutz, *Die Psalmen* (1925)
DTTM	M. Jastrow, *A Dictionary of the Targumim, the Talmud Babli and Yerushalmi, and the Midrashic Literature* (1950), 2 vols.
EP	H. Gunkel and J. Begrich, *Einleitung in die Psalmen*, 2nd edn (1966)
ERE	*Encyclopaedia of Religion and Ethics*, ed. by J. Hastings (1908–26), 13 vols.
ET	*Expository Times*
ETKD	Chr. Barth, *Die Errettung vom Tode in den individuellen Klage- und Dankliedern des Alten Testaments* (1947)
EUT	M. H. Pope, *El in the Ugaritic Texts* (*SVT* II) (1955)
fg.	fragment
FI	H. H. Rowley, *The Faith of Israel* (1956)
FP	H. Ringgren, *The Faith of the Psalmists* (1963)
GAB	L. H. Grollenberg, *Atlas of the Bible*, Eng. tr. by Joyce M. H. Reid and H. H. Rowley (1956)

GB	D. Baly, *The Geography of the Bible* (1957)
GK	*Gesenius' Hebrew Grammar*, ed. by E. Kautzsch; Eng. tr. by G. W. Collins, revised by A. E. Cowley, 2nd English edn (1910)
GT	R. E. Clements, *God and Temple* (1965)
HAL	*Hebräisches und Aramäisches Lexikon zum Alten Testament*, ed. by W. Baumgartner, Lieferung 1 (1967)
HAT	*Handbuch zum Alten Testament*
HB	N. Glueck, *Hesed in the Bible*, Eng. tr. by A. Gottschalk (1967)
HCW	L. I. J. Stadelmann, *The Hebrew Conception of the World* (*Analecta Biblica* XXXIX) (1970)
HDB	*Dictionary of the Bible*, ed. J. Hastings (1898–1904), 5 vols.
HGBH	A. Sperber, *A Historical Grammar of Biblical Hebrew* (1966)
HI	J. Bright, *A History of Israel* (1960)
HS	C. Brockelmann, *Hebräische Syntax* (1956)
HTR	*Harvard Theological Review*
HUCA	*Hebrew Union College Annual*
ICC	*The International Critical Commentary*
IDB	*Interpreter's Dictionary of the Bible* (1962), 4 vols.
IEJ	*Israel Exploration Journal*
ILC	J. Pedersen, *Israel: its Life and Culture* (1926–40), 4 vols.
IP	C. F. Barth, *Introduction to the Psalms*, Eng. tr. by R. A. Wilson (1966)
IPH	*Israel's Prophetic Heritage*, ed. by B. W. Anderson and W. Harrelson (1962)
IR	H. Ringgren, *Israelite Religion*, Eng. tr. by D. Green (1966)
ISS	H. H. Guthrie, jr., *Israel's Sacred Songs* (1966)
IYOT	C. J. Labuschagne, *The Incomparability of Yahweh in the Old Testament* (Pretoria Oriental Series v) (1966)
JAB	M. H. Pope, *Job* (*AB* 15, 1965)
JAOS	*Journal of the American Oriental Society*
JBL	*Journal of Biblical Literature*
JBR	*Journal of Bible and Religion*
JCS	*Journal of Cuneiform Studies*
JJR	J. Gray, *Joshua, Judges and Ruth* (*Cent. B.*, new edn, 1967)
JNES	*Journal of Near Eastern Studies*
JQR	*Jewish Quarterly Review*
JSS	*Journal of Semitic Studies*
JTS	*Journal of Theological Studies*
KBL	L. Koehler and W. Baumgartner, *Lexicon in Veteris Testamenti Libros* (1953)

LAT M. A. Klopfenstein, *Die Lüge nach dem Alten Testament* (1964)
LBCP A. B. Rhodes, *Psalms* (1961)
LN N. H. Snaith, *Leviticus and Numbers* (*Cent. B.*, new edn, 1967)
LP J. Calès, *Le livre des Psaumes* (1936), 2 vols.
LPA *D. Martin Luthers Psalmen-Auslegung* (1959–65), 3 vols.
LPOBL *Le Psautier* (*Orientalia et Biblica Lovaniensia* IV), ed. by R. de Langhe (1962)
LPOE M. Noth, *The Laws in the Pentateuch and Other Essays*, Eng. tr. by D. R. Ap-Thomas (1966)
MK A. Jirku, *Der Mythus der Kanaanäer* (1966)
MMJA D. S. Russell, *The Method and Message of Jewish Apocalyptic* (*OTL*) (1964)
MTI B. S. Childs, *Memory and Tradition in Israel* (*SBT* XXXVII) (1962)
NBD *The New Bible Dictionary*, ed. by J. D. Douglas (1962)
N.F. Neue Folge
NHTS S. R. Driver, *Notes on the Hebrew Text and Topography of the Books of Samuel*, 2nd edn (1913)
n.s. new series
OMICG A. R. Johnson, *The One and the Many in the Israelite Conception of God*, 2nd edn (1961)
OOTT Th. C. Vriezen, *An Outline of Old Testament Theology*, Eng. tr. by S. Neuijen (1958)
OTI O. Eissfeldt, *The Old Testament: an Introduction*, Eng. tr. by P. R. Ackroyd (1965)
OTL *Old Testament Library*
OTMS *The Old Testament and Modern Study*, ed. by H. H. Rowley (1951)
OTS *Oudtestamentische Studiën*
OTT G. von Rad, *Old Testament Theology*, Eng. tr. by D. M. G. Stalker. I (1962); II (1965)
PAB M. Dahood, *Psalms I: 1–50* (*AB* 16, 1966); *Psalms II: 51–100* (*AB* 17, 1968)
PAP E. A. Leslie, *The Psalms* (1949)
PBK H.-J. Kraus, *Psalmen* (*BK* XV) (1960)
PBP J. Wellhausen, *The Book of Psalms*, Eng. tr. by H. H. Furness (1898)
PCB *Peake's Commentary on the Bible*, rev. ed. by M. Black and H. H. Rowley (1962)
PCD N. J. Tromp, *Primitive Conceptions of Death and the Nether World in the Old Testament* (1969)
PCT M. Buttenwieser, *The Psalms* (1938)
PEB F. Nötscher, *Die Psalmen* (*Echter-Bibel*) (1959)

PEPC	C. S. Rodd, *Psalms 1–72* (1963); *Psalms 73–150* (1964)
PGHAT	H. Gunkel, *Die Psalmen* (*Göttinger Handkommentar zum Alten Testament*), 4th edn (1926)
PGP	C. Westermann, *The Praise of God in the Psalms*, Eng. tr. by K. R. Crim (1966)
PHAT	H. Schmidt, *Die Psalmen* (*HAT*) (1934)
PHOE	G. von Rad, *The Problem of the Hexateuch and other Essays*, Eng. tr. by E. W. Trueman Dicken (1966)
PIB	W. R. Taylor *et al.*, *The Book of Psalms* (*The Interpreter's Bible* IV) (1955)
PIW	S. Mowinckel, *The Psalms in Israel's Worship*, Eng. tr. by D. R. Ap-Thomas (1962), 2 vols.
PNWSP	M. Dahood, *Proverbs in Northwest Semitic Philology* (1963)
POM	L. Sabourin, *The Psalms: Their Origin and Meaning* (1969), 2 vols.
POTL	A. Weiser, *The Psalms* (*OTL*), Eng. tr. by H. Hartwell (1962)
PSon	A. Cohen, *The Psalms* (Soncino Bible) (1945)
PStud	S. Mowinckel, *Psalmenstudien* I–VI (1921–4)
PSVP	P. Boylan, *The Psalms* (1949), 2 vols.
PTBC	J. H. Eaton, *Psalms* (*Torch Bible Commentary*) (1967)
PWC	W. E. Barnes, *The Psalms* (*Westminster Commentary*) (1931), 2 vols.
PWdB	A. Deissler, *Die Psalmen* (*Die Welt der Bibel*) (1963–5), 3 vols.
RAI	Th. C. Vriezen, *The Religion of Ancient Israel*, Eng. tr. by H. Hoskins (1967)
RB	*Revue Biblique*
RHPR	*Revue d'Histoire et de Philosophie religieuses*
RQM	A. R. C. Leaney, *The Rule of Qumran and its Meaning* (1966)
SBA	*Studies in Biblical Archaeology*
SBL	J. Barr, *The Semantics of Biblical Language* (1961)
SBT	*Studies in Biblical Theology*
SJT	*Scottish Journal of Theology*
SKAI	A. R. Johnson, *Sacral Kingship in Ancient Israel* (1955)
ST	*Studia Theologica*
SVT	*Supplements to Vetus Testamentum*
SWSLSD	Y. Yadin, *The Scroll of the War of the Sons of Light against the Sons of Darkness* (1962)
TD	C. H. Spurgeon, *The Treasury of David* (1878)
TDNT	*Theological Dictionary of the New Testament*, ed. by G. Kittel, Eng. tr. by G. W. Bromiley (1964– ; in progress)

TGUOS	*Transactions of the Glasgow University Oriental Society*
TH	M. Mansoor, *The Thanksgiving Psalms* (Studies on the Texts of the Desert of Judah III) (1961)
ThLZ	*Theologische Literaturzeitung*
ThWB	*Theologisches Wörterbuch zum Neuen Testament*, ed. by G. Kittel and G. Friedrich (1932– ; in progress)
ThOT	P. van Imschoot, *Theology of the Old Testament*, Eng. tr. by Kathryn Sullivan and F. Buck. I (1965)
ThZ	*Theologische Zeitschrift*
TOT	W. Eichrodt, *Theology of the Old Testament* (*OTL*), Eng. tr. by J. A. Baker. I (1961); II (1967)
TOTe	E. Jacob, *Theology of the Old Testament*, Eng. tr. by A. W. Heathcote and P. J. Allcock (1958)
TP	W. O. E. Oesterley, *The Psalms* (1939)
TPst	*The Psalmists*, ed. by D. C. Simpson (1926)
TRP	D. Winton Thomas, *The Text of the Revised Psalter* (1963)
TS	*Theological Studies*
UHP	M. Dahood, *Ugaritic-Hebrew Philology* (1965)
UT	C. H. Gordon, *Ugaritic Textbook* (1965)
UTH	S. R. Driver, *The Use of the Tenses in Hebrew* (1892)
VITAI	A. R. Johnson, *The Vitality of the Individual in the Thought of Ancient Israel*, 2nd edn (1964)
VT	*Vetus Testamentum*
WAI	H. H. Rowley, *Worship in Ancient Israel* (1967)
WCB	*World Christian Books*
WI	H.-J. Kraus, *Worship in Israel*, Eng. tr. by G. Buswell (1966)
WMANT	*Wissenschaftliche Monographien zum Alten und Neuen Testament*
WO	*Die Welt des Orients*
WUS	J. Aistleitner, *Wörterbuch der Ugaritischen Sprache*, 3rd edn (1967)
ZAW	*Zeitschrift für die alttestamentliche Wissenschaft*
ZThK	*Zeitschrift für Theologie und Kirche*
ZLH	F. Zorell, *Lexicon Hebraicum et Aramaicum* (1946– ; in progress)

SELECT BIBLIOGRAPHY

COMMENTARIES

G. W. Anderson, 'The Psalms', *PCB*, pp. 409–43

W. E. Barnes, *The Psalms* (*Westminster Commentaries*) (1931), 2 vols.

C. A. Briggs and E. G. Briggs, *The Book of Psalms* (*ICC*) (1907), 2 vols.

J. Calès, *Le livre des Psaumes* (1936), 2 vols.

M. Dahood, *Psalms I: 1–50* (*AB* 16) (1966); *Psalms II: 51–100* (*AB* 17, 1968)

J. H. Eaton, *Psalms* (Torch Bible Commentaries) (1967)

H. Gunkel, *Die Psalmen* (*Göttinger Handkommentar zum Alten Testament*), 4th edn (1926)

H. Herkenne, *Das Buch der Psalmen* (*Bonner Bibel*) (1936)

C. C. Keet, *A Study of the Psalms of Ascents* (1969)

A. F. Kirkpatrick, *The Book of Psalms* (*Camb. B.*) (1902)

E. J. Kissane, *The Book of Psalms* (1964)

H.-J. Kraus, *Psalmen* (*BK* xv) (1960), 2 vols.

C. Lattey, *The First Book of Psalms* (1939)

F. Nötscher, *Die Psalmen* (*Echter-Bibel*) (1959)

W. O. E. Oesterley, *The Psalms* (1939)

E. Podechard, *Le Psautier*, I (1949); II (1954)

C. S. Rodd, *Psalms 1–72* (1963); *Psalms 73–150* (1964)

L. Sabourin, *The Psalms: Their Origin and Meaning* (1969), 2 vols.

W. R. Taylor *et al.*, *The Book of Psalms* (*The Interpreter's Bible* IV) (1955)

A. Weiser, *The Psalms* (*OTL*), Eng. tr. by H. Hartwell (1962)

GENERAL AND SPECIAL STUDIES

C. F. Barth, *Introduction to the Psalms*, Eng. tr. by R. A. Wilson (1966)

K. R. Crim, *The Royal Psalms* (1962)

P. Drijvers, *The Psalms: their Structure and Meaning* (1965)

H. H. Guthrie, jr., *Israel's Sacred Songs* (1966)

A. R. Johnson, *Sacral Kingship in Ancient Israel* (1955)

R. de Langhe (ed. by), *Le Psautier* (*Orientalia et Biblica Lovaniensia* IV) (1962)

S. Mowinckel, *The Psalms in Israel's Worship*, Eng. tr. by D. R. Ap-Thomas (1962), 2 vols.

H. Ringgren, *The Faith of the Psalmists* (1963)

C. Westermann, *The Praise of God in the Psalms*, Eng. tr. by K. R. Crim (1966)

INTRODUCTION

to

The Book of Psalms

I. THE PSALTER AND ITS FORMATION

1. NAMES OF THE PSALTER

The words 'psalms' and 'psalter' are anglicized forms of the Latin *psalmi* and *psalterium*, which in turn are derived from the Greek *psalmoi* and *psaltērion*. The Greek *psalmos* denotes the music of a stringed instrument, or a song which is sung to the accompaniment of such music. *Psaltērion* originally referred to a stringed instrument (cf. Dan. 3:5), but later it came to mean also a 'collection of songs', and it was used in the Codex Alexandrinus as the title of the Book of Psalms (cf. Gunkel, *EP*, p. 433). The *NT* employs either *biblos psalmōn* (Lk. 20:42; Ac. 1:20) or *psalmoi* (Lk. 24:44). These Greek terms, apparently, translate the Hebrew *mizmôr*, which is usually taken to mean 'a (religious) song accompanied by stringed instrument(s)' (Mowinckel, *PIW*, II, p. 208), which occurs some 57 times in the titles of the Psalms. Thus the Greek translator(s) must have taken the translation of the most common Hebrew term for a particular kind of song, using it as a title for the whole collection. R. H. Pfeiffer (*Introduction to the Old Testament*, 2nd edn (1952), p. 619) points out that 'the Hebrew title defines the *contents* of the book, or at least an important part of it, as praises to God . . . whereas the Greek and English titles define the *form* of the book as hymns sung to the accompaniment of stringed instruments'.

In the Hebrew Bible the title of the Book of Psalms is *sēper tᵉhillîm* ('book of praises') or simply *tᵉhillîm* ('praises'), which comes from the same root as the word 'Hallelujah', a transliteration of the Hebrew *halᵉlû yāh* ('praise the Lord' (or '. . . Yāh')). Although not all psalms are praises, this term is a fitting name for the Psalter as a whole because the theme of praise and thanksgiving recurs again and again. *Tᵉhillāh* ('praise') is found only once, in the title of Ps. 145, but it occurs in the Book of Psalms some 28 times. Philo, the Jewish scholar of Alexandria, referred to the Psalter by using the term *humnoi* ('hymns, songs of praise'), which points to the Hebrew *tᵉhillîm*.

In 72:20 we find a note which presumably marks the end of an older collection: 'The prayers of David, the son of Jesse, are ended.' This implies that 'prayers' (*t*^{e}*pillôṯ*) may have been the title of this particular Davidic collection, but only five psalms in the whole Psalter are designated by this title (Ps. 17, 86, 90, 102, 142). Not all psalms could be regarded as prayers, even in the widest sense of the term, and therefore *t*^{e}*pillōṯ* was not an adequate designation of the Psalter.

The usual word, *t*^{e}*hillîm*, may well be a technical term for the Book of Psalms, because the normal plural form of *t*^{e}*hillāh* ('praise') is *t*^{e}*hillôṯ*.

2. THE PLACE OF THE PSALMS IN THE OLD TESTAMENT CANON

The Hebrew Bible is divided into three parts: the Law, the Prophets, and the Writings, and it is commonly supposed that this threefold division represents the successive stages in the growth of the Hebrew scriptures, as well as the order in which these three groups came to be recognized as sacred and authoritative. These three stages do not necessarily reflect the date of origin of the respective books, and therefore the Writings may contain materials which may be older than certain sections of the first part of the Hebrew canon, the Law.

This particular arrangement of the *OT* is not followed in the English versions, where the order is essentially that of the Greek and Latin scriptures; there the division between the Prophets and Writings has disappeared, and the new arrangement probably rests on a topical and chronological basis.

In the Hebrew Bible the Book of Psalms belongs to the Writings. The order of the books in this group may vary from manuscript to manuscript, but the Psalter is nearly always first in the Writings. In Lk. 24:44 the name 'psalms' is used, apparently, for the whole of the third part of the canonical Scriptures, probably because it was the first book in this section. According to the Talmudic tradition (*Baba Bathra* 14b) the Book of Ruth was placed before the Psalms 'because of the theory that it gave the genealogy of David, and therefore should precede the Psalms of David' (Briggs, *CECBP*, I, p. xix).

3. COMPILATION AND FORMATION OF THE PSALTER

The Psalter is clearly neither the work of one single author, nor the result of one single act of compilation. It appears to be a collection of various smaller collections and of individual songs. The formation of the Psalter must have undergone a complicated process which can no longer be reconstructed with any certainty.

The main reasons for arguing that the Book of Psalms was composed of earlier collections are as follows:

(i) The Psalter contains a number of doublets (Ps. 14=53; 40:13–17=70:1–5 (M.T. 40:14–18=70:2–6); Ps. 108=57:7–11 (M.T. 8–12)+60:5–12 (M.T. 7–14)), and it is unlikely that such duplications would have originated had the Psalter been gathered into one collection by one editor.

(ii) It has been noticed that some parts of the Psalter show a preference either for the name 'Yahweh' (*RSV* 'the LORD') or for 'God'. Rhodes (*LBCP*, p. 11) has drawn attention to the following statistics: in Ps. 1–41 'the LORD' occurs some 278 times, and 'God' only 15 times; in Ps. 42–83 the figures are 44 and 201 respectively. In Ps. 84–9 and 90–150 these two words occur 31 and 7, and 339 and 9 times respectively. This variation can hardly be accidental and without any significance. The predominance of either 'Yahweh' or 'God' need not be original; rather it reflects editorial activity, as suggested by Ps. 14 and 53, which are doublets. This phenomenon points to at least two collections, a Yahwistic and an Elohistic, otherwise it is incomprehensible why the Elohistic revision was confined to *one* section of the Psalter.

(iii) In 72:20 we have the statement: 'The prayers of David . . . are ended'. The Psalm itself is attributed to Solomon, but the phrase 'by Solomon' (*RSV* '. . . of Solomon') may mean '(by David) for the King's son [cf. verse 1] Solomon'(so Mowinckel, *PIW*, II, p. 194). Whether the concluding note in 72:20 was taken over from an earlier collection, or whether it was inserted at this point by the editor, it implies that either he did not know of any other Davidic psalm, or that this particular collection contained no more. Actually the Psalter has well over ten Davidic psalms after Ps. 72, and in particular Ps. 86 which is called 'A Prayer of David'.

(iv) Another important point is the noticeable presence or absence of the Psalm titles. Most Psalms in the first part of the Psalter (Ps. 1–89) are ascribed to David, Asaph, the sons of Korah, etc., while the second part (Ps. 90–150) is largely anonymous, i.e. there are few indications as to the supposed author or collector, and many Psalms lack musical or liturgical instructions.

In view of all this, it seems very likely that the present Psalter is composed of earlier collections. It does not follow that the Book of Psalms is the sum total of all Israelite religious songs; most likely it represents only a part of the liturgical poetry of the people of Israel. The selection must have been determined by the needs of the post-Exilic community and by the relevance of the psalms concerned. The Psalter was not an equivalent of the *Oxford Book of Christian Verse*, but it was, primarily, a liturgical manual. Consequently psalms which could no longer be adapted or re-interpreted must have been excluded.

It is impossible to reconstruct the history of the compilation of the Psalter with any degree of certainty but, on the basis of the available indications, the most likely hypothesis is as follows:

(i) At an early stage there must have existed several smaller collections; it may well be that every sanctuary had its own collection or collections based on subject matter (cf. the Lamentations of Jeremiah), cultic usage, etc. The Book of Psalms points to several compilations: (a) the first Davidic psalter consisting of Ps. 3–41 (Ps. 33 may have been a later insertion, since it has no title); (b) the Korahite psalter (containing Ps. 42–9) which may have included also Ps. 84–5 and 87–8; (c) the Asaphite psalter (Ps. 73–83 + Ps. 50); (d) the second Davidic psalter (Ps. 51–71, and probably also Ps. 72 which is attributed to Solomon).

(ii) The next stage in the process probably involved the combination of some of the smaller collections into larger compilations. One result of this editorial activity must have been the so-called Elohistic psalter, consisting of the Korahite psalms (42–9), the Davidic psalms (51–71 and 72), and the Asaphite psalms (73–83, and 50). It was, perhaps, at this time that in most places the divine name Yahweh was altered into 'God' (*ᵓᵉlōhîm*). Barth (*IP*, p. 3) places this activity sometime *before* the Exile. The first Davidic psalter (Ps. 3–41) remained untouched by this editorial alteration, and therefore it must have existed separately.

(iii) The third stage probably involved the joining of the first Davidic psalter with the Elohistic collection, and this new compilation may have been introduced by Ps. 2, while at the end there were added Ps. 84–9 (which are Yahwistic psalms).

(iv) During the fourth stage the combined Psalter (Ps. 2–89) was gradually enlarged by the addition of smaller collections (of different origins and dates), such as the Songs of Ascents (Ps. 120–34), and the Hallelujah psalms (Ps. 146–50), and various individual psalms. At some point Ps. 1 was added to the whole collection 'as a kind of "motto" for the aim and use of the whole Psalter' (Mowinckel, *PIW*, II, p. 197).

(v) Finally there came the division of the Psalter into five books, although some of the groupings may have already existed (e.g. that between Ps. 3–41 and 42–72). These five books consist of Ps. 1–41; 42–72; 73–89; 90–106; 107–150, but the reason for this fivefold division is no longer known; the pattern may have been provided by the Pentateuch. Thus the Midrash on Ps. 1.1 explains that 'Moses gave the Israelites the five books of the Law, and to correspond to these David gave them the Book of Psalms containing five books' (quoted from Kirkpatrick, *BPCB*, p. xvii). It is highly unlikely that David had anything to do with this arrangement, but the ancient tradition may be right in suggesting that the fivefold division is an imitation of the Pentateuch. This five-book scheme of the Psalter does not rest on a grouping according to the literary types, because psalms of different *Gattungen*, or psalm-types, are found in all five books of the Psalter; it seems rather arbitrary, determined by no clear principle (cf. Gunkel, *EP*, pp. 435f.; Mowinckel, *PIW*, II, p. 197). Each book in the present Psalter ends with a doxology (see 42:13 (M.T. 14), 72:18f., 89:52 (M.T. 53), 106:48); there is no doxology at the end of Ps. 150, but it is generally thought that this Psalm itself is the concluding doxology to Book V, and to the whole Psalter. It is possible that some of these liturgical formulae were already found at the end of earlier collections; it is less likely that *every* Psalm ended with a doxology (cf. Briggs, *CECBP*, I, p. lxxxiii).

Our Psalter contains 150 Psalms or units, and this figure must have been fixed before the Greek translation of the Psalter. LXX contains also Ps. 151, but it is described as being 'outside the number' (*exōthen tou arithmou*); the Hebrew version of this Psalm has been found in Qumran Cave 11 (cf. J. A. Sanders, *The Psalms Scroll of Qumrān Cave* 11 (1965), pp. 54–64). The reason why only 150 Psalms were included in the Psalter is not known, but the number is reminiscent of the 153 sections of the Torah, or Law; it is not improbable that each reading of the Torah may have been accompanied by one Psalm (cf. Briggs, op. cit., pp. lxxxviii–ix). This would be, however, a late practice. Both M.T. and LXX have the same number of Psalms but the actual extent of particular psalms is not always identical. Thus LXX seems to be right in joining Ps. 9 and 10, but there is less reason for linking

Ps. 114 and 115. Ps. 42 and 43 may well have formed a single Psalm, although M.T. and the versions treat them separately.

The actual compilation of the Psalter was probably complete by the end of the third century B.C. (cf. J. Hempel, 'Book of Psalms', *IDB*, III, p. 943).

4. TEXT AND ANCIENT VERSIONS

The Psalms were originally written in Hebrew, and most of the modern translations of the Psalter are based on the official or canonical text known as the 'Massoretic text' (M.T.). The extant manuscripts of the Massoretic tradition are comparatively late, dating from the end of the first millennium A.D. (for details and references, see Eissfeldt, *OTI*, pp. 679–93). The Massoretic text goes back to the Hebrew consonantal text (the vowel signs were added roundabout the middle of the first millennium A.D.), which was standardized about A.D. 100 (cf. Eissfeldt, *OTI*, pp. 684f.). Other text forms (some of which may well represent the original reading) are occasionally preserved in the ancient versions and various fragments. Of special importance is the Biblical material from Qumran (cf. J. A. Sanders, op. cit.; J. M. Allegro (and A. A. Anderson), *Qumrān Cave* 4 I (4Q158–4Q186) (1968), pp. 42–50, 51–3); these fragments could hardly be later than the middle of the first century A.D., yet they do not offer many *important* variations.

The oldest and the most important version is the Greek translation of the *OT* books called the Septuagint (LXX), which was completed in Egypt at the beginning of the second century B.C. (see Eissfeldt, pp. 701–15). Among the later Greek versions of some interest are those of Aquila (Aq), Theodotion (Theod), and Symmachus (Sym). Next in importance are the Syriac version (S) or the so-called Peshitta, and the Aramaic version or the Targum (T) which is often characterized by a paraphrastic style (see Eissfeldt, pp. 696–701). The last version of some greater relevance is the Vulgate (V) which is Jerome's Latin translation from the Hebrew text. Jerome's version of the Psalter could not, however, displace the familiar Gallican psalter, and consequently the Vulgate Book of Psalms is in fact the Gallican psalter which was a revision of the Old Latin version based on the Septuagint (for more information, see Kirkpatrick, *BPCB*, p. lxxii). In Dahood's opinion (*PAB*, I, p. xxiv) the Ugaritic studies have brought about a devaluation of the ancient versions, undermining their authority 'as witnesses to the original text'. This may be partly true; but the testimony of the Ugaritic texts and the versions is not of the same nature, and each case must be judged on its own merits.

II. PSALM TYPES AND THEIR SETTING IN LIFE

Traditionally, most Psalms were regarded as composed by David (cf. Ac. 2:25,34, 4:25; Cohen, *PSon*, p. xi) and therefore the main task of the commentator was to determine what event in David's life had given rise to the particular Psalm. This method is well illustrated by the so-called historical notes found in the superscriptions of certain Psalms (see Ps. 3, 7, 18, 34, 51, 54, 56, 57, 59, 60, 63, 142); they must have been added by some later compiler or editor whose intention was to supply (what seemed to him) the appropriate historical setting for the Psalms concerned. Even when the Davidic authorship of the majority of the Psalms was rejected, the same basic assumption that the Psalms had arisen out of particular experiences of the nation or the individual continued to determine the exegesis. The Psalms were occasionally classified according to various principles, such as topics (cf. J. E. McFadyen, *Introduction to the Old Testament* (1932), pp. 272f.), the nature of their contents (cf. Barnes, *PWC*, 1, pp. xv–xvii), etc.

The real turning point in psalm interpretation was the work of H. Gunkel (for references, see *WAI*, p. 178) during the early part of this century. He attempted to classify the Psalms according to their literary types (*Gattungen*), and to reconstruct their situation in life (*Sitz im Leben*). In his opinion the various psalm-types had their origin in the cult, and were associated with certain cultic situations. In his posthumous introduction to the Psalter (*EP*), he distinguished six main types: Hymns of Praise, Enthronement Psalms, Laments of the Community, Royal Psalms, Laments of the Individual, and Individual Songs of Thanksgiving. Among the minor categories he listed Pronouncements of blessings and curses, Pilgrimage Songs, Victory Songs, National Songs of Thanksgiving, Sacred Legends, and Torah Psalms, as well as Wisdom Psalms and Prophetic elements (for an excellent summary, see A. R. Johnson, 'The Psalms', *OTMS*, pp. 166–81). Although

Gunkel recognised that the psalm-types originated in the cult, he believed that most *OT* Psalms were free compositions expressing the feelings and thoughts of their authors, and that they were more 'spiritual' in their outlook than their earlier cultic counterparts.

In the light of more recent *OT* study, it seems far more likely that the large majority of *OT* Psalms were cultic in origin and in their usage during the *OT* period. It is possible that *some* Psalms were created by certain great crises in the life of the nation, or that *some* songs in the Psalter reflected the actual experiences of a particular poet, but even in such cases the conventional language must have exercised some influence, and the subsequent use of such Psalms by later generations may also have left its mark upon these poems.

Exegetically it is often *convenient* to attempt a reconstruction of the Psalmist's 'experiences', but the resultant picture may well be, in most cases, a description of a typical situation encountered by a hypothetical person. The reason for this is to be found in the purpose of the Psalms: they were, primarily, intended as vehicles to convey the feelings and attitude of *any* worshipper in a similar situation. Thus even the Psalms of the individual have a collective character, or 'the poet is above all an interpreter of the soul of his people. *He* says what *they* think and feel' (P. Drijvers, *The Psalms: their Structure and Meaning* (1965), p. 38). It is very likely that most Psalms were composed by skilled poets for the use of other people less able to clothe their experiences in a poetical language. Therefore it is fairly clear that any reconstruction of the particular circumstances (such as often attempted in the exegesis of the Psalms) presents us with a generalization of what often happens in typical cases, rather than with a factual description. The aim of these frustrating efforts is to determine, as far as possible, the *type* of man envisaged by the Psalmist, and the Psalm's possible situation in life.

Gunkel's epoch-making method was further elaborated by S. Mowinckel, a younger contemporary. In his opinion, most Psalms had their setting in the worship of Israel, and therefore the main task of the commentator was to describe the cultic setting of the various poems. One of the main contributions of Mowinckel was the reconstruction of the New Year Festival, of which an important part was the Enthronement Festival of Yahweh (cf. *PIW*, I, pp. 106–92; for a brief summary, see A. R. Johnson, 'The Psalms', *OTMS*, pp. 189–97; Rowley, *WAI*, pp.

184–95). Mowinckel assigned a large number of Psalms to this cultic festival, and it is this special emphasis on the New Year Festival which may well be one of the 'weaknesses' of his outstanding work.

Another important contribution was made by Weiser (*POTL*, pp. 23–52) who postulated a Covenant Festival of pre-monarchical origin, celebrated at New Year in the autumn (op. cit., p. 27). An essential aspect of this Festival was the renewal of the Sinaitic Covenant and the cultic re-presentation of the salvation-history of the nation. In Weiser's view, the Covenant Festival of Yahweh provided the setting for the majority of Psalms.

In a similar way, Kraus (e.g. in *WI*, pp. 179–222) has drawn our attention to the Royal Zion Festival in which the election of David and of Jerusalem played an important role.

These three festivals do not represent contradictory views, but rather various stages in the history of the great Autumn Festival and/or different aspects of it. Furthermore, we must not overlook the complexity of Israel's cultic life by overemphasizing *one* festival and some of its various aspects. It is very likely that the major Israelite festivals formed the background not only of most of the National Psalms but also of the majority of the Psalms of the individual. The three pilgrimage festivals may have been the only occasions when most of the Israelites had opportunity to worship in the Temple or sanctuary.

Any discussion of the psalm-types is bound to start with some such scheme as that suggested by Gunkel (cf. J. W. Wevers, *VT*, VI (1956), p. 80; A. Descamps, 'Les genres littéraires du Psautier', *LPOBL*, pp. 73–88). Westermann (*PGP*, p. 153) has argued that the various psalm-types represent two basic ways of praying: plea and praise, which were eventually expanded and changed. This may be right (cf. R. E. Murphy, *CBQ*, XXI (1959), pp. 83–7), but essentially it does not alter Gunkel's main outline; Westermann has demonstrated, however, that the difference between Hymns and Psalms of Thanksgiving is very small although the two are not identical (*PGP*, pp. 25–30).

A possible outline of the main types of *OT* Psalms may be as follows:

1. THE PRAISES OF GOD
   - a. Hymns or Descriptive Praises
     - (i) Praises of God in general
     - (ii) Psalms celebrating Yahweh's kingship
     - (iii) Songs of Zion (or Indirect Praises of God)

b. Declarative Praises of the Individual, or Individual Songs of Thanksgiving
c. Declarative Praises of the People, or National Songs of Thanksgiving

2. LAMENTS

a. Laments of the Individual
  (i) Prayers of the Unjustly Accused Man
  (ii) Psalms of Penitence
b. Laments of the Nation
c. Psalms of Confidence

3. ROYAL PSALMS

4. MINOR TYPES

It is important to stress that any classification of psalms according to their categories, or *Gattungen*, is not an exact science, and it is bound to involve a subjective judgment. In the *OT* there are comparatively few examples of pure psalm-types, and the *Sitz im Leben* of most Psalms is far from certain. We must also reckon with the possibility that in the course of the history of the Psalter some psalm-types may have disintegrated, or that some Psalms lost their original cultic setting, as in the case of the Royal Psalms. This may well have affected the form and contents of the Psalms concerned. On the other hand, irrespective of the weaknesses and difficulties of this method of interpretation, this seems to be the right approach to the Psalter.

1. The Praises of God

This group of Psalms includes three main types: Hymns, and Declarative Praises of the Individual and of the Nation; in essence they are the response of the worshipper or the cultic community to the works of God, or to his saving intervention. This cultic answer takes the form of praise for what God had done, and since the possible situations can be varied we shall consider the main types and their subdivisions separately.

a. HYMNS OR DESCRIPTIVE PRAISES

Gunkel defined this category as Hymns of Praise, or simply Hymns (cf. *EP*, pp. 32–94), while Westermann (*PGP*, pp. 25–35) preferred to speak about Descriptive Praises. The principal aim of this psalm-type is to declare Yahweh's greatness which he has manifested both in nature and in the history of Israel; thus the main theme is his praise. The subject of the Hymns is God, his nature, or his mighty deeds, and he is usually spoken of in the third person; the use of the second person is rare (cf. 65:1 (M.T. 2)).

The formal structure of Hymns is often made up of three parts: introduction, main section, and conclusion.

The introduction usually begins with an exhortation to praise and bless Yahweh, e.g. 'Praise the LORD . . .' (113:1). This imperative call to praise God may be expanded by describing the object of praise (150:1), or by defining the people addressed (cf. 134:1), etc. The main section of the Hymn gives the grounds for the introductory exhortation, and quite frequently this 'corpus' of the Hymn begins with the so-called hymnic *kî* ('for' or 'because') (cf. 33:4; see on 89:2). Another characteristic of this section is the hymnic participle, which is usually translated by a relative clause (cf. 103:3ff.). Sometimes the main section consists of short sentences which describe certain actions, deeds, or qualities of Yahweh (cf. 29:3–10). The conclusion of the Hymn often re-echoes the introductory formula (cf. 8:1 (M.T. 2) and 8:9 (M.T. 10)) with greater or lesser variations (cf. 136:1 and 136:26). Occasionally the Psalm of Descriptive Praise may end with a prayer or wish (cf. 19:14 (M.T. 15), 29:11).

Mowinckel (*PIW*, ii, p. 85) distinguishes two main types of Hymns: the more general category which deals with the works of God as a whole, and the more special type which depicts a particular work of salvation. For the former, see Ps. 136; for the latter, Ps. 114 (cf. Ps. 46 and 48). Eissfeldt (*OTI*, p. 108) points out that although the Hymns are cultic in origin, it is no longer possible to ascertain their exact place in the cultus. They may have been sung on more than one occasion: any situation where the works of Yahweh were re-presented, or brought to mind, could provide a setting for the Hymns (cf. C. Westermann, *Der Psalter* (1967), pp. 70f.; A. Szörényi, *Psalmen und Kult im Alten Testament* (1961), pp. 507–21).

Among the Hymns or Praises of God we may distinguish two sub-types: namely, Psalms which praise God as king, or the Psalms Celebrating Yahweh's Kingship, and the Songs of Zion.

Psalms Celebrating the Kingship of Yahweh

This psalm category is often called the Enthronement Psalms, but since this descriptive title is slightly misleading it is better to use some other definition. To this group are usually assigned Ps. 47, 93, 96–9, and Gunkel spoke of them as 'eschatological songs of Yahweh's enthronement' (cf. *EP*, pp. 329, 345). But it was

Mowinckel who paid a special attention to this type (*PStud*, II; *PIW*, I, pp. 106–92). In his view the main characteristic of these Psalms is that 'they salute Yahweh as the king, who has just ascended his royal throne to wield his royal power' (*PIW*, I, p. 106). He also included in this group Ps. 95 and 100, and linked with them a second, closely associated group of songs consisting of Ps. 8, 15, 24, 29, 33, 46, 48, 50, 66a, 75, 76, 81, 82, 84, 87, 114, 118, 132, 149 (for a further discussion, see J. D. W. Watts, '*Yahweh Mālak* Psalms', *ThZ*, XXI (1965), pp. 341–8). The particular feature of the so-called Enthronement Psalms is the phrase *yhwh mālak* rendered by *RSV* as 'the LORD reigns' (*PNT* and *NEB* 'the LORD is king'). Mowinckel argues that this translation is misleading because it is not a lasting condition which is thus described, but rather 'something new and important which has just taken place: Yahweh has now become king' (*PIW*, I, p. 107). Therefore he suggests that the right rendering is 'Yahweh has become king' (for further information, see 93:1), although the linguistic arguments are far from conclusive (cf. A. Gelston, *VT*, XVI (1966), pp. 507ff.).

Mowinckel proceeded to reconstruct the Enthronement Festival of Yahweh, on the basis of the so-called Enthronement Psalms, Near Eastern analogies, and various hints found in post-biblical Hebrew literature; he regarded this Festival as 'another aspect of the harvest and new year festival itself' (*PIW*, I, p. 124). The principal motifs associated with this cultic occasion were the kingship of Yahweh, the defeat of the primeval enemies, the creation of the world, and the judgement of the nations. It is questionable, however, how far it is right to speak of an *enthronement* of Yahweh. In the Babylonian myth Marduk could be acclaimed by other gods (cf. *ANET*, p. 66a) and, possibly, also Baal could be hailed as king by other members of the pantheon (cf. Driver, *CML*, p. 83; W. H. Schmidt, *Königtum Gottes in Ugarit und Israel* (*BZAW*, 80 (1966)), pp. 12, 72) but it is difficult to see who would be in position to enthrone Yahweh. Although he is thought to be surrounded by his heavenly court (see on 89:5ff.), none of them was equal to him. Even less likely is the possible implication that Yahweh had relinquished his kingship for a time, or that he was subject to the cycle of death and resurrection, like Baal. This is not to say that Mowinckel or other exegetes would subscribe to these views, but it seems that the term 'Enthronement Psalms' (or '. . . Festival') is a misleading phrase. Was there ever a time when Yahweh was not king? In any case, it seems more plausible to speak about the celebrating of Yahweh's kingship. The occasion would have been the New Year Festival, i.e. the Feast of Tabernacles, and the actual setting could have been the renewal of the people's allegiance to Yahweh.

Songs of Zion

The Descriptive Praises or Hymns usually extol God, his character, and so on, but occasionally this praise may be expressed indirectly by praising the Temple or the Holy City. Consequently there is some justification for regarding these implicit praises of Yahweh as a subdivision of the ordinary Hymns. The term 'Songs of Zion' is derived from 137:3, where the captors of the Jewish people asked them to sing 'the songs of Zion', which probably were a group of songs composed for the glorification of Jerusalem, and ultimately for the praise of Yahweh—for the glory of Zion is Yahweh.

Kraus (*PBK*, p. liv) includes in this group Ps. 48, 76, 84, 87, 122, and possibly also Ps. 46 and 132. These psalms lack the usual hymnic Introduction (cf. Gunkel, *EP*, p. 81).

b. DECLARATIVE PRAISES OF THE INDIVIDUAL

This psalm-type is better known as Individual Songs of Thanksgiving, or Private Hymns of Thanksgiving. Declarative Praises presuppose Laments, and they are man's response to God's gracious intervention. Their aim is not only to offer praises or thanks to God, but they are also intended as a testimony to the saving work of God, declared before the whole congregation. Thus also the private thanksgiving is a communal act of worship. In the Declarative Praises, the worshipper addresses God directly (in the second person), while the Hymns or Descriptive Praises speak *about* God. Another difference is that the former are composed for, and used on, specific occasions, while the latter refer to the great works of God in general.

Structurally the Declarative Praises consist of three main parts: introduction, main section, and conclusion. The introduction contains an invocation of Yahweh's name (this can be expanded by various hymnic additions, as in 18:2 (M.T. 3), 92:5–8 (M.T. 6–9)) and the declaration of intent (cf. 34:1 (M.T. 2), 116:1f., 138:1f.). The main section is essentially an account of the distress experienced and of the subsequent divine deliverance; occasionally the writer may quote the prayer (or its summary) uttered during the time of need (cf. 116:4), and a description of the fulfilment of the vow (116:12–19). The conclusion often includes an invitation to praise Yahweh (116:19*c*, 118:29), or a repetition of the self-exhortation to thank Yahweh (18:49 (M.T. 50)). For more details, see Gunkel, *EP*, pp. 265-92; H. H. Guthrie, jr., *ISS*, pp. 147–57; Westermann, *PGP*, pp. 102–16.

In comparison with Laments, there are few Declarative Praises but this is no reflection of the Israelite spirituality or the lack of it. It is possible that Descriptive Praises or Hymns may have equally well served the same purpose, and many Laments contain also an element of thanksgiving. The *Sitz im Leben* of the Declarative Praises or Songs of Thanksgiving must have been the sacrifice of thank-offering; this is suggested by the Psalms themselves (cf. 66:13–19, 116:12ff.) and by their Hebrew designation (*tôḏāh*), which may denote both a thank-offering and a Song of Thanksgiving (see on 69:30). The song may have been sung or recited by the delivered man himself (see Job 33:26ff.) or by 'persons skilled in liturgical singing' (Rowley, *WAI*, p. 182). The actual occasion may have been either during the sacrifice itself (cf. Mowinckel, *PIW*, II, p. 31) or during the sacrificial meal which followed (cf. 22:22–26 (M.T. 23–27)).

To this category of songs are usually assigned Ps. 9–10, 18, 32, 34, 92, 116, 118, and 138.

C. DECLARATIVE PRAISES OF THE PEOPLE

This *Gattung*, or psalm-type, is often called the National Songs of Thanksgiving, and very few of them are found in the Psalter; Gunkel (*EP*, p. 315) suggests Ps. 66: 8–12, 67, 124, and 129, while Weiser thinks that only Ps. 124 is a genuine thanksgiving (*POTL*, p. 83). C. Westermann (*Der Psalter*, 1967, p. 43) accounts for this lack by suggesting that, since the Psalter is a post-Exilic collection, and since there were no great national deliverances during this period, National Songs of Praise or Thanksgiving were not transmitted. This is possible, but it is more likely that the explanation is similar to that above, concerning the Declarative Praises of the Individual. See also F. Crüsemann, *Studien zur Formgeschichte von Hymnus und Danklied in Israel* (*WMANT*, 32, 1969).

2. LAMENTS

This type of psalm is the most common category in the Psalter, and nearly a third of the Psalms belong to this *Gattung*. Laments could be subdivided into Individual or Communal Lamentations, but the distinction between the two is not always clear. Some Individual Laments may well have been used by the king, and therefore such Psalms would really be communal lamentations rather than individual. On the other hand, it is possible that elements and features of Royal Psalms could have been adapted to the songs of the private individual, especially in post-Exilic songs.

a. LAMENTS OF THE INDIVIDUAL

Lamentation was man's response to God, in a situation of need and affliction. In such circumstances the sufferer might go to the sanctuary to offer prayers or lamentations, and to perform the appropriate ritual acts. It is very likely that in most cases the Laments were uttered by the cultic staff of the sanctuary, on behalf of the needy man.

The Laments usually consist of two main parts: introduction and main section, or 'corpus'; to this is occasionally added an expression of certainty and thanksgiving.

The introduction includes the invocation of Yahweh, and often it is no more than a mention of the divine name (cf. 143:1). This contrasts with the Babylonian practice where the invocation is frequently expanded by a hymnic recitation of the divine attributes and deeds (see the 'Prayer of Lamentation to Ishtar', *ANET*, pp. 383–5). Only occasionally a similar practice, on a much smaller scale, is found in *OT* (cf. 86: 2–13). The introduction also contains a call for help, usually in the imperative (cf. 5:1f. (M.T. 2f.), 6:1f. (M.T. 2f.), etc.).

The main section of the Lament consists of a number of elements, the order of which may vary from time to time; and some of them may be lacking in certain Psalms. Most Lamentations would have a description of the distress or misfortune, which may be of a very varied nature (cf. 22: 6–18 (M.T. 7–19), 38: 2–12 (M.T. 3–13), etc.). Normally this would be followed by a prayer and a cry for help and deliverance (cf. 38:15f. (M.T. 16f.), 39:7–10 (M.T. 8–11), 41: 4,10 (M.T. 5,11), 86:16, etc.). Occasionally the Psalmist gives a motivation or reason for appealing to Yahweh, such as his need (54:3 (M.T. 5)), the nature of God (86: 2, 15), the honour of God (42:10 (M.T. 11)), etc. In some Lamentations we find either a confession of sin (cf. 51: 3f. (M.T. 5f.)), or a protestation of innocence (59: 3f. (M.T. 4f.)), also wishes and curses (55:15 (M.T. 16), 61:4 (M.T. 5), 109: 6–20), as well as a vow to praise God (cf. 61:8 (M.T. 9), 109: 30f.).

Not infrequently the Lamentation changes from supplications to thanksgiving, and there may be several explanations for this transition. One possibility is that two Psalms of different types have accidentally been joined together, but in most cases this is rather unlikely (cf. 3: 7 (M.T. 8), 13: 5f. (M.T. 6f.), 22: 22–31 (M.T. 23–32), etc.; cf. also Westermann, *PGP*, pp. 79ff.). A more likely suggestion is the view that the Laments which contain elements of thanksgiving are in actual fact Declarative Praises in which the 'lament section' merely recalls the past experience and dramatizes it (cf. E. Podechard, *Le Psautier* (1949) I, pp. 33f.). Another plausible proposal is to assume that the transition is due to a priestly oracle which promised the deliverance of the afflicted person; cf. 22: 21 (M.T. 22). See also W. Beyerlin, 'Die tôdā der Heilsverkündigung in den Klageliedern des Einzelner', *ZAW*, LXXIX (1967), pp. 208–24.

For more details on Lamentations, see Gunkel, *EP*, pp. 172–265; Guthrie, jr., *ISS*, pp. 120–45; Westermann, *PGP*, pp. 64–81.

The following Psalms are often attributed to the Laments of the Individual: 3, 5, 6, 7, 17, 22, 25, 26, 27, 28, 35, 39, 41, 42–3, 51, 54, 55, 56, 57, 59, 61, 63, 64, 69, 71, 86, 88, 102, 109, 130, 140, 141, and 143.

It is probable that among the Laments of the Individual we should distinguish two sub-types: the Prayers of the Unjustly Accused Man and Psalms of Penitence. This differentiation is not based on different literary forms but on the contents of the Psalms. The former group was treated in detail by H. Schmidt (*Das Gebet der Angeklagten im Alten Testament* (*BZAW*, XLIX, 1928)) who thought that these Psalms belonged to a procedure of legal examination; they would be recited by (or 'for') the accused man in the sanctuary, and the aim was to obtain a favourable divine judgement; cf. J. W. Wevers, *VT*, VI (1956), p. 88; see Ps. 7, 17, 26, 35, 57, and 69.

The classic example of the Psalms of Penitence is Ps. 51. Here we could include those songs where the confession of sin receives a special emphasis. According to the tradition of the early Church, Ps. 6, 32, 38, 51, 102, 130, and 143 are the Penitential Psalms, although some of them contain no explicit confession of sin. It may be surprising that so few Psalms show true penitence, but it is possible that the very description of the distress is an implicit admission of guilt. If God is just and responsible for the affliction, then an account of the misfortune is tantamount to penitence. See also E. R. Dalglish, *Psalm Fifty-One* (1962), pp. 4ff.; Wevers, op. cit., pp. 91f.

b. LAMENTS OF THE NATION

The Communal Laments are less numerous than the Individual Songs of Lamentation; the following Psalms are often reckoned as Laments of the Nation: 60, 74, 79, 80, 83, 85, 90, 124, 126, 137 (?), and 144 (?). There is little if any structural difference between the two types of Laments.

The background of the National Laments is some disaster—such as defeat in war, epidemic, drought, etc.—which affects the whole people; on such occasions it would be fitting to hold a day of fasting and prayer (cf. 1 Kg. 8: 33–40, 21: 9–12; Jer. 36:1–10; Jl 1:13f., 2:12–17). There may have been also certain fixed days of prayer and penitence during which the nation would remember a particular catastrophe (cf. Zech. 7) and would, no doubt, sing psalms of Lamentation. It is not impossible that national lamentation may have been part of certain annual rituals (cf. Guthrie, jr., *ISS*, pp. 136–40); for the possible royal ritual of humiliation, see Johnson, *SKAI*, pp. 102–11.

c. PSALMS OF CONFIDENCE

Occasionally certain aspects of the Lamentations may be particularly emphasized, giving rise to a new psalm-type or a new subdivision in the existing category. One such group is the Psalms of Confidence or Trust; we may include in it such Psalms as 4, 11, 16, 23, 27, 62, 131, and 125 as an example of a Collective Song of Trust (so Eissfeldt, *OTI*, pp. 114f.). The difference between the individual and collective Psalms is not very clear, in some cases at least.

3. Royal Psalms

Gunkel regarded these Psalms as one of the main types (cf. *EP*, pp. 140–71), but in actual fact they do not form an independent literary type; rather they comprise Psalms of *various* categories. Their distinguishing feature is the subject matter which concerns the relationship between God and the King. Also their *Sitz im Leben* is greatly varied, depending upon the basic psalm-type used. Mowinckel (*PIW*, 1, p. 47) includes among the Royal

Psalms the following songs: Ps. 2, 18, 20, 21, 45, 72, 101, 110, 132, as well as 28, 61, 63, 89, and others unspecified. It is clear that exegetes will differ on this point, finding either less or more royal songs: for further information, see Eissfeldt, *OTI*, pp. 102ff.; K. R. Crim, *The Royal Psalms* (1962).

Most if not all Royal Psalms belong to the pre-Exilic period, although it is not absolutely impossible that some of them are post-Exilic Messianic Psalms following the pattern of Royal Psalms (cf. Deissler, *PWdB*, 1, pp. 20f.). In any case, it is difficult to draw the line between Royal and Messianic Psalms, since the former survived because they could be adapted to the use of the individual (or community) or re-interpreted in a messianic sense. It is quite possible that certain parts of the older Psalms were omitted or changed in the course of adaptation.

4. Minor Types

In most cases minor categories do not possess clearly defined structure but are linked together by their common contents, aims, etc. The more important classes are the Entrance Liturgies (Ps. 15 and 24), which may have been used by pilgrims wishing to enter the Temple; the Wisdom Psalms or Reflective poems (cf. Ps. 1, 37, 49, 73, 112, 127, 128, and 133), which are reminiscent of the Wisdom literature, as regards their style, language, and subject matter. There are also the so-called Prophetic Psalms or Liturgies. A. R. Johnson ('Psalms', *DB*, p. 818b) describes as 'Oracular Psalms' the following poems (or parts of them): Ps. 2, 12, 50, 60, 75, 81, 82, 85, 91, 95, and 110. Further, one could mention the Sacred Legends (Ps. 78, 105, and 106), Pilgrimage Songs (Ps. 84 and 122), Mixed Poems (e.g. Ps. 119), and others.

III. HEBREW POETRY

Poetry occupies a considerable part of the *OT*, and some books are poetic in their entirety, e.g., Psalms, Proverbs, Lamentations, Song of Songs and Micah. Hebrew poetry is characterized by the so-called parallelism (either actual or formal) and rhythm; occasionally it exhibits a strophic arrangement (cf. Ps. 119), refrain (see Ps. 42–3), and acrostic structure (cf. Ps. 9–10).

Parallelism is essentially a rhythm of meaning, or the repetition of meaning in a parallel form. The basic unit of poetic composition could be described as 'the line which constitutes normally one half (sometimes one third) of the parallelism' (N. K. Gottwald, 'Hebrew Poetry', *IDB*, III, p. 831a). There are three main categories of parallelism: complete, incomplete, and formal.

1. COMPLETE PARALLELISM

Here belong instances where every single term or thought unit in one line is parallel to an equivalent term or unit in the other line (cf. G. B. Gray, *The Forms of Hebrew Poetry* (1915), p. 59). Complete parallelism can be subdivided into:

(a) *synonymous parallelism*, where the same thought is repeated by the other line, in different but synonymous words.

'Then Israel | came | to Egypt;
Jacob | sojourned | in the land of Ham.' (105:23)

The order of the parallel terms need not be the same in both lines;

(b) *antithetic parallelism* balances the parallel lines through the opposition or contrast of thought, as in 90:6:

'in the morning | it flourishes | and is renewed;
in the evening | it fades | and withers';

(c) *emblematic parallelism* employs a simile or a metaphor, so that the thought of the first line is compared to that of the second. E.g.,

'As a father | pities | his children,
so the LORD | pities | those who fear him' (103:13);

(d) *inverted or chiastic parallelism* is strictly speaking a form of synonymous parallelism; the main difference is that the former involves the inversion of terms in the second line. A clear example is found in Isa. 11:13*b*:

'Ephraim | shall not be jealous of | Judah,
and Judah | shall not harass | Ephraim.'

2. INCOMPLETE PARALLELISM

This type of parallelism is very frequent, and it offers a considerable number of variations. Here only some of the respective terms are parallel, and we can distinguish:

(a) *incomplete parallelism with compensation* where only some of the terms are parallel, but each line has the *same* number of terms.

'You will destroy | their offspring | from the earth,
and their children | from among the sons of | men'
(21:10 (M.T. 11)).

A variation of this is the so-called *step-parallelism*, or *repetitive parallelism*, where the thought is developed by repetition and extension, as in 29:1f.:

'Ascribe | to the LORD, | O heavenly | beings,
ascribe | to the LORD | glory | and strength.
Ascribe | to the LORD | the glory of | his name;
worship | the LORD | in holy | array';

(b) *incomplete parallelism without compensation*, where the second line contains a smaller number of terms, as in 6:2 (M.T. 3):

'O Lord, | rebuke me not | in thy anger,
nor chasten me | in thy wrath.'

3. FORMAL PARALLELISM

Strictly speaking, this type is no parallelism at all, because the second line simply continues the thought of the first, or the second line is *all* compensation. On the other hand, the two lines are usually balanced quantitatively, and the usual pattern is observed. E.g.,

'I have set | my king
on Zion, | my holy hill.' (2:6)

Or 'The fool | says | in his heart,
"There is no | God" ' (14:1).

The three main categories of parallelism described above could be called *internal parallelism*, which is found in the verse consisting of two or three lines. Occasionally we also find *external parallelism*, where the correspondence occurs between the successive verses, as in Isa. 1:3:

'The ox | knows | its owner,
and the ass | its master's | crib;
but Israel | does not | know,
my people | does not | understand.'

4. METRE

The other main characteristic of Hebrew poetry was metre or rhythm. This metre has little in common with its classical counterparts, because in Hebrew poetry we often find a succession of accented monosyllabic words without any intervening unaccented syllables; on the other hand, two stressed syllables are sometimes separated by four or even five unstressed syllables. N. K. Gottwald (p. 834b) has suggested that Hebrew rhythm 'is not due to syllabic quantities, but to the less definable instinct of balancing parts whose exact accentual values are not measurable and probably never were'. Although it is possible to observe in the Psalms certain metric patterns, there are very few poems in the Psalter which follow consistently *one* pattern; hence one may quote Gordon's remark (*UT*, p. 131) that the poets of the ancient Near East 'did not know of exact metre. Therefore emendations *metri causa* are pure whimsy'; as a generalization, this view is right.

Some of the more common metric patterns are 3+2, 3+3, 4+4, but we also find 2+2, 2+2+2, 4+2, etc. (for more information, see Mowinckel, *PIW*, II, pp. 159–75; Eissfeldt, *OTI*, pp. 57–63).

The strophic arrangement is comparatively rare in the Psalter, but its existence cannot be doubted. Thus Ps. 119 contains 22 strophes, each consisting of eight verses (or *bicola*, i.e. two-line units). This is made clear by the acrostic scheme (see introduction to Ps. 9–10), with the result that all the eight verses of each strophe begin with the same Hebrew letter. The strophic arrangement is occasionally marked out by the refrain, as in Ps. 42–3, 80.

IV. PSALM TITLES

The study of psalm titles or headings is a very inconclusive work, and Rowley (*WAI*, p. 212) has well summed up the situation, saying: 'We have no evidence on which to base our conjectures, and it seems profitless to speculate'. Consequently the following notes are merely indications of the more common or, seemingly, more likely suggestions.

Most of the terms in the psalm headings and others, such as 'Selah', are technical expressions, the meanings of which have been lost. Even the ancient versions are of little help; in some cases LXX lacks some of the notifications found in M.T., while in other instances it adds many others; the Syriac version is even more divergent.

These terms can be classified according to what is believed to be their purpose, nature, etc.; but, since quite often we do not know the meaning and function of particular expressions, it follows that the categories are rather subjective.

1. TERMS INDICATING COLLECTIONS, COMPILERS OR AUTHORS

(i) **of David:** this term occurs 72 times in *RSV*, but it is omitted from the heading of Ps. 133; in LXX there are 14 other Psalms which have this title. Its interpretation is problematic, because both the preposition *l*ᵉ (*RSV* 'of') and the word 'David' are capable of more than one interpretation. The preposition may suggest such meanings as 'by' (of authorship), 'to' (of ownership), etc., while 'David' refers in the first place to King David; but the term could also denote any king of the house of David, as in Hos. 3:5: '. . . the children of Israel shall return and seek the LORD their God, and David their king', who is hardly a David *redivivus*, but a Davidic king (cf. Ezek. 34:23). Some scholars have argued that 'David' is to be linked with the word *dawidum* found in the Mari texts (for references, see K. A. Kitchen, *Ancient Orient and Old Testament* (1966), pp. 84f.) meaning, perhaps, 'a commander'; this identification has not found, however, a wide acceptance.

From this brief survey it is clear that the phrase 'of David' can have a number of possible interpretations:

(a) The traditional view is that it denotes authorship, and this finds some support in the Jewish and Christian traditions. The *OT* itself refers to David as a musician and poet (1 Sam. 16:17–23, 18:10; 2 Sam. 1:17–27, 3:33f., 23:1–7; Am. 6:5), and in 11QPsᵃ Dav. Comp. it is said that David composed 3,600 psalms plus many other songs. In *Aboth* vi:9 David is called the author of the Book of Psalms, and a similar view is reflected in the *NT* (cf. Mk 12:36f.; Rom. 4:6ff., 11:9f.). Furthermore, David is credited with the organization of the cultic worship in Israel (cf. 2 Chr. 29:30; Ezr. 3:10; Neh. 12:24; Sir. 47:7ff.), and in thirteen Psalms we find the so-called historical notes, which purport to give information about the incidents in David's life with which the Psalms in question are associated. Thus they are meant to provide the historical setting in which David either composed or recited these Psalms. Theoretically the phrase 'of David' may well indicate authorship, as in Hab. 3:1, where we find a similar phrase 'A prayer *of Habakkuk* the prophet'.

In view of all this, there is no reason to doubt that David actually composed certain psalms and songs, but it is wellnigh impossible to say which of them, if any, were preserved in the Psalter. Many scholars regard the historical notes as based on 'speculative exegesis of disconnected details' in a midrashic style (so Mowinckel, *PIW*, II, p. 100), and a number of Psalms bearing the phrase 'of David' seem to be later than the reign of David, or the speaker is a descendant of David (cf. 89:3, 19, 49 (M.T.

4, 20, 50), 132:1, 10); sometimes the Temple is already in existence (cf. 24:7, 9) and the social and religious conditions point to a later date (cf. 51:16–19 (M.T. 18–21)). Consequently 'of David' can hardly mean that David was the author of *all* these Psalms, although later generations came to think that the reference is to authorship.

(b) It is possible that in some instances 'of David' means 'on behalf of David' (i.e. the Davidic king), as in Ps. 20, which is an intercession for the king. In the majority of cases the Davidic Psalms may have been composed '*for* David', i.e. for the use of the Davidic king (so Mowinckel, *PIW*, I, p. 77). On the other hand, one has to bear in mind that not all the Psalms marked 'of David' must be Royal Psalms.

In the Ugaritic texts we have notes such as *lʾqht*, *lbʿl*, *lkrt*, at the top of some texts. Here the preposition *l–* seems to introduce the principal person or hero of the particular poem (i.e. 'about Aqhat', 'about Baal', 'about Keret'). Weiser (*POTL*, p. 96) argues that 'of David' may be an analogous construction, suggesting that the Psalm was intended for 'the Davidic ruler who exercises certain functions in the cult and appears there in the role of the ancestor as the bearer of the promises made to David. . .'.

(c) Perhaps the most likely explanation is that in the majority of Psalms we should render our phrase by 'belonging to David', i.e. to the Davidic collection of songs. It is not impossible that this collection included some poems composed by David himself, as well as others written for the use of the Davidic kings (cf. McCullough, *PIB*, p. 8), or derived 'from the archives of the royal palace at Jerusalem' (L. A. F. Le Mat, *Textual Criticism and Exegesis of Psalm XXXVI* (1957), p. 36).

(ii) **of the Sons of Korah:** this term probably indicates that the so-called Korahite Psalms (Ps. 42–3, 44–9, 84–5, 87–8) formed the repertoire of this family of Temple singers (cf. Mowinckel, *PIW*, II, p. 97). It is possible that these poems originated in their circles (see G. Wanke, *Die Zionstheologie der Korachiten* (*BZAW*, 97 (1966), pp. 23–31).

(iii) **of Asaph:** according to Ezr. 2:40, Asaph was the ancestor of Temple singers; the Chronicler (1 Chr. 6:39 (M.T. 24), 15:17, 16:5f.; 2 Chr. 5:12) makes him one of David's chief musicians. 'Asaph' in the Psalm heading may be an abbreviation for 'the sons of Asaph' (so Oesterley, *TP*, p. 16), and it may suggest that the

Asaphite Psalms may have been either composed or handed down by this guild of Temple singers.

(iv) **of Solomon:** see introduction to Ps. 72. Two Psalms (72 and 127) are attributed to Solomon, but this seems to be a late tradition. The Solomonic 'authorship' of Ps. 72 may have been suggested by verses 1, 10, and 15, while that of Ps. 127 may have been deduced from verse 1, assuming that the 'house' is the Temple.

(v) **Heman the Ezrahite:** according to 1 Kg. 4:31 (M.T. 5:11) Heman was one of the famous sages of Solomon's time. In 1 Chr. 15:17, 19 Heman (the same person?) was a Temple singer of David's time, and in 1 Chr. 25:5 he is called 'the king's seer'. It is not clear why Ps. 88 should have been attributed to Heman (or to his collection).

(vi) **Ethan the Ezrahite:** to him is attributed Ps. 89. He is mentioned together with Heman in 1 Kg. 4:31 (M.T. 5:11) and 1 Chr. 15:17, 19.

(vii) **of Moses:** this can hardly be a serious indication of the authorship of Ps. 90; it is probably a late speculation (cf. Mowinckel, *PIW*, II, p. 101f.). This and similar ancient guesses imply that the headings of the Psalms must not always be taken at their face value.

(viii) **to Jeduthun:** this term is found in Ps. 39, and 'according to Jeduthun' in Ps. 62 and 77. In 1 Chr. 16:41 Jeduthun was one of David's chief musicians, and in the Psalms the allusion may be to the family of singers of that name. Mowinckel (*PIW*, II, p. 213) thinks that the term is not a personal name, but means something like 'confession'; hence the Psalms denoted by 'Jeduthun' would be sung at some penitential ritual.

2. TERMS INDICATING THE TYPE OF PSALM

(i) **Psalm** (*mizmôr*) occurs some fifty-seven times; it is a technical term used only in the Psalter. Probably it denotes a cultic song sung to the accompaniment of stringed instruments (cf. Mowinckel, *PIW*, II, p. 208; Kraus, *PBK*, p. xix).

(ii) **Shiggaion** (*šiggāyôn*) is found only in Ps. 7. Mowinckel (*PIW*, II, p. 209) takes it to mean 'a psalm of lamentation'. The noun could also be associated with the verb *š-g-h* ('to err' or 'to wander'), hence a song characterized by a variety of feeling, or irregularity of construction (cf. Davison, *Cent. BP*, I, p. 16); this is, however, dubious. Some exegetes think that *šiggāyôn* is a corruption of *higgāyôn* (so Oesterley, Snaith *et al.*).

(iii) **Miktam** (*miktām*): this term is found in six Psalms (16, 56–60), and Mowinckel (*PIW*, II, p. 209) takes it to mean 'a Psalm of atonement' (connected with the Akkadian *katāmu*, 'to cover (atone)'. For other views, see Kraus, *PBK*, p. xxii).

(iv) **Prayer** (*t^epillāh*): see on 65:2. It is found in the headings of Ps. 17, 86, 90, 102, and 142 (cf. 72:20). In its technical sense it may denote psalms of lamentation.

(v) **Song** (*šîr*): see on 69:30. *Šîr* is a common term for both cultic and secular songs, but in the psalm titles it must have a more specialized meaning which is no longer known; it is found in the headings of some thirty Psalms. A psalm could be both a *šîr* and *mizmôr* (cf. Ps. 65, 75, 76, 92), but the difference beween the two is not clear.

(vi) **Maskil** (*Maśkîl*): this is the designation of a special type of psalm but there is no agreement concerning its translation. Mowinckel (*PIW*, II, p. 209) suggests 'efficacious song', while some of the other proposals are 'a didactic poem', 'a meditation' (Delitzsch), 'a skilful psalm' (Ewald), etc. See Kraus, *PBK*, pp. xxii-xxiii.

(vii) **A Song of Praise** (*t^ehillāh*): see on 65:1, 119:171. This term occurs only in the title of Ps. 145.

(viii) **a love song** (*šîr y^edîdôt*), lit. 'a song of loves' (*AV*): this seems an appropriate designation of Ps. 45 (see Delitzsch, *BCP*, II, pp. 77f.).

(ix) **A Song of Ascents** (*šîr hamma^calôt*): see introduction to Ps. 120; also C. C. Keet, *A Study of the Psalms of Ascents* (1969), pp. 1–17.

3. TERMS INDICATING THE LITURGICAL AIM AND USAGE

(i) **for the thank offering** (for *tôdāh*, see on 69:30). *RSV* links Ps. 100 with the offering of the *tôdāh*; Mowinckel (*PIW*, II, p. 212) thinks that the reference is to a 'congregational festal offering' rather than to a private sacrifice. *RV* offers a possible alternative 'a Psalm of Thanksgiving'.

(ii) **Leannoth** (*l^e^cannôt*; found in Ps. 88): Mowinckel (*PIW*, II, p. 212) understands it as 'for penance' (i.e. from *^c-n-h* III, 'to be afflicted'), while Kraus (*PBK*, p. xxvi) links it with *^c-n-h* IV, 'to sing'. It is not impossible that the phrase **Mahalath Leannoth** constitutes the opening words of a well-known song, to the tune of which the Psalm was to be performed. Mowinckel, however, is dubious of such a usage.

(iii) **for the memorial offering** (*l^ehazkîr*): this term is used in the headings of Ps. 38 and 70, and it may be associated with the so-called *ʾazkārāh* offering or 'memorial' sacrifice (see R. de Vaux, *Studies in Old Testament Sacrifice*, Eng. tr. by J. Bourke and R. Potter (1964), p. 30). Mowinckel (*PIW*, II, p. 212) thinks that the purpose of this song was to 'remind' Yahweh of the distress of the worshipper(s).

(iv) **at the dedication of the Temple:** see introduction to Ps. 30.

(v) **for instruction** (*l^elammēḏ*), *AV* 'to teach': Mowinckel (*PIW*, II, p. 217) thinks that this phrase may not be a liturgical term but that its meaning may be 'to goad on', i.e. to encourage the people. It is unlikely that this expression suggests that the psalm is to be learnt by heart (cf. Kirkpatrick, *BPCB*, p. xxviii).

(vi) **for the Sabbath:** see introduction to Ps. 92.

4. TECHNICAL MUSICAL EXPRESSIONS

(i) **To the choirmaster** (*lam^enaṣṣēaḥ*): this term is found in fifty-five psalms and in Hab. 3:19. The word seems to be a *pi^eʿēl* participle of *n-ṣ-ḥ*, 'to be pre-eminent', etc.; *AV*, *RV* render it by 'the chief Musician', while T suggests 'for praise' (cf. Kirkpatrick, *BPCB*, p. xxi). Mowinckel (*PIW*, II, p. 212) has proposed 'for the merciful disposition (of Yahweh)' taking the verb in its primary sense: 'to beam, shine'; similarly Eaton (*PTBC*, p. 16) who suggests 'for propitiation'. It is quite possible that this term denoted an older collection of psalms (cf. Briggs, *CECBP*, I, p. lxxii-iv. For more details, see E. R. Dalglish, *Psalm Fifty-One* (1962), pp. 234–8). I. Engnell was of the opinion that *lam^enaṣṣēaḥ* was the North-Israelite equivalent of the Jerusalem term *l^eḏāwīḏ* ('to David') (cf. Rowley, *WAI*, p. 210, n.1).

(ii) **with stringed instruments** (*bin^egînôṯ*): this is found in Ps. 4, 6, 54, 55, (61), 67, 76; the note is probably meant to exclude percussion and wind instruments.

(iii) **for the flutes** (*ʾel hann^eḥîlôṯ*): Mowinckel (*PIW*, II, p. 210) points out that the Babylonians had a special kind of lamentation called 'flute psalms of lamentation'. This may be true of Ps. 5.

(iv) **Selah** (*selāh*): this term is found some 74 times in the *OT*: 71 times in the Psalter and 3 times in the book of Habakkuk. Most of the occurrences are in the first three books of the Psalter, and Kirkpatrick (*BPCB*, p. xxii) infers from this that 'Selah is a technical term of great antiquity', while *BDB* (p. 700) suggests that it 'probably came into use in late Persian period'. It seems reasonably clear that 'Selah' was found in the relatively older collections of psalms, but it is less certain that its usage in these collections is as old as the psalms themselves.

In spite of the frequency of 'Selah' in the *OT*, its interpretation is uncertain. Even the ancient versions and writers were not agreed as to its right meaning. On the whole, there are two main ancient traditions of interpreting the word:

(a) LXX (always), Sym and Theod (generally) render it by *diapsalma*, which according to most scholars marks an interlude of some kind in which something else was either sung or played; cf. N. H. Snaith, *VT*, II (1952), p. 54. The Vulgate omits the word entirely.

(b) Most ancient Jewish traditions interpret it as meaning 'for ever' or 'always, everlasting'; so Aquila has *aei* ('for ever'), T uses *lᶜlmyn* and *tdyrᵓ*, while Jerome employs *semper*.

Of the more recent suggestions, two seem more reasonable than others:

(a) 'Selah' could be derived from *s-l-l* ('to lift up'); in which case it might mean 'to lift up one's voice' (i.e. to sing louder), or 'to lift up one's eyes' (i.e. to repeat the verse); the allusion may also be to music (i.e. to come in with loud music), or to some benediction sung by the choir.

(b) Another suggestion is that the term is derived from *s-l-h* which is taken to correspond with the Aramaic *ṣ-l-ᵓ* ('to turn, bend, pray'). If this is right, 'Selah' would indicate the points at which the congregation fell prostrate in respectful homage and submission to God (cf. Mowinckel, *PIW*, II, p. 211). Kraus (*PBK*, p. xxv) draws our attention to certain Sumerian cult poems consisting of ten main sections called *kirugu* ('obeisance'), which seems to suggest that at the end of each section there was kneeling and bowing down.

(v) **Higgaion** (*higgāyôn*): this term is used in 9:16 (M.T. 17); see on 92:3. Mowinckel (*PIW*, II, p. 211) thinks that it indicated some kind of 'musical flourish'.

(vi) **. . . the Sheminith** (*ᶜal haššᵉmînîṯ*): lit. 'on the eighth'. This was often taken as a reference to men's voices an octave lower but this is unlikely (cf. E. Werner, *IDB*, III, p. 459b). The term may refer to some stringed instrument with eight strings (perhaps a harp), or to the eighth stage of some particular ritual (cf. Eaton, *PTBC*, p. 16); cf. also 4Q177 5–6 line 13.

(vii) **the Gittith** (*haggittîṯ*): this is found in Ps. 8, 81, and 84. Its meaning is obscure, but some of the suggestions are 'the Gittite (lyre)', 'for the wine-press' (LXX), 'a vintage melody' (Snaith), etc.; cf. *HAL*, p. 198b.

(viii) **. . . Muth-labben** (*ᶜal mûṯ labbēn*): its literal meaning might be 'for the occasion of death of the son'. The text is, however, suspect; it may be a corruption of *ᶜal ᶜᵃlāmôṯ* (see below); cf. Mowinckel, *PIW*, II, p. 217; S. Jellicoe, *JTS*, XLIX (1948), pp. 52f.

(ix) **The Hind of the Dawn:** see introduction to Ps. 22.

(x) **to Alamoth** (*ᶜal ᶜᵃlāmôṯ*; in Ps. 46): Aquila and Jerome took it to mean 'maidens', but it is doubtful whether women took part in Temple services. LXX suggests 'hidden things, mysteries' (from *ᶜ-l-m* I, 'to hide'), and Mowinckel regards it as a plausible possibility (*PIW*, II, p. 216); cf. *PStud* IV, pp. 35–40.

(xi) **. . . to Lilies** (*ᶜal šōšannîm*): this is used in Ps. 45, 69, and 80, while Ps. 60 has **to Shushan Eduth** (*ᶜal šûšan ᶜēḏûṯ*; Mowinckel renders it 'over the lily of revelation' (*PIW*, II, p. 214)); he thinks that the allusion is to a rite in which omens were taken from lilies, or, in case of Ps. 45, lilies may be symbols of love and fertility. Johnson (*DB*, p. 817a) follows the more usual interpretation, and assumes that the above expressions may be different ways of citing one and the same song. The flower mentioned may be the anemone rather than the lily.

(xii) **. . . Mahalath** (*ᶜal māḥᵃlaṯ*): this term is used in Ps. 53, while **Mahalath Leannoth** is found in Ps. 88. The meaning of these expressions is obscure. Mowinckel (*PIW*, II, p. 210) suggests 'to the flute', which may indicate that the Psalms in question were Laments. It is also possible that the reference is to the tune of the songs.

(xiii) **. . . The Dove on Far-off Terebinths** occurs in the title of Ps. 56, and it is often taken as an indication of the tune (cf. Kraus, *PBK*, p. xxvii), while Mowinckel (*PIW*, II, p. 213, n.16) is sceptical of this suggestion. He sees here a possible allusion to a ritual act associated with atonement; hence the reference would be to a 'psalm of atonement'.

(xiv) **Do Not Destroy:** (*'al tašḥēṯ*; in Ps. 57, 58, 59, and 75). Mowinckel (*PIW*, II, p. 215) argues that the term indicates some ritual act, while Kraus (*PBK*, p. xxviii) finds here a possible allusion to the mode of singing; cf. also Isa. 65:8.

5. HISTORICAL NOTES

Such notes are found in Ps. 3, 7, 18, 34, 51, 52, 54, 56, 57, 59, 60, 63, and 142. For these historical indications, see the respective Psalms; they all seem to be later additions, and they help to understand the interpretation of these psalms by post-Exilic Jewish exegetes (cf. E. R. Dalglish, *Psalm Fifty-One* (1962), pp. 240–8).

V. ISRAELITE FESTIVALS

The Israelite religious calendar contained a number of holy days, such as the New Moon and the Sabbath; but of special importance were the three great annual festivals: the Passover and the Feast of Unleavened Bread, the Harvest Festival, and the Feast of Tabernacles. It seems that these three cultic occasions provided the background for most of the Psalms in the Psalter; the worshippers would take part not only in the annual celebrations, but they would also perform any personal religious obligations, such as votive sacrifices, prayers, etc.

1. THE PASSOVER AND FEAST OF UNLEAVENED BREAD

The earliest list of cultic festivals, in Exod. 23:14–17 does not mention the Passover, but it does not mean that this feast was a late institution; it simply suggests that at this time the Passover was not one of the pilgrimage festivals. It is very likely that the Passover was an ancient Israelite pastoral festival, and originally different from the three agricultural feasts of the Canaanite cultic calendar. The Passover was not only a time when the events of the Exodus would be remembered, but also an occasion on which the deliverance from Egypt would be re-enacted. It is not clear, however, when the Passover was first associated with the Exodus story (cf. Rowley, *WAI*, p. 88; Ringgren, *IR*, pp. 187f.). It was celebrated on the 14th of Nisan (i.e. the first month of the Babylonian calendar, where the year began in the spring).

At some point the Passover was linked with the Feast of Unleavened Bread, which lasted seven days. During the latter festival a sheaf of barley was presented before Yahweh, as well as other offerings (cf. Lev. 23:9–14), and only unleavened bread made from the new grain was eaten. Although the Feast of Unleavened Bread was adopted from the Canaanites (so also the other agricultural festivals), it was greatly modified; now it was kept 'unto Yahweh' (Exod. 23:14), and at an early date it must have been historicized, thus breaking the links with the nature myths. For further details, see Kraus, *WI*, pp. 45–55; de Vaux, *AI*, pp. 484–93, 550f.

2. THE FEAST OF WEEKS

It was also called the Harvest Festival (Exod. 23:16) or the Wheat Harvest (Exod. 34:22), and it was known in NT times as Pentecost. Originally it may have been a one-day festival but later it was extended into a seven-day celebration (Num. 28:24). During the festival sacrifices were offered, and the firstfruits of the wheat harvest were presented; on the whole it was a joyful occasion (cf. *IDB*, IV, p. 828).

Eventually this festival too was related to the salvation history of the nation. Kraus (*WI*, p. 59) thinks that 'in the third century B.C. the solemn renewal of the Covenant with God was part of the Feast of Weeks...'. It is very likely that in the pre-Exilic period this Covenant ceremony was linked with the Feast of Tabernacles. For further details and bibliography, see de Vaux, *AI*, pp. 493ff., 551.

3. THE FEAST OF TABERNACLES

This is the last festival in the cultic calendar, and also the most important one. Even in the time of Josephus, it was regarded as 'the holiest and the greatest of Hebrew feasts' (*Antiquities* VIII, iv. 1). In the earliest lists in the OT, it is referred to as the 'Feast of Ingathering' (cf. Exod. 23:16) or the 'feast of Yahweh' (Jg. 21:19); sometimes it is simply called the 'Feast' (1 Kg. 8:2; Neh. 8:14). Later it came to be known as the Feast of Booths or Tabernacles (cf. Dt. 16:13). At one time it may have been the only Israelite pilgrimage festival (cf. 1 Sam. 1:3,21). It was held at the end of the year (Exod. 34:22), and it began on the 15th day of the seventh month (September/October), and it lasted for seven days.

Since this feast was celebrated at the turn of the year, it is very likely that it possessed the character of the New Year Festival also. The term 'New Year' is found only in Ezek. 40:1, but even here it is dubious; yet this is no proof that there was no New Year in the pre-Exilic Israel. As Mowinckel has pointed out (*PIW*, II, p. 230), 'we are not dealing with a new, as yet unknown and just postulated festival, but with a hitherto unnoticed aspect of the well-known main festival of the year . . .', i.e. the Feast of Tabernacles. Thus the real point of any relevant argument is the *nature* of the great Autumnal Festival. In Mowinckel's opinion the Israelite New Year was primarily concerned with the enthronement of Yahweh, and therefore he speaks about the so-called Enthronement Festival (see Introduction, p. 33ff.); for a brief summary on this subject, see Rowley, *WAI*, pp. 184–92; cf. also E. Lipiński, 'Les psaumes de la royauté de Yahwé dans l' exégèse moderne', *LPOBL*, pp. 133–272; de Vaux, *AI*, pp. 551f.

It is very likely that another aspect of the Feast of Tabernacles was the Covenant Renewal, which originally may have taken place every seventh year (Dt. 31:10). The main aspects of this ritual would be a re-presentation of the Sinai events, a recital of the Law, a promise of blessings, and a threat of curses for the disobedient, as well as the conclusion of the Covenant (cf. Exod. 19–24; Jos. 24). For more details, see Weiser, *POTL*, pp. 23–52.

Kraus has rightly stressed yet another aspect of this great Festival, namely the choice of Jerusalem and the election of the Davidic dynasty (see Kraus, *WI*, pp. 179–222).

At a later time the Feast of Tabernacles was split into three parts: the (New Year's) Day on the first of the seventh month (Lev. 23:23ff.), the Day of Atonement on the tenth day of Tishri (i.e. the seventh month) (cf. Lev. 23:26–32), and the Feast of Tabernacles itself on 15–21st Tishri (cf. Lev. 23:33–6).

COMMENTARY ON THE BOOK OF PSALMS

Psalms 1–72

BOOK I

Psalm 1 The Two Ways of Mankind

This Psalm is regarded as a prologue or an introduction to the whole Psalter, and Dahood calls it 'a précis of the Book of Psalms' (*PAB*, I, p. 1). At one time it was either not numbered at all or it was combined with Ps. 2 (cf. Briggs, *CECBP*, I, p. 3). Thus in the Western texts of Ac. 13:33 a quotation from Ps. 2 is cited as from Ps. 1; in the Talmud (*Berakoth*, 9b) it is stated that the first and second psalms (according to our numbering) formed one division or lesson. Neither the first nor the second psalm has a title or superscription, and this may have facilitated the confusion. Psalm 1 may have been added to the Psalter by the final editor but it does not necessarily follow that *he* must have composed it for the purpose of providing a preface to the whole collection; it could have been taken from some other source, and it may predate the final edition of the Book of Psalms.

This poem is rather unusual; its style is more didactic than psalmodic, and therefore it has been described as a 'reflective poem rather than a psalm for use in public' (G. W. Anderson, *PCB*, 361a). Some exegetes (e.g. S. Bullough, 'The Question of Metre in Psalm 1', *VT*, XVII (1967), pp. 42–9) are of the opinion that our Psalm is a *prose* account of the happiness of the righteous and the doom of the wicked, yet the traditional view may well be right. Although the Psalm hardly fits into any of the better known literary types, its connexion with the cult is not improbable. It could be a more recent variation of the ancient curses and blessings, of which some examples are found in Dt. 27:11–28:6; Jer. 17:5–8.

The general impression of the Psalm is that it represents a comparatively late stage in the history of *OT* religion, and therefore it must belong to the post-Exilic period. The choice of the vocabulary and the contents of the Psalm point to a connexion with the Wisdom literature; its emphasis on the written Law and the teaching about reward and punishment is reminiscent of the later Jewish piety. Also the similarity with Jer. 17:5–8 implies the priority of the passage from the Book of Jeremiah, rather than vice versa, thus suggesting a post-Exilic date. See also E. P. Arbez, *CBQ*, VII (1945), pp. 398–404; P. Auvray, *RB*, LIII (1946), pp. 365–71.

The Psalm can be divided into two main parts: verses 1–3 depict the attractiveness of the godly life, while verses 4–6 describe the ultimate futility of the godless existence.

The metre, if any, is irregular.

THE PORTRAIT OF THE RIGHTEOUS **1–3**

1. Blessed is the man: this formula of joyful affirmation is found mainly in the Book of Psalms and in the Book of Proverbs, and therefore it is more at home in the so-called Wisdom literature. It is always found in connexion with people but never with reference to God, because this blessedness may have been regarded as the gracious gift of God. A similar formula is found in the beatitudes of Mt. 5 which may be based on the *OT* pattern. The etymology of *ʾašᵉrê* ('blessed') is uncertain, and no translation is able to reproduce the full significance of the Hebrew term. Some translators prefer 'happy' (*NEB*) or 'Oh the blessedness of', but on the basis of the various texts in which this word occurs (cf. 41:1ff. (M.T. 2ff.), 94:12f., 127:3ff., 128:1–4, 145:12–15, etc.) we may paraphrase this joyous exclamation as 'how rewarding is the life of'. W. Janzen ('ʾAšrê in the Old Testament', *HTR*, LVIII (1965), pp. 215–26) regards *ʾašᵉrê* as an expression of 'envious desire' and renders it 'To be envied is the man . . .'. See also J. Alberto Soggin, 'Zum ersten Psalm', *ThZ*, XXIII (1967), pp. 81f. In the above-mentioned phrase the emphasis is on the material side of human existence, but spiritual blessings are not excluded because true welfare and prosperity are the echo of a righteous life. This formula is not addressed to men in general but to that kind of person who is described in verses 1–3. Women and children are included because, in the Israelite view, part of man's true happiness is his family—a good wife and many children—and so *his* blessings (as well as his responsibilities) are shared by the whole family.

The description of the happy man in verse 1 consists of three phrases, and the respective terms are thought to form a climax: 'wicked', 'sinners', 'scoffers' and 'walks', 'stands', 'sits'. On the other hand, the three clauses form a synonymous parallelism, and therefore the corresponding terms merely repeat the same thought in different words without any intentional grading of the godless and their actions. The main point of this threefold picture is to show that the truly righteous man does not follow the godless way of life.

the wicked: the Hebrew *rᵉšāʿîm* may have originally denoted men who had been proved guilty of a particular charge (cf. L. Koehler, *Old Testament Theology* (1957), p. 171), but in the Psalter this term usually refers to men who are the enemies of God, and therefore also the adversaries of his people. They may consist not only of the ungodly in Israel but also of the Gentiles or foreign enemies (cf. Mowinckel, *PIW*, I, p. 208). 'To walk in the counsel of the wicked' means to follow their advice rather than the guidance of God.

sinners: the term *ḥaṭṭāʾîm* signifies those men who miss the mark (or 'their way'; cf. Prov. 19:2), or who deviate from the accepted standards. The intensive form of the Hebrew word may indicate that their straying from the right path has become a habit and is no longer an accidental error. 'To stand in the way of sinners' is to share their way of life (cf. Prov. 1:10–19; Jer. 23:18).

the seat of scoffers: the Hebrew *môšāḇ* means not only 'seat' or 'place of sitting down' but also 'session' or 'assembly'. The latter connotation is, perhaps, more appropriate to verse 1, and a parallel to this usage is found in 1QS VI:8,11; VII:10, etc. 'Scoffers' (*lēṣîm*) are the self-sufficient who act with haughty pride (Prov. 21:24), and who refuse to accept instruction both from God and from men (cf. Prov. 15:12; Mal. 3:13ff.). They scoff at the ways of the wise and of the righteous, and thereby they set themselves against God and incur *his* scorn (Prov. 3:34). 'To sit in the seat of the scoffers' amounts to making light of God's law which ought to be one's delight; it also means identifying oneself with the thinking and planning of the godless (cf. Isa. 5:11f.).

2. **the law of the LORD:** the Hebrew *tôrāh* is usually rendered by 'law' although this is hardly an adequate translation to convey the full meaning of the Hebrew equivalent (see on 119:1). In our context 'law' is not primarily something which has to be adhered to, word for word, but it is the revelation of the will of Yahweh, which is both demanding and liberating. It was perhaps this 'law' that Jesus said he had not come to abolish but to fulfil (cf. Mt. 5:17). Such a 'law' is not opposed to grace, because it presupposes both the grace of God and his mercy. 'The law of the LORD' in this verse probably refers to a written document, but it would be pointless to attempt its identification. This 'law', far

from being a burden or an unbearable yoke, is the 'delight' of the godly man. Perhaps we should render 'his delight . . .' as 'his concern (or 'preoccupation') is with the law of the LORD'; this might give a slightly better parallel to the following line (cf. also Isa. 58:3,13 margin). N. H. Snaith (*The Distinctive Ideas of the Old Testament* (1944), p. 98) describes this man as a scribe 'whose full-time occupation is in the Law of the LORD', but this need not be the case (see 1QS VI:6ff.).

he meditates: this same verb *h-g-h* is used of a young lion growling over his prey (Isa. 31:4), of the moaning of a dove (Isa. 38:14), and as a synonym of 'to speak' (37:30, 71:24) or 'to remember and to muse on' (143:5). In CD X:6, XIII:2 we find 'the book of *hgw*', which is sometimes rendered as 'the book of recitation'. 'He meditates' may mean in our context 'he reads to himself in a low tone', and the purpose of this activity is clear from Jos. 1:8: '. . . you shall meditate on it day and night, that you may be careful to do according to all that is written in it; for then you shall make your way prosperous . . .'. So this 'meditation' is not merely an intellectual exercise but, above all, it is a study of the will of God for the purpose of doing it.

day and night: i.e. continually. L. Köhler (*Hebrew Man* (1956), p. 101) thinks that 'one who cannot sleep—usually the fate of the old—may "meditate in his law day and night" '. It is more likely, however, that the righteous man's dependence upon the revealed will of God must be *unbroken*, whether he is old or young. This regulation (or a similar one) was taken quite literally by the Qumran sectarians (cf. 1QS VI:6f.), so that in each of their communities there always was a man studying the Law.

3. The comparison of the godly man with a luxuriant tree is a well-known picture in the *OT* (cf. 92:12ff. (M.T. 13ff.); Jer. 11:19, 17:8; Ezek. 17:5–10,22ff., 19:10). A similar metaphor is also found in the *Wisdom of Amen-em-ope* (an Egyptian text dated between c. 1000 and c. 600 B.C.; see *DOTT*, p. 178) as well as in 1QH X:25, etc. We can only guess what kind of tree the Psalmist had in mind, but it may have been a palm tree, as in 92:12 (M.T. 13).

planted: lit. 'transplanted'. This may be intended to imply that the happiness of the godly man is entirely due to God's action. Dahood (*PAB*, I, p. 3) argues that it suggests that the righteous man will be transferred to the Elysian Fields or its Hebrew equivalent. It is far more likely that the allusion is to the *present*

life; furthermore, the Elysian Fields are not attested in the *OT* and their 'discovery' rests on dubious interpretation.
streams of water (*palᵉgê mayim*): may refer to artificial irrigation channels such as are found in Egypt and Mesopotamia. This need not suggest that the metaphor was not 'at home' in Palestine; there the difference between trees by the water-side and those in less favourable places would be equally noticeable. The well-watered tree follows the pattern of its kind, undisturbed by any capricious weather, and therefore it yields abundant fruit **in its season**, i.e. at the proper time as well as regularly, unfailingly; **its leaf** or foliage does not wither during the drought. The point of the metaphor is to stress the fruitfulness and vitality of the life of the godly man, as well as its stability, rather than to providc a symbol of immortality (so Dahood).
In all that he does, he prospers: this is often regarded as a later addition, derived from Jos. 1:8, because the subject is no longer the tree but the righteous man himself. The phrase could also be rendered 'and whatever he does, it prospers' (cf. Oesterley, *TP*, p. 121). This is primarily a statement of faith rather than the result of the observation of human fortunes. The image of the luxuriant tree need not suggest the idea of reward but it may point to the fact that the tree is fulfilling the function for which it was created. Similarly the life of the righteous man could be regarded as reflecting human existence as God meant it to be (cf. Weiser, *POTL*, pp. 105f.).

THE PORTRAIT OF THE GODLESS **1:4–6**

4. The wicked are not so: lit. 'Not so the wicked'. LXX adds after this phrase an emphatic repetition 'not so' (so also V); this may well be the original reading.

The godless are **like chaff**, and this simile is probably intended to describe both the men themselves and their destiny. They are thought of as having become worthless in themselves, and their life as empty and without permanence, as long as they continue their present way of life. It is only the relationship with God that can give true substance and dignity to human life. The word-picture was familiar to the contemporaries of the Psalmist; every harvest-time they saw the corn being threshed and winnowed on the local threshing floor situated on some open, elevated site. During the winnowing, the corn, still mixed with broken straw and chaff, was thrown into the wind, which separated the heavy grain from the lighter straw, while the chaff was blown far away. Thus 'chaff' provided a good description of all that was passing and useless. The metaphor of winnowing is not infrequently used of divine judgement (cf. 35:5; Hos. 13:3; 1QH VII:23).

5. This verse creates considerable difficulties for the exegete, and the main problem is the interpretation of **judgment.** Some of the suggestions are as follows: 'the great Messianic Assize' (Boylan, *PSVP*, I, p. 3), 'the dispensation of divine judgment in this life' (G. W. Anderson, *PCB*, 361a), 'every act of judgment by which Jehovah separates between the righteous and the wicked' (Kirkpatrick, *BPCB*, p. 4). Dahood (*PAB*, I, p. 4) takes *mišpāṭ* ('judgment') to mean 'the place of judgment', and argues that the wicked will not be admitted to the final judgment in the heavenly council, but that they will be condemned *in absentia.* Thus they will have no chance of being in the congregation of the righteous. It is possible that **judgment** in this verse refers both to the continuous divine judgment as well as to that at the end-time (cf. Mal. 3:2). God continually removes the sinners from the congregation of the righteous, and this process will be brought to completion at the coming day of the Lord (cf. 1QS II:11–18).

Consequently also the meaning of **will not stand** depends largely upon the interpretation given to 'the judgment'. Most of the ancient versions saw here a reference to the resurrection from the dead, and some have argued (e.g. Briggs) that the wicked would have no part in the resurrection because only the righteous would rise (cf. Isa. 26:14–19). In spite of the antiquity of this and similar interpretations, the more likely view is that 'to stand' (*ḳ-w-m*) simply means 'to last, endure' in God's judgment, as in Nah. 1:6: 'Who can stand before his indignation? Who can endure the heat of his anger?'

the congregation of the righteous: the meaning of this phrase is also linked with the understanding of verse 5*a*, but the allusion probably is to the worshipping community (cf. 111:1) which would eventually become the Messianic community. For *'ēḏāh* ('congregation)', see on 74:2.

the righteous: the Hebrew *ṣaddîḳîm* describes persons who are what they should be. The criterion is not primarily certain ethical norms as such, but the fulfilment of the demands of the relationships within which one finds oneself. The Israelite stood in a particular relationship to his God, his fellow men, and his world in general, and each of these relationships made certain demands upon him from day to day. The righteous man accepted his responsibilities and carried them out accordingly. The same term (*ṣaddîḵ*) can also be used of God (cf. 7:9,11 (M.T. 10, 12), 11:7, 119:137, 129:4).

6. knows: the verb *y-d-*ᶜ suggests not merely intellectual knowledge, for in this sense God would also know the way of the wicked, but it implies a personal relationship and points to God's care for the existence of the righteous (as in 3:17 (M.T. 8), 144:3). *RP* renders 'preserveth', while Soggin (op. cit., p. 88) suggests 'loves'; *NEB* has 'watches over'.

the way of the righteous is contrasted with that of the wicked, which turns out to be a sort of *cul-de-sac* because in the end it perishes. Since the godless have no regard for the Law of God, God cannot have a real regard for their way, because the Law is the God-given guide to his people, and consequently those who reject that guidance also repudiate God's concern for them, and thereby they cut the very ground from under their own feet. They say to God 'Depart from us! We do not desire the knowledge of thy ways' (Job 21:14). For *dereḵ* ('way'), see on 103:7, 146:9.

Psalm 2 Man Proposes, God Disposes

This Psalm has no superscription, and it may not have belonged to the original Davidic Psalter. Although occasionally it has been linked with Ps. 1 (see introduction to Ps. 1), the contents of the two Psalms are quite different, and therefore it is unlikely that they ever formed a literary unity. It may be said that, just as Ps. 1 presents before us the Two Ways for individuals, so Ps. 2 deals with the Two Ways for nations (cf. Cohen, *PSon*, p. 3); but this similarity may be purely accidental.

Ps. 2 can be classed as a Royal Psalm (see Introduction, pp. 39f) in which the King is unmistakably in the foreground. Its cultic setting was either the enthronement of the King or the yearly celebration of his accession, and it was, apparently, a part of the ritual used on such regular festive occasions, which were not merely political in nature but also important religious events (cf. Johnson, *SKAI*, pp. 118ff.). Mowinckel (*PIW*, I, p. 64) tries to be more explicit by suggesting that in its form the Psalm is 'the king's first proclamation to his subjects' (see verse 7).

The older commentators used to attribute this Psalm to David or Solomon (cf. Kirkpatrick, *BPCB*, p. 5), but at the present time the general opinion is that although Ps. 2 is of pre-Exilic origin, it is impossible to be more exact. Its author may have been the reigning King (cf. verse 6) or, more likely, a cultic (or 'court') prophet. The speaker in the Psalm seems to be the King, but some scholars have argued that this poem was part of a coronation ritual with different speakers (so e.g. Barnes). More recently Marco Treves ('Two Acrostic Psalms', *VT*, xv (1965), pp. 81–5) has argued that Ps. 2 is an acrostic psalm containing the phrase: 'Sing ye to Jannaeus the First and his wife.' This view is, however, unlikely (see also B. Lindars, 'Is Psalm II an Acrostic Psalm?', *VT*, xvii (1967), pp. 60–7), although a few scholars, with some justification, have assigned the Psalm to the post-Exilic period (e.g. Deissler), in which case it would be a prophetic-eschatological song describing the *coming* 'David' (cf. Jer. 23:5, 30:9; Ezek. 34:23, 37:24). The author may have adapted an earlier Royal Psalm. The messianic interpretation of the Psalm is also supported in the *NT* (cf. Ac. 4:25f., 13:33; Heb. 1:5, 5:5; Rev. 2:27, 19:18), which applies it to Jesus of Nazareth. The most likely view seems to be the cultic interpretation which associates the poem with the ritual of the enthronement of the successive Davidic monarchs.

Another problem is the universal setting, which implies that the Psalmist could hardly be describing any specific historical situation, even though David's kingdom might have ranked as an empire. This idealistic framework has partly contributed to the messianic understanding of the Psalm. It is possible, however, to account for the so-called unrealistic picture by supposing that the author was following a well-established foreign pattern, and that the apparently arrogant language was simply that of the traditional court style; e.g., Cyrus speaks of himself as 'the king of the world' and 'the king of the four quarters' (see *DOTT*, p. 93); yet even his kingdom did not include all the inhabited world as known at that time. An alternative or supplementary view is provided by the Israelite belief that Yahweh, who is the Lord of the whole world and all its history, is also present at the enthronement of his regent. Therefore, however insignificant might be the actual kingdom of the Davidic king, behind him was Yahweh, the Creator and the actual Lord of all the kingdoms of this world. As God's regent (and adopted son), the King 'exercised' a universal rule, even though to his contemporaries it appeared that his dominion extended only over Judah. Thus the glory of the Davidic king was a hidden one, made real only in the cult. Consequently the Psalm need not have sounded presumptuous coming from the lips of the King of Judah, which was unimportant in comparison with the great empires of the ancient Near East.

The Psalm consists of four strophes, and the metre is mainly 3+3. The first strophe (verses 1–3) describes the futile conspiracy of the nations of the world against the Lord and his anointed. The second strophe (verses 4–6) expresses the reaction of Yahweh who views their rebellious plans with utter derision. The third strophe (verses 7–9) declares the decree of Yahweh concerning his anointed one and outlines the regent's authority. The final strophe (verses 10–12) consists of an ultimatum to the leaders of the peoples and an exhortation to serve Yahweh.

THE FUTILE PLANNING OF THE NATIONS **1–3**

1. The Psalm opens with a rhetorical question expressing astonishment at the pointless plotting of the peoples, but at the same time it voices a quiet confidence in God.

Why do the nations conspire: the death of the old King and the accession of the new one were frequently the signal for a rebellion among the subject nations, and this familiar political pattern provided the Psalmist with a suitable word-picture. It is less likely that the writer had in mind a particular historical situation (see above), such as the revolt of states like Ammon, Edom, and Moab; rather the existence of Israel was continually threatened by the nations, and the universal rule of God was challenged by the worship of other gods. Hence Ps. 2 is essentially a statement of faith.

plot in vain: or 'scheme to no purpose'. The verb 'plot' is the same as 'meditate' in 1:2, and it may suggest the murmuring of the conspirators as they forge their futile plans. Dahood (*PAB*, I, p. 7) suggests 'number their troops', and he finds some support for this in the Ugaritic literature where the cognate verb may have the meaning 'to count', and in Gen. 14:14; Jg. 9:4, 11:3 which, in his opinion, offer instances of the word *rîḳ* (*RSV* 'in vain') used in the sense of 'troops'.

2. The interrogative force of 'why' in verse 1 may also extend to this verse, thus providing a parallel to verse 1.

the kings . . . the rulers are synonyms, and denote the leaders of the enemies of God (cf. 76:12 (M.T. 13), 102:15, 148:11; see also Jg. 5:3; Isa. 40:23; Hab. 1:10).

set themselves: rather than 'stand up' (*RP*). The underlying thought is that of preparing for a battle (cf. 1 Sam. 17:16; Jer. 46:4; 1QM VIII:3, XVI:5, XVII:11).
and his anointed: lit. 'and against his anointed'. Ritual anointing was neither a strictly royal practice nor a rite peculiar to Israel (cf. de Vaux, *AI*, pp. 104ff.). In the *OT* anointing was used to consecrate objects, such as an altar (Exod. 29:36; Num. 7:10), the Ark (Exod. 30:26), or the Tabernacle (Lev. 8:10), as well as persons, e.g., priests (Exod. 28:41; Num. 3:3), prophets (1 Kg. 19:16; 1 Chr. 16:22; Ps. 105:15), and kings (1 Sam. 10:1, 16:3; 1 Kg. 1:39; 2 Kg. 9:6; etc). In Ps. 2 the anointed one is the Davidic king who, as the Lord's anointed, is regarded as sacrosanct (cf. 1 Sam. 24:6,10; 26:9,11,23; 1 Kg. 21:10,13). See also E. Kutsch, *Salbung als Rechtsakt*, (*BZAW*, 87 (1963)), pp.52–66.
saying: this word is supplied by the translators.

3. bonds . . . cords: the reference is probably to the leather thongs which lashed the yoke-bar(s) to the horns or neck of the animal (cf. Jer. 27:2). Here they are used by metonymy for 'yoke' (cf. the use of 'crown' for 'king') which provides an appropriate symbol of subjection and servitude. The possessive pronoun **their** refers to Yahweh and his regent. Verse 3 is a figurative description of a rebellion against authority (as in Jer. 2:30, 5:5).

YAHWEH'S RESPONSE **4–6**

4. He who sits: (*RP* 'He that dwelleth') or better 'He who sits enthroned (as king)' (cf. 1 Kg. 7:25; Am. 1:8). Yahweh's throne is in heaven (11:4, 103:19), and thus it is the divine King who speaks, and who is infinitely superior to all earthly rulers.
laughs . . . has in derision: these anthropomorphic descriptions of God express the belief that the Almighty is able to share in human feelings, but that he is not reduced to the level of human beings (cf. 37:13, 59:8 (M.T. 9)). The picture of the scornful God ought not to be taken as a credal statement, because it is primarily a poetic description; it is meant to show that the hostile efforts of God's enemies are simply laughable (cf. Isa. 40:22ff.).
the LORD: the M.T. has *ʾaḏōnāy*, although a number of Hebrew MSS. have the tetragrammaton (*yhwh*), of which 'Jehovah' was the traditional but incorrect pronunciation; the generally accepted rendering of the divine name is 'Yahweh', while 'Jehovah' is made up of the tetragrammaton read with the vowels of *ʾaḏōnāy* ('lord').

5. Then: this marks the turning point at which the hidden God will make himself known as the God who intervenes in history—the point where cultic experience will be substantiated by actual events.

he will speak . . . in his wrath: the divine word is power and it will accomplish what it says. Dahood (*PAB*, I, p. 6) puts forward the ingenious rendering: 'Then he drives away their lieutenants in his ire . . .'. This translation is possible linguistically, but it seems less suited to the general context (cf. verses 9 and 12) which speaks of the vain planning but not of an actual defeat.

6. I have set my king: some scholars (e.g. Kissane, *BP*, p. 6) follow LXX, V, and render 'And I have been set up as king upon Sion His holy mountain', reading *nissaḵtî meleḵ . . . ḳoḏšô* for M.T. *nāsaḵtî malkî . . . ḳoḏšî* ('I have set my king . . . my holy (mountain)'). Dahood (*PAB*, I, p. 10) suggests 'I have been anointed (*neSūḵōṯî*) his king', and he regards the suffix of *malkî* (*RSV* 'my king') as the third person singular masculine, and equivalent to the Phoenician *-y*, meaning 'his' (or 'hers'). These suggestions are not impossible, but M.T. seems to give the most likely reading, underlining the contrast between the words of the kings of the earth and those of the King of kings.

Zion, my holy hill: LXX and V have '. . . his holy hill'. In the time of David the stronghold of Zion was identified with the city of David (2 Sam. 5:7), but later the name 'Zion' (see on 65:1) was transferred to the Temple hill (cf. 132:13; Mic. 4:2) and to the whole city of Jerusalem (cf. Isa. 10:24; Jer. 3:14; Am. 6:1). In the present verse it is used of Jerusalem (cf. 48:1f. (M.T. 2f.)) and it points to the election of Jerusalem, just as verse 6 expresses the election of the Davidic dynasty.

YAHWEH'S DECREE 7–9

The speaker of verses 7–9 (and 10–12?) is the King, but if we follow the rendering of LXX and V, then the whole Psalm may have been uttered by the King (cf. Mowinckel, *PIW*, I, p. 64ff.).

7. the decree of the Lord: most recent exegetes take it to be the royal protocol giving the substance of the Davidic covenant. The form and contents of this may have been reminiscent of those found in Eygpt, and the Canaanite royal ritual may have played a mediating role. The Egyptian protocols contain in particular the ancient titles and sovereign rights and duties conferred on the Pharaoh by the god. For various parallels, see G. v. Rad, 'The

Royal Ritual in Judah', *PHOE*, pp. 225ff.; K. A. Kitchen, *Ancient Orient and Old Testament* (1966), pp. 106–11. For *ḥōḳ* ('decree'), see on 119:5.

You are my son: this is a formula of adoption (cf. the Code of Hammurabi 170–1, in *ANET*, p. 173), but it does not imply that the king was deified (cf. 2 Sam. 7:14; 1 Chr. 28:6). It is noteworthy that, although the *OT* prophets often criticized the kings, they were not accused of claiming divinity. In Mowinckel's opinion it is 'the election, the anointing and the installation which are viewed as an adoption' (*PIW*, I, p. 65).

today I have begotten you: (cf. Num. 11:12; Dt. 32:18). 'Today' probably refers to the day of coronation or, perhaps, to its re-enactment during the annual autumn festival. In M.T. the emphasis is not on 'today' but on '*I myself* (have begotten you this day)'. The idea of begetting may be part of the non-Israelite prototype of the royal document, but in our context it can only refer to the adoption of the King and the declaration of his sonship. Weiser (*POTL*, p. 113) points out that by this act 'special importance is attributed not to the person of the King but to his office'. Cf. L. Sabourin, *The Psalms*, II (1969), p. 215.

8. Ask of me: Dahood (*PAB*, I, p. 12) reads *māmōnî* for M.T. *mimmennî*, and he renders: 'Ask wealth of me'; this, however, is hardly an improvement. Some scholars delete the phrase because it is 'unnecessary to the sense, since the inheritance is the consequence of the sonship, and not of the request, or to the parallelism . . .' (H. H. Rowley, 'The Text and Structure of Psalm II', *JTS*, XLII (1941), p. 150). *NEB* gives an interpretative rendering: 'Ask of me what you will'.

the nations your heritage: i.e. the King as a son is the heir (cf. Gal. 4:7; also Mt. 21:28; Mk 12:7) and, since Yahweh is the Lord of all the world, the son's inheritance consists of all peoples and their lands (cf. Gen. 48:4; Dt. 20:16).

the ends of the earth: i.e. all the earth (see on 59:13, 72:8; cf. Mic. 5:4 (M.T. 3); Zech. 9:10).

9. You shall break them: LXX, S, and Jerome read: 'you shall shepherd (or 'rule') them' (i.e. *tirʿēm* for M.T. *tᵉrōʿēm*; see also Rev. 2:27, 19:15), but M.T. is supported by the parallelism of verse 9*b*. The substance of this verse is that, if need be, the King will defeat all his enemies and will be able to establish a righteous rule (cf. Isa. 11:4).

a rod of iron: this may be the royal sceptre in the form of a long

staff or a short-handled battle mace. Here it serves as a symbol of the might of the Lord's anointed. For 'iron', see on 107:10.
dash them in pieces . . .: the smashing of a vessel is a descriptive picture of an effortless but complete destruction (see Isa. 30:14; Jer. 19:11). The shattered vessel could not be mended, and the tiny fragments were of no use; such will be the fate of the King's enemies (i.e. the adversaries of God) if they continue in their state of rebellion.

THE WARNING **10–12**

10. The ultimatum is addressed to the kings of the world (for the form, see Prov. 8:32). If they wish to avoid destruction, they must serve Yahweh (verse 11); this is the beginning of all wisdom. It is possible that the Psalmist was thinking of the conversion of the Gentiles (cf. Weiser, *POTL*, p. 115). The speaker is probably the king as Yahweh's representative; similar expressions are also attributed to Yahweh (cf. Jer. 6:8; see also Wis. 6:1).
rulers: lit. 'judges'. E. A. Speiser (*Genesis* (*AB* 1 (1964)), p. 134) points out that the basic sense of *šāpaṭ* ('judged') is 'to exercise authority', hence 'to govern, decide'; see on 72:2.

11. Serve the Lord: in its religious aspect it means to worship Yahweh, while politically it implies a submission to his vicegerent. There may be a word-play on *ᶜ-b-d* ('to serve') in verse 11, and *ʾ-b-d* ('to perish') in verse 12; unless the nations decide to serve Yahweh, they shall perish.
with trembling kiss his feet: this phrase is a well-known *crux interpretum*, and it may be the result of a textual corruption. M.T. reads: 'and rejoice with trembling. Kiss the son'. The first part of this rendering provides a poor parallel to verse 11*a*, while 'rejoicing' and 'trembling' form an odd pair. Furthermore, the word used for 'son' is the Aramaic *bar* instead of the Hebrew *bēn* (used in verse 7). Although Aramaisms as such are not surprising, the present one is somewhat unexpected. These and other difficulties have been reflected in the great variety of renderings among the ancient versions; e.g., LXX translates: 'and rejoice in him with trembling. Lay hold of instruction', while T has: 'and pray with trembling. Receive instruction'. For the last phrase Sym and Jerome have 'worship purely'. *RSV* and most recent commentators have followed the emendation proposed by Bertholet, reading, with a slight variation, *ûḇirᶜāḏāh naššᵉḳû ḇᵉraḡlāyw*. Dahood (*PAB*, I, p. 6) proposes 'and live in trembling, O mortal men', taking *gîl*

('to rejoice') in the sense of 'to live' (cf. ibid., p. 13) and changing *naššᵉḳû ḇar* ('kiss the son') into *nᵉšê ḳāḇer* ('men of grave'). It seems, however, that the usual emendation is the simplest solution of the *crux*. The kissing of the feet is a well-known act of self-humiliation and homage (cf. 72:9; Isa. 49:23; Mic. 7:17; Lk. 7:38,45); e.g., the Assyrian king, Sennacherib (705–681 B.C.), reports how the kings of Syria and Palestine brought gifts to him and kissed his feet (see *ANET*, p. 287b; *ANEP*, Pl. 351). It is possible that *naššᵉḳû ḇar* may mean 'kiss the field', i.e. the ground before the king, as a gesture of submission (cf. H. Ringgren, *The Messiah in the Old Testament*, *SBT*, XVIII (1956), p. 12h, n.l.), but this would not solve *all* the problems of this verse.

12. lest he be angry: the subject of the verb is Yahweh, as in verse 5.

and you perish in the way: for the thought, cf. Dt. 6:15. Dahood (*PAB*, I, p. 6) renders 'and your assembly perish'. His translation is based on the assumption that the Ugaritic *drkt* ('dominion, throne') underwent a semantic transition from 'dominion' to 'the place where it is exercised', i.e. 'assembly' (see ibid., p. 2). It is, however, more convincing to take *dereḵ* ('way') to mean 'in respect of (your) way' (cf. Gunkel, *PGHAT*, p. 12).

Blessed: see on 1:1. This last sentence is often regarded as a later addition to the Psalm, but there is no valid reason why its originality should be doubted. It provides an appropriate conclusion to the final verse, as well as to the whole poem.

Psalm 3 'In Trouble But Not Afraid'

This Psalm is generally classed as a Lament of the Individual (see Introduction, pp. 37ff); but Mowinckel (*PIW*, I, p. 220) has defined it as a 'protective psalm', voicing a prayer for God's protection against imminent danger. H. Schmidt (*Das Gebet der Angeklagten im Alten Testament*, *BZAW*, 49 (1928), p. 26) regards the Psalm as a prayer of an accused man, but this view seems less likely.

According to the superscription of the Psalm, its author was David, who composed it during his flight from Absalom (cf. 2 Sam. 15–19). This historical note seems to be a later interpretation, which derives little support from the contents. In fact, the reference to 'his holy hill' (verse 4) may well indicate a later date, because it is far from certain that Zion was thought of as Yahweh's holy mountain in the time of David (cf. Gunkel, *PGHAT*, p. 13). Even more perplexing is the mention of the enemies in general; in particular, one misses any allusion to Absalom. David would have given not only his kingdom but even his own life for Absalom, and he would have regarded it a profitable exchange (cf. 2 Sam. 18:33). The martial language of the Psalm may indicate that its author was a Davidic king or a leader of the community, but, on the other hand, it is not impossible that some ordinary Israelite appropriated the 'court style' to express his own personal experiences. Buttenwieser (*PCT*, p. 397) argues that the 'I' of the Psalm personifies the experience of the whole country. Thus if the speaker in the Psalm was King, then the cultic setting must have been a day of national lamentation; if it was spoken by an ordinary Israelite then the lament may have been used in time of personal trouble, such as illness or false accusation.

The 3+3 metre of the Psalm is almost regular. Occasionally the poem is divided into four strophes, but it is doubtful whether such a division was original to it. The Psalm opens with an appeal to Yahweh, and is followed by a description of the plight. In verses 3–6 the tone changes, and the writer expresses his confidence in God. In verse 7 there is a cry for help, and the final verse voices the certainty that victory belongs to Yahweh alone.

A Psalm of David: see Introduction, pp. 46 and 43ff.

Absalom: the third son of David. His mother was Maacah, the daughter of Talmai, King of Geshur in Aram (cf. 2 Sam. 3:3).

THE PRESENT DISTRESS **1–2**

1. how: instead of a straightforward account of the trouble, we have an exclamation which serves to emphasize the seriousness of the situation. The force of 'how' probably extends also to verses 1*b* and 2*a*.

many: the threefold repetition of the same stem in verses 1–2 stresses the magnitude of the Psalmist's misfortune.

my foes are not further defined (for *ṣar* ('foe'), see on 107:2). According to the Psalm title the enemies would be David's own subjects, but, since the historical note seems to be a late conjecture (see introduction to the Psalm), the more likely view is to regard the speaker in the Psalm as a Davidic king, and his enemies as foreign invaders. When there was no longer a King in Judah, the Psalm must have been reinterpreted and applied to the individual and his adversaries.

Many are rising against me: this is an appropriate expression of the activities of rebels (cf. 2 Sam. 18:31,32), but with equal justification it could also be used of personal enemies (cf. Jg. 20:5; Ps. 54:3 (M.T. 5), 86:14) or of foreign peoples (Ob. 1). Perhaps we should read 'How many . . .!' (so also in verse 2*a*).

2. are saying: Dahood (*PAB*, I, p. 16) takes ʾ*-m-r* ('to say') as meaning 'to see' (as in Akkadian and Ugaritic), and renders 'who eye (my life)'. This is possible, but it would leave verse 2*b* in the air.

of me: lit. 'of my soul' (*AV*). It is unlikely that 'soul' (for *nep̄eš*, see on 33:19) in this particular context has any specific implications; it is simply used as an alternative of the Hebrew *lî*, 'of me'.

help: lit. 'salvation' (see on 35:3); *NEB* 'victory'. The enemies of the Psalmist, and perhaps even his apparent friends, are convinced that he is beyond any help, including that of God. The severity of the distress seemed to suggest that the forsaken person must have been a great sinner (cf. Job 8:6). See on 35:3.

in God: LXX and V read 'in his God', which brings out the irony implicit in the hostile comments. This may be, however, a later interpretation of the original reading. Dahood (*PAB*, I, p. 16) takes the preposition *b*ᵉ (*RSV* 'in') in the sense of 'from' as in Ugaritic; this is possible but not imperative.

Selah: see Introduction, pp. 48f.

THE PSALMIST'S EXPRESSION OF CONFIDENCE **3–6**

Ultimately the situation is not what it appears to be. He who is regarded as abandoned by God is actually the one who has God at his side. Therefore his enemies may well find themselves fighting against the Almighty himself.

3. But thou: this is strongly emphatic, and it introduces the contrast to verses 1–2.

shield: the Hebrew *māḡēn* was a smaller type of defensive armour (in contrast to *ṣinnāh*, see on 35:2), probably round-shaped and made either of metal or, more often, of a wooden frame covered with leather which was coated with fat or oil (cf. Isa. 21:5; for further details, see de Vaux, *AI*, p. 245). In this verse 'shield' is used figuratively to describe God's protection against the attacks of the enemies (cf. Gen. 15:1; Dt. 33:29; Ps. 18:2 (M.T. 3) 28:7, 33:20). Dahood (*PAB*, I, pp. 16ff.) argues that there is a need to distinguish between *māḡēn* ('shield') and *māḡēn*, or *māḡān* ('suzerain') (cf. 84:9 (M.T. 10) where it is parallel to 'the anointed' (*māšîaḥ*), and 89:18 (M.T. 19) where it is synonymous with 'our king'). Consequently he translates: 'But you . . . are my Suzerain as long as I live'. This involves a repointing of *ba*^{ca}*ḏî* ('about me') into *b*^{ec}*ōḏî* ('as long as I live'), while the pronoun in the phrase 'my Suzerain' is 'obtained' from 'my glory' (verse 3*b*) on the principle of the double-duty suffix (i.e., two parallel nouns or other parts of speech need not necessarily have more than *one* pronoun (or preposition, etc.) because its force may extend to the parallel noun, etc.).

my glory: i.e. God is either 'the one in whom I glory' (so Briggs) or, more likely, 'the one who restores my honour (or 'dignity')' (cf. 21:5 (M.T. 6), 62:7 (M.T. 8)). Dahood (*PAB*, I, p. 18) thinks that 'my glory' is a divine appellative and that it should be rendered 'my Glorious One'; the following conjunction *w*^{e} ('and') could be taken as an explanatory *wāw*, meaning 'namely (the one who lifts up my head)'.

the lifter of my head: this may be a metaphor derived from the court of law (cf. Kraus, *PBK*, p. 27) describing the action of a judge who lifts the accused from the ground, as a sign of his acquittal (cf. Schmidt, *PHAT*, p. 7). It is, however, far from certain that the accused waited during the court session either kneeling or lying down (see L. Köhler, *Hebrew Man* (1956), p. 155). The phrase may have originally denoted the act of releasing a person from prison (cf. Gen. 40:13,20; 2 Kg. 25:27; Jer. 52:31), but in this verse it may mean no more than that God is the one who can reverse the fortunes of an afflicted man and raise him to honour. The Psalmist regarded himself as hemmed in by the troubles and enemies, but he was sure that God would free him from his prison-like existence.

4. I cry: or 'as often as I cried', if the Hebrew imperfect is to be taken as denoting a repeated action; thus the Psalmist would base his confidence in Yahweh upon his past experience (so also Weiser, *POTL*, p. 117).

aloud: lit. 'with my voice' (cf. 142:1 (M.T. 2)).

he answers: or 'he answered', either by means of an oracle or through giving actual help; see on 119:26.

from his holy hill: i.e. from Mount Zion (see on 2:6). Its holiness was due, not only to the presence of the Ark of the Covenant or to the Temple, but also to the idea, common in the ancient Near East, that the sacred mountain was the abode of the deity or 'the symbol, or representation, of the cosmos which formed the true abode of the deity whom men worshipped. It was thus the part which represented the whole' (Clements, *GT*, p. 3). So also Mount Zion was thought to represent both the heavenly abode of Yahweh before men, and the whole land before Yahweh (cf. 14:7, 20:2 (M.T. 3)).

5. In verses 3–4 the Psalmist stated the truths which he had learnt from his past life, while in verse 5 he describes the night just passed. In view of what his enemies had been saying, he ought to have spent a restless night, yet his confidence in God was such that he had been able to have both peace of mind and sound sleep. In other words, the night and all that it symbolized could do him no harm.

I: this is emphatic and it could be paraphrased 'so I, in spite of my enemies'.

sleep: the reference is probably to the Psalmist's restful night, rather than to the practice of incubation or the technique whereby an oracle might be sought by sleeping in a sacred place in the hope of receiving a dream.

for the LORD sustains me: this is the foundation of the Psalmist's peace and confidence. The tense of 'sustains' (in Hebrew an imperfect) may imply that God's care has been and ever will be unceasing.

6. With God at his side, the Psalmist is not dismayed by the numerical strength of his enemies, nor by their hostility.

ten thousands: or 'myriads' (so *NEB*), i.e. countless in number (cf. 91:7). Dahood (*PAB*, I, p. 19) derives *rib̲ᵉb̲ôṯ* from *r-b-b*, 'to shoot arrows', hence 'the shafts of (the people)', but the usual interpretation is by no means inferior.

people: the Hebrew *ʿam* may refer to people in general (*NEB* 'the nations') or to 'fighting men', 'warriors' (cf. Num. 20:20) which may be more appropriate to the warlike situation of this verse.

set themselves against me: this is probably a military term, as in Isa. 22:7, elaborating the martial picture of the preceding line.

THE PSALMIST'S PRAYER 7–8

It is difficult to determine the relationship between verse 7*a* and 7*bc*. Oesterley (*TP*, p. 129) takes verse 7*a* as 'an exclamation denoting the Psalmist's affirmation of trust, rather than in the

nature of an appeal', but most recent scholars take it rightly as a prayer which forms an integral part of this lamentation. Verse 7*bc*, on the other hand, may describe the Psalmist's past experience. There may have been times when his enemies had been put to shame and when he had experienced God's mighty deeds of salvation re-presented in the cult of the Covenant people. It is also possible that the verse refers to future events, in which case the Hebrew verbs should be taken as prophetic perfects.
Arise, O Lord: this is probably a kind of Israelite war cry, associated with the Ark of the Covenant (cf. Num. 10:35; Ps. 68:1 (M.T. 2)), which may have been regarded as the symbol of Yahweh's presence or as his throne (cf. Kraus, *PBK*, p. 27; Clements, *GT*, pp. 28ff.).
thou dost smite . . . on the cheek: or 'thou hast smitten . . .' (*AV*). This was an expression of contempt and insult (cf. 1 Kg. 22:24; Job 16:10; Lam. 3:30; Mic. 5:1 (M.T. 4:14); Mt. 5:39; Jn 19:3), and it suggests that the enemies are no longer in a position to offer any resistance. Dahood (*PAB*, I, pp. 19ff.) takes the verbs as precative perfects introduced by *kî* (*RSV* 'for'). This would be an appropriate continuation of verse 7*a*; thus the whole verse would form a brief prayer or wish: 'O that you would smite . . . O that you would break . . .'.
thou dost break the teeth: here the metaphor is changed and the foes are likened to wild beasts; to break their teeth means to deprive them of their power to do harm (cf. Job 29:17; Ps. 58:6 (M.T. 7)).
the wicked: see on 1:1.

AN EXPRESSION OF CERTAINTY 8

8. Men can prepare themselves for war, but victory belongs to God alone (cf. Prov. 21:31).
Deliverance: lit. 'salvation' or 'victory' (so *NEB*). Kissane (*BP*, p. 11) reads: 'For me, Yahweh, there will be salvation' (i.e. *lî yhwh* for *l^eyhwh*, 'to Yahweh' (*RSV* 'to the Lord')); this involves a slight emendation, but it provides a better parallelism with the second line.
to the Lord: Dahood (*PAB*, I, p. 21) interprets the preposition *l^e* (*RSV* 'to') as a *lāmeḏ vocativum*; for various examples, see op. cit., p. 21 and *VT*, XVI (1966), pp. 299–311. It is doubtful, however, whether the rendering 'O Yahweh, salvation!' is in any way preferable to that of *RSV*.

thy blessing be upon thy people: this need not imply that the speaker must be a high priest or some other cultic official (cf. B. Duhm, *Die Psalmen* (1922), p. 15). Verse 8*a* is a confession of faith, while verse 8*b* is a prayer for the people of God.

Psalm 4 God is My Joy and Safety

This Psalm is a Lament of the Individual (see Introduction, pp. 37f.), but since the note of trust in God is so prominent it could be classed as a Psalm of Confidence (see Introduction, p. 39). Its setting may be a particular cultic act in the Temple (see verse 5), associated with some such situation as that described in Dt. 17:8–13 (cf. also Dt. 19:16–21) where complicated legal cases are decided in the central sanctuary. Dahood (*PAB*, I, p. 23) considers the Psalm as a prayer for rain, and he compares it with other Psalms (such as 65:9–13 (M.T. 10–14) and Ps. 67, 85) which, in his opinion, were meant for the same purpose. This suggestion is doubtful, although the exegesis of our Psalm is difficult.

It has been often suggested that Ps. 3 and 4 may have formed at one time a literary unity, and that both must have been written by the same author. On the other hand, the points of contact between the two are not sufficiently great to demand a common authorship, and some of the similarities may be due to their common psalm-type, or *Gattung*.

It is also far from certain that the speaker in the Psalm is a king (so Baethgen, Eaton, *et al.*), a leader of the people (so Wellhausen), or a high priest (as suggested by Duhm). The language of the Psalm is equally appropriate to any ordinary Israelite, and so are its sentiments. There is little justification for interpreting this lament in terms of David's experience while fleeing from Absalom, especially if Ps. 4 is not an integral part of Ps. 3. A more likely exegesis is the view that the author was falsely accused of some crime (which is not further defined in the Psalm), and that, even after he had been acquitted, certain people were scheming against him. Verse 6 may refer to certain difficulties facing the Psalmist's adversaries, which could be interpreted as the consequence of their lack of trust in God.

The metre of the Psalm is mainly 4+4.

To the choirmaster: see Introduction, p. 48.

with stringed instruments: see Introduction, p. 48.

A Psalm of David: see Introduction, pp. 43ff and 46.

INVOCATION AND CRY FOR HELP 1

1. **Answer me** by giving me the help needed. See on 119:26. **God of my right:** lit. 'God of my righteousness' who vindicates my right or upholds my just cause, hence 'God of my vindication'. **Thou hast given me room:** or 'You have delivered me from distress'. Any calamity could be regarded as a condition of being hemmed in by enemies or trouble in general (cf. 18:19 (M.T. 20), 119:45). Therefore the above-mentioned phrase is a synonym for 'saved' or 'delivered'. If we adopt the *RSV* rendering, then the reference is to the Psalmist's former experiences, but the Hebrew verb can be taken as a precative perfect (equivalent to an imperative), meaning 'give me room', i.e. in trouble deliver me. In the light of recent study there is no real reason to doubt that such precative perfects did exist in Biblical Hebrew; see Dahood, *PAB*, I, p. 20.

Be gracious to me: this is an appeal to the unmerited favour of God; see on 6:2, 57:1.

my prayer: i.e. my plea for deliverance or my cry for vindication in face of the false accusations brought against me. For *tᵉp̱illāh*, 'prayer', see on 65:2.

THE DESCRIPTION OF THE PLIGHT **2–6**

Unfortunately the Psalm does not provide any clear indication as to the identity of the speaker and his adversaries, or of the specific circumstances which form the background of this lamentation; consequently the interpretation of many details must remain speculative.

2. **O men:** lit. 'sons of men' (*bᵉnê ʾîš*). Buttenwieser (*PCT*, p. 405) renders 'O fellow men', but it is more likely that the reference is to men of substance or to the influential members of the community (cf. 49:2 (M.T. 3), 62:9 (M.T. 10)). The equivalent phrase is also found in Egyptian and Babylonian literature, with a similar meaning (for references, see Kraus, *PBK*, p. 33). *NEB* has 'Mortal men'.

my honour can be taken as the author's personal dignity or as his faith in God (so Weiser, *POTL*, p. 120). Cheyne (*BPPI*, p. 9) thinks that it is a synonym for 'my God', in which case the verse could be regarded as a reproof to the apostates among the people (similarly Dahood; see on 3:3). But, if so, the rebuke would have been expressed, most likely, in much sterner language. 'My honour' need not imply that the author must have been a person of high rank.

vain words: they may refer to idols and their worship (cf. 40:4 (M.T. 5); Am. 2:4) as well as to 'lies', but in this verse the allusion may be to the false and unfounded accusations brought against the Psalmist (cf. 31:18 (M.T. 19)). We are not told the substance of this malicious charge.

Selah: see Introduction, pp. 48f.

3. The Psalmist appeals to his adversaries to face the fact that Yahweh has been gracious to him, thus suggesting that he had been righteous.

has set apart the godly for himself: or with a slight alteration, 'Yahweh has shown to me his covenant loyalty in a wonderful way', reading *hiplî*ʾ *yhwh ḥasdô lî* for M.T. *hiplāh yhwh ḥāsîḏ lô* (cf. Kraus, *PBK*, p. 30); this conjectural reading finds a good parallel in 31:21 (M.T. 22). In either case the main point seems to be the same: Yahweh has marked out the godly for a different treatment. One aspect of this special care is that God hears and answers the prayers of his loyal worshipper.

godly: *ḥāsîḏ* is one who practises *ḥeseḏ* ('covenant loyalty'), i.e. one who is loyal to the Covenant relationships both in respect of God and of men (cf. 18:25 (M.T. 26); see on 30:4, 86:2).

hears . . . call: this is rendered by some exegetes 'heard . . . called', and taken to refer to past events (for such a usage see Job 3:3; Ps. 116:1). Dahood (*PAB*, I, p. 24) suggests 'will hear me' by applying the double-duty rule on suffixes (see on 3:3).

4. Some commentators have resorted to emendations or transpositions (cf. Weiser, Kraus), yet M.T. gives a reasonable sense, although the two lines are metrically unbalanced.

Be angry: lit. 'tremble' (in fear and dismay at Yahweh's goodness to the godly; cf. Exod. 15:14) or 'be disquieted' (so Dahood). Verse 4*a* is quoted in Eph. 4:26 as a warning against harbouring anger.

but sin not: or 'and stop sinning' (see on 32:1, 119:11).

commune with your own hearts: lit. 'say in your heart' or simply 'think'. What is said, or thought about, depends upon the larger context; perhaps we should paraphrase as: 'ponder in your heart on the goodness of God towards the righteous' (referring back to verse 4*a*). Dahood (*PAB*, I, p. 24) proposes 'examine your conscience' (for this use of ʾ*-m-r* (usually 'to say')

in the sense 'to see, look', see on 3:2; cf. M. Dahood, 'Hebrew-Ugaritic Lexicography, I', *Biblica*, XLIV (1963), pp. 295ff.).
and be silent: or 'and be still' (i.e. cease from seeking after lies or from bringing forth your false accusations; cf. Jos. 10:13). Dahood (*PAB*, I, pp. 24f.) suggests 'upon your beds weep' (cf. 6:6 (M.T. 7)). The Hebrew *d-m-m* usually means 'to be silent, dumb', but there may be another verb *d-m-m* cognate with the Ugaritic *dmm* ('to cry, weep'). If this proposal is adopted, then the conjunction *w*ᵉ ('and') before *dommû* ('weep') could be taken as an emphatic *wāw* (i.e. '(upon your beds) do indeed (weep)').

5. Most exegetes rightly regard this verse as addressed to the opponents of the Psalmist (i.e. to the men of importance).
right sacrifices: or 'sacrifices of righteousness'. The reference is either to sacrifices offered with the right ritual or to those brought in the right spirit (cf. Dt. 33:19; Ps. 51:19 (M.T. 21)). In this verse 'right sacrifices' seem to be implicitly contrasted with 'vain or wrong sacrifices'. This is also implied by the challenge in verse 5*b*, where the adversaries are asked to put their trust in God. Therefore 'right sacrifices' are offerings presented by men who have not disregarded their responsibilities to God and men. An acceptable sacrifice can only be offered in the context of right living.
put your trust in the Lord: i.e. make an obedient and humble response to the word of Yahweh. 'Trust in God' is one of the key concepts of the Psalter, and it is practically equivalent to Isaiah's concept of faith (cf. H. W. Robinson, *Inspiration and Revelation in the Old Testament* (1946), p. 266).

6. The older exegetes were apt to take verse 6*a* as an expression of the disheartened followers of David (cf. Delitzsch, *BCP*, I, p. 116), or of the grumbling adherents of Absalom (cf. Cohen, *PSon*, p. 9), while verse 6*b* was attributed to David as a prayer for himself and his people. It is more likely, however, that the *whole* verse reports the words of the opponents of the Psalmist, because no change of speakers has been indicated.
O that we might see some good: Dahood (*PAB*, I, p. 22) renders 'who will show us rain', and he produces a number of examples where *ṭôḇ* ('good') may possibly mean 'rain' (cf. Dt. 28:12; Jer. 17:6; for further instances, see *Biblica*, XLV (1964), p. 411). Although Dahood's general argument may be right, his translation of this verse is less convincing.
Lift up: this may be a reminiscence of the priestly blessing in

Num. 6:24ff. (*n^esāh* is apparently an alternative form of *n^eśā'* or *śā'* ('lift up')). Some commentators render verse 6*b* 'the light . . . has departed (*nās^e'āh*) from us' (cf. Kraus, *PBK*, p. 31), but the simplest solution is to read *nāsāh*, 'has fled' (from *n-w-s*), for M.T. *n^esāh* ('lift up'), and to take it either as an archaic third person masculine singular (so Dahood, *PAB*, I, p. 26) or as the third person feminine singular, even though the subject (*'ôr*, 'light') is masculine in gender; hence we could render: 'The light of your presence, O Yahweh, has fled (from) upon us' (similarly also *NEB*).

the light of thy countenance: this phrase may denote the favour and love of God (so Calvin) or simply 'the presence of God'. The point of verse 6, in its wider context, seems to be that, although many long for the blessings of God, they do not want to accept the truth that such a boon is the consequence of a right relationship with God (cf. verse 5).

THE JOY AND PEACE THAT COMES FROM GOD **7–8**

The Psalmist contrasts his own experience with that of his opponents who long for good but are stubbornly wrong about the nature of God. The writer is not primarily comparing spiritual and material blessings or the enjoyment of them, but he uses the picture of rejoicing at the harvest time as a metaphor for great joy (cf. Isa. 9:3 (M.T. 2)). The gladness which God has put in his heart is far greater than any other joy he has known. It is doubtful if we are justified in arguing from this verse that the Psalmist was a poor man (so Kraus), persecuted by the rich who had an abundance of corn and wine but a famine in their soul. Nor is there sufficient evidence to say that there had been a bad harvest and that consequently many had lost their faith in the providence of Yahweh.

8. I will both lie down and sleep: I shall have no sleepless hours full of worry and fear, but as soon as I lie down I shall sleep, because God is my safety. Dahood (*PAB*, I, p. 27) regards the word *yaḥdāw* (*RSV* 'both') as a noun meaning 'his face', and connects it with the Ugaritic *ḥdy* ('to see, gaze'), which he takes as a dialectal form of the Hebrew *ḥ-z-h*, 'to see'; his rendering would be 'In his peaceful presence (i.e. in the peace of his face) I shall lie down and sleep'.

for thou alone: this is an emphatic statement in which 'alone' adds a further stress to the personal pronoun 'thou'.

Psalm 5 Judgment Belongs to God

This Psalm is an Individual Lament (see Introduction, pp. 37ff.), or a prayer of a falsely accused man (see verse 9). The accusers or enemies are the Psalmist's fellow Israelites (cf. verses 4*b* and 5*a*), who are not only boasters (verse 5) and slanderers (verse 6) but also 'bloodthirsty men' (verse 6*b*) who would not shrink from any violence to accomplish their unprincipled designs. On the other hand, some scholars (e.g. Eaton) regard the Psalm as 'a prayer of the Davidic dynasty' (*PTBC*, p. 38), offered in the Temple courts.

If the *RSV* rendering of verse 3*b* is right, then the Psalm was recited or sung during the offering of morning (?) sacrifice; this would hardly be the customary sacrifice, for it must have had some specific significance. In actual fact, the Psalm does not mention sacrifice at all, and the object of the verb *ᶜ-r-k* ('to prepare') is not expressed; it could equally well be 'my case' or 'arguments for my defence'. If this latter suggestion is correct, then the cultic situation may have been the presentation of the defence and the awaiting of the decision. In the end the accused would either be admitted to the sanctuary or be excluded, apart from any other consequences.

It is impossible to determine the date of the Psalm, but many modern scholars assign it to the post-Exilic period.

The prevailing metre of the lament is 3 + 2.

To the choirmaster: see Introduction, p. 48.
for the flutes: see Introduction, p. 48.
A Psalm of David: see Introduction, pp. 43ff. and 46.

AN APPEAL TO YAHWEH 1–3

1. Give ear to my words: this and the following invocations emphasize the magnitude of the affliction, even though these expressions are a characteristic part of the style of laments (cf. the Babylonian parallel, 'Prayer of Lamentation to Ishtar', *ANET*, pp. 384f.).

give heed to my groaning: or '. . . to my utterance', linking the Hebrew *hāḡîḡ* ('groaning') with *h-g-h* ('to meditate, speak') (cf. *ZLH*, p. 184b). *AV*, *RV*, *RP* have 'my meditation', which is less suited to the general sense of the verse; *NEB* 'my inmost thoughts'.

2. my cry: lit. 'the voice of my crying'. This need not be a reflection of the naïve, primitive idea that gods could be wakened with piercing cries; rather it is the natural expression of one's inward anguish irrespective of the original significance of the phrase.

my King: this form of address may suggest that, just as the Israelite king was the final court of appeal in his realm (cf. 2 Sam. 14:1ff., 15:2ff.), so, in the Psalmist's view, Yahweh is the supreme judge *par excellence*. For *meleḵ* ('king') as Yahweh's title, see on 68:24.

my God: in this expression, the pronoun 'my' seems to bridge the gulf between the almighty sovereign and the humble petitioner (see on 91:2; cf. 44:4 (M.T. 5), 68:24 (M.T. 25), 72:12, 84:3 (M.T. 4)). This is favour indeed to be able to address the King of the whole world as '*my* God'.

3. O Lord: Dahood (*PAB*, I, p. 28) adds this vocative to the end of verse 2, while Kraus (*PBK*, p. 36) deletes it for metrical reasons (i.e. to retain the 3+2 metre); the former alternative is preferable.

in the morning: this was one of the usual times appointed for sacrifice and prayer (cf. 2 Kg. 3:20, 16:15; Am. 4:4). It was also believed that the early morning was the time when one could expect God's help (see on 46:5).

thou dost hear my voice: the Hebrew imperfect *tišmaᶜ* ('you will hear') may be equivalent to an imperative (i.e. 'hear (my voice)') in view of the preceding imperatives in verses 1–2.

I prepare a sacrifice: lit. 'I arrange (or 'set in order')', while the object must be inferred from the context. *AV*, *RV*, *RP* have 'my prayer', but a reasonable rendering might be 'my case' (so also Dahood). Gunkel (*PGHAT*, p. 19) points out that in the *OT* the verb *ᶜ-r-k* ('to prepare') is not used of prayers, but it could be applied to legal cases or to sacrifices; it is also found in military contexts. Consequently the alternative seems to be between 'my case' and 'my sacrifice'; perhaps the former is more likely (cf. Job 23:4, 32:14, 33:5, 37:19). In both alternatives the essential thing is the hope to receive a favourable divine revelation. It is unlikely that the oracle was obtained by means of inspecting the sacrificial victim, as was often the practice in the ancient Near East (cf. Kraus, *WI*, p. 124). The divine will may have been communicated by a priestly oracle; there is little evidence for a 'sacrifice for omens' as suggested by Mowinckel (*PIW*, II, p. 54). He takes *bōḵer* (*RSV* 'morning') as the object of the verb, meaning 'omen sacrifice'; but even if this use of *bōḵer* were attested in *OT* it would be rather unlikely in this verse, because it would involve the use of *bōḵer* in two different senses in the same verse and in similar constructions.

and watch: the verb *ṣ-p-h* is employed in Hab. 2:1, where the prophet is looking for a revelation (cf. also Isa. 21:6; Mic. 7:7). It may have a similar meaning here.

GOD AND EVIL ARE INCOMPATIBLE **4–6**

4. For thou art not a God: since verse 4*a* is rather long, some scholars (Budde, Gunkel, *et al.*), omit 'God' (*ʾēl*), following some Hebrew MSS. Dahood (*PAB*, I, p. 30) renders: 'A no-god delights in evil'. The excesses of the Canaanite deities are well illustrated by the Ugaritic texts, but little is gained by introducing them into this verse. Barnes (*PWC*, I, p. 23) may be right in reminding us that, although the thought expressed by verse 4 is a truism for Christians, it was not self-evident to the peoples of the world of antiquity.

evil: or 'an (or 'the') evil man' as in LXX, V, Jerome *et al.*

may not sojourn with thee: or 'cannot be your guest'. In the ancient Near East a guest usually enjoyed hospitality and protection (see Pedersen, *ILC*, I–II, pp. 356ff.), but an evil man does not qualify for such a privilege in the household of God (cf. Ps. 15 and 24).

5. The boastful: cf. 73:3ff., 75:4 (M.T. 5). They are the arrogant whose boast is not in the Lord but in themselves.

may not stand before thy eyes: i.e. as worshippers in the Temple (cf. Jos. 24:1; 1 Sam. 10:19). Dahood (*PAB*, I, p. 31) is of the opinion that the word-picture is that of a court of law where the enemies press their charges against the Psalmist (cf. Job 33:5), but this is less likely than the former alternative (cf. verses 4*b* and 7).

thou hatest all evildoers: Yahweh dislikes both the sinner and his sin, because the deed can hardly be separated from the doer. The link between sin and sinner ceases only when the guilty man puts an end to his wrongdoing (cf. N. H. Snaith, *The Seven Psalms* (1964), p. 20). Dahood (*PAB*, I, p. 31) repoints *śānēʾṯā* ('you hate') and reads *śānēʾtī* ('I hate (all evildoers)'); he regards the expression as a technical term derived from the formula of the repudiation of false gods, and he believes that the Psalmist was accused of idolatry. This seems plausible, but the emendation is not justified by the result.

6. those who speak lies: the reference is not to occasional 'terminological inexactitudes', but to something far more sinister. It may refer to the bearing of false testimony (cf. Exod. 20:16; Dt. 5:20) in legal cases involving capital punishment.
bloodthirsty: (cf. 2 Sam. 16:7,8; Ps. 139:19), lit. 'a man of blood' or 'a man guilty of bloodshed'. They need not have been actual murderers, although they were potential ones.

ONLY THE UPRIGHT CAN WORSHIP GOD **7–8**
Obviously sinners also may find their way into the Temple, but their worship would be meaningless and unacceptable to God (cf. Isa. 1:12ff.) as long as they were determined to continue their perverted way of life.

7. I . . . will enter thy house: if the allusion is to a future event, then the Psalmist may still be awaiting the decision in his case. For 'thy house', see on 122:1.
I will worship: lit. 'I will prostrate myself' (see on 29:2). In ancient times this was an attitude which fittingly expressed one's homage to God or to a person of great importance (cf. *ANEP*, pl. 351).
toward thy holy temple: cf. 1 Kg. 8:35,38,42; Ps. 28:2, 134:2, 138:2; Dan. 6:10. It was also the custom of the Jews of the Diaspora, or the Dispersion, during their prayers to turn towards the Holy City (cf. G. A. Smith, *Jerusalem*, II (1908), pp. 396ff.). In our context the worshipper is pictured as being in the forecourt of the Temple facing towards the sanctuary with its Holy of Holies where God was thought to be present in a very special sense (cf. Rowley, *WAI*, pp. 79ff.).
in the fear of thee: this is not a feeling of dread but one of awe and reverence. Dahood (*PAB*, I, p. 32) suggests 'among those who fear you' (see 119:38), arguing that the abstract noun 'fear' (*yirʾāh*) has assumed a concrete significance due to the parallelism and context.

8. Lead me . . . in thy righteousness: i.e. lead me by means of your righteous acts of salvation (cf. v. Rad, *OTT*, I, pp. 370ff.). Dahood (*PAB*, I, p. 33) regards the Hebrew *ṣᵉdāḳāh* ('righteousness') as a poetic term for 'paradise' or 'the Elysian Fields'; he finds a similar usage in 23:3, 69:27 (M.T. 28), 143:11; Prov. 21:21 (*RSVm*). This suggestion is unlikely; cf. 1:3.
my enemies: see on 54:5; cf. 27:11, 56:2 (M.T. 3), 59:10 (M.T. 11).

make thy way straight: Davison (*Cent. BP*, I, p. 61) explains it as making the way 'straight, easy to travel', but the intended meaning may suggest *ability* to tackle the problems rather than 'ease', or 'lack of difficulties' (cf. 27:11, 32:8).

THE DESCRIPTION OF THE ENEMIES **9–10**

9. in their mouth: M.T. '. . . in his mouth'. *RSV* is right in following the ancient versions and reading *b^e^p̱îmô* for M.T. *b^e^p̱îhû*. The adversaries are liars and therefore there is no truth in their mouth. The word used for 'truth' is the Hebrew *n^e^ḵônāh*, which suggests 'what is firm, established' or 'what is right', hence 'truth' (cf. Dhorme, *CJ*, p. 648).
their heart is destruction: or, to paraphrase, 'their inner being brings forth nothing but destruction' (cf. 52:1 (M.T. 3)). 'Their heart', lit. 'their inward part' (*ḳirbām*), may form a word play with 'sepulchre' (*ḳeḇer*) in verse 9*b*.
their throat is an open sepulchre: their speech is deadly (cf. Jer. 5:16). These enemies in their desire to do harm resemble Sheol or the underworld, which is never satisfied in its greed for more victims (Prov. 27:20).
they flatter with their tongue: Dahood (*PAB*, I, p. 35) renders: 'with their tongue they bring death', taking the verb *ḥ-l-ḳ* ('to flatter') in the sense of 'to die, perish' (as in Ugaritic, where the verb *ḫlḳ* is used as a synonym of *mt* ('to die')). This would provide a good parallel to verse 9*c*.

10. Make them bear their guilt: the verb *ʾ-š-m* probably means 'to perish, destroy' (cf. 34:21,22 (M.T. 22,23); Isa. 24:6; Jer. 2:3; Ezek. 6:6; Hos. 5:15, 10:2). Another verb (?) *ʾ-š-m* occurs often in the sense 'to be, or become, guilty'. The attitude of the Psalmist is considerably different from that of Jesus, who prayed: 'Father forgive them . . .' (Lk. 23:34).
let them fall: this can hardly mean 'into Sheol' (as suggested by Dahood, *PAB*, I, p. 36); rather it is a picture of misfortune in general (cf. 20:8 (M.T. 9), 27:2, 36:12 (M.T. 13)) caused, primarily, by their own scheming.
cast them out: or 'banish them (from your presence)'; cf. verse 4; Jer. 8:3, 24:9, 27:10,15; Dan. 9:7.
they have rebelled against thee: i.e. they have distorted the God-established relationships between man and man, and therefore they have set themselves, not only against their fellow Israelite, but also against God himself.

GOD BLESSES THE RIGHTEOUS **11–12**

11. let all . . . rejoice: cf. 2:11. The reason for this rejoicing is not so much the impending punishment of the wicked as the fact that Yahweh is a righteous God (cf. 64:9f. (M.T. 10f.); see also 58:10 (M.T. 11) where vengeance is an important factor in the thinking of the author).

ever sing for joy: because God is their refuge. For 'ever' (*l^eᶜôlām*), see on 9:5. It is unlikely that the allusion is to an eternal rejoicing in the celestial paradise.

and do thou defend them: many scholars transfer this phrase to verse 12*b*, rendering: 'and you cover him (as with a shield, and you crown him with (your) gracious favour)'. This improves the structure of both verses.

who love thy name: cf. 69:36 (M.T. 37), 119:132. It was believed in Israel, as also elsewhere, that a close relationship existed between a person and his name, so much so that it could be regarded as a double of one's self (cf. v. Rad, *OTT*, I, p. 183). Thus to love the name of Yahweh means to love him or as much as is known of him. For *šēm* ('name'), see on 20:1.

12. thou dost bless the righteous: Yahweh gives success to his people in everything they do (cf. 29:11, 67:6 (M.T. 7), 107:38, 128:5). For 'righteous', see on 1:5.

shield: see on 3:3, 35:2. The reference here is, apparently, to the large rectangular shield that provided protection for practically the whole body (cf. Yadin, *SWSLSD*, pp. 115ff.).

dost cover him with favour: or 'you crown him . . .'; see also verse 11. The Hebrew *rāṣôn*, 'favour', is a synonym for 'blessing' (cf. Dt. 33:23; Ps. 30:5 (M.T. 6), 106:4f., 143:10).

Psalm 6 A Prayer in Time of Trouble

This is the first of the so-called Penitential Psalms which include Ps. 32, 38, 51, 102, 130, 143. This designation may be slightly surprising, because there is no explicit expression of penitence and confession in Ps. 6; but the Early Church must have felt that the spirit of contrition was there. Psalm 6 is usually classed as a Lament of the Individual (see Introduction, pp. 37ff.), except by some older commentators (such as Smend, Briggs, *et al.*) who regarded it as a description of the experience of the community. It could also be defined as a Psalm of Illness (so

Mowinckel, *PIW*, II, pp. 1ff.), but there is the possibility that illness is simply used as a metaphor of great misfortune. Any disaster brings with it weakness and loss of vitality, and this can be taken as a form of illness.

The setting of the Psalm, or its *Sitz im Leben*, is the cult; the afflicted person offers his prayers and/or sacrifice, for his deliverance or healing. See 2 Sam. 12:16; 1 Kg. 8:37f.; of special interest is Sir. 38:9ff., which, although of a later date, is instructive in that the sick person is reminded to offer prayers and sacrifices. Mowinckel (*PIW*, II, p. 5) describes the Psalms of Illness as 'prayers to be used at the cleansings from illness and at sin-offerings and atoning offerings'.

The date and authorship of the Psalm are impossible to determine. Some (e.g. Kissane) argue that there are no solid grounds for disputing the Davidic origin, but a post-Exilic date is far more likely. This is also suggested by the similarities that exist between our Psalm and other late pre-Exilic or post-Exilic poems: compare verse 1 and 38:1 (M.T. 2), verse 2 and 41:4 (M.T. 5), verse 4 and 109:26, verse 6 and Jer. 45:3, verse 7 and 31:10 (M.T. 11), verse 8 and 119:115, verse 10 and 35:4,26, 83:13 (M.T. 14).

The Psalm is often divided into four strophes (so *RSV*) of unequal length. In the first three strophes lamentations alternate with petitions; the total impact of this pattern is quite impressive, and a reasonable substitute for a climactic movement of thought. A point of special interest is the abrupt change of tone after verse 7. The difference is so great that some exegetes (e.g. Oesterley, Cohen) have considered the last three verses as a postscript by the same author, added when the crisis had passed. Schmidt (*PHAT*, p. 11) thinks that verses 8–10 constitute a new prayer in a new situation. There may be several possible explanations for this sudden transition (see Introduction, p. 38), but a likely suggestion is that at a certain point during the recitation of the Psalm the petitioner was granted an oracle from Yahweh mediated by a priest or a cultic prophet, which brought about the sudden change of mood. Thus these verses (8–10) could be taken as the afflicted man's response to the word of God.

The metre is, for the greater part, 3+3.

To the choirmaster: see Introduction, p. 48.

with stringed instruments: see Introduction, p. 48.

The Sheminith: see Introduction, p. 49.

A Psalm of David: see Introduction, pp. 43ff. and 46.

A PRAYER FOR DELIVERANCE **1–5**

1. rebuke me not in thy anger: this expression ascribes human passions to God, but a reverent anthropomorphism does no harm and is actually indispensable. God's anger is both just and rational, but the Psalmist feels that he needs mercy more than justice (cf. 38:1ff. (M.T. 2ff.); Jer. 30:11, 46:28). It is very seldom that we find in the *OT* occasions where the wrath of God is portrayed as well-nigh irrational, e.g., when Yahweh sought to kill Moses (Exod. 4:24), or when his anger was kindled against Uzzah (2 Sam. 6:7) who, well-intentioned, had touched the Ark. Such instances are probably to be understood as the popular explanations of certain happenings rather than what might be called the 'Biblical faith'. In a way we may regard God's anger or wrath as the indication that human failings have become rebellion against him (cf. Job 5:17; Prov. 3:11,12). Cf. also 4Q177, XII–XIII, 1:2f.

nor chasten me in thy wrath: this is simply a parallel to the preceding line. The Psalmist is aware (at least implicitly) that he has done wrong and that he fully deserves a corrective punishment, but he is afraid to experience the justice of God outside the covenant relationship (cf. Dt. 11:16f., 29:20; 2 Kg. 22:16f.).

2. Be gracious to me: the Hebrew verb *ḥ-n-n* and its derivatives carry with them the idea of 'unmerited favour, or of supreme graciousness and condescension on the part of the giver, who is superior' (N. H. Snaith, *The Distinctive Ideas of the Old Testament* (1944), p. 128; cf. also K. W. Neubauer, *Der Stamm CHNN im Sprachgebrauch des Alten Testaments* (1964), pp. 73–105).

I am languishing: or 'I have no strength left' (*PLE*). This is the result of the Psalmist's illness or misfortune. It would be futile to attempt a diagnosis of the disease on the basis of the symptoms described, because in this type of poetry the word-pictures may have been drawn from the experiences of many people with different afflictions. The problem becomes even more complex when we accept the possibility that the descriptions, in some cases at least, should be taken metaphorically.

O LORD, heal me: i.e. only God is the true healer (cf. Exod. 15:26; 2 Kg. 5:7). Since all disease and misfortune were thought to be closely linked with sin, it follows that healing or deliverance implies also forgiveness (see 41:4 (M.T. 5)).

my bones are troubled: or 'my bodily frame is . . .'. There is no need to emend the verb (cf. 32:3), because the Hebrews often ascribed feelings to various parts of the body (cf. Johnson, *VITAI*, pp. 64ff.). The same verb is repeated in the following verse, but this raises no serious problem.

3. **My soul:** i.e. I myself. For 'soul', see on 33:19.

is sorely troubled: the author feels like the brothers of Joseph in Egypt, who were speechless and dismayed at his presence (Gen. 45:3), and the Psalmist's stammering 'But thou, O LORD – how long?' fits the situation (cf. Jg. 20:41; 2 Sam. 4:1).

how long: this is an expression characteristic of many laments (cf. 74:10, 79:5, 80:4 (M.T. 5), 90:13, 94:3). For some Babylonian parallels, see G. R. Driver, 'The Psalms in the Light of Babylonian Research', *TPst*, p. 131.

4. **Turn, O LORD:** (cf. 90:13). This may be a plea to Yahweh to turn away from his wrath (so Gunkel; cf. Exod. 32:12; 2 Kg. 23:26; Jon. 3:9), or an appeal to him to turn to the sufferer (so Briggs, Kraus, *et al.*) who has been seemingly abandoned by him (cf. 80:14 (M.T. 15), 90:13). Moffatt renders 'save my life once more' (i.e. the two imperatives are co-ordinated, and the principal idea is expressed by the second verb; for the construction, see *GK* 120g).

my life: lit. 'my soul'; see verse 3.

deliver me . . .: the Psalmist's only hope lay in the faithfulness of God and in his covenant loyalty. See on 26:3.

5. **in death there is no remembrance of thee:** this does not mean that the dead are unable to remember anything (cf. Isa. 14:13–17), but rather that they cannot share in the praise of Yahweh which is a characteristic feature of Israel's worship (cf. Childs, *MTI*, p. 71). The dead, being unclean, are outside the cultic sphere. The gravity of the situation is a constant reminder to the Psalmist that he is near the underworld, and that he already experiences something of the Sheol-existence. Therefore he longs for a fresh lease of life in order that he might be able to glorify God. This seems to be his conception of a worthwhile existence. It is unlikely that he wants to convince Yahweh that he would greatly miss the praises of his minstrel (so Leslie, *PAP*, p. 393).

Sheol: this is the name of the Hebrew realm of the dead, the counterpart to the Greek Hades. The word 'Sheol' is a transliteration of the Hebrew *š*^{e}*ʾôl*, the etymology of which is uncertain (see on 88:3). It was the home of the departed (49:11 (M.T. 12)) and a land of no return (Job 7:9, 10:21, 16:22). It was the abode of all, rich or poor, Israelite or foreigner, and it was characterized by silence (94:17), darkness (143:3), weakness and helplessness (88:4ff. (M.T. 5ff.)). Its inhabitants were cut off from the land of the living, and also from fellowship with God (88:5 (M.T. 6)). And herein lay the bitterness of death (cf. v. Rad, *OTT*, I, pp. 275ff.). Occasionally we find certain variations in the descriptions of Sheol and its conditions (cf. 139:8); but these inconsistencies, apparent or real, can be explained as due to a subjective evaluation of the ideas concerning the underworld. Thus to the wealthy man, who is enjoying all that life can offer, the prospect of Sheol-existence is a terrifying outlook, while for the poor man whose health and strength are failing, death may be a welcome friend (cf. Sir. 41:1ff.). See also Tromp, *PCD*, pp. 21ff.; Stadelmann, *HCW*, pp. 165–76.

THE DISTRESS OF THE PSALMIST **6–7**

6. I am weary . . .: or 'I am exhausted . . .'. The same phrase is also found in Jer. 45:3, but there is no reason to suppose that one is quoting the other (cf. 69:3 (M.T. 4)).
I flood my bed with tears: this poetical exaggeration helps to stress the seriousness of the affliction. Similar expressions are also used in the literature of other peoples: e.g., in the story of Keret it is said that when 'he entered his chamber, he wept . . . his tears streamed down like shekels to earth, the covering of his bed was soaked with his weeping . . .' (Driver, *CML*, p. 29a (Keret I, i: 25–31)).
my couch: the Hebrew *miṭṭāh* is one of various terms for 'bed'. Only the rich would have proper beds standing on legs (cf. 2 Kg. 1:4; Am. 6:4). Usually a bed was simply the place where one slept, whether on the floor or on a ledge near the wall (cf. Exod. 22:26f.), with or without a straw mat, rug or a simple wooden frame. One's outer garment might serve as a covering, but more affluent people would have special coverings (cf. Prov. 7:16).

7. My eye wastes away: it is possible that the crying (or illness as such) has affected the sufferer's sight, but it is more likely that the expression is a metaphor indicating the loss of vitality. 'My eye' may be another way of saying 'I' (i.e. a part is mentioned when the whole is to be understood; cf. Dt. 7:16:

'. . . you shall destroy all the peoples . . . your eye shall not pity them').

it grows weak: some scholars follow LXX, Aq, Sym, in reading *ᶜāṯaḳtî* for *ᶜāṯᵉḳāh,* and rendering: 'I have grown old (or 'weak')'. The versions probably give an interpretation rather than the original reading.

THE CERTAINTY OF BEING HEARD **8–10**

8. Depart from me: the same words are used in Mt. 7:23, and they mark the turning point at which the cry of anguish changes into a shout of triumph. The reason for this transition is found in the twice-repeated 'the LORD has heard' (verses 8*b* and 9*a*). This could be illustrated from 107:17ff. where the afflicted men cried to Yahweh who 'sent forth his word and healed them' (verse 20). It is possible that a similar experience is reflected in this Psalm: an oracle may have been imparted to the petitioner (cf. 22:24 (M.T. 25), 28:6, 34:6 (M.T. 7), 66:19), and this would account for the sudden change from the feeling of rejection to the certainty of being accepted. The fact that God has heard the supplication means that the suppliant has been forgiven and that his troubles are at an end. Consequently his enemies now have no case against him, even if they had previously (cf. 139:19).

workers of evil: for *pōᶜᵃlê ᵓāwen,* see on 28:3. Mowinckel (*PIW,* II, p. 11) regards them as sorcerers, as men who use their spells to do harm to their opponents (cf. *ANET,* p. 328). The suggestion may be right only when it is taken in a very general sense as denoting people who cause suffering by the use of various means.

9. the LORD accepts my prayer: for *tᵉpillāh,* 'prayer', see on 65:2. Much argument has surrounded the change of tenses: from 'has heard' (in Hebrew a perfect) to 'accepts' (which represents the Hebrew imperfect). The most likely explanation is that this is one of the cases where the Hebrew imperfect is used to describe a past event. A. Sperber (*A Historical Grammar of Biblical Hebrew* (1966), p. 591) would go as far as to argue that *both* tenses are used to indicate present, past or future, and that therefore they are interchangeable.

10. All my enemies shall be ashamed: whether they were the cause of the Psalmist's misfortunes or whether they only aggravated his distress, they will now be put to shame themselves (cf. 35:4).

sorely troubled: for the verb *b-h-l*, see on 90:7.
they shall turn back: Dahood (*PAB*, I, p. 39) sees here the motif of 'return to Sheol', and he cites other possible instances in Job 1:21, 30:23, 34:15; Ec. 3:20f., 5:15, 12:7. This view is interesting, but it is doubtful if one can use 139:15 as the basis for such an interpretation. According to Gen. 3:19 man must return to the ground from which he has been taken, but it is far from certain that in *this* verse 'ground' is identical with Sheol. In 139:13 it is clearly stated that man is formed in his mother's womb, but it is uncertain what is meant by 'intricately wrought in the depths of the earth' (139:15); here the allusion may be to the creation of the first man. For more details, see A. Bentzen, *King and Messiah* (1955), p. 88, n. 14; Eichrodt, *TOT*, II, p. 141.

Psalm 7 THE LAMENT OF THE ACCUSED MAN

This Psalm belongs to the category of the Laments of the Individual (see Introduction, pp. 37ff.) although its literary unity is not undisputed. An important place in this lament is taken by the so-called protestation of innocence, and consequently it could be described as a Psalm of Innocence or a Prayer of the Accused (so Schmidt, Deissler, *et al.*). Its setting may be similar to the situation described in 1 Kg. 8:31f. (cf. also Exod. 22:7f.; Num. 5:11ff.; Dt. 17:8). The accused man has come (or he may have fled) to the Temple to find protection and to obtain Yahweh's decision on his case. At some point during the proceedings, the person charged with the crime(s) would recite the Psalm (or have it said for him) and would await the divine acquittal. On the other hand, it is not impossible that this Psalm is simply an imitation of a prayer of the accused, and as such it may be merely a general lament. Eaton (*PTBC*, p. 42) regards it as a royal prayer in time of national distress.

Occasionally some exegetes have thought it to be composite and have considered verses 6–11, in particular, as a later addition (cf. Briggs, *CECBP*, I, p. 52). This literary fragmentation is based on the differences of metre, the use of the divine names and the subject matter, and Gunkel (*PGHAT*, p. 25) provides a brief history of the treatment of this poem. It is doubtful, however, if the Psalm is composite; the above differences may well have other explanations.

According to the superscription, the Psalm is of Davidic origin (so Kirkpatrick, Cohen, Kissane); but actually it may be of a later date, not necessarily post-Exilic. Deissler, however, thinks that its post-Exilic origin is practically certain (*PWdB*, I, p. 43). 'Cush the Benjaminite' and the event alluded to in the title of the Psalm are unknown, but the editor may have had access to a more detailed account of David's life or to legends about the great king of Israel. This mysterious Benjaminite has sometimes been identified with Saul (as suggested by T) or Shimei, who also was of the tribe of Benjamin (cf. 2 Sam. 16:5ff.) and was an enemy of David. Yet these and similar suggestions are mere guesses.

The metre of the Psalm is mixed, but nearly a half of it is 3+3. An outline of its structure is as follows: verses 1–2 form the introduction and contain an invocation of Yahweh and an appeal for help. Verses 3–5 consist of a declaration of the Psalmist's innocence, while in verses 6–11 we have a further petition to God, who is pictured in the role of a judge of all peoples. Verses 12–16 describe the wicked man and his impending doom, and the poem ends with a brief praise of Yahweh, or with a vow (verse 17).

A Shiggaion: see Introduction, p. 46.
of David: see Introduction, pp. 43ff.

THE INVOCATION OF YAHWEH **1–2**

1. in thee do I take refuge: this is a favourite theme in the Psalter, and it is found in the opening lines of many Psalms (11:1, 16:1, 31:1 (M.T. 2), 57:1 (M.T. 2), 71:1). Calvin and some other commentators took it to mean: 'in you do I trust'. This is obviously true, but it may also imply the seeking of protection in the sanctuary (see on 16:1).

from all my pursuers: many exegetes read *mērōḏ^e^pî* ('from my pursuer') for M.T. *mikkol rōḏ^e^pay* ('from all my pursuers') to make it correspond with the singular verb in verse 2*a*. Such a transition from the singular to the plural, and vice versa, is quite frequent in the *OT*, and consequently the emendation is scarcely justified.

and deliver me: see on 59:1. This may be the beginning of verse 2 (so, e.g., Dahood).

2. lest like a lion they rend me: lit. '. . . he rends me'. The enemies of the Psalmists are often likened to wild animals or to hunters (cf. 9:15 (M.T. 16), 31:4 (M.T. 5), 35:7f., 57:5 (M.T. 6), etc.). Another frequent metaphor is that of an attacking army (cf. 3:6 (M.T. 7), 27:3, 55:18 (M.T. 19), etc.). In most cases these descriptions are word-pictures, and as such they should not be taken literally. In Ps. 7 the actual hostility of the enemy (or enemies) expressed itself (at least primarily) in the form of false accusations which could have had serious consequences if not disproved.

The 'lions' mentioned in the *OT* were, apparently, the Asiatic or Persian lions, and they were quite common during the Biblical period, although extinct since the Crusades (cf. G. R. Driver, 'Lion', *DB*, p. 587).

dragging me away: the pronoun 'me' is supplied from the context. T suggests *yiprōḳ* ('(lest) he drag (me) away') for M.T. *pōrēḳ*; cf. Isa. 5:29.

A PROTESTATION OF INNOCENCE **3–5**

Verses 3–5 form a sort of oath of purgation or clearance (cf. Job 31) whereby the Psalmist attempts to prove his innocence (for a contrast see 143:2). The oath is made valid by the invocation of Yahweh who, as the guardian of the oath, would either fulfil or annul the self-cursing (verse 5) according to the integrity of the accused. A guilty man might break down under the strain, but it is likely that in ancient Israel, too, there were people who feared neither God nor men (cf. Lk. 18:2). Oaths were often accompanied by symbolic actions (cf. Dan. 12:7) and in this instance it might have involved the washing of hands (cf. 26:6; Isa. 1:15f.).

3. if I have done this: either 'this' points to the allegations against the Psalmist or it (i.e. the Hebrew *zō'ṯ*) conceals the object of 'I have done', which must be synonymous with 'wrong' (*ʿāwel*) in verse 3*b*. Dahood (*PAB*, I, p. 42) proposes that *zō'ṯ* (*RSV* 'this') is a substantive with the meaning 'indignity, insult' (and possibly connected with *ṣō'āh*, 'filth'), which may also occur in 44:17 (M.T. 18); Job 2:11; Zeph. 2:10. This explanation is plausible, but in the absence of more evidence the usual rendering could well be retained.

if there is wrong in my hands: this ought not to be taken as a claim to moral perfection, but it refers to the alleged offences.

4. From the structure of the two halves of this verse, it seems that they must be synonymous, and the following rendering may reproduce what appears to be the thought of this ambiguous verse: 'If I have (as much as) requited (evil) to him who was my treacherous partner, or (if) I have spoiled him who was my foe for no reason whatsoever'.

if I have requited . . .: there are several possible translations, e.g. 'if I have injured him who (now) requites' (Weiser, *POTL*, p. 134), or 'if I have requited him that rewarded me evil' (cf. Kirkpatrick, *BPCB*, p. 31).

or plundered . . .: *RV* 'Yea, I have delivered him that without cause was my enemy'; this affirms that the psalmist's behaviour has been the very opposite of that of which he is accused (cf. G. R. Driver, 'Notes on the Psalms. I 1–72', *JTS*, XLIII (1942), p. 151). The parallelism, however, seems to be against this rendering. Sabourin (*POM*, II, p. 10) suggests: 'I who spared those who without cause were my enemies'.

5. let the enemy pursue me: this is the beginning of the three-fold self-imprecation or self-cursing which was intended as a proof that the speaker's assertions were true.

me: lit. 'my soul'; see on 33:19.

to the ground: Dahood (*PAB*, I, p. 40) renders 'into the nether world'. 'Earth' (*ʾereṣ*) may indeed have such a connotation, and a reasonable parallel is found in 143:3: 'For the enemy has pursued me; he has crushed my life to the ground; he has made me sit in darkness like those long dead'. This quotation also provides a commentary on verse 5*c* (**and lay my soul in the dust**). For 'soul' M.T. has *k*ᵉ*ḇôḏî* ('my glory'), which is altered by some commentators into *k*ᵉ*ḇēḏî* ('my liver') (so Gunkel, Dahood, *et al.*). It is possible that such a confusion between 'liver' and 'glory' has occasionally taken place in some *OT* passages, because this is attested by the variant readings of the ancient versions; in this passage, however, 'my glory' may be 'a sort of glorified personal pronoun' (Johnson, *VITAI*, p. 75 n.5). The verse seems to describe in a graphic manner the different stages in the hypothetical punishment; first the pursuing, then the trampling down (cf. 2 Kg. 7:17,20), and finally the death (cf. 22:15 (M.T. 16), 30:10 (M.T. 11)).

Selah: see Introduction, pp. 48f.

AN APPEAL TO THE RIGHTEOUS JUDGE **6–11**

6. Arise, O LORD: this phrase is reminiscent of the old battle-cry found in the traditions associated with the Ark and Holy War (cf. Num. 10:35; Ps. 3:7 (M.T. 8), 9:19 (M.T. 20), 17:13, 44:26 (M.T. 27), 102:13 (M.T. 14); see also Isa. 33:10).

thy anger: see on 6:1.
lift thyself up . . .: (cf. 94:2; Isa. 33:10). Gunkel, Oesterley, *et al.* regard the scene in verses 6–10 as eschatological in nature, yet the Psalmist expects an answer here and now, not a final judgment in the messianic age. Yahweh is still the judge of all the earth (Gen. 18:25) even when he intervenes in the life of a single man.
awake: Kraus (*PBK*, p. 58) points out that the thought underlying 'awake' may have originated in the fertility cult of Canaan, and that this call may have belonged to the ritual awakening of the vegetation deity (cf. 1 Kg. 18:27); but there is no need to assume that the *OT* writers actually imposed this aspect of the cult of Baal upon that of Yahweh. It is possible that the *terminology* was of Canaanite origin, although the associations with the fertility myths were no longer there. See on 44:23.
my God: so also *NEB*; *AV*, *RV*, *RSVm* have 'for me'; but the former rendering is more likely and no change is required in the pointing of *ʾēlay*, which may be a plural of majesty (cf. *GK* 124g).
thou hast appointed a judgment: the Hebrew *ṣiwwîṯā* may be regarded as a precative perfect, equivalent to an imperative (i.e. 'appoint a judgment!') and as a stylistic variation of the preceding three imperatives.

7. the assembly of the peoples: Briggs (*CECBP*, I, p. 54) argues that this is a judgment of the nations gathered from all parts of the world, but since it would be alien to the thought of the previous verses (so Briggs), it must belong to a different psalm. It is more likely that we have here a picturesque description of Yahweh as the Judge of one and all. Gunkel, Weiser, *et al.* read: 'the assembly of the heavenly host' (i.e. *ʾelōhîm* for M.T. *leʾummîm*, 'peoples'); cf. Job 1–2; Ps. 82:1.
take thy seat on high: reading *šeḇāh* ('be enthroned'?) for M.T. *šûḇāh*, 'return', as in *RSVm* (*AV*, *RV*). Dahood (*PAB*, I, p. 44) sees no need for the emendation because, in his opinion, *š-w-b* may be a by-form of *y-š-b* ('to sit, dwell'), and not necessarily the verb 'to return'. He also regards 'on high' (*lammārôm*) as a divine epithet 'Exalted One', and he takes the preposition *le* as a sign of the vocative case. His translation of verse 7*b* would be: 'and over it preside, O Exalted One'.

8. The LORD judges the peoples: Yahweh, as the sole deity, administers justice to all nations, and the case of the Psalmist is only one particular instance of this judicial activity of God. The verb *d-y-n*, 'to judge', need not imply only condemnation, for it is both the vindication of the innocent and the punishment of the guilty (see on 72:2).

judge me: or 'vindicate me' or even 'help me' (cf. L. Köhler, *Hebrew Man* (1956), pp. 156ff.). The verb used is *š-p-ṭ*, see on 72:2. Cf. Isa. 1:17: '. . . defend (lit. 'judge') the fatherless' (see also Ps. 72:4, 82:3).

according to my righteousness: this is no more an expression of arrogance or Pharisaism than the plea of 'not guilty' by an innocent person in our courts.

the integrity that is in me: i.e. 'my integrity' (cf. 25:21, 26:1). It is very likely that the Psalmists had no illusion about man's true nature (cf. 130:3, 142:2), but a man could be guiltless of particular charges brought against him by his false accusers. Dahood (*PAB*, I, p. 45) may be right in taking the preposition *ᶜālāy* (*RSV* 'that is in me') as a divine name, 'Most High', which could be considered as an abbreviation of *ᶜelyôn*, 'Most High' (cf. H. Cazelles, *Mélanges André Robert* (1957), pp. 138ff.; cf. also Driver, *CML*, p. 43, n.7, and Keret, II. iii. 6,8, where *ᶜal* occurs as a name or title of Baal).

9. let the evil . . . come to an end: Dahood (*PAB*, I, p. 40): 'Avenge the treachery of the wicked' (for this use of the verb *g-m-r*, see *TS*, XIV (1953), pp. 595ff.). Both renderings express the idea that God's vindication will manifest itself in the cessation of the activities of the evildoers and in the establishing of the righteous (verse 9*b*; cf. 90:17).

who triest the minds and hearts: lit. '. . . hearts and kidneys'. 'Heart' (*lēḇ*) approximates to what we call 'mind, intellect' while 'kidneys' (*kelāyôṯ*; see on 139:13) could be described as the seat of one's emotions (cf. Johnson, *VITAI*, pp. 74ff.). For the phrase, see also 17:3; Jer. 11:20, 17:10, 20:12. The judgment of God is unlike that of men who judge according to appearances (cf. 1 Sam. 16:7); God takes into the reckoning also man's inmost motives.

thou righteous God: or 'art a righteous God' (cf. 129:4). Mowinckel (*PIW*, I, p. 203) offers a paraphrase: 'is a God who vindicates the right'.

10. My shield is with God: lit. 'my shield is upon God'. S reads 'my shield is God' (omitting the preposition *ᶜal*, 'upon'), similarly also *NEB*, while Kraus (*PBK*, p. 53) renders 'my shield over me is God' (reading *ᶜālay* for M.T. *ᶜal*), i.e. God is the protector of the accused man. Dahood (*PAB*, I, p. 45) proposes:

'My suzerain is the Most High God'; he reads *m^e^ḡānî* ('my suzerain') (see on 3:3) for M.T. *māḡinnî* ('my shield'), and he takes the preposition *ʿal* as the divine name 'Most High' (see verse 8).
the upright in heart is a favourite expression of the Psalmists. See 11:2, 36:10 (M.T. 11) where it is synonymous with 'those who know thee', and 32:11, 64:10 (M.T. 11), 97:11 where it is parallel to 'the righteous'; see note on 94:15.

11. God is a righteous judge: this is a continuation of the praise of God as the one who upholds justice, and it is reminiscent of the so-called doxology of judgment (cf. Jos. 7:19ff.; v. Rad, *OTT*, I, pp. 357ff.).
and a God: or 'and El' (so Dahood).
who has indignation: or 'who passes sentence' (cf. *KBL*, p. 262; see on 38:3).

THE BOOMERANG EFFECT OF SIN **12–16**

12. This and the following verse are very problematic. Is the subject God (so Kirkpatrick, Oesterley, Dahood, *NEB*, *et al.*) or the wicked man (so Gunkel, Nötscher, Weiser, Mowinckel)? Probably the latter since verse 14 obviously refers to the evildoer, and no change of subject is indicated.
If a man does not repent: or 'he will certainly (sharpen his sword) again' (for this use of the verb *š-w-b* ('to return, do again'), see *GK* 120d). G. W. Anderson (*PCB*, 362c) renders: 'If he (the evildoer) does not repent, but whets his sword', while Dahood (*PAB*, I, p. 41) suggests: 'O that the Victor would again . . .' and for M.T. *lōʾ* ('not') he reads *lēʾ* ('Victor') which he derives from the Ugaritic *lʾy*, 'to be strong, prevail'; this is, however, doubtful. Sabourin (*POM*, II, p. 10) has 'Unless they be converted'.
God will whet his sword: the word 'God' is not in M.T. but is an interpretative addition. The subject of the verb 'to whet' may be the wicked man (see *supra*).
he has bent . . . his bow: i.e. he is ready to shoot. For 'bow', see on 44:6.

13. his deadly weapons are his sharp sword and his bow. The enemy is described by means of military metaphors which should not be pressed too far. Perhaps we should render: 'But against himself has he prepared his . . .' (cf. Eaton, *PTBC*, p. 43); this is implied by verses 15–16.
fiery shafts: the allusion may be either to the incendiary arrows (tipped with tow or pitch), which were often used by the besiegers

to set the beleaguered city on fire (cf. 76:3. (M.T. 4)), or to the lightnings if the reference is to God (cf. 18:14 (M.T. 15); Zech. 9:14).

14. This verse portrays graphically the growth of evil by using metaphors of conception, pregnancy and birth (cf. for a similar use Job 15:35; Isa. 33:11, 59:4). Some have described this comparison as 'extremely distasteful' (Oesterley, *TP*, p. 139), but for all that the description is very apposite. In this context, 'evil', 'mischief' and 'lies' may be used for the sake of parallelism, and need not necessarily represent a progression.

15. He makes a pit: this word-picture is taken from hunting by means of pitfalls. These pits (the Hebrew *bôr* and *šaḥaṯ*) were, probably, lightly covered and served as traps for bigger animals (cf. 9:15 (M.T. 16), 35:7,8, 57:6 (M.T. 7), 141:9f.; Prov. 26:27; Ec. 10:8); see on 94:13.

digging it out: Dahood (*PAB*, 1, p. 47) renders it by 'it pitted him' (i.e. the subject is the pit, and the verb is taken as a causative or *hip̄ʿîl* in form). This would give a better parallel to verse 15*b*, but there is no clear indication of a change in subject.

16. on his own pate . . .: this description reminds us of Sir. 27:25: 'Whoever throws a stone straight up throws it on his own head' (cf. Prov. 26:27). Verses 15–16 show that the deed and its consequences form a unity (cf. v. Rad, *OTT*, 1, p. 386), but it is unlikely that in the *OT* the link between the two amounted to an impersonal law. Evil is self-destructive because it is opposed to God.

DOXOLOGY **17**

It is difficult to decide whether this verse is a *vow* to praise Yahweh for the future deliverance, or whether it is a thanksgiving in itself. The latter alternative is preferable, and it assumes that in the course of the ritual an oracle or assurance has been granted to the petitioner.

his righteousness: Calvin (*A Commentary on the Psalms*, revised and edited by T. H. L. Parker, 1 (1965), p. 87) has summed up its meaning as follows: 'God's righteousness is in this place taken for His faithfulness, which he performs towards His servants in saving their lives'.

the name of the Lord: see on 5:11.

the Most High: (*ʿelyôn*), see on 47:2. *ʾĒl ʿelyôn* is often regarded as the chief deity of the pre-Israelite Jerusalem who, after the conquest of the city, was identified with Yahweh. The epithet *ᶜelyôn* probably means 'exalted, high' and it can also be used independently, as in 9:2 (M.T. 3); Isa. 14:14. Cf. M. Haran, 'The Religion of the Patriarchs', *ASTI*, IV (1965), pp. 30–55.

Psalm 8 All Creation Reflects the Majesty of God

This Psalm belongs to the Hymns or Songs of Praise (see Introduction, pp. 32f.). The emphasis upon the motif of creation may suggest that it could better be described as a Psalm of Creation, i.e. a hymn praising God in creation (cf. Ps. 19, 104, 139). The cultic setting of the Hymns is, on the whole, uncertain because they may have been used on more than one cultic occasion (cf. Eissfeldt, *OTI*, p. 108), and therefore it is difficult to be specific in the description of the *Sitz im Leben* of the Hymns or of their setting. The theme of creation may link Ps. 8 with the Feast of Tabernacles or some particular aspect of it, during which the creation of the world and of all that is in it was relived in the cult. The mention of the starry sky and the moon may indicate that the hymn was sung at night time, as e.g. Ps. 134 (cf. 1 Chr. 9:33; Isa. 30:29). It was probably chanted antiphonally, although the alternation between 'we' and 'I' need not necessarily be a proof of this.

Traditionally the Psalm was attributed to David, but it may be of a later date; it is impossible to be more explicit. The question may be raised as to whether the Psalm presupposes the priestly account of creation in Gen. 1, or whether the dependence is the other way round. Probably both come from the same circles, and the Psalm need not be subsequent to the time of Ezra (so Briggs, *CECBP*, I, p. 62).

The metre is varied, and the strophic arrangement (if any) is difficult to determine. Verse 1*a* may be the introduction to the hymn, and it is repeated in the conclusion (verse 9). The rest of the Psalm is, more or less, equivalent to the hymnic main section dealing with the glory of God, as seen in his creation (verses 1*b*–2), and with the paradox of man (verses 3–8). Comparatively man is of little account, yet God has bestowed upon him kingship over the whole earth. This, too, is a glorification of Yahweh, for the greater man's status is, the more awestruck should be his attitude to God who is the source of man's glory.

To the choirmaster: see Introduction, p. 48.

The Gittith: see Introduction, p. 50.
A Psalm of David: see Introduction, pp. 43ff. and 46.

THE INTRODUCTION **1a**

O LORD, our Lord: the Hebrew uses two *different* words; the first is *yhwh* ('Yahweh'), the proper name of the God of Israel (see on 140:7), while the second one is the honorific title *ʾāḏôn*, indicative of the bearer's position and authority, and as such particularly fitting to one who can be described as 'the Lord of all the earth' (97:5) and the 'Lord of lords' (136:3).
how majestic: the sovereign power of God is more majestic than 'the everlasting mountains' (76:4 (M.T. 5)) or anything else in the whole universe. C. H. Spurgeon (*The Treasury of David* (1869), I, p. 89) once remarked that 'no words can express that excellency; and therefore it is left as a note of exclamation'.
thy name: a name (see on 20:1) is more than merely the designation by which a person or thing is known, because in Hebrew thought the name and its bearer are inseparably associated. Thus to praise one's name means to glorify the person concerned. See Ps. 148, where the praising of Yahweh alternates with the praising of his name. For other examples, see Imschoot, *ThOT*, I, pp. 195ff.

THE GLORY OF GOD **1b–2**

Much speculation has surrounded this section, because M.T., as it stands, is probably textually corrupt. A reasonable solution is offered by Dahood (*PAB*, I, p. 49), who reads *ʾašārᵉṯannāh* for M.T. *ʾašer tᵉnāh* (*AV* 'who hast set'), which he derives from *š-r-t* 'to serve, worship, adore', and takes it as an energetic form of the *piʿēl* imperfect. He translates: 'I will adore your majesty above the heavens, with the lips of striplings and sucklings'. In other words, the Psalmist feels inadequate to praise God, just like an infant of a few months; when he tries to glorify God, even the best he can do is little more than the babbling of a baby. Weiser (*POTL*, p. 139) renders verse 1*b*: 'Thou whose glory is praised (from *tānāh*, 'to be repeated in an antiphonal song') in the heavens', while verse 2 forms a new sentence. The verb *tānāh* is, however, problematic, and the verse remains awkward.

2. by the mouth of babes and infants: the *RSV* rendering suggests that God is praised by infants, and the thought is unique in the *OT* although it is supported by Mt. 21:16, which is based upon the LXX interpretation of our passage. Equally unique

is the translation of *RV*: 'Out of the mouth of babes . . . hast thou established strength'. Eaton (*PTBC*, p. 44) is of the opinion that the reference may be to the 'heavenly beings as "sons of God" '.
thou hast founded a bulwark: or (a new sentence) 'You built a fortress for your habitation . . .' (Dahood, *PAB*, I, p. 50); this involves the reading of *l^{e}mā^{c}ōn* ('for (your) habitation') for M.T. *l^{e}ma^{c}an* ('because of'). The 'fortress' (*^{c}ōz*) may be a poetic name for 'heaven', as probably in 78:26, 150:1, and the act of building or founding may refer to the creation of the heavens (see verse 3). If this is so, then the 'enemies' could be the powers of Chaos which were subdued at the creation of the world (according to some traditions). Similarly in Canaanite mythology Baal builds himself a palace after he had subdued his opponent, the god of the sea or Yam (cf. Driver, *CML*, pp. 83ff.). *NEB* renders 'thou hast rebuked the mighty'.
the enemy and the avenger: in 44:16 (M.T. 17) the same phrase is used of the foes of Israel, but in this verse they may form a poetic parallel to the adversaries in verse 2*b*. A number of these primeval opponents of Yahweh are mentioned in the *OT*, e.g. Rahab (Job 26:12; Ps. 89:10 (M.T. 11); Isa. 51:9), the helpers of Rahab (Job 9:13), the sea (Job 26:12; Ps. 74:13, 89:9 (M.T. 10); Isa. 51:10), the great deep (Isa. 51:10), the floods (93:3), Leviathan (74:14) and the dragons (74:13; Isa. 51:9).

INSIGNIFICANT YET MADE GLORIOUS 3–8

3. thy heavens: i.e. as created by Yahweh (cf. 33:6, 96:5, 102:25 (M.T. 26), 136:5).
the moon and the stars: they probably represent (together with the heavens) all created things. The sun is not mentioned but this may suggest that the Psalm was meant for some cultic act at night time when the fathomless immensity of the starry sky was the most impressive factor. The heavens as well as the whole creation were the 'work of thy fingers', and this expression seems to stress the fact that the creation was a *personal* work of God, and is not meant to describe the actual manner in which God made the world (cf. 102:25 (M.T. 26)).

4. what is man: in this rhetorical question 'what' (*māh*) forms an antithesis to 'how' (*māh*) in verse 1, and the point of contrast is the majesty and power of God, and the relative littleness of man (cf. 144:3). Man in himself is puny, even in comparison with other created things and beings, but God's word has made him into the crown of creation (cf. verses 5–8). It is possible that the particular choice of terms, 'man' (*ᵓᵉnôš*) and 'son of man' (*ben ᵓāḏām*), was intended to convey the sense of human frailty, but, on the other hand, they may be merely synonyms of 'man' (*ᵓîš*) without any specific emphasis (cf. Barr, *SBL*, pp. 144ff.). In this instance the former alternative may be preferable (cf. 9:20 (M.T. 21), 90:3, 103:15).

that thou art mindful of him: lit. 'that you remember him'. This is no mere recollection, but it implies that God is continuing to act on behalf of mankind (cf. Childs, *MTI*, pp. 31ff.). This is supported by the parallel phrase: 'that thou dost care for him' (verse 4*b*).

the son of man: this is an alternative expression for 'man' in verse 4*a*, and it does not possess the special significance which it came to have in post-*OT* literature. The word *ben* ('son of . . .') is used to denote a member of a class or group, and is not to be taken literally in its usual sense as a 'male child'. The question may be raised as to what is meant by 'man' or 'son of man' ('mortal man'?) in this verse. A. Bentzen (*King and Messiah* (1955), p. 42) argues that the reference is to the 'First Man' who is both 'First King' and 'Man in General'. The author of the Letter to the Hebrews saw in this Psalm a picture of Jesus Christ and his rule (2:5ff.). It is more likely that we should understand 'man' as 'man in general' which would include Adam or the First Man as the traditional patriarch of mankind. It would also justify its application to Jesus Christ who descended to the depths of human experience and also ascended on high to reign over creation.

5. little less than God: a problem is caused by the Hebrew *ᵓᵉlōhîm* which may mean 'God' (so it was understood by Aq, Sym, Theod) or 'angels' (so LXX, T, S, V). The latter alternative is more likely, because the Psalmist had been at pains to stress the infinite greatness of God and the comparative insignificance of man. The first alternative would have the effect of practically contradicting the essence of verses 3–4, and therefore the comparison must be between man and the heavenly beings or God's messengers who surround his throne (cf. 1 Kg. 22:19; Job 1:6; Ps. 82:1, 86:8, 89:6 (M.T. 7)).

glory and honour are frequent royal attributes (see on 96:6).

6. Thou hast given him dominion: the same thought is also expressed in Gen. 1:26ff. and Sir. 17:1ff.

all things under his feet: man is the undoubted master of them (cf. 18:38 (M.T. 39), 110:1). For the application of this phrase in the *NT*, see 1 C. 15:27; Eph. 1:22.

7. sheep . . . oxen . . . beasts: man's rule is exercised not only over domestic animals, but it also extends over the wild creatures.

8. birds . . . fish: these, too, are under the dominion of man. The creatures mentioned in verses 7–8 are the more obvious representatives of the world of living things.

whatever passes along . . .: some scholars see here an allusion to the sea monsters mentioned in Gen. 1:21, and to Leviathan (104:26), while Wellhausen takes this as a description of the fish in verse 8*b* (i.e. 'which dart through . . .'; cf. *PBP*, p. 7). The former alternative is, however, more plausible.

THE CONCLUSION **9**

The concluding words of the Psalm re-echo the introduction in verse 1, on which see.

Psalms 9–10 Yahweh is the Hope of the Oppressed

Most scholars agree that originally these two Psalms formed a literary unity, and the argument is based on the following factors: (i) some Hebrew MSS, LXX and V treat Ps. 9–10 as one Psalm; (ii) there is no title or superscription to Ps. 10, and this lack is rather noteworthy in the first book of the Psalter; (iii) an acrostic scheme seems to embrace both Psalms, although textual corruption and/or editorial activity may have disturbed the alphabetic sequence, especially at the beginning of Ps. 10; (iv) the presence of 'Selah' in the final verse of Ps. 9 may suggest that this verse is not the conclusion of the poem, because 'Selah' is not found elsewhere at the end of a Psalm; (v) both Psalms exhibit a considerable similarity in language and contents, e.g. 'times of trouble' is found both in Ps. 9 (verse 9 (M.T. 10)) and in Ps. 10 (verse 1), so also 'Arise, O Lord' (9:19 (M.T. 20) and 10:12), 'for ever and ever' (9:5 (M.T. 6) and 10:16).

The main objection against the literary unity is the change of mood, tone and *Gattung*, or psalm-type. Thus Ps. 9 resembles a Thanksgiving of the Individual (or of the Community), while Ps. 10 reminds us of a Lament. Such a mixing of psalm-types is not unknown in the Psalter (cf. Ps. 22, 36, 52, 77, etc.) but the odd feature is the fact that the lamentation follows the thanksgiving. Kraus (*PBK*, p. 79) has suggested that thanksgiving psalms may occasionally have provided an opportunity for the instruction of the hearers, as in Ps. 34, where the Psalmist, after exalting God and his gracious help, exclaims: 'Come, O sons, listen to me, I will teach you the fear of the LORD' (verse 11 (M.T. 12)). Similarly also the writer of Ps. 9–10 passes from thanking God to other related themes, such as Yahweh's judgment of the nations and the problem of the prosperity of the wicked. Consequently there is no need to assume that an original Psalm of thanksgiving has been re-worked and expanded by another author (cf. Schmidt, *PHAT*, p. 18). Another view is represented by Dahood (*PAB*, I, p. 54) who regards the verbs in 9:4–6 as precative perfects and consequently the Psalm itself is taken as a lament; the opening verses, in such a case, would contain a promise to thank Yahweh once the enemies are destroyed. Such vows or promises need not be regarded as a kind of bargain: if God will deliver the Psalmist, then he, on his part, will give thanks. A promise could be viewed as an expression of confidence or faith in God; the Psalmist is *certain* that he will have opportunity to give thanks to God. Since Yahweh is both just and the Lord of all, the cause of the oppressed will be vindicated whatever the immediate circumstances might be. It is also possible that both Psalms could be understood as forming, essentially, a prayer of supplication in which the speaker repeatedly returns to the theme of the salvation-history as the source of his inspiration and confidence. The Psalmist can thank or praise Yahweh for the past manifestations of his saving power, but implicit in this praise is the hope that the same power will prove effective in the present situation (cf. W. Beyerlin, 'Die *tôdā* der Heilsvergegenwärtigung in den Klageliedern des Einzelnen', *ZAW*, LXXIX (1967), pp. 208–24.)

The speaker in the Psalm is probably an individual and the references to the nations may belong to the liturgical setting or they may be derived from the Communal Laments. The life-situation, or the *Sitz im Leben*, of the Psalm may be some cultic act in the Temple during which the needy person presents his prayers to God.

The older generation of commentators attributed the Psalm to David (so Delitzsch, Davison, Kirkpatrick) who was thought to be celebrating his victories over the Philistines or other enemies. On the other hand, the use of the acrostic structure and the possible mixing of psalm-types may indicate a later date, though not necessarily the Greek period.

The metre of the Psalm is varied, but most verses exhibit either 4+4 or 4+3 metre. The acrostic arrangement of the psalm is such that the first letters of the successive strophes (?), consisting of two verses each, appear in alphabetic order (for a similar arrangement see Ps. 25, 34, 37, 111, 112, 119, 145). The reason for the use of such artificial acrostic schemes is unknown. It is possible that sometimes the acrostic was invested with a magical significance, or that it was used as a pedagogic device by means of which boys were taught the alphabet. In the type of literature which is found in the Psalter, the acrostic scheme may have been either a mnemonic aid or, perhaps, another way of saying that the subject matter has been dealt with from A to Z. For a more detailed discussion, see N. K. Gottwald, *Studies in the Book of Lamentations* (*SBT* 14, 1954), pp. 23ff.

In Ps. 9, verses 1–4 express the certainty of the Psalmist that he will have cause to praise Yahweh, and verses 5–6 describe the source of that conviction. In verses 7–10 the writer explains the reasonableness of his confidence by affirming that Yahweh is not only the king of the whole world, but also the protector of the oppressed. Verses 11–12 are an invitation to glorify Yahweh, while verses 13–14 are a prayer of the needy person. In verses 15—18 we find further thoughts on the salvation-history, followed by another supplication (verses 19–20). Ps. 10:1–11 is concerned with the evildoers and their prosperity, while verses 12–15 consist of brief appeals to God. The Psalm ends with a further expression of a courageous faith (verses 16–18).

To the choirmaster: see Introduction, p. 48.
Muth-labben: see Introduction, p. 50.
A Psalm of David: see Introduction, pp. 43ff. and 46.

THE PROMISE TO PRAISE YAHWEH **1–4**

1. I will give thanks . . .: practically the same phrase is also found in 111:1. More frequent is the expression 'I will thank you, O LORD', and therefore some scholars read with LXX, 'I will thank you' (*'ôḏeḵā*) and treat 'LORD' as a vocative. The emendation is hardly required, because the pronoun 'you' may have been understood from the context (see on 3:3 concerning the double-duty suffix).

with my whole heart: i.e. sincerely. The opposite is to honour

God with one's lips only while the heart is far away from him (cf. Isa. 29:13), or to offer him a formal homage without a true allegiance.

I will tell: or 'declare, recount'. This indicates that the Psalm was not meant for a private meditation, but that it was used before a congregation, as were most Psalms (if not all).

thy wonderful deeds: the Hebrew *niplāʾôṯ* is a familiar term in the Psalter (27 times, out of a total of some 45 occurrences in the whole *OT*), and in most instances it refers to God's acts of creation (cf. 136:4), judgment and redemption (cf. 26:7, 71:17, 75:1 (M.T. 2), 78:4,11, etc.). Kissane (*BP*, p. 41) sees here an allusion to the works of creation and to the favours shown to Israel, but it is possible that the author had in mind also the deliverance that would be granted to him. This is seen, however, in the wider context of God's mighty deeds in general (see 40:5 (M.T. 6)).

2. I will sing praise . . .: nearly the same expression is also found in 7:17 (M.T. 18), 92:1 (M.T. 2).

thy name: i.e. God as he has made himself known through his word and acts. For *šēm* ('name'), see on 20:1.

Most High: (*ᶜelyôn*), see on 7:17, 18:13, 46:4, 47:2.

3. When my enemies turned back: better '. . . turn back' (in defeat; cf. 44:10 (M.T. 11), 56:9 (M.T. 10), 129:5), looking forward to God's deliverance.

they stumbled and perished: or '(when) they stumble and perish' (cf. 27:2; Jer. 20:11).

before thee: lit. 'from your face' or, perhaps, 'because of your hostile presence', as in Lam. 4:16 where the 'face of Yahweh scatters the faithless leaders. Dahood (*PAB*, I, p. 53) translates 'by your fury'.

4. For thou has maintained: this verse should, probably, be linked with verse 2; when the enemies are scattered, the Psalmist will praise God who has upheld justice (cf. 140:12 (M.T. 13)).

my just cause: lit. 'my right and my cause' (so *NEB*). The victory over the enemies is seen as an intervention by the Righteous Judge. The Psalmist's case is won, not because he knows the right formulae, but because his cause is a just one.

on the throne: see on 93:2. The 'throne' is often used as a symbol of the judicial power of God (or of a King), and therefore in this verse it is, primarily, a throne for judgment (cf. 122:5; Prov. 20:8; Dan. 7:9; Mt. 19:28; Rev. 20:4).

giving righteous judgment: or 'a judge of righteousness' (so Ḳimḥi).

THE SALVATION-HISTORY AS THE SOURCE OF CONFIDENCE **5–6**

The Hebrew perfects of this passage can be taken either as expressing a wish or as referring to past events, i.e. to the *Heilsgeschichte*, or the salvation-history, of Israel.

5. **Thou hast rebuked the nations:** or 'Rebuke the nations . . .' (so Dahood). God's rebuke is not simply a verbal censure but it can be described as a 'word in action' (cf. 104:7; Isa. 17:13; Nah. 1:4). The verb 'rebuke' is not infrequently found in a mythological setting (cf. 104:7), and it is possible that the author of this Psalm is drawing upon the language of old cultic traditions associated with Jerusalem. It is unlikely that verse 5 (and the following verses) describes an eschatological scene (as suggested by Oesterley, Leslie, *et al.*), rather this passage is part and parcel of the cultic glorification of Yahweh as the 'Mighty in battle' (24:8, 76:6 (M.T. 7)) and a 'Judge of the world' (9:8 (M.T. 9)).

thou hast blotted out their name: or 'blot out . . .'. This means to destroy one's existence, as in 83:4 (M.T. 5): '. . . let us wipe them out as a nation; let the name of Israel be remembered no more.' In the other extreme, the act of creation is not quite complete until the beings or things created have received their names (cf. Gen. 2:18–23). In the Akkadian Epic of Creation, the opening line reads: 'When on high the heaven had not been named (i.e. created)' (cf. *ANET*, p. 60b).

for ever and ever: the first word (*ᶜôlām*) refers to the remotest time in the past or in the future, and its duration may sometimes be limited by the context, e.g. 'he shall be slave for ever' (i.e. as long as he lives; cf. Exod. 21:6). The second word (*ᶜaḏ*) is sometimes said to denote 'the time which carries on to the uttermost thinkable limits' (so Orelli, quoted in J. Barr, *Biblical Words for Time* (*SBT* 33, 1962), p. 86). In actual usage the difference between the two may have been small, if any. The above-mentioned phrase, by linking the two nouns together, emphasizes the thought of perpetuity. Dahood (*PAB*, I, p. 66) regards it as a composite noun; see also E. Jenni, 'Das Wort *ᶜôlām* im Alten Testament', *ZAW*, N.F., XXIII (1952), pp. 197–248; XXIV (1953), pp. 1–35.

6. **The enemy:** (*hāʾōyēḇ*) is a collective noun in an emphatic

position, and it probably refers to the foreign nations which were subdued at the time of the Conquest (i.e. as depicted in the traditions).

in everlasting ruins: the preposition 'in' is not in M.T. Some exegetes prefer to re-arrange the verse as follows: 6*a*, *d*, *c*, *b* because the metaphor of ruins would be more appropriate to the cities than to the enemies. Nevertheless, the verb *ḥ-r-b* (cf. *ḥ*ᵒ*rāḇôṯ*, 'ruins'), 'to be waste, desolate', can be applied to nations and persons (cf. 2 Kg. 19:17; Isa. 37:18, 60:12).

their cities thou hast rooted out: Dahood (*PAB*, I, p. 55) renders: 'Root out their gods', taking *ʿîr* (usually 'city') as related to the Ugaritic *ǵyr* ('to protect'), hence the noun would mean 'protector' or 'god'. Several scholars have recognized similar examples elsewhere in the *OT*, and for references, see *PAB*, I, p. 56. Dahood's suggestion is a possibility, but it is hardly an improvement on the *RSV* rendering. The mention of 'ruins' in the previous sentence, may favour 'cities' here.

the very memory of them: i.e. of the enemies. This is the result of their name being blotted out (verse 5*b*); since they no longer exist, the memory of them, too, comes to an end. Cf. Dt. 32:26: 'I will scatter them afar, I will make the remembrance of them cease from among men'.

At the end of this verse (in M.T. verse 7) there is the word *hēmmāh* (lit. 'they'), which *RSV* has taken as emphasizing the pronoun 'them'; but J. H. Patton (*CPBP*, p. 37), and others have pointed out that it can be an equivalent to the Ugaritic *hm* ('behold'), and that it may belong to verse 7 (see below).

THE DIVINE KING IS THE PROTECTOR OF THE NEEDY **7–10**

7. But the LORD: better 'Behold, the LORD . . .' (see verse 6), and the conjunction 'and' (*w*ᵉ), if authentic here, may be the emphatic *wāw*.

enthroned for ever: or 'enthroned from the primeval time', taking the preposition *l*ᵉ in the sense of 'from' (as in Ugaritic; cf. Patton, *CPBP*, p. 41). Gunkel (*PGHAT*, p. 35) has argued that the reference is not to the past but to the present, and in view of 29:10, 93:2 the latter alternative is preferable (cf. 102:12 (M.T. 13)). Verses 7–8 give the reasons for God's actions described in verses 5–6.

he has established his throne: Yahweh's throne is in heaven (cf. 11:4, 103:19; also 1 Kg. 22:19; 2 Chr. 18:18; Isa. 6:1,

66:1; Lam. 5:19; Ezek. 1:26, 10:1), but it could be symbolized by the Ark of the Covenant or even Jerusalem (Jer. 3:17).

8. This verse is practically identical with 98:9 (cf. 96:10). Yahweh's rule is both universal and just, and consequently the oppressed can be sure of his help.

9. The Lord is: lit. 'and let Yahweh be', but most scholars read *way^e^hî* ('and . . . is ('was')') for M.T. *wîhî* ('and let . . . be').

a stronghold for the oppressed: what an inaccessible place is to the refugee in time of war, God is to the oppressed. Cf. 46:7,11 (M.T. 8,12): 'The Lord of hosts is with us; the God of Jacob is our refuge' (i.e. stronghold).

in times of trouble: as in 10:1.

10. who know thy name: i.e. those who not only know Yahweh's nature and his demands but also live according to the will of Yahweh. 'Because he cleaves to me in love, I will deliver him; I will protect him, because he knows my name' (91:14).

put their trust in thee: see on 4:5.

who seek thee: i.e. who depend upon Yahweh. The expression may be used with a variety of meanings, e.g. 'to seek an oracle' (cf. 1 Kg. 14:5) or 'to seek in worship' (e.g. 105:4), 'to resort to a sacred place' (Dt. 12:5). For the verb *d-r-š*, 'to seek', see also on 24:6, 142:4.

SING TO THE LORD **11–12**

11. Sing praises to the Lord: this is a characteristic call to praise, and it is common in the Psalter (cf. 30:4 (M.T. 5), 47:7, 66:2, 68:4,32 (M.T. 5,33), 98:5, 105:2,1 35:3, 147:7). See on 66:4.

who dwells in Zion: better 'who sits enthroned . . .'. There is no contradiction between this statement and the belief that the throne of God is in heaven. Both ideas are found side by side (according to the usual interpretation) in 11:4: 'The Lord is in his holy temple, the Lord's throne is in heaven'. The earthly abode of Yahweh, or his throne, was but a counterpart of his heavenly abode (cf. Clements, *GT*, p. 68). In a sense the symbol not only points beyond itself, but it also shares in the reality of the thing or person symbolized.

Tell among the peoples . . .: i.e. declare the saving deeds of Yahweh, which are not some sort of esoteric knowledge, but which are to be made known to all (cf. 1 Chr. 16:8; Ps. 105:1; Isa. 12:4).

12. he who avenges blood: *OT* makes it clear that 'blood and life belong to God alone; whenever a man commits murder he attacks God's very own right of possession' (G. v. Rad, *Genesis*, Eng. tr. by J. H. Marks (*OTL*, 1961), p. 102). Consequently God requires a reckoning from the guilty, either by the hand of another man (Gen. 9:2) or by his (i.e. God's) own hand (cf. 2 Sam. 12:14ff.). The verb 'avenges' translates the Hebrew *dōrēš*; see on verse 10.
is mindful of them: i.e. of the afflicted. Dahood (*PAB*, I, p. 53). renders verse 12*a*: 'For he cares for those who mourn, their lament he remembers', reading *dammîm* (from *d-m-m*, 'to weep, mourn') for M.T. *dāmîm*, 'blood', and *ʾawwōṯām* (a *piʿēl* infinitive, from *ʾ-w-h*, 'to lament') for M.T. *ʾōṯām*, 'them'. This gives a better parallel to verse 12*b*, but is not otherwise superior to the traditional reading.
he does not forget: he does not disregard the cry of the oppressed; he will act as circumstances may demand (cf. 10:12).
the afflicted: see on 34:2. They do not constitute a special class or party within Judaism, but are simply those who are oppressed or who are the victims of some misfortune.

THE PRAYER OF THE AFFLICTED **13–14**

13. Be gracious to me: see on 51:1. Some scholars (e.g. Weiser, Kraus) read, following Aq and Jerome, *ḥᵃnānanî* ('he was gracious to me'), and similarly *rāʾāh* ('he saw') (for the M.T. imperative *rᵉʾēh*, 'behold'). It is doubtful, however, whether this and other emendations (such as the deletion of 'those who hate me') are fully justified.
those who hate me: Dahood (*PAB*, I, p. 57) takes the Hebrew *śōnᵉʾāy* ('my haters') as a plural of majesty, rendering 'my Enemy', i.e. the chief enemy of the Psalmist, Death. Yet the affliction was brought on, primarily, by the enemies, and not by Death as such.
O thou who liftest me up: the participle *mᵉrômᵉmî*, which follows two imperatives, may have the force of an imperative itself, hence 'lift me up . . .' (so also Dahood).
from the gates of death: in the *OT* the experience of disease, calamity, etc. is tantamount to being in Sheol or on the very threshold of death. Although the afflicted man's experience of death is a partial one, it is none the less real. Cf. 107:18; Job 38:17; Mt. 16:18.

14. that I may recount . . .: i.e. that I may declare Yahweh's saving deeds before other worshippers (cf. verse 1).

the gates of the daughter of Zion: this expression recalls the opposite sphere, the gates of death (verse 13), thus emphasizing, by contrast, the greatness of the deliverance. He has passed from death to life. 'The daughter of Zion' occurs only here in the Psalter, but it is found frequently in Isaiah and Lamentations, denoting the people of Jerusalem. Cities could be regarded as mothers of their people, while the inhabitants could be described as the sons and daughters of a city (e.g. 'sons of Zion' in 149:2; Lam. 4:2; Jl 2:23; and 'daughters of Zion' in Isa. 3:16, 4:4; Jer. 4:31, 6:2). For 'gates', see on 87:2.

FURTHER REFLECTIONS ON THE SALVATION-HISTORY **15–17**

15. The nations have sunk . . .: the reference is to Israel's *Heilsgeschichte* ('salvation-history') which is able to inspire new hopes in the heart of the needy. To the Israelite the salvation-history was a certainty; the very fact that he was worshipping in Jerusalem was to him a proof that God *had acted* on behalf of his people.

the pit which they made: seen on 7:15f.; cf. also 35:7, 57:6 (M.T. 7).

the net: in the ancient Near East nets were usually made of such materials as flax, hemp or palm fibre. They could be used for catching birds, fish and smaller animals. In the *OT* 'net' is often used as a figure of speech, suggesting the plotting of the enemy or similar hostile activities.

16. he has executed judgment: this probably describes the way in which Yahweh has made himself known, i.e. by the judgment which he has carried out. This was the experience of the Egyptians during the Exodus events as they are described in the *OT* traditions (cf. Exod. 7:5, 14:4,18).

the wicked are snared . . .: Calvin (p. 108) comments: '. . . this happened not by chance, but was the work of God, and a notable proof of God's judgment' (cf. 141:10). A similar example of being hoist with one's own petard is found in 1QH ii:29: 'the net which they spread for me has ensnared their own feet'.

Higgaion: see Introduction, p. 49.

Selah: see Introduction, pp. 48f.

17. The wicked shall depart to Sheol: Dahood (*PAB*, I, p. 54) translates: 'Let the wicked return to Sheol', and he argues that, since man was created 'in the lowest regions of the nether world', one may properly speak of a 'return to Sheol' (op. cit., p. 58). It is doubtful, however, whether we ought to press the literal sense too far. The phrase may simply mean that the wicked shall perish, without suggesting that the first man or men in general have been formed in Sheol. See on 6:10.

that forget God: this means to forsake God (cf. Isa. 65:11; also Job 8:13; Ps. 50:22).

18. the needy shall not always be forgotten: although for the time being the needy appear to be disregarded by Yahweh, this is not a permanent situation. An example is the deliverance of the Israelites from Egypt; see note on 35:10.

the hope . . . shall not perish for ever: this is an illustration of the extension of the force of the negative ('not') from the first half of the verse to the second; there is no negative in verse 18*b*, although it is clearly required by the context.

THE SUPPLICATION **19–20**

19. Arise, O Lord: see on 7:6. Weiser (*POTL*, pp. 38ff.) sees here and in similar passages, a reference to the epiphany of Yahweh above the Ark of the Covenant; if so, it would be both a cultic and spiritual experience.

let not man prevail: see on 8:4. Man (*ʾᵉnôš*) whose frailty is so obvious in comparison with God, should not be allowed to boast of his apparent superiority (cf. 2 Chr. 14:11; Job 4:17).

let the nations be judged: they have set themselves up against God; let them now realize their absurd position (cf. 2:4f.). For *gôyīm*, 'nations', see on 59:5, 106:5.

20. Put them in fear: LXX, S and V render: 'Appoint a lawgiver . . .' (or 'teacher' (*môreh*)), while Aq, T and Jerome suggest 'fear' (*môrāʾ*) which is read by some Hebrew MSS. for M.T. *môrāh* (a variant on *môrāʾ*?). The reference is, apparently, to some manifestation of God's power.

Psalm 10

See introduction to Ps. 9–10.

THE WICKED AND THEIR PROSPERITY **1–11**

1. Why dost thou stand afar off: this thought of the apparent aloofness of God is a recurrent theme in the Psalter (cf. 13:1 (M.T. 2), 22:1f. (M.T. 2f.), 35:22, 38:21 (M.T. 22), 42:9f. (M.T. 10f.), 43:2, 71:12, 88:14 (M.T. 15)). It is not so much the misfortune itself that worries the Psalmist, but rather the seeming separation from God.

Why dost thou hide thyself: i.e. 'Why do you take no notice of the distress?' (cf. Isa. 1:15; Lam. 3:56). The help which the author expects is not simply an inner assurance of God's presence, but an actual intervention in the situation. Therefore, in this sense, when God manifests his power by saving the afflicted, he is near to the needy person; cf. 34:17f. (M.T. 18f.).

in times of trouble: as in 9:9.

2. the wicked: for *rāšā*ᶜ, see on 1:1, 28:3, 140:4.

hotly pursue . . .: cf. Gen. 31:36; 1 Sam. 17:53; Lam. 4:19. *PNT* reads: 'The poor man is devoured by the pride of the wicked', which is a possible literal rendering.

let them be caught: i.e. let the wicked be trapped by their own scheming (cf. 9:15; see on 7:15f.). LXX and V suggest '(the poor) are caught by the schemes which (the wicked) had thought out', and this provides a good parallel to verse 2*a*. The plural verbs in M.T. refer to the collective noun 'the wicked' (*rāšā*ᶜ) in the previous line.

3. . . . boasts of the desires of his heart: i.e. the wicked brag that whatever they desire they also achieve. The text of this verse is in some disorder, and perhaps 'his heart' (lit. 'his soul', *napšô*) belongs to the next line, while 'renounces the LORD' is to be transferred to verse 4. Hence 'Indeed, the wicked brags about (his) desire(s), and it is himself that the unscrupulous profiteer blesses' (cf. 49:18 (M.T. 19)).

4. The verse is textually uncertain; a possible paraphrase might be: 'The wicked spurns the Lord (cf. verses 3 and 13) because (even when) his anger is high [infinitive construct], he does not, so the wicked argues, require justice (cf. verse 12); consequently the reasoning (of the godless) amounts to this, "There is no God"' (cf. 14:1, 53:1 (M.T. 2)). This is not an expression of theoretical atheism, but an assertion that God is not concerned with human affairs.

5. His ways prosper: this is the vexing problem. The wicked not only ill-treat the defenceless, but they also reject the belief that God judges the world and its peoples with justice and equity (cf. 9:8 (M.T. 9)). Yet the only tangible result is that they become more and more affluent. *NEB* reads: 'His ways are always devious'.

thy judgments are on high, out of his sight: i.e. the wicked man thinks that, whatever criticisms God might have concerning his activities, they are ineffective (cf. Job 22:12ff.).

all his foes: i.e. the ones who are not weak enough to be an easy prey.

he puffs at them: this is probably an idiom expressing contempt (cf. Mal. 1:13), but some exegetes (e.g. Gunkel, Mowinckel) see here a possible allusion to magic; this, however, seems less likely.

6. thinks in his heart: lit. 'he says . . .'. For *lēḇ* ('heart'), see on 27:3, 51:10.

I shall not be moved: he looks forward to an undisturbed prosperity which is, strictly speaking, the type of existence promised to the righteous (cf. 15:5, 16:8, 21:7 (M.T. 8), 62:2 (M.T. 3), 112:6). Perhaps we should render the verse: 'I shall not falter throughout all generations, because the curse (of my enemies or that of the Covenant) does not (have the power to show itself) in adversity' (i.e. it does not bring any misfortune). The word 'curse' (*ʾālāh*) has been transferred from verse 7 to verse 6 (so also in *RSV*). For covenant curses, see Dt. 27:15ff.; D. R. Hillers, *Treaty-Curses and the Old Testament Prophets* (1964), pp. 30–42. A similar type of wicked man is described in Dt. 29: 18ff., who also assures himself (when he hears the words of the covenant curse) that he will enjoy well-being (cf. 1QS ii:11ff.).

7. His mouth is filled with cursing . . .: 'cursing' (*ʾālāh*) probably belongs to the preceding verse. The Psalmist shows the absurdity of the wicked man's confidence. Only a man loyal to God and his Covenant can hope for a blessing and peace (*šālôm*), while the man who is described in verses 7–11 can expect nothing but justice.

under his tongue are mischief . . .: either they are ready to be uttered, or his speech is characterized by deceit and wickedness (cf. Ca. 4:11). It is unlikely that 'mischief' (see on 55:10) and 'evil' (see on 36:4) are to the wicked like a delicious morsel, kept under the tongue for a prolonged enjoyment (cf. Job 20:12; Ps. 140:3 (M.T. 4)).

8. The various 'portraits' of the wicked are only a series of metaphors. The evildoers are not necessarily robbers or 'powerful nobles who plundered their poorer neighbours' (so Kirkpatrick, *BPCB*, p. 53), although the word-pictures themselves may have been derived from such and similar situations. If the Psalmist had any actual murderers in mind, they might have been involved in judicial murders, of which the classic example is the case of

Regina *versus* Naboth (1 Kg. 21). The different figures of speech may imply that a certain amount of secrecy surrounded the misdeeds of the godless, which in turn may suggest that although, at the most, the letter of the law may have been observed, its inner meaning and function were deliberately perverted.
the villages were, most likely, smaller, unwalled settlements with simpler administration than a city. In Talmudic times a village was defined as a place which had no synagogue (cf. C. U. Wolf, 'Village', *IDB*, IV, p. 784).
His eyes stealthily watch . . .: this phrase is textually problematic, but *RSV* seems to be a reasonable rendering. LXX renders: 'his eyes gaze at the poor'.
the hapless: this word occurs only here and in verses 10 and 14; its exact connotation is obscure. Yet some such meaning as the one in *RSV* is required by the context. The same word (*ḥlkʾym*) is found also in 1QH iii:25,26; iv:25,35, where it is variously translated as 'the wicked tyrant' (Mansoor), 'the damned' (Vermes), etc.; but these are obviously not the meanings required by our passage.

9. like a lion in his covert: such similes are frequent in the *OT*, e.g. in 7:2 (M.T. 3), 17:12, 22:13 (M.T. 14); Isa. 15:9, 31:4; Jer. 2:30, 4:7, 5:6, 25:28.
he lurks that he may seize the poor: this phrase may be a variant on verse 9*c* because of the repetition of the same terms (cf. Oesterley, *TP*, p. 143). Perhaps verse 9*bc* could be translated: 'he lies in wait to seize the afflicted one, in his bag' (cf. R. Gordis, JQR, XLVIII (1947), pp. 116ff.). The words 'into his net' could be transferred to the beginning of verse 10.

10. The hapless: see verse 8. Strictly speaking, this word belongs to verse 10*b*, while the subject in verse 10*a* is, apparently, missing. Hence some exegetes supply 'the righteous' (*ṣaddîḳ*), which would also provide the letter of the alphabet lacking in the acrostic scheme at this particular point. *NEB* adds 'the good man'.
by his might: Briggs (*CECBP*, I, p. 69) renders: 'because of his great numbers', while Dahood (*PAB*, I, p. 63) suggests 'into his pit' (from *ʿ-ṣ-m*, 'to dig', as in Ugaritic), which would give a good parallel but, unfortunately, the evidence for the existence of this verb in Hebrew is rather slender. The appeal to the parallelism is a useful guide, but in itself it proves nothing.

11. He thinks in his heart: lit. 'He says . . .'. The subject

of the verb is either the evildoer (so Calvin, Briggs, Weiser, Kraus, *et al.*) or the afflicted man (so Kissane *et al.*). The former alternative seems more likely.
God: the Hebrew *ʾēl* is found in the Ugaritic texts as a personal name of the chief deity of the pantheon, who was, at least nominally, its head (cf. Pope, *EUT*, pp. 1–21). In this verse *ʾēl* is a synonym of *ʾᵉlōhîm*, 'God'; see on 52:5.
has forgotten: see on 9:12; cf. 13:1 (M.T. 2), 44:24 (M.T. 25), 74:19,23, 77:9 (M.T. 10).
he has hidden his face: (cf. 13:1 (M.T. 2), 22:24 (M.T. 25), 27:9, 30:7 (M.T. 8), 51:9 (M.T. 11), 69:17 (M.T. 18), 88:14 (M.T. 15), 102:2 (M.T. 3), 143:7). This is a graphic description of displeasure; here, if the speaker is the wicked, it suggests that God is disinterested and that he has turned his back on human affairs, therefore 'he will never see' the injustice.

THE APPEAL TO GOD **12–15**

12. Arise, O Lord: see on 7:6; the same phrase occurs also in 9:19 (M.T. 20).
O God, lift up thy hand: Dahood (*PAB*, I, p. 64) adds 'O God' to 'O Lord', and regards them both as forming a composite name, representing the original form of the tetragrammaton (see on 2:4), which he renders: 'El brings into being'. Although not entirely improbable, this suggestion is only one hypothesis among many. The lifting up of one's hand can be a symbolic act used in oaths (cf. Exod. 6:8; Num. 14:30), but here it denotes hostility. In 2 Sam. 20:21 it is said concerning the rebellious Sheba, the son of Bichri, that he 'has lifted up his hand against King David'. *NEB* has: '. . . set thy hand to the task'.
forget not the afflicted: this is not a good verbal parallel to verse 12*a*, although essentially they mean the same thing: 'May Yahweh manifest his power in delivering the oppressed.'
13. Why . . .: Dahood (*PAB*, I, p. 64) suggests: 'Must the wicked man condemn God for ever?', and he takes 'why?' (*ʿal meh*) as 'for ever' (*ʿōlāmāh*). Ugaritic literature may provide some parallels, but this is not good enough reason to alter M.T., which yields a satisfactory sense.
renounce God: a similar phrase is found in verse 3. In Dt. 31:20 Yahweh accuses his people, saying that they 'despise (i.e. renounce) me and break my covenant'. Also in Jer. 14:21 'to renounce, spurn' is linked with the breaking of the Covenant

(cf. Isa. 1:4; for a further discussion, see H. Wildberger, *Jesaja* (*BK* 10, 1965), pp. 20ff.).

say in his heart: i.e. think.

Thou wilt not call to account: cf. verse 4 and 9:12 (M.T. 13). The wicked assumes that God will overlook his misdeeds which may suggest that his crimes were committed with an air of respectability, and within the letter of the law (cf. verse 8).

14. Thou dost see; yea, thou dost note . . .: either *kî* ᵓ*attāh* ('for you') is used to emphasize *rā*ᵓ*iṯāh* ('you have seen') or, more likely, the former is a dittograph of the latter. Perhaps verse 14*ab* could be paraphrased: 'You have seen (all) mischief and grief, and (therefore) you will show regard (for this state of affairs) by taking matters into your own hand'. Any rendering is, however, rather forced.

the hapless: see on verse 8. *NEB* renders: 'The poor victim'.

commits himself to thee: or 'he leaves (his cause) to you'.

the helper of the fatherless: see on 82:3. The 'fatherless' represent all oppressed and needy people; God is the helper of such persons lacking protection (cf. Exod. 22:21ff.).

15. Break thou the arm of the wicked: i.e. deprive them of their power to do harm. The phrase is not to be taken literally for, in any case, the wicked more often than not resorted to indirect means rather than to brute force (cf. Job 38:15; Ps. 37:17).

seek out his wickedness: probably 'requite, punish, his crimes' (cf. 9:12 (M.T. 13)).

till thou find none: i.e. no unrequited evil. Aq, Sym and Theod suggest 'till (the evildoer) is found no more', reading *timmāṣē*ᵓ for M.T. *timṣā*ᵓ ('you find').

THE LORD WILL HEAR **16–18**

16. The LORD is king: see on 93:1. For the idea, cf. 5:2 (M.T. 3), 29:10, 44:5 (M.T. 6), 47:7, 48:2 (M.T. 3), 68:24 (M.T. 25).

the nations shall perish: i.e. the peoples shall come to an end, in as far as they are enemies of God (cf. 2:1ff.), and not because they are non-Israelites. *RV*, *RP*, and others have: '. . . are perished'; this may be right if the allusion is to the salvation-history.

17. the desire of the meek: i.e. the prayer of the afflicted who long for deliverance. Their desire will be granted while that of the wicked, for all his boasting, will ultimately come to nothing (cf. verse 3).

thou wilt strengthen their heart: or 'you will give them a new determination'. Calvin (op. cit., p. 125) remarked: 'he upholds our understanding in temptation, and suffers it not to be led another way'.

thou wilt incline thy ear: i.e. God will give heed to the supplications of the oppressed.

18. to do justice: perhaps, 'by doing justice'.

the fatherless and the oppressed: i.e. the underprivileged and the wronged (see on 82:3). As such they are an object of special concern; cf. Exod. 22:21ff.; Lev. 19:33ff.; Dt. 10:18f., 16:11,14, 24:16ff.; Isa. 1:17; Jer. 7:6, 22:3. Such a regard for the weak is also found in the literature of other ancient peoples. E.g. in the Ugaritic Legend of Aqhat it is said that Danel the Rephaite 'judged the cause of the widow and tried the case of the orphan' (cf. Driver, *CML*, p. 53a; see also F. C. Fensham, 'Widow, Orphan, and the Poor in Ancient Near Eastern Legal and Wisdom Literature', *JNES*, XXI (1962), pp. 129ff.).

man who is of the earth: probably 'a mere mortal man'. It is possible that 'no more' (*bal yôsîp̱ ᶜôḏ*) is a later gloss and that verse 18*b* could be rendered: 'to frighten (or 'drive away in terror') the feeble (but insolent) man from the land.' Dahood (*PAB*, I, p. (61) reads: 'no more shall the arrogant (i.e. taking *ᶜôḏ* as from *ᶜ-d-d* 'to swell up') frighten men from the earth.' *NEB* gives an interpretative rendering: 'that fear may never drive men from their homes again.'

Psalm 11 The Lord is My Refuge

The situation in which the Psalmist finds himself is reminiscent of that of the authors of the Psalms of Lamentation, yet our Psalm is not a lament or a prayer because it is not addressed to God but refers to him in the third person. Since Ps. 11 is characterized by a trust in Yahweh, it could be described as a Psalm of Confidence or Trust (see Introduction, p. 39), and under this heading we might include such Psalms as 4, 16, 23, 27, 62, 131. It is less likely that this poem is a Royal Lamentation which accompanied the ritual combat during the New Year Festival (cf. A. Bentzen, *King and Messiah* (1955), p. 25), or that it was a prayer of one falsely accused.

Verses 1 and 4 imply that the Psalmist has sought refuge in the Temple, where he now addresses his friends who had advised him to flee from his enemies. He also explains why he declined their suggestion, and why he had chosen to trust Yahweh rather than to take any other alternative. It is far from certain that the Psalmist was a leader of the people, or that his times were marked by a complete breakdown of social order, so that there was no firm basis for justice or personal integrity (cf. Rodd, *PEPC*, I, p. 23).

It is impossible to assign any particular date to this Psalm but many scholars (e.g. Oesterley, Kraus) see no reason why it could not be of pre-Exilic origin. Few (e.g. Davison, Kirkpatrick, Cohen) would contend for a Davidic authorship, and associate it with the situation depicted in 1 Sam. 18.

The metre of the Psalm is varied. Structurally, the poem consists of two main parts: verses 1–3 which give a glimpse of the Psalmist's plight, and verses 4–7 which, in a hymnic style, affirm the author's faith in Yahweh as the Righteous Judge and Vindicator.

To the choirmaster: see Introduction, p. 43.
of David: see Introduction, pp. 48ff.

IF YOU HAVE TO FLEE – FLEE TO GOD **1–3**

1. In the LORD I take refuge: this phrase could almost be regarded as the title of the psalm. The writer has found protection in the Temple (verse 4), and the very flight to the sanctuary is a manifestation of his trust in Yahweh. It is not improbable that the Psalmist's case had some similarity to the situation described in Exod. 21:12ff. and 1 Kg. 1:50, where persons in mortal danger fled to the altar or sanctuary (cf. J. Gray, *I & II Kings* (*OTL*, 1964), p. 94).

how can you say to me: lit. 'to my soul'; cf. 33:19. Dahood (*PAB*, I, p. 69) suggests: 'How can you lie in wait for my life . . .', taking *ʾāmar* (which usually means 'to say') in the sense of 'to see, watch for' (cf. *Biblica*, XLIV (1963), pp. 295ff.). This rendering does not, however, offer any real advantage, and it breaks the connexion between verses 1 and 2.

Flee like a bird to the mountains: similarly also LXX, T and S; but this presupposes a change from *harᵉḵem* ('your mountain') to *har kᵉmô* ('(to the) mountain(s) like . . .'). M.T. could be rendered: 'Flee to your mountain, O bird (i.e. you, defenceless creature)' (cf. 55:6 (M.T. 7), 124:7). Since the 'fire and brimstone' in verses 6 is reminiscent of the story of Sodom and Gomorrah (Gen. 19:24), it is of some interest that also Lot was advised (by the angels) to flee to the mountains, although he preferred to escape to the nearby city (Gen. 19. 17ff.). Probably a flight to the mountains was a proverbial expression for a measure of desperation (cf. 1 Sam. 26:20). For 'bird' (*ṣippôr*), see on 84:3.

2. *RSV*, *NEB* and many exegetes take verses 2–3 as part of the warning to flee to the hills, giving the reason why he should decamp. On the other hand, these two verses could be viewed as the Psalmist's explanation why the advice of his friends was unacceptable.

the wicked: for *r*^{e}*šā*^{c}*îm*, see on 1:1, 28:3, 92:7.

bend the bow: lit. 'tread . . .'. The bow was bent or strung only when a hostile action was imminent, and this was done by treading on the lower end of the bow while pressing upon the other end. See on 44:6. The arrows were usually made from light wood or reed, and their tips or heads were of flint, bone or bronze (and later also of iron).

the string: the material used for the bowstrings could be flax cords, plaited hair, ox gut or the like.

to shoot in the dark: Dahood (*PAB*, 1, p. 69) proposes: 'To shoot from ambush' (for the use of the preposition *b*^{e} with the meaning 'from', see on 64:4). In 64:3f. a similar word-picture is employed to depict the malicious slanders of the enemies. If the term 'dark' (or 'ambush') has any *particular* significance in this context, it may well point to the underhand methods of the foes.

the upright in heart: i.e. who think and act rightly; see on 7:10; cf. 73:1.

3. if the foundations are destroyed: most interpreters explain 'the foundations' as the 'fundamental principles of law and justice' (so Kissane, *BP*, p. 47), or as 'the established institutions, the social and civil order of the community' (Briggs, *CECBP*, 1, p. 89). For similar metaphors, see 82:5; Isa. 19:10; Ezek. 30:4; but all these instances are rather ambiguous.

what can the righteous do: or 'the righteous, what has he done?' that he has deserved all this misfortune. Dahood (*PAB*, 1, p. 68) suggests 'what is the Just One doing?' but this seems to contradict the very spirit of trust and confidence which characterizes this Psalm.

the righteous: see on 1:5.

THE CONFIDENCE IN THE RIGHTEOUS JUDGE **4–7**

4. in his holy temple: (=Hab. 2:20). This could denote the heavenly abode of God, as is implied by the parallelism (so Wellhausen, Davison, Gunkel, *et al.*), but it may equally well refer to the Temple on Mount Zion, which was a representation of Yahweh's dwelling place in heaven (cf. 150:1; Clements, *GT*, p. 68). Sperber (*HGBH*, p. 660) renders verse 4*a*: 'The LORD, His sanctuary is in the temple', and this would agree with the structure of verse 4*b*.

the LORD's throne: see on 9:6, 47:8.

his eyes behold: the object of the verb may have fallen out, due to some scribal error; S[h] suggests *l[e]ḥeleḏ*, 'the world'.

his eyelids: or 'his pupils', which is possible but not certain. The picture is probably derived from the contraction of the eyelids during a close scrutiny of some object, but, in any case, it is used as a synonym for 'eyes'.

test: the metaphor must have originated from the process of refining metals (see Jer. 6:27–30). God judges between the righteous and the wicked like an assayer who separates the pure metal from the worthless dross.

5. his soul: i.e. he himself (see on 33:19).

him that loves violence: this is a fitting description of the godless. The opposite type of man is the one who loves Yahweh, and whose love is expressed, primarily, by keeping God's commandments (cf. Dt. 10:12, 11:22, 19:9, 30:16; Jos. 22:5).

6. coals of fire: lit. 'snares, fire'. *RSV* follows Sym in reading *paḥ[a]mê* ('coals of . . .') for M.T. *paḥîm* ('snares'). The Biblical references to coal can only mean charcoal, because mineral coal is not mined in Palestine.

brimstone: or 'sulphur', is often found in regions of volcanic activity. 'Fire and brimstone' recalls the punitive destruction of Sodom and Gomorrah, and in 1QpHab x:5 there is a reference to divine punishment by means of 'fire of brimstone' (cf. also 140:10 (M.T. 11); Ezek. 38:22). The description in verse 6 could also be an echo of a theophany (cf. 18:12f. (M.T. 13f.)).

a scorching wind: it has been suggested that the reference is to a volcanic storm or to the dry, suffocating wind, *simoom*. Yet the real significance of this metaphor is that it serves as a figure of speech for the divine punishment (cf. Isa. 21:1, 40:7; Jer. 4:11; Hos. 13:15).

the portion of their cup: destruction will be the lot of the wicked, while Yahweh is the chosen portion of the righteous (cf. 16:5). For the ungodly there is only the cup of wrath (cf. Lam. 4:21; 1QpHab xi:14); for the loyal servants of God there is the cup of salvation (cf. 116:13; Isa. 51:17).

7. he loves righteous deeds: either God delights to perform deeds of righteousness or he loves the righteous way of life of the godly. The latter alternative may well be right (cf. Isa. 33:15, 64:5).

the upright shall behold his face: or 'his countenance doth behold the upright' (*AV*). Most commentators adopt the former rendering, but the latter finds some support in 17:2: 'Let thy eyes see the right'. Dahood (*PAB*, I, p. 68) translates it as 'Our face shall gaze upon the Upright One', and he argues that this vision of God implies a belief in after-life in the presence of Yahweh. Even if this rendering were right, it need not suggest the concept of after-life in the divine presence, but rather a change in one's fortunes here on earth. So far the righteous has suffered afflictions but now he will experience God's favour (cf. 17:15).

Psalm 12 YAHWEH'S ANSWER IN TIME OF NEED

This Psalm seems to be a Lament of the Community (see Introduction, p. 39), although in view of verses 5 and 7 it could be regarded as an Individual Lament (see Introduction, pp. 37ff.). Verse 5 is in the form of an oracle, and consequently the whole Psalm has occasionally been defined as a prophetic liturgy.

Some scholars (e.g. Cohen) have contended for a Davidic authorship, and have seen in the Psalm a reflection of the society during the last years of Saul's reign; yet the language is very general, and could belong to almost any age. But since there is a similarity with Isa. 33:7–12, and since the conditions of the Psalmist's time are reminiscent of those found in other prophetical books (e.g. Hos. 4:1ff.; Mic. 7:2ff., etc.), the Psalm may be of pre-Exilic origin. The prophetic element is against a late date, unless it is merely a quotation or imitation of Isa. 33:10.

Little can be said about the author of this lament, except that H. Schmidt's view that the writer is an old man who is disgruntled and suspicious of new ways and means is unsatisfactory; it does not necessarily need an old man to be able to recognize perversion.

The poem can be divided into three parts. The first comprises verses 1–4, and begins with a cry for deliverance, followed by a description of the situation out of which it arose. In verses 3–4 the writer expresses his wish that the power of the mischief-makers might be brought to an end. The second and the central part consists only of verse 5 which, in the form of an oracle, declares that Yahweh will intervene on behalf of the needy. The last part, verses 6–8, affirms that God's word is dependable and that he both can and will protect the afflicted, whatever the circumstances.

The metre of the Psalm is mainly 4 + 4.

To the choirmaster: see Introduction, p. 48.

The Sheminith: see Introduction, p. 49.

A Psalm of David: see Introduction, pp. 43ff. and 46.

A CRY FOR HELP 1–4

1. Help, LORD: the lament begins with this abrupt cry for succour, and in the following lines the author describes the reason for his supplication. See also 3:7 (M.T. 8), 6:4 (M.T. 5), 7:1 (M.T. 2), 118:25.

for there is no longer any that is godly: some commentators (e.g. Briggs, Leslie) read 'for kindness is no more' (*NEB* 'loyalty') (i.e. they alter *ḥāsîḏ* into *ḥeseḏ*), and this would match 'faithfulness' or 'good faith' (so *NEB*) (a possible rendering of *ʾemûnîm*, 'the faithful') in verse 1*b*. This, however, would not avoid the poetical exaggeration, and similar sentiments have been uttered by other men of God; e.g. in Mic. 7:2: 'The godly man has perished from the earth . . .' (cf. Isa. 57:1) and, above all, it brings to mind the well-known words of Elijah: 'I, even I only, am left' (1 Kg. 19:10). 'The godly' (*ḥāsîḏ*) is the man who is loyal to God's Covenant or to the revealed will of Yahweh; therefore he is also a righteous man.

from among the sons of men: the reference is, primarily, to Israel; but it may well be true of the world as a whole. Of some interest is the Egyptian text, 'A dispute over Suicide' (see J. A. Wilson, *ANET*, p. 406), which is dated *c.* 2000 B.C. and which portrays a similar situation. The writer complains: 'The gentle man has perished, (But) the violent man has access to everybody . . . Goodness is rejected everywhere . . . There are no righteous; The land is left to those who do wrong . . .'.

2. Every one utters lies . . .: i.e. words are no longer a way of sharing, but have become the means of ensnaring the unsuspecting victim. For *šāwᵓ* ('falsehood, lie'), see on 119:37.

with flattering lips: (cf. Isa. 30:10; Dan. 11:32). The purpose is not so much to ingratiate oneself, but rather to exploit and even to destroy while displaying a mock humility and hypocritical sympathy. Dahood (*PAB*, I, p. 73) suggests 'with pernicious lips' (cf. the Ugaritic *ḫlq*, 'to perish'). In the Dead Sea Scrolls there are frequent references to 'seekers of *smooth things*' (*ḥᵃlāḳôṯ*), who are occasionally found in the company of the 'interpreters of lies' (cf. 1QH ii:32, iv:10; CD i:18; 4QpNah 3–4 i:7, ii:2,4, iii:3,6f.).

a double heart: in 1QH iv:14 there is a reference to those who seek God with 'a double heart' and who are not established in God's truth. Such men are hypocrites or double minded (cf. Jas. 1:8). The expression 'double heart' (lit. 'heart and heart') resembles that in Dt. 25:13: 'You shall not have in your bag two kinds of weights (i.e. 'a stone and a stone'), a large and a small'; the writer is obviously thinking of false weights. Hence the double-minded man is the one who is motivated by falsehood, and not one who is always in two minds.

3. **cut off all flattering lips:** the allusion is not to some devilish punishment (cf. 2 Mac. 7:4) in the literal sense, but to the destruction of the wicked, as in Am. 2:3: 'I will cut off the ruler from its midst, and will slay all its princes with him.'

the tongue that makes great boasts: the tongue represents the *whole* man, as do the 'flattering lips'. This literary device (synecdoche) mentions a part when the whole is to be understood. Dahood (*PAB*, I, p. 73) proposes 'distortions' for 'great boasts' (lit. 'great things'), deriving it from *g-d-l*, 'to spin, weave' (cf. also Jastrow, *DTTM*, I, p. 213).

4. **With our tongue we will prevail:** (so T). Dahood (*PAB*, I, p. 73) renders: 'By . . . we are powerful' (i.e. *naḡbîr* is viewed as a denominative verb from *geḇer*, 'man, hero'; cf. also *Biblica* XLV (1964), p. 396). That denominative verbs existed in classical Hebrew is clear, but it is not certain to what extent we are justified in transforming all the verbal 'geese' into 'swans'. An expression similar to verse 4*a* is found in 1QH viii:35: 'You (i.e. God) have made mighty (my) tongue in my mouth'.

our lips are with us: Kraus (*PBK*, p. 93) paraphrases: 'our lips help us', and similarly Eaton (*PTBC*, p. 51): 'our lips are our means of success', while Dahood (*PAB*, I, p. 73) takes *ʾittānû* ('with us') as a noun *ʾēṯ* with the pronominal suffix, translating it 'our weapon'. This noun is found in the *OT* with the meaning 'ploughshare' (cf. 1 Sam. 13:20; Isa. 2:4; Mic. 4:3). Another possibility is to assume that the Hebrew *ʾtnw* (i.e. 'with us') is a denominative verb from *ʾôṯ* ('sign, wonder'), and could be rendered '(with our lips) we have worked wonders' (for this usage, see Dahood, *PAB*, I, p. 246). If this is right, then the clever schemers have, in a way, usurped the place of God, being like the wicked in 10:3 who curse and renounce God. Consequently they are so self-confident as to ask 'Who is our master?'. The answer expected is: 'No one'; they are a masterless race. They do not question the existence of God in a theoretical sense, but they simply deny his power to intervene in human affairs.

THE ANSWER OF GOD **5**

This verse is the focal point of the whole Psalm, and in its form it is an oracle. When the Psalm was used in a cultic setting, the oracle may have been uttered by a priest or a cultic prophet, while the rest of the Psalm was repeated by the congregation.
because the needy groan: similarly in Exod. 2:24 where God heard the cries of his people and remembered his Covenant with their fathers.
I will now arise: so also in Isa. 33:10, which envisages a similar situation; but there is no need to assume a direct dependence by the Psalmist upon the Isaiah passage, or vice versa.
I will place him in the safety: this clause is ambiguous, and the suggested translations are many. Mowinckel (*PIW*, II, p. 60) renders: 'I will set in freedom (the poor oppressed), him that (the wicked) has blown upon', assuming that 'has blown upon' refers to witchcraft and that it amounts to 'afflicting one with a curse'. Yet the *RSV* rendering (=*NEB*) is as reasonable as any.

THE TRUSTING RESPONSE OF THE CULTIC COMMUNITY **6–8**

6. The promises of the Lord: i.e. those expressed in verse 5, although the writer may have thought of the promises of Yahweh in general (cf. 105:42, 119:140; 4Q 177 10–11, line 1).
are pure: i.e. are true. God's promises or words are compared with purified silver, which is in a sense true silver, i.e. its quality can be relied upon. This word-picture would have been well known, because the purity of silver had a great importance in

business transactions, for silver was one of the main media of exchange.

silver: see on 105:37. It was one of the precious metals in antiquity, and at times, and in certain places, it was valued even above gold.

a furnace on the ground: this is an obscure phrase which has caused difficulties both to the ancient versions and modern exegetes. Some (e.g. Gunkel, Kraus) omit it as a gloss and this would help to retain the usual 4+4 metre of the Psalm. The gloss, if such it is, may have been intended to describe in greater detail the process of purification. Some other scholars (see Winton Thomas, *TRP*, p. 4) read *ḥārûṣ* ('gold') for M.T. *lāʾāreṣ* ('on the ground'), regarding the preposition *le* ('on') as a dittograph of the letter *l* at the end of the preceding word. So *NEB*: 'gold seven times purified.'

7. protect us: so some Hebrew MSS., LXX and Jerome. M.T. has 'you will protect them' (i.e. the poor and the needy) or the object ('them') may refer to the promises of Yahweh in verse 6 (so Kraus); cf. Jer. 1:12.

guard us . . . from this generation: (so some Hebrew MSS., LXX and Jerome). M.T. could be rendered 'you will guard (or 'save') him . . .', probably alluding to each one of the oppressed who long for deliverance (cf. verse 5). Dahood (*PAB*, I, p. 72) regards the Hebrew *zû leʿôlām* ('ever') as a divine name, 'O Eternal One'. This would provide a good parallel to the vocative 'Yahweh' in verse 7*a*. A possible translation might be: 'You will guard us from this generation, O Eternal One' (with a *lāmeḏ vocativum*; see on 75:9).

8. On every side the wicked prowl: this seems to suggest that even when the godless *surround* the righteous, God is fully able to protect them.

as vileness is exalted: or '(even) when worthlessness is highly praised by the sons of men' (cf. Ec. 8:11). Some scholars (e.g. Kissane) argue that M.T. provides a weak conclusion to the poem, but if we accept the above interpretation, then we have an appropriate ending, stating that God will keep his own in spite of anything the wicked might do or think. For another possible interpretation of this verse, see G. R. Driver, 'Notes on the Psalms. I 1–72', *JTS*, XLIII (1942), p. 152.

Psalm 13 How Long, O Lord?

The Psalm is a Lament of the Individual (see Introduction, pp. 37ff.), although Rashi and Ḳimḥi, the medieval Jewish commentators, regarded it as a description of Israel's sufferings caused by the hostile neighbours. Also Bentzen's view that Ps. 13 is a Royal Psalm of Lamentation, accompanying the ritual combat, is rather forced (see *King and Messiah* (1955), p. 25). The actual situation of the Psalmist is not, however, clear. He appears to be near death (verse 3) and troubled by his foes (verses 2 and 4), and there seems to be no end to his distress. He may have been a sick man but his primary concern is the apparent separation from God. For some Near Eastern parallels, see G. R. Driver, *TPst*, p. 131; Widengren, *AHPL*, p. 94.

There is little indication as to the date of the Psalm. The metre of the lament is irregular.

To the choirmaster: see Introduction, p. 48.

A Psalm of David: see Introduction, pp. 43ff. and 46.

THE LAMENT OF A MAN IN DESPAIR **1–2**

1. How long: the fourfold repetition of this interrogative in verses 1–2 voices the extreme perplexity and despondency to the Psalmist. For a similar expression, see 6:3 (M.T. 4); 4Q177 10–11, ll. 8f.

Wilt thou forget me for ever?: the reference is not to an unintentional failure to call to mind the plight of the sufferer, but rather to a deliberate aloofness on the part of God for some unspecified reason. Cf. 10:1; Widengren, *AHPL*, p. 94f. The Hebrew *neṣaḥ* (*RSV* 'for ever') probably means 'utterly' (cf. Winton Thomas, *TRP*, p. 4); *NEB* 'quite'.

. . . hide thy face: or '. . . turn your face' following the rendering of LXX, and deriving the verb from *s-w-r*, 'to turn aside', and regarding it as an 'infixed *-t-* conjugation' (for further details, see Dahood, *PAB*, I, p. 64). In both cases the phrase denotes divine displeasure or even punishment (see Isa. 54:8, 57:17, 59:2; Ezek. 39:23). For the opposite thought, see the Aaronic blessing in Num. 6:24ff.

2. pain: as suggested by S (reading *ᶜaṣṣāḇôṯ* for M.T. *ᶜēṣôṯ*, 'counsels'). M.T. could be rendered: 'How long shall I go on placing (perplexing) counsels in my soul' (cf. Sir. 30:21). Perhaps no emendation is necessary, because it has been shown (cf. G. R.

Driver, *WO* I (1947–52), p. 410) that the Hebrew *ʿēṣāh* can also mean 'anguish, pain'; *NEB* has 'anguish'.
all the day: lit. 'by day'; it might be better to read with some Greek MSS. 'day and night' (so *NEB*) (i.e. adding *wālaylāh*, 'and night').
my enemy: the Hebrew *ʾōyēḇ* may be understood in a collective sense (cf. verse 4). Dahood (*PAB*, I, p. 77) argues that the foe is Death itself, the enemy *par excellence*.

THE FINAL PETITION 3–4

3. Consider: or 'Look upon me', assuming that the object of the verb 'answer' serves both verbs. God is implored to consider the plight of his servant, instead of turning his face away from the afflicted man (cf. verse 1).
answer me: either by removing the misfortune or, literally, by giving a favourable oracle (see v. Rad, *OTT*, I, p. 401).
lighten my eyes: a man's eyes can be regarded as a 'barometer' of vitality. Grief, illness and other troubles dim a man's eyes (cf. Job 17:7; Ps. 6:7 (M.T. 8), 38:10 (M.T. 11); Lam. 5:17), while the restoration of his health, strength or fortunes makes the eyes bright (cf. 1 Sam. 14:27,29; also Dt. 34:7; Ps. 19:8 (M.T. 9); Ezr. 9:8).
lest I sleep the sleep of death: in the *OT* 'sleep' is one of the metaphors used to describe death (cf. Job 3:13, 14:12; Ps. 76:5 (M.T. 6); Jer. 51:39,57). The different *OT* word-pictures of the after-life are only different ways of looking at death, and they are complementary rather than contradictory. It is to be noted that for the Psalmist death would mean a final separation from Yahweh, and *this* is the real bitterness of dying.

4. my enemy: this is to be taken in a collective sense, as is implied by 'my foes' in the parallel line. The chief concern of the author is not the triumph of the enemies in itself but its theological implications. If the dead cannot share in the saving acts of God, then justice must be done on this earth, and if the sufferer is a righteous man (in the *OT* sense of the word) then God is certain to answer by restoring the afflicted man to his former fortunes. Cf. Job 42:7–17.
lest my foes rejoice: probably because they would have been proved right in their judgment of the sufferer by the events (cf. 38:16 (M.T. 17)).
I am shaken: this may be a euphemistic expression for dying (so

Nötscher); so also in 38:16 (M.T. 17) (cf. 121:3; Prov. 24:11). Usually it is a picture of misfortune in general (cf. 15:5).

AN EXPRESSION OF HOPE **5–6**
It is not easy to account for the change of mood (if it is such) and consequently there are numerous explanations. It has been argued that the change is the result of a psychological process or due to actual healing; one could also assume that the transition was effected by an oracle of salvation. Yet another possibility is to regard verses 5–6 as a continuation of the petition and as a statement of faith. See Introduction, p. 38.

5. thy steadfast love: or 'your covenant loyalty' (see on 26:3). The foundation of the author's hope is Yahweh's promise to be the God of his people, with all that it involves.
my heart shall rejoice: perhaps, 'let my heart (i.e. me) rejoice'. For 'rejoice', see on 89:16.
thy salvation: or 'your saving help' (see on 35:3).
6. I will sing: perhaps, 'let me sing'.
because he has dealt bountifully: the Hebrew verb may be a perfect of certainty expressing the conviction that God will be merciful to the stricken man (cf. 116:7). Dahood (*PAB*, I, p. 79) regards the word *ᶜālāy* ('with me') as a divine appellative, 'the Most High', yet this suggestion does not seem convincing in this context; the preposition *ᶜal* (*RSV* 'with') is often found after the verb *g-m-l* ('to deal bountifully'), e.g. in 2 Chr. 20:11; Ps. 103:10, 116:7, 119:17, 142:7 (M.T. 8).

LXX adds: 'and I will sing to the name of the Lord, the Most High'. but this may have been derived from 7:17 (M.T. 18).

Psalm 14 Is God Relevant?

Another version of this Psalm is found in the so-called Elohistic Psalter (Ps. 42–83) as Ps. 53, a fact which points to the independent existence of both the First Davidic Psalter (Ps. 3–41) and of the Elohistic.

The psalm-type, or *Gattung*, of this Psalm is not clear, but it has many points of contact with Prophetic and Wisdom literature. Certain themes in the Psalm are reminiscent of Jer. 5:1ff., 8:6ff. (cf. also Isa. 59:4ff., 64:6ff.; Hos. 4:1ff.), while the contrast between the 'fool' (verse 1) and those who 'act wisely' (verse 2) reminds us of the Wisdom writers. The Psalm has occasionally been described as a prophetic liturgy (so Leslie, Rhodes, *et al.*) or as a lament (so Dahood). In view of this uncertainty, the life-situation of the Psalm is not clear. Rashi and Ḳimḥi thought that the writer was describing the hardships of Israel in a godless and hostile world, while others have suggested that the evildoers were the ruling classes in Israel whose victims were the faithful Israelites (so Kissane, Weiser).

Most commentators (e.g. Oesterley, Kraus, Deissler) would place the Psalm in the post-Exilic period, and the practical atheism in verse 1, as well as the language of the Psalm, seem to point in the same direction.

The Psalm could be divided into three parts. Verses 1–3 are an account of the well-nigh universal godlessness, while in verses 4–6 we find a rhetorical question expressing the amazement at the 'could-not-care-less' attitude of the wicked, followed by a threat. The Psalm concludes with a prayerful wish (verse 7) expressing hope for the restoration of the well-being of the people of God.

The metre of the Psalm is mainly 3 + 2 which befits the tone of the poem.

To the choirmaster: see Introduction, p. 48.

Of David: see Introduction, pp. 43ff.

A LAMENT ABOUT THE STATE OF THE NATION **1–3**

1. The fool: *nāḇāl* is to be taken collectively as describing a type of man. Such people are not simpletons by nature but they have deliberately closed their minds to God and to all instruction. W. A. L. Elmslie (*Studies in Life from Jewish Proverbs* (n.d.), p. 129) comments on this sort of person saying that having made the fundamental error in thinking that there is no God, 'his whole judgment of life has become perverted. Probably he is an astute person; but the greater his ability, the greater and more pernicious will be his folly'. Isa. 32:6 provides a fitting description of the *nāḇāl* as the man who speaks folly and whose mind plots iniquity ('to practise ungodliness, to utter error concerning the Lord, to leave the craving of the hungry unsatisfied, and to deprive the thirsty of drink'). The same term can also be applied to the whole nation (cf. 74:18).

says in his heart: or 'thinks'; his way of life clearly expresses what is in his mind.

There is no God: this phrase is usually taken as a statement of practical atheism. The question of God's existence is apparently ignored, and the main emphasis seems to be on the conviction that there is no need to reckon with God in any sphere of one's existence, i.e. for practical purposes God does not matter. The same phrase and similar thoughts are also found in 10:4, 73:11; Jer. 5:12; Zeph. 1:12; Rom. 1:28; and in more recent literature. For further discussion, see J. Barr, *SBL*, p. 62; he thinks that the Hebrew *ʾên* (*RSV* 'there is no . . .') may 'perfectly well mean "absolute non-existence" '.

do abominable deeds: T and 53:1 (M.T. 2) read 'doing abominable iniquity' (i.e. *ʿāwel* for *ʿalîlāh*), which sounds more forceful. The Psalmist may have had in mind the situation which existed (according to Gen. 6:1ff.) immediately before the Deluge, and which may have suggested a parallel to his own times.

none that does good: cf. Isa. 59:4, 64:7; Jer. 8:6. It is not clear whether the phrase means that there is none among the wicked that does any good (so S. J. De Vries, 'Sin, sinners', *IDB*, IV, p. 365) or whether it suggests that sinfulness is a universal characteristic of the human race. The latter view is found explicitly in several *OT* books, e.g. Ec. 7:20: 'Surely there is not a righteous man on earth who does good and never sins' (cf. also 1 Kg. 8:46; 2 Chr. 6:36; Ps. 143:2; Prov. 20:9). The present verse is probably a generalization: the nation as a whole has become corrupt, but this does not imply that *all* members of Israel are godless.

2. The LORD looks down . . .: cf. 102:19 (M.T. 20); Lam. 3:50. A more anthropomorphic expression is found in Gen. 11:5 where Yahweh *comes down* to see the city and the tower which the sons of men had built (cf. Gen. 18:21).

the children of men may well refer to mankind in general (so Kirkpatrick), but it seems that the Psalmist had in mind the people of Israel. It would not be surprising if the Gentiles did not seek after God (i.e. Yahweh; cf. 7:7f. (M.T. 8f.)), but it is unbelievable that the *chosen* nation as a whole has disregarded its God.

that act wisely: the wisdom of such a man is that he seeks after God, and this, in its turn, will colour all his activities. The term *maśkîl* is used in Dan. 11:33 in the sense of one who is endowed with divine wisdom and who is also able to instruct others in that knowledge (cf. G. Vermes, *The Dead Sea Scrolls in English* (1962), pp. 22ff.). It occurs also in the Scrolls from Qumran with a similar connotation (cf. 1QS iii:13, ix:12,21; CD xii:21), and is often rendered 'instructor'.

that seek after God: cf. 1QS i:1. In the Dead Sea Scrolls the same verb (*d-r-š*) can describe the seeking of God, by studying the Scriptures (cf. P. Wernberg-Møller, *The Manual of Discipline* (1957), p. 44, n.3), but it is unlikely that this is the meaning of the verb here, where it may denote the worship of Yahweh. For *d-r-š*, see on 24:6.

3. They . . . all: or 'every one' (cf. Gen. 16:12; Ec. 10:3).

gone astray: the verb is usually derived from *ś-w-r* ('to turn aside'), but it could also come from *ś-r-r* ('to be stubborn, rebellious') (so Dahood). In 53:3 (M.T. 4) we have 'fallen away' (i.e. *śāḡ*).

corrupt: this word is found elsewhere only in 53:3 (M.T. 4) and Job 15:16. The cognate Arabic verb sometimes means 'to turn sour' (of milk).

Certain parts of verses 1–3 have been quoted in Rom. 3:10ff. where they are followed by a series of phrases taken from different parts of the *OT*. Some Greek MSS. have inserted Rom. 3:13–18 after verse 3 here.

THE REBUKE AND THREAT **4–6**

4. Have they no knowledge: either of their impending punishment or of their responsibility towards Yahweh (cf. H. B. Huffmon, 'The Treaty Background of Hebrew YĀDA^{c}', *BASOR*, no. 181 (1966), pp. 37ff.). In this respect they are almost more ignorant than the ox or the ass (Isa. 1:3). Winton Thomas (*TRP*, p. 5) links the Hebrew *y-d-*^{c} (*RSV* translates as 'to know') with the Arabic *wadu^{c}a* ('to be still, submissive'). If we follow this suggestion, we could render: 'Shall all the evildoers not be punished?' reading *yēḏe^{c}û* for M.T. *yāḏe^{c}û* (*RSV* 'Have they (no) knowledge'). *NEB* has 'Shall they not rue it'.

evildoers: see on 28:3. They are those Israelites who have no regard for the welfare of the weaker members of the community, rather than foreign oppressors (so Kirkpatrick, Davison, *et al.*) or 'sorcerers' (so Mowinckel).

my people: either the people of Yahweh or those of the Psalmist (so Kraus). In verses 5–6 they are defined as the 'righteous' and the 'poor', and the two terms are synonymous.

as they eat bread: some commentators (e.g. Gunkel, Schmidt) suggest: 'They eat the bread of Yahweh, but do not call upon his name', taking *šām* ('there') from verse 5, and reading it as *šᵉmô* ('his name'), or assuming that *šᵉmô* had been omitted due to haplography. If this interpretation is correct, then the evildoers are priests, because sacrifices can be described as the bread of God (cf. Lev. 21:6,8,17; Num. 28:2) and the priests are permitted to eat of it (Lev. 21:22). Most exegetes, however, prefer a rendering which is more or less similar to that of *RSV*, and which would suggest that to the wicked the oppression of their fellows is as commonplace as the eating of bread. Perhaps we could paraphrase verse 4: 'Have all the evildoers no awareness (of the authority of Yahweh)? The destroyers of my people eat the food (provided by) Yahweh (yet) they do not call upon (his name).'

Verses 5–6 correspond to 53:5, but the variations at this point are considerable.

5. There . . . in great terror: the word **There** may belong to verse 4 (see above). Dahood (*PAB*, I, p. 80) renders verse 5*a*: 'See how they have formed a cabal' (cf. the Ugaritic *pḫd*, 'flock'), but the usual translation may be right in describing the effect of the intervention of Yahweh who is **with** (or 'in') **the generation** (or 'assembly') **of the righteous**. For *dôr* as 'assembly', see F. J. Neuberg, *JNES*, IX (1950), p. 216. The parallel in 53:5 (M.T. 6) could be rendered 'There they shall be greatly afraid, (although) there was no fear (previously), for God will scatter the bones of him who encamps against you; (but) you will put him to shame (reading *hᵉḇîšōṯōh*) for God has rejected them'. Perhaps we could alter *ᶜaṣᵉmôṯ* ('bones') into *ᶜēṣôṯ* ('plans').

6. You would confound . . .: or, perhaps, we could follow Dahood (*PAB*, I, p. 80) and suggest 'The council of the poor will put him (i.e. the evildoer or his clique) to shame', reading *tᵉḇîšēhû* for M.T. *tāḇîšû* (*RSV* 'you would confound'); cf. Exod. 22:30 (M.T. 29).

but the LORD is his refuge: or 'for the LORD . . .'. Cf. also 46:1 (M.T. 2), 61:3 (M.T. 4), 62:7,8 (M.T. 8,9), 71:7, 73:28.

THE HOPE OF RESTORATION 7

This final verse may be a later addition to the psalm when it was re-interpreted and applied to a new situation, to make it a truly national lament (cf. Nötscher, *PEB*, p. 37). But, in any case, the main point is that help can be expected only from Yahweh.

out of Zion: it is here in particular that one finds the presence of Yahweh (see 20:2 (M.T. 3), 128:5, 134:3). Clements (*GT*, p.

49, n.1) argues that Mount Zion became a source of blessing to Israel 'as a result of the belief in Yahweh's presence, mediated through his sacred mountain'. See on 3:4.

restores the fortunes of his people: rather than: 'bringeth back the captivity of his people' (*AV*). The former rendering is the generally accepted translation although the etymology of the phrase is still a matter of dispute. For a brief discussion, see Johnson, *CPAI*, p. 67, n.4; cf. also 85:1 (M.T. 2), 126:1.

Jacob shall rejoice: or, more likely: '(Then) let Jacob rejoice, (since the verb is jussive in form). For 'Jacob', see on 20:1, 85:1.

shall be glad: or 'let . . . be glad'.

Psalm 15 Who can be Yahweh's Guest?

Most exegetes regard this Psalm as a liturgy, and it has been described as a 'Torah Liturgy' (F. James), 'Entrance Torah' (Weiser) or an 'Admission Torah' (Eissfeldt). Since the Psalm exhibits a certain didactic tendency, some scholars (e.g. Dahood) have assigned it to the Wisdom Psalms. Perhaps it is best to define it as an Entrance Liturgy which also had (or came to have) a didactic purpose. It is not impossible that the Psalm was linked with the right of asylum.

Archaeology has provided us with a number of texts and inscriptions (for references, see Kraus, *PBK*, p. 111) which are more or less reminiscent of the Entrance Liturgies (Ps. 15 and 24), and which suggest that it was customary to inform the worshippers of the cultic requirements necessary for the admission to the temple. Thus an Egyptian inscription in the temple of Horus at Edfu states:

> 'O, you prophets and priests,
> all you who enter before gods . . .
> Do not appear with sin.
> Do not enter in uncleanness.
> Do not speak lies in his house.
> Do not embezzle the provisions!'

(quoted from H. Ringgren, *FP*, p. 120). It is very likely that in Jerusalem also, when a festive procession or a group of pilgrims wished to enter the sanctuary, they would ask the Temple gatekeepers for the conditions of entry (see verse 1). Thereupon the answer would be given by some priest or Levite; in Ps. 15 the reply is found in verses 2–5*b*. Mowinckel and others have pointed out that the qualifications required are precisely ten in number, reflecting what might be called the decalogical tradition of Israel. On the other hand, the total of *ten* conditions may be simply a coincidence; it is a question how far the parallel halves of a verse should be regarded as independent commands (cf. Kraus, *PBK*, p. 112). It is also very unlikely that the requirements mentioned were exhaustive; they may have been typical of, and may have represented, the sum total of Yahweh's demands. The declaration of the conditions for the entry into the Temple had an instructive function as well as an admonitory purpose (at least theoretically); one could be excluded (as in 2 Chr. 23:19) or Yahweh himself would punish the deceiver. It has been suggested (e.g. by König) that the Psalm refers not to the admission to the Temple but rather to God's companionship, but it is unlikely that this was the original intention. When, at a later time, the Psalm was detached from its cultic setting, then it probably was taken in such a sense.

Taylor (*PIB*, p. 78) argues for a late post-Exilic date, and points to the catechetical character of the Psalm. On the other hand, this poem has considerable similarities with such passages as Jer. 7:1ff.; Ezek. 18:5–9; Mic. 6:6ff., and especially Isa. 33:14ff. We need not argue for an interdependence, but the similarities may at least imply that the prophetic passages show some acquaintance with a psalm-type not unlike that of Ps. 15 and 24; therefore these two Psalms may also belong to the same period. Jer. 7:1ff. seems to suggest that by this time the Entrance Liturgies had ceased to function in their proper setting or that they were used purely formally.

The author of the Psalm may have been a priest, but, whoever he was, he must have been dependent upon older cultic traditions.

The poem quite naturally falls into three main sections: verse 1 contains the question of the worshippers, while verses 2–5*b* give the answer in the form of a series of descriptive commands; the Psalm concludes with a promise to the righteous (verse 5*c*).

The dominant metre of the Psalm is 3 + 3.

A Psalm of David: see Introduction, pp. 43ff. and 46.

THE QUESTION OF THE PILGRIMS 1

1. who shall sojourn . . . dwell: the prospective worshippers are primarily concerned with the privilege to enter the

Temple, but this may also have further implications. Both the Temple and the holy mountain had a symbolic significance; at the risk of oversimplification we could say that the former could be viewed as representing the dwelling place of God before men, while the latter represented the land (or the whole earth) before the deity. Hence the desire of the pilgrims is not only to worship Yahweh in his Temple, but also to have the privilege of dwelling in his land. For a detailed discussion on this subject, see R. E. Clements, 'Temple and Land: A Significant Aspect of Israel's Worship', *TGUOS*, XIX (1963), pp. 16ff. One who is not fit to enter the sanctuary (or to dwell on his holy hill) is not entitled to enjoy the blessings of Yahweh's land (cf. Jer. 7:15). The actual implementation of the exclusion may well have been left to Yahweh unless the case was very obvious.

thy tent: i.e. 'your Temple' (cf. 27:5f., 61:4 (M.T. 5); Isa. 33:20). The term is not so much an archaic expression as a reflection of the Tent tradition (cf. 2 Sam. 7:4ff.).

thy holy hill: or 'Mount Zion'; see on 2:6; cf. 3:4 (M.T. 5), 43:3, 48:2 (M.T. 3), 99:9.

YAHWEH'S ANSWER **2–5b**

The question of the worshippers in verse 1 is directed to Yahweh, and the answer is given through the representatives of the cult (priests ?). The actual reply is given in verse 2, while verses 3–5*b* provide a number of concrete examples. The choice of these conditions may have been determined by the current neglect of certain aspects of righteousness. The Psalmist does not mention the more serious sins such as apostasy, murder, adultery, or stealing (cf. Jer. 7:8ff.), but the observance of these basic commands may have been taken for granted. It is of some interest that the Psalm does not refer to purely cultic requirements (e.g. sacrifices, offerings, etc.), and this may reflect the attitude that obedience is better than sacrifice (1 Sam. 15:22), although the question would not be of an 'either-or' type. It does not necessarily follow that the Psalm must have been influenced by prophetic teaching, because the prophets of Israel were not so much revolutionary teachers of morality as preachers of repentance, pleading with their people to return to Yahweh by obeying his commands *already* known. Therefore both Ps. 15 and the prophets may belong to the same stream of Yahwism which was firmly rooted in the Covenant traditions.

2. who walks blamelessly: i.e. who is loyal to the revealed will of Yahweh. Cf. 119:1, 'whose way is blameless, who walk in the law of the LORD' (cf. 84:11 (M.T. 12)). Similar expressions are frequently found in the Dead Sea Scrolls, e.g. 1QS i:8, ii:2, iii:9, viii:18,21, ix:6,9,19; CD i:21, ii:15. See on 18:23.
does what is right: this is synonymous with 'walking blamelessly' (cf. Ac. 10:35; 1 Jn 3:7). The opposite of such a righteous man is the evildoer (cf. 5:5 (M.T. 6)).
speaks truth from his heart: or '. . . in his heart' (*AV*, *RV*). They are unlike the people mentioned in Isa. 29:13 who honour God 'with their lips' only, while their hearts (i.e. their real selves) are far from him, and whose words are meant to disguise their thoughts and their nature.

3. slander with his tongue: rather than 'trip over his tongue' (so Dahood, *PAB*, I, p. 84). *RP* renders: 'hath used no deceit in his tongue', or we might translate 'who does not go about (with slander) on his lips' (cf. 2 Sam. 19:27; Ps. 101:5; Sir. 5:14).
his friend: i.e. his fellow-man.
nor takes up a reproach: the exact meaning is not clear. Kissane (*BP*, p. 60) takes it to mean that the God-fearing man does not rejoice over another's misfortune, while Calvin suggests that the righteous man does not listen to evil reports of his neighbours. C. H. Spurgeon (*TD*, I, p. 199) remarks that 'in slander as well as robbery, the receiver is as bad as the thief.' The above phrase probably means that the godly man does not make his neighbour an object of scorn (cf. 1QH ii:9).

4. a reprobate: Weiser (*POTL*, p. 170) argues that the term includes not only the notorious evil-doers, but also those whose sinfulness is inferred from some great misfortune of theirs. It is more likely, however, that the Psalmist had in mind the former type of person. The idea of honouring the godly and of despising the reprobate finds its echo in 1QS i:9f. which demands from the Qumran covenanters that they should love all the sons of light (i.e. their fellow covenanters) but hate all the sons of darkness. Ps. 15:4 may allude to a situation where the reverse was true, where there was a danger that some Israelites might be 'carried away' by the attractiveness of evil and perversion, so that the evil-doer appeared to be the clever man while the honest servant of God was thought to be the fool. Another possible rendering is: 'he is despised in his own eyes and rejected' (cf. G. R. Driver,

'Notes on the Psalms. I 1–72', *JTS*, XLIII (1942), p. 152); this would give an ideal picture of a truly humble man (cf. 1 Sam. 15:17; 2 Sam. 6:22).

who swears to his own hurt: (=*NEB*) lit. 'who swears to do evil', but this seems obviously wrong. LXX, S, V read 'he swears to his neighbour' (*l^ehārēa^c* (?) for M.T. *l^ehāra^c* ('to (his own) hurt')). Dahood (*PAB*, I, p. 84) suggests: 'he swore to do no wrong', taking the preposition *l^e* as expressing a separation; cf. on this point *CBQ*, XVI (1954), p. 302. None of the suggestions is very satisfactory, and the phrase parallel to verse 4*c* may be missing. The general meaning seems to be that the righteous man honours his oath.

5a,b. at interest: the lending of money and other things to fellow Israelites was viewed as an opportunity to help them in their need, and not as an occasion for making a profit out of their misfortune (cf. Exod. 22:25 (M.T. 24), 25:36; Dt. 23:19). On the other hand, it is clear that this law was not always observed in practice (see Neh. 5:6ff.; Prov. 28:8; Ezek. 18:13, 22:12). In antiquity the rates of interest were often exorbitant; e.g. in Babylon the common rate for loans in kind was as high as 33⅓% p.a., while in Nuzi the rate charged for loans of 'money' was up to 50% p.a. (cf. G. A. Barrois, 'Debt', *IDB*, I, p. 809). In Israel one could lend on interest (the rate is not stated) to a foreigner (see Dt. 23:30), but this law may be a provision for business transactions, and therefore the financial position of the borrower might be different from that of the needy person.

a bribe against the innocent: the reference may be to judges and witnesses, because both could easily pervert the course of justice (cf. Exod. 23:8; Dt. 16:19). Such an abuse was not infrequently rebuked by the prophets (cf. Isa. 1:23, 5:23; Mic. 3:11, 7:3). Dahood (*PAB*, I, p. 83) proposes: 'nor accept compensation from the hungry'; for this use of *šōḥaḏ* ('bribe'), see Prov. 6:35, and for *nāḳî* (*RSV* 'innocent') in the sense of 'hungry', see Am. 4:6 ('cleanness of teeth'). Although this rendering is possible and might provide a reasonable parallel to verse 5*a*, it does not really improve the meaning of the line.

THE RIGHTEOUS MAN IS BLESSED **5c**

shall never be moved: this is often taken to mean that the upright man will not meet with adversity and that one who is admitted to the divine fellowship will enjoy unbroken prosperity (cf. 24:5; Isa. 33:16). Thus what the wicked man has vainly hoped for will become a reality for the loyal Israelite. The expression 'to be shaken' is a figure of misfortune; see on 13:4; cf. Prov. 10:30: 'A good man can never be shaken, but the wicked have no permanence in the land' (R. B. Y. Scott, *Proverbs and Ecclesiastes* (*AB* 18, 1965), p. 83).

Psalm 16 YAHWEH IS MY PORTION

Although the text of certain verses (especially 3–4) is in some confusion, the general sense of the Psalm is reasonably clear. It is usually described as a Psalm of Confidence or Trust (see Introduction, p. 39). This psalm-type may have developed out of certain elements of the Lamentations; but its *Sitz im Leben* or its life setting is difficult to define, though it may well have been in the cult. Weiser (*POTL*, p. 172ff.) finds the origin of the Psalm in the 'pre-Exilic cult of the Covenant Festival', and he interprets the poem as a personal confession of the worshipper. Among other suggestions we may note that of Dahood, who describes the author as a Canaanite convert to Yahwism, though this seems unlikely; and the view of Kraus, who thinks that the Psalmist was a Levitical priest; Eaton (*PTBC*, p. 58) is of the opinion that the speaker is the King. These different views simply show that the detailed interpretation of the Psalm is ambiguous, and therefore one's judgment should be exercised with great caution. The *NT* writers must have regarded the Psalm as a messianic poem, and a similar view is also held by some more recent exegetes (cf. Calès, *LP*, I, p. 201ff.). Neither is there any agreement as to the situation of the Psalmist. Kittel, Kraus, *et al.* argue that the author of the Psalm was in a grave danger, while other scholars (e.g. Oesterley, James) assume that the trouble, if any, is long past. The general tone of the Psalm seems to support the latter alternative.

Little can be said about the date of the Psalm. Duhm contends for a late date, while Gunkel, Deissler, *et al.* have assigned the Psalm to the early post-Exilic period. There are certain similarities between verse 4 and Isa. 57:5ff., 65:1ff., and some interpreters have detected the influence of the Wisdom style (so McCullough, *PIB*, p. 82). In contrast, Weiser (*POTL*, p. 172) draws attention to various allusions to particular aspects of the Covenant Festival, e.g. the presence of God (verses 1, 8, 11), the renunciation of foreign gods (verse 4), the bestowal of land (verses 5ff.); all these points may suggest a pre-Exilic date for the origin of the poem. See also Sabourin, *POM*, II, pp. 97f.

The Psalm opens with a brief prayer and a statement of faith (verses 1–2); verses 3–4 are textually uncertain and their interpretation is problematic. According to *RSV*, they describe the saints and sinners, but it is more likely that these two verses give us an account of the fate of the apostates. In verses 5–8 the author depicts *his* good fortune: Yahweh is the giver of his portion, and his real portion is Yahweh; consequently his life cannot be shaken by adversity. Verses 9–11 stress the fact that nothing can separate the loyal worshipper from Yahweh; therefore he can live his life in a joyful confidence, for Yahweh will give what is needful and what is best for him, even though this might mean in the end death, when he will be sated with years and when he will have fulfilled his God-given destiny. Perhaps we may remark that Sheol cannot snatch the godly from the presence of Yahweh but Yahweh can give rest to his faithful servant when he has completed his task to the best of his ability.

The metre of the Psalm is irregular, but a number of verses belong to the 4+3 pattern.

A Miktam: see Introduction, p. 47.

of David: see Introduction, pp. 43ff.

THE PRAYER AND CONFESSION OF FAITH **1–2**

1. Preserve me: this opening petition recalls the Psalms of Lamentation (cf. 17:8, 140:4 (M.T. 5), 141:9) but in the present context it need not imply that the author is in any serious trouble (as suggested by Kraus *et al.*). The meaning of the above phrase may be: 'keep on protecting me as in the past'.

in thee I take refuge: this metaphor may have been derived from the tradition which regarded the sanctuary as a place of asylum (see on 63:7); Yahweh was the refuge *par excellence*. The expression could be taken either literally or metaphorically; the latter alternative seems more likely in this context (cf. also 7:1 (M.T. 2), 11:1, 25:20, 31:1 (M.T. 2)).

2. I say: so also the ancient versions; M.T. has: 'you (feminine singular) said', which may be a defective spelling of the first person singular.

to the Lord: or 'O Yahweh' (so Dahood; he regards the preposition as a *lāmed vocativum*, see on 75:9).

Thou art my Lord: rather than '. . . the Lord' (*RVm*). This offers a striking contrast to the reasoning of the godless who say: 'Who is our master?' (12:4; cf. 140:6 (M.T. 7)).

I have no good apart from thee: M.T. could be translated: 'my good (is) not upon you' which is obviously wrong; consequently most renderings involve either a re-interpretation or an emendation. The simplest solution may be to assume that in this verse the Hebrew *bal* ('not') has a positive meaning, expressing affirmation (cf. R. T. O'Callaghan, 'Echoes of Canaanite Literature in the Psalms', *VT*, IV (1954), pp. 164ff.), so we could render: 'my welfare surely (rests) upon you (alone)'. G. R. Driver has suggested: 'my good is all upon you' (reading *kullāh* for *bal*), i.e. my well-being is entirely dependent upon God. Cf. M. Scott, *Textual Discoveries in Proverbs, Psalms, and Isaiah* (1927), p. 108.

THE FATE OF THE WORSHIPPERS OF OTHER GODS **3–4**

These two verses are textually uncertain, and their interpretation is dubious; therefore it is wellnigh impossible to avoid emendation. Cf. *ZAW*, LXXVI (1964), pp. 171–5.

3. the saints: *NEB* has 'The gods'. The Hebrew *ḳ^{e}ḏôšîm* may denote the pious folk in Israel (so LXX), the Levitical priests (so Kraus), Canaanite gods (so Dahood), foreign deities in general (as suggested by Wellhausen, Kissane, Mowinckel). The last possibility seems preferable because it offers a slightly better coherence between verses 3 and 4, rendering verse 3: 'As for the so-called holy ones who are in the land, cursed (i.e. *waʾ^{a}rûrê* for M.T. *w^{e}ʾaddîrê*, 'and the majestic ones of . . .') are all who delight (reading *hōp̄^{e}ṣê* for M.T. *hep̄ṣî*, 'my delight') in them' (similarly also Kissane and *NEB*). This verse occurs also in 4Q177 14 line 2.

4. Those who choose another god: or 'those who lust after other gods' (deriving the verb from *h-r-r*, 'to lust after' (as in Ugaritic), and reading *ʾ^{a}ḥērîm hārû* for M.T. *ʾaḥēr māhārû*, lit. 'they hasten after'; cf. Dahood, *PAB*, I, p. 88; Driver, *CML*, p. 71 (H i:39)).

multiply their sorrows: or 'let their sorrows be great'.

their libations of blood: the exact nature of these offerings is not clear. Some of the proposed interpretations are: 'libations accompanying human sacrifices' (cf. Isa. 57:5); 'offerings brought by men whose hands are "blood-stained"' (cf. Isa. 1:15); or libations of blood, to which were ascribed special powers (so

Weiser, *POTL*, p. 174). Another possible rendering might be 'libations of blood to them' (i.e. to the other gods, taking the pronominal suffix as datival in meaning).

their names upon my lips: the reference is to the names of the foreign deities, and the author may have thought, primarily, of the cultic use of these names (cf. Hos. 2:17 (M.T. 19); Zech. 13:2).

TRUST AND CONFIDENCE IN YAHWEH **5–8**

5. Kraus sees in verses 5–6 a reminiscence of the traditions of the allotment of land (cf. Jos. 13:14ff., 18:2ff.) which was done by means of the sacred lots (cf. Gray, *JJR*, pp. 158ff.). Of some relevance for our passage is the fact that the tribe of Levi was given no land (cf. Jos. 13:14, 14:4); its portion and inheritance were the LORD himself (cf. Num. 18:20; Dt. 10:9), i.e. they were entirely dependent upon Yahweh for their living. Kraus comes to the conclusion that the speaker must be a Levite, although at a later time the Psalm could have been used in a more spiritual sense by any true worshipper. On the other hand, it is equally true that Israel was a kingdom of priests (Exod. 19:6) and therefore, in this sense, Yahweh was the portion of his people (Jer. 10:16*a*) and also of the individual (cf. 73:26, 119:57, 142:5 (M.T. 6); Lam. 3:24).

The LORD is my chosen portion: or 'O Yahweh, you have allotted my portion' (reading *minnīṯā* or *mānīṯā* ('you have allotted') for M.T. *mᵉnāṯ* ('portion')). In view of the above argument, the speaker may be a priest, but not necessarily so.

my cup: this, too, may belong to the same set of ideas as 'portion', 'lot', 'heritage', and it may be a synonym of 'lot' (cf. 11:6). Weiser (*POTL*, p. 175) associates it with the festal cup of Yahweh, 'which was passed round at a cultic meal of those who participated in the feast'. The former alternative is, however, more plausible.

thou holdest my lot: Weiser (*POTL*, p. 171) reads: 'thou art my lot for ever' (i.e. he changes *tômîḵ* into *tāmîḏ* ('for ever')), while Dahood (*PAB*, I, p. 89) suggests: 'you yourself have cast my lot', and he derives the verb *tômîḵ* ('you hold') from *y-m-k*, which he regards as a by-form of *m-k-k* ('to sink, fall'). The Hebrew *tômîḵ* may be a participle (written fully for *tômēḵ*) from *t-m-k*, 'to support, uphold', and thus Yahweh has not only apportioned the Psalmist's inheritance but he also upholds it (i.e. his good fortune).

6. The lines: better 'the portion (measured out for me)' (similarly also *PNT*). The word for 'measuring line' has become the designation of the plot or territory thus marked out (see also Jos. 17:5,14 where 'lot' (*gôrāl*) is synonymous with 'portion' (*ḥeḇel*)).

yea: (*ʾap̱*) or 'and' (so Dahood, who argues that it could lose its emphatic quality, as in Ugaritic).

I have a goodly heritage: Dahood (*PAB*, I, p. 86) suggests 'the Most High (i.e. *ʿēlî* for M.T. *ʿālāy* (*RSV* 'I have', lit. 'upon me')) has traced out my property', and he regards the Hebrew verb *šāp̄ᵉrāh* ('is goodly') as an archaic third person singular masculine, related to *š-b-r*, 'to measure' (see also A. Guillaume, 'The Arabic Background of the Book of Job', *Promise and Fulfilment*, ed. by F. F. Bruce (1963), p. 123). The Psalmist may have intended to point not only to his heritage in Yahweh's land, but also to Yahweh himself, who is the ground of all existence.

7. I bless the LORD: since God is the source of all that is good, and is 'exalted above all blessing and praise' (Neh. 9:5), man can add nothing to the power and majesty of God. Yet man can bless God in the sense of acknowledging his blessings and praising his wonderful deeds. 'It is good to praise God and to exalt his name, worthily declaring the works of God' (Tob. 12:6). In a way, to bless God means to thank him.

counsel: cf. 73:24. The essence of the counsel is, apparently, the path of life which Yahweh has made known to his servant (verse 11). This could refer, among other things, to an oracle which the worshipper had received from God. Others have seen Yahweh's guidance as the law in general.

in the night: the Hebrew *lêlôṯ* is plural in form, hence some commentators render 'during the watches of the night' (so Dahood), 'every night' (so Kissane), or 'in the dark night' (as an intensive plural; so Briggs).

my heart instructs me: 'heart' (lit. 'kidneys' or 'reins') is the centre of emotions or one's innermost self (cf. Johnson, *VITAI*, pp. 74ff.). Dahood (*PAB*, I, p. 90) takes the pronominal suffix of *kilᵉyôṯāy* ('my kidneys') as the third person singular (as in Phoenician), and consequently it is God's heart that instructs the Psalmist (cf. 33:11). This reading would offer a good parallel with verse 7*a*; the *RSV* gives, however, a satisfactory sense, and here it is the poet's own conscience that bears witness to the divine word.

8. I keep the LORD always before me: i.e. by observing his commands (cf. 119:30). The characteristic of the insolent and ruthless men is that they do not set God before them, as in 54:3 (M.T. 5), 86:14.

he is at my right hand: this rendering supplies the pronoun *hûʾ* ('he') after *mîmînî* ('at my right hand'); perhaps we should read: 'Indeed (Yahweh) is at my right hand . . .' (for this use of *kî* (*RSV* 'because'), see on 118:10).

I shall not be moved: i.e. I shall not meet with adversity (see on 10:6, 30:6; cf. Prov. 10:30).

THE BLESSINGS OF GOD'S PRESENCE **9–11**

9. my soul rejoices: lit. 'my glory . . .' (so *AV*, *RV*) but a number of scholars read *k*^{e}*ḇēḏî* ('my liver') for M.T. *k*^{e}*ḇôḏî* ('my glory'); for the idiom, see Driver, *CML*, p. 71 (H i:13); H. W. Robinson, *The Christian Doctrine of Man* (1911), p. 23.

my body . . . dwells secure: it is unlikely that the reference is to the body in the grave, as suggested by LXX and the *NT* (Ac. 2:26: 'my flesh will dwell in hope'). This expression usually denotes the undisturbed security in Yahweh's land (cf. Dt. 33:12,28; Jer. 23:6, 33:16).

10. This verse is quoted in Ac. 2:27, and it is interpreted in 2:31 as referring to the resurrection of Jesus Christ. A similar interpretation was also adopted by the older exegetes including Luther and Calvin. In more recent times, scholarly opinion has been divided on this subject. A number of exegetes (e.g. Kirkpatrick, Gunkel, Chr. Barth, Kraus, Mowinckel) find no mention of life after death in Ps. 16, while the opposite view is held by such scholars as S. R. Driver, Weiser, Dahood, *et al.* Rowley (*FI*, p. 175 n.2) points out that the different interpretations indicate 'that no clear doctrine is here enunciated, and it is unwise to press the interpretation on either side'. Therefore he rightly prefers to speak of 'a glimpse, rather than of a firm faith'.

thou dost not give me up to Sheol: probably God will deliver his servant from an untimely death, or from the danger of death during his allotted span of life. Yet it is just possible that the Psalmist may have hoped that, in some way or other, his fellowship with God would not come to an end. But since such a view would have been a novelty, one would have expected a more explicit description of this daring faith, which would show that the writer was not simply following the traditional beliefs about the after-life. For 'Sheol', see on 6:5.

or let thy godly one see the Pit: either the word 'Pit' (for *šaḥaṯ*, see on 49:9) is a synonym of 'Sheol', or it means 'corruption, destruction' as suggested by the ancient versions. If we accept the suggestion that the Psalmist was thinking of a *worthwhile* after-life, then the first alternative might imply that the godly (see on 4:3) will be granted the same (or similar) privilege as that accorded to Enoch and Elijah (so Dahood); while, if we follow the second alternative, then the allusion might be to the belief of the resurrection of the body (cf. W. E. Barnes, *Lex in Corde* (1910), pp. 48ff.). The best solution may be to regard verse 10*a* and *b* as the two parallel lines in a synonymous parallelism, expressing the conviction that the author will be delivered from all possible mortal perils until he is ready to die in a good old age.

11. the path of life: this may be the content of God's counsel (see verse 7), while Dahood (*PAB*, I, p. 91) argues that 'life' (*ḥayyîm*) means in this setting 'eternal life' (cf. also *ANET*, p. 151 (AQHT A vi: 27ff.), M. Dahood, *Biblica*, XLI (1960), pp. 176ff.). Weiser also takes it as 'a life lived in communion with God which will be carried on even after death' (*POTL*, p. 178). In view of our interpretation of verse 10, the 'path of life' may be that course of life which enables the godly to fulfil his destiny (cf. Prov. 5:6, 9:23, 10:17, 15:24). Perhaps the most significant factor for the Psalmist is not the contrast between life and death, but rather between life *with* God and life *without* him. If the author were hoping for a life to come, even then the emphasis would be upon the quality of the present existence which is the pledge of anything else to come.

in thy presence: Leslie (*PAP*, p. 406) sees here an allusion to the worship in the Temple but the expression may well be even more general. In terms of one's earthly existence, to be in God's presence means to experience his favour in all its aspects. The same thought is more or less expressed by verse 11*c* (cf. 145:16; Prov. 3:16).

for evermore: (for *neṣaḥ*, see on 74:1). This need not suggest eternity, but it can simply mean 'as long as life lasts' (cf. Exod. 21:6, where the slave is described as serving his master 'for ever', i.e. for life).

Psalm 17 The Innocent Man's Cry for Help

Verses 1–2 and 6–9 contain expressions characteristic of an Individual Lament (see Introduction, pp. 37ff.), while the declaration of innocence in verses 3–5 suggests that this Psalm could be described more specifically as a Psalm of Innocence. The generalities of the Psalm could be due to its use in the cult. Weiser (*POTL*, p. 180) contends that its *Sitz im Leben* or cultic setting was 'the celebration of the cult of the Covenant Festival', yet it seems more likely that this poem, as a prayer of an accused man, was used whenever the need arose, irrespective of any particular festival. Dt. 17:8–11 mentions certain legal cases which were transferred from the local community to the central sanctuary, and in which the verdict of God (in whatever way it may have been communicated) played an important role. It is therefore possible that the Psalms of Innocence (cf. Ps. 7, 26, 35) are the petitions of a falsely accused man, and their setting is some such situation as the one envisaged by the above passage (cf. G. v. Rad, *Deuteronomy*, Eng. tr. by Dorothea Barton (*OTL*, 1966), p. 118; see also 1 Kg. 8:31ff.). Verses 3 and 15 may suggest that the accused man spent the night in the sanctuary and that in the morning he was given the divine answer which may have been communicated to him by means of an oracle (cf. Dt. 17:11). Eaton (*PTBC*, p. 60) considers the psalm as a *royal* prayer and he regards the interpretation suggested above as seemingly unwarranted. It is probable that the heading 'A Prayer of David' should be given due consideration, but, on the other hand, there is no need to assume that all the Davidic Psalms of our Psalter were originally used in connexion with the royal rites (cf. also Rowley, *WAI*, pp. 205f.), and therefore the alternative interpretation cannot be excluded.

There is little that we can say about the Psalmist himself; he may have belonged either to the late pre-Exilic period or to the early post-Exilic times.

The structure of the Psalm is comparatively simple. In verses 1–2 we find an introductory appeal to God, and verses 3–5 declare the Psalmist's innocence and loyalty to Yahweh. In verses 6–9 the author offers further supplications to God for his deliverance from the enemies, and verses 10–12 give a description of the adversaries. Verses 13–14 are textually problematic, but they

may contain a prayer for the punishment of foes while the concluding verse (15) is an affirmation of the writer's conviction that he will continue to enjoy the favour of God.
A Prayer: see Introduction, p. 47.
of David: see Introduction, pp. 43ff.

AN APPEAL TO YAHWEH **1–2**

1. Hear a just cause: lit. 'Hear, O Yahweh, righteousness' (perhaps '. . . O Yahweh, Righteous One'). LXX has '. . . my righteousness', while Briggs (*CECBP*, I, p. 128) proposes '. . . a righteous man'. The parallelism, however, supports the *RSV* rendering, and requires a synonym of 'my cry' and 'my prayer'. The Hebrew *ṣeḏeḳ* ('righteousness') could be rendered '(my) just plea', the pronoun being implied by the parallel in verse 1*b*.
my cry: i.e. the shrill cry for help (cf. 61:1 (M.T. 2), 106:44, 142:6 (M.T. 7)); for *rinnāh* ('cry'), see on 88:2.
lips free of deceit: a prayer must be sincere and not uttered by lying lips (i.e. by a deceitful man as long as he remains a liar). Prayers of two-faced men are not accepted by God (cf. Isa. 1:15; see also Ps. 31:18 (M.T. 19)).

2. From thee let my vindication come: or 'Let my justice shine before you' (so Dahood, *PAB*, I, p. 92) which is a possible translation, but it is more likely that the suppliant awaits the divine decision through a priest. See Hab. 1:4, where the prophet complains that law has become ineffective and 'justice never goes forth'.
Let thy eyes see the right: LXX has 'let my eyes . . .' but M.T. is preferable; the meaning may be 'to see in order to test the accused man's integrity' (cf. 11:4).

THE DECLARATION OF INNOCENCE **3–5**

3. If thou triest my heart: it may be better to follow Dahood's suggestion (*PAB*, I, p. 94) and regard the verbs as precative perfects equivalent to the preceding imperatives and jussives of M.T. The 'heart' (see on 27:3) often denotes will and reason in Hebrew idiom, and it is frequently regarded as the very centre of one's being; as is a man's heart, so is the man himself. For the verb *b-ḥ-n* ('to try'), see on 66:10.
if thou visitest me by night: or 'testest me at night' (cf. Job 7:18). The pronoun 'me' is not in M.T. but it is suggested by the parallel clauses. Although nothing is hidden from God at

any time, it was at night or in sleep that man was thought to be particularly open to the divine scrutiny. This is, however, no proof that an oracle was sought by means of incubation, i.e. by sleeping in the Temple precincts in order to receive a divine communication in sleep (cf. F. F. Bruce, 'Dreams', *DB*, pp. 221f.; J. Lindblom, 'Theophanies in Holy Places in Hebrew Religion', *HUCA*, XXXII (1961), pp. 91–106).

thou wilt find no wickedness in me: Dahood (*PAB*, I, p. 94) suggests that the Psalmist was accused of worshipping idols, and he reads *zimmāṯî* (so also the ancient versions) for M.T. *zammōṯî* (lit. 'I am purposed' or 'my wickedness' (?)), and translates it by 'idolatry'. The *RSV* rendering seems more likely, since there is nothing in the Psalm to lend a further support to Dahood's proposal.

my mouth does not transgress: this phrase may belong to the beginning of verse 4; see below.

4–5. These verses are textually difficult (if not corrupt); the following translation is a tentative rendering: 'My mouth (i.e. 'I, myself') has not transgressed according to (or 'after the manner of') the doings of (other) men (cf. verse 10) but I have kept the word of your lips (cf. 119:101); (otherwise in) the ways of the lawbreaker(s) my steps (i.e. 'I') would have been humbled (from *m-k-k*, 'to be low, humiliated'; cf. 106:43) but in *your* paths my feet can never falter'.

A FURTHER SUPPLICATION TO GOD **6–9**

6. I call upon thee: *PNT* 'I am here and I call', yet the pronoun *ʾănî* ('I') may not be emphatic but used simply for metrical reasons. See on 141:1.

for thou wilt answer me: the Hebrew *kî* ('for') can be taken as an emphatic particle ('O that') (so Dahood), and this would fit well into the general background of this section. The *RSV* rendering may express either the certainty that God will answer the suppliant, or the experience of Yahweh's continual help in the past.

my words: i.e. my cause and my prayers.

7. Perhaps we should render this verse 'Set apart (cf. 4:3 (M.T. 4)) your godly one (reading *ḥăsîḏeḵā* for M.T. *ḥăsāḏêḵā* (*RSV* 'thy steadfast love'); cf. also S), O Deliverer of those who seek refuge (in you), from those who rebel against your might (i.e. your right hand)'; see also 89:1.

8. the apple of the eye: lit. 'the pupil, the daughter of (your) eye'. It serves as a symbol of what is to be guarded with the greatest care (cf. Dt. 32:10; Prov. 7:2).

in the shadow of thy wings: i.e. in your protective power (cf. Isa. 49:2, 51:16; Lam. 4:20; Hos. 14:7). Most scholars assume that the metaphor is suggested by the watchful care of a mother bird, but the reference may also be to the wings of the cherubim above the Ark of the Covenant (so Weiser, Kraus); cf. 36:7 (M.T. 8), 57:1 (M.T. 2), 61:4 (M.T. 5), 63:7 (M.T. 8), 91:4. It is less likely that the word-picture is of Egyptian origin (so Oesterley, *TP*, p. 160) and that it is to be associated with the winged solar disc (cf. *ANEP*, Pll. 320, 321). See on 36:7.

9. from the wicked: or 'from the fury of the wicked' (so Dahood, *PAB*, I, p. 92). For this use of *pānîm*, 'face', see *Biblica* XLIV (1963), p. 548. The 'wicked' are apparently the false accusers.

who despoil me: or 'who (seek to) destroy me'.

my deadly enemies: or '(from) my enemies (who) in (their) greed . . .'. The Hebrew *b^{e}nep̱eš* may mean 'against my soul' (i.e. against my very life) or 'in greed' (see on 33:19), cf. 27:12: 'Give me not up to the greed of my adversaries; for false witnesses have risen against me'.

who surround me: Dahood detects here the language of the chase, but it could well allude to the enemies encircling the accused man like a besieged city (cf. 2 Kg. 6:14).

THE DESCRIPTION OF THE ENEMIES **10–12**

10. They close their hearts to pity: lit. 'they have closed their fat'. Dahood (*PAB*, I, p. 97) has suggested that the verb *sāḡ^{e}rû* ought to be read as a *qal* passive (a pausal form) *sūḡārû*; if this is right, we could render: 'they are closed up (in) their own fat'. In the *OT* obesity is often linked with a rebellious spirit (e.g. in Dt. 32:15; Ps. 73:7; Jer. 5:28). Thus the above-mentioned phrase probably means that the foes have become rebellious against God, and verse 10*b* seems to support this interpretation. See on 119:70. 'Fat' may stand for a 'fat heart' (i.e. a disobedient will); cf. Isa. 6:10: 'Make the heart of this people fat . . .'. Cf. also Winton Thomas, *TRP*, p. 6.

11. The translation of this verse is uncertain, but *RSV* may be right.

They track me down: reading *ʾiššᵉrûnî* for M.T. *ʾaššūrênû*

('Our steps'); also the versions suggest a verb, e.g. LXX reads 'they cast me out'.

they set their eyes: probably 'they pay the greatest attention (to destroy me)', i.e. they are determined to bring me down.

to cast me to the ground: the pronoun 'me' is derived from the parallel phrase (see on 3:3 for the double-duty suffixes). 'The ground' (*hāʾāreṣ*) may be a synonym of the underworld (see on 7:5). The Hebrew *linṭôṯ* ('to bend down') should probably be changed into the causative *lᵉhaṭṭôṯ* ('to cast down').

12. They are like a lion: lit. 'his likeness (is) like . . .' which may simply mean 'he is like . . .' (cf. *BDB*, p. 198a). The enemies of the Psalmists are frequently compared to wild animals and the point of comparison is usually their cruelty and fierceness (cf. 7:2 (M.T. 3), 10:9, 22:12 (M.T. 13)).

young lion: in this verse *kᵉp̄îr* is probably a synonym of the more common term *ʾaryēh* ('lion') (verse 12*a*). Lions must have been common in Palestine during the biblical period and they are usually represented as destructive, fear-inspiring animals (see on 7:2).

MAY THE WICKED BE PUNISHED **13–14**

13. Arise, O Lord: see on 3:7, 7:6; cf. also 9:19 (M.T. 20), 10:12.

confront them: *RVm* 'forestall him', but this pronoun ('him') as well as the following ones may refer to the collective noun *rāšāʿ* (see on 1:1) in verse 13*b*. For the verb *ḳ-d-m*, see 18:5 (M.T. 6); Job 30:27.

my life: lit. 'my soul', i.e. me (see on 33:19).

by thy sword: i.e. the Hebrew *ḥarbeḵā* is taken as an accusative of instrument. Dahood (*PAB*, i, p. 98) links it with the preceding noun ('the wicked') but reads it as a participle *ḥōrᵉḇeḵā* (a pausal form), 'who wars on you'. This conjecture compares favourably with the *RSV* rendering.

14. This verse is in some disorder and/or corrupt; consequently most translators resort to emendations. *AV*, *RV* take the verse to mean that while the wicked enjoy only the *gifts* of God, the Psalmist will be satisfied with nothing less than the *presence* of God. *RSV* and *NEB* understand this verse as a prayer for vengeance.

from men by thy hand: Dahood (*PAB*, i, p. 98) reads: 'Slay them (with) . . .', altering *mimᵉṯîm* ('from men') into *mᵉmīṯām*, a participle used with the force of an imperative and thus

continuing verse 13; this seems to be an improvement on the usual emendations, although the resultant translation itself is not new (cf. Gunkel, *PGHAT*, p. 55); similarly *NEB*.
from men whose portion . . .: perhaps we should render (following Dahood) 'destroy them from the world, make them perish (*ḥalleḳēm* for *ḥelḳām* ('their portion')) from among the living' (the preposition b^e is taken to mean 'from', as in Ugaritic). For the meaning of the verb *ḥ-l-ḳ*, 'to perish', see M. Dahood, *Biblica*, XLV (1964), p. 408; cf. also 5:9 (M.T. 10).
May their belly . . .: or 'Fill them (i.e. their belly) with (the punishment) which you have stored up for them, and may even their sons be sated (with it)'. For the thought, see Job 21:19: 'God stores up their iniquity for their sons'.
may they leave . . .: or 'and they (i.e. the sons) shall leave what remains (of the punishment) to their (own) children'. If correct, this would reflect the teaching that the sins of the fathers are visited upon their descendants (cf. Exod. 20:5; Dt. 5:9). For a different rendering, see Dahood, *PAB*, I, p. 93; Eaton, *PTBC*, p. 61. It is hardly fair to charge the Psalmist with expressing 'the bitterness of a revengeful spirit' (so Oesterley, *TP*, p. 161), because he is simply expounding the implications of the blessings and curses inherent in the covenant. Since it is unlikely that the writer held a belief in a satisfactory after-life where justice might triumph, the consequences of obedience and rebellion must be seen here and now.

AN AFFIRMATION OF HOPE **15**

15. in righteousness: or 'at (the time of my) vindication'. Many of the older commentators and some more recent ones (e.g. Dahood) have thought that the reference is to the final judgment, but the ancient versions give no indication of such an interpretation, at least not explicitly. The phrase may allude to the vindication of the accused man, or to God as the 'one who manifests himself as the Righteous One'; for this interpretation of *b^eṣeḏeḳ*, see *GK* 119i.
when I awake: Dahood (*PAB*, I, p. 99) translates: 'At the resurrection' which is, theoretically, a possible rendering. The verb *ḳ-y-ṣ* ('to awake') is used with such a connotation in Isa. 26:19 and Dan. 12:2. Yet if our understanding of verse 15*a* is right, then verse 15*b* may give us a similar thought. Therefore the Psalmist is probably referring to the night spent in the

Temple precincts (see verse 3) and not to the 'resurrection morn'. Kissane (*BP*, p. 67) follows the construction suggested by LXX and V, rendering: 'I shall be satisfied when Thou awakest' (i.e. when God will intervene in punishing the adversaries of the Psalmist). The *RSV* rendition seems preferable.

Psalm 18 A Royal Psalm of Thanksgiving

This Psalm has been transmitted in two versions, the second being found in 2 Sam. 22. Commentators differ as to which of the two is closer to the original; the differences between the parallel versions are, however, small.

Another important point is the unity of the Psalm. Some exegetes (e.g. Schmidt, Taylor) have argued that it is a composite poem consisting of a lament of a man falsely accused by his enemies (verses 1–30) and of a royal thanksgiving (verses 31–50). Yet, in spite of the varied contents, the Psalm may be a literary unity. It can be described as an Individual Psalm of Thanksgiving (see Introduction, pp. 35f.), but, in so far as the speaker is the king (cf. verses 43ff., 50), it belongs also to the Royal Psalms.

According to the title of the Psalm, its author was David; a similar view has been held by a number of more recent scholars (e.g. Briggs, Albright, Kissane). On the whole it is more likely that the poem was composed by a court poet for the use of the Davidic kings; the time of David himself seems too early, yet the reign of Josiah (640–609 B.C.), as suggested by Kittel, Gunkel, Oesterley, *et al.*, may be too late. The Psalm contains a number of archaic features, such as orthography, the literary associations with Exod. 15; Hab. 3; Dt. 32–33, and the account of the theophany (verses 7–15), with its points of contact with the Canaanite literature; consequently it may belong, in its original form, to the early part of the pre-Exilic period (cf. F. M. Cross jr and D. N. Freedman, 'A Royal Song of Thanksgiving', *JBL*, LXXII (1953), pp. 15ff.). During the post-Exilic period the Psalm must have been adapted for the use of the community, and it is possible that certain alterations and additions were made to the text.

Concerning the *Sitz im Leben* of the Psalm, there are two main possibilities. It could have been recited by the King on his return from the battlefield, at a service of thanksgiving for victory (cf. Eissfeldt, *OTI*, p. 104), or it may have been part of the dramatic ritual performed at one of the yearly festivals, most likely at the Feast of Tabernacles (cf. Johnson, *SKAI*, p. 107).

Verses 1–2 form the introduction to the song, and verses 3–6 provide a description of the past plight and affliction. In verses 7–15 we find an account of Yahweh's theophany, and the result of this divine intervention is the deliverance of the King (verses 16–19). This salvation was essentially an act of vindication (verses 20–30), and verses 31–45 recount in more detail the triumphs of Yahweh's loyal servant over the peoples of the earth. The recital is sufficiently general to be applicable to successive occasions. The song concludes with a praise of Yahweh (verses 46–50).

The Psalm is characterized by a fairly regular 3 + 3 metre.

the choirmaster: see Introduction, p. 48.

A Psalm of David: see Introduction, pp. 43ff. and 46.

the servant of the Lord: for the various uses of the phrase, see W. Zimmerli and J. Jeremias, *The Servant of God* (*SBT* 20, 1965), pp. 11–36. In the present context the expression denotes the King as the servant of Yahweh. See on 27:9, 36:1.

when the Lord delivered him: it is unlikely that the Psalmist had in mind any particular victory; rather the song had arisen out of the cult and for use in it.

from the hand of . . .: i.e. from their oppressive power.

from the hand of Saul: this may well be a later addition still. Dahood (*PAB*, I, p. 104) suggests 'Sheol' (*šᵉʾôl*) for 'Saul' (*šāʾûl*). This gives a good sense but it need not be the original reading.

THE PRAISE OF YAHWEH'S SAVING POWER **1–2**

1. I love thee: this expression is not found in 2 Sam. 22:2, and consequently it is regarded as a later gloss. The *qal* form of the verb *r-ḥ-m* occurs only here, while the intensive form is usually used of God's compassion for his people (see on 116:5). Many exegetes follow F. Hitzig's suggestion to read *ʾărōmimᵉḵā* ('I will exalt you') for M.T. *ʾerḥomᵉḵā* ('I love you'), as in 30:1 (M.T. 2), 145:1; Isa. 25:1 (*Die Psalmen*, 1863, p. 98).

my strength: i.e. the source of my strength.

2. my rock: see on 42:9. This is a figure of security and refuge; cf. 31:2: 'Be thou a rock of refuge for me'.

my fortress: cf. 31:2,3 (M.T. 3,4), 71:3, 91:2. Since the author of the Psalm is not David, it is unlikely that the imagery was derived from the landmarks or actual places of refuge which David used during his flight from Saul (so Kirkpatrick). The descriptions belong to the language of the cult and some of them may be divine appellatives of great antiquity.

my deliverer: since the other appellatives are metaphors, some commentators delete this term or read for it: 'my place of refuge' (*miplāṭî*); but see also verse 48. It is possible that some of the titles in verse 2 are later additions but it is difficult to say which.

my rock: or 'my mountain' (so Dahood). Johnson (*SKAI*, p. 107) reads: 'My God is my rock', which balances: 'Yahweh is my rock (or 'crag')' in verse 2*a*. This rock-imagery is also reflected by early personal names such as Elizur ('my God is a Rock'; Num. 1:5) and Pedahzur ('May the Rock redeem'; Num. 1:10). This title is also one of Baal's appellatives, and in the Akkadian prayers the term 'great mountain' is often used as a title of a deity (cf. *ANET*, p. 390a).

my shield: i.e. God is the protector of his servant. See on 3:3.

the horn of my salvation: or 'my saving horn' (so Johnson, *SKAI*, p. 107). The phrase occurs only here and in 2 Sam. 22:3 (also in Lk. 1:69). 'Horn' was a symbol of strength, and the metaphor was most likely derived from the horns of animals rather than from the horns of the altar (cf. *NDB*, p. 537b) and denoting 'my place of asylum'. See on 75:4; W. Foerster, '*Keras*', *TDNT*, III, pp. 669ff.

my stronghold: or 'my high tower' (*RV*); cf. 9:9 (M.T. 10), 46:7 (M.T. 8).

AN ACCOUNT OF THE DISTRESS 3–6

3. who is worthy to be praised: some scholars attach this phrase to the end of verse 2, or emend it, because it does not provide a good parallel to verse 3*b*. Kraus (*PBK*, p. 136) reads 'Being wounded (I called unto Yahweh)' (i.e. *m*ᵉ*ḥōlāl* for M.T. *m*ᵉ*hullāl* ('worthy to be praised'); cf. Isa. 53:5). Perhaps we should read 'on account of the boastful (*mēhōlēl*) I cried unto Yahweh'. Eaton (*PTBC*, p. 63) suggests *m*ᵉ*hêlîl* (from *y-l-l*, 'to howl'), '(with) lamentation (I called . . .)'.

. . . from my enemies: Dahood (*PAB*, I, p. 105) takes 'enemies' as a plural of excellence, denoting Death, the arch-enemy of the Psalmist. This seems plausible in view of verses 4–5.

4. The cords of death: most exegetes read with 2 Sam. 22:5 'The breakers of . . .' (i.e. *mišb*ᵉ*rê* for M.T. *ḥeḇ*ᵉ*lê* ('the cords of . . .')).

'The cords of death' may also mean 'most terrible pains (or 'sorrow')' (cf. Winton Thomas, *VT*, XVIII (1968), p. 123). For the expression see also 116:3, 119:61.

the torrents of perdition: or '. . . of Belial'. Cross jr. and Freedman (p. 22, n.6) interpret 'Belial' (*b*^{e}*liyya*^{c}*al*) as '(place from which) none arises', and they take it as a euphemism for 'Sheol'. *B*^{e}*liyya*^{c}*al* could also be derived from *b-l-*^{c} ('to swallow'), meaning 'the Swallower' (i.e. the abyss) (so Winton Thomas, *TRP*, p. 6). More than once the *OT* writers speak of the greed of Death (cf. Job 18:13; Hab. 2:5). The King's fight with his enemies is also, in a sense, a struggle with Death. Weiser (*POTL*, p. 188) remarks that the realm of the dead is conceived as 'a river or an ocean', but it is more likely that the breakers and torrents of Death form only part of the total concept of the underworld. The metaphor itself may come from the Tiamat myth (cf. 93:3; G. R. Driver, 'The Psalms in the Light of Babylonian Research', *TPst*, p. 146).

5. the cords of Sheol . . . the snares of death: the mysterious netherworld is depicted as a hunter laying traps and snares (see on 64:5) for the righteous. See also 116:3; 1QH ii:21, iii:9,28; CD xiv:2; Widengren, *AHPL*, p. 118.

6. In my distress: the King is in a deadly peril, and verses 4–5 show that he felt himself to be in the very clutches of Death. The vivid descriptions of the trouble point to the awareness that only God could deliver his servant from this overwhelming disaster.

from his temple: most commentators take it as a reference to God's palace/temple in heaven (cf. 11:4) while some (e.g. Kraus) see here an allusion to the Temple in Jerusalem (cf. Jon. 2:4,7 (M.T. 5,8)).

. . . my cry to him: probably we should omit 'to him' (*l*^{e}*p̄ānāyw*) as being a variant reading of 'his ears', so *NEB*.

THE THEOPHANY OF YAHWEH 7–15

It is possible that the language which is used to portray the *OT* theophanies, was originally borrowed from the accounts of the epiphany of the storm-god, as well as from the descriptions of volcanic activity (cf. Kraus *PBK*, p. 145). The *OT* theophanies often refer to certain natural phenomena which are interpreted as Yahweh's intervention (cf. Jg. 5), to some visionary experiences (e.g. Isa. 6), to a cultic representation of a particular theophany, such as that of Sinai (Exod. 19), or, perhaps, to certain symbolic actions or words; cf. Westermann, *PGP*, pp. 98ff.; see also Eichrodt, *TOT*, II, pp. 16–45; J. Jeremias, *Theophanie, die Geschichte einer alttestamentlichen Gattung* (1965).

In our Psalm the epiphany may be a picturesque way of stating that it was Yahweh who had granted the deliverance to the King, and that *all* his acts of salvation form a single, never-ending whole.

7. the earth reeled: or 'the netherworld . . .' (so Dahood, *PAB*, I, p. 106). For the latter alternative, see 1QH xvii:13, where the 'foundations of the mountains' is synonymous with 'Sheol' (cf. also Dt. 32:22; Jer. 31:37; Jon. 2:7 (M.T. 8)).
the foundations . . . of the mountains: 2 Sam. 22:8 has: '. . . of the heavens'; but the former reading is more likely (cf. Isa. 24:18; Hab. 3:6). Even those things which are usually symbolic of all that is enduring and permanent, are shaken because of the wrath of God for the ill-treatment of his chosen one. Implicitly it suggests that the only stability is to be found in the doing of Yahweh's will.

8. from his nostrils: the preposition b^e (usually 'in') has also the force of 'from', as in Ugaritic.
devouring fire from his mouth: the reference may be to the lightning-flashes since a number of the following metaphors are derived from the experience of thunderstorms. For a somewhat similar description (i.e. that of Leviathan), see Job 41:18–21. It is also said that when Marduk, the chief god of the Babylonian pantheon, 'moved his lips, fire blazed forth' (*ANET*, p. 62).

9. He bowed the heavens: or '. . . spread apart . . .' (so Cross jr. and Freedman, op.cit., p. 24); see on 144:5; cf. Isa. 64:1.
thick darkness: or 'a storm-cloud'. The epiphany of Yahweh is frequently associated with a cloud (cf. v. Rad, 'The Tent and the Ark', *PHOE*, p. 117).

10. He rode on a cherub: see on 99:1. In this verse 'cherub' is synonymous with 'the wings of the wind', and may be a personification of the storm-cloud or 'the cloud-chariot of Yahweh' (cf. Clements, *GT*, p. 31). It seems that the functions of the cherubim and their significance were not the same during all the *OT* periods. Baal, too, is often described as 'the Rider of the Clouds' (cf. Patton, *CPBP*, p. 20); similarly in 68:4 Yahweh is the one 'who rides upon the clouds' (cf. 68:33 (M.T. 34)). In 104:3 Yahweh makes the clouds his chariot.
and flew: i.e. by means of the cherub-chariot or cherubim (so LXX, S, V). Cf. W. H. Schmidt, *Königtum Gottes in Ugarit und Israel*, *BZAW*, 80 (1966), pp. 49, 85, 89.

11. He made darkness his covering: although Yahweh manifests himself to men, at the same time, he is still the hidden God who cannot be seen by human eyes. The text of this verse may be in some disorder, and, perhaps, we should omit 'his covering' (*sitrô*) as a variant reading; it is lacking in 2 Sam. 22:12. If so, we could render: 'He set darkness round about him, his canopy (was) the dark rain-cloud (lit. 'darkness of waters'), even the thick clouds without brightness' (reading *ᶜabî* ('thickness') for *ᶜābê* ('clouds of . . .') and transferring *minnōgah* ('without brightness') from verse 12*a* to verse 11*b*).

before him there broke through . . .: or, perhaps, 'His clouds passed before him (as well as) hailstones . . .'. The epiphany of Yahweh is announced or accompanied by frightening natural phenomena which put to flight the enemies of God and those of his people (cf. 2 Sam. 5:20).

13. The LORD also thundered: i.e. the thunder is often described as the voice of Yahweh (cf. 29:3, 104:7; see also Dt. 5:22; Sir. 45:5; Jn 12:28f.).

in the heavens: or 'from . . .' (so *NEB*) (see verse 8); 2 Sam. 22:14 has the preposition *min* ('from') instead of *bᵉ* (*RSV* 'in').

the Most High: see on 47:2. Yahweh is the Most High because he is exalted above all the earth (83:18 (M.T. 19)) and above all the gods or divine beings (97:9). According to Gen. 14:19 'God Most High' is also the maker of heaven and earth.

hailstones and coals of fire: this phrase is usually deleted (so *NEB*) as an intrusion from verse 12; it is lacking in 2 Sam. 22:14

14. he sent out: Dahood (*PAB*, I, p. 109) suggests 'he forged', and he finds the same meaning of *š-l-ḥ* in Ugaritic also; yet both points are far from certain.

his arrows are his lightnings (cf. 77:17 (M.T. 18); 144:6; Hab. 3:11); see on 97:4.

scattered them: some interpreters take 'them' as referring to the enemies (so Kirkpatrick, Kissane, Cohen, *et al.*), but it may equally well describe the arrows (so Graetz, Duhm, Gunkel, Winton Thomas *et al*,).

and routed them: this translation is more appropriate to the enemies than to the lightnings, and therefore Johnson (*SKAI*, p. 109) renders 'making them resound' which gives a good sense.

15. the channels of the sea: so 2 Sam. 22:16, while M.T. of Ps. 18 reads *mayim* ('. . . of water'). It is possible that the initial

mēm of *mayim* should be added to the preceding word (*ᵓᵃpîḳê*), as a *mēm* enclitic, and the resultant reading would be practically the same as that of 2 Sam. In our context the phrase probably refers to the fountains of the sea, which are exposed at the rebuke of God (see also Exod. 15:8; Ps. 104:7, 106:9). The verse may also call to mind the breakers of death and the torrents of Sheol in verse 4. In the Ugaritic myths the abode of El is situated 'at the source of the rivers (in) the midst of the channels (*ᵓapq*) of the two oceans' (*Baal* II, iv: 21f.; III, i: 5f.; Pope, *EUT*, pp. 62f.).
at thy rebuke: or 'at your roar' (cf. H. G. May, 'Some Cosmic Connotations of *Mayim Rabbîm*, "Many Waters" ', *JBL*, LXXIV (1955), p. 17); see on 9:5.
at the blast of the breath . . . : this may simply mean: 'at your great anger' (cf. M. Noth, *Exodus*, Eng. tr. by J. Bowden (*OTL*, 1962, p. 124). Johnson (*SKAI*, p. 109) suggests: 'At the tempestuous breathing of Thy Nostril'.

YAHWEH'S DELIVERANCE **16–19**

16. He reached from on high: perhaps 'He stretched forth (his hand) . . .', as in 144:7. For 'on high' (*mārôm*), see on 68:18; cf. Patton, *CPBP*, pp. 19f.
he took me: or 'delivered me'.
he drew me out of many waters: the author may be thinking not only of the waters of the netherworld (so Dahood), but also of the whole sphere of influence of the Chaos (cf. Kraus, *PBK*, p. 145) which both is and symbolizes the powers hostile to God's people and to God himself. The verb *m-š-h* is found elsewhere only in the parallel passage in 2 Sam. 22:17 and in Exod. 2:10; it has been suggested that the use of this verb serves as a pointer to the Mosaic stories and to the Salvation-history as a whole. See on 69:1, 144:7.

17. my strong enemy: most versions read the plural 'enemies' thus balancing 'those who hated me'. Dahood regards them as plurals of excellence, denoting Death (cf. *Baal* III, vi: 20). It is possible that the foes are both the national enemies and the forces of darkness.
they were too mighty for me: this emphasizes that the victory is due to God alone. Without the divine help the King (as well as the nation) would have been engulfed by the destructive foes.

18. They came upon me . . .: or '. . . confronted me' (*NEB*). Dahood (*PAB*, I, p. 110) follows the reading suggested by the

consonantal text of 2 Sam. 22:19, and he renders 'He went before me' (*y^e^ḳadd^e^mēnî*), but the M.T. of Ps. 18 may well be right.
the day of my calamity: i.e. when I was practically overpowered by my enemies (cf. Dt. 33:35; Job 21:30; Jer. 18:17, 46:21).
my stay: or 'my support' (cf. 23:4) upon which I could lean (Isa. 10:20).

19. into a broad place: in the Hebrew idiom 'distress' is a condition of being hemmed in by trouble, while 'deliverance' is to be brought out of the affliction, out of the stranglehold of distress, into a broad place, to be set at liberty (cf. 4:1 (M.T. 2)). Dahood (*PAB*, I, p. 111) argues that 'the broad place' (*merḥāḇ*) is a poetic name for the underworld, and he adduces a number of references which describe the vastness of the abode of the dead. His description of Sheol is, of course, right, but it is not certain that 'the broad place' must be the netherworld.
he delighted in me: this is the reason for the divine help; one could argue that the salvation proves that Yahweh is pleased with his servant (cf. 41:11 (M.T. 12)).

THE PROFESSION OF RIGHTEOUSNESS AND LOYALTY **20–30**

This is no self-righteous boasting, but an indirect affirmation of faith in the covenant loyalty of Yahweh.

20. The LORD rewarded me . . .: the obedience to the covenant, and the consequent blessings, do not stress the merits of man, but rather the graciousness of God. Loyalty to him may become a legal righteousness, but its misunderstanding does not discredit its true function. Verses 20-4 are reminiscent of the Entrance Liturgies (Ps. 15, 24).
righteousness is fidelity to God's Covenant and to the divinely established relationships, and thus it is part of the right response to God's love which is prior to both the Covenant and obedience. See on 33:5.
the cleanness of my hands: i.e. the integrity of my conduct (cf. 24:4; 1QS ix:15).

21. the ways of the LORD: i.e his commandments (cf. Dt. 8:6, 10:12, 11:22, 19:9, 26:17, 30:16; Jos. 22:5).
have not . . . departed from my God: Dahood (*PAB*, I, p. 102) reads: '. . . have not been guilty, O my God', and he takes the preposition 'from' as an enclitic *mēm* belonging to the preceding verb (i.e. *rāšaʿtî-m*). This produces a reasonable rendering and improves the construction; that of M.T. is not attested elsewhere.

22. all his ordinances were before me: i.e. they continually determined my way of life (cf. Dt. 6:6–9; Ps. 119:30).

I did not put away . . .: 2 Sam. 22:23 has 'I did not turn aside', but the former reading seems more likely (cf. Job 27:5).

23. I was blameless: see Dt. 18:13; Ps. 15:2. G. v. Rad (*Deuteronomy* (1966), p. 123) comments: 'It is not moral and religious "perfection" which is demanded from Israel, but rather an undivided commitment . . . to the conditions of fellowship with Yahweh'.

I kept myself from guilt: or, better, '. . . from all that would render me guilty' (so Johnson, *SKAI*, p. 111), since the King has been affirming his innocence.

24. See verse 20.

25. the loyal: (*ḥāsîḏ*) this is the man who is faithful to his covenant obligations because God has been gracious to him; he is not looking for merit but he is honestly trying to respond to the grace of God by means of a gracious living. See on 145:17.

with the blameless man: perhaps omit 'man' (*g*ᵉ*ḇar*) (so also S).

26. With the pure . . .: G. R. Driver (*HTR*, XXIX (1936), pp. 172ff.) renders: 'With the boorish Thou dost show Thyself boorish' (i.e. the Hebrew *b-r-r* is associated with the Syriac *b*ᵉ*rîrā*ʾ ('simple, rude')). This would provide a good parallel to verse 26*b*, and the whole verse would form a contrast to verse 25 (but see also Johnson, *SKAI*, p. 111, n.2).

thou dost show thyself perverse: Johnson (*SKAI*, p. 111) suggests: 'Thou dost prove ready to wrestle' (cf. Gen. 30:8).

27. thou dost deliver a humble people: Kraus (*PBK*, p. 147) points out that the deliverance of the King is not due to his special relationship with God, but to his solidarity with the righteous and the humble in Israel.

the haughty eyes: this is another way of saying 'the proud men' (cf. 131:1). The haughty and the proud, in the *OT* sense, are those who act as if they were God (cf. Isa. 2:11,12,17). 'Haughty eyes' are one of the seven things which God abominates (Prov. 6:16ff.).

28. thou dost light my lamp: in 2 Sam. 22:29 'thou art my lamp, O LORD'. The former reading can be explained as a corrupt conflation of two variants: 'my lamp' and 'my light' (i.e. ʾ*ôrî* ('my light') probably became *tā*ʾ*îr* (*RSV* 'thou dost light')). In the Ugaritic texts the god Shapash is called the lamp of the gods or 'the divine lamp' (cf. *Baal* II, viii:21; III, ii:24, iv:8,17). Light is usually a symbol of life and prosperity while darkness represents disaster and death. Following 2 Sam. 22:29, it seems that the writer regards Yahweh as the source of light (or 'life') who has lightened his servant's darkness and has brought him back to the fulness of life (cf. Job 18:5f.; Prov. 13:9, 20:20, 24:20). Just as Yahweh is the lamp of the King, so the King can be regarded as the lamp of his people (2 Sam. 21:17).

29. The translation of this verse is uncertain, but Kraus and v. Rad see here an allusion to the Holy War. It is less likely that it refers to certain incidents in the life of David (so Kirkpatrick, Oesterley).

by thee I can crush a troop: or, with Johnson (*SKAI*, p. 112): '. . . I break down the fence', by taking *g*^{e}*d̲ûd̲* (*RSV* 'troop') to mean 'section, division' hence also 'fence'.

I can leap over a wall: this probably refers to the scaling of the walls of hostile cities. Barnes (*PWC*, I, p. 85) sees here a reference to David's escape from Keilah (1 Sam. 23:7–13), but this suggestion is a mere guess.

30. This God: or 'As for God'.

his way is perfect: Dahood (*PAB*, I, p. 114) suggests 'his dominion is complete', but this provides no improvement. Rather the dealings of God with his people are irreproachable, without blemish, as in Dt. 32:4.

the promise . . . proves true: whatever Yahweh says is reliable (119:140), and his word has stood the test like pure gold or silver, which is without any dross (see on 12:6).

he is a shield: see on 3:3. Verse 30*bc* is practically identical with Prov. 30:5.

DELIVERANCE AND VICTORY COME FROM YAHWEH **31–45**

31. For who is God . . .: this rhetorical question introduces a hymnic confession of the uniqueness of Yahweh. Cf. Exod. 15:11: 'Who is like thee . . . among the gods'. In essence the Psalmist means that Yahweh is the sole God (cf. Labuschagne, *IYOT*, pp. 116f.).

rock: see on 42:10; cf. Dt. 32:4; 1 Sam. 2:2. Here it is used as a divine appellative, and is parallel to 'God' (verse 31*a*).

32. who girded me with strength: in 2 Sam. 22:33 '(is) my strong refuge', but the former alternative may be preferable. For the opposite view, see Cross jr. and Freedman, p. 30. The meaning of the phrase is: 'You have made me strong'; cf. 30:11 (M.T. 12): 'girded me with gladness', i.e. made me glad.

made my way safe: Dahood (*PAB*, I, p. 114) takes 'way' (*dereḵ*) in the sense of 'dominion, power' (as in Ugaritic; see on 10:5); he renders: '. . . whose dominion is complete'. If this change is acceptable, then it might be better to translate 'and made my power complete' which offers a reasonable parallel to verse 32*a*.

33. my feet like hinds' feet: in ancient warfare, swiftness was an important qualification of a successful warrior (cf. 2 Sam. 1:23, 2:18; 1 Chr. 12:8). Yet it was not regarded as a personal attainment, but as a gift of Yahweh.

set me secure on the heights: reading *bāmōṯ* ('heights') for M.T. *bāmōṯay* ('my heights'). The description probably parallels the thought of verse 33*a*, and the writer may have had in mind the sure-footed gazelle upon the mountain heights (cf. 1 Chr. 12:8). Briggs (*CECBP*, I, p. 147) interprets 'heights' as 'battle-fields'; but this seems less likely.

34. He trains my hands for war: (=144:1*b*), i.e. for warlike skills such as the use of sword, spear, and bow.

a bow of bronze: see on 44:6. The term 'bronze' probably refers to the bronze-tipped arrows (cf. G. R. Driver, *WO*, v (1950), p. 410) rather than to the bow itself. Dahood (*PAB*, I, p. 115) proposes the view that we should translate 'the miraculous bow', deriving *nᵉḥûšāh* (*RSV* 'bronze') from *n-ḥ-š*, 'to practise divination, enchant'. In the Aqhat legend (*Aqhat* II, v; Driver, *CML*, p. 53) we find a mention of a miraculous, god-made bow, but it is not very likely that our verse refers to a similar weapon.

35. the shield of thy salvation: or 'your saving shield' rather than 'shield of victory' (so Dahood).

thy right hand supported me: the subject of the verb may be Yahweh (as in verse 35*a*), hence 'with your right hand you upheld me' (cf. 63:8 (M.T. 9)).

thy help: the Hebrew *ᶜanāwāh* is problematic. *RSVm* renders 'thy gentleness' (=*AV*, *RV*) while Dahood (*PAB*, I, p. 116) derives it from *ᶜ-n-w*, 'to conquer', hence 'your triumph'. A reasonable suggestion is to regard the word as associated with *ᶜ-n-h*, 'to answer', and to translate 'by your answering (you have made me great)', reading *ᶜanôṯᵉḵā* for M.T. *ᶜanᵉwaṯᵉḵā* (cf. also Winton Thomas, *TRP*, p. 7). The opposite thought is found in verse 41, where the enemies cry for help but Yahweh does not answer.

36. This verse refers either to the deliverance from trouble (cf. 4:1*b* (M.T. 2*b*)) or it resumes the thought of verse 33 (cf. Job 18:7; Prov. 4:12).

37. I pursued my enemies: (cf. Exod. 15:9). This and the following verses sound like a self-glorification; yet essentially they show forth the praise of God who has turned defeat into victory.

till they were consumed: this is a far cry from turning the other cheek (Mt. 5:39), but the Psalm must be seen against its own background. The Psalmist lived in a world of sharp contrasts, and he who was not for Yahweh, was against him; he who rejected life, chose death.

38. Here we have a continuation of the description of the overthrow of the enemies who are shattered once for all (cf. 110:5; Hab. 3:13).

they fell under my feet: this is not an expression of homage, but a portrayal of the death of the foes (cf. *Aqhat* I, iii:3,10,18, 24,32,38).

39. The first half of the verse takes up the theme of verse 32*b*.

my assailants sink under me: or 'you made my opponents to sink down in death beneath me (i.e. on the ground before my feet)'.

40. . . . my enemies turn their backs . . .: (cf. Exod. 23:27). This is usually taken to mean that the enemies have been made to flee (Jos. 7:8,12), but Dahood argues that the picture suggests a victor placing his foot on the neck of the defeated foe (similarly *NEB*), as in Jos. 10:24; after this symbolic expression of victory, the enemies are put to death (Jos. 10:26).

I destroyed: lit. 'I destroyed them'; but the suffix (i.e. 'them') may be the enclitic *mēm*, and so the direct object of the verb would be 'those who hated me'.

41. The second half of the verse seems to imply that the adversaries were Israelites. This may be a later alteration or addition when the Psalm was used in the post-Exilic period by the worshipping community; it does not, however, exclude non-Israelites (cf. 1 Sam. 5:12; Jon. 1:14, 3:8ff.).

they cried to the LORD: M.T. has 'unto (?) Yahweh'. Dahood may be right in treating the Hebrew *ʿal* (which could be the preposition 'upon') as a divine title, 'the Most High' (see on 7:8,10). If this proposal is accepted, we could render: '(even) the Most High, Yahweh, did not answer them'; and the conjunction *w*^e^ (*RSV* 'but') might be taken as an emphatic *wāw* (see P. Wernberg-Møller, *JSS*, III (1958), pp. 321–6).

42. as dust before the wind: 2 Sam. 22:43 has: 'as the dust of the earth', which may be the original reading. Dahood (*PAB*, I, p. 117) changes *rûaḥ* ('wind') into *rewah* ('square', i.e. broad place; see on verse 10); his rendering '(in the) square' gives a good parallel to the 'streets' in verse 42*b*. The metaphor describes the destruction of the enemies (cf. 2 Kg. 13:7).

I cast them out: (*ʾarîḳēm*) 2 Sam. 22:43 has 'I crushed them' (*ʾaḏaḳḳēm*) or 'I trampled them' (*NEB* 'I trample . . .') which seems more appropriate to the present metaphor. The former reading may have arisen due to a confusion between the Hebrew letters *r* and *d*.

like the mire of the streets: is a simile of humiliation or defeat (cf. Isa. 10:6; Mic. 7:10).

43a,b. strife with the peoples: (=2 Sam. (LXX)). 2 Sam. 22:44 has '. . . my people'. Some scholars read: 'You have delivered me from a myriad (*mēribbô*) of people (or 'warriors')' (cf. Dt. 32:30).

the head of the nations: Dahood (*PAB*, I, p. 103) suggests '. . . protected me (so 2 Sam. 22:44) from the venom of nations' (cf. Dt. 32:33). The Hebrew *rōʾš* can be either 'head' or 'venom', and the preposition *l*^e^ can occasionally mean 'from', as in Ugaritic (cf. Driver, *CML*, p. 158). The *RSV* rendering is possible, and the thought expressed is reminiscent of Ps. 2.

43c. This line could be taken with verse 44, and it would refer to the world dominion of Yahweh's vicegerent. Verses 44–5 continue the same theme. The King's fame is so great that nations surrender without a battle. A similar incident is described in 2 Sam. 8:9ff., where the king of Hamath seeks to win David's friendship by sending him gifts. It is unlikely, however, that the Psalm refers to this or a similar event during the reign of David. The language of the poem is strongly reminiscent of the court style (see introduction to Ps. 2), and the victories described are, primarily, cultic experiences and realities.

THE PRAISE OF YAHWEH **46–50**

46. The LORD lives: Dahood (*PAB*, I, p. 118), following Ewald, regards this phrase as 'an archaic formula of a precative type'; hence he renders it: 'May Yahweh live'. Some other interpreters have associated this phrase with the dying and rising god of the fertility cult (cf. Baal III, iii:1ff.); Widengren (cf. A. Bentzen, *King and Messiah* (1955), p. 27) takes it as a cultic word which proclaims the resurrection of the god. We may assume that the formula itself is of Canaanite origin, but its present purpose is to emphasize Yahweh's unchanging vitality and power. As the living God he can intervene in history; perhaps there is also an implicit contrast with the deities of other peoples (cf. Vriezen, *OOTT*, p. 171).

blessed: see on 16:7.

my rock: see verse 2.

God of my salvation: i.e. the God who has saved me. See 25:5, 27:9, 88:1 (M.T. 2); Mic. 7:7; Hab. 3:18.

47. who gave me vengeance: vengeance belongs to God alone (Dt. 32:35), but he can execute it by various means, e.g. by his people Israel (Ezek. 25:14). The motive underlying vengeance is that the guilty might know that Yahweh is the true God (cf. Ezek. 25:17). Yahweh's actions are governed by his justice and not vindictiveness.

subdued peoples under me: this triumph was probably a cultic experience, but none the less real because this cultic symbolism rests upon the mighty deeds of Yahweh in the past, and it points to what Yahweh is doing now and will do in the future. For the verb *d-b-r* ('to subdue'), see G. R. Driver, *JTS*, XXXI (1929–30), pp. 283ff.; cf. also 47:3 (M.T. 4), 144:2.

48. who delivered me: or 'my deliverer' (cf. verse 2).

my enemies: they are, most likely, the hostile nations; see also verse 3.

men of violence: lit. 'man of . . .' but it could be understood collectively as a synonym of 'enemies' (verse 48*a*) and of 'adversaries' (verse 48*b*). Cf. 140:1,4,11 (M.T. 2,5,12); Prov. 3:31, 16:29; 1QpHab viii:11.

49. I will extol thee: or '(Therefore) I will thank thee'. See 1QH for this common introductory formula (ii:30,31, iii:19, iv:5, v:5, vii:6, xi:3,15). According to Westermann (*PGP*, p. 27) 'The expression of thanks to God is included in praise, *it is a way of praising*'.

O LORD: it would be better to take this vocative with verse 49*b* (for metrical reasons) and to regard the conjunction *wᵉ* ('and') as an emphatic *wāw* (cf. verse 41*b*), hence 'O Lord, to your name (alone) I will sing praises'.

50. Great triumphs . . .: rather '(To) him who makes

great the victories of his King', or 'Who made his King famous through victories' (so Dahood, *PAB*, I, p. 104).

shows steadfast love to . . .: or 'who keeps his covenant promises to . . .' (cf. Gen. 24:14; Exod. 20:6; Dt. 5:10).

his anointed: see on 2:2, 89:20.

to David and his descendants: it is unlikely that these words meant that the author of the Psalm was David (so Kirkpatrick); rather the opposite was the case. The reference is, apparently, to the promises made to the Davidic dynasty, in 2 Sam. 7 (cf. 144:10).

Psalm 19 The Glory of God in Nature and in His Law

It has been argued that Ps. 19 consists of two more or less independent poems. The main reasons for this suggestion are the differences in the contents, style, and metre. The first poem, Ps. 19A, is contained in verses 1–6, and could be described as a nature Psalm or a hymn in praise of God. The second poem, Ps. 19B, comprises verses 7–14, and extols the law of Yahweh. Ps. 19A is characterized by word-pictures drawn from mythology, and the prevailing metre is 4+4, while Ps. 19B praises the law by enumerating its various aspects and their significance for the godly man. The dominating metre is 3+2.

Ps. 19A is usually regarded as of great antiquity, and it is possible that it is but a fragment of a larger work which dealt in detail not only with the sun but also with other works of God. It may well belong to the pre-Exilic period and, with its glorification of the creator, it could have had its life setting in the New Year Festival (see Introduction, pp. 52f.). It has certain affinities with Ps. 8, 104, and 148. J. Morgenstern ('Psalm 8 and 19A', *HUCA*, XIX (1945–6), p. 515) has suggested that since Ps. 19A does not mention Yahweh, it (or its primary source) must have been of non-Israelite origin, and must have dealt only with El as the supreme world-deity. The reason for joining the two poems is not clear, but it could hardly be accidental. A likely explanation is that the author of Ps. 19B used certain fragments of an older poem (Ps. 19A) as an introduction for his own work. In ancient Near Eastern thought, 'sun' and 'justice' belong together, and this may account, at least partly, for the collocation of the two poems. In a way, both parts speak of the divine will: nature is not only created by God but it is also ordered and maintained by him, and therefore it truly proclaims the glory

of God. This same function is also performed by anyone who keeps the divine law. See also Sabourin, *POM*, I, pp. 185f.
To the choirmaster: see Introduction, p. 48.
A Psalm of David: see Introduction, pp. 43ff. and 46.

THE HEAVENS DECLARE THE GLORY OF GOD **1–6**
This hymn begins rather abruptly without the usual exhortation to praise God.

1. In this verse the Hebrew text shows a chiastic arrangement – i.e. the respective terms in the parallel phrases occur in a reversed order. This cannot very well be reproduced in the translation without introducing some ambiguity.
The heavens: this is probably the canopy of the earth, or the sky, and so possibly a synonym of 'the firmament' (see on 150:1). The latter was conceived of as having the structure of a metal plate. In Job 37:18 the writer says: 'Can you, like him, spread out the skies, hard as a molten mirror'. Mirrors were often made of polished bronze (cf. Exod. 38:8). In Dt. 28:23 the heavens are compared to 'brass' (*RSV*) or 'bronze'. The Hebrew *šāmayim* ('heavens') can also denote the dwelling place of God and of the heavenly beings (cf. 123:1). In this verse 'heavens' are personified or, perhaps, the allusion is to the divine beings serving God (see on 89:5).
are telling: or 'keep on telling' (and 'keep on proclaiming' in verse 1*b*).
the glory of God: see on 104:31. In general, 'glory' (*kāḇôḏ*) is 'that asset which makes peoples or individuals, and even objects, impressive . . .' (v. Rad, *OTT*, I, p. 239), and so the glory of God is his power and majesty, or their manifestation in nature and in history (cf. 84:11 (M.T. 12)).
his handiwork is either the created world (cf. Weiser, *POTL*, p. 198), or the stars and the moon (so Kraus), as in 8:3 (M.T. 4).

2–4b. Day to day pours forth speech: without a pause, like a fountain or spring (cf. Prov. 18:4). Although their language is not *heard* by the ear of man (i.e. it is not fully comprehended), their message reaches to the ends of the world (verse 4*ab*). Primarily this account of God's glory is addressed by nature to nature (i.e. day proclaims it to day, and night to night), but something of it is perceived by the poet. The *AV* rendering of verse 3 suggests that this confession of the glory of the creator reaches all peoples of every tongue, but this translation is rather forced. Weiser (*POTL*, p. 199), rather enthusiastically, affirms that the 'heavens are the book from which the whole world can derive its knowledge of God'. On the other hand, whatever we can learn from the nature, cannot be compared to the law of the Lord.

their voice: (*ḳawwām*), *AV*, *RV* render 'their line', but the sense suggested by the parallelism supports *RSV*. The Hebrew word (*ḳaw*) may mean, perhaps, 'call' (so Dahood, following Jacob Barth), and it may be associated with *ḳ-w-h*, 'to call, collect' (for other possible examples, see Dahood, *PAB*, I, p. 122). Weiser (*POTL*, p. 197) suggests 'their law', but the evidence for this rendering is very slight; cf. Isa. 28:10,13.

to the end of the world: lit., perhaps, 'in the end . . .', hence some exegetes read *weliḳeṣēh* ('and to the end . . .') for M.T. *ûḇiḳeṣēh* ('and in the end . . .'), yet the preposition *be* may have the meaning 'to' (cf. Kraus, *PBK*, p. 153).

4c. In them: i.e. in the heavens or firmament (see verse 1). Some commentators (e.g. Weiser, Leslie, Taylor) emend it to 'in the sea' (*bayyām*); this may be right mythologically but it is far from clear that *bayyām* is the original reading. Verse 4*c* may mark the beginning of the fragment of a hymn to the sun; Dahood thinks that it may have been of Canaanite origin.

a tent for the sun: it is of some interest that out of the many works of God, only the sun is dealt with in some detail; and one of the reasons may have been a polemic tendency. The sun was regarded by many ancient peoples as a very important deity, and there is a considerable amount of information on this subject from Egypt and Mesopotamia (for references, see Kraus, *PBK*, p. 157). In Mesopotamia the sun-god, Shamash, was considered to be the upholder of justice and righteousness; e.g. on the stele which contains the well-known Code of Hammurabi, Shamash is pictured as giving the law (or the commission to write the law-book) to Hammurabi (cf. *ANET*, p. 163; *ANEP*, pl. 246). In the *OT*, on the other hand, the sun (*šemeš*) is but the work of God's hands, and all worship is to be given to the creator alone. The sun has a 'tent' and not a 'palace', and this may point to the antiquity of the metaphor. The tent is, apparently, the place where the sun 'spends' the night (cf. *ANET*, p. 391a).

5. like a bridegroom: Gunkel (*PGHAT*, p. 75) points out that the Babylonian Shamash is often called 'bridegroom', and he sees here an allusion to the myth of the marriage of the sun, or to the idea that 'the sun-god rests during the night in the sea, lying in the arms of his beloved' (cf. Weiser, *POTL*, p. 199). The 'chamber' (*ḥuppāh*) may mean 'marriage-tent' (as in Jl 2:16) but in this verse it is simply part of the simile derived from some ancient mythology. Any intended allusion to such a myth would only serve as poetic imagery, while the myth itself could not have had any religious significance for the Psalmist. The word-picture in verse 5 probably means that the sun goes to its task strong and radiant. Cf. Jg. 5:31: '. . . like the sun as he rises in his might'.

like a strong man: or 'hero'. Similar descriptions of the sun or Shamash are found in the literature of the Near East; e.g., he is called 'valiant Shamash' (cf. *ANET*, pp. 89, 91, 115, etc.), 'lordly hero Shamash' (*ANET*, p. 337b), etc.

runs its course: speed was one of the necessary qualifications of a good fighting man (see on 18:33) in ancient times. The swiftness of the sun is also mentioned in 1 Esd. 4:34.

6. from the end of the heavens: or 'from the extreme East'. **its circuit:** perhaps, 'its return' (so Dahood) or 'turning about' (so Morgenstern) which is to be found in the other extreme of the heavens, in the West. Cf. Ec. 1:5: 'The sun rises and the sun goes down, and hastens to the place where it rises'.

from its heat: or 'from its light' (so Morgenstern, pp. 512ff.); cf. Job 30:28.

YAHWEH'S LAW IS PERFECT **7–14**

The second poem (Ps. 19B) could be subdivided into a hymn, the object of which is to praise the law (verses 7–10), and a prayer for pardon and guidance (verses 11–14). The poem contains many similarities with Ps. 119.

The Praise of the Law **7–10**

In verses 7–8 we find an account of four different aspects of the Law, and each of them is followed by a description of the effects produced upon the godly man. This differentiation is primarily a literary device, and it is difficult to discern these distinctions in actual usage. The 'law' in this Psalm is the written expression of Yahweh's will, which can be read and studied (see on 1:2), but which has not, as yet, become 'an absolute quantity'; this happened 'when it ceased to be understood as the saving ordinance of a special racial group (the cultic community of

Israel) linked to it by the facts of history . . .' (v. Rad, *OTT*, I, p. 201).

7. perfect: this term is frequently used in reference to sacrificial animals, as being without blemish. The same adjective (*tāmîm*) can also describe the work of God (Dt. 32:4), his way (18:30 (M.T. 31)), the perfection of his knowledge (Job 37:16), etc. When used of man, it may suggest uprightness or blamelessness (cf. Gen. 6:9; Job 1:1,8).

reviving the soul: when a man loses his strength or dies, the soul (*nep̄eš*) is said to depart (Gen. 35:18), or is poured out (Lam. 2:12). On the other hand, the restoration of life (cf. 1 Kg. 17.22) or vitality (Lam. 1:11) can be described as the return of the soul or its reviving. For a detailed discussion on this subject, see Johnson, *VITAI*, pp. 9ff.

the testimony like the 'precepts' and 'commandments' in verse 8, is a synonym of the 'law' (see on 119:2). Weiser (*POTL*, p. 202) finds here a reference to the manifestation of Yahweh's will in history.

is sure: or 'is reliable'.

making wise the simple: i.e. by imparting them understanding (cf. 119:130). In the Book of Proverbs 'the simple' are usually the gullible, simpletons, and even the wayward (Prov. 1:32). If the word (*peṯî*) has a similar connotation in this verse, then we should render 'making wise (even) the simple'.

8. are right: i.e. there is nothing crooked in them (cf. Prov. 8:8f.).

rejoicing the heart: i.e. the law imparts not only instruction but also gladness, thus enabling one to enjoy the fulness of life. Dahood (*PAB*, I, p. 123) quotes, in comparison, from the Amarna Letters (CXLII:7–10): 'When I heard the words on the tablet of the king, my lord, my heart rejoiced and my eyes became radiant.'

is pure: or 'is bright (or 'radiant')'. For this use of *bārāh* ('pure'), see Ca. 6:10: 'bright as the sun'. Consequently the law or commandment (see on 119:6) enlightens the eyes or gives understanding. Similarly in Prov. 6:23: 'For the commandment is a lamp and the teaching a light . . .' (cf. also 119:105,130).

9. the fear of the LORD: some scholars (e.g. Kissane, Kraus) assume that the present phrase is an error for 'the word of Yahweh' (*ʾimraṯ yhwh*) (cf. 119:38), which would fit in the series of the synonyms for 'law'. Yet M.T. may be right. Just as the

testimony of Yahweh can make wise even the simple, so also the fear of Yahweh is the beginning of wisdom (111:10; Prov. 1:7, 9:10) or the controlling principle. Thus the 'fear of Yahweh' may be a synonym of the 'law'; see on 25:12.
is clean: i.e. in contrast to the immoralities of heathenism (so Kirkpatrick). Perhaps the expression points to the finality of the Law; it is pure like refined silver (cf. 12:6 (M.T. 7)) and there is no dross in it, therefore it is 'enduring for ever'. For a contrast, see Isa. 10:1: 'Woe to those who decree iniquitous decrees . . .'.
are true: lit. 'are truth'; cf. Jer. 17:17: 'thy word is truth'. For *ʾemeṯ*, 'truth', see on 25:5.

10. The law in all its aspects is more precious than the finest gold (cf. 119:72,127), and it is more enjoyable than the best honey (cf. 119:103).

The Psalmist's Prayer **11–14**

11. warned: or 'is enlightened' (from *z-h-r* I; so Dahood).
great reward: this consists, in the first place, of the experience derived from the enjoyment of the law: there is new strength and joy, wisdom and enlightenment (verses 7–8); there is also the relief and gladness in being saved from going astray. It is very likely that obedience to the law was expected to bring riches and honour (so Prov. 22:4) as a natural consequence, but they need not have been the main motive for loyalty. See on 119:112.

12. But who can discern his errors: the 'reward' for keeping the law is great, but there are many pitfalls. One must take into account the hidden, inadvertent sins, and consequently any form of self-righteousness is out of place (cf. also Lev. 4:1ff., 13ff.; Num. 15:22ff.). Instead of clamouring for a reward, one must depend upon God for one's very existence.

13. Keep back thy servant . . .: the author is aware that his own efforts to observe the divine law would come to nothing (cf. 119:133) but for the help of Yahweh.
presumptuous sins: i.e. deliberate disobedience. The Hebrew *zēḏîm* can also mean 'arrogant men' (so G. W. Anderson) or 'presumptuous ones', which Dahood (*PAB*, I, p. 124) regards as 'idols or false gods' (cf. 40:4 (M.T. 5)). LXX suggests 'strangers' (which points to the Hebrew *zārîm*) or 'foreign gods' (as in Dt. 32:16). The *RSV* rendering may well be right; a good parallel is found in Gen. 20:6 where God says to Abimelech: '. . . it was I who kept you from sinning against me'.

I shall be blameless: when God has dealt with the sins of ignorance and when he has upheld his servant.
great transgression: see on 51:1. Dahood (*PAB*, I, p. 125) argues that the phrase refers to idolatry (cf. also W. L. Moran, *JNES*, XVIII (1959), pp. 280f.). A similar expression occurs in Exod. 32 where the making and worshipping of the golden calf is described as 'a great sin' (Exod. 32:21,30,31); Jeroboam, too, is said to have made the Israelites to commit 'a great sin' (2 Kg. 17:21). For **transgression** (*pešaᶜ*) see on 32:1.

14. This final verse is in the form of a dedicatory formula (cf. 104:34, 119:108). A similar expression may have been used at the offering of sacrifices, but it does not follow that 'the prayer is offered in place of the sacrifice' (so Weiser, *POTL*, p. 204), in spite of the possible support found in 141:2. Similarly Delitzsch (*BCP*, I, p. 289), who states that 'prayer is a sacrifice offered by the inner man'. Dahood (*PAB*, I, pp. 121:125) has proposed a reasonable rendering of verse 14: '. . . be according to your desire. And the thoughts of my heart according to your will . . .'. The preposition *lᵉ* (in *lᵉp̄ānêḵā* (*RSV* 'in thy sight')) may have the proposed connotation (cf. *BDB*, p. 516a). For a similar example, see Gen. 10:9, where *lip̄ᵉnê yhwh* (*RSV* 'before the LORD') is rendered by E. A. Speiser (*Genesis* (*AB* I, 1964), p. 67) as 'by the will of Yahweh'.
my rock: see on 42:9.
my redeemer: cf. Job 19:25. The term *gōʾēl* ('redeemer') was usually applied to the nearest kinsman, and it was his duty to look after the interests of his less fortunate relative(s). This might involve the redeeming either of the relative himself or his property, and sometimes he would act as the avenger if the kinsman was killed. When the term is used of Yahweh, it may imply that he is a kinsman of his people, not 'by the law of blood, but by that of election' (O. Procksch, '*Luō*', *TDNT*, IV, p. 330). See A. R. Johnson, 'The Primary Meaning of the Root Gʾ L', *SVT*, I (1953), pp. 67–77.

Psalm 20 'Give Victory to the King, O Lord'

Verses 1–5 form a prayer of intercession by the community on behalf of the King, while verses 6–9 are reminiscent of a thanksgiving Psalm. Verse 5 suggests several speakers (the Temple singers?) but in verse 6, at least, there is only one, unless he is simply the representative of the worshipping community. These and other factors imply that this Psalm is a liturgy which belongs to the Royal Psalms (see Introduction, pp. 39f.). Mowinckel (*PIW*, I, p. 225) describes it as 'a national psalm of intercession for the King before he goes to war', and it may have formed part of the ritual during which prayers and sacrifices were offered to Yahweh. Thus the *Sitz im Leben* or the setting of the Psalm may have been a day of preparation for the battle. It was customary to offer sacrifices before the beginning of a battle (cf. 1 Sam. 7:9, 13:9–12), and of particular interest is 2 Chr. 20 which tells us of the invasion of Judah by the united forces of the Ammonites, Meunites, and Moabites. When the news of this aggression reached Jehoshaphat, the King (873–849 B.C.), he proclaimed a fast. During the ritual appropriate to such a day, the King offered a prayer to Yahweh before the congregation, asking for his help. Thereupon Yahweh's answer was given by Jahaziel, an Asaphite, who delivered an oracle of salvation, stressing that the war is Yahweh's war. The main duty of the people was to believe in God and in his promises. It is quite possible that Ps. 20 was used on a similar occasion, but it would be futile to guess which was the original event that gave rise to this poem. Its title in the Syriac version ascribes it to the time of David's war with the Ammonites, while Theodore of Mopsuestia, and others after him, have thought of the time of Hezekiah (715–687/6 B.C.). Briggs (*CECBP*, I, p. 176) suggests the above-mentioned event during Jehoshaphat's reign, but all that one can reasonably say is that the Psalm belongs to the late pre-Exilic period, because it reflects a more advanced theology. E.g., Yahweh does not go into battle in 'person' (cf. 1 Sam. 4:3) as in the olden days, but he sends help from Mount Zion. There is also a certain stress upon the *name* of Yahweh, which is reminiscent of Deuteronomy, although it need not be post-Deuteronomic. A Maccabean date seems to be out of the question.

In the second part of the Psalm we find an expression of certainty which contrasts with the prayer at the beginning of the poem. This transition was probably brought about by an oracle (cf. 2 Chr. 20:14ff.; E. Würthwein, *ThLZ*, LXXII (1947), pp. 147ff.); or it could be the result of a cultic theophany (so Weiser).

The metre of the Psalm is mainly 3+3.

the choirmaster: see Introduction, p. 48.

A Psalm of David: see Introduction, pp. 43ff. and 46.

THE INTERCESSION FOR THE KING **1–5**

1. answer you: i.e. by giving his help and victory; see verse 6. Dahood (*PAB*, I, p. 127) renders: 'grant you triumph', deriving the verb from *ᶜ-n-w*, 'to conquer'; cf. also R. T. O'Callaghan, *Orientalia*, XVIII (1949), p. 186, yet *RSV* provides the more fitting translation.
day of trouble: or 'the time of crisis'. For the use of this phrase, see Gen. 35:3; Ps. 50:15, 77:2 (M.T. 3), 86:7.
the name is not to be associated with some magical incantation of the divine name (cf. Ac. 19:13), but in this context 'the name of God' may mean 'God in action'. Where the name of God is, there one also finds his presence which is made known through the help and deliverance bestowed upon the needy. Thus 'the name' is 'a symbol summing up his activity in revelation' (Eichrodt, *TOT*, II, p. 42). The 'name' is often described as an extension of Yahweh's personality (cf. Johnson, *OMICG*, p. 17), but sometimes it may simply be a circumlocution for Yahweh himself (cf. 68:4 (M.T. 5), 145:1,2). Occasionally the name exhibits a certain degree of independent existence, e.g., in Exod. 23:21: 'Give heed to him' (i.e. the angel of Yahweh) '. . . for my name is in him'. We may also note the Ugaritic story of Keret (II, vi:56), which mentions 'Ashtoreth-name-of-Baal' (Driver, *CML*, p. 47); this seems to describe the goddess as a manifestation of Baal.
the God of Jacob: (also in 84:8 (M.T. 9)). The name 'Jacob', in this verse, refers primarily to a theological entity rather than to a political unit (cf. Isa. 41:14, 43:1,22,28, 48:12; cf. also G. Wanke, *Die Zionstheologie der Korachiten*, *BZAW*, 97 (1966), pp. 54–8). It may well allude to the *Heilsgeschichte*, or the salvation-history, of the nation; the people of Israel or the house of Jacob had experienced God's deliverance from Egypt (see Exod. 19:3), when Yahweh, the God of Jacob, manifested himself as a deliverer. It is to this very God that the Psalm appeals (cf. 146:5). Originally 'Jacob' was the name of one of the sons of Isaac, and once upon a time it must have been a theophoric name, meaning perhaps 'May God protect'; the present form is only a shortened version (cf. Bright, *HI*, p. 70). The name 'Jacob' could be used of the whole nation of Israel (78:5,71; Isa. 2:5f.; Jer. 30:7,10,18) or of northern Israel (cf. Mic. 1:5); sometimes it denotes the southern kingdom (Jer. 5:20; Mic. 4:2).

protect you: or 'set you on high (beyond the reach of your enemy)' (cf. 69:29 (M.T. 30), 91:14, 107:41).

2. May he send you help: lit. '. . . your help'; but here the pronoun (i.e. the pronominal suffix) has, apparently, a datival force.

the sanctuary: lit. 'holy place' (S 'his sanctuary'). The parallel phrase indicates that the writer must have thought of the Temple in Jerusalem rather than of Yahweh's dwelling place in heaven (cf. verse 6*b*); on the other hand, the two ideas are not mutually exclusive (cf. 11:4).

give you support from Zion: it is possible to argue from this expression that it is an advance on the more ancient belief according to which Yahweh went into battle at the head of the armies of his people (cf. 1 Sam. 4:3–9; 2 Sam. 15:24–29; Ps. 44:9 (M.T. 10)). In this Psalm, Yahweh sends his help from the place where his name dwells, i.e. from the Temple. For 'Zion', see on 65:1.

3. May he remember: this is no mere reflection on Yahweh's part (see on 79:8), but it implies both thought and action (see 119:49). God accepts the offerings as a sincere expression (if such it is) of the people's cry for help, and he acts accordingly. The sacrifices mentioned are probably those offered before the battle or military operation in general (cf. 1 Sam. 7:9ff., 13:9ff.).

your offerings: or 'your gifts'; see on 40:6. The Hebrew *minḥāh* can denote any kind of sacrifice or gift, but in the post-Exilic period it became restricted to oblations of flour and oil.

regard with favour: lit. 'regard as fat' or 'find fat'. According to Lev. 3:16: 'All fat is the LORD's. It shall be a perpetual statute throughout your generations . . . that you eat neither fat nor blood'. Hence it seems that to regard an offering as fat would mean to accept it favourably. In this phrase the intensive form of the verb (*d-š-n*) is used in a declarative sense.

burnt sacrifices: these are offerings the whole of which are burnt upon the altar, and nothing is given back to the worshipper or to the priests; see on 51:16; cf. R. de Vaux, *Studies in Old Testament Sacrifice* (1964), pp. 27–51.

Selah: see Introduction, pp. 48f.

4. your heart's desire: lit. 'according to your heart' (similarly *AV*). For 'heart' (*lēḇ*), see on 27:3, 51:10.

fulfil all your plans: i.e. in as far as they are in harmony with

Yahweh's purposes. The 'plans' may be the council of war for the forthcoming battle (cf. 2 Sam. 16:20; 2 Kg. 18:20).

5. May we shout for joy: the speakers are either the Levitical singers or the whole community. Some (e.g. Kissane) regard this verse as a promise of thanksgiving rather than a prayer. For the verb *r-n-n* ('to shout in joy', or 'in grief') see on 33:1.
your victory: the Hebrew *y*ᵉ*šûᶜāh* means, in this verse, a salvation from enemies, hence 'victory' (see on 35:3).
set up our banners: if M.T. has preserved the right reading, then the reference may be to a cultic act in which some symbol of Yahweh's presence was set up, perhaps as a sign of the forthcoming victory (so Weiser, *POTL*, p. 207; cf. also Exod. 17:15f.; Num. 21:8f.; 2 Kg. 18:4). The use of the banners by the Qumran community may provide some parallel (cf. Yadin, *SWSLSD*, pp. 38–64). LXX (and similarly S and V) has preserved a different reading: *megalunthēsometha* ('we shall be magnified') which points to the Hebrew *g-d-l*, 'to be great' (the verb in M.T. comes from *d-g-l*). G. R. Driver (*HTR*, xxix (1936), p. 174) suggests that the Hebrew *d-g-l* (*RSV* 'to set up a banner') may be related to the Assyrian *dagālu*, 'to look upon, wait for', hence 'and we will wait upon the name of our God'. Winton Thomas (*TRP*, p. 8) follows the versions, in reading *nagdīl*, '(let us) triumph'.

THE CONFIDENCE IN GOD'S HELP **6–8**

6. Now I know: this new-found confidence is probably the result of a divine oracle promising salvation. It is less likely that this transition was due to the latest news from the battlefield, telling that the King has just achieved a great victory (so Dahood). It is possible that during the ritual not only the mighty deeds of Yahweh in the past were represented in some dramatic form but also some symbolic promise of victory may have been granted to the King (cf. 1 Kg. 22:11f.; Ps. 44:1–8 (M.T. 2–9)). The principle involved is expressed in Dt. 7:17ff.: '. . . you shall remember what the LORD your God did to Pharaoh and to all Egypt . . . so will the LORD your God do to all the people of whom you are afraid'.
will help: lit. 'has saved' or 'granted victory'. The Hebrew verb is, apparently, a prophetic perfect which describes an event in the future with such certainty as if it had already taken place (cf. *GK* 106n; D. Michel, *Tempora und Satzstellung in den Psalmen* (1960), pp. 90ff.).
his anointed: see on 2:2, 89:20.

from his holy heaven: i.e. his celestial dwelling place. Yahweh is present in the sanctuary on Mount Zion through his name, and his help could be described as coming from Zion. It is unlikely that there was a contradiction between the belief in the transcendent God in heaven, and the faith in the immanent deity on earth, in the Temple; these seem to be two ways of thinking of God. See also Clements, *GT*, pp. 68f.

with mighty victories: Dahood (*PAB*, I, p. 128) suggests '. . . from his fortress has given victory', regarding *g*^{e}*ḇûrôṯ* ('mighty victories' (*RSV*)) as a poetic name for heaven, and taking the preposition *b*^{e} in the sense of 'from' (see on 18:8). The *RSV* rendering, however, seems more likely (cf. 106:2, 150:2).

his right hand stands for Yahweh himself as *pars pro toto*, or a part denoting the whole. The right hand is usually the more active one, and therefore the more significant. In this phrase it serves as an accusative of means. It can also denote the might or power of a person (89:25 (M.T. 26), 118:15f.) or of a people (89:42 (M.T. 43)).

7. chariots . . . horses: this seems to support the interpretation that the Psalm must be seen against the background of war. The reference may be to chariotry (see on 68:17) and cavalry respectively or, perhaps, only to the chariot force, since cavalry was not widely used in warfare except by a few peoples (cf. de Vaux, *AI*, p. 224; see on 147:10).

we boast of the name . . .: or 'we remember . . .' (so Weiser). Dahood (*PAB*, I, p. 129) derives the verb *z-k-r* from *zāḵār*, 'male', and suggests as its meaning 'to be powerful'. The evidence for this denominative verb is slender, although S renders the Hebrew verb by 'we shall prevail'. The conviction that victory can be gained only by the help of God is reminiscent of the traditions of the Holy War (cf. Isa. 30:15,17; 31:1; Zech. 4:6). The most formidable weapon of the Israelites was their trust in Yahweh (Jos. 23:10). For the *RSV* rendering, see G. R. Driver, 'Hebrew Homonyms', *Hebräische Wortforschung* (*SVT*, 16, 1967), p. 53.

8. They will collapse: or '. . . will be bowed down' (cf. 18:39*b* (M.T. 40*b*)).

but we shall rise: this may point to the present superiority of the enemy, as far as their numerical strength is concerned; but through Yahweh's intervention the tables will be turned. The experience of 'the day of trouble' (verse 1) will have been a lesson in dependence upon Yahweh.

THE CONCLUDING PRAYER 9

Give victory to the king, O LORD: the punctuation of M.T. suggests 'Grant victory, O Yahweh, let the King hear us when we call' (cf. *RSVm*). The *RSV* translation is supported by LXX and V, and it provides the more natural conclusion to the Psalm which is, essentially, an intercession for the King. In a way, the conclusion resumes the opening theme of the poem, as in 8:1,9 (M.T. 2, 10).

Psalm 21 KING BY THE GRACE OF GOD

The reference to the King in verses 1 and 7 suggests that this Psalm is a Royal song, but its more specific classification is problematic. The Psalm consists of two main parts: verses 1–7 and 8–12. The first part reminds us of a Thanksgiving Psalm, and it enumerates the various blessings which Yahweh has bestowed upon the King, and, indirectly, also upon the whole people. These verses were probably uttered by a priest or the whole congregation. The second part of the Psalm is more complex: either it was addressed to the King as a kind of oracle promising success in his future ventures; or it was directed toward Yahweh, as an expression of confidence in his power. The Psalm concludes with an ascription of praise to Yahweh (verse 13). All these various elements imply that we are dealing with a liturgy, but it is difficult to know what was its life-setting. Mowinckel (*PIW*, II, p. 62) thinks that Ps. 21 (and also Ps. 20) was probably uttered *before* a military expedition, while Briggs, Dahood, *et al.* regard it as a thanksgiving for royal victory; it seems, however, that verses 8–12 look *forward* to the defeat of the enemy. Perhaps the most likely explanation is that Ps. 21 belongs to the ritual of the coronation of the King, or to the annual celebration of the King's accession. Verse 3 actually mentions the royal crown, and verse 5 speaks of the kingly attributes of splendour and majesty which God has bestowed upon the monarch. It is possible that this occasion was also connected with the renewal of the Covenant, and that the blessings and curses (which form an integral part of the Covenant) are reflected in the two main sections of the Psalm (cf. F. C. Fensham, *ZAW*, LXXVII (1965), pp. 193–202).

The date of the Psalm is in the pre-Exilic period.

The metre is uneven, but 4 + 4 and, especially, 3 + 3 predominate.

the choirmaster: see Introduction, p. 48.
A Psalm of David: see Introduction, pp. 43ff. and 46.

THE BLESSINGS OF THE KING **1–7**

1. In thy strength: or 'In your triumph' (so Dahood, *PAB*, I, p. 130) which may also be suggested by the parallel term 'help' or 'victory' (*y^e^šû^c^āh*, see on 35:3). Gunkel derives the Hebrew *^c^ōz* (*RSV* 'strength') from *^c^-w-z*, 'to seek refuge', hence 'protection' (cf. 28:7f.).
how greatly he exults: or 'he shall greatly exult' omitting 'how' (*māh*) with the versions.

2. his heart's desire: we must assume that Yahweh had granted the prayers of the King, because he had been a man 'after God's own heart' (cf. 1 Sam. 13:14); Yahweh and the King were, so to speak, of one heart (cf. Jer. 32:39; Ezek. 11:19). He who loves God and walks in his statutes is given the promise: 'Ask what I shall give you' (1 Kg. 3:5; cf. Ps. 2:8, 20:4 (M.T. 5)).
request: *ᵓ^a^rešet* is a *hapax legomenon* in the *OT*, but a cognate of the same root is attested in Ugaritic; cf. Aqhat II, vi: 25, 26. 'Ask (*erš*) for life, O hero Aqhat, ask for life . . .' (cf. Driver, *CML*, p. 55a).

3. thou dost meet him: this may be an allusion to the incident after the Exodus from Egypt, when the Moabites instead of *meeting* the Israelites with bread and water (cf. Dt. 23:4; Neh. 13:2; Isa. 21:14) hired Balaam, the seer, to curse them. Yet God turned the curses into blessing (Dt. 23:5). Similarly in Ps. 21 Yahweh is seen as having transformed a possible disaster into a 'goodly blessing' (cf. Prov. 24:25) consisting of welfare and prosperity.
crown of fine gold: this may suggest the coronation of the King or his annual enthronement festival (so Duhm). The crowns of antiquity had a great variety of forms, and were not always made of metal. Essentially it was a headdress symbolic of royal rank or some other special distinction. For some examples, see *ANEP*, pll. 395, 422, 442. In 2 Sam. 12:30 David is said to have placed the crown of the Ammonite deity upon his own head, and its weight is given as a talent of gold, which would be some 130 lbs (cf. H. W. Hertzberg, *I & II Samuel* (*OTL*, 1964), p. 319) or, on a different reckoning, some 75–80 lbs (cf. de Vaux, *AI*, p. 206). It is doubtful, however, that the usual royal crowns were of such a weight.

4. He asked life of thee: the meaning of 'life' (*ḥayyîm*) creates certain problems. It may refer either to a long life (so most scholars) or to eternal life (so, e.g., Dahood). The former alternative seems more likely, although it needs some further qualification; what was expected could be described as a life characterized by vitality and prosperity. It is possible that the King (as well as any other person) could be thought of as living on in his descendants (see Kirkpatrick, *BPCB*, p. 111), and so 'for ever and ever' might allude to the dynastic line. Cf. 2 Sam. 7:29, where David asks Yahweh 'to bless the house of thy servant, that it may continue for ever before thee . . .' (cf. 72:17). Dahood (*PAB*, I, p. 132), in support of his view, quotes from the Legend of Aqhat: 'Ask for life eternal (i.e. *ḥym*), and I will give it to you; immortality, and I will bestow it upon you', and he argues that it is probable that the Hebrew *ḥayyîm* in verse 4 also means 'eternal life'. It seems, however, that, in the context of the Israelite beliefs, the King was more concerned with the permanence of his dynasty than with eternal life. It is also far from certain that a concept of a worthwhile eternal life was already part and parcel of the Israelite understanding of life and death, during the pre-Exilic period. Consequently Weiser (*POTL*, p. 213) is right in saying that the idea of immortality is unknown in the *OT*, and that this type of language (i.e. wishing the King 'length of days for ever and ever') belongs to the ancient court style and etiquette (cf. also E. Nielsen, *The Ten Commandments in New Perspective*, Eng. tr. by D. J. Bourke (*SBT*, 2nd ser., 7, 1968), p. 104). A good example of such language of the court is found in Neh. 2:3, where Nehemiah says to Artaxerxes, the Persian king: 'Let the king live for ever' (cf. also Dan. 2:4).

5. His glory . . . splendour . . . majesty are all divine attributes. They characterize the King only as far as he has received them from Yahweh; thus the King's majesty and glory is a derived splendour. See also on 90:16, 96:6.

6. . . . most blessed for ever: or 'you make him (a channel of) blessings for ever'. The Israelite King receives God's favour or blessings (see on 24:5) not only for himself but he is also the means whereby God brings peace, prosperity, and fruitfulness upon the whole land and all its people (72:15ff.). The opposite may be equally true; national disasters and calamities could be explained as due to the King who had lost favour with God, as in the case of Saul (cf. 2 Sam. 7:15).

make him glad . . .: Dahood (*PAB*, I, p. 133) renders 'you will make him gaze . . . upon your face', and he regards the Hebrew verb *ḥāḏāh* as a Canaanite form of *ḥzy*, 'to see' (cf. *Biblica*, XLV (1964), pp. 407ff.). In such a case, the reference would be to after-life, but the *RSV* rendering seems far more appropriate in this context (see verse 4).

with the joy of thy presence: or '. . . joy from Thy very presence' (Leslie, *PAP*, p. 93); similarly T.

7. trusts in the LORD: this is the necessary condition for all blessings. Some scholars have drawn attention to the covenantal character of this verse, and F. C. Fensham (p. 197) suggests that this phrase alludes to the Covenant relationship. This receives further support from the reference to 'the steadfast love' (*ḥeseḏ*) or 'the covenant-solidarity between God and his people' (Fensham, *art. cit.*, p. 197) or between God and the King. Weiser (*POTL*, p. 214) affirms that it is no longer the priest who speaks in this verse, but rather the whole worshipping community who 'give their assent to the coronation of their King (ibid. p. 215), yet the change from the second person to the third (in reference to Yahweh) need not imply a different speaker.

the Most High: see on 46:4, 47:2.

shall not be moved: see on 15:5.

THE INVINCIBLE MIGHT OF YAHWEH **8–12**

Although some commentators consider these verses to be addressed to the King, wishing him success in his reign, yet it may well be that the background of this section is the Covenant curses for those who break the Covenant or who intend to destroy it, whether from within (by disobedience) or from without (by attacking the Covenant people). For the former, see 89:30–3 (M.T. 31-4), and, for the latter, cf. Exod. 23:22.

8. Your hand: i.e. you yourself. Dahood (*PAB*, I, p. 133) translates 'your left hand', thus balancing 'your right hand' in verse 8*b* (cf. Jg. 5:26; 2 Sam. 20:9f.). This shade of meaning (if Dahood is right) is due, mainly, to the colouring given by the immediate context.

will find out: or 'may your hand find out . . .'. The verb *m-ṣ-ʾ*, 'to find', may mean, perhaps, 'to reach', as in 1 Sam. 31:3; *NEB* 'shall reach'.

right hand: see on 20:6.

will find out: the verb used is the same as that in verse 8*a*.

Unless this repetition is due to a scribal error, it may be used for the sake of emphasis, or with a slightly different shade of meaning.

9. as a blazing oven: i.e. enemies will burn like a fiery furnace (cf. Mal. 4:1; also Ps. 18:8 (M.T. 9); Isa. 30:27). F. C. Fensham (p. 199) suggests that the writer may have had in mind 'a burned-down city with the enemy inside it'. G. R. Driver (*HTR*, XXIX (1936), p. 175) proposes 'thou puttest them in a furnace' (deleting 'fire' (*ʾēš*), and changing the preposition k^e ('as') into b^e ('in')).

when you appear: lit. 'in the time of your presence'. *AV*, *RV* have '. . . of thine anger' as in 34:16, where the 'face' (or 'presence') of Yahweh is against the evildoers. Similarly also in Lam. 4:16 the 'face' (or 'anger') of Yahweh scatters the disobedient people. Johnson (*VITAI*, pp. 44f., n.3) suggests: 'In Thine own good time' for 'in the time of your presence'.

The LORD will swallow them up: as in Isa. 25:8 which looks forward to the time when God will swallow up death for ever.

10. You will destroy their offspring: lit. '. . . their fruit'; cf. Lam. 2:20. F. C. Fensham (p. 199) has pointed out that the destruction of the descendants of the enemies or of the disobedient vassals is a common feature in the vassal treaties. See also 37:28; Hos. 9:11–14.

11. If they plan evil: or 'For they planned . . .' thus giving the reason for the punishment; cf. 2:2.

they will not succeed: i.e. they will not be able to accomplish their rebellious schemes against the King of kings (cf. 2:4) or against his vicegerent and the Covenant people. In the latter case, too, the attack would ultimately be against Yahweh, for the enemies of his people are also the adversaries of their God.

12. you will put them to flight: lit. 'you will make them (turn their) backs'; *NEB* '. . . will catch them round the shoulders'.

aim at their faces: the expression does not necessarily refer to an episode *during* or *after* the flight of the enemies, and therefore there is no need to emend it into '. . . at their back' (so e.g. Gunkel, Leslie). 'Their faces' may simply be a roundabout expression for 'them' (i.e. the men themselves).

your bows: lit. 'your bowstrings' but it may probably suggest 'arrows' (so Nötscher).

WE WILL PRAISE YAHWEH **13**

The Psalm concludes with this hymnic ascription of praise to God for his strength and power.

13. Be exalted, O Lord . . .: this phrase is exegetically difficult, and a number of solutions have been suggested. It may be best to take the imperative 'be exalted' as an emphatic statement 'You shall be exalted' (cf. Gen. 12:2; Brockelmann, *HS*, p. 2). Both 'strength' and 'power' may refer to Yahweh's might in battle, and he will be exalted when he triumphs over his enemies. To this, the fitting response on the part of his people will be praise.

praise: for *z-m-r*, see on 66:4.

Psalm 22 God is Able to Deliver

The Psalm consists of two parts: verses 1–21, which resemble a lament; and verses 22–31, which express praise and thanksgiving. In view of this contrast, some exegetes (e.g. Duhm, Cheyne and Schmidt) have come to the conclusion that two different and originally independent Psalms must have been placed together by some later editor. This is possible, and some clear examples come to light when we compare the numbering of the Psalms in M.T. and LXX (see Introduction, pp. 27f.). Nevertheless, it is more likely that the Psalm is a literary unity, and that there are other reasons for the composite character of the Psalm (see introduction to Ps. 28). One possible explanation is the view that the lamentation was followed by a favourable priestly oracle, and that therefore the Psalmist was able to give thanks to God (see verse 21). Another likely suggestion is that the poem is essentially a thanksgiving in which the lamentation section describes the trouble which the author had experienced, and from which he has been delivered; if this view is correct, then the life-setting of the Psalm would be the offering of the votive sacrifice. This occasion was not so much a private act of devotion as a communal act of worship. The other worshippers shared not only in the sacrificial meal but also in the experiences of the delivered man. More recently some exegetes (e.g. Bentzen, Eaton) have argued that this poem is a Royal Psalm (see Introduction, pp. 39f.) which accompanied the symbolic humiliation of the King and his restoration. This tentative suggestion, in its more moderate form, is a reasonable possibility.

In view of all this, it is unlikely that the Psalm portrays the trials of David's life (so Delitzsch) or the deliverance of Hezekiah, the trials of Jeremiah, or the Babylonian exile and return of the Jewish people. Although the Psalm has certain points of contact with the Passion narrative in the *NT*, it is unlikely that the poem was ever intended as a prophecy of the sufferings of Christ. The real point of contact between the Psalmist and Christ is the reality of suffering and faith, not simply the poetic language.

Structurally, the Psalm falls into two main parts: verses 1–21 and 22–31. The first part consists of three smaller sections, each of which contains a lament and a petition. Verses 1–5 contrast the situation of the writer with that of the fathers who trusted and were delivered from their adversities. There is also the implicit prayer to God: '*I* trust in you, therefore deliver *me*'. Verses 6–11 give a more detailed description of the plight of the Psalmist, and end with a petition for help. Verses 12–21 resume the account of the trouble, and the problem is where to draw the line between the metaphors and factual descriptions of symptoms. The more or less stereotyped language could have been used for various kinds of misfortune. If we are allowed a guess, the original cause of the distress may have been illness aggravated by the attitude of the Psalmist's fellow men, as well as by his own doubts and the spiritual dilemma: God is a saving God, yet he has forsaken his loyal servant. At the end of verse 21 we have the solution: God did answer! Therefore verses 22–31 can serve as an expression of praise and thanksgiving to God.

The metre of the Psalm is varied, but the 3 + 3 rhythm could be regarded as the dominant one.

To the choirmaster: see Introduction, p. 48.

The Hind of the Dawn: this phrase is often taken as a 'cue word' suggesting a song popular at the time of the Psalmist or of the editor. LXX renders it: 'concerning the help (that is given in) the early morning', and it is a plausible explanation; it is a common theme in the Psalter that God's help comes to the needy in the morning (see on 46:5).

A Psalm of David: see Introduction, pp. 43ff. and 46.

THE UNBEARABLE SILENCE OF GOD **1–5**

1. My God, my God: this repetition of 'my God' may be an expression of the depth of the Psalmist's suffering and spiritual agony, while the pronoun 'my' provides the bridge between utter despair and hope. As a member of the Covenant people he recalls Yahweh's promise to be their God (cf. Dt. 26:17ff.; Jer. 7:23), and therefore also *his* God. This brings to mind the words of Martin Luther who, when he was assailed with doubts, used to say, 'I am baptized' (cf. R. H. Bainton, *Here I Stand* (1951), p. 367) which, as an unchangeable fact, provided a ray of light in the dark night of anguish.

. . . why hast thou forsaken me: these words have a special significance for the Christian reader because of their association with the Crucifixion of Jesus Christ; it is quoted in Mt. 27:46; Mk 15:34. To the Psalmist, this forsakenness was an inexplicable fact. Since the nearness of God was not only a spiritual experience but also manifested itself in actual help to the needy (according to contemporary beliefs), the present situation drove the Psalmist to the conclusion that God was aloof (cf. 10:1, 13:1 (M.T. 2), 35:22, 38:21 (M.T. 22), etc.).

Why art thou so far from helping me: *RVm* gives a possible literal translation: 'far from my help are the words of my roaring', i.e. my crying seems pointless. The *RSV* rendering assumes that the force of the interrogative 'why' (*lāmāh*) extends also to verse 1*b*.

the words of my groaning: lit. 'the words of my roaring' (cf. 32:3, 38:8 (M.T. 9)). The same verb is also used of the roaring of a lion (Isa. 5:29) and in 11QPs[a] Plea (xix:8) we find the phrase: 'my soul cries out (i.e. 'roars out') to praise thy name' (cf. J. A. Sanders, *The Psalms Scroll of Qumrân Cave 11* (1965), p. 78). See on 38:8.

2. O my God is probably outside the metre and may be a later addition.

I cry by day . . . and by night: i.e. continually (cf. Jer. 14:1; Lam. 3:49).

thou dost not answer: this is the real cause of the writer's anguish. The silence of God is more unbearable than the vociferous mockery of the foes.

3. This verse, as also verses 4–5, is in a hymnic style, and the interpretation is rather difficult as is indicated by the variety of possible renderings. The word *ḳāḏôš* ('holy') may be an adjective used predicatively as in *RSV*: 'Yet thou art holy'. Dahood (*PAB*, I, p. 139) argues that 'holy' has become by metonymy (i.e. by the substitution of an attribute for the thing meant) the name for God's throne, and so he translates 'While you sit upon the holy throne'. Others (e.g. Kissane) following some Greek MSS. and

V, render: 'And thou abidest in the sanctuary' (i.e. *baḳḳōḏeš* for M.T. *ḳāḏôš*). The *RSV* rendition (or that of Kraus, 'Yet you are enthroned as the Holy One, you praise of Israel') is preferable because it brings out the author's perplexity. Here is a man who had committed himself to God but who is now in great calamity for no apparent fault of his own (cf. verses 8 and 10). He has cried to God, yet the only answer has been mute silence. Nevertheless, God is holy, he is 'of purer eyes than to behold evil' (Hab. 1:3), and the one who has manifested his holiness by restoring his people (cf. Ezek. 20:41, 28:25, 36:23). He is the Lord who 'is exalted in justice' and who 'shows himself holy in righteousness' (Isa. 5:16). This is no mere private belief, but it is supported by the experience of the past generations (verses 4–5).

enthroned on the praises of Israel: cf. 'He sits enthroned (upon) the cherubim' (80:1 (M.T. 2), 99:1). The expression suggests that Yahweh is the object of his people's praises (so *NEB*) and the reason is stated in verses 4–5 (cf. Dt. 10:21: 'He is your praise; he is your God'; see also Ps. 71:6, 109:1; Jer. 17:14).

4. In thee our fathers trusted: in a way, the reality of Israel's deliverance is the source of the individual's comfort in adversity. The threefold repetition of 'they trusted' may be more than a stylistic feature and it may be intended to stress the condition on which one can expect Yahweh's help. So in 1QM xi:2 the author states that God gave David victory over Goliath 'because he trusted in thy great name, and not in sword and lance' (Yadin, *SWSLSD*, p. 308). In the case of the Psalmist, to trust means to believe that Yahweh does not change and that his promises are reliable.

5. . . . were not disappointed: i.e. '. . . they were not put to shame', because God came to their aid (cf. Isa. 50:7).

BE NOT FAR FROM ME, O GOD **6–11**

6. But I am a worm: here 'worm' serves as a metaphor of lowliness and humiliation (cf. Isa. 41:14: 'Fear not, you worm Jacob'; see also Job 25:6; 11QPs[a] Plea (xix:1)).

and no man: perhaps 'an unwanted nobody', one who does not belong anywhere, and who has become an island in a sea of hostility. Cf. the description of the Servant of the Lord in Isa. 53:2ff.

scorned . . . despised because of his calamities, which were interpreted as a manifestation of God's disfavour. Consequently the enemies need not be called 'godless' in the strict sense of the word; rather, they were men whose piety had turned sour because of their dogmas.

7. mock at me: cf. Lk. 23:35.

they make mouths at me: this expression is found only here in the *OT*, but it is obviously a gesture of scorn, although its exact nature is unknown. Some suggest 'they gape (in sadistic enjoyment)'.

they wag their heads: either in mock sympathy and surprise or in an expression of their approval at the supposed punishment (cf. Job 16:4; Ps. 64:8 (M.T. 9), 109:25; Lam. 2:15).

8. He committed his cause to the Lord: so *RSV*, following LXX, S, and V, in reading *gal* for *gōl* which could be rendered 'roll (upon Yahweh your cause)'. The object of the verb ('your cause') is implied by the context (cf. 37:5; Prov. 16:3). Dahood (*PAB*, I, p. 139) suggests: 'he lived for Yahweh' (i.e. *gāl* for M.T. *gōl*, deriving it from *g-y-l*, 'to live') but this is no improvement on *RSV*. This verse is quoted in Mt. 27:43, and an interesting parallel is found in Wis. 2:16ff.

for he delights in him: this sarcastic expression states that Yahweh delights in the sufferer (cf. also the parallel expression in 2 Sam. 22:20). We could paraphrase: 'for God obviously takes a great pleasure in him, that's why he is in trouble!' The implication is that the afflicted man is not only a sinner, but also a hypocrite.

9. In this and the following verses the Psalmist refutes the implicit accusation. God has been the protector of his life from his very birth, and that is, in a way, a proof that he had been loyal to his Master.

he took me from the womb: this rendering probably conveys the right meaning although the etymology of *gōḥî* ('who drew me forth' ?) is uncertain. The phrase may suggest that the Psalmist had been accepted into the family of God's people (cf. Gen. 50:23; Job 3:12). This imagery is appropriate to the King, but also to the whole nation (cf. Isa. 44:2, 46:3) and the ordinary Israelite (cf. Jer. 1:5).

thou didst keep me safe . . .: LXX suggests '(thou art) my hope from my mother's breasts', while G. R. Driver renders 'you laid me upon my mother's breasts' (cf. *Studies in Old Testament Prophecy*, ed. by H. H. Rowley (1950), p. 59); similarly *NEB*.

10. Upon thee was I cast: the words 'upon thee' are in an emphatic position (cf. 71:7). Dahood (*PAB*, I, p. 139) provides a good paraphrase: 'I was placed in your custody'.
thou hast been my God: this does not mean that as an infant he had exercised faith, but rather that God had watched over him.

11. Be not far from me: this resumes the perplexed cry of verse 1, but with a difference. Having reviewed the past goodness of Yahweh, he has derived a new hope, however faint (cf. verse 19).
for trouble is near: Dahood (*PAB*, I, p. 136) renders: 'for the adversaries . . .', which balances 'none to help' in verse 11*c*; he regards *ṣārāh* (*RSV* 'trouble') as an abstract noun with a concrete meaning.

HAS TROUBLE NO END? **12–21**

12. Many bulls encompass me: better, 'mighty bulls . . .' parallel to 'strong bulls of Bashan'. The metaphors describing the enemies are frequently derived from the world of wild animals. This language is not meant to be derogatory but points, primarily, to the strength and cruelty of the foes. Some scholars have pointed out that in the Near Eastern literature similar metaphors are often used of demonic powers, and that it is not improbable that a similar usage may sometimes be found in the Psalter (cf. Kraus, *PBK*, p. 180).
Bashan was situated East of Jordan between Mount Hermon in the N. and the river Yarmuk in the S. The major part of it was a table land between 1600 and 2300 feet in height, well suited for the growing of wheat and raising of cattle; it was also famous for its oaks (cf. Isa. 2:13); see D. Baly, *The Geography of the Bible* (1957), pp. 219ff. The rich pastures would help to produce prime cattle, and consequently the strong bulls of Bashan would be an appropriate picture of mighty enemies. Likewise also the 'cows of Bashan' must have been a fitting portrayal of the well-fed women of Samaria (Am. 4:1).

13. they open their mouths at me: the enemies (and not the bulls) appear to the sufferer like ravening lions. For 'lions', see on 7:2.

14. I am poured out like water: (cf. Jos. 7:5). This, and the following description in verses 14*b*–15, need not necessarily refer to the consequences of an illness, but it may denote the physical expressions of fear and anxiety. The above-mentioned word-picture probably means that the Psalmist regards himself as good as dead.

all my bones are out of joint: this is a graphic description of utter helplessness, and is an equivalent to 'paralysed with fear'.

my heart is like wax: the Psalmist has become greatly afraid and fainthearted (as in Dt. 20:8; Jos. 2:11).

15. my strength is dried up: Gunkel, Weiser, *et al.* read *ḥikkî* ('my throat' or 'my palate') for M.T. *kōḥî* ('my strength'), and it would give a better parallel to 'my tongue' in verse 15*b* (cf. Lam. 4:4). *NEB* 'my mouth'.

my tongue cleaves to my jaws: it is not necessary to think of the Psalmist as suffering from fever (so Davison), but this may simply be part of the effects of his mental agony (cf. 69:3 (M.T. 4)).

. . . in the dust of death: possibly 'death' in this phrase is a synonym of Sheol. The expression suggests that behind the hostility of his enemies the author perceives the hand of God. Either God uses the adversaries as instruments of the perplexing punishment or he has given them a free hand by forsaking the Psalmist (cf. verses 1ff.). The expression itself indicates the nearness of death, as in 107:18: 'they drew near to the gates of death'.

16. dogs: the foes are contemptuously likened to the prowling dogs which haunt the streets and refuse dumps, ready to devour any edible thing (cf. 59:6,14 (M.T. 7,15)), including a human carcass (1 Kg. 14:11, 16:4, 21:19,23–24, 22:38; 2 Kg. 9:10,36; Ps. 68:23 (M.T. 24); Jer. 15:3). Similarly the 'company of evildoers' or 'his enemies' can hardly wait for the Psalmist's death.

they have pierced my hands and feet: some of the older commentators thought that this passage predicted the Crucifixion of Jesus, but no such interpretation is given in the Passion narratives of the *NT*. The phrase is a continuation of the graphic description of the Psalmist's distress. The reading in M.T. may be textually corrupt; it could be rendered: 'like a lion (at ?) my hands and my feet'. It is possible that the Hebrew *kā'ᵃrî* ('like a lion') conceals a verb, and the two most likely suggestions are either 'they bind together' (for burial ?) (cf. G. R. Driver, *ET*, LVII (1945–6), p. 193, who proposes the verb *k-r-h* ('to bind together')) or 'they have dug' (from *k-r-h*, 'to dig'), i.e. they have pierced. The latter alternative finds some support in LXX, S, and V, and the former in Aq and Sym.

17. I can count all my bones: i.e. the distress has reduced the Psalmist (either literally or metaphorically) to a bag of bones (cf. Job 33:21; Ps. 102:5 (M.T. 6)); to the enemies of the Psalmist this wretched condition provides a ghoulish entertainment.

18. they divide my garments: i.e. either the sufferer is pictured as already robbed of his only belongings or his enemies cast lots in anticipation of his death (cf. Jn 19:23f.; also Mt. 27:35). As far as the foes are concerned the afflicted person is already dead. In the Middle Assyrian laws (cf. *ANET*, p. 183, par. 40) there is a provision that the offender's clothes are given to the prosecutor or to the one who arrested the culprit. In our verse 'garments' and 'raiment' are synonymous, and do not refer, in this context, to two different items of clothing.

19. But thou is an emphatic expression and probably implies that God is his only hope, and that he cannot expect help from any other quarter.

O thou my help: or 'O thou my strength' (cf. 88:4 (M.T. 5)).

20. from the sword: i.e. from a violent death before one's due time.

my life: *NEB* 'my very self'; *RSVm* 'my only one' (=M.T.), which is probably a description of life as the only thing left to the sufferer.

the dog: this refers back to verse 16, and may be a collective designation of the enemies. *NEB* reads 'the axe'.

21. from the mouth of the lion: this is yet another reference to the enemies who have been previously referred to by the same term (verse 13), as well as by 'bulls' (verse 12) and 'dogs' (verse 16).

the wild oxen: *AV* 'unicorns' (as in LXX and V). The former rendering is preferable (cf. verse 12), because verses 20–1 seem to resume the *previous* metaphors used to describe the adversaries.

my afflicted soul: similarly LXX, S and V. M.T. may mean: 'You have answered me' (cf. 120:1), and this phrase could form the link between the two parts of the Psalm, and it could explain the abrupt transition from lamentation to thanksgiving. Cf. *VT*, XXI (1971), pp. 91ff. Dahood (*PAB*, I, p. 142) suggests 'make me triumph' (from *ᶜ-n-h*, 'to conquer'; cf. R. T. O'Callaghan, *Orientalia*, XVIII (1949), p. 186). The M.T. (if it refers to the divine oracle) may well be right and it would account for the change of mood at this point in the Psalm. The parallelism seems to favour *RSV*; *NEB* has 'my poor body'.

THE DESPAIR IS PAST **22–31**

22. It is possible that verses 1–21 were the prelude to the thanksgiving, enabling the other worshippers to have a meaningful share in the thanksgiving because they would also have shared, in some small measure, the experience of the suffering.

I will tell of thy name: or 'I will recount your gracious deeds' (see on 8:1, 20:1). Cf. 66:16: 'Come and hear . . . and I will tell what he has done for me'.

my brethren: not simply actual brothers and friends, but also the members of the congregation (see verse 22*b*).

in the midst of the congregation: Yahweh's saving work, even if it concerns primarily the individual, is not a private matter; it is relevant not only to the person concerned, but also to the whole congregation (cf. Ringgren, *FP*, p. 21; see also 1QH xii:3). For *ḳāhāl*, 'congregation', see on 89:5.

23. You who fear the Lord: i.e. who practise religion in sincerity and truth, or who worship Yahweh meaningfully (cf. 2 Kg. 17:25).

sons of Jacob: this is parallel to 'you who fear the Lord' and to 'sons of Israel'. If so, the reference may be to the true Israel and not to the whole ethnic unit (cf. Kraus, *PBK*, p. 182). For 'Jacob', see on 20:1, 85:1.

stand in awe of him: this is similar in meaning to 'fear him' (cf. 33:8).

24. he has not despised . . .: i.e. he has accepted the prayer of the sufferer (cf. 51:17 (M.T. 19), 69:33 (M.T. 34), 102:17 (M.T. 18)).

the affliction of the afflicted: Dahood seems right in rendering 'the song of . . .' (deriving the Hebrew *ᶜᵉnûṯ* (*RSV* 'the affliction of . . .') from *ᶜ-n-h* IV ('to sing')). Thus the reference would be to the lamentation(s) used during the time of distress. The LXX and T have 'the prayer of . . .'.

he has not hid his face: see on 10:11. The important point is that Yahweh had not turned away from the sufferer for ever and that he *had heard* the cry of the unfortunate man.

25. From thee comes my praise: Graetz, Leslie, Nötscher, *et al.* render: 'Your (or 'his') faithfulness (*ʾᵃmittᵉḵā* or *ʾᵃmittô*) is my praise', but M.T. gives a reasonable sense. God is both the source and object of the writer's praise, which is the only right response to the work of God.

the great congregation: (see 35:18, 40:9,10 (M.T. 10, 11)). Kraus (*PBK*, p. 183) sees here a reference to the assembly of the Israelites during the great annual pilgrimage festivals.
my vows I will pay: i.e. I will bring the votive offerings which I have promised during the time of trouble (cf. 50:14, 61:8 (M.T. 9), 66:13, 116:14,18).
before those who fear him: Calvin (I, p. 264) points out that 'the chief part of the service of God consists in this, that the faithful should openly shew that they acknowledge God to be the author of all good things'.

26. The afflicted: or 'the poor' (see on 34:2); *NEB* 'the humble'.
shall eat and be satisfied: this need not be taken in a figurative or a spiritual sense only; just as the widow, the fatherless, and the sojourner share in the tithes (Dt. 14:29, 26:12) and in the offerings at the annual festivals (Dt. 16:10f.,14) so also they are invited to take part at the sacrificial meal. They are shown kindness because the host himself has been the recipient of God's help. The principle is not 'Give in order that you may receive', but rather 'Share because you have already received' (cf. 142:7 (M.T. 8)).
may your hearts live for ever: it is possible that here the guests at the fellowship meal are addressed by the host. His wish is that the needy might be strengthened not only in body but also in spirit by sharing both in the meal and in the experience of God's saving help (cf. Gen. 45:27; see also Ps. 21:4).

27. All the ends of the earth: i.e. the whole world or its inhabitants (cf. 2:8, 67:7 (M.T. 8), 98:3; also Gen. 12:3, 22:18).
shall remember: the meaning is not so much to bring to mind what they have forgotten (cf. 9:17 (M.T. 18)) as to worship God, to acknowledge him (cf. 119:52). The reason for this unbelievable change is not the testimony of the Psalmist (cf. Taylor, *PIB*, p. 122), but the fact that Yahweh is the creator and ruler of the whole world. The cosmic kingship of Yahweh must eventually lead to a universal worship of him.
before him: (=*NEB*) so LXX, S, and Jerome; M.T. has 'before you' which may be the original reading. Such unexpected changes of person are not infrequent in the *OT* (cf. verse 25).

28. For dominion belongs to the LORD: Dahood (*PAB*, I, p. 138) offers a possible alternative rendering: 'For truly is Yahweh the king', and he takes *mᵉlûḵāh* (*RSV* 'dominion') in a concrete sense as 'king', regarding the preposition *l*ᵉ ('to') as an emphasizing particle. This would balance verse 28*b*: 'and (he is) the ruler over the nations', so M.T., and similarly *PNT*.

29–30. Yea, to him: (reading *ʾak̠ lô*), while M.T. (see *RSVm*) could be rendered 'They have eaten and . . .' which hardly fits the context; it seems that a scribe must have wrongly joined together two separate words. Winton Thomas (*TRP*, p. 8) suggests *ʾēk̠ lô*, '(As for them . . .) how (shall they worship) him?' Similarly *NEB*.

all the proud of the earth: lit. 'all the fat ones of . . .'. Yet neither of these translations provides a satisfactory parallel to 'who go down to the dust'. The similarity of construction may suggest a similarity of thought between the parallel lines, and therefore most commentators emend *dišᵉnê* ('the fat ones of') into *yᵉšēnê* ('those who sleep (in the earth)'). Dahood (*PAB*, I, p. 143) arrives at the same rendering without resorting to an emendation, by taking *d* as a relative particle (as in Ugaritic and Aramaic) and regarding *šny* as a syncopated form of *yᵉšēnê*. The real problem is whether this means that the dead will join in the worship of God, in Sheol (cf. Oesterley, *TP*, p. 181) or whether they will serve God only in as far as they live on in their descendants (so Kissane, *BP*, p. 102). To some Psalmists at least, Sheol was outside the sphere of the cult (see on 6:5, 30:9), and consequently it is possible that this verse speaks not of those long dead in Sheol but of those who are about to descend into the underworld, i.e. people who are near to death (cf. verse 15). A good parallel is found in 30:3: 'O Lord, thou hast brought up my soul from Sheol, restored me to life from among those gone down to the pit'. Perhaps we may paraphrase verse 29*ab* 'Even all those who were about to sleep in Sheol will pay homage to him, and all those who were nearly gone down to the dust (of the underworld) will bend their knee before him.' The Psalmist himself is a good example of such people. For 'dust', see on 119:25.

and he who cannot keep himself alive: (*NEB* has 'But I shall live for his sake'). This phrase is often regarded as a later gloss or a 'doctrinal addition' (so Weiser), and it is difficult to make sense of it. A possible solution is to join verse 29*c* to verse 30*a* (so LXX), and verse 30*b* to verse 31 (cf. Cohen, *PSon*, p. 66), and to render 'and (when one) is no longer able to keep himself alive (i.e. when his time to die has come), then (his) descendants shall serve him (i.e. Yahweh)'. Although no man lives for ever, the story of God's saving works knows no end. It will be transmitted by posterity (cf. verse 23), and they will also add their own testimony.

men shall tell of the LORD: or 'it shall be told of...' (cf. 145:4).

the coming generation: so LXX, suggesting *laddôr yāḇōʾ* (cf. 71:18); M.T. takes the verb *yāḇōʾû* (*AV* 'They shall come') with verse 31.

31. his deliverance: lit. 'his righteousness' (*RV*).

a people yet unborn: or 'a people that will yet be born', i.e. the future generations.

that he has wrought it: or 'Indeed, he has acted!', i.e. he has intervened on behalf of his people, on behalf of their fathers. Cf. verses 3–5, and 52:9 (M.T. 11); Isa. 44:23. *NEB* 'that this was his doing'.

Psalm 23 The Lord is My Shepherd

This is, perhaps, the best known Psalm in the whole Psalter, or 'the pearl of Psalms' (so C. H. Spurgeon), yet its interpretation is by no means certain. The oriental imagery found in this well-loved poem makes it difficult to separate facts from verbal images.

First of all there is the question of how many metaphors are used to describe the relationships between the Psalmist and his God. Some exegetes (e.g. L. Koehler, 'Psalm 23', *ZAW*, LXVIII (1956), pp. 229f.) argue that the background of the *whole* Psalm is the scene of the change of pastures, but this involves a forced interpretation, especially of verses 5–6. The more usual view is to find in Ps. 23 two main word-pictures of Yahweh, namely those of the caring shepherd and the gracious host. The third suggestion is that, alongside the two above-mentioned metaphors, there is another one depicting Yahweh as the guide of the wanderer (in verses 3–4). Of these three interpretations the second seems the most likely.

This poem could be classified as a Psalm of confidence or trust but it is less easy to define its *Sitz im Leben*. The reference to the 'house of the LORD' (verse 6) points to a cultic setting, and the meal before the enemies may imply a thanksgiving banquet (for a detailed discussion, see E. Vogt, 'The "Place in Life" of Ps. 23', *Biblica*, XXXIV (1953), pp. 195–211). As is obvious from the exegesis of the Psalm, the available evidence is far from being unambiguous, but this interpretation seems a reasonable working hypothesis. We do not know the actual experiences of the Psalmist (or what he envisaged in his poem), but he may have been unjustly accused (or he may have suffered at the hands of his adversaries in some other way). After his acquittal or deliverance, he is offering thanks to God, and this Psalm is an expression of his confident trust in Yahweh, being the outcome of a bitter experience transformed by the help of God. The Psalm may have been uttered either before or during the sacrificial meal, and the speaker may be an 'ordinary' Israelite. It is less likely that the Psalmist was a priest (so Schmidt) or that he belonged to a group of spiritual writers who found their 'consolation in the lofty mystical experience of the cultus' (v. Rad, *PHOE*, p. 260). Eaton (*PTBC*, pp. 76f.) believes that the Psalm was recited by 'a royal head and representative of the community'. This is a plausible explanation of the original use of the Psalm, but it would not apply to its application in the post-Exilic period.

The metre is mainly 3+2.

A Psalm of David: see Introduction, pp. 43ff. and 46.

YAHWEH AS SHEPHERD **1–4**

1. The LORD is my shepherd: in Israelite cultic traditions Yahweh is not infrequently described as 'Shepherd of Israel' (80:1 (M.T. 2), cf. also 28:9) or depicted as the shepherd of his people (74:1, 77:20 (M.T. 21), 78:52, 79:13, 95:7, 100:3; Isa. 40:11; Jer. 23:3; Ezek. 34:11–16; Hos. 4:16; Mic. 7:14; Zech. 9:16). Similar language can be used to describe the King (cf. 2 Sam. 5:2, 7:7; Jer. 3:15, 10:21, 22:22; Ezek. 34:23; Mic. 5:4; in CD xiii:9 the overseer of the camp is likened to a shepherd of a flock). This terminology is not, however, peculiar to Israel, but it is also found among other nations of the ancient Near East; e.g. Hammurabi is called 'the shepherd' (*ANET*, p. 164b) or 'the shepherd of the people' (*ANET*, p. 165b; cf. also p. 177b). In the Hymn to the Sun-God (*ANET*, p. 387b, line 26), Shamash is designated as 'shepherd of (the people of the world)'.

It is noteworthy that in Ps. 23 Yahweh is the shepherd of the individual (unless he represents the people). Oesterley (*TP*, p. 183) sees here an indication of what he calls the 'growing sense of the importance of the individual in contrast to the traditional conception of the community as the unit of divine solicitude'.

I shall not want: or 'I shall lack nothing'. This confidence of the Psalmist is further strengthened by the implicit allusion to the salvation-history of the people. Even in the wilderness during the forty years, the Israelites lacked nothing, for God was with them (Dt. 2:7). Dahood (*PAB*, I, p. 146) argues that the Psalmist means that he will lack neither in this life nor in the next, but this view seems unlikely.

2. This verse elaborates further the metaphor of the shepherd. Perhaps the writer intended to state an implicit contrast: what for him had been merely a hope, had become a reality through God's help and guidance.

He leads me like an eastern shepherd who gently guides his sheep, going before the flock. Cf. Isa. 49:9f.

still waters: or 'waters of rest'; some exegetes (e.g. Taylor) regard this as an inversion of 'resting places by water'. The reference is more likely to the waters that bring refreshment, being parallel to 'he restores my soul' (verse 3*a*; cf. also Ezek. 34:13). Eaton (*PTBC*, p. 77) thinks of a pool of still waters, formed by making a small dam in a wadi.

3. he restores my soul: or 'he brings back my vitality', or simply 'he restores me' (cf. 19:7 (M.T. 8); Lam. 1:11,16,19). For 'soul' (*nep̱eš*), see on 33:19. A. Sperber (*HGBH*, p. 660) suggests 'he calms down my soul'.

paths of righteousness: these are sometimes taken to mean 'straight (or 'right') paths' (so Briggs, Taylor, *et al.*). Kissane (*BP*, p. 104) is nearer the mark when he suggests 'paths which lead to happiness', i.e. the way which leads to deliverance, and thus to welfare and blessedness (cf. 5:8 (M.T. 9)).

for his name's sake: or 'he acts for the sake of his "reputation".' Yahweh's name is often associated with his self-revelation (cf. 106:8), and consequently whatever he does is done in order to be true to himself or to his self-manifestation (cf. 25:11, 31:3 (M.T. 4); Isa. 43:25, 48:9).

4. The reference to the 'rod' and 'staff' suggests that this verse also is part of the word-picture found in the preceding verses.

the shadow of death: the Hebrew *ṣalmāweṯ* is either a compound noun (so *RSV*, following the ancient versions), or it could be read as *ṣalmûṯ* ('darkness') (so Gunkel, Oesterley, *et al.*). If it is a compound noun, the word *māweṯ* ('death') may be a means to express the superlative, i.e. 'total darkness' (so D. Winton Thomas, *JSS*, VII (1962), pp. 191–200). Such a valley of deep darkness, both in its literal and metaphorical sense, may fill one's heart with dread and fear, but the Psalmist can affirm that he fears no evil even in such circumstances. The basis of his confidence is the conviction that Yahweh is with him (cf. Gen. 26:3,24, 28:15, 31:3; Dt. 31:6; Jos. 1:5,9).

rod (*šēḇeṭ*) was a club used in defence, to drive away the wild animals or any other enemy (cf. 2 Sam. 23:21; Mic. 7:14). It could occasionally be tipped with metal or studded with nails (cf. G. Dalman, *Arbeit und Sitte in Palästina* (1932), VI, pp. 238ff.); see on 45:6.

staff was probably a wooden rod, longer than the club, which could be used as a support.

they comfort me: Gunkel *et al.* read *yanḥûnî* ('they lead me') for M.T. *yᵉnaḥᵃmûnî* ('they comfort me').

YAHWEH AS HOST **5–6**

The metaphor changes from that of the shepherd and his sheep, to the word-picture of the host and his guest. It is very likely that the author had in mind the sacrificial meal which followed the sacrifice of thanksgiving; cf. 116:17f.: 'I will offer to thee the sacrifice of thanksgiving . . . I will pay my vows to the LORD in the presence of all his people' (cf. also 1 Sam. 1:3,9; Ps. 22:25f. (M.T. 26f.), 63:4f. (M.T. 5f.)). E. Vogt (p. 202) may be right when he states that 'God is really the Psalmist's host in the Temple, because the sacrificial meal is offered as a gift by God to him who in turn had offered God the victim and his own devotion'. This is far more reasonable than Schmidt's suggestion (*PHAT*, p. 41) that the picture is that of a traveller pursued by a hostile tribe, and who has now found protection and provision in the tent of his host. See also Sabourin, *POM*, II, p. 101.

5. a table: the cognate of the Hebrew *šulḥān* is also found in the Ugaritic texts (cf. Driver, *CML*, p. 152), and therefore the connexion with the Arabic *salaḫa*, 'to strip off the hide' (cf. *KBL*, p. 190a), is unlikely.

in the presence of my enemies: i.e. either those who had been responsible for the Psalmist's distress, whatever its nature, or those who had increased his suffering by their dogmatically correct but inhuman attitude. They, too, would be found in the Temple, especially if the occasion of paying one's vows took place during the pilgrimage festivals.

oil: for *šemen*, see on 104:15. Oil and perfumes were symbolic of rejoicing, and as such they would be used on festive occasions;

even the arrival of a guest might come into this category (cf. 45:7 (M.T. 8), 92:10 (M.T. 11), 133:2; Ec. 9:8; Am. 6:6; Lk. 7:46). Eaton (*PTBC*, p. 78) finds here an allusion to 'God's anointing of the King', but this seems less likely.

my cup overflows: i.e. the cup given by the host. This suggests a picture of a generous host who makes abundant provision for the needs of his guest (cf. 116:13).

6. goodness and mercy: or 'welfare which is the result of God's covenant loyalty'. This verse stresses the great transformation of the circumstances. The Psalmist is no longer hunted down by his enemies, but he is literally pursued by the goodness of God. Furthermore, this is no temporary situation but it is going to be the characteristic of his whole life.

I shall dwell: (=*NEB*) i.e. *wᵉšiḇtî* (or *wᵉyāšaḇtî*) for M.T. *wᵉšaḇtî* ('and I shall return'); the *RSV* rendering is also supported by the ancient versions. If correct, it could be taken literally as the expression of trust and confidence by a Levite who had found happiness in residing in the Temple. More commonly, the phrase is understood as a metaphor referring to a continual communion with God, or as belonging to the language of cult-mysticism, i.e. originally the expression applied to the actual situation of the Levites, but later it was taken over by worshippers in general who wished to stress the protection and blessings offered by Yahweh. The best solution to date seems to be provided by R. E. Clements ('Temple and Land', *TGUOS*, XIX (1961–2), pp. 16–28), who suggests that the dwelling in the Temple is associated with the right to enter the Temple (cf. Ps. 15, 24:3–6) and to participate in its worship. This carries with it, so it was believed, the privilege of dwelling on Yahweh's land, and all the blessings associated with it.

If, on the other hand, we follow M.T., then verse 6*b* could be paraphrased: 'I shall keep on returning to the Temple and I shall keep on sharing in its worship (and so also in all the associated blessings) as long as I shall live (and by God's mercy it will be a long life)'. The regular return to the Temple could have the same significance as that suggested by Clements, or the reference might be to the thank-offerings which the Psalmist will repeat year by year, because there will be ample cause to praise God for his mercy throughout his long life. Thus the present sacrificial meal is only the beginning of a series of such occasions. See also A. R. Johnson, 'Psalm 23 and the Household of Faith' in *Proclamation and Presence*, ed. by J. I. Durham and J. R. Porter (1970), pp. 261–71.

Psalm 24 YAHWEH IS THE KING OF GLORY

Although the Psalm consists of three distinctive elements, it may well be a literary unity (so Kraus, *PBK*, p. 195), being part of a processional liturgy which, apparently, accompanied the bringing of the Ark into the holy city or into the sanctuary. Some other scholars (e.g. Taylor) regard the three sections of this liturgy as originally independent songs, but the former view seems preferable.

With which festival this Psalm was originally connected is a matter of speculation. According to its superscription in LXX, it was used on the first day of the week, and the same view is also suggested by T. The reason for this association may have been the traditional belief that the creation of the world began on the first day of the week (cf. Gen. 1). This evidence concerns, however, only the usage of this Psalm at the end of the pre-Christian era; originally it may have been linked either with the festival celebrating Yahweh's kingship or with the autumn festival in general. The theme of God as Creator and Saviour may favour this suggestion.

The older exegetes used to associate the Psalm with the removal of the Ark by David from the house of Obed-edom (cf. 2 Sam. 6:12–19; 1 Chr.13:1–28) to Jerusalem, but the cultic interpretation is more likely. The references to the 'ancient doors' and 'gates' (verses 7 and 9) suggest the existence of the Temple, and the limited nature of the entrance qualifications (verse 4) may imply a later date, when this aspect of liturgy had become more formal than didactic. Most scholars assign the Psalm to the monarchical period, some time after the reign of Solomon. A Maccabean date is highly unlikely, at least on the grounds suggested by M. Treves (*VT*, x (1960), p. 430).

The structure of the Psalm is comparatively simple. Verses 1–2 form a brief hymn celebrating Yahweh's rule and his creative power, while verses 3–6 can be described as a *Tôrāh* liturgy, dealing with the question concerning the conditions of entry into the sanctuary (verse 3), followed by the answer (verses 4–5) which gives an account both of the moral qualifications required and of the blessedness of the loyal man. Verse 6 concludes this

Admission *Tôrāh*. In verses 7–10 we find the so-called 'gate-liturgy' (so Kraus) with alternating questions and replies. This section of the Psalm is usually linked with the procession of the Ark representing the presence of Yahweh, although Weiser (*POTL*, p. 234) doubts whether the Ark actually belonged to 'the sacred equipment for processions'; he suggests that the climax of the Psalm was the epiphany of Yahweh in the Temple. See also D. R. Hillers, 'Ritual Procession of the Ark and Ps. 132', *CBQ*, xxx (1968), pp. 48–55; he is not convinced that the Ark was used on such regularly recurring festivals.

The metre of the Psalm is irregular.

A Psalm of David: see Introduction, pp. 43ff. and 46.

YAHWEH AS LORD AND CREATOR **1–2**

1. The earth is the LORD's: or 'To Yahweh (alone) belongs the earth' (cf. Exod. 19:5; Dt. 10:14; Ps. 50:12, 89:11 (M.T. 12)). He is the Lord of all the world (97:5) because he is its Creator.
the fulness thereof: i.e. all the created things and beings in God's universe (cf. Dt. 33:16; Isa. 34:1; Mic. 1:2).
the world: the Hebrew *tēḇēl* is a poetic synonym of *ʾereṣ*, 'earth'; it is doubtful if, in this context, the former is any more cosmological than the latter. Occasionally *tēḇēl* is regarded as the habitable part of the earth (cf. 9:8 (M.T. 9)) or the cultivated land (cf. Isa. 14:17).

2. This verse gives the explanation why Yahweh is the undisputed Lord of the world. He, and no one else, is the world Ruler because he alone is the world Creator. According to the cosmology of the Psalmist, the earth rests upon the waters of the great cosmic ocean (Gen. 7:11, 49:25; Exod. 20:4; Dt. 33:13; Job 26:10; Ps. 136:6), being supported by pillars which are, at the same time, the bases of the mountains (cf. 1 Sam. 2:8; Prov. 8:29; Jon. 2:6 (M.T. 7)). For a further discussion on this point, see Johnson, *VITAI*, pp. 91f.; Stadelmann, *HCW*, pp. 126–60.
the rivers are most likely part of the cosmic waters upon which the earth is established (Isa. 44:27; Hab. 3:8), and not rivers such as Jordan, Euphrates, etc. Some render the Hebrew *nᵉhārôṯ* by 'currents of the sea (or 'ocean')' (so W. H. Schmidt, Dahood); see on 46:4, 72:8. 'River' and 'sea' are frequently parallel terms in the Ugaritic literature (cf. W. H. Schmidt, *Königtum Gottes in Ugarit und Israel* (*BZAW*, 80, 1966), pp. 37ff.).

THE ENTRANCE LITURGY **3–6**
At this point in the procession, the prospective worshippers ask for a guidance or *Tôrāh*, as to who is fit to take part in the Temple worship. The answer is supplied by the priest in charge (the keeper of the threshold?), but it is not to be regarded as the sum total of God's requirements (cf. v. Rad, *PHOE*, p. 245). The conditions stated are representative and not exhaustive (cf. E. Nielsen, *The Ten Commandments in New Perspective* (*SBT*, 2nd ser., 7, 1968), pp. 23f.). What is required is purity in thought and deed (see 15:2–5*b*). If any one was conscious of having broken the Covenant law, he could, apparently, humble himself, confessing his sins and hoping for divine forgiveness (cf. 32:3, 103:10–14; Sir. 17:29).

The question about the entrance conditions may belong to an ancient tradition, and its origin may be found in the rules regulating the admission to different sanctuaries. The worshippers would be expected to make sure that they knew the laws and customs of the sanctuary they attended. An example of a similar Temple rule is the well-known inscription of the Jerusalem Temple: 'No alien may enter within the barrier and wall around the Temple. Whoever is caught (violating this) is alone responsible for the death (-penalty) which follows' (quoted from G. E. Wright, *Biblical Archaeology*, rev. edn (1962), p. 227). It seems that in Israel the rules governing the right to worship in the Temple were linked with the Covenant. Such questions and answers as found in Ps. 15 and 24 (cf. also 118:19–20) served the purpose of guidance and instruction, but it is possible that in course of time they became a sacred rite which was regularly repeated although the requirements were known. It is plausible that during certain periods the conditions stated were not observed in actual practice (cf. Jer. 7:1ff.; Isa. 33:14ff.).

3. Who shall ascend: the verb *ᶜ-l-h* can be used in a technical sense for a pilgrimage to the sanctuary (cf. 1 Sam. 1:3,22; Ps. 122:4; Isa. 2:3). Here it is synonymous with participating in worship.

the hill of the Lord is Mount Zion (see on 2:6; cf. also 3:5 (M.T. 6), 15:1, 43:3; Isa. 2:3 (=Mic. 4:2), 30:29). This is not simply an ancient cultic place of great fame, but rather the holy mountain of Yahweh.

who shall stand: i.e. who is fit to be confronted with the almighty God? Similarly in 1 Sam. 6:20 the men of Beth-shemesh exclaim: 'Who is able to stand before the LORD, this holy God?'.

4. clean hands: this phrase occurs only here in the *OT* (cf. 1QS ix:15), and it denotes a person whose conduct is blameless, and who can affirm: 'I have not transgressed any of thy commandments, neither have I forgotten them' (Dt. 26:13). In cultic terms such a person is righteous or loyal to Yahweh.

a pure heart is a characteristic of those who not only do what is right but also do it for the right motives (cf. 73:1).

his soul: (*NEB* 'his mind'); so a number of Hebrew and Greek MSS., also V (cf. 25:1); M.T. has 'my soul' which is, perhaps, a substitute for 'my name' (cf. Exod. 20:7; Nielsen, op. cit., p. 101).

what is false: or 'an idol' (so Dahood, Treves, *et al.*); cf. 31:6 (M.T. 7); Jer. 18:15; Jon. 2:8 (M.T. 9); see on 25:1.

swear deceitfully: i.e. perjure himself by making a false declaration upon oath. Dahood (*PAB*, I, p. 150) renders '. . . sworn by a fraud' (referring to an idol).

5. The priestly answer is followed by a promise (cf. 15:5) of blessing and vindication, to those who are faithful to God's Covenant (cf. Exod. 20:6; Dt. 5:10).

blessing is ultimately the privilege of enjoying God's gracious presence or living in the light of his countenance (Num. 6:23–26), and its natural consequence is usually a prosperous and happy life.

vindication: lit. 'righteousness' or 'due reward' (so Taylor); Dahood, following Zorell (*ZLH*, p. 684a), translates it by 'generous treatment'. In other words, he who does what is right (15:2) shall obtain righteousness, and he who is truly faithful to God's Covenant shall receive the Covenant promises of God (cf. *TDNT*, II, p. 195).

God of his salvation: see on 18:46.

6. the generation: or 'the type of man', perhaps, '(such is) the lot of . . .' (cf. G. R. Driver, *JBL*, LIII (1934), p. 285); *NEB* 'the fortune of'. Mowinckel (*PIW*, I, p. 179) takes this verse as the answer of the worshippers (cf. also E. Vogt, 'Psalm 26, ein Pilgergebet', *Biblica*, XLIII (1962), p. 330), and it means, more or less: 'we are confident of fulfilling the demands' or to paraphrase 'this *is* the assembly of those who have followed Yahweh's commands (i.e. we are the faithful ones) . . .'.

those who seek him: or (following some Greek MSS.) '. . . seek

Yahweh' (*dōrᵉšê yhwh*). The verb *d-r-š*, 'to seek', may denote both a visit to a sanctuary (as in Am. 5:5: 'do not seek (i.e. frequent) Bethel') and the worship of God in general (as in Am. 5:6: 'seek the LORD and live'; cf. 69:32 (M.T. 33)). In this verse the Psalmist may have had in mind both meanings—namely, to visit the Temple for the purpose of worshipping God. The verb *d-r-š* is also the regular term for consulting an oracle (Gen. 25:22; 1 Sam. 9:9). In 77:2 (M.T. 3) it describes the desperate search for the presence of God or his help, while in 78:34 it denotes a less sincere turning to Yahweh. The passive participle of the verb is applied to the works of Yahweh (111:2) depicting them as something to be *studied* (so *RSV*) or as something that can be cultically experienced. For *d-r-š* in the sense of 'to care for', see on 142:4.

the face of the God of Jacob: so *RSV*, *NEB*, following LXX and V; M.T. could be translated 'thy face, O Jacob' (so *AV*) or '(those who seek) your face, (they are the descendants of) Jacob'. The parallelism seems to support the *RSV* rendering, or we may follow S in reading *pānêḵā ᵓᵉlōhê yaᶜᵃḳōḇ*, 'your face, O God of Jacob'.

Selah: see Introduction, pp. 48f.

THE ANTIPHONAL SONG AT THE TEMPLE GATES **7–10**

Those who assign this Psalm to the time of David see here a reference to the historic occasion when the Ark was brought for the first time into Jerusalem (so Cohen, *PSon*, p. 70). It seems far more likely that Ps. 24 belongs to the ritual of an annual festival (cf. also Sabourin, *POM*, II, pp. 328f.).

7. Lift up your heads is taken to mean 'extend your height' (so Cohen) because the King of glory is too lofty to enter the low and narrow gates. It is difficult to say to what part of the gates the 'heads' refer, but it is possible that the phrase is to be taken metaphorically as a command to rejoice (cf. Lk. 21:28; *Keret* II, iii:11), and that the gates are personified, as in Isa. 14:31: 'Wail, O gate; cry, O city'. This would also be reminiscent of Zech. 9:9: 'Rejoice greatly, O daughter of Zion . . . Lo, your king comes to you . . .'.

and be lifted up: or 'be exalted' by the great honour bestowed upon you. This interpretation of verse 7 modifies only the understanding of what was expected of the gates, and does not alter the overall exegesis of the Psalm. The traditional view is equally possible, as seen in Ezek. 44:1f.

ancient doors: or 'everlasting doors' (*AV*, *RP*, *NEB*). Dahood (*PAB*, I, p. 153) takes *ʿôlām* as a divine appellative, and renders 'gates of the Eternal', yet the *RSV* rendering makes better sense. Some scholars (cf. Kraus, *PBK*, p. 205) have raised the question whether the reference may not be to the 'gates of heaven' (cf. Gen. 28:17), since in antiquity the earthly Temple was usually associated with its heavenly counterpart.

King of Glory: or 'glorious king' (so Johnson). Glory along with splendour and majesty are royal attributes (cf. Est. 1:4; Ps. 21:5 (M.T. 6); Isa. 6:3). At this point it might be asked how ancient is the concept of Yahweh as king. M. Buber (*Kingship of God*, Eng. tr. by R. Scheimann (1967), pp. 136–62) *et al.* have argued that this idea is as old as the time of Moses, and some support for this view may be found in the suggestion that the Mosaic Covenant is analogous to the suzerainty treaties of the second millennium B.C., thus implying that Israel's relationship with Yahweh may have been regarded as similar to that of a vassal with his overlord or king. Other scholars have thought that the kingship of Yahweh was originally derived from Canaanite sources (for references, see Kraus, *PBK*, p. 197f.). It is indeed very likely that the Canaanite religion has exercised a considerable influence upon the faith of Israel and its institutions (cf. W. H. Schmidt, pp. 85ff.), but it is possible that the so-called Mosaic religion prepared the way for the kingship of God which received a more definite form *after* the Settlement in Canaan. See also J. Gray, 'The Kingship of God in the Prophets and Psalms', *VT*, XI (1961), pp. 1ff.

8. Who is . . .: this could be regarded as a rhetorical question, or it could be taken emphatically as: 'Who then is . . .' (cf. *GK* 136c). The answer was the pass-word, 'The LORD . . . he is the King of glory' (verse 10).

strong and mighty are the qualities of a warrior (cf. Dt. 10:17; Neh. 9:32; Isa. 10:21; Jer. 32:18). These descriptions of Yahweh were probably derived from the language and concepts of the Holy War (cf. Ringgren, *IR*, pp. 53f.; G. v. Rad, *Der Heilige Krieg im Alten Testament* (1951), pp. 81ff.).

9. and be lifted up: so many Hebrew MSS. and the ancient versions. M.T. has 'lift (them) up' (but cf. verse 7).

10. The LORD of hosts: this is the traditional rendering of the Hebrew *yhwh ṣᵉḇāʾôṯ*, although it is misleading because the word 'the LORD' (i.e. Yahweh) is not a noun in construct state. The actual significance of this phrase is rather uncertain, but there are several possibilities. It could be an abbreviated form of 'Yahweh, the God of Hosts' (cf. 2 Sam. 5:10; 1 Kg. 19:10,14; Ps. 89:8 (M.T. 9); Am. 5:14,15,16, 6:8, etc.) but it is usually thought that the longer form was a later interpretation of the shorter version. The main problem is the meaning of *ṣᵉḇāʾôṯ* (*RSV* 'hosts'). Sometimes this term is clearly used of the armies of Israel (cf. Exod. 7:4, 12:41; Ps. 44:9 (M.T. 10)) and in the light of 1 Sam. 17:45 it could be interpreted as a description of Yahweh, meaning: 'the God of the armies (of Israel)'. Yet since the phrase *yhwh ṣᵉḇāʾôṯ* occurs primarily in the prophetic writings, and since the armies of Israel played a comparatively small role in the thought of the canonical prophets, the suggested interpretation seems hardly adequate, at least for the period of the classical prophets. A variation of this interpretation would be to apply the term 'hosts' to the heavenly bodies or to the armies of the angels and other spiritual beings. Another possibility is to take *ṣᵉḇāʾôṯ* as an abstract or intensive plural, in the sense of 'might', hence 'Yahweh, the Almighty' or 'Yahweh who is almighty' (cf. Johnson, *SKAI*, p. 65, n. 1). This is partly supported by the LXX rendering *pantokratōr* ('all-powerful', 'all-mighty'). Perhaps the most likely explanation is the rendering 'Yahweh (whose are) the hosts (i.e. all the powers on earth and in heaven)' (cf. Eichrodt, *TOT*, I, pp. 192ff.). It is quite possible that this phrase may have had more than one interpretation in the course of its history during the *OT* period. See also O. Eissfeldt, *Kleine Schriften*, III (1966), pp. 103–23; J. P. Ross, *VT*, XVII (1967), pp. 76–92.

Psalm 25 Remember Me, O Lord

This is one of the nine acrostic Psalms of the Psalter (see the introduction to Ps. 9–10), although there are some slight irregularities in the alphabetic scheme. In the present text there are no verses beginning with the letters *w* and *ḳ*, while there are two verses with an initial *p* (one of them is at the end of the poem), and two verses start with the letter *r*. A similar irregularity is also found in Ps. 34, and some scholars have suggested that both Psalms must have been written by the same author.

In spite of the artificial structure of the composition, it resembles a Lament of the Individual (see Introduction, pp. 37ff.), but it is wellnigh impossible to define with any reasonable certainty its *Sitz im Leben* or setting in life. Weiser (*POTL*, p. 238) assigns it to the Covenant Festival, but the evidence is rather vague. The description of the Psalmist's enemies and troubles is in very general terms, and consequently it has been argued that the author was not appealing to God on his own behalf, but that he composed this lament for any one in need (cf. Taylor, *PIB*, p. 135). This may be right, because it is plausible that most Psalms were composed by 'experts' for the use of worshippers of no special ability. Ps. 25 probably belongs to the post-Exilic period, and this is partly suggested by the acrostic scheme, as well as by its subject matter.

According to its contents, the Psalm can be roughly divided into three main sections. Verses 1–7 contain a prayer or series of petitions to God for help, guidance, and forgiveness. In verses 8–14 the theme is the nature and the attributes of God, and some of the verses are reminiscent of certain elements in the Hymns (cf. verses 8–10). The last section (verses 15–22) opens with an expression of assurance (verse 15) which is followed by another series of petitions for deliverance from trouble, concluding with a prayer for Israel.

The dominant metre is 3 + 3.

A Psalm of David: see Introduction, pp. 43ff. and 46. M.T. has only 'Of David' but the term 'A Psalm' may be implied; it is found in LXX.

A PRAYER OF PETITION **1–7**

1. I lift up my soul: just as the needy man sets his heart (i.e. his soul) upon his wages which are the means of his existence (cf. Dt. 24:15), so the godly man directs his whole being towards God, who alone is his trust and the object of his longings. This is to worship God in spirit and truth (Jn 4:23) and to lift up hearts, not merely hands, to God in heaven (Lam. 3:41; cf. N. K. Gottwald, *Studies in the Book of Lamentations* (*SBT* 14, 1954), p. 14). Cf. 86:4, 143:8.

This verse seems to lack the second line, and consequently some scholars have proposed to transfer verse 5*c* to verse 1 (so Kirkpatrick *et al.*).

2. O my God: (see on 91:2). This may belong to the preceding verse because the first line of verse 2 should begin with the Hebrew letter *b*.

in thee I trust: this implies that the writer takes seriously the

Covenant promises of God (cf. 21:7 (M.T. 8), 22:4f. (M.T. 5f.)) and, on the basis of this, he can pray for deliverance.

let me not be put to shame in the eyes of my foes. Since God does not go back on his word, misfortune could only be understood (according to the traditional view of that time) as a just punishment.

exult over me: or 'gloat . . .' (so Dahood), because God has proved by this treatment (so it seemed to the enemies) that the sufferer had been a fake and a hypocrite (cf. 31:1,17 (M.T. 2,18); Mic. 7:8).

3. that wait for thee with hopeful expectancy, i.e. that are attuned to thy will (see on 40:1). There is often a tension between one's hope and the present reality, yet those who wait upon Yahweh will never be disappointed, at least ultimately (cf. Isa. 49:23). Dahood (*PAB*, I, p. 155) renders the verb *ḳ-w-h* (*RSV* 'to wait') by 'to invoke' (i.e. '(who) invoke (you aloud)'); for this use of the verb, see on 19:4.

let them be ashamed: this expression repeats the same verb as in verse 3*a*, and therefore it is textually suspect. Some commentators (e.g. Gunkel, Schmidt, Kraus) adopt the change of *yēḇōšû* into *yāšūḇû*, rendering: 'only the deceitful shall return empty' (cf. Isa. 55:11; Jer. 50:9). The verb *b-g-d* ('to deal treacherously') may imply, at least in some cases, a previously existing relationship (cf. Jg. 9:23; Ps. 78:57; Jer. 3:20; Hos. 6:7). In CD i:12f. the writer describes the treacherous as those 'that backslide from the way' (cf. also CD viii:4f.).

4. thy ways . . . thy paths are the conduct which Yahweh prescribes for his people (Dt. 9:12,16; 1 Kg. 2:3; Jer. 5:4) and thus they are closely linked with the law or *tôrāh*. Cf. Widengren, *AHPL*, pp. 187f.; N. H. Ridderbos, 'The Psalms: Style-Figures and Structure', *OTS*, XIII (1963), pp. 65ff.

5. Lead me in thy truth: (cf. Jer. 16:13); or 'Make me walk in faithfulness to you' (as in 26:3); perhaps: 'Lead me by means of your truth (or 'because of your fidelity')'. 'Truth' (*ʾemeṯ*) in this verse ought not to be taken in the sense of abstract verities but rather as the dependability of God. Imschoot (*ThOT*, I, p. 66) suggests that *ʾemeṯ* 'expresses that the thing or the person is as it should be, that is true . . .'; cf. 145:18, 146:6.

the God of my salvation: i.e. the God who has saved me in the past and who will deliver me also in the future (cf. 18:46 (M.T. 47), 24:5).

for thee I wait: see on verses 1 and 3. The position of the words 'for thee' is emphatic, and a possible rendering might be: 'It is for you alone that I wait'.
all the day: i.e. continually.

6. Be mindful: or 'Remember (your mercy)', i.e. be merciful.
mercy . . . steadfast love: see on 51:1, 89:1.
from of old: this implies that God's nature is unchangeable and that therefore his people can depend upon him from 'everlasting to everlasting' (cf. 103:17). The stress is not upon the antiquity (as suggested by Dahood (*PAB*, I, p. 156)) but rather upon the enduring character of Yahweh's mercy and Covenant loyalty.

7. Remember not: i.e. do not remember in my disfavour (cf. Childs, *MTI*, p. 32).
the sins of my youth: this probably means 'the faults committed before I was fully responsible' (cf. Job 13:26; Kissane, *BP*, p. 112), or 'the inadvertent errors of his youth'.
my transgressions: or 'my acts of rebellion'; see on 51:1.
. . . remember me: i.e. deal with me according to your own Covenant promises (cf. Gunkel, *PGHAT*, p. 107); see on 119:49.
for thy goodness' sake: or in other words, the plea for pardon does not rest upon any merits of the Psalmist but solely upon the nature of God. Similarly in Isa. 43:25: 'I, in very truth I, do wipe out your transgressions, because I am what I am, and your sins I shall remember no more' (quoted from C. R. North, *The Second Isaiah* (1964), p. 42).

THE NATURE OF YAHWEH **8–14**

8. Good and upright: these are characteristic descriptions of God. In his actions towards men, God is beneficent yet he is not a 'sentimental philanthropist' because he is also upright and just in his well-doing. Therefore he shows the right way even to those who miss it, in order that they may return to him. A similar thought is expressed in 51:13: 'Then I will teach transgressors thy ways, and sinners will return to thee'.
sinners: see on 1:1.

9. the humble: for *ᶜᵃnāwîm*, see on 34:2.
what is right: (*mišpāṭ*), or 'the conduct of life fitting to God's people' rather than 'in judgment' (so *AV*, *RV*). See Ringgren, *IR*, p. 132.
he teaches the humble: some exegetes (e.g. Gunkel, Oesterley) regard the repetition of 'humble' (see above) as due to a scribal

error, and suggest 'the poor' (*'eḇyônîm*) (so also S). This is a stylistic improvement, but it is not necessarily the original reading; LXX follows M.T.

his way is parallel to 'what is right' (cf. verse 4).

10. All the paths of the LORD: or, paraphrasing: 'All the dealings of Yahweh (with his people) are characterized (as seen in the salvation-history) by a loyalty to his Covenant promises and by an absolute trustworthiness'. Cf. 89:33f.: '. . . but I will not remove from him my steadfast love, or be false to my faithfulness. I will not violate my covenant, or alter the word that went forth from my lips'. It is less likely that the 'paths of Yahweh' are the conduct which he teaches to his people (so Briggs).

who keep his covenant: or 'who observe his Covenant stipulations' (cf. Dt. 33:9). For a brief discussion on the covenant, and the relevant bibliography, see K. A. Kitchen, *Ancient Orient and Old Testament* (1966), pp. 90–102; see also on 55:20.

his testimonies: *NEB* 'his charge'. This term and 'his covenant' probably make up a hendiadys, i.e. the two phrases form one idea, 'his Covenant obligations'.

11. For thy name's sake: i.e. for the sake of your self-revelation. God will vindicate his words by his deeds (cf. Ezek. 36:22f.). See on 23:3.

pardon my guilt: (cf. Hos. 14:1f.). The plea for forgiveness is usually preceded by a turning from sin to God, and by a confession of the transgression; see on 130:4.

for it is great: Dahood (*PAB*, I, p. 157) argues that the sin of the Psalmist was idolatry because the expression 'great sin' is often used to describe the worship of idols or strange gods (cf. Exod. 32:21,30,31; 2 Kg. 17:21). In itself this suggestion is feasible, but the Psalm does not provide explicit evidence on this particular point.

12. Who is the man . . .: this should be taken, probably, as a very emphatic expression, because the enclitic pronoun *zeh* adds a special stress.

that fears the LORD: i.e. who shows reverence and obedience towards God. In a similar manner Job is described as a man 'who feared God, and turned away from evil' (Job 1:1,8). The 'fear of the Lord' includes both the experience of awe and the irresistible attraction to the graciousness of God, but it is *not* a state of anxiety. G. v. Rad (*Genesis* (*OTL*, 1961), p. 237) suggests that the phrase 'fear of God' could be interpreted 'simply as a term for obedience to the divine commands'. This is, of course, true but it represents only one aspect of the whole concept.

Him will he instruct: see verse 8.

the way that he should choose: i.e. the right way. Some take Yahweh as the subject of this relative clause, i.e. the way which Yahweh will choose for the godly man, but the former alternative seems more likely (cf. Isa. 48:17).

13. He himself: lit. 'His soul' (see on 33:19).

shall abide in prosperity: i.e. the consequence of walking in God's ways is a life of blessings. Similarly in 34:10: '. . . those who seek the LORD lack no good thing' (cf. 37:25). From our point of view such an affirmation can only be sustained if it is applied, primarily, to the spiritual realm.

his children shall possess the land because a man's blessing (or for that matter also his curse, if this is the case) involves not only the individual himself but also his family and sometimes even the whole community. A similar phrase is found in 4QpPs. 37 ii:4–5, where it is interpreted as referring to the 'congregation of his elect who do his will' (cf. CD i:7), while in Mt. 5:5 it is the meek who will inherit the earth. In our Psalm it means to enjoy the privilege of dwelling in Yahweh's land (cf. Gen. 17:8; Dt. 4:1; Ps. 140:13 (M.T. 14)).

14. The friendship of the LORD: or 'The secret of . . .' (*AV*, *RV* and similarly *RP*). The Hebrew *sôḏ*, which is here translated as 'friendship', may also mean 'secret' (Am. 3:7), 'secret plot' (64:2 (M.T. 3)), 'counsel' (83:3 (M.T. 4); Prov. 15:22), 'assembly' (89:7 (M.T. 8), 111:1), or 'an intimate circle of friends' (Job 19:19; Jer. 6:11). The parallel term 'covenant' (i.e. the Covenant obligations) may imply that *sôḏ* means here 'counsel' (not necessarily secret). See on 55:14.

who fear him: see verse 12.

A SERIES OF PETITIONS FOR HELP **15–22**

15. My eyes . . . toward the LORD: cf. 141:8. The Psalmist turns continually to God for guidance and succour. As the servant and maidservant look to their master and mistress, 'so our eyes look to the LORD . . . till he have mercy upon us' (123:2).

out of the net: i.e. out of the troubles and perplexities of life (cf. 9:15 (M.T. 16), 31:4 (M.T. 5)). The metaphor is derived from a hunting scene (see on 9:15).

16. Turn thou to me is equivalent to 'be gracious to me' (cf. 86:16, 119:132) which is an appeal to God's unmerited favour (see on 57:1). The opposite of this expression is the hiding of one's face (cf. 22:24 (M.T. 25), 69:17 (M.T. 18); see on 10:11).
for I am lonely: or 'solitary', 'friendless'. Probably, due to his troubles, he has been regarded as forsaken by God, and as such he was shunned by his fellows, who in turn were determined by the current 'theology' of their times.
afflicted: see on 34:2.

17. Relieve the troubles of my heart: reading *harḥēḇ* for M.T. *hirḥîḇû* ('(the troubles of my heart) are enlarged') (so *AV*, *RV*, *RSVm*). The M.T. reading does not give a satisfactory sense because 'enlarged' cannot very well mean 'become many', consequently the emendation presupposed by *RSV* may be right; it provides a suitable parallel to verse 17*b*. For a similar expression, see 4:1: 'Thou hast given me room when I was in distress', i.e. trouble is seen as a condition of being hemmed in, while deliverance consists of 'giving freedom' by bringing the oppressed into a broad place (18:19 (M.T. 20)). Dahood (*PAB*, I, p. 158) has suggested that the Hebrew verb should be taken in a privative sense, rendering: 'Anguish cramps my heart'. Although privative usage of certain verbs is known in Hebrew, there is no clear evidence for it in the case of the verb *r-ḥ-b* ('to be large').
bring me out: or 'deliver'.

18. my affliction and my trouble: they are not more closely defined, but they appear to be connected with 'sin' (verse 18*b*), perhaps as a punishment for it. Calvin (*Commentary on the Psalms*, ed. by T. H. L. Parker (1965), I, p. 297) remarks that 'as long as God is angry and displeased, all things must needs fall out unhappily to us'.
forgive all my sins: lit. 'take away . . .', and the meaning of sins (*ḥaṭṭā'ōṯ*) may well be that of guilt or the consequences of sins (cf. Zech. 14:19). They are thus a burden too heavy for a man to bear (38:4 (M.T. 5)).

19. violent hatred: or 'hatred that leads to violence'. Dahood (*PAB*, I, p. 159) takes this phrase in a concrete sense, 'my treacherous enemies', parallel to 'my foes' in verse 19*a*.

20. my life: lit. 'my soul'; essentially it is a synonym of 'me' (cf. 16:1, 86:2).
put to shame: see verses 2–3.
I take refuge in thee probably means: 'I trust in you and I seek

protection in your house' (see on 11:1; cf. 7:1 (M.T. 2), 31:1 (M.T. 2), 71:1, 141:8).

21. The interpretation of **integrity and uprightness** is problematic. Briggs, Dahood, *et al.* regard them as two messengers of God, sent to protect the afflicted (cf. 37:37), but the reference may be to the attributes of Yahweh, which give substance to the hope for deliverance (see verse 8). Some other scholars have taken 'integrity and uprightness' as the qualities of the Psalmist himself without any suggestion that he was a paragon of all virtues. Davison (*Cent. BP*, I, p. 137) points out that the essence of these two traits is 'an honest determination to do right', and even this is ultimately derived from God. A similar phrase is used to describe David's life (1 Kg. 9:4) but, in spite of all his greatness, he was neither sinless nor perfect.

I wait for thee: see verses 3 and 5.

22. This verse may be a later liturgical addition (so Briggs, Taylor, Weiser, *et al.*) in order to make the Psalm suitable for a congregational use. It also stands outside the acrostic scheme; otherwise it would reduplicate the line which begins with the letter *p* (in verse 16). Eaton (*PTBC*, p. 81) is of the opinion that verse 22 is a choral refrain, and therefore not included in the alphabetic arrangement.

Psalm 26 The Prayer of an Innocent Man

This Psalm is usually regarded as an Individual Lament (see Introduction, pp. 37ff.), although one of the main elements of this psalm-type—namely, the description of the misfortune—is lacking. Mowinckel (*PIW*, I, pp. 219f.) has defined this song as a Protective Psalm, distinguishing it from laments proper; its main characteristics are the prayer for divine protection and the absence of any account of the plight because the danger is not, as yet, a present reality; it only threatens the life of the Psalmist.

The *Sitz im Leben* of this Psalm may be similar to that of Ps. 7 (see its Introduction), and the Psalmist appears to be unjustly accused of some crime or of a breach of the sacral law (so Sabourin), rather than afflicted with some grievous illness (as suggested by Gunkel). He has taken refuge in the Temple, where he protests his innocence and appeals to Yahweh for deliverance. This situation is reminiscent of that described in 1 Kg. 8:31f. (cf. also Exod. 22:7–11 (M.T. 6–10); Num. 5:11–31); yet on the other hand, the life-setting of the Psalm is far from being obvious. It could be objected that the Psalm does not mention, at least explicitly, the accusation (cf. 7:3ff. (M.T. 4ff.), 69:4 (M.T. 5)) or the accusers, and therefore other explanations are not impossible. It could be argued that it was a pilgrim's confession at the Temple gates, in response to the priestly direction, such as is described in Ps. 15, 24 (cf. E. Vogt, 'Psalm 26, ein Pilgergebet', *Biblica*, XLIII (1962), pp. 328–37). Eaton (*PTBC*, pp. 83f.) considers the poem more suited 'to the worship offered by congregation, priest, or King' than to a legal setting being used as a formulary by an accused man.

The speaker of the Psalm seems to be an ordinary Israelite rather than a Levite (so Briggs) or the King. There is little evidence for the date; Oesterley would assign it to the Greek period, but there is nothing in the poem to contradict a pre-Exilic origin.

The Psalm opens with a prayer for vindication, which also includes an assertion of the author's integrity and loyalty to God (verses 1–3). This is followed by a protestation of innocence, unless verses 4–5 are taken as a continuation of the account of the author's faithfulness to God, in a negative form. The same theme is continued by the symbolic act of washing hands and of circling (?) the altar (verses 6–7). Finally, in verses 8–12 we find a further prayer for protection and an affirmation of fidelity.

The metre is mainly 3 + 3.

A Psalm of David: see Introduction, pp. 43ff. and 46. M.T. has 'Of David' (so also in Ps. 27–8; see the title of Ps. 25).

AN APPEAL FOR THE JUDGMENT OF GOD 1–3

1. Vindicate me: lit. 'Judge me' (see on 72:2), perhaps, 'Acknowledge my righteousness' (cf. E. Vogt, p. 335) or, paraphrasing: 'See for yourself (that my actions have been characterized by integrity)'. Cf. 7:8 (M.T. 9), 35:24, 43:1.

for: or 'On my word' (so Dahood *PAB*, I, p. 161), taking the Hebrew *kî* as an emphatic particle (see on 118:10).

I have walked in my integrity: see on 7:8 (cf. Prov. 10:9, 19:1, 20:7, 28:6). 'Integrity' is not to be judged by some ideal or absolute standard, but by one's relationship to God within the framework of his revelation (cf. L. Koehler, *Old Testament Theology*, Eng. tr. by A. S. Todd (1953), pp. 166ff.).

I have trusted . . .: i.e. I have believed that Yahweh is able to do what he has promised (see on 78:22). Man's trust in God is matched by God's *ḥeseḏ* or his faithfulness to his word (cf. 21:7 (M.T. 8), 32:10, 33:21f., 143:8).

without wavering: either 'I have not wavered (in my reliance upon Yahweh), or '(my steps) have not slipped (from your way)' (cf. 18:36 (M.T. 37), 37:31).

2. Prove me ... try me: the Psalmist offers his life to God for a fresh scrutiny, or it may be another way of saying: 'You *know* that I have been faithful to you.'

test ...: the metaphor may be derived from the process of testing silver. See on 66:10.

my heart and my mind: lit. 'my reins and my heart' (*AV*, *RV*). For the use of these two terms, see on 7:9; in this context they denote 'my whole being'.

3. steadfast love: *ḥeseḏ* is primarily a Covenant word, as suggested by 1 Sam. 20:8: 'Therefore deal kindly (lit. 'do *ḥeseḏ*) with your servant, for you have brought your servant into a sacred covenant with you'. In 89:28 *ḥeseḏ* is synonymous with 'Covenant', and in Dt. 7:9 God is described as one 'who keeps covenant and steadfast love with those who love him' (cf. 1 Kg. 8:23; 2 Chr. 6:14; Dan. 9:4). This *ḥeseḏ* or 'Covenant loyalty' is the unceasing outworking of the Covenant relationship, the essence of which is summed up in 'I will be your God and you shall be my people' (Jer. 7:23; cf. Jer. 11:4, 24:7, 30:22, 31:33, etc.). When referring to Yahweh, *ḥeseḏ* means, in the first place, his Covenant promises and all that they imply; while the *ḥeseḏ* of the Israelite consists, primarily, of his loyalty to his Covenant obligations. Consequently the meaning of this term is closely associated with the significance and interpretation of the Covenant. See Nelson Glueck, *HB*, pp. 56–102.

before my eyes: i.e. God's (objective genitive?) *ḥeseḏ* is a present reality to the Psalmist, in that he has constantly been true to his Covenant responsibilities.

I walk in faithfulness to thee: or 'I have acted in (the light of) your truth' (cf. Kissane, *BP*, p. 114). See on 25:5.

THE PROTESTATION OF INNOCENCE 4–7

4. This and the following verses remind us of 1:1 which gives a similar description of a righteous man. It is possible that verses 4–5 are an implicit account of the accusation brought against the Psalmist.

false men: or 'idol-worshippers' (so Dahood, *PAB*, I, p. 162) but the latter rendering, although not impossible, seems too specific (cf. Job 11:11). For *šāwʾ* ('vanity'), see on 119:37.

nor do I consort: perhaps 'nor have I entered' (together with the dissemblers their houses or gatherings) (cf. Prov. 22:24).

dissemblers (*NEB* 'hypocrites') are either those who conceal their thoughts and motives or those who hide themselves (i.e. their activities). In 1QH iii:28, iv:13, vii:34 the Hebrew word *naʿalāmîm* is translated by such terms as 'hypocrites', 'those who do evil', etc. In 1QH iv:13 they are described as seeking God with a double heart (i.e. dishonestly, under false pretences), and as not established in God's truth.

5. the company of evildoers is probably contrasted with 'the great congregation' in verse 12. Instead of seeking the companionship of the godless and participating in their activities, the righteous man enjoys the fellowship of God's people. See on 64:2.

the wicked: for *rešāʿîm*, see on 1:1.

6. The first part of this verse may refer to the ritual purification prescribed by the law for the priests (Exod. 30:19ff.), and therefore some exegetes have contended that the Psalm is a profession of integrity by a Levite (so Briggs). It is more likely, however, that the washing of hands is connected with the oath of purification, being symbolic of guiltlessness, and thus part of the appropriate ritual for such occasions (as in Dt. 21:6; Mt. 27:24). It is less certain that verses 3–5 form the oath of purification itself (cf. Weiser, *POTL*, p. 243), because such oaths usually involve a conditional self-cursing (e.g. 'May God do so to me and more also . . .'; cf. Ru. 1:17; 1 Sam. 3:17, 14:44; 2 Sam. 3:35, etc.). Cf. L. A. Snijders, 'Psaume XXVIet l' innocence', *OTS*, XIII (1963), pp. 120ff.

go about thy altar: i.e. to take one's place among those who offer their sacrifices, or to join in the solemn procession around the altar (similarly *NEB*). Kraus (*PBK*, p. 217) links the going round the altar with the prayers for divine help (so also Deissler), and this may be right, although the relevant evidence is rather slender (cf. 1 Kg. 18:26; Ps. 118:27).

7. The understanding of this verse is connected with the exegesis of verse 6. If we follow Kraus, then verse 7 would express the goal of the prayers of the godly man: having received his vindication, the suppliant is offering a song of thanksgiving. On the other hand, this verse may be an expression of hope, faith, and promise, rather than a description of an actual thanksgiving for the help already received.

thy wondrous deeds are the main content of the Psalmist's praise, and they include both the salvation events manifested in the life of the nation, and the help received or hoped for, by the individual worshipper. See on 9:1.

FURTHER PRAYERS **8–12**

8. I love . . .: this is the positive aspect of the right attitude to God; the negative one is expressed in verse 5: 'I hate the company of evildoers'. The whole verse may simply be a roundabout way of saying that the Psalmist loves God. The authors of the Psalms do not usually speak of man actually loving God (cf. 31:23 (M.T. 24), 97:10 (?), 116:1 (?), 145:20), although quite often man is said to love God's name (5:11 (M.T. 12), 69:36 (M.T. 37)), his law (119:47,48,97,113,119,127,159,163), or his salvation (40:16 (M.T. 17), 70:5 (M.T. 6)). This relative reluctance to state explicitly that man should love God (so characteristic of the Book of Deuteronomy) may be due to the Psalmists' sense of awe, when they speak about the King of glory. The verb ᵓ-*h-b* ('to love') can be used of God loving the righteous (146:8; Prov. 3:12), his people, his city, etc. (cf. Dt. 7:8,13; Ps. 47:5, 78:68, 87:2; Isa. 43:4; Hos. 3:1; etc.).

the habitation of thy house: this can be understood in several ways. It may mean: 'the house which is God's habitation', 'the divine abode in the Temple' (i.e. the Holy of Holies (so Briggs)), or 'the abiding (of the worshipper) in God's house' (cf. 23:6, 27:4, 84:4 (M.T. 5)); similarly also Dahood (*PAB*, I, p. 162): 'I love to live in your house', reading *ᵓāhaḇtî-m ᶜûn bêṯeḵā*, and regarding the *mēm* of the M.T. *meᶜôn* ('the habitation of . . .') as an enclitic particle.

thy glory: i.e. the glory of Yahweh which is frequently associated with his self-manifestation, inspiring respect and awe, and which represents the very presence of God. His glory dwells in the Temple (1 Kg. 8:11), but it can also be manifested in the whole world (57:5,11 (M.T. 6,12); Isa. 6:3, 40:5). The same glory can depart from the Temple (Ezek. 10:18f., 11:22f.) or it can return to it once more (Ezek. 43:4), thus symbolizing the absence or presence of God, respectively. Imschoot (*ThOT*, I, p. 200) defines the glory of God as 'divine holiness and power manifested' (cf. L. H. Brockington, 'The Presence of God: A Study of the Term "Glory of Yahweh" ', *ET*, LVII (1945), p. 21f.).

9. sinners: see on 1:1. These are the men who intentionally miss the way of God, and love doing so; but it is far from certain that this term, in this particular context, refers to polytheists (so Dahood). In Israel it was a common belief that the wicked will perish (1:6) or that God will cut off the evildoers before their time (55:23 (M.T. 24)). It is with such men that the Psalmist apparently has been classed.

my life: (*ḥayyîm*) is parallel to 'me' (lit. 'my soul') in verse 8. See on 21:4, 143:3.

bloodthirsty men: lit. 'men of blood'—i.e. people who have no hesitation to use murder as a means to an end. See on 5:6.

10. hands: Dahood (*PAB*, I, p. 163) reads 'left hand'; see on 21:8.

evil devices: the Hebrew *zimmāh* can denote sexual immorality (cf. Lev. 18:17, 19:29, 20:14; Job 31:11; Jer. 13:27, etc.), but it is doubtful whether this specific meaning should be found in this verse. The same is true of Dahood's rendering 'idols'; although idolatry is not infrequently described as adultery or harlotry (cf. Jer. 13:27; Ezek. 16:23–29; etc.), the parallel in verse 10*a* suggests a more general evil.

full of bribes: *PLE* has a fitting paraphrase: 'palms ever itching for a bribe'. The men guilty of perverting the course of justice were probably those in authority, in whose hands was the administration of the law. Briggs (*CECBP*, I, p. 234) suggests that the author had in mind the criminals who offered the bribes, but possibly both groups were meant because both would be distorting justice.

11. See verse 1. For **redeem** (*p-d-h*), see on 119:134.

be gracious to me: for this appeal to God's unmerited favour, see on 51:1.

12. level ground: or 'uprightness' (cf. 45:6 (M.T. 7), 67:4 (M.T. 5); Isa. 11:4; Mal. 2:6). The Psalmist may have intended a play on both meanings of the word: as he had walked in integrity or uprightness (cf. verses 1,3,11), so now he can stand on level ground (in the Temple courts? cf. 122:2); *NEB* 'firm ground'. There is some uncertainty concerning the tense of the verb *ᶜāmeḏāh* (*RSV* 'stands'): it could be taken as a perfect of certainty, meaning 'shall stand', or as an ordinary perfect (cf. verse 1) describing the past fidelity of the Psalmist (so Dahood).

the great congregation: lit. 'assemblies'; the reference is probably to the worshipping community.

I will bless the LORD: see on 104:1; cf. Widengren, *AHPL*, pp. 311ff.

Psalm 27 CONFIDENCE IN YAHWEH AND A PRAYER FOR HELP

This Psalm is marked by a clear break between verses 6 and 7, with the result that verses 1–6 appear to form a Psalm of Confidence or Trust, while verses 7–14 bear the characteristics of an Individual Lament (see Introduction, pp. 37ff.), ending with an oracle (verse 14; cf. J. Begrich, '*Das priesterliche Heilsorakel*', *ZAW*, LII (1934), pp. 81–92). The main problem is whether this Psalm consists of two originally independent poems (so Weiser, Taylor, Leslie, *et al.*) or whether it forms a literary unity (as suggested by Schmidt, Birkeland, Kraus, Eaton, *et al.*). There are several reasons for separating the two parts:

(i) There are differences in tone between the two sections; one voices confidence and trust, while the other is full of lamentation and petitions.

(ii) Both parts seem to be reasonably self-contained, and they belong to different psalm-types. The first part is a Psalm of Confidence, and Yahweh is spoken of in the third person, whereas the second part is a Lamentation or a prayer of an unjustly accused person, and Yahweh is addressed in the second person in most verses.

(iii) The sequence of the two sections is rather unusual, in that the cry for help follows expressions of confidence and certainty; there is no real parallel to this in any other Psalm (cf. H. Birkeland, 'Die Einheitlichkeit von Ps. 27', *ZAW*, LI (1933), p. 220).

The collocation of two different Psalms is not an unknown phenomenon in the Psalter; e.g., Ps. 114, 115 are regarded as one unit in LXX, although they are two separate poems.

It is just possible that Ps. 27 is essentially a lament in which the element of trust has been particularly emphasized. Eaton (*PTBC*, p. 85) regards the Psalm as a literary unity but treats it as a Royal Psalm, and there is a reasonable justification for this view. The title and certain expressions lend support to this interpretation, but other details, e.g. the references to the false witnesses (verse 12), and to the abandonment of the speaker by his father and mother (verse 10), may suggest that an ordinary Israelite has applied royal metaphors to his own experiences.

The Psalm offers little evidence to date it; Oesterley suggests a post-Exilic date, but a pre-Exilic origin is not excluded.

The metre of the Psalm is 3 + 2, with a few exceptions.

A Psalm of David: see Introduction, pp. 43ff. and 46. M.T. has only 'Of David', while LXX adds 'before he was anointed'; but this seems to be a late interpretation.

THE LORD IS MY LIGHT **1–6**

The background of this Psalm (or section) is the aggression of the enemies (verses 2–3); but, despite the odds, the Psalmist is confident in Yahweh and in his protection. It is possible that the warlike metaphors were borrowed from the language of the Royal Psalms, especially if the composition originated during the post-Exilic period.

1. The LORD is my light: i.e. he 'lightens my darkness' (18:28 (M.T. 29)). Only here in the *OT* is Yahweh described as 'my light' (cf. Jn 8:12: 'I am the light of the world'); in Isa. 10:17 he is called 'the light of Israel', and in Isa. 60:19,20 he is described as the 'everlasting light' of his people. It is probable that the Psalmist has applied to the individual a metaphor that was more appropriate to describe Yahweh's relationship with his people. A parallel to this would be the use of the 'shepherd-image' in 23:1. 'Light' can be symbolic of all that is good (see on 56:13, 97:11).

my salvation is here a synonym of 'my light', meaning 'my saviour', i.e. the source of my deliverance (cf. 62:7 (M.T. 8)). Yahweh had manifested himself to his people through the great historical events of deliverance, but his saving activity is not at an end. He is still the saviour of his people, and the deliverer of the individual in particular.

whom shall I fear is a rhetorical question expressing a daring trust in God. It is reminiscent of Rom. 8:31: 'If God is on our side, who is against us?' (*NEB*).

the stronghold: the Hebrew *mā*ᶜ*ôz* is derived from ᶜ-*z*-*z* ('was strong'), while *RSVm*, *NEB* (also Gunkel, Briggs, *et al.*) link it with ᶜ-*w*-*z* ('sought refuge'), rendering the noun by 'refuge'. The former alternative seems more likely (cf. 90:1; Isa. 25:4; Jer. 16:19).

2. evildoers are synonymous with 'my adversaries' and 'foes', and they are more likely the enemies of the individual rather than the national enemies of the people of God or of the King. See on 64:2.

uttering slanders against me: lit. 'to devour my flesh'. The exact meaning of the metaphor is not clear. Most commentators think that the enemies are likened to wild beasts, whose only concern is to devour their prey (cf. 7:2 (M.T. 3), 14:4, 17:12; Jer. 30:16, 50:7), i.e. to destroy the victim utterly. 'My flesh' may simply mean 'me' (so *NEB*) as *pars pro toto*. Eaton (*PTBC*, p. 86) thinks that the reference is to 'demonic beast-like powers which prey on the life of the king and his society'. The *RSV* rendering finds its parallel in Dan. 3:8, 6:24, where the phrase: 'to eat the pieces of . . .' means: 'to denounce, slander' (cf. J. A. Montgomery, *A Critical and Exegetical Commentary on the Book of Daniel* (*ICC*, 1950), pp. 204f.). In Syriac the 'eater of pieces' is an accuser, and can also denote the 'devil'.
they shall stumble and fall: or 'they stumbled and fell' (*AV*, *RV*). But the Hebrew perfects may express confidence and certainty: 'they shall certainly stumble . . .'. The picture is that of an overthrow by means of a divine intervention (cf. Isa. 3:8, 8:15, 31:3; Jer. 6:21, 46:6).

3. a host: or 'an army', lit. 'a camp'. The martial language need not be taken literally as if the speaker were a king or a military commander; it may well be used metaphorically indicating a very great danger and an extremely grave situation. Ultimately the metaphor may have been derived from National or Royal Psalms. Cf. 2 Kg. 6:14ff.
my heart: or simply 'I', an idiomatic substitute for the personal pronoun. 'Heart' (*lēḇ* or *lēḇāḇ*) is one of the most frequent anthropological terms in the *OT*, and it occurs some 850 times. Its real physiological significance was not understood, and it is rarely used in a purely physical sense (cf. 2 Kg. 9:24). The term often denotes the seat of psychic life, the emphasis being on the intellectual (cf. 83:5 (M.T. 6)) and volitional aspects (cf. 141:4) rather than on the emotional activities. It can also signify one's whole personality or the whole man (cf. 77:6, 102:4 (M.T. 5)). In a way the heart is the quintessence of man, so that the quality of the heart is also the measure of the man himself. For more details, see Johnson, *VITAI*, pp. 75–87; also Eichrodt, *TOT*, II, pp. 142ff.; F. Baumgärtel, '*Kardia*', *TDNT*, III, pp. 606f.
war: (*milḥāmāh*) is taken by Dahood (*PAB*, I, p. 167) as meaning 'the participants in war', i.e. troops; *NEB* 'armed men'. This rendering may be supported by the parallel term 'host' (verse 3*a*),

although it is not attested elsewhere in the *OT* in an unambiguous way.

4. One thing . . .: or 'One thing alone . . .'. This resembles Mt. 6:33: 'Set your mind on God's kingdom and his justice before everything else, and all the rest will come to you as well' (*NEB*).

that I may dwell in . . .: or 'that I may worship in . . .' and so receive all the attendant blessings; see on 23:6. Some commentators consider this phrase as a later addition from 23:6 (cf. Kraus, *PBK*, p. 224). It is unlikely that by **the house of the Lord** the Psalmist meant 'the heavenly habitation of Yahweh' (so Dahood, *PAB*, I, p. 167).

all the days of my life: i.e. as long as I live.

the beauty of the Lord: or 'the graciousness of Yahweh' as in 90:17: 'Let the favour (i.e. the graciousness, beauty) of Yahweh . . . be upon us' (cf. 135:3). It is possible that the origin of this metaphor is to be found in the non-Israelite world where various idols were carried around, and where the worshipper would actually behold the face of the deity—i.e. the unveiled statue (cf. *ANET*, pp. 330, 342). If indeed this word-picture was derived from the sphere of iconolatry, then it was used, quite obviously, in a spiritual sense as a description of Yahweh's graciousness. Mowinckel (*PIW*, I, p. 142) points out that 'even in Israel this "beholding" was attached to a visible symbol, namely to the holy ark of Yahweh . . .'. G. v. Rad (*PHOE*, p. 258) regards 'the beauty of Yahweh' as more or less synonymous with 'the glory of Israel'.

to inquire is a problematic term. Mowinckel (*PIW*, II, p. 54) relates it to 'some sort of interpretation of signs in connexion with the sacrifices . . .' something like 'taking omens' (see on 5:3). This may suggest some kind of divination, perhaps, by means of the entrails of the sacrificial animal, the behaviour of the victim, or a similar practice (cf. J. Gray, *I & II Kings*, (*OTL*, 1964), p. 578); it is doubtful, however, whether this is what the Psalmist had in mind. It is more likely that he may have looked for an oracular sign or an oracle (not unlike the one quoted in verse 14). Weiser (*POTL*, p. 245) has suggested that 'to inquire' may mean 'to say prayers', while Cohen (*PSon*, p. 79) renders 'to visit early (in His temple)' (cf. V 'to visit his sanctuary'). Dahood (*PAB*, I, p. 167) has taken the verb as denominative of *bōḳer* ('morning, dawn') and translates the above phrase 'awakening each dawn'. Out of this medley of suggestions, the most appropriate meaning seems to be: 'to ask for a divine answer or decision', without specifying as to how it was obtained (cf. v. Rad, *PHOE*, p. 257, n.21).

5. **he will hide me in his shelter:** this metaphor seems to be based on the ancient belief that the sanctuary offered a right of asylum. The underlying principle was not so much that of a divine hospitality as the holiness of the sanctuary, the dwelling place of the deity (cf. W. Robertson Smith, *Religion of the Semites*, rev. edn. (1894), pp. 148f.). 'Shelter' (*sukkāh*; cf. 15:1) and 'tent' (*ᵓōhel*; cf. 76:2 (M.T. 3); Lam. 2:6) are two archaic terms used to denote the Temple; it is unlikely that the reference is to the time when Yahweh actually 'dwelt' in a tent (cf. 2 Sam. 7:2), i.e. the time of David or earlier.

the day of trouble: as in 41:2 (M.T. 3). It may point to the day when the enemies present their accusations (cf. Kraus, *PBK*, p. 225) rather than to 'the day of death' (so Dahood).

a rock: this is, according to Gunkel, an allusion to the rock-sanctuary of Jerusalem. It is more probable, however, that the expression is used as a symbol of defence and security; hence to be set high upon a rock means to be outside the reach of the enemies. For *ṣûr* ('rock'), see on 28:1, 42:9.

6. **And now:** this probably introduces the conclusion of the Psalm, as in 2:10. Briggs (*CECBP*, I, p. 240) suggests that the sequence implied is logical and not temporal.

my head shall be lifted up: or, following LXX, S, and V, 'he shall lift up (*yārîm*) my head' (*RP*). M.T. may well be the original reading, while the versions provide an interpretative rendering. The lifting-up of the head may be a sign of triumph or indicate the reversal of fortunes (see on 3:3).

in his tent: i.e. in the Temple (cf. verse 4); see on 61:4.

sacrifices with shouts of joy: or 'sacrifices of joy' (so Weiser). The Hebrew *tᵉrûᶜāh* ('shout of joy') can also denote a 'war cry' (1 Sam. 17:20), a 'signal' (Lev. 25:9), or an 'alarm' (Num. 10:5,6); it could also be a 'cry of homage' (47:5 (M.T. 6)). For a detailed discussion, see P. Humbert, *TEROUᶜA: Analyse d'un rite biblique* (1946). The Psalmist promises this homage because he is quite convinced that God will help him; thus his attitude is not determined by a *quid pro quo* mentality, but by an unshakable faith in God.

FORSAKE ME NOT, O GOD 7–14

This second part of Ps. 27 may well be an independent lament; the speaker is probably unjustly accused of some sin, with the result that he has become an outcast even from his own family (verse 10), and his very life seems to be in danger. The 'royal' interpretation of this section is possible, but hardly any more convincing than the view followed in the exegesis.

7. The Psalm opens with the usual petition for hearing and for help (cf. 4:2 (M.T. 3), 5:2f. (M.T. 3f.), 17:1, 28:2, 55:1f. (M.T. 2f.), etc.).

Hear, O Lord, when I cry aloud: this sentence is divided differently by Dahood (*PAB*, I, p. 168) who reads: 'Hear, O Yahweh, my voice; when I call have pity . . .'. For **be gracious to me,** see on 6:2, 57:1.

answer me by giving the help required, either by removing the particular misfortune, or by granting a favourable oracle which would have the same effect.

8. The translation of this verse can be only tentative. A possible literal rendering might be: 'To you, says my soul, belongs (the command), "Seek (plur.) my face" . . .' (cf. F. James, *Thirty Psalmists* (1965), p. 146) or perhaps: 'To you, O my heart, has he said: "Seek (sing.) my face" . . .' (reading *baḳḳēš ûp̱ānāy* for M.T. *baḳḳ^ešû p̱ānāy*, 'seek (plur.) my face', and regarding the conjunction *wāw* as an emphatic particle (see on 18:41)).

Thy face . . . do I seek: i.e. he is about to offer sacrifice; for other possible meanings of the verb *b-ḳ-š*, see on 40:16. In 2 Chr. 11:16 we read: 'And those who had set their hearts to seek the Lord . . . came . . . to Jerusalem to sacrifice to the Lord' (cf. Hos. 11:16). The same expression can be used of worship in general, as in Jer. 50:4f.; Hos. 3:5; Zech. 8:22. The 'face' of Yahweh may be a symbolic description of his self-manifestation or of his cultic presence, which is experienced through one's participation in the worship. It can also be a circumlocution for Yahweh himself (cf. 139:7f.).

9. Hide not thy face: (cf. 102:2 (M.T. 3), 143:7) or 'do not withdraw your favour'; this is further explained by the parallel clause: 'Turn not thy servant away in anger'. The hiding of one's face is a graphic picture of displeasure or even of hostility; see on 13:1.

Turn not . . . away may be derived from the sphere of legal activity. In Isa. 29:21 there is a reference to men who, with specious arguments, 'turn aside', or deny justice to, the innocent man. See also the legal maxim in Prov. 18:5: 'It is not good to be partial to a wicked man, or to deprive (lit. 'to turn away') a righteous man of justice'.

thy servant is a more polite way of saying 'me'. Such a usage is frequent in epistolary style and in prayers (cf. 19:11,13 (M.T. 12,14), 31:16 (M.T. 17), 35:27, 69:17 (M.T. 18), etc.).

God of my salvation: i.e. the God who is the source of my deliverance; see on 65:5.

10. This verse presents a picture of extreme loneliness and forsakenness. Even his own kith and kin have given him up (cf. Job 19:13f.; Ps. 38:11 (M.T. 12), 69:8 (M.T. 9); Isa. 49:15), because he is regarded as a guilty man under divine wrath manifesting itself in the particular misfortune or trouble.

the LORD will take me up: or '. . . will gather me (to himself)' as a father or foster-father might pick up his child. A. Bentzen (*King and Messiah* (1955), p. 25) sees here an allusion to the adoption theme (cf. 2:7); this is possible, although it does not follow that this lament *must* be a Royal Psalm. The expression may mean that in the deepest trouble Yahweh will side with the afflicted man, and will declare him to be his own thereby giving him a place in the family of God's people (cf. Mt. 12:48ff.).

11. Teach me thy way: i.e. not my will but yours be done (cf. Lk. 22:42). The writer may imply that he is conscious of some past failures to keep the divine commands, although his false accusers (verse 12) are obviously wrong in their charges. Whatever may be the evaluation of the past, the Psalmist prays for a new beginning.

lead me on a level path: not so much a way that is cleared of all possible obstacles and made easy, but a way of life that is right in the sight of God (see on 26:12).

because of my enemies: meaning either 'lest they have a *real* cause to accuse me', or 'lest they attack me from their ambush'. The former alternative may be right; see on 54:5.

12. Give me not up . . .: or 'Do not put me into the throat of . . .' (so Dahood, *PAB*, I, p. 166). The Hebrew *nep̄eš* is rendered by *RSV* as 'will' but it may well be translated as 'greed' (*PNT*, *NEB*); see on 41:2, also on 33:19.

false witnesses: they were probably the witnesses for the prosecution, or they could be taken in a less technical sense as 'slanderers' or as people who infer from the sufferer's misfortunes that he has sinned (so Kissane). The first suggestion seems to be more appropriate. Although witnesses, especially in capital cases, carried a grave responsibility, this did not prevent the miscarriage of justice (cf. 1 Kg. 21:10–13). If one was proved to be a malicious witness, he received the punishment which would have been inflicted upon the accused had he been found guilty (so Dt. 19:18f.). According to Josephus (*Antiquities* IV, viii:15), neither women nor slaves were qualified to give a testimony in a court of law. Contradictory testimony would normally be ruled invalid, at least according to the Mishnah (*Sanhedrin* V:2; cf. also Mk 14:56–59).

have risen against me: i.e. they are testifying against me.

and they breathe out violence: reading *weyāpîḥû* for M.T. *wîpēaḥ*, as suggested by S. A good parallel is found in Prov. 6:19, 14:5 where a false witness is said to breathe out (*yāpîaḥ*) lies (cf. also Prov. 14:25, 19:5,9; Ac. 9:1).

13. The beginning of this verse is textually difficult. Literally it could be read 'Unless I had believed . . .' or 'Had I not had the courage to believe that I shall see . . .'; the apodosis of the conditional sentence, perhaps something like 'I am afraid to think of what would have happened . . .', has apparently been suppressed (cf. *GK* 159dd). This abbreviated sentence probably amounts to an emphatic statement: 'I *have* believed . . .'. The *RSV* rendering simply omits the conditional particle *lûlē'* ('unless'), which is lacking in some Hebrew MSS.

the land of the living: (cf. 142:5 (M.T. 6); Jer. 11:19); the reference is to this life as distinguished from the existence in Sheol or the underworld (see on 52:5). If he could not have believed that justice might be done during this life, there would have been no hope at all, because there could be no vindication in Sheol after death. This was, at least, the traditional view of after-life at that time (see 30:9 (M.T. 10), 115:17).

14. This concluding verse is probably a priestly oracle of hope promising deliverance, rather than a self-encouragement to hope in God (cf. Weiser, *POTL*, p. 254), or a 'conversation' between the Psalmist and his own soul (so F. James, p. 148). The oracle was presumably part of the answer hoped for in verse 7. Similarly in 1 Sam. 1:17 Eli says to Hannah: 'Go in peace, and the God of Israel grant your petition which you have made to him'; this seems to be not simply a wish, but a real promise (of God).

wait for the Lord: i.e. wait for his answer (cf. 40:1 (M.T. 2)) or his intervention which is sure to come (Hos. 12:6 (M.T. 7)).
be strong . . . take courage: for a similar expression of assurance, see Dt. 31:7; Jos. 1:6,7,9,18, 10:25; Ps. 31:25 (M.T. 26).

Psalm 28 The Silence of God means Death

Most exegetes have described this Psalm as a Lament of the Individual (see Introduction, pp. 37ff.), consisting of two distinct sections: verses 1–5 which are the lament proper, asking God for deliverance and for the punishment of the wicked, while verses 6–9 form a hymnic thanksgiving to Yahweh, or a declarative praise. This transition from lamentation and petition to thanksgiving and praise is 'a development which is peculiar to the Israelite Psalms' (Westermann, *PGP*, p. 79). There are several possible reasons for this change of mood (see introduction to Ps. 22) and a reasonable suggestion is proposed by Westermann (*PGP*, pp. 79f.); he thinks that the decisive event is the fact that God has heard the prayer and has had pity on the afflicted man. The actual change in circumstances will therefore inevitably follow and it can be regarded, in faith, as a present reality. Thus the Psalm is no mere lament, but a 'lament that has been turned into praise' (*ibid.*, p. 80). Another plausible view is that the lament was followed by an oracle of weal uttered by a priest or a cultic prophet. This word from Yahweh promised salvation, and it formed the basis of the thanksgiving; the Psalmist could praise God, because he had heard the afflicted man's prayer and had answered it (cf. 1 Sam. 1:17f.; Mowinckel, *PIW*, 1, p. 219). A good parallel is provided by Lam. 3:55ff. where the writer describes how he called upon the name of Yahweh and how he heard his plea. Then he goes on to say: 'Thou didst come near when I called on thee; thou didst say: "Do not fear" .'

Verses 8–9 are essentially an intercession for the people as a whole, and there is also the mention of God's anointed who is usually taken to be the King or the people (cf. Taylor *PIB*, p. 150). The allusion to the anointed one does not make the poem into a Royal Psalm (so Bentzen, Mowinckel, Eaton), for it is probable that these two verses are a later liturgical addition to adapt the Psalm for congregational worship. Yet even if these verses are an integral part of the original Psalm, it does not follow that the speaker must be the King. It is not improbable that a

Psalm of an ordinary Israelite should contain a reference to the nation and its King, because the welfare of the individual was inseparably linked with that of the people and their monarch; one could only enjoy the fulness of life within the fellowship of God's people.

The life-setting of the Psalm may be the Temple worship (cf. verse 2), and the annual pilgrimage festivals may have provided a good opportunity (although not exclusively so) to offer prayers and thanksgiving to Yahweh. The nature of the Psalmist's distress is not clear. Mowinckel, Schmidt, *et al.* are of the opinion that the author of the lament was suffering from a grave illness, but there may also be other possibilities, such as unjust accusation, oppression, etc. (cf. Kraus, *PBK*, p. 229).

The Psalm is probably of pre-Exilic origin, but hardly as early as the time of David.

The dominant metre of the Psalm is 3+2.

A Psalm of David: see Introduction, pp. 37ff. and 46.

THE CRY TO YAHWEH **1–5**

1. To thee . . . I call: i.e. to you and to no other do I appeal for help.

my rock: see on 42:9. This divine title is a metaphor of power and strength, reliability and unchangeableness. Jacob (*TOTe*, p. 62) has suggested that the origin of this divine name is, perhaps, linked with 'the worship of divine power enclosed within the sacred stones . . .', while Kraus (*PBK*, p. 230) points to the possibility that 'my rock' may refer to the sacred rock over which the Temple was built; there is, however, no *OT* evidence for this (cf. W. F. Stinespring, 'Temple, Jerusalem', *IDB*, IV, p. 542a; de Vaux, *AI*, pp. 318f.). Cf. 18:2 (M.T. 3), 19:14 (M.T. 15).

be not deaf to me: i.e. do not give me up (just as 'to hear' means 'to help'). This is an expression found in a number of Psalms (cf. 35:22, 39:2 (M.T. 3), 83:1 (M.T. 2), 109:1). See also 1 Sam. 7:8 which could be paraphrased: 'Do not give us up (i.e. 'do not be deaf to us') by ceasing to cry to Yahweh our God for us'.

who go down to the Pit: i.e. those who are about to perish or those who are already dead. This is a common phrase in the *OT* (cf. 30:4 (M.T. 5), 88:4 (M.T. 5), 143:7; Prov. 1:12; Isa. 38:18; Ezek. 26:20, 31:14,16, 32:18,24f.,29f.), and it is synonymous with 'going down to Sheol' (Job 7:9) and 'going down to the dust' (22:19 (M.T. 20)). The Hebrew *bôr* can denote a hole in the ground or a cistern for storing water (cf. Lev. 11:36); it could also serve as a grim dungeon (Isa. 24:22; Jer. 37:16, 38:6). The term is once used of a quarry (Isa. 51:1), and metaphorically it describes trouble (40:2 (M.T. 3)). It is employed by many *OT* writers as a synonym of Sheol or the underworld (cf. 30:3 (M.T. 4), 88:6 (M.T. 7), 143:7; Prov. 1:12; Isa. 14:15, 38:18; Ezek. 31:14,16, 32:18; *ANET*, p. 135 (viii 8–11)). See also Tromp, *PCD*, pp. 66–9.

2. the voice of my supplication is a circumlocution for 'my supplication' (cf. 116:1, 130:2, 140:6 (M.T. 7); see on 86:6).
I lift up my hands: this represents the usual attitude of the worshipper in prayer; he may be either standing (1 Kg. 8:22) or kneeling (1 Kg. 8:54; Ezr. 9:5). For references to various Near Eastern parallels, see Gunkel, *PGHAT*, p. 119. The hands are lifted up either toward heaven (1 Kg. 8:22; Lam. 2:19, 3:14) or toward the Temple (1 Kg. 8:35,38,42; Ps. 5:7 (M.T. 8), 134:2) as the 'earthly dwelling place' of God or as the representation of his heavenly abode.
thy most holy sanctuary: not 'thy holy oracle' (as *AV*, *RV*). The reference is to the *d^{e}ḇîr* ('the Holy of Holies'), which has no semantic relationship with *dāḇār* ('word, oracle'); cf. J. Barr, *SBL*, p. 136. The *d^{e}ḇîr* was the inmost shrine of the Temple, while the other two main parts of the sanctuary were the porch or vestibule, and the Holy Place or the main room. The Holy Place measured some 30 by 60 feet, and the porch was about 15 by 30 feet; the Holy of Holies was formed in the shape of a cube, some 30 feet in each dimension. The latter had no windows, and it contained the Ark and the cherubim with their outstretched wings, as if guarding the Ark (1 Kg. 8:6). After the Exile the Holy of Holies was, apparently, empty since the Ark and the cherubim must have perished during the destruction of the Solomonic Temple in 587 B.C. For a more detailed account, see A. Parrot, *The Temple of Jerusalem* (*SBA*, 1957).

3. Take me not off . . .: i.e. do not drag me away to doom (appointed for the wicked). The Psalmist seems to be in danger of sharing the same fate as the evildoers, but there is no explicit indication as to how he had come into that situation. The Psalmist's petitions in verses 3–4 are an implicit protestation of innocence; he is *not* one of the mischief-makers.
the wicked: (*r^{e}šā^{c}îm*) are those who have no regard for God; therefore they have no standing before God. They are men who

insist on sawing off the branch on which they are sitting. In their arrogance they trust in themselves rather than in God; that they do not acknowledge God and consequently all that God is is their loss (cf. also Widengren, *AHPL*, pp. 143f.); see on 1:1.

workers of evil: (*pōᶜᵃlê ᵓāwen*) this is a frequent description of the enemies of the Psalmists, and many important discussions have dealt with the meaning of this term (see G. W. Anderson, 'Enemies and Evildoers in the Book of Psalms', *BJRL*, XLVIII (1965), pp. 18–29; K.-H. Bernhardt, *Theologisches Wörterbuch zum Alten Testament*, I (1970), coll. 151–9.) but no *single* solution has been reached on this matter. Consequently it might be better to recognize that the 'workers of evil' may refer to several categories of evildoers, and that each occurrence of the term must be judged on its own merits. It may well be that in some psalms the term refers to national enemies (cf. H. Birkeland, *The Evildoers in the Book of Psalms* (1955)), while in some others the expression may even describe 'workers of magic' (for references, see Johnson, 'The Psalms', *OTMS*, p. 199) and those whose weapon was their false accusations and the potent word of a slanderer. It is difficult to say to which group we should assign the 'workers of evil' in Ps. 28; if it is a Psalm of the individual, then the reference may be to the Psalmist's own countrymen whose one weapon, at least, was deceit (see below).

who speak peace: i.e. they appear as friends, but in actual fact they work for the downfall or the destruction of their neighbour; cf. 12:2 (M.T. 3); Jer. 9:8.

4. This petition for retribution on the evildoers may not be in accord with twentieth-century Christian thought, but it was reasonable enough in its own setting. This prayer is not an expression of a vindictive personal revenge, but it is rather a longing for divine justice and for a society where a man can trust his fellow, and where they can serve the same Lord. The Psalmist, too, would accept the dictum that God has no pleasure 'in the death of the wicked, but that the wicked turn from his way and live' (Ezek. 33:11). To requite sin means to strip off its outward attractiveness and to make the guilty man to experience sin in all its reality.

5. Here we find the main reason why God should intervene. The actions of the evildoers toward their fellows are not motivated by mere personal incompatibility but by their self-centred existence. Instead of having regard for the works of God or for what God has done for them, their one and only stimulus is their own desires, the objects of which do not include God. Therefore God will break them down (cf. Jer. 24:6, 42:10, 45:4) and they will perish, for they have chosen to defy the law of 'spiritual gravity'.

THE THANKS AND INTERCESSION **6–9**

6. Blessed be the LORD: or 'Let Yahweh be praised'. This phrase is, more or less, a shout of praise and an expression of gratitude for the blessings received (see on 16:7, 124:6; cf. Westermann, *PGP*, pp. 88f.). It is quite frequent in the Psalter (cf. 31:21 (M.T. 22), 41:13 (M.T. 14), 66:20, 68:19,35 (M.T. 20, 36), 72:18, 89:52 (M.T. 53), 106:48, 118:26, 124:6, 135:21, 144:1).

for he has heard . . .: this may refer to the divine answer in the form of an oracle of salvation (see the introduction to this Psalm); **my supplication** is probably the prayer mentioned in verse 2.

7. my strength: Yahweh is the source of the strength of the Psalmist (cf. Exod. 15:2; Ps. 59:17 (M.T. 18); Isa. 49:5; Jer. 16:19). Dahood (*PAB*, I, p. 173) takes 'my strength' and 'my shield' as forming a hendiadys, the two nouns expressing one idea: 'my strong shield'. For 'shield', see on 3:3.

my heart trusts: i.e. 'I trust'. The verb *b-ṭ-ḥ* describes man's proper attitude to God (see on 78:22; cf. H. W. Robinson, *Inspiration and Revelation in the Old Testament* (1956), pp. 266f.).

so I am helped: this is rendered by Dahood (*PAB*, I, p. 173) as 'I have been rejuvenated', and he regards the verb *ᶜ-z-r* as from the same root as the Ugaritic *ǵzr* ('lad, warrior'). The theme of renewal is not unknown in the *OT*, e.g. in Job 33:25; Ps. 103:5; Isa. 40:31; the proposed reading is just possible (cf. *JBL*, LVII (1938), p. 211).

my heart exults: (cf. 1 Sam. 2:1), or 'I am very glad' because Yahweh has sided with me (cf. 5:11 (M.T. 12)).

with my song: this is either the thanksgiving which will accompany the thank-offering, or it may refer to the present Psalm.

8. the strength of his people: lit. 'their strength', or 'a strength unto his people' (*RVm*). *RSV* and *NEB* follow some Hebrew MSS., LXX and S in reading *leᶜammô* ('to his people') for M.T. *lāmô* ('to them') (cf. 29:11). This verse may allude to Exod. 15:2.

the saving refuge of his anointed: or, perhaps, 'refuge' should be taken with the previous line (so also Dahood), rendering verse 8: 'Yahweh is the strength of his people and (their) stronghold (see on 27:1), the salvation of his anointed is he'. Dahood (*PAB*, I, p. 173) takes 'salvation', not as an abstract plural but as a plural of majesty, with the meaning of 'Saviour'.

His anointed is usually regarded as the reigning King (see on 2:2), but some have suggested that the reference is either to the High Priest or to the people as a whole (cf. 105:15; Hab. 3:13).

9. save thy people: (=*NEB*) or 'give victory to your people'. The actual meaning depends, of course, upon the situation out of which the Psalm has arisen or to which it is applied.

bless thy heritage: or 'grant happiness to your special possession, (to your people)' (cf. 1QM xii:11; Yadin, *SWSLSD*, p. 318). This is a petition to God to manifest his favour and goodness to his nation and to all that is theirs (see Dt. 7:12–16). God's heritage or possession, in this case, is the people of Israel. So in 1 Kg. 8:35: 'For thou didst separate them from among all the peoples of the earth, to be thy heritage . . .' (cf. 1 Sam. 10:1). Also the land of Israel can be described as Yahweh's heritage (cf. 79:1).

be . . . their shepherd: or 'feed them'; see on 23:1.

carry them for ever: this is a continuation of the picture of the shepherd of Israel. See Isa. 40:11, where Yahweh is described as a shepherd, gathering the lambs in his arms and carrying them in his bosom.

Psalm 29 Hymn to the Awesome Majesty of God

This Psalm is clearly a Hymn (see Introduction, pp. 32ff.) in praise of the greatness and power of Yahweh. Weiser (*POTL*, p. 261) describes it as a 'theophany psalm' which was the 'hymnic response to the appearance and revelation of God at the climax of the festival cult'. According to the LXX addition (*exodiou skēnēs*, '(belonging to) the finale of the Feast of Tabernacles'), the Psalm was sung on the last day of the great Autumnal Harvest Festival, while according to the Talmudic tradition it belonged to the Feast of Weeks (see Introduction, p. 52). Most modern scholars associate Ps. 29 with the Feast of Tabernacles, which may have included as one of its aspects the so-called New Year Festival. Due to the references to Yahweh's kingship and other related themes, some commentators have linked this hymn with the ceremony of the *enthronement* of Yahweh; but this point is rather dubious.

The Psalm contains a sevenfold repetition of the phrase 'the voice of Yahweh', and consequently Delitzsch has entitled the poem as the 'Psalm of Seven Thunders'. This phrase is, obviously, a keyword in the Psalm, but it is not certain that the number seven has any special significance. It is not impossible that the mention of the voice of Yahweh brought to the minds of the Israelites the concept of the Word of Yahweh, so powerful and diverse.

Most commentators regard this Psalm as one of the oldest in the whole Psalter, and in recent years it has been customary to stress the similarities between this poem and the Ugaritic literature (as well as other Near Eastern parallels). It was H. L. Ginsberg who first suggested that Ps. 29 was an ancient Canaanite hymn to Baal, which was adapted to suit Israelite worship (for references on this subject, see Johnson, *SKAI*, p. 54, n.2. Cf. also H. Strauss, *ZAW*, LXXXII (1970), pp. 91–102; B. Margulis, *Biblica*, LI (1970), pp. 332–48.) It seems quite likely that the pattern and metaphors of this hymn were provided by a Baal-Hadad song which extolled the might of the Phoenician storm god. Psalm 29 is often dated *c.* 10th cent. B.C., and this may be a reasonable estimate; Deissler (*PWdB*, I, p. 116) *et al.* place the Psalm in the post-Exilic period, because its thought and vocabulary have many points of contact with the prophetic literature.

The Psalm consists of three main parts. Verses 1–2 form the characteristic introduction to the hymn, summoning the heavenly host to pay homage to Yahweh. The main section, or corpus, of the hymn comprises verses 3–9, which depict the majestic power of God and his awe-inspiring epiphany described in terms of a violent thunderstorm. Verses 10–11 supply the conclusion, but it is possible that this section begins with verse 9*c* which is an echo of the introduction (verses 1–2). The Psalm ends with an intercession for the people of God, and it may be a later addition.

The metre of the Psalm is irregular, and a similar feature is not unusual also in the Ugaritic poems.

A Psalm of David: see Introduction, pp. 43ff. and 46.

THE CALL TO PRAISE YAHWEH **1–2**

1. Ascribe to the LORD: lit. 'Give . . .' (*AV*, *RV*; cf. 115:1). This exhortation urges the heavenly beings to recognize and to extol the might of Yahweh. The object of the verb is supplied in the second line—'glory and honour'. This ascription of majesty to God reminds us of Isa. 6:3, where the cry of the seraphim was

'Holy, holy, holy is the LORD of hosts'. In the Babylonian creation epic, Marduk is extolled by the other gods who recount his fifty names (see *ANET*, pp. 69b–72b). In a sense, all this praise involves also a declaration (or renewal) of allegiance. Verse 1 is reminiscent of the Ugaritic El-tradition, and it serves as an example of the way in which Yahwism was able to adapt many characteristics of El and Baal, and yet remain victorious over syncretism (cf. Vriezen, *RAI*, p. 170; W. H. Schmidt, *Königtum Gottes in Ugarit und Israel*, 2nd edn (*BZAW*, 80, 1966), pp. 26f.)

heavenly beings: or 'sons of gods' (*RSVm*); *NEB* 'gods'. The exact translation of *bᵉnê ʾēlîm* is not clear, but this and similar phrases are also found in Gen. 6:2,4; Dt. 32:8 (LXX); Job 1:6, 2:1, 38:7; Ps. 82:6, 89:6 (M.T. 7); in 1QH fg. ii:3 it probably refers to angels. There is little doubt that in the *OT* Yahweh is God (cf. Johnson, *OMICG*, pp. 22ff.), while all other heavenly beings are but his messengers or servants subordinate to him. None of them is equal to him, as in 89:6: 'For who in the skies can be compared to the LORD? Who among the heavenly beings is like the LORD . . .'. In the Ugaritic texts 'the sons of El' were the minor deities of the pantheon but nevertheless they were gods (cf. *Baal* II, iii:13, IV, i:3). It is possible that the 'heavenly beings' (or 'the sons of God' or '. . . of gods') in this verse is a 'demythologized' form of the assemblies of gods, such as are found in the Babylonian and Canaanite myths (cf. H. W. Robinson, 'The Council of Yahweh', *JTS*, XLIV (1943), pp. 151–7). 'The sons of God' can sometimes mean 'stars' (cf. W. F. Albright, *From the Stone Age to Christianity* (1957), p. 296), as in Job 38:7, but also the stars can be regarded as divine beings (cf. Dt. 4:19). In various Near Eastern cults the stars were important deities (cf. 2 Kg. 17:16, 21:3), but in the *OT* they were relegated to the ranks of Yahweh's celestial attendants (Isa. 40:26). It should be noted, as pointed out by Vriezen (*OOTT*, p. 180), that the idea of heavenly beings does not detract from the uniqueness of Yahweh, but rather emphasizes it. The reason why these divine beings (and not the people of God) are called to praise him, may be found in the Psalmist's view that human language is inadequate to describe the glory of God (cf. Weiser, *POTL*, p. 262); or it is possible that the author of this Psalm simply followed the prototype.

The whole Psalm serves to emphasize the majesty of Yahweh. That mere human beings should praise him is not very surprising; but when all the heavenly hosts and even the stars join in singing his praise, then indeed God has no equal. LXX and V add after verse 1*a* the phrase 'bring (i.e. offer) to Yahweh young rams', but this seems to be an alternative (and inferior) interpretation of the preceding line.

glory and strength: i.e. the glorious manifestation of God's power in nature (cf. 96:7).

2. the glory of his name: i.e. the glory (see on 57:5) due to his name (cf. 66:2, 79:9) or to himself.

worship: or 'bow down'. The Hebrew verb is apparently derived from *ḥ-w-y* (and not from *š-ḥ-w*), with the prefix *hišt-* (cf. M. H. Pope, *Job* (*AB* 15, 1965), p. 16). This worship involved an act of prostrating before the person honoured (cf. Gen. 33:3; 1 Sam. 20:41; Ps. 72:11; *ANEP*, pl. 355). In the letters from Tell El-Amarna the vassals of the Pharaoh speak of falling down at the feet of the King 'seven times and seven times' (cf. *DOTT*, pp. 39, 43).

in holy array: or 'at (his) holy theophany' (cf. *Keret* I, iii:51; H. H. Guthrie, jr., *Israel's Sacred Songs* (1966), p. 75). Weiser renders this phrase: 'when he appears in his sanctuary' (*POTL*, p. 259). See on 96:9; W. H. Schmidt, op. cit., p. 56; H. Donner, 'Ugaritismen in der Psalmenforschung', *ZAW*, LXXIX (1967), pp. 324–7.

THE THEOPHANY OF YAHWEH **3–9**

3. The voice of the LORD: i.e. thunderclap (cf. Exod. 9:23; Job 37:4f.; Ps. 18:13 (M.T. 14); Isa. 30:30). Some exegetes have argued that 'voice' (*ḳôl*) is to be understood as an interjection: 'hark' (so Kissane) or 'hear' (cf. E. Vogt, 'Der Aufbau von Ps 29', *Biblica*, XLI (1960), p. 17); this is possible, and it would make Yahweh the subject of the verbs in verses 3–9. Also in the Ugaritic texts 'thunder' is understood as the voice of the deity (i.e. that of Baal); cf. *Baal* II, v:8–9: '. . . and he will utter his voice in the clouds, his flashing (and) lightnings on the earth' (Driver, *CML*, p. 97). Dahood (*PAB*, I, p. 176) has pointed out that thunder could be regarded not only as the voice of Baal but also as that of El.

upon the waters: this could mean either the Mediterranean Sea or the waters of the primeval flood (see verse 10; Jer. 10:13, 51:16); it is less likely that the reference is to the rain clouds (so Kirkpatrick). Dahood suggests that in the original Canaanite setting this phrase would have meant 'against the waters', being an allusion to Baal's fight against the Sea (cf. *Baal* III* A). Perhaps we should also read in this verse 'against the waters'; the new rainy season could be regarded as a sign of Yahweh's primeval victory over the waters of Chaos, and of his mastery over the whole realm of nature.

the God of glory: or 'the most glorious God' (cf. 24:7; Ac. 7:2). Verse 3*b* probably belongs after verse 7.

upon many waters: or '. . . the great (or 'mighty') waters' (cf. H. G. May, 'Some Cosmic Connotations of *Mayim Rabbîm*, "Many Waters",' *JBL*, LXXIV (1955), pp. 9–21). This may be a pointer to Yahweh's triumph over the cosmic waters (cf. 93:3), although the immediate reference is, apparently, to the flood over which was firmly established Yahweh's palace or heavenly dwelling.

4. is powerful: i.e. manifests itself in power (taking the preposition as a *bêṯ essentiae*, cf. *GK* 119i), or *bakkōaḥ* could be rendered as '. . . is strength itself' (i.e. b^e is regarded as an emphasizing particle; so Dahood, *PAB*, I, p. 177).

is full of majesty: lit. 'is with (or 'in') majesty'. Perhaps we should translate '(shows itself) in majesty' or '. . . is majesty itself' (see above).

5. . . . breaks the cedars: i.e. if a causal link is intended, then the lightning and its effects are attributed to the thunder, or it simply means that if the *voice* of Yahweh has such awesome effects, then how much more terrifying must be his actual intervention.

cedars of Lebanon: see on 37:35. The cedar was the prince of trees (so Tristram), and its strength and durability as well as its grandeur were proverbial. Lebanon and Anti-Lebanon were the two mountain ranges dominating Syria; sometimes 'Lebanon' denotes the adjoining regions (cf. Jos. 13:5). The mountain range itself is some 100 miles long, reaching in places the height of some 10,000 feet or more. The term 'Lebanon' may be derived from *l-b-n* ('to be white'), and the connexion could be either the greyish limestone which often forms the upper layer of the mountain range, or the snow-covered peaks.

6. The collocation of Lebanon and Sirion, the Phoenician name of Mt. Hermon (according to Dt. 3:9) makes a well-known pair which is mentioned also in *Baal* II, iv:18–21. Some have suggested that 'Sirion' is the name of the Anti-Lebanon (so Perowne, Calès, Gordon, *et al.*), of which Mt. Hermon forms a part. The word-picture of this verse is nearly grotesque: the

massive mountains are pictured as skipping and leaping like frightened calves; yet it makes its point.
he makes . . . to skip: lit. 'he makes them to skip' (similarly *AV*, *RV*) but the Hebrew verbal suffix (*m*), here translated by 'them', may well be an enclitic letter, as assumed by *RSV* (cf. Dahood, *PAB*, I, p. 178). See 114:4.

7. Dahood (*PAB*, I, p. 178) places this verse before verse 6, but it is equally probable that verse 3*b* should follow verse 7 (cf. Kraus, *PBK*, p. 237). It is also possible that a line could easily have been omitted due to a homoioteleuton, a scribal error of omission where the eye of the copyist has 'jumped' a word, or any number of words, found between two identical (or similar) words (cf. B. J. Roberts, *The Old Testament Text and Versions* (1951), p. 96).
flashes forth: or 'cleaves'. The 'flames of fire' (probably a poetic description of the lightnings) may be the object of the verb (so Kissane, Johnson) or the phrase could be an accusative of means.

8. Weiser sees in this verse a link with the Sinai tradition, and locates 'Kadesh' on the way from Egypt to Palestine. Yet in the Ugaritic texts we find a reference to *mdbr qdš* (cf. *Shachar and Shalim* ii:31; Driver, *CML*, pp. 124, 125) which can hardly mean the wilderness near Kadesh Barnea, S. of Judah. Ginsberg renders it by 'Syrian desert' (in the vicinity of Kadesh on the Orontes?) which is far more likely (cf. Driver, *CML*, p. 125, n.3). Probably the same meaning should be assigned to the 'wilderness of Kadesh' in verse 8, since the geographical setting of this Psalm is Syria.
. . . shakes the wilderness: or, perhaps, 'makes the wilderness tremble (in fear)'; the verb is used in this sense in 96:9, 97:4, 114:7. The description probably refers to the animals and vegetation (?) of this particular steppe, which is not a literal desert, but primarily a 'land without permanent settlements' (Dahood, *PAB*, I, p. 178).

9. makes the oaks to whirl: the *RSV* rendering is a well-established emendation, while M.T. could be rendered 'makes the hinds to calve' (similarly *NEB*), i.e. they bring forth their young prematurely. It does not follow that the hinds were particularly susceptible to this predicament, but they simply represent all female animals as *pars pro toto*. The 'oaks' (*RSV*) provides a better parallel to the 'forests' (verse 9*b*) but, on the other hand, the parallelism is not always strictly synonymous. It is possible to translate verse 9*b*: 'and he causes premature birth of kids' (cf. *NEB*) reading *way*^{e}*ḥaśśēp̱* for M.T. *wayyeḥ*^{e}*śōp̱*; cf. G. R. Driver, *JTS*, XXXII (1930–1), pp. 255f.

Verse 9*c* may well belong to the conclusion of the Psalm (so Kraus), or we may assume that the abrupt transition from verse 9*b* to 9*c* is due to a scribal omission.

in his temple: i.e. in Yahweh's heavenly dwelling (cf. 11:4; Mic. 1:2). This takes us back to the beginning of the Psalm which envisaged the heavenly assembly praising the glorious King. Consequently some commentators suppose that verse 9*c* was preceded by a line stating how the sons of God (verse 1) acclaimed Yahweh (cf. H. H. Guthrie, jr, op. cit., p. 79), but obviously we can only speculate.

all cry: or 'everyone says' (so Kissane), but it is probable that 'all' refers to the Temple, i.e. in his *whole* Temple (they) utter the shout 'Glory' (cf. 19:1 (M.T. 2), 150:1; Isa. 6:3).

THE CONCLUSION TO THE HYMN **10–11**

10. The LORD sits enthroned . . .: cf. *Baal* IV, iii:14 (*CML*, p. 118a); *Keret* II, vi:24 (*CML*, p. 45b). For the kingship of Yahweh, see on 24:7, 93:1.

over the flood: Dahood (*PAB*, I, p. 180) suggests 'from the flood', taking the preposition *l*^{e} in a temporal sense. This would balance 'from eternity' (*RSV* 'for ever'), i.e. from the primeval time (verse 10*b*), and would draw attention to Yahweh's victory over the waters of Chaos (cf. 93:3f.). The word *mabbûl* ('flood') is used in the *OT* of the deluge in Noah's time (Gen. 7–8), and therefore it has been suggested that *mabbûl* has a similar meaning also in this verse. The underlying thought may be that as Yahweh was King then, so he will be King for ever (cf. Weiser, *POTL*, p. 265). It is possible that the 'flood' is synonymous with the waters above the firmament (cf. Gen. 1:7; Ps. 148:4) in which were laid the foundations of Yahweh's palace or temple; cf. 104:3; E. Vogt, p. 22.

11. Some interpreters (e.g. Gunkel) have suggested that this verse is a later, patriotic addition, expressing a prayerful wish for the welfare of the people. This may be, however, an integral part of the Psalm. Yahweh, who is so powerful and majestic, is also the God of Israel, his people, and therefore they can base their hopes for their welfare on him. Yahweh's lordship over the whole of nature means that he is indeed able to care effectively for his people, and that he *can* provide the seasonal rains that are so indispensable for the prosperity of the nation. Therefore the Psalm would fit well into the setting of the great Autumnal Festival.

bless his people: i.e. grant happiness and welfare to his people, or simply prosper them. Delitzsch has well remarked that the Psalm begins with: '*Gloria in excelsis*' and ends with 'peace on earth' (*pax in terris*) (*BCP*, I, p. 373). For the verb *b-r-k*, 'to bless', see on 67:1. *Šālôm* ('peace') is discussed on 119:165, 147:14.

Psalm 30 His Anger is but for a Moment

The strongly personal terms of this Psalm suggest that it is a Thanksgiving of the Individual or a Declarative Psalm of Praise of one who has been restored from a serious but unspecified illness. The title, on the other hand, states that it was used as a communal song at the dedication of the Temple. Most exegetes have little doubt that this explanatory note, 'A Song at the dedication of the Temple', is a later addition which intrudes awkwardly between 'A Psalm' and 'of David' (see M.T.). It seems that some time after the composition of this poem, it was re-intrepreted and understood in terms of the people as a whole.

This 'dedication of the Temple' is generally thought to be the same event as the purification of the Temple in the time of Judas Maccabaeus (cf. 1 Mac. 4:42–60), *c.* 164 B.C. (cf. F. F. Bruce, *Israel and the Nations* (1963), pp. 152f.). It is unlikely that the reference is to the dedication of the site of the future Temple by David, or to the re-consecration of David's palace after Absalom's revolt, although the re-dedication of the second Temple in the sixth century B.C. (cf. Kirkpatrick, *BPCB*, p. 151) is a possible alternative; it would mark the restoration of the nation from the deadly grip of the Babylonian Exile.

Thus it seems that after 164 B.C. the life-setting of the Psalm was the Feast of Dedication, or *Hanukkah* (for a brief discussion of this festival and for relevant references, see Kraus, *WI*, pp. 88ff.); before this date it may well have accompanied the thanksgiving sacrifices offered by men who had been brought back from the door of death. Although the poem must have been composed before 164 B.C., there is no clear indication whether its origin is to be sought in the pre-Exilic or early post-Exilic period.

The structure of the Psalm is not easy to determine but it could be divided into three parts. Verses 1–3 extol Yahweh for healing the singer and for delivering him from death. This leads the author to exhort the faithful to praise God for his unfailing favours (verses 4–5). In the third part (verses 6–12) the writer gives a detailed description of his past experiences, and he concludes his song with a praise and thanks, which are the characteristics of a life lived in dependence upon God.
A Psalm of David: see Introduction, pp. 43ff. and 46.
. . . the dedication of the Temple: see above.

THE PRAISE TO GOD FOR HEALING **1–3**

1. I will extol thee is a hymnic introduction. To extol or exalt Yahweh means to recognize him as the Exalted One in all his graciousness (cf. Isa. 25:1). To extol and to thank go together: God exalts men by reversing their misfortune and by prospering them, while men can only exalt God by realizing that he is the source of their blessing, and by declaring this to their brethren.
for thou hast drawn me up: this gives a brief summary of the deliverance which God has wrought in the Psalmist's life, and provides the reason for exalting God. The verb *d-l-h*, 'to draw up', can also be used of drawing water from a well (cf. Exod. 2:16,19); one of its cognates is *d^{e}lî* ('bucket') (cf. Isa. 40:15). In this verse the implied 'well' is the 'Pit' (verse 3) which is a synonym of the underworld.
my foes: this is taken by Dahood (*PAB*, 1, p. 182) as a plural of excellence, denoting 'Death', the foe *par excellence*. Yet the traditional reading seems more likely; the writer probably had in mind those fellow men of his who had misinterpreted his illness as a divine punishment for sin, and who had rejoiced at this supposed unmasking of a dangerous hypocrite (cf. 38:16 (M.T. 17); Lam. 2:17). Also Job's 'friends' could be described as enemies, for they offered to him, in the hour of his greatest distress, a devastating criticism instead of sympathy. Even if their criticism were right, the unfortunate man might not always survive such shock tactics, or find them helpful.

2. thou hast healed me: Yahweh alone is the great healer (see Exod. 15:26). The Israelites believed that both sickness and health came from God, as in Dt. 32:39: 'I kill and I make alive; I wound and I heal . . .', and therefore the sick person came to God for help. Any healing or 'medical treatment' would be done within the context of dependence upon Yahweh (cf. 2 Kg. 20:1–7; Sir. 38:1–8). To seek other help, outside the sphere of Yahweh's influence, as in 2 Kg. 1:2–8, was a sign of disloyalty. It was a common belief that there existed a close connexion between sin and disease but, as the example of Job clearly shows, the relationship between the two was not always apparent to human beings. Roughly speaking, sin brings disease and misfortune in its train, but not every illness and tragedy is the result of the sufferer's *own* actions, although many were tempted to argue along these lines. See also 107:20.

3. The experience of illness is tantamount to being in Sheol or in the netherworld, and therefore healing can be described as a deliverance from the underworld. Sheol was not so much a geographical location as a sphere of influence: wherever one finds the characteristics of Sheol, such as weakness, disease, misery, forsakenness, etc., there is Sheol also. The stricken man's experience of the underworld is partial, but it is none the less very real. Unless he was rescued from this situation by God, he would become fully dead and not simply '*like* the slain' (88:5 (M.T.6)). For those who are actually dead, Sheol is their home for ever (49:11 (M.T. 12); Job 30:23), and they can no longer share in the life of the living (see on 40:2).

my soul: i.e. 'me' and not some immortal part of me (cf. R. Laurin, 'The Concept of Man as a Soul', *ET*, LXXII (1961), pp. 131–4; and W. D. Stacey, 'Man as a Soul', vol. cit., 1961, pp. 349f.). See on 33:19.

Sheol: see on 6:5, 88:3.

restored me to life: i.e. to a full life or existence which is not marked by God-forsakenness (the essence of the Sheol-existence). In a sense 'any weakness in life is a form of "death"' (A. R. Johnson, 'Jonah 2:3–10: a study in Cultic Phantasy', *Studies in Old Testament Prophecy*, ed. by H. H. Rowley (1950), p. 98). Thus life and death are often used by the *OT* writers in a relative sense; so H. Birkeland ('The Belief in the Resurrection of the Dead in the O.T.', *ST*, III (1949), p. 70) suggests that life and death are the positive and negative aspects of existence, respectively. See also on 119:25.

Pit is another name for Sheol (see on 28:1). The *RSV* rendering 'from among those gone down to the Pit' follows the *Keṯîḇ* variant and most of the ancient versions (reading *miyyôreḏê*), while the *Kerê* has *miyyoreḏî* ('from my going down to . . .'), similarly T,

Jerome, *AV*, *et al.* The former rendering seems more likely (cf. 28:1).

THE INVITATION TO PRAISE GOD 4–5

4. **Sing praises:** this is a characteristic call to praise, the object of which can be the acts of God in history and in nature, as well as the helping deeds of Yahweh both in the life of the individual and in that of the nation.

his saints are those who have experienced God's redeeming grace and who have been loyal to God in terms defined by the Covenant relationship (cf. 86:2). The term *ḥāsîḏ* is a familiar word in the Psalter (occuring some 25 times); frequently the emphasis is on the favours received rather than on the loyalty rendered, although the latter is obviously presupposed (145:10). In this verse 'his saints' may refer to the fellow-worshippers who were the witnesses to the Psalmist's thanksgiving to God, and who probably took part in the sacral meal which followed (cf. 22:22–26 (M.T. 23–27), 35:18, 40:9 (M.T. 10), 116:14). The deliverance of Yahweh is not purely a private affair between God and man, but the glad news is also to be shared by his people.

his holy name: i.e. God himself; lit. 'the remembrance of his holiness' (*AV*, *RP*). The *RSV* rendering is more plausible, and it is supported by cases where *zēḵer* ('remembrance') is parallel to *šēm* ('name'), as in Exod. 3:15; Job 18:17; Ps. 135:13; Prov. 10:7; Isa. 26:8. See also Childs, *MTI*, pp. 70-3.

5. Weiser (*POTL*, pp. 269f.) has well stated that this verse does not minimize God's wrath but rather shows that its motivation is the desire to help a man to give up his ways of sin and error. The primary purpose of the divine anger is to teach the wayward, and not to destroy them.

For his anger is but for a moment: this is rendered by Dahood (*PAB*, I, p. 182) 'For death is in his anger'. This interpretation of *rega*ᶜ (*RSV* 'moment') may be implied by the corresponding term 'life' in the antithetic parallelism. It is not impossible that *rega*ᶜ is a synonym of 'death', in as far as it suggests what is transient and changes suddenly. LXX (similarly also S and V) reads: 'For anger is in his wrath' (*rōgez* (?) for *rega*ᶜ). *NEB* has 'In his anger is disquiet'. It is unlikely that 'life' (*ḥayyîm*) in this verse means 'eternal life' (so Dahood); see on 21:4.

Weeping may tarry for the night . . .: or 'In the evening one settles down crying, but in the morning there are shouts of joy'.

This seems to suggest the suddenness of God's help (cf. Isa. 17:14), and therefore it may lend some weight to the *RSV* translation of verse 5*a*. Some scholars (e.g. Gunkel, Kraus) delete, with some justification, the verb *yālîn* ('tarry'). Dahood (*PAB*, I, p. 181) takes this same verb as 'to fall asleep' (i.e. die) and in the word 'morning' (*bōḳer*) he sees an allusion to immortality or resurrection. This interpretation is, however, rather forced, and therefore unlikely.

A REVIEW OF THE PAST EXPERIENCE **6–12**

6. in my prosperity: i.e. in the state of affluence the Psalmist had lost sight of the Giver of all prosperity. Dt. 8:11–20 envisages a similar situation: the Israelites are told to beware lest they become too self-confident in their good fortune so that they forget God who had blessed them. There is often the temptation to interpret the blessings of God as exclusively human achievements and the net result is ingratitude which opens the way to apostasy (cf. Dt. 32:15; Dan. 4:28–37).

I shall never be moved: this may be either a description of the arrogant man's confidence, or an account of the righteous man's faith in the divine promises (see 10:6; also 15:5, 16:8, 21:7 (M.T. 8), 62:2 (M.T. 3)). In this verse the reference is to the former alternative.

7. The writer realizes that his welfare is entirely in the hands of God, who 'makes poor and makes rich' (1 Sam. 2:7).

established me as a strong mountain: the M.T. of this phrase is difficult, and this is reflected in the great variety of the renderings, both ancient and modern. Dahood (*PAB*, I, p. 181) suggests: 'you made me more stable than the mighty mountains'. 'The mighty mountains' is a possible translation, and it is confirmed by T, while the preposition *l*ᵉ may be taken in a comparative sense, and the pronoun 'me' is supplied on the basis of the context. For other possible emendations, see Kraus, *PBK*, p. 240. *NEB* has 'But, LORD, it was thy will to shake my mountain refuge'.

thou didst hide thy face: this is either a temporal clause ('then (or 'when') you hid . . .') (cf. *PNT*), or a hypothetical one (so Briggs). The phrase is a picturesque expression of displeasure and of the withdrawal of the divine favour.

I was dismayed: i.e. my whole existence was threatened. So in 90:7: '. . . we are consumed by thy anger; by thy wrath we are overwhelmed' (i.e. utterly dismayed). Cf. Jg. 20:41; 2 Sam. 4:1; Ps. 6:2,3 (M.T. 3, 4), 83:17 (M.T. 18).

8. I cried . . . made supplication represent Hebrew imperfects, which may suggest frequentative actions or be equivalent to historic presents giving a vivid description of the supplications in progress. Gunkel (*PGHAT*, p. 129) describes the tenses as 'poetic aorists'. For the verb *ḥ-n-n* ('to make supplication'), see on 142:1.

9. What profit is there in my death: this is usually taken to mean that it is to the advantage of Yahweh to preserve the life of the sufferer. Taylor (*PIB*, p. 161) suggests that to 'the ancient mind a god with none to praise him was an extinct deity', but it is unlikely that this was the Psalmist's own view. It is possible that 'my death' (lit. 'my blood') means 'imperilled life' (as in 2 Sam. 23:17; 1 Chr. 11:19) and that the question amounts to 'What advantage do I gain if I imperil my life (by an arrogant and self-confident attitude to life)' (see verses 6–7). His only achievement would be a premature death or descent into Sheol, and there he would be for ever outside the care of God. The point is not that God would lose one of his songsters who would praise his name, but rather that God does not perform his saving miracles in the land of forgetfulness (88:10ff. (M.T. 11ff.); Isa. 38:18). Therefore the chastised man turns to God while there is yet time.
the Pit: (*šaḥaṯ*) see on 49:9.
dust is either the 'grave' (so Kirkpatrick, Cohen; cf. 22:15,29 (M.T. 16, 30)) or 'my dead body' (or 'those whose bodies have turned to dust'). Perhaps it simply means 'those who dwell in the dust', i.e. the dwellers of the underworld (cf. 88:10 (M.T. 11), 115:17; Isa. 38:18); see on 119:25.
thy faithfulness: or 'thy truth' (*AV*, *RV*, *NEB*); see on 25:5. The dead appear to be outside the Covenant relationship with God (cf. 88:11 (M.T. 12)), but it does not follow that Sheol is under the jurisdiction of another deity. Yahweh has given no promises to the dead to which they might appeal (cf. G. Quell, '*Alētheia*', *TDNT*, I, p. 236).

10. be thou my helper for there is no other deliverer. Cf. 54:4 (M.T. 6).

11. The verbs of this verse are renderings of the Hebrew perfects. The *RSV* translation implies that the prayer has been answered and that the divine favour has become manifested in the change of the visible fortunes of the Psalmist. Dahood (*PAB*, I, p. 184) takes the verbs as precative perfects expressing wishes, but *RSV* seems preferable, since the Psalm is a thanksgiving for the deliverance already experienced.

dancing: (*māḥôl*) was one of the ways of expressing rejoicing. It could be used to celebrate a national victory (1 Sam. 18:6), or to express joy at the time of the annual festivals (Jg. 21:19ff.); it could be used at worship in general, as in 149:3, 150:4. See on 87:7.

sackcloth was a garb or symbol of penitence and mourning. It was usually made of goat's hair, and was dark in colour. Sometimes it was in the form of a loin-cloth (cf. 1 Kg. 20:31f.; Isa. 3:24, 20:2) and was worn next to the skin (2 Kg. 6:30), but there is no indication that it caused great physical discomfort. At other times it may have been rectangular in form, like a sack, with openings for head and arms (cf. 2 Kg. 19:1f.; Ps. 69:11 (M.T. 12)).

12. my soul: lit. 'my glory'. Most commentators assume that this reading is due to a confusion between *kāḇôḏ* ('glory'; LXX has 'my glory') and *kāḇēḏ* ('liver'). In any case, the term would be a circumlocution for 'I' (see on 7:5). The pronoun 'my' may be presupposed from the context, and Dahood (*PAB*, I, p. 184) suggests that as in Ugaritic, so also in Hebrew, the pronominal suffixes (i.e. personal pronouns) with the names of parts of the body are sometimes omitted.

I will give thanks to thee: this is a recognition of God's help and a declaration of what he has done for his servant. The emphasis is, to some extent, upon what God has given rather than upon what man has received (see on 18:49).

Psalm 31 INTO YOUR HAND I COMMIT MY SPIRIT

In many ways Ps. 31 is a problematic song, and even its *Gattung* or psalm-type is not easy to determine. It contains a number of different elements such as lamentation (verses 9–13), expressions of trust (verses 3, 5, 14–15), thanksgiving (verses 7–8, 19–20), etc.; and consequently some scholars have suggested that the Psalm is a composite work. Taylor (*PIB*, pp. 162f.) sees Ps. 31 as a combination of three different laments: a 'protecting psalm' (verses 1–8), a lament of a sick man (verses 9–12), and a lamentation of an unjustly accused person (verses 13–18). Verses 19–24 contain a thanksgiving for the deliverance from such troubles as are mentioned in the three laments.

H. Schmidt (*PHAT*, pp. 57f.) regards the Psalm as consisting of two parallel but independent prayers (so also Leslie, Rhodes), in verses 1–8 and 9–24. It is possible that this collocation of two seemingly independent laments is intentional; the first one offers a shorter version of the writer's experiences, while the second one gives a more detailed account of the distress, and the subsequent thanksgiving (cf. Kraus, *PBK*, p. 247). Consequently the composition may be a literary unity (see also Ps. 18, 30, 102).

Most scholars describe this Psalm as a Lamentation (see Introduction, pp. 37ff.), or as a prayer of lamentation and thanksgiving; the transition from the former to the latter could be attributed to an oracle of hope, delivered after verse 18. It is equally possible that the Psalm may be a Thanksgiving of the Individual (see Introduction, pp. 35f.) *after* his prayers have been answered; the lamentation would simply describe the distress from which he had been delivered. This seems reasonable because even individual thanksgiving was a public affair, in that the delivered man uttered his gratitude to God before his fellow-worshippers. Consequently a vivid account of the past afflictions and troubles would be as important as the thanksgiving itself.

Eaton (*PTBC*, p. 93) thinks that this poem may have been used 'by or for the Davidic king or a similar representative'. The date of the Psalm is uncertain. The earlier commentators used to assign it to David, and the same view is suggested by the LXX addition to the title of the Psalm: *ekstaseōs* which probably means '(written in time of) extreme fear', and which may allude to some incident in David's life. Since there are certain similarities between this Psalm and other *OT* writings, especially the Book of Jeremiah, Kirkpatrick (*BPCB*, p. 155) argues that the author may have been Jeremiah or some other prophet. These similarities do not, however, demand a direct dependence or a common authorship; the various authors may well have drawn upon a common liturgical language.

The metre of this Psalm is varied.

the choirmaster: see Introduction, p. 48.

A Psalm of David: see Introduction, pp. 43ff. and 46.

THE TRUST IN GOD **1–8**

1. I seek refuge: this is a well-known theme in the Psalter (see on 7:1, 16:1) and a familiar beginning of a lament. Verses 1–3*a* are practically identical with 71:1–3, but it is generally thought that Ps. 31 is more likely to be original. The idea of seeking refuge in Yahweh may suggest that the Psalmist had sought asylum in the sanctuary according to the age-old custom (cf. Exod. 21:12ff.; 1 Kg. 1:50), or this expression is to be taken in a spiritual sense (cf. Isa. 57:13).

let me never be put to shame: see on 25:2. 'Never' (*leᶜôlām*), lit. 'for ever', may mean 'as long as I live' (cf. Exod. 21:6). Dahood (*PAB*, I, p. 187) takes *leᶜôlām* as a divine name in the vocative, i.e. 'O Eternal One'; the preposition *le* would be employed to denote the vocative case (see on 3:8).

in thy righteousness: J. Lindblom (*Prophecy in Ancient Israel* (1962), p. 382) defines it as God's 'faithfulness to the Covenant and the obligation that He has imposed upon Himself by virtue of the covenant'. Some exegetes add at the end of verse 1 the phrase 'and save me' (*wehaṣṣîlēnî*), following LXX and 71:2.

2. Incline thy ear: i.e. 'hear (and answer my prayer)' (as in 102:2).

rescue me speedily: this stresses the urgency of the situation. Ps. 71:2 omits 'speedily', while Sperber (*HGBH*, p. 660) reads, 'make haste to deliver me', taking the Hebrew *mehērāh* (*RSV* 'speedily') as an imperative.

a rock of refuge: or 'my strong rock' (*RP*), i.e. a rock which is like a stronghold in itself (so Perowne). Ps. 71:3 reads 'a sheltering rock' (i.e. *māᶜôn* ('dwelling') for M.T. *māᶜôz* ('refuge')) but this seems less likely. Dahood (*PAB*, I, p. 187) regards this phrase, as well as 'strong fortress', as divine names used in the vocative. For 'rock' (*ṣûr*), see on 18:2, 42:9; and for 'refuge' (*māᶜôz*), see on 27:1.

3. Yea, thou art my rock . . .: this is an expression of trust. The Hebrew *selaᶜ* ('rock') is merely a synonym of *ṣûr* (see verse 2). **my fortress** is the same noun as in verse 2*b* (see on 18:2). All these divine titles in verses 2–3 serve to characterize God as one who provides safety and protection for those who seek refuge in him (cf. 1QH ix:28).

for thy name's sake: i.e. true to your own self-revelation (cf. 23:3, 106:8).

lead me . . . guide me may be an assertion of the author's confidence in God rather than a petition (as in *RSV*). Only divine guidance and protection can prevent him from ever being put to shame (cf. verse 1). Perhaps the allusion is to Yahweh as the Shepherd, as in 23:1ff. (cf. Wellhausen, *PBP*, p. 177).

4. take me out of the net: or 'you will free me . . .' (so Dahood, *PAB*, I, p. 185). For 'net' (*rešeṯ*), see on 9:15. Here it is a metaphor of present or impending trouble. The enemies are pictured as hunters seeking to catch their victim by means of hidden nets (cf. Isa. 51:20; Ezek. 19:8).

my refuge: see on 27:1. LXX adds 'O Yahweh' (cf. Calès, *LP*, I, p. 342).

5. The first part of this verse has been made immortal by Jesus, who used these words to express his self-committal to God, in the hour of his death (Lk. 23:46), and they have been repeated by many of his followers in similar circumstances. In our Psalm these words do not refer to an impending death but to the preservation of the life of the Psalmist. They are not an expression of 'aquiescent fatalism' but an affirmation of faith and trust.

my spirit: better, 'my life' or simply 'me'. The Psalmist entrusts himself to Yahweh who has redeemed him from his distress. Gunkel takes the verb 'redeemed' as a perfect of certainty, implying that the deliverance is yet to come although the writer has no doubts about it. It is more likely, however, that the salvation from the calamity has already taken place.

O Lord, faithful God: or '. . . God of truth' (*AV*, *RV*, *RP*, *PNT*, *NEB*). The latter rendering may well be right, for it seems that the 'true God' (cf. 2 Chr. 15:3) is contrasted with the 'vain idols' in verse 6. Dahood (*PAB*, I, p. 188) transfers 'truth' (*ʾemeṯ*) to the next verse, treating it as an emphatic substantive, meaning 'truly'; yet *RSV* seems superior on this point. Some commentators (e.g. Gunkel, Weiser) omit 'O Lord' for metrical reasons.

6. Thou hatest: so one Hebrew MS. and the versions; M.T. has 'I hate' or '. . . have hated' (*AV*). The *RSV* translation is more likely because verse 6*b* ('but as for me . . .') seems to introduce a contrast to verse 6*a*, or may be a continuation of verse 5*b*. G. R. Driver ('Abbreviations in the Massoretic Text', *Textus I* (1960), p. 119) regards the M.T. *śānēʾṯî* as an abbreviation for *śānēʾṯā yhwh* ('you have hated, O Yahweh . . .'). Kraus (*PBK*, p. 249) suggests that the M.T. reading may be reminiscent of an oath of purification while the other variant might be linked with the renunciation of idols. Dahood (*PAB*, I, p. 188) regards the verb 'I hate' as a technical term used 'in the formal repudiation of idolatry or charges of idolatry'.

vain idols: or 'false gods' (cf. Dt. 32:21; Jer. 10:15, 14:22, 18:15; Jon. 2:8 (M.T. 9)). Delitzsch (*BCP*, I, p. 385) calls them

'beings without being'; they are worse than nothing because they only create false hopes.
but I trust: see on 26:1, 28:7. This phrase (verse 6*b*) is probably the parallel to verse 7*a*, while verses 4*b* and 5*a* 5*b* and 6*a* are the other pairs of lines.

7. I will rejoice: or 'Let me rejoice'. Weiser (*POTL*, p. 277) sees here a vow to offer joyful thanks for the anticipated help, but it is more plausible that the Psalmist is rejoicing in God because he has already been helped.
thy steadfast love: or 'your Covenant loyalty'; see on 26:3.
because thou hast seen . . .: i.e. you have taken notice (cf. Exod. 3:7); it could be regarded as a temporal clause linked with what follows (so Dahood). It seems, however, that verse 7*bc* gives the reason for the gladness (verse 7*a*), and therefore the *RSV* rendering is preferable.
thou hast taken heed . . .: lit. 'you know . . .'. This implies not only cognition, but also effective help—'you have cared for me in my adversities' (cf. *RP*; see on 1:6).
adversities is a general term like 'affliction', and does not help in determining the exact nature of the Psalmist's trouble. Dahood (*PAB*, I, p. 188) translates it as '(against) the Adversary', taking the noun as a plural of excellence and as referring to 'Death'. The parallelism may favour the usual rendering; see also verse 15.

8. into the hand of the enemy: i.e. into his power. Dahood, as might be expected, regards the 'enemy' as yet another name for 'Death' (cf. 49:15 (M.T. 16) where God delivers the Psalmist 'from the power of Sheol'); this is a possible alternative to the more common view that the 'enemy' (*ʾôyēḇ*) is a collective noun designating the human foes of the author.
a broad place may be a figure of speech describing the condition of being freed from the restrictions of trouble and misfortune (cf. 1QH v:33), while some have suggested that it is a poetic synonym of Sheol (see on 18:19). If so, the force of the negative in verse 8*a* would also extend to verse 8*b* the meaning of which would be that God has not abandoned the Psalmist to the netherworld. Cf. Tromp, *PCD*, pp. 47–50.

THE LAMENTATION **9–18**

9. Be gracious to me: or 'grant me your favour'; see on 6:2 (cf. 1QH xiv:25, xvi:9).
for I am in distress: which may mean that the writer is

grievously ill. On the other hand, it is always possible that this language should not be taken literally (cf. Kraus, *PBK*, p. 250) and that the various descriptions serve as metaphors for *any* great calamity (cf. 69:17 (M.T. 18)).

my eye is wasted from grief: as in 6:7 (M.T. 8) (which reads *mikkaᶜas* for *bᵉḵaᶜas* where the preposition *bᵉ* seems to have the meaning 'from', as in Ugaritic). Some commentators retain only the verb, but delete the rest of the phrase (so Briggs) for metrical reasons, while others apply a similar treatment to verse 9*c* regarding it as a later addition (so Kittel, Gunkel, Oesterley, *NEB*, *et al.*).

my soul: or 'my throat' (so Dahood) which seems less likely; it may simply mean 'my vitality (has diminished)'. For *nep̱eš* ('soul') see on 30:3, 33:19; Johnson, *VITAI*, pp. 6–22.

my body: lit. 'my belly' (so *AV*). It is possible that 'soul' and 'body' represent the whole man.

10. This verse continues the description of the affliction caused, apparently, by some prolonged disease, unless the author is using stereotyped language which should not be taken literally.

because of my misery: so LXX, S, and V (i.e. *boᶜᵒnî* of which the consonantal text (*bᶜwny*) may be a *scriptio plena* (cf. *GK* 8i–l), i.e. an orthographical variant where the vowels are represented by the so-called vowel letters (cf. B. J. Roberts, *The Old Testament Text and Versions* (1951), pp. 15f.)). M.T. could be rendered '. . . my iniquity' (so also T, Aq, and Theod). The former alternative fits better into the context which does not state anywhere (except, perhaps, here) that the suffering was due to the Psalmist's own sins. Some exegetes (e.g. Cohen, Weiser) follow M.T. and suggest that the affliction was bound with the Psalmist's own guilt, but the *RSV* interpretation is more plausible.

my bones waste away: or '. . . have become weak' (so Kraus, following *KBL*, p. 745a); another possibility is: '. . . are diseased'. Perhaps we should read: 'my strength (i.e. *ᶜoṣmî* for M.T. *ᶜᵃṣāmay*, 'my bones') wastes away' (cf. Gunkel, *PGHAT*, p. 133).

11. . . . of all my adversaries: or 'Because of all my . . .' (so Kirkpatrick, Oesterley, Cohen), perhaps: 'It is at the hands of my adversaries that I have become a reproach' (cf. 74:22).

a horror: lit. 'exceedingly', which does not make much sense. A possible suggestion is to read *ʾēḏ* ('calamity') for *mᵉʾōḏ* ('exceedingly'), adding the letter *m* to the preceding word either as enclitic or as the last letter of the masculine plural ending (cf. Dahood, *PAB*, I, p. 189), rendering the phrase 'even to my neighbours (or 'the neighbours') I have become an example of calamity'. In Prov. 1:26,27 the word *ʾêḏ* is associated with *paḥaḏ*, 'dread', as in this verse (if we adopt the above-mentioned emendation). Yet another possibility is to regard the M.T. *mʾd* as a noun from the same root as *ʾêḏ* ('burden') (so Delitzsch, G. R. Driver, *NEB*).

those who see me . . . flee from me: (cf. 38:11 (M.T. 12), 88:8,18 (M.T. 9, 19)); the reason for this is not so much the illness as such but the fact that he was believed to be a man marked out by God (and by his enemies) for a fitting punishment. Therefore it was neither wise nor safe to associate with him.

12. I have passed out of mind: i.e. I have been forgotten. Yet the Psalm makes it plain that the sufferer has been anything but forgotten by his foes; the verse probably means that his name is no longer mentioned because it could do only harm. It is also possible that the verb *š-k-ḥ* should be linked with the Ugaritic *ṯkḥ* ('to wither'), hence we could render 'I have withered (or 'become powerless') like one long dead (i.e. out of mind, forgotten)'. For the construction, see verse 12*b*.

like a broken vessel: useless and no longer needed by anyone. Cf. Jer. 22:28: 'Is this man Coniah a despised broken pot, a vessel no one cares for?' (cf. also Jer. 48:38; Hos. 8:8).

13. terror on every side: this is a favourite expression of Jeremiah's (Jer. 6:25, 20:3f.,10, 46:5, 49:29; also in Lam. 2:22). J. Bright (*Jeremiah* (*AB* 21, 1965), pp. 132f.) suggests that the phrase may have become a nickname for Jeremiah, so that the people would point to him, saying: 'There goes the old "Terror-on-every-side" '. LXX misunderstood the phrase, rendering 'those who dwell round about' (so also V).

they plot to take my life: or '. . . my soul' (cf. Jer. 11:19, 18:23). Nötscher (*PEB*, p. 71) points out that this may imply either an accusation (a false one?) or a plain murder, perhaps the former.

14. In spite of all the deadly danger and ostracism, the Psalmist puts his trust in God all the more (see 37:5).

thou art my God: this is a trusting and confident statement; it is also an affirmative of loyalty. See on 143:10; cf. 86:3; Isa. 25:1; Jer. 31:18.

15. My times: 'my varying fortunes' (so Cohen), or 'fate, destiny' (so Oesterley). Luther (*LPA*, I, p. 33) sees here an allusion to life and death, while Taylor (*PIB*, p. 166) understands it as an expression for the 'time set for rendering judgment on a case'. Perhaps the phrase simply means 'my whole life' (cf. verse 5*a*).

16. Let thy face shine: this is a familiar expression in the Psalter (cf. 67:1 (M.T. 2), 80:3,7,19 (M.T. 4, 8, 20), 119:135; see also 4:6 (M.T. 7), 118:27). The light of the face or a 'beaming face' is a sign of pleasure, and to cause one's face to 'shine' upon some one else, is a picturesque description of a favourable attitude to that person. It is thought that the idiom may be of comparatively late origin, perhaps of the post-Exilic period (cf. Oesterley, *TP*, p. 207), but the idea itself must be ancient (cf. 67:1). In Prov. 16:15 'the light of the King's face' is synonymous with 'his favour' (cf. also Num. 6:25).

thy servant: this is a polite self-designation (see on 27:9).

steadfast love: see on 26:3.

17. let the wicked be put to shame: (cf. Jer. 17:18), i.e. let them experience the disgrace which is the companion of sin. The pious would have been put to shame, had God not answered their prayers (see on 25:2). For the 'wicked' (r^{e}*šā*^{c}*îm*), see on 1:1, 28:3.

let them go dumbfounded to Sheol: or 'let them be hurled into Sheol'. Dahood (*PAB*, I, p. 190) derives the verb *yidd*^{e}*mû* (*RSV* 'let them be dumbfounded') from *n-d-h*, 'to hurl', which is attested in Akkadian and Ugaritic. M.T. could be translated 'let them perish (as they go down) to Sheol' (similarly LXX and V; cf. 55:15 (M.T. 16)); for this use of the verb, see Jer. 8:14, 48:2. Sheol (see on 6:5) is a land of silence (94:17, 115:17) and there the harmful activities of the wicked come to an end.

18. . . . insolently against the righteous: this is sometimes omitted as a gloss (so Oesterley, Taylor), since the line is clearly overloaded. There are also other variations as to what should be deleted (cf. Kraus, *PBK*, p. 247). Dahood (*PAB*, I, p. 191) translates this phrase '. . . against the Ancient Just One' (cf. Dan. 7:9,13,22). This involves the repointing of ^{c}*āṯāḳ* into ^{c}*attīḳ* ('old, ancient'), yet the *RSV* rendering seems more likely (cf. Klopfenstein, *LAT*, p. 371, n. 190). For 'righteous' (*ṣaddîḳ*), see on 1:5.

THE PRAISE AND THANKSGIVING 19–24

19. O how abundant is thy goodness is reminiscent of the Hymns (and so also are the following lines); cf. 38:7 (M.T. 8), 145:7. LXX and V add 'O Lord' (i.e. 'Yahweh') at the end of

the verse, thus improving the balance between the two lines.
who fear thee: see on 25:12. Cf. S. Plath, *Furcht Gottes* (1963), pp. 84–103.
in the sight of the sons of men: the goodness of God is not merely a subjective experience, but it can also be observed objectively by all concerned. It may have been hidden, stored up for a time (verse 19*b*) but sooner or later it will be manifested openly (cf. 23:5).

20. In the covert of thy presence: i.e. in your personal protection or in the refuge provided by the place where your presence dwells (cf. 27:4f.). The former alternative may be more likely. In 65:4 (M.T. 5) we have a reference to the 'shelter of thy wings', but this is no reason to emend the present verse (as is done by Oesterley, Taylor; cf. 32:7, 91:1).
from the plots of men: this phrase occurs only here. Dahood (*PAB*, I, p. 191) suggests 'slanderings of men' which is preferable to Weiser's 'hordes of men' (*POTL*, p. 274); *NEB* '. . . men in league together'.
thou holdest them: or 'you hide (or 'shelter') them' (from the accusations of men). Cf. Job 31:35.
the strife of tongues: hardly 'a noisy debate' (*PLE*) but rather '(their) accusation' (cf. B. Gemser, 'The *Rîb*—or Controversy—Pattern in Hebrew Mentality', *SVT* III (1955), pp. 120–37).

21. Blessed be the Lord: see on 28:6.
he has wondrously shown . . .: or, perhaps, 'he has set apart his loyal servant for himself', reading *ḥ^{a}sîḏô lô* ('his loyal servant for himself') for M.T. *ḥasdô lî* ('his steadfast love to me', *RSV*). See on 17:7; cf. 31:23 (M.T. 24).
when I was beset . . .: lit. 'in the fortified city'. Winton Thomas (*TRP*, p. 11) reads *b^{ec}ēṯ māṣôḵ* ('in time of trouble') for M.T. *b^{ec}îr māṣôr* (cf. also Calès, *LP*, I, p. 343); similarly *NEB*.

22. I had said: or 'And yet I actually thought'.
in my alarm: or 'when I was terrified' (cf. 116:11).
I am driven far: lit. 'I am cut off (from your care)'. The verb *g-r-z* occurs only here, but this is not sufficient ground for emendation. There is, however, a noun from the same root, namely, *garzen* ('axe') (cf. *BDB*, p. 173b) and this lends some support to M.T.
But thou didst hear . . . i.e., you answered my cry for help in spite of my wavering trust in you (cf. 116:10).

23. Love the Lord: see on 26:8, 119:47; cf. Dt. 6:5, 10:12.
his saints: for *ḥ^{a}sîḏîm*, see on 30:4, 86:2.

the faithful: or 'his faithful', deriving the suffix from the preceding line on the principle of the double-duty suffix (see on 3:3). This may also be a possible instance where the abstract noun has acquired a concrete meaning from the context of the whole sentence (cf. 'his saints' in verse 23*a*). It could also be reap with Wellhausen (*PBP*, p. 29) as: '(Yahweh keeps) faith' (cf. Isa. 26:2), or '. . . faithfulness' (see Kirkpatrick, *BPCB*, p. 161; cf. also LXX and V).

who acts haughtily: or 'acts with pride'. Human pride is essentially a self-exaltation, but since the only truly exalted one is God, it follows that the proud man is often in danger of setting himself in opposition to God. Therefore the Wisdom writers emphasize the destructive nature of pride and arrogance; so in Prov. 16:18: 'Pride goes before destruction, and a haughty spirit before a fall' (cf. Prov. 29:23).

24. Be strong: see on 27:14.

who wait for the LORD: i.e. those who hope for the fulfilment of God's promises, and who trust in him (cf. 33:18, 69:3 (M.T. 4), 147:11). This is equivalent to waiting for his 'loving kindness' (1QH vii:18, ix:10) or 'goodness' (1QH xi:31).

Psalm 32 The Blessings of Repentance and Forgiveness

According to the tradition of the Christian Church, this is one of the seven Penitential Psalms (which include Ps. 6, 32, 38, 51, 102, 130 and 143) but in actual fact it is a Psalm of Thanksgiving. It could also be described as a Wisdom poem because it is reminiscent of sapiential literature; cf. the so-called Beatitudes in verses 1–2, or the instruction in verses 6–7, 10. This feature, as well as the language of the Psalm as a whole, may imply that it is relatively late, but it is difficult to be more specific.

Its *Sitz im Leben*, or life-situation, is to be found in the Temple worship (cf. 22:22 (M.T. 23)), during which the Psalmist offered his song of thanks in the presence of his fellow-worshippers. This circumstance would also account for the didactic element in the Psalm. Since the poem emphasizes the themes of sin and forgiveness, it is not impossible that it was connected with the bringing of the sin offering or with the rites of purification (cf. Lev. 4:27–5:19; 14:1–57). The Psalm may imply that at one point the Psalmist had been grievously ill, and that only through repentance and forgiveness has he attained healing (cf. Schmidt, *PHAT*, p. 60).

The structure of the Psalm presents a clear picture. Verses 1–2 describe the blessedness of the forgiven man, while in verses 3–5 we find an account of the Psalmist's past experiences: sin and its consequences, repentance and the miracle of forgiveness. In verses 6–7 the writer draws certain conclusions from his personal trials and the subsequent deliverance, and he also expresses his trust in God. The next section (verses 8–9) may well be a divine oracle which the Psalmist received when he asked for forgiveness. Other exegetes (Gunkel, Weiser, Kissane, *et al.*) regard the Psalmist himself as the speaker in this particular part, in the role of a Wisdom teacher. Finally, verses 10–11 present a brief summary of the Psalmist's 'lesson', and the song concludes with an exhortation to be glad and to rejoice in Yahweh.

The metre of the Psalm is uneven, mainly a mixture of 3+2 and 2+2.

A Psalm of David: see Introduction, pp. 43ff. and 46.

A Maskil: see Introduction, p. 47.

THE BLESSEDNESS OF BEING FORGIVEN **1–2**

1. Blessed is he: or 'How rewarding is the life of the man . . .' (see on 1:1). This joyful exclamation is based on personal experience but it has a universal application.

In verses 1–2 we find three different terms for sin (see the discussion in R. Knierim, *Die Hauptbegriffe für Sünde im Alten Testament* (1965), pp. 245–51); they are matched by three expressions describing the ways of God in dealing with man's transgression. It is unlikely that the writer intended to use the various terms to describe *different* aspects of sin and forgiveness. The purpose of the threefold repetition may be both to serve the requirements of style and to stress the totality of the themes mentioned. Etymologically, 'transgression' (*pešaᶜ*) is a rebellion against the divine authority (see on 51:1), while 'sin' (*ḥaṭṭā'āh*) is a faulty action, often deliberate, with the result that one misses both God and his way (see on 51:2). The third term, 'iniquity' (*ᶜāwōn*) can mean either 'crookedness' or 'going astray'. It can also be used to denote the effects of sin or guilt (see on 51:2). In Ps. 32 all these three terms are probably used as synonyms and, if anything, the emphasis is on the nature of guilt, which is like an oppressive burden too heavy for one to bear (cf. Gen. 4:13; Ps. 38:4 (M.T. 5)), and suffering is often one of the ways in which it is manifested. This is only what can be expected, because all sin is a separation between man and God who is the source of life and blessing. Therefore, as long as this gulf exists, man's existence is thought to be endangered, whether this is immediately apparent (cf. verse 3) or not (cf. Ps. 37 and 73). Since all sin is essentially against God (cf. Rowley, *FI*, p. 89), he is the only one who can remove the existing barrier, the necessary precondition being repentance and confession (see verse 5).

The triad of terms used for pardon consists of 'forgiving the transgression', 'covering the sin', and 'not imputing the iniquity'. The first expression uses the verb *n-ś-ʾ* ('to bear, carry'), and it depicts sin and its consequences as a burden which can be lifted up from the penitent sinner and be carried away (see on 85:2). 'To cover (one's sin)' (*k-s-h*) suggests the 'covering up of something that offends the eye' (Kissane, *BP*, p. 141) but it may well be more than that, because certain aspects of sin remain or must be attended to; e.g., the act itself cannot be undone, and there is also a restitution wherever it applies (cf. Lev. 5:5f.; Num. 5:5–8). The third phrase 'to impute no iniquity' seems to imply that God no longer considers the repentant man a sinner (cf. 2 Sam. 19:19). Others have seen here an allusion to a release from a debt (so Kirkpatrick, Davison). Verses 1–2 are also quoted by St. Paul in Rom. 4:6ff.

2. in whose spirit there is no deceit: or 'one whose actions are not characterized by guile' (cf. 1QH iv:21). LXX reads 'in whose mouth there is . . .' implying that the reference might be to a 'deceitful tongue', or to a 'speech full of falsehood'.

THE WONDER OF FORGIVENESS **3–5**

3. Most commentators assume that the Psalmist had committed a particular sin or sins which he had refused to acknowledge before God and men. Rhodes (*LBCP*, p. 63) suggests that this unwillingness 'to confess his sin resulted in what we would call a psychosomatic illness'. This may be so; it is equally possible that the process was the other way round: the Psalmist was afflicted by a severe illness (or some other misfortune), and he came to the conclusion that he must have committed some sin. Hence the way to deliverance or healing would be through repentance and confession. This was exactly the argument of Job's friends; see also the Plague Prayers of Mursilis (*ANET*, pp. 394–6).

When I declared not my sin: lit. 'When I was silent' but this is usually understood as a refusal to confess one's transgressions.

Dahood (*PAB*, I, p. 194) takes the verb *ḥ-r-š* as a denominative from *ḥereś* ('potsherd'), and proposes 'But I had become like a potsherd' (cf. 22:15 (M.T. 16)). This gives a reasonable sense but there is no evidence that this denominative verb actually existed.

my body wasted away: lit. 'my bones . . .' which seems to imply that the description is not to be taken literally. In a sense, the bones are the very last part of the body to disintegrate, and therefore the phrase may serve as a word-picture of a most serious and hopeless human situation, irrespective of the actual causes. Ezekiel's vision of the valley of the dry bones (chapter 37) is an example of such a usage. Some Hebrew MSS. read *kālû* ('were spent, finished') for M.T. *bālû* ('wasted away'), but the general meaning of the idiom remains unchanged.

4. The affliction was regarded as the visible sign of the divine wrath—as the hand of God put forth in punishment, striking heavy blows (cf. 38:2 (M.T. 3), 39:10 (M.T. 11)).

my strength was dried up . . .: lit., perhaps, 'my moisture (vitality?) was changed (into dryness)'. Olshausen, followed by Gunkel, Kraus, *et al.*, suggests *lᵉšōnî* ('my tongue (is changed)') for M.T. *lᵉšaddî* ('my moisture').

Selah: see Introduction, pp. 48f.

5. I acknowledged my sin: i.e. I made a confession of my offences. Sometimes this may involve, first of all, the finding out of the particular cause of the distress (cf. 2 Sam. 21:1; also 1 Sam. 14:36–45). Confession is more than merely informing God of one's sins. It is also a turning away from the transgression to God. So in Prov. 28:18: 'He who conceals his transgressions will not prosper, but he who confesses and forsakes them will obtain mercy'.

I did not hide my iniquity: meaning perhaps 'I have finished hiding . . .', i.e. I have decided to give up concealing my perversity, my self-deception.

the guilt of my sin: (Ḳimḥi 'my very great sin'). This is rather an unusual expression, and therefore some exegetes follow Duhm's proposal to read *sālaḥtā* (for M.T. *selāh*, 'Selah'), rendering verse 5*c* 'you have pardoned (my) iniquity, my sin you have forgiven'. This is obviously the easier reading, but it is not thereby the right one.

THE ADVICE **6–7**

6. every one who is godly: or 'loyal to Yahweh's Covenant'. For *ḥāsîḏ* ('godly'), see on 30:4. They are encouraged to turn to Yahweh for help whenever they are in trouble; the experience of the Psalmist is yet another proof of God's faithfulness to his loyal servants.

at a time of distress: reading *leᶜēṯ māṣôḵ* for M.T. *leᶜēṯ meṣōʾ raḵ* ('at a time of finding only') (=*RSVm*). V renders *in tempore opportuno* ('in due season'), while Dahood (*PAB*, I, p. 193) suggests 'when an army approaches', taking M.T. *raḵ* as *rīḵ* ('troop'; for this use of *rīḵ*, see on 2:1). The emendation assumed by *RSV* may be the simplest solution; similarly *NEB*.

in the rush of great waters: this is a word-picture derived from the heavy downpour during a storm when, in a short time, the dry wadis become raging torrents. Perhaps we could paraphrase verse 6 as: 'Therefore in a time of trouble let every loyal (servant of God) pray to him, (with the result that) when the floods of many waters (i.e. trouble) (will sweep everything before them) they will not reach him' (cf. 18:16 (M.T. 17); Isa. 28:2,17, 30:28; Nah. 1:8; Lk. 6:48).

7. In view of the preceding verse, it is tempting to read the third person singular pronouns instead of the first person singular in M.T. Yet M.T. may be right, and the Psalmist may be once more referring to his own knowledge of God.

a hiding place: see on 27:5.

from trouble: this is better than 'from the besieger' (so Dahood), deriving *ṣar* ('trouble') from *ṣ-w-r*, 'to besiege'.

with deliverance: lit. 'with shouts of deliverance'. LXX and V have '(you are) my joy, deliver me (from those that surround me)'. Dahood (*PAB*, I, p. 196) regards *rny* ('shouts of') as a noun in the vocative, 'My refuge' (cf. LXX and V), from a postulated root *r-n-n*, 'to find refuge', while *pallēṭ* (*RSV* 'deliverance') is parsed as an imperative: 'save!'.

Selah: see Introduction, pp. 48f.

THE DIVINE ORACLE **8–9**

It is possible that in these two verses the author is quoting the word of Yahweh which he received when he besought God during the time of affliction. Some scholars (e.g. Delitzsch, Weiser, Kissane) think that the speaker is not Yahweh, but the Psalmist himself; but verse 8*b* may favour the former alternative.

8. instruct . . . teach: this may be an instance of the co-ordination of complementary verbal ideas (cf. *GK* 120d), hence: 'I will give you a wise instruction . . .' (cf. 16:11, 25:4f.).
I will counsel you with my eye upon you: or, better, 'I will counsel you, my eye (will be) upon you' (cf. 33:18; 1QH ii:31 '. . . for you have set(?) your eye upon my soul (i.e. me)'.

9. Be not like: (the verb is in the second person plural). Two Hebrew MSS. (so *BH*) have the singular verb which is suggested by the second person singular pronouns in verse 8. Dahood explains the plural verb as an archaism, standing for the singular (*PAB*, I, p. 196).
like a horse or a mule: perhaps 'like a mulish horse' (cf. Brockelmann, *HS*, p. 64), who always needs to be controlled by physical means because he has no 'sense' (cf. Prov. 26:3; Sir. 30:8).
which must be curbed . . .: or 'the obstinacy of which must be held in check with . . .' (cf. M. H. Pope, *Job* (*AB* 15, 1965), p. 79); G. R. Driver (*JTS*, XLIII (1942), p. 153) 'whose course (*ʿaḏyô* for M.T. *ʿeḏyô* ('ornament', a gloss on 'bit and bridle' (?)) is for checking . . .' (similarly *NEB*).
else it will not keep with you: M.T. could be paraphrased 'then nothing can approach you (to do you any harm)', but the text may be corrupt. Gunkel, Snaith, *et al.* think that this phrase, in its present position, is an intrusion; the ancient versions offer little help. *NEB* omits it.

THE SUMMARY AND THE CONCLUDING PRAISE **10–11**

10. The writer states once more the orthodox belief that numerous troubles will pursue the wicked, while God's steadfast love (*ḥeseḏ*; see on 26:3) or his unfailing providential care within the Covenant context will surround the man who directs his way according to the divine will.

11. Be glad: this is a call to rejoice, and a characteristic feature of the Hymns. The Deuteronomist chides his contemporaries, saying, '. . . you did not serve the LORD your God with joyfulness and gladness of heart' (Dt. 28:47). Similarly the author of Neh. 8:10 states: 'the joy of the LORD is your strength'. Thus joyful service of God is not an optional extra, but it is of the essence of all true service.
righteous: for *ṣaddîḳîm*, see on 1:5.
upright in heart: this is a synonym of 'righteous'. The expression is found only in the Psalter and in 2 Chr. 29:32. See on 7:10.

Psalm 33 Praise to the Creator and Lord

Most commentators class this Psalm as a Hymn (see Introduction, pp. 32f.). It begins with the customary call to praise Yahweh (verses 1–3), which is followed by the main section (verses 4–19), giving the reasons for the rejoicing. The principal themes mentioned are the nature of Yahweh and the creative power manifested in his word (verses 4–9), the relative futility of human plans as against those of God (verses 10–12), the providence of God and the ineffectiveness of human resources (verses 13–19). The hymn concludes with an affirmation of faith, and with a brief petition (verses 20–2).

This song was probably used at the great Autumnal Festival at which both the traditions of creation and of the salvation-history were recounted and relived. The reference to the 'new song' (verse 3) is occasionally taken to mean that it was intended for the ritual of the renewal of creation at the turn of the year (cf. Leslie, *PAP*, p. 84) but it could also be linked with the renewal of the Covenant (so Weiser); it is less likely that it was written 'in commemoration of deliverance from some threatened national peril' (Oesterley, *TP*, p. 210), such as the threat to Jerusalem in 701 B.C. Equally unlikely is a *purely* eschatological interpretation.

Some scholars have seen a connexion between the twenty-two verses of this Psalm and the twenty-two letters of the Hebrew alphabet (cf. Gunkel, *PGHAT*, p. 139) yet this similarity may be more of a coincidence than a deliberate feature of the style. The Psalm has no title, but LXX attributes it to David. This may be either a later addition, or it could have been accidentally omitted from M.T. It is difficult to determine the date of the hymn; it may belong to the post-Exilic period although not necessarily to the Greek period (so Briggs).

The metre of the Psalm is mainly 3+3.

THE EXHORTATION TO PRAISE YAHWEH **1–3**

1. Rejoice in the Lord: i.e. utter your praise to Yahweh with ringing cries of joy (cf. 20:5 (M.T. 6), 92:4, 145:7). Sometimes the verb *r-n-n* may express also a cry in distress (Lam. 2:19) or in supplication (1 Kg. 8:28).

righteous . . . upright are generally regarded as honorific names of the cultic community. At least theoretically these qualities should characterize the worshippers of Yahweh (cf. Ps. 15,

24). For *ṣaddîḳîm*, see on 1:5. The 'upright' (*y^e^šārîm*) are those who do what is right in the sight of God (Dt. 6:18, 12:25, 21:9).
Praise befits . . .: it is right and proper that the people of God should sing praises to him. The failure to do so would be not only churlish but also deliberately offensive. For 'praise', see on 119:171.

2. Musical instruments were used to accompany the songs of the worshippers. The Psalmist mentions only the lyre and the harp; but they probably represent *all* the instruments used in public worship, such as are mentioned in Ps. 150. For 'lyre', see on 98:5. The Hebrew *nēḇel* is usually identified with the harp, and this may well be right, even though the ancient versions often employ different terms to translate it. In any case, it is in this instance a ten-stringed instrument (cf. 144:9); Josephus (*Antiquities*, VII,xii.3) speaks of a harp with twelve strings; but it is possible that their number was not always identical, and may have changed from time to time, and from place to place. What the relationship was, if any, between *nēḇel* ('skin-bottle, pitcher') and *nēḇel* ('harp') is impossible to say. Delitzsch (*BCP*, I, p. 402) thought that they resembled each other in shape, and that therefore the same name was used for both.

3. a new song: this can suggest one of several things. It may refer to a newly composed poem meant for a particular occasion, or it may be associated with the 'renewal' of the Covenant, etc. Another alternative is that its newness may be found in the celebration of the ever-new acts of God: the same old words could allude to fresh experiences of God's providence; it may also have an eschatological undertone (cf. Kraus, *PBK*, p. 262; also Isa. 42:10; Rev. 5:9). See on 96:1, 149:1.
with loud shouts: or 'at the shouts of joy' referring to the accompanying shouts of rejoicing rather than to the music itself (cf. *AV*, *RV* 'with a loud noise'). The Hebrew *t^e^rû^c^āh* may have a number of possible connotations; see on 27:6.

THE WORKS OF YAHWEH 4–19

This main part of the hymn provides the reasons for the previous exhortations by elaborating certain representative acts of God in creation and history.

The Description of the Nature of God 4–5

4. the word of the LORD is upright: i.e. it says what he means and there is no crookedness in it (Prov. 8:8); it 'holds true' (*NEB*).

his work is done in faithfulness: or '. . . is faithfulness itself' (similarly Perowne, Dahood). All that Yahweh does is an expression of his faithfulness (cf. 1QH vi:9); see on 36:5.

5. He loves righteousness and justice: i.e. loves to perform righteous and just deeds (cf. 99:4; Jer. 9:24). This may also imply that God is concerned both to do and to uphold righteousness and justice. 'Righteousness' (*ṣ*ᵉ*ḏāḳāh*) is a term of relationships, denoting that kind of conduct which serves to maintain the established ties. In certain specific contexts it would amount to 'deliverance' (cf. 22:31 (M.T. 32), 40:9 (M.T. 10), 51:14 (M.T. 16), 65:5 (M.T. 6)), 'salvation' (cf. 69:27 (M.T. 28)), 'victory' (cf. Isa. 41:2), 'vindication' (103:6), 'righteous help' (71:24), 'healing' (40:10 (M.T. 11)), perhaps even 'reward' (106:31). On the negative side it means punishment to the wicked (cf. 119:75). In a Covenant context 'righteousness' signifies faithfulness to the obligations stipulated by the Covenant, but in general it may imply a behaviour which is right according to the standards accepted by the community. (For bibliography, see H. H. Rowley, *FI*, p. 65, n.3.) 'Justice' (*mišpāṭ*) may be the decision given by the judge (*šōp̄ēṭ*), or it may denote what has become a custom or habit. See on 36:6, 119:7.

the steadfast love . . .: see on 26:3. The *ḥeseḏ* of Yahweh embraces the whole world (cf. 36:5 (M.T. 6), 119:64, 136:1–9; Isa. 6:3) although not in the same way as it surrounds Israel (see Eichrodt, *TOT*, I, p. 239).

The Creative Word **6–9**

6. 'Creation' is a frequent motif in the *OT* hymns (cf. Gunkel, *EP*, p. 74); this and the following verses seem to be a poetic reflection of Gen. 1. Creation by means of the divine word was not, strictly speaking, unique to Israel (cf. W. H. Schmidt, *Die Schöpfungsgeschichte der Priesterschrift* (*WMANT*, 17, 1964), pp. 173ff.), but it is not certain that the concept was actually borrowed from the neighbours of Israel. It may well be the result of the emphasis upon the divine word in the prophetic preaching. Gen. 1 and the related accounts of creation do not stress a *creatio ex nihilo* (nor do they necessarily suggest it); rather the emphasis is upon the awe-inspiring might of God. The distant stars were beyond man's reach; yet Yahweh was their creator, and infinitely greater than any of his works (cf. Sir. 43:28). Verses 6–7 were intended to provide only a few representative examples of Yahweh's creative power.

all their host: i.e. the sun, moon, and the stars (cf. Jg. 5:20; Ps. 147:4; Isa. 40:26, 45:12) which do his bidding, rather than the angels and other heavenly beings (cf. 103:20).

the breath of his mouth: this is parallel to 'the word of the LORD' and is not to be understood as the '(holy) spirit (*rûaḥ*) of his mouth' (so Luther). Cf. 147:18. *NEB* 'his command'.

7. the waters of the sea are not the seas in general but the 'waters which were above the firmament' (Gen. 1:7). Thus the reference is not to the separation of the waters from the dry land (Gen. 1:9f.), nor to the crossing of the Sea of Reeds (Exod. 15:8), but to the miraculous storing of the waters above the dome of heaven.

as in a bottle: so *RSV* following most of the ancient versions, reading *kannōḏ* (or *kannʾōḏ*) for M.T. *kannēḏ* ('as (in) a heap'). Dahood (*PAB*, I, p. 201) is probably right in regarding the Hebrew *knd* as associated with the Ugaritic *knd* ('jar, pitcher'), and the Akkadian *kandu* which has a similar meaning (cf. also Aistleitner, *WUS*, p. 152). So we could render verse 7*a*: 'He gathers (i.e. he has gathered and still keeps control of) the waters of the sea (in) a pitcher', assuming that the force of the preposition in verse 7*b* extends also to the parallel phrase, verse 7*a*. A similar idea is found in Job 38:37 which refers to the 'water jars of heaven'.

the deeps: the Hebrew *tᵉhôm* is a synonym of the 'waters of the sea' and also an etymological equivalent of the Babylonian sea monster or primeval ocean, Tiamat (cf. G. R. Driver, 'The Psalms in the Light of Babylonian Research', *TPst*, pp. 140f.). The actual relationship between the two is, however, difficult to determine, yet whatever was the original mythological significance of the 'deep', in the *OT* passages it was largely 'demythologized'. Ringgren (*FP*, p. 49) sees in this verse an allusion to Yahweh's 'victory over the powers of chaos'.

in storehouses: i.e. just as the wind was stored in its repository (cf. 135:7; Jer. 10:13) and the hail and snow in theirs (Job 38:22), so were the waters of the deeps collected in their storehouses.

8. all the earth: i.e. all its inhabitants, as is clear from the parallel phrase (verse 8*b*). This verse (see also verse 5) suggests that Yahweh stands in a particular relationship to all the peoples of the world as their creator and sustainer, whether they actually worship him or not. Therefore it is not unreasonable to expect also from them a joyous response.

fear the LORD: see on 25:12. The reference may be to that kind of fear which drives one to submission.

stand in awe of him: cf. 22:23 (M.T. 24). The verb *g-w-r* III usually means 'to be afraid', as in Dt. 1:17: '. . . you shall not be afraid of the face of man'.

9. This verse reminds us of the recurrent formula 'And God said . . . And it was so' (Gen. 1).

it stood forth: i.e. it was created (so LXX and V); cf. 148:5: 'For he commanded and they were created'.

Only the Counsel of Yahweh will Endure **10–12**

10. The Psalmist expresses a general truth rather than an observation based on some recent deliverance. The Hebrew verbs of this verse are perfects; but they may describe not only past events but also facts which are of common knowledge (cf. *GK* 106k) or repeated actions (cf. Brockelmann, *HS*, p. 39f.). LXX and V add at the end of this verse 'he sets at nought the counsel of the princes' which is, probably, a variant of verse 10*b* (cf. Calès, *LP*, I, p. 359).

11. No power in the world can frustrate the purposes of God (cf. Prov. 19:21; Ec. 3:14; Isa. 8:10).

The counsel of the LORD stands in the sharpest contrast to the decisions of the nations. The schemes of the peoples, in as far as they are contrary to the divine will, must come to nothing.

the thoughts of his heart: i.e. his plans. The heart is frequently used to denote the seat of the intellect (see on 27:3).

12. Blessed is the nation: (i.e. Israel), or 'how rewarding is the life of . . .' (see on 1:1). This fortunate situation is primarily due to Yahweh, the God of Israel; and only secondarily does it depend upon the obedience of the people. See the parallel in 144:15. Cf. also W. Käser, *ZAW*, LXXXII (1970), pp. 239ff.

the people whom he has chosen: this is a reference to the doctrine of election. R. E. Clements ('Deuteronomy and the Jerusalem Cult Tradition', *VT*, XV (1965), pp. 305f.) argues that the Deuteronomists were the first 'to use the terminology of election in defining the relationship between Yahweh and his people'. Instead of proclaiming the divine election of the monarchy, they affirmed that Yahweh had chosen the nation as his own possession. See also 65:4 (M.T. 5).

as his heritage: better 'as his special possession' (see on 28:9, 105:11).

The Providence of God **13–19**

13. Yahweh is not an 'absentee landlord', but he is acquainted with everything that goes on in his world. Being the creator of all, he rules over all, and sees all.

14. from where he sits enthroned: lit. 'from the place of his habitation' (*AV*, *RV*). Dahood (*PAB*, 1, p. 200) suggests that the Hebrew *mākôn* (usually 'place, foundation') means here 'throne', on the principle that a part of a thing can occasionally be used to denote the whole. Cf. 85:15 (M.T. 16) which speaks of the 'foundation (*mᵉkôn*) of your throne'.

he looks forth: the Hebrew *š-g-ḥ* is a rare verb, and it serves as a poetic synonym of the two verbs in verse 13 (cf. Isa. 14:16).

15. he who fashions . . .: or '(Yahweh is the one) who forms their hearts all together'. The Hebrew *yaḥaḏ*, here rendered as 'all together', does not yield a satisfactory meaning, and so far it remains unexplained in spite of various suggestions. LXX has *kata monas* ('alone'), which may suggest the Hebrew *yāḥīḏ*, and consequently we could render: 'who alone (*yāḥīḏ*) forms their minds (i.e. their hearts)'. For 'heart', see on 27:3. God, being the creator of men's minds, is the only one who knows what is in the heart of man (i.e. what determines his actions), and therefore he is able to judge between appearance and reality (cf. 1 Kg. 3:9).

16. A king is not saved . . .: or, in a reflexive sense, '. . . does not give himself victory' (so Dahood; cf. Zech. 9:9). It is unlikely that the author alludes to any particular king, because verses 16–17 may simply stress that all human power, however great, does not determine history. The same thought is re-echoed in 1 Mac. 3:19: 'It is not on the size of the army that victory in battle depends, but the strength comes from Heaven'.

a warrior: the Hebrew *gibbôr* is often translated as 'mighty man'. LXX (also V) has *gigas* ('giant') which is more suited to the Arabic equivalent of *gibbôr* than to the Hebrew word itself. J. Gray (*I & II Kings* (*OTL*, 1964), p. 81) suggests that the word meant primarily a 'man of substance' who was able to equip himself, and sometimes also his followers, for war. The same word is also used of 'professional soldiers' (1 Kg. 1:10) or 'picked warriors' (Am. 2:14); occasionally it may denote a man of special rank, such as a 'potentate' (Gen. 10:8; so E. A. Speiser, *Genesis* (*AB* 1, 1964), p. 67) or 'military leader' (1 Chr. 5:24; so Yadin, *SWSLSD*, p. 305).

17. The war horse may be taken collectively as 'the mounted cavalry (of the king)' or '(his) chariotry'; it may also be taken symbolically of military power as a whole. So in 20:7: 'Some boast of chariots, and some of horses' (cf. Isa. 31:1; Ezek. 17:15). Even the most formidable weapons of that time were ultimately nothing more than a lie (*šeḳer*), a deceptive hope, if they were wielded *against* the purposes of God (cf. 147:10).

and by its great might . . .: this refers to the war horse (verse 17*a*), while some exegetes make the King the subject of 'cannot save'. The latter view is supported, to some extent, by LXX, T, and V, which have 'he shall not be delivered' (*yimmālēṭ* for M.T. *yᵉmallēṭ* ('. . . save')).

18. the eye of the Lord: this is the providential care of Yahweh (cf. Ezr. 5:5; Job 36:7; Ps. 34:15 (M.T. 16), 1 Pet. 3:12). LXX and S have 'the eyes of . . .' (i.e. *ᶜênê*), and some commentators have suggested that we should read *ᶜênāyw* ('his eyes') for M.T. *ᶜên yhwh*, deleting 'Yahweh' for metrical reasons.

who fear him: see on 25:12.

his steadfast love: for *ḥesed̲*, see on 26:3.

19. their soul: i.e. 'their life' or simply 'them'. The Hebrew *nep̄eš* occurs some 755 times in the *OT*, and its usage is roughly divided into three main groups. It can denote the life principle in man, the essential vitality, life itself (cf. 107:5) or it can be used in a psychical sense, and various emotional states can be attributed to it. In some 200 instances it is employed (together with the respective pronominal suffixes) as a periphrasis, or even as an emotional substitute for the personal pronouns (e.g. in 78:50, 120:2). Some of the less common uses of *nep̄eš* include such meanings as 'throat' or 'neck' (69:1 (M.T. 2), 105:18, 106:15; Isa. 5:14; Jon. 2:5 (M.T. 6)), 'greed' (17:9, 27:12, 41:2 (M.T. 3)), 'appetite' (78:18), 'desire' (35:25), 'courage' (107:26), 'slave, person, individual' (Gen. 14:21; Lev. 22:11), and even 'corpse' (Lev. 19:28, 21:1; Num. 6:6). For a more detailed discussion and bibliography, see Johnson, *VITAI*, pp. 4f.

in famine does not necessarily imply that the Psalm was actually composed in a time of famine. 'Death' (verse 19*a*) and 'hunger' are simply typical examples of affliction; the point is that God can deliver and preserve his faithful ones in *any* circumstances. Dahood (*PAB*, I, p. 203) takes the M.T. *bārā*[c]*āḇ* as meaning 'from the Hungry One', a poetic synonym of 'Death'. The preposition *b*[e] is given the sense 'from', as in Ugaritic. Nevertheless, *RSV* provides the more likely alternative.

Yahweh is Our Help and Shield **20–2**

20. Our soul waits . . .: i.e. 'We wait . . .'. This verb involves a whole complex of attitudes, such as hope, trust, obedience. The opposite can be seen in 106:13 where the author writes concerning the fathers: '. . . they soon forgot his works; they did not wait for his counsel'.

help and shield: or 'our protective shield' (a hendiadys?). See Dt. 33:29 where Yahweh is called 'the shield of your help' (cf. 115:9–11). For 'shield', see on 3:3.

21. Yea, our heart is glad . . .: i.e. in none but him we are glad. For 'heart', see on 27:3.

trust is the right attitude to him who has said, 'I am the LORD your God' (Exod. 20:2), who both gives and demands. 'Trust', strengthened by the knowledge of the past, looks forward with confidence; at the same time, it enables men to take seriously the claims of God (cf. 9:10 (M.T. 11)).

in his holy name: or 'in Yahweh himself', the never-absent God whose presence is manifested in his providential care. See on 20:1.

22. steadfast love: *ḥeseḏ* is discussed on 26:3, 51:1.

even as: better, 'since' (with a causal force); *NEB* 'as'.

Psalm 34 O MAGNIFY THE LORD WITH ME

This Psalm is an acrostic poem, in that the first letters of the successive verses (or lines) appear in alphabetical order. In some ways this Psalm is similar to Ps. 25 because both lack a verse beginning with the sixth letter of the Hebrew alphabet (*wāw*), and both have an additional verse with the initial letter *pê*, at the end of the poem. For this and other reasons, it has been suggested that both Psalms must have been written by the same author (cf. Schmidt, *PHAT*, p. 64); such a view is not improbable.

Ps. 34 is usually classed as a Thanksgiving of the Individual, with a strongly marked didactic element (verses 11–22). In spite of its more or less artificial structure, its *Sitz im Leben* may well be the same as that of other Psalms of Thanksgiving (see Introduction, pp. 35f.). Mowinckel (*PIW*, II, p. 114) has suggested that Psalms such as 34, 37, 49, 73 may have been 'deposited as a votive and memorial gift to Yahweh and a testimony to future generations'. At some later time they were, apparently, included in the existing collections of Psalms. For some Near Eastern parallels, see *PIW*, II, pp. 41f.

According to its title, the Psalm was written by David, with reference to the episode described in 1 Sam. 21:11–16, when he feigned madness at the court of Achish, the king of Gath. In our Psalm, however, the king is called Abimelech, and some scholars have suggested that this contradiction, if such it is, must have been due to a scribal error. Dahood (*PAB*, I, p. 205) suggests the possibility that Abimelech may have been the Semitic name of the king of Gath, while Kirkpatrick speculates that Abimelech could be a dynastic name or a royal title (cf. Gen. 26:1). Vulgate reads 'Ahimelech' which is, apparently, an error of transcription (cf. Calès, *LP*, I, p. 367). The Psalm itself shows no real connexion with the event described, and it is very likely that the 'historical note' is a later interpretation. The Psalm may be of post-Exilic origin; this is implied, to some extent, by the acrostic scheme, as well as by the didactic element; cf. also Sabourin, *POM*, II, p. 123.

The Psalm consists of three main parts. It opens with a hymnic introduction, praising God and calling upon others to join in glorifying him (verses 1–3). The second part (verses 4–10) offers a testimony to the goodness of God, and the Psalmist tries to share the fruits of his experience with his fellow-worshippers. In the third section (verses 11–22) the author appears in the role of a Wisdom teacher, and he elaborates the meaning of the fear of Yahweh, and the consequences of its absence or presence.

Most of the lines in the Psalm are in the 3+3 metre.

A Psalm of David: lit. 'Of David'; see Introduction, pp. 43ff. and 46.

when he feigned . . .: lit. 'when he disguised his judgment' or '. . . altered his behaviour'. In 1 Sam. 21:13 this is expanded by 'and he feigned himself mad in their hands'. For *ṭaʿam*, 'judgment', see on 119:66.

he drove him out because David appeared to the Philistine lord to be insane, and as such, according to the ancient beliefs, under the protection of the god or gods.

THE HYMNIC INTRODUCTION 1–3

1. I will bless the Lord: this is an expression both of gratitude and praise. None can add anything to the power of God but every one can and should acknowledge his majesty and graciousness. See on 16:7.

his praise . . .: i.e. I shall utter the praise of Yahweh continually. Thus the true meaning of life is to glorify God in word and deed.

2. My soul: this may be a substitute for the personal pronoun 'I'. See on 33:19.

makes its boast: the godly person does not draw attention to his own qualities, but to the attributes of God. The Psalmist does not mean to say that he is arrogant in God, but that he gives praise to God (cf. 105:3). Some boast of the abundance of their riches (49:6 (M.T. 7)); others make their boast in their idols (97:7) or in their own cleverness (Prov. 20:14) and might (Jer. 9:23). But true boasting or glorying in God is this: that one 'understands and knows me, that I am the Lord who practise kindness, justice, and righteousness . . .' (Jer. 9:24).

the afflicted: the Hebrew *ʿānāw* has been given several interpretations during the past half century or so. A. Rahlfs (*ʿānî und ʿānāw in der Psalmen* (1892)) argued that the poor and their enemies formed two parties, opposed to each other, within the Jewish community; similar views were also held by a number of other exegetes (Baethgen, Briggs, Duhm, *et al.*). In more recent years commentators have tended to see in the term 'humble' an individual rather than the personification of a group or party. This is not, of course, the only current view; so H. Birkeland (*The Evildoers in the Book of Psalms* (1955)) has suggested that the pious or the afflicted one represents the Covenant people of God, while their enemies are the foreign nations. This view leads to the asumption that most of the individual Psalms of Lamentation, if not all, are Royal Psalms. Very similar is the argument of Mowinckel (*PIW*, I, p. 229), who writes: 'The "oppressed", or "humble" . . . are no party or class, but Israel, or her representative men in times of emergency, "oppressed" by external enemies, "helpless" in their own power, "in need of help", and "humbly" hoping for the interference of Yahweh'. The various interpretations, of which the above is but a sample, become suspect when one proposal is taken as the *only* explanation of all the afflicted and their enemies. The right solution may well be found in a synthesis of the various views, because the Psalter spans more than one century and the different psalms must have had varying backgrounds, although they employed the same terminology but not necessarily the same shades of meaning. Snaith (*LN*, p. 235) has pointed out that there is a frequent confusion between *ᶜānāw* and *ᶜānî*, both of which could be translated: 'poor, afflicted' (cf. *BDB*, p. 776b); he suggests that the former denotes a state of mind, while the latter a situation in life; and as a generalization this may be right, although in many cases both terms are synonymous. For a brief summary on this subject, see Johnson, 'The Psalms', *OTMS*, pp. 198–203; R. Martin-Achard, *Approche des Psaumes* (1969), pp. 18–25.

3. O magnify the LORD: or 'Glorify . . .', by praising Yahweh (69:30 (M.T. 31)) and by acknowledging his greatness.
exalt his name: see on 30:1.

THE TESTIMONY TO THE GRACE OF GOD **4–10**

4. I sought the LORD: the Hebrew *d-r-š* is frequently used as a technical term for visiting the sanctuary, and this may be its meaning here; the purpose of the Psalmist was to seek Yahweh's help (see on 24:6).
he answered me: either by a favourable oracle (cf. J. Begrich, 'Das priesterliche Heilsorakel', *ZAW*, LII (1934), pp. 81–92) or by delivering the worshipper from his distress.
from all my fears: or 'from all the things I dread' (Prov. 10:24; Isa. 66:4).

5. Look to him: lit. 'They looked to him (i.e. Yahweh)'; the subject is not further defined. *RSV* follows some Hebrew MSS., S, and Jerome in reading the imperative *habbîṭû* for M.T. *hibbîṭû*. Perhaps we should read with M.T. '(Those who) look (an equivalent to the gnomic aorist?) to him shall be radiant and their faces (i.e. they themselves) shall never be ashamed', because they will receive the help for which they long.

6. This poor man: or 'Here is a humble man' (so Weiser, Kraus). This expression is similar to that in Lam. 3:1: 'I am the man who has seen affliction'. Verse 6 gives a personal witness to the truth of the general statement in verse 5.
the LORD heard him and answered him by delivering him from all his troubles (verse 6*b*). The accusative 'him' is not expressed in M.T., but it is to be understood (cf. 'saved *him*' in verse 6*b*).

7. The angel of the Lord: or 'The messenger of Yahweh' is mentioned in the Psalter only here and in 35:5,6. Sometimes it is difficult to distinguish between Yahweh and his messenger (cf. Gen. 31:11ff.; Jg. 6:11–23), so that in some instances one could nearly say that 'the angel of Yahweh' is a manifestation of Yahweh himself (cf. v. Rad, *OTT*, I, p. 287). This may be the case also here, although Gunkel *et al.* think of the 'angel' as an individual divine being who (together with the heavenly host) surrounded the pious (cf. Jos. 5:14; 2 Kg. 6:17). Johnson (*OMICG*, p. 31) suggests that the Psalmist had in mind not a mere individual messenger of God but a *host*, 'a collective unit or corporate personality'.

who fear him: i.e. Yahweh. S. Plath (*Furcht Gottes* (1963), p. 103) has shown that in most cases the phrase 'those who fear him' is a technical term for the pious community, those faithful to God. S. Terrien ('Fear', *IDB*, II, p. 258) argues that the fear of the Lord 'is not merely to be equated with reverence, piety, or religion', because in our usage these terms have lost their ancient connotation of awesomeness. See on verse 9.

8. taste: or 'judge' as in Prov. 31:18: 'she judges that her profit is good', so R. B. Y. Scott, *Proverbs, Ecclesiastes* (*AB* 18, 1965), p. 187. Cf. 1 Pet. 2:3.

and see: or 'and drink deeply' (so Dahood, *PAB*, I, p. 206) deriving the verb not from *r-ʾ-h* ('to see') but from *y-r-ʾ* II ('to be fat, sated; drink deeply'), cognate with *r-w-h* ('to drink one's fill'). Another possible occurrence of this verb *y-r-ʾ* II is in Prov. 23:31.

that the Lord is good: V has '. . . is kind'. The singer of this Psalm invites his fellow-worshippers to share in his experience of deliverance so that they, too, might become partakers of Yahweh's salvation.

Happy is the man . . .: see on 1:1.

who takes refuge in him: this is a frequent expression in the Psalter (cf. 2:12, 5:11 (M.T. 12), 7:1 (M.T. 2), 11:1, 16:1, etc.). The refuge may be the sanctuary where, in a special way, one may find the presence of Yahweh and asylum.

9. fear the Lord: an attitude of reverence and awe, which does not become terror or dread but finds expression in praise and prayer, obedience and loyalty.

his saints: better 'his holy ones' (see on 16:3); *NEB* 'his holy people'. According to Noth (*LPOE*, p. 218), this is the only certain example in the *OT* where the phrase denotes the pious; usually it refers to the divine beings (so also Mowinckel). 'Holy' (*ḳāḏôš*) is that which belongs to Yahweh alone and stands in a special relationship to him. The people of God are holy because they have been chosen by him, and in as far as they have responded to him by giving him their absolute allegiance.

have no want: cf. 23:1. The Psalmist does not base his argument upon a doctrine of rewards and punishments, but upon his own experience. He argues from the particular to the general, because God is absolutely trustworthy.

10. The young lions: LXX has *plousioi* ('the rich'; similarly also S and V) and this seems a possible reading, although it is not clear what Hebrew word was read by the Greek translator; perhaps *kabbîrîm* ('mighty men') for M.T. *kᵉp̄îrîm*. Some scholars (e.g. Weiser, Cohen) retain the M.T. reading, and assume that 'the young lions' is used either metaphorically or to represent mere physical strength apart from the care of God (cf. 104:21). *NEB* has 'Unbelievers'. See on 35:17, 58:6.

who seek the Lord: i.e. who worship him (see on 24:6). The affirmation that the loyal servants of Yahweh will lack nothing must be a generalization. The Psalmist could hardly say that the righteous have *never* experienced hardship and trouble, but his own life and the belief in the goodness of God enable him to deduce that, with God on his side, blessings are sure to come.

THE MEANING OF THE FEAR OF YAHWEH **11–22**

11. O sons: this was a customary form of address of the Wisdom teachers to their pupils, not only in the *OT*, but also in Egyptian and Babylonian Wisdom literature (cf. e.g. the 'Words of Ahiqar', *ANET*, pp. 427–30). The origin of this convention may be found in the teaching which parents imparted to their children from time immemorial (cf. Exod. 12:26; Dt. 6:6–9).

listen to me: i.e give heed to practise it.

the fear of the Lord is a frequent theme in the Book of Proverbs, where it occurs well over a dozen times (e.g. 1:7,29, 2:5, 8:13, 9:10, etc.). See also verses 7 and 9.

12. What man is there . . .: this may be an emphatic way of saying: 'Who is the man . . .? Let him do the following . . .' (cf. 25:12). There is none (or very few) who would not desire life characterized by 'fulness of joy' (16:11) and other blessings of God (34:10 (M.T. 11)), but not all are prepared to accept it on

God's terms. For an Egyptian parallel, see *RB*, LVII (1950), pp. 174ff.

many days: or 'a long life' (cf. Prov. 3:2, 10:27).

13. Keep your tongue . . .: this does not refer so much to the making of rash promises or disclosures which might lead to ruin (cf. Prov. 13:3, 21:23) as to that malicious use of words which harms one's fellows, and in the end also oneself (cf. 15:3; Jas. 3:2–12), for 'death and life are in the power of the tongue' (Prov. 18:21; cf. Sir. 28:13–18).

14. Depart from evil: also in 37:27; cf. Job 1:1,8, 28:28; Prov. 16:17. It is by 'the fear of the LORD' that 'a man avoids evil' (Prov. 16:6; cf. Prov. 3:7).

do good: (as in 37:27). The author refers, apparently, not only to particular deeds of kindness and righteousness, but to the whole way of life which is marked by these qualities (cf. Isa. 1:16f.; 1QS i:2).

seek peace: this phrase occurs only here in the *OT*, while Rom. 14:19 may provide a commentary on it: 'Let us then pursue the things that make for peace' (*NEB*).

pursue it: (cf. 23:6). This means a single-minded devotion to the cause of harmony between man and man, which is, at the same time, one of the aspects of the fear of the Lord.

15. The eyes of the LORD: he cares in a special way for the righteous (see on 33:18; cf. Sir. 15:19).

righteous: see 1:5.

his ears . . .: i.e. he is ready to answer the appeal of the needy.

16. The face of the LORD: or 'the fury of Yahweh' (so Dahood, *PAB*, I, p. 133). The face is usually the mirror of one's feelings and dispositions. Very often 'to behold one's face' means to receive favour (see on 31:16), but sometimes the result may be less pleasing. In Gen. 31:2 we read that, when Jacob saw the face of Laban, it was no longer friendly as formerly (cf. Exod. 14:24). The evildoers in Ps. 34 will have a similar experience when they see the face of Yahweh.

to cut off the remembrance of them is to destroy them so that no trace or influence of them is left in the place they lived. Even their name will be mentioned no more (cf. Job 18:17; Jer. 11:19). They are not only forgotten, but their name has also become a sign of ill-omen and objectionable; therefore it is deliberately shut out of active memory (cf. 109:15).

17. When the righteous cry for help: so *RSV*, following LXX,

T, S, and V; lit. 'When they . . .'. The addition of 'the righteous' may be a correct interpretation of M.T. On the other hand, Ibn Ezra *et al.* have thought that the Psalmist spoke of the evildoers who turned from their evil ways and repented (cf. Cohen, *PSon*, p. 101).

18. the brokenhearted: cf. 51:17 (M.T. 19), 147:3. This expression is probably the opposite of having a heart of stone (Ezek. 11:19, 36:26). It seems that the Psalmist is stating that none is beyond the saving help of God, as long as the afflicted person turns to God in humility and trust. The important factor is not the circumstances of the person concerned but rather his attitude to God.

19. Many are the afflictions . . .: or 'Even though the trials of the righteous might be many . . .'. This may suggest that either the righteous will not be exempt from trials but will be delivered out of them, or they will be helped in all circumstances.

20. He keeps all his bones: i.e. he preserves the godly even in the most disastrous situation. To 'break one's bones' means to afflict one with disease (51:8 (M.T. 10); Isa. 38:13) or to oppress (Mic. 3:3); consequently to *keep* one's bones must mean the opposite —to protect one from such and similar calamities. On the possible allusion to this verse in Jn 19:36, see C. H. Dodd, *The Interpretation of the Fourth Gospel* (1953), p. 234.

21. Evil shall slay the wicked: this may mean that the evildoers (verse 16) will be destroyed by their own deeds, or it may refer directly to the punishment of God. On the 'wicked', see 1:1, 28:3.

righteous: see on 1:5.

will be condemned: or 'are brought to ruin' (*NEB*); 'will perish' (so Dahood; see on 5:10), which seems to be supported by verse 22*b*, in that it repeats the same verb (with the negative); there is no reason why those who take refuge in Yahweh should be condemned, although there was a possible danger that they might *perish* unless Yahweh intervened.

22. The LORD redeems: Dahood (*PAB*, I, p. 207) sees here a metaphor depicting Yahweh as paying ransom to Death, but this is rather unlikely. The verb *p-d-h* can indeed mean 'to ransom by means of a payment' (as in Exod. 13:13; Lev. 27:27), but the context of this phrase does not demand such an interpretation; it may simply mean 'to deliver' (see on 119:134).

the life: the Hebrew word used is *nep̄eš* which often means 'soul', but the *RSV* rendering is a frequent connotation of it (some 171 times out of some 756 occurrences, according to *BDB*, p. 659a). See on 33:19.

who take refuge in him: see verse 8.

Psalm 35 A Prayer for Deliverance

Most recent commentators assign this Psalm to the Laments of the Individual (see Introduction, pp. 37ff.), while Mowinckel (*PIW*, I, p. 219) regards it as a National or Congregational Psalm. If so, the personal traits of the poem would point to the King or the leader of the people as the speaker in this Psalm. Although a number of the so-called 'I-Psalms' may be Royal Psalms, it is not certain that this is true of Ps. 35.

The lament is made up of three petitions, each followed by a promise to give thanks for the deliverance, or by an expression of certainty that God will save the Psalmist in the time of his need. This structure of the Psalm has led some exegetes (e.g. Taylor) to the conclusion that its constituent parts were originally independent laments, either relating to three different episodes in the life of the Psalmist, or suggesting separate authors. On the other hand, Psalms in general are characterized by the use of stereotyped forms and language, and therefore it is unwise to apply strict modern criteria to these ancient songs. Furthermore, troubles do not always come singly, nor are all the word-pictures statements of fact. Therefore it may well be that the Psalm is a literary unity, describing the Psalmist's experience from three different angles, with some overlapping. Verses 1–10 are a prayer for the divine help, using metaphors derived from warfare and hunting. In verses 11–18 we find a further petition, but the main theme is the complaint about the ingratitude of the Psalmist's former friends, who have become his enemies when he needed them most. The last section (verses 19–28) continues the series of appeals to Yahweh, giving a further description of the dire need. Probably Schmidt (*PHAT*, p. 67) is right in regarding this poem as a prayer of an accused man, and the experiences of Job show that such accusations need not be confined to actual legal proceedings. The author is looking forward to the deliverance from this particular calamity, which is unjustly interpreted as the consequence of a supposed wicked sin on the part of the Psalmist, or as a divine punishment. Eaton (*PTBC*, p. 103) thinks that 'the enemies may be rival states with allies among the King's subjects', and he regards the lament as a Royal Psalm.

There is little evidence for determining the date of this composition; in its present form it may belong to the early part of the post-Exilic period. The metre of the Psalm is uneven, chiefly 3 + 2.

A Psalm of David: see Introduction, pp. 43ff. and 46.

THE PETITION FOR PROTECTION **1–10**

1. Contend: the Hebrew verb is derived from *r-y-b* ('to strive, contend'), and in this verse the meaning may be either: 'Plead my cause (in a lawsuit)' (so most scholars), or: 'Attack' (so Dahood). Although the forensic usage is more common, the verb is also used for contending on a battlefield. In Jg. 11:25 we read: 'Did he ever strive against Israel, or did he ever go to war with him?' The martial language of verses 1–3 may imply that the metaphor in verse l*a* also, is derived from the battlefield background. Yahweh is depicted as a warrior, a man of war (Exod. 15:3; Dt. 32:41ff.). Some commentators (e.g. Oesterley) have regarded these warlike word-pictures applied to Yahweh as unseemly and as an expression of 'an undeveloped conception of God' (*TP*, p. 218). Although modern theology may be more developed, the language of the Psalmist could hardly be described as unseemly, because it is obviously metaphoric, and the underlying thought is simply a cry for help.

2. shield: for *māğēn*, see on 3:3.

buckler: the Hebrew *ṣinnāh* was a shield larger than the *māğēn*, perhaps similar to the covering shields of the Assyrians, which protected the whole body (see *ANEP*, pll. 368, 373). The *ṣinnāh* of Goliath was carried by his 'shield-bearer' (1 Sam. 17:7,41). The buckler was probably rectangular in shape, and made of a wooden frame covered with leather. Metal shields must have been comparatively rare (cf. 1 Kg. 10:16f.).

and rise for my help: (so LXX) or '. . . as my help'. Dahood (*PAB*, I, p. 210) proposes '. . . to my battle', and he derives the noun *ᶜezrāh* from *ᶜ-z-r*, which he takes as a cognate with the Ugaritic *ģzr* ('warrior, hero'). For the construction of 'for my help', see *GK* 119i.

3. Draw the spear: either from the spearholder or from the armoury; the former alternative is more likely. The spear was a weapon consisting of a wooden shaft (some four feet in length?) on which was mounted a spearhead of stone, bronze, or iron (cf.

de Vaux, *AI*, p. 242). It could be thrown like a javelin (1 Sam. 18:11, 20:33), or used at close range (1 Sam. 26:8).

and javelin: the Hebrew reads *ûsᵉgōr*, which was understood by the ancient versions as an imperative: 'Stop!'. We expect, however, the name of a weapon, and 1QM v:7 offers the solution. There we find a noun *sgr* meaning 'the socket or clasp of the blade (of the spear)', and consequently the corresponding word in our Psalm probably means 'javelin' or 'spear', i.e. it is denoted by metonymy, just as 'the cloth' can be used to refer to the clergy. See also Yadin, *SWSLSD*, p. 137.

my soul: this may be an idiomatic expression for 'I'; see on 33:19.

I am your deliverance: lit. 'I am your salvation'. This is regarded by Kraus as an example of a priestly oracle of salvation which offers assurance to the afflicted man. 'Salvation' (*yᵉšûᶜāh*) can have a theological or a non-theological usage (as in Gen. 47:25; Jos. 6:25; 1 Sam. 23:5). In the former sense 'salvation' is the work of God, and its content may vary according to the circumstances (cf. F. F. Bruce, '"Our God and Saviour": a Recurring Biblical Pattern', *The Saviour God*, ed. by S. G. F. Brandon (1963), pp. 54–65). It can denote victory over historical enemies (Ps. 60:11, 144:10) or the forces of Chaos at the creation (65:5–8 (M.T. 6–9)); it can also signify vindication (72:4, 76:9 (M.T. 10)), help (69:14 (M.T. 15), 119:81), or freedom from troubles and calamities (Job 30:15, Ps. 18:19 (M.T. 20), 85:7 (M.T. 8), 91:16). Occasionally it has eschatological undertones (67:2 (M.T. 3)). S. R. Driver (*NHTS*, p. 119) suggests that salvation and deliverance 'seldom, if ever, express a spiritual state *exclusively*: their common theological sense in Hebrew is that of *a material deliverance attended by spiritual blessings* (e.g. Isa. 12:2, 45:17)'. Man's role in this work of salvation is one of trusting response to God: 'Fear not, stand firm, and see the salvation of the Lord, which he will work for you today' (Exod. 14:13). See also G. Fohrer, '*Sōzō*', *TDNT*, VII, pp. 970–80.

4. This verse is practically identical with 40:14 (M.T. 15), 70:2 (M.T. 3).

Let them be put to shame by being disappointed in their expectations (so Kissane) or, more likely, continuing the martial description, by being defeated (either in battle or in a lawsuit); cf. 127:5.

my life: lit. 'my soul'; see on 33:19, 34:22.

Let them be turned back: cf. Isa. 41:11, 42:17.

who devise evil against me: or 'who plan my discomfiture' (cf. Jer. 17:18; see also Ps. 140:2) continuing the series of military metaphors.

5. like chaff: this presents a picture of helplessness and worthlessness; see on 1:4.

the angel of the LORD: some read 'your angel' (cf. *BH*) to avoid its repetition in the following verse. See on 34:7; M. Mansoor, *The Thanskgiving Hymns* (1961), pp. 77–84.

driving them on: the accusative 'them' is not in M.T. but it is to be supplied from the context (see verse 6*b*). The angel of Yahweh will hurl the enemies before him like chaff driven by the wind. See also 104:4 where the winds are described as God's messengers.

6. Let their way be dark . . .: i.e. let misfortune or punishment come upon them as certainly as a man would fall on a dark and slippery path (cf. 73:18; Jer. 23:12). Dahood's translation: 'Let their destiny be Darkness and Destruction' is a good paraphrase (*PAB*, I, p. 208) but it is doubtful whether 'Darkness' and 'Destruction' in this verse are poetic names for the underworld.

7. without cause: this is rendered by Dahood (*PAB*, I, p. 211) as 'secretly, stealthily', dissociating the Hebrew *ḥnm* from the root *ḥ-n-n* ('to be gracious'), and linking it with the Ugaritic *ḫnn*, which suggests something done stealthily or secretly. In view of verses 12–14, the *RSV* rendering is preferable, for the enemies are repaying good with evil.

they hid their net for me: i.e. they are represented as hunters planning to catch their victim in their nets or pits (see on 7:15). M.T. could be rendered literally, 'they hid for me the pit, (even) their net', but this overloads verse 7*a*, and therefore most recent scholars (so also *NEB*) transpose 'the pit' (*šaḥaṯ*) to verse 7*b* (perhaps in place of 'without cause' (*ḥinnām*) which might be deleted).

they dug a pit for my life: lit. 'they dug for my soul' (i.e. for me). The *RSV* reading finds some support in S.

8. This verse is reminiscent of Isa. 47:11 and Ps. 9:15 (M.T. 16) but the exact relationship is not clear. Briggs (*CECBP*, I, p. 304) regards our verse as dependent upon the other two passages.

Let ruin come upon them: lit. '. . . upon him' but the datival verbal suffix may be taken collectively rather than as referring to the chief opponent. LXX (also S) has the plural forms of the respective verbs and pronouns.

the net: see on 9:15, 31:4. This refers figuratively to the plots of the enemies, but it is impossible to be sure about the nature of the hostile schemes. If 'contend' in verse 1 is taken in a forensic sense, then verses 1–8 may be a poetic description of the enemies seeking the death of the Psalmist by supposedly legal means. In that case the punishment which they hoped would come upon the innocent man, would fall upon them, and thus they would be truly ensnared in their own nets. See on 27:12.

to ruin: the Hebrew *beššôʾāh* is occasionally emended into *bešûḥāh* ('into a pit'). Dahood (*PAB*, I, p. 212) attributes the same meaning to *šôʾāh*.

9. Then my soul shall rejoice: i.e. after the maledictions have been answered. It is clear that such an attitude is not identical with Christian *ideals* but, on the other hand, the Psalmist lived in the pre-Christian era.

exulting in his deliverance: or '. . . his victory'; see on verse 3.

10. All my bones shall say: or 'My whole being . . .'. Gunkel (*PGHAT*, p. 148) thinks that the reason why the reference is made to the bones, is that they had been 'broken' by illness (see on 31:10, 51:8).

who is like thee in power and majesty? (cf. Exod. 15:11; Mic. 7:18; IQM x:8, xiii:13; 1QH vii:28.) For this use of a rhetorical question to express Yahweh's incomparability, see Labuschagne, *IYOT*, pp. 22f., 65.

the weak: (*ʿānî*), see on 34:2.

the weak and needy: the repetition of 'the weak' is stylistically suspect, and therefore it is often deleted (cf. Gunkel, Weiser, Kraus, *et al.*). Dahood retains M.T. but describes the phrase as a 'ballast variant' to compensate for the absence of a parallel term which might be expected in this line. The 'needy' (*ʾeḇyôn*) is a frequent word in the Psalter, where it is found some 23 times. It can denote one who is actually poor in material things (cf. Dt. 15:7f.; 1 Sam. 2:8; Ps. 112:9, 113:7, 132:15) and hence it can come to mean 'one who needs help' (12:5 (M.T. 6), 140:12), in particular the succour of God. At the same time it can indicate not only the nature of the situation, but also an attitude to God; thus in 37:14 the poor and needy are parallel to those 'who walk uprightly' and in 86:1f. they are synonymous with 'the godly'. Ps. 69:33 (M.T. 34) describes the needy as 'his (i.e. God's) own', and it is possible that in some instances the word signifies the servants of God as a whole. In the Qumran community the expression had become one of its self-designations. According to K. Elliger (*Studien zum Habakkuk-Kommentar vom Toten Meer* (1953), p. 222) it was nearly a proper name for the sectarian community. Cf. also the name 'Ebionites', the name of the early Jewish Christian sect (cf. G. R. Driver, *The Judaean Scrolls* (1965), pp. 160f.).

THE FORMER FRIENDS TURNED ENEMIES **11–18**

11. Malicious witnesses: lit. 'Witnesses of violence'. According to Dt. 19:15 a charge can be sustained only if there are at least two witnesses. A false witness, if he is found out, receives the same punishment as would have been inflicted upon the accused man (Dt. 19:19). This is a form of *lex talionis* or the law of retaliation (or 'tit for tat'). Cf. M. A. Klopfenstein, *LAT*, p. 68.

rise up to testify against me (see Mk 14:57; cf. also 1Kg. 21:13).

they ask me . . .: or 'they charge me . . .' (so Kissane). Dahood (*PAB*, I, p. 208) renders: 'they whom I know not interrogate me', but this seems less suitable. It is more likely that the accused was charged with crimes of which he had no knowledge.

12. evil for good: the enemies return ingratitude for sympathy and kindness (see verses 13–14). Some exegetes have suggested that 'evil for good' is not only the general principle involved, but that it implies the reversal of the actual circumstances. Once the enemies (i.e. the former friends) were afflicted with disease, but the Psalmist identified himself with them in their distress. Now the Psalmist is stricken, while his one-time associates deduce from his illness that he must have committed some awful crime or sin which must be severely dealt with. This would also be a means of dissociating oneself from the crime (in this case an imaginary sin) and of protecting oneself and the community from any possible divine punishment (see Jos. 7; 2 Sam. 21:1–9).

my soul is forlorn: lit. 'childlessness for my soul', which seems to be a textual corruption. Kraus (*PBK*, p. 275), following Perles and Gunkel, suggests *śāḵû lᵉ* ('they seek for (my life)') for M.T. *šᵉḵôl* ('childlessness'), deriving the verb from *ś-k-h* ('to look'), which is not used in the *OT*, although there are some nouns from this root (cf. *BDB*, p. 967b). This seems a reasonable conjecture; *NEB* has 'lying in wait to take my life'.

13. But I: this emphasizes the contrast between the behaviour of the Psalmist and that of his present enemies.

when they were sick: rather than 'when they played the pipe' (i.e. rejoiced) as suggested by Dahood (*PAB*, I, p. 209). The latter rendering would destroy the contrast, and would leave verse 12 in the air.

I wore sackcloth: 'I became involved in the misfortunes of my friends as if they were members of my own family' (cf. 2 Sam. 12:16); this seems to be a good example of righteousness in action. Sackcloth was a sign of grief, mourning, and penitence (see on 30:11).

I afflicted myself with fasting: lit. 'I afflicted my soul . . .'. 'To afflict oneself' is wellnigh a technical term for fasting (cf. Lev. 16:29,31; Isa. 58:3,5). The purpose of fasting may have been the desire to awaken the pity and compassion of Yahweh either for the individual or the nation. It is unlikely that in the pre-Exilic period, or even in the early part of the post-Exilic times, fasting was regarded as a meritorious practice by the *OT* writers, although the popular view may have been less noble (cf. Isa. 58:3). Sometimes fasting was a preparation for the reception of a divine communication (cf. Exod. 34:27f.; Dan. 10:3). In order that fasting might be meaningful, it had to be accompanied by the right attitude of mind and heart (cf. Jer. 14:12; Zech. 7:4ff.) and therefore, essentially, it was a vehicle of the right spirit rather than an end in itself. Cf. also J. Behm, '*Nēstis*', *TDNT*, IV, pp. 927–31.

I prayed with my head bowed . . .: lit. 'And my prayer returned into mine own bosom' (*AV*, *RV*). Nötscher, Kraus, *et al.* take this phrase as a parenthesis expressing the wish that the prayer for the enemies might become ineffective. See Mt. 10:13: '. . . if it is not worthy, let your peace return to you' (cf. also Isa. 55:11). Some scholars (e.g. Gunkel, Kissane, Taylor) read: 'and my prayer (for them) kept on returning upon my mouth' (i.e. 'I kept on praying for them'). This involves a change of *ḥêḳî* ('my bosom') into *ḥikkî* ('my mouth'). *NEB* renders: 'When my prayer came back unanswered'.

14. He was grieved over the illness of his fellow-men even as much as he would have grieved over the death of the nearest of his kin.

bowed down is one of the outward expressions of mourning.

in mourning: the Hebrew verb is *ḳ-d-r*, 'to be dark', and it is often used figuratively of mourning. S. R. Driver and G. B. Gray (*The Book of Job*, *ICC*, 1921, p. 53) have remarked that *ḳ-d-r* 'does not denote a state of mind (sorrowing or grieving), but (meaning properly *to be dirty*) has reference to the squalid person and dark attire . . . of a mourner in the East'. Cf. 2 Sam. 12:16–20, 13:19; Est. 4:1; Ps. 38:7 (M.T. 8).

15. But at my stumbling . . .: i.e. when calamity befell me (cf. Job 18:12; Jer. 20:10). 'Stumbling' is a figure of speech describing disaster, a sudden change in one's fortunes, etc.

cripples whom I knew not does not give a satisfactory sense. The problem is the Hebrew word *nēḵîm* (*RSV* 'cripples', i.e. smitten ones). Although the *qal* form of the verb *n-k-h*, 'to smite', is not found in the *OT*, Dahood may be right in suggesting that it may have been used in addition to the causative form; hence we could translate: 'smiters (*nōḵîm*) whom I did not know' (cf. *PAB*, I, p. 213) or paraphrasing: 'smiting (me with their words) although I have not been involved (i.e. I did not know) (in the things of which I am accused)'. T renders: 'who smite me with their words', while *NEB* has 'nameless ruffians'. Some commentators emend *nēḵîm* into *noḵrîm* ('strangers').

slandered me: lit. 'they tore (me) to pieces', a well-known and appropriate figurative description of slander.

without ceasing: lit. 'and they were not silent'.

16. they impiously mocked . . .: the meaning of this phrase is problematic. A possible literal rendering might be 'with (or 'like') the profanest mockers of a cake', and some take this as an allusion to knaves who mock at their neighbours for a piece of cake. Dahood (*PAB*, I, p. 214) argues that the Hebrew *ḥ-n-p* can also mean 'to slander', hence 'when the encircling mockers slandered me (*b*^{e}*ḥon*^{e}*pî*)', deriving *mā*^{c}*ôḡ* (*RSVm* 'cake') from ^{c}*-g-g* or ^{c}*-w-g* ('to draw (a circle)', 'to make a cake') (cf. Jastrow, *DTTM*, II, p. 1040b). For another possible interpretation, see Winton Thomas, *TRP*, p. 13 and *NEB*. Eaton (*PTBC*, p. 104) sees here an allusion to sorcery.

gnashing . . . with their teeth: for similar picturesque accounts of anger, see Job 16:9; Ps. 37:12, 112:10; Lam. 2:16.

17. look on: with indifference and without intervening.

from their ravages: the Hebrew *miššōʾêhem* is problematic (for various conjectures, see Kraus, *PBK*, p. 275). Dahood (*PAB*, I, p. 214) connects the word with *šōʾāh* ('pit'), hence 'from your pits', which seems as good as any of the proposed emendations.

my life: lit. 'my only one'. The same expression is also used in 22:20 (M.T. 21).

the lions: *RP* reads *kôp̄*^{e}*rîm* ('the ungodly') for M.T. *k*^{e}*p̄îrîm* ('lions', see on 58:6), which is associated with the Arabic *kafara*, 'to become an unbeliever' (cf. *TRP*, p. 12); *NEB* 'the unbelievers'.

18. This verse concludes the second section of the lament, and it is in the form of a vow of thanksgiving.

Then I will thank thee . . .: i.e. I will gratefully declare your gracious help, to my fellow-worshippers (see on 18:49).

the great congregation was probably the cultic assembly in the Temple during a pilgrimage festival (cf. Mowinckel, *PIW*, II, p. 87). Yahwism was a religion of fellowship; the glad news of the deliverance of one is the cause for rejoicing of all. For *ḳāhāl*, 'congregation', see on 89:5.

GOD DELIGHTS IN THE WELFARE OF HIS SERVANT **19–28**

19. who are wrongfully my foes: or 'my treacherous foes' (so Dahood, *PAB*, I, p. 214) which takes *ᵓōyᵉḇay šeḳer* as a genitive construction in which the noun in the construct state has the pronominal suffix.

wink the eye finds explanation in Sir. 27:22: 'Whoever winks his eye plans evil deeds' (cf. Prov. 6:13, 10:10).

who hate me without cause: i.e. the reason for the enmity is not to be found in the behaviour of the Psalmist, but in the character of those who hate him (cf. 38:20 (M.T. 21), 69:4 (M.T. 5)).

20. they do not speak peace: i.e. they behave like foes; cf. 28:3; Jer. 9:8 (M.T. 7).

but against those . . .: Dahood (*PAB*, I, p. 215) takes the preposition *ᶜal* as a verb, reading *wᵉᶜālū* ('but they attack'), from *ᶜālāh*, 'to attack'; cf. Prov. 21:22; *JAOS*, LXVII (1947), p. 155.

who are quiet in the land: this expression is a *hapax legomenon* in the *OT*, and Mowinckel (*PIW*, II, p. 87) regards it as a poetic term for the congregation or the people of God. T renders 'the righteous in the land'; *NEB* 'peaceable folk'.

words of deceit: or 'deceitful schemes'. For *mirmāh* ('deceit'), see on 52:4.

21. They open wide their mouths: this may be a gesture of mockery and contempt, as in Isa. 57:4. Dahood sees here a word-picture depicting a ravenous monster (cf. Isa. 5:14 where Sheol is described as a monster with mouth wide open, ready to swallow up its victims), yet the former alternative seems more likely.

our eyes have seen it: i.e. the fall or the misfortune of the Psalmist (so most exegetes). It is possible that this expression was an echo of a similar legal statement whereby the witnesses affirmed their testimony. If so, then the enemies are claiming that they witnessed the accused commit the crime(s).

22. Thou hast seen: this is an appeal to Yahweh as the truly reliable eye-witness, as over against all the false ones. This is also a statement of innocence, for only a man who need not fear the truth, can invoke the all-seeing Witness and Judge.

be not silent: see on 28:1.

be not far from me: i.e. 'help me in my need'. For the ancient Israelites the situation of being forsaken by God was often identical with being beset by troubles; see on 22:11.

23. Bestir thyself is synonymous with **awake.** The construction of the verse is rather unusual because it has two imperatives in the first half and two vocatives in the second. However, this may be intentional, and no emendation is required (cf. *BH*). A similar arrangement is also found in 27:2*b*. For a brief discussion on the anthropomorphic expressions, see on 7:6, 44:23. It is unlikely that these word-pictures were taken literally, rather they conveyed vividly the intended thought. Not infrequently the *OT* stresses the otherness of God, lest some people might be tempted to think of God purely anthropomorphically; so in Job 10:4 the writer exclaims: 'Hast thou eyes of flesh? Dost thou see as man sees?'. In Hos. 11:9 Yahweh says: '. . . I am God and not man'; he is the one who 'will neither slumber nor sleep' (Ps. 121:4), and who 'does not grow faint or grow weary' (Isa. 40:28). It is probable that most 'of the anthropomorphisms we find in the Bible are mere accommodations to human speech, or vivid pictures used for their psychological effect rather than theological in significance' (Rowley, *FI*, p. 75). See also Eichrodt, *TOT*, I, p. 211ff.

for my cause: see on verse 1.

24. Vindicate me: lit. 'Judge me' or 'help me' (cf. 7:8 (M.T. 9), 26:1, 43:1), so that my enemies have no longer any reason to gloat over my misfortunes.

according to thy righteousness: similarly in 7:8 (M.T. 9), where the Psalmist pleads to be judged 'according to my righteousness'. Some scholars delete this phrase for metrical reasons.

25. . . . say to themselves: or '. . . say in their heart'. Some exegetes (so also *NEB*) regard verse 25*a* as a variant of verse 25*c*. For 'heart', see on 27:3.

Aha, we have our heart's desire: lit. 'Aha, our soul'; for *nepeš* ('soul, desire'), see on 33:19.

We have swallowed him up: i.e. we have destroyed him (cf. 124:3; Prov. 1:12; Jer. 30:16; Lam. 2:16).

26. The Psalmist prays for a reversal of fortunes, and re-echoes verse 4; cf. 40:14 (M.T. 15), 70:2 (M.T. 3).

clothed with shame and dishonour: i.e. surrounded by calamities. For a contrast, see 132:16 where Yahweh speaks of the priests as being clothed with salvation. Similarly, Yahweh can be described as clothed, figuratively, in majesty and strength (93:1), or in honour and majesty (104:1).

27. who desire my vindication: or 'righteousness' (see on 33:5). They need not necessarily be his friends in the literal sense of the word, but simply Israelites who delight in righteousness wherever it is manifested (cf. 40:16 (M.T. 17)). In this verse 'righteousness' and 'welfare' ('peace', see on 119:165) are probably synonymous; in *OT* thought the one could hardly exist without the other.

28. thy righteousness: (see 31:1, 119:40), i.e. your conformity to your own self-revelation. In this instance God's righteousness is seen in the vindication of the oppressed one (cf. G. Schrenk, '*Dikaiosunē*', *TDNT*, II, p. 195).

thy praise: i.e. my gratitude to you and my public witness to your saving help.

Psalm 36 In Thy Light do We see Light

Most commentators agree that this Psalm includes elements from different psalm-types. Verses 1–4 could be part of a lament, although Weiser *et al.* see in them a reflection of Wisdom literature. Such a difference of opinion is due to the fact that the different types of literature may share many common features. Verses 5–9 are clearly hymnic in style, while verses 10–12 are in the form of a prayer. Some exegetes (e.g. Duhm, Schmidt, Taylor) have concluded that the literary relationship between the various parts is so weak that originally they must have formed at least two independent compositions. Theoretically this is possible, yet mixed types are common in the Psalter, and, on the whole, it is more likely that Ps. 36 is a literary unity. Mowinckel (*PIW*, I, p. 220) would assign it to the National Laments in the 'I'-form (similarly also Eaton), but it could well be an Individual Lament (see Introduction, pp. 37ff.). If we emphasized the Wisdom elements of this poem, it could be classed, with certain reservations, as a Wisdom Psalm, reminding us of such poems as Ps. 1 and 14. The noticeable lack of personal characteristics may support this suggestion.

If the Psalm is a lament, then the speaker seems to be a man pursued by arrogant oppressors (verse 11); it is less likely that he is a national figure, or that he represents the community as a whole. According to Weiser the setting of the Psalm was the cult of the Covenant Festival, but this is far from certain, especially if verse 11 is directly relevant to the author's circumstances.

The date of the Psalm is a matter of conjecture, but the post-Exilic period is a reasonable suggestion.

The metre is mainly 3 + 3.

To the choirmaster: see Introduction, p. 48.

A Psalm of David: see Introduction, pp. 43ff. and 46.

the servant of the Lord: this is one of the honorary titles of David (cf. 78:70, 89:3 (M.T. 4)). The phrase can also be used to denote Israel as the people of God (Isa. 41:19) or certain distinguished persons, such as Moses (Dt. 3:4,5; Jos. 1:1,13, 12:6; 2 Kg. 18:12), Joshua (Jos. 24:29; Jg. 2:8). The term 'servant' (*ᶜeḇeḏ*) can suggest a variety of other shades of meanings, e.g. 'slave', 'worshipper' (102:14 (M.T. 15), 116:16), 'official', etc. It can also be used as a polite or humble self-designation (69:17 (M.T. 18)). See W. Zimmerli and J. Jeremias, *The Servant of the Lord* (*SBT* 20, 1965), pp. 11–36. Roughly speaking, the term *ᶜeḇeḏ* denotes a relationship (or a Covenant relationship) of the weaker member to the stronger party. The relation of dependence may be either enforced (as the slavery in Egypt) or it may be voluntary (cf. Exod. 21:5f.). The plural noun (*ᶜaḇāḏîm*) may denote the whole worshipping community.

A DESCRIPTION OF THE GODLESS LIFE 1–4

1. Transgression: or 'rebellion'; see on 32:1. The phrase 'transgression speaks' (*neʾum pešaᶜ*, lit. 'an oracle of rebellion') is a *hapax legomenon* in the *OT*. The Hebrew *neʾum* usually means 'utterance, whisper, oracle', and in most cases it is linked with God as the subject (cf. 110:1). In Num. 24:3,15 it is associated with Balaam, and in 2 Sam. 23:1 with David. In view of all this, the present usage is suspect because what follows could hardly be described as an oracle of rebellion. Consequently some scholars (e.g. Kraus) have emended *neʾum* into *nāᶜēm* ('pleasant (is rebellion to the wicked)'). Most of the ancient versions suggest that *nʾm* is probably a verb, and if so, we could render: 'The rebel (*pōšēaᶜ*) speaks wickedly (*lᵉrešaᶜ*) deep in his heart (*libbô*)', i.e. he plans evil. See also L. A. F. Le Mat, *Textual Criticism and Exegesis of Psalm XXXVI* (1957), pp. 4–9.

fear of God: the word used for 'fear' is *paḥaḏ* ('dread'). This is not so much reverence for God as terror inspired by God (cf. Isa. 2:10, 19:21). In other words, the wicked man neither reveres God nor fears him, and for the time being he behaves as if God did not exist (cf. 10:4, 14:1, 53:1 (M.T. 2)).

before his eyes: i.e. he is not afraid of God, because for him God is not a living reality which should be taken into account. See Rom. 3:18.

2. This verse is textually difficult, and all the suggested renderings, including those of the ancient versions, are hypothetical. Probably the general idea of the verse is that the godless person deludes himself in believing that God will neither find out his sin nor hate it (or him). Perhaps we should render: '. . . he flatters himself . . . as regards the finding out of his iniquity, and as regards the hating (of it (or 'of him'))'. For 'iniquity' (*ᶜāwōn*), see on 32:1.

3. mischief and deceit may form a hendiadys 'mischievous deceit' (cf. 10:7). For 'deceit' (*mirmāh*), see on 52:4.

to act wisely and do good: or 'to act wisely so as to do good' (cf. Isa. 1:16f.). The first verb, *ś-k-l* (see on 101:2), is well known from Wisdom literature (cf. Prov. 10:5,19, 14:35, 15:24, etc.).

4. He plots mischief . . .: or 'he devises wickedness . . .'. Instead of devoting himself to the study of God's word day and night, i.e. continuously (see on 1:2), he plans evil schemes even on his bed so that he may perform them in the morning (cf. Mic. 2:1). 'Mischief' (*ʾāwen*) can denote that 'operative, evil power, pregnant with disaster and everything connected with it' (Mowinckel, *PIW*, II, p. 7); it can also signify calamity, divine punishment (90:10), or a thing of nought, such as an idol (Isa. 66:3). H. Wildberger (*Jesaja* (*BK* 10, 1965), p. 43) points out that *ʾāwen* does not belong to the terminology of the Covenant traditions, but rather to Wisdom literature.

a way that is not good: or 'the path of crime' (so Dahood, *PAB*, I, p. 219) who regards 'not good' (*lōʾ ṭôḇ*) as a composite noun, 'no-good'. For this kind of way of life, see Prov. 1:10–18, 16:29; Isa. 65:2.

he spurns not evil: instead of refusing evil and choosing good (Isa. 7:15f.) he spares no effort to pursue mischief.

THE NATURE OF GOD AND ITS MEANING FOR THE GODLY **5–9**
Schmidt sees as the main theme of these hymn-like verses the praise of God as the giver of rain, but Kissane (*BP*, p. 159) is nearer to the mark when he describes this section as the Psalmist's confession of faith.

5. This verse is practically the same as 57:10 (M.T. 11), which see.
steadfast love: or 'Covenant loyalty'; see on 26:3.
extends to the heavens: so *RSV* reading *ᶜaḏ šāmayim* for M.T. *bᵉhaššāmayim* which is taken by Dahood (*PAB*, I, p. 217) as: 'from the heavens'. Yet the *RSV* rendering may be more likely, in view of the parallels in 57:10 (M.T. 11), 108:4 (M.T. 5). The Psalmist probably does not mean that God's Covenant loyalty extends *from* the heavens, but that it is immeasurable. The same is also true of God's faithfulness (*ʾᵉmûnāh*) which is, in this verse, a synonym of *ḥeseḏ* ('Covenant loyalty'). Not infrequently it signifies 'trust' (Prov. 12:22), 'reliability' (2 Kg. 12:15), 'what is self-consistent and dependable' (40:10 (M.T. 11), 89:2 (M.T. 3), 119:86; Isa. 25:1), or 'truth' (2 Chr. 19:9; Jer. 5:1). It is a word that often belongs to the Covenant terminology, suggesting Yahweh's dependability in the Covenant relationship. He has promised to bless his loyal servants and to punish the offenders, and in his faithfulness he implements his word (89:28–37 (M.T. 29–38), 119:75). In LXX the usual translation of *ʾᵉmûnāh* is either *pistis* ('faith'; some 20 times) or *alētheia* ('truth'; some 22 times); for further details, see *TDNT*, VI, p. 197.

6. righteousness: see on 31:1, 33:5.
the mountains of God: or, more likely, 'the mighty (or 'the highest') mountains . . .'. D. Winton Thomas (*VT*, III (1953), p. 215) points out that the presence of the divine name may raise 'a person or subject to a pre-eminent degree by virtue of the fact that the person or subject in question is brought into relationship with God' (cf. also *VT*, XVIII (1968), p. 123). This is one of the ways used by the *OT* writers to express the superlative degree. For a Ugaritic example, cf. *Aqhat* II, vi:22 (Driver, *CML*, p. 55, n.3).
thy judgments: the Hebrew *mišpāṭ* can mean a number of things, such as judgment, verdict, decision based on precedent, custom, justice; in a sense it is what God (King, or judge) both

demands and gives, hence it can also mean salvation or help (cf. Isa. 30:18f.). H. S. Gehman (*Biblical Studies in Memory of H. C. Alleman* (1960), p. 121) remarks that 'acting in accordance with *mišpāṭ* is a form of *imitatio Dei* . . .'. See also 119:7.

the great deep is found elsewhere in the *OT* in Gen. 7:11; Isa. 51:10; Am. 7:4. It is doubtful whether the author is referring to the mythological significance of the deep (*teĥôm*); rather he depicts the opposite to the 'mighty (or 'highest') mountains', and consequently it could be translated 'the deepest depths'. For *tehôm*, see on 104:6.

thou savest: probably '. . . you help'. Mowinckel (*He That Cometh* (1956), p. 47) has pointed out that 'salvation' means 'not only deliverance from earthly, cosmic, and demonic enemies, and from distress and misfortune, but good conditions, well-being, outward and inward prosperity, fertility in the field, flock, nation . . .'. Hence 'to save' in this verse may mean 'to preserve the life of . . .' or 'to provide for every need (of both man and beast)'.

7. steadfast love: see on 26:3. It is precious because it has no match, and is beyond all comparison.

O God: some commentators (e.g. Le Mat, Dahood, also *NEB*) take it as a plural, suggesting that both *gods* and men seek refuge in Yahweh. If so, 'gods and men' may be a stereotyped phrase which should not be taken literally (cf. Jg. 9:9,13; possibly also Gen. 32:28; cf. E. A. Speiser, *Genesis* (*AB* 1, 1964), p. 255). The *RSV* seems more likely.

the shadow of thy wings: i.e. in your protective care. See on 17:8. Le Mat (op. cit., p. 23) argues that the expression 'thy wings' is not to be identified with the wings of the cherubim over the Ark. He believes that behind this metaphor is the symbol of the winged disc of the sun, so well known in Egypt and in Mesopotamia (cf. Mal. 4:2; *ANEP*, pll. 320, 493, 536). This origin of the word-picture is not impossible, but it is unlikely that the original significance, whatever it might have been, was retained throughout the history of this phrase. G. v. Rad (*OTT*, 1, p. 402) links the idea of seeking refuge in Yahweh with 'the function of the sanctuary as asylum for one who was being pursued. But it became divorced from this sacred institution and, given a spiritual sense, passed over into the general language of prayer'.

8. the abundance of thy house: lit. 'from the oil of . . .' (*middešen bêṯeḵā*). 'Your house' is usually understood as the

Temple of Jerusalem, although Gunkel, Le Mat, *et al.* are doubtful on this point, since the verb seems to refer to 'the children of men' (verse 7). This phrase may suggest, however, the worshipping community, or such as take refuge in Yahweh. The Hebrew *dešen* may denote 'oil' (Jg. 9:9), 'fat' (63:5 (M.T. 6)), 'food' in general, or 'rich food' (Job 36:16); figuratively it could be used of spiritual blessings (Isa. 55:2), or of blessings in a more material sense (65:11 (M.T. 12)). It could even signify 'the refuse or ashes from the altar' (Lev. 1:16). In this Psalm the reference seems to be to the sacrificial meal in the Temple (cf. Ringgren, *IR*, p. 155), which is, at the same time, a symbol of spiritual blessings, or it could be a word-picture describing the goodness of God to all who worship him.

thou givest them drink . . .: this seems to support the metaphorical interpretation of this verse. Yahweh is the generous host who supplies all the needs of his guests (cf. 23:5).

the river of thy delights may allude to the 'river whose streams make glad the city of God' (46:4 (M.T. 5); cf. Ezek. 47:1ff.). Literally, the Hebrew *naḥal* (*RSV* 'river') can be either the practically dry river bed, or the same valley filled with waters to the brim during the rainy season; sometimes it may denote a brook (fed by a spring?), as in 74:15. The Psalmist may have had in mind the second connotation. The word *ʿēḏen* ('delights') may be etymologically associated with '(the garden of) Eden', the 'home' of Adam and Eve; cf. the Apocalypse of Abraham xxi. Dahood (*PAB*, I, p. 222) thinks that these verses may have provided the background of the messianic banquet, which is frequently mentioned in the Qumran literature and in the *NT*.

9. the fountain of life may be a stock phrase (like 'the tree of life') to denote the never-failing source of life (Prov. 10:11, 13:14, 14:27, 16:22). What appears to be a fuller form of the same expression is found in Jer. 2:13, 17:13: 'the fountain of living water' (cf. also Jn 4:10ff., 7:38; 1QH viii:14). Dahood takes 'life' in this phrase as an equivalent to 'eternal life', but most exegetes would differ from him.

in thy light: probably 'in the light of your countenance' (as in 4:6 (M.T. 7)), i.e. 'in your favour and love' (cf. 89:15 (M.T. 16)). Dahood (*PAB*, I, p. 222) suggests 'in your field' (reading *ʾûreḵā*), i.e. in the eternal abode of the righteous; his argument seems ingenious but not convincing.

see light: this may mean 'to live', as in Job 3:16; Ps. 49:19

(M.T. 20), and it may refer to a full and satisfying life; Dahood, as might be expected, sees here a reference to the reward of eternal life (cf. Isa. 53:11 (LXX, 1QIs[a]); 1QS iv:6ff.).

THE CONCLUDING PRAYER **10–12**

10. O continue: or 'Prolong'. For a contrast, see 109:12; cf. 85:5 (M.T. 6).

steadfast love: see on 26:3.

those who know thee: i.e. who recognize your authority. The verb *y-d-*[c] ('to know') may belong to the Covenant terminology (see H. B. Huffmon, 'The Treaty Background of Hebrew YĀDA[c]', *BASOR*, 181 (1966), p. 3).

thy salvation: lit. 'your righteousness' (see on 33:5). It is parallel to *ḥesed̲* in verse 10*a*, and it probably suggests Yahweh's faithfulness to his Covenant promises.

the upright of heart is a frequent expression in the Psalter to denote the worshippers of Yahweh (see on 7:10).

11. the foot of arrogance: Dahood may be right in suggesting that the abstract 'arrogance' is paired with the concrete 'wicked ones' (verse 11*b*), with the result that the former also has come to have a concrete meaning, hence 'the foot of the arrogant'. The metaphor may be derived from the ancient practice in which the victorious king or the commander of the forces placed his foot upon the neck of the subdued enemy; see note on 110:1; cf. *ANEP*, pl. 308.

the wicked: see on 28:3.

drive me away: either from the protection of the Temple (so Kraus) or from one's own home so as to make one homeless (cf. 2 Kg. 21:8; Job 15:23; Mic. 2:8).

12. There: or 'See' (so Dahood), linking it with the El Amarna *šumma* ('behold'). M.T. is difficult, because there is nothing to which 'there' could refer.

the evildoers: see on 28:3.

lie prostrate: the verb is probably a perfect of certainty (cf. *GK* 106n). When the wicked attempt to harm the godly, they will most certainly fall; they will be thrust down never to rise again. The latter allusion is not to resurrection (so Davison), but simply to their final overthrow.

Psalm 37 Nothing but God is More than Everything and No God

Mowinckel (*PIW*, II, p. 111) has described this Wisdom Psalm as 'a non-cultic poem'. It consists of 22 strophes (usually containing four lines each) forming an alphabetic acrostic—the successive strophes begin with the letters of the Hebrew alphabet in their appropriate order (see introduction to Ps. 9–10). Each strophe is, more or less, an independent unit, so that the whole poem approximates to a collection of proverbs (cf. Weiser, *POTL*, p. 315). Nevertheless, the main theme of the Psalm—recompense and retribution—forms an underlying unity.

The author of this composition may well have been an old man of considerable experience (verse 25), and he could be described as a Wisdom teacher. His aim was to impart his hard-won knowledge to the younger generation, to impress upon them that any seeming injustice in this life is of a transitory nature.

The Psalm offers little help in dating it. Weiser (*POTL*, p. 316) argues that the Psalm contains references to the tradition of the Covenant cult (e.g. the curses and blessings (verse 22), the possession of the land (verses 9, 11, 18, 22, 29, 34)), and therefore it may well be a pre-Exilic work. The majority of scholars prefer, however, a later date, *c.* fourth century B.C. or so.

There is little progression of thought in the Psalm but it could be divided into four main sections. Verses 1–11 stress the need for trusting in Yahweh, and verses 12–20 illustrate the inevitable reversal of the fortunes of the wicked man. Verses 21–31 show that sooner or later the future of the righteous will be a time of blessing, while verses 32–40 re-emphasize retribution and recompense. Essentially each section is little more than a variant of the main theme of the Psalm.

The metre of this composition is, on the whole, 3 + 3.

A Psalm of David: see Introduction, pp. 43ff. and 46.

1. Fret not yourself . . .: there is no need to be angry at the prosperity of the wicked, or to envy the success of those who practise injustice. Both they and all that is theirs will soon perish. To continue in this spirit of resentment would be tantamount to doubting Yahweh's justice (cf. 73:21f.). The same phrase is also found in Prov. 24:19 (cf. Prov. 3:21, 23:17, 24:1). See also *TPst*, pp. 120f.

wrongdoers: (see on 28:3, 119:3), they are the opposite of those who trust in Yahweh and who do good (cf. Zeph. 3:5,13).

2. the grass . . . the green herb are often used as similes to depict that which is temporary (cf. Job 14:2; Ps. 90:5ff., 103:15, 129:6; Isa. 40:6; Mt. 6:30; Jas 1:10,11), especially that type of transitoriness which is not renewed by God.

3. Trust in the LORD: this provides the antidote to envy and resentment (cf. 4:5 (M.T. 6); Prov. 3:5, 16:20, 28:25f.; Isa. 26:4).

so you will dwell in the land . . .: lit. 'dwell (imperative) in . . .' (as a result of your obedience). Loyalty to Yaweh brings with it the blessing of dwelling in his land, i.e. in Canaan, and so also in his care.

and enjoy security: *NEB* 'and find safe pasture'. This is the rendering of an ambiguous Hebrew phrase and consequently there are numerous alternative suggestions. Dahood (*PAB*, I, p. 228), following LXX, proposes 'feed on its riches' (i.e. those of the promised land); he postulates a noun *ʾāmôn* ('riches') identical in meaning with *hāmôn* in verse 16.

4. Take delight in the LORD: v. Rad (*OTT*, I, p. 382) suggests that the verb *ʿ-n-g* expresses the bold idea of 'letting oneself be spoiled by Yahweh' (cf. Job 22:26, 27:10; Isa. 58:14). The emphasis is not so much on the spiritual aspect as on the material welfare (verse 11).

the desires of your heart are attained through the reliance upon Yahweh who will fulfil the hopes and expectations of his people (cf. 20:4f. (M.T. 5f.), 21:2 (M.T. 3); Mt. 6:33; Lk. 12:31).

5. Commit your way to the LORD: lit. 'roll your way upon Yahweh' (see on 22:8; cf. Prov. 16:3; 1 Pet. 5:7). The basic idea is probably the same as in 55:22: 'Cast your burden on the LORD'. The 'way' (see on 103:7) here is one's life or destiny.

trust in him: i.e. direct your whole life according to the ways of God (cf. Prov. 16:20, 28:26); see on 78:22.

and he will act: or 'he will turn (to you)'. For this use of the verb *ʿ-ś-h* (*RSV* 'act'), see G. R. Driver in *Studies in Old Testament Prophecy*, ed. by H. H. Rowley (1950), pp. 53ff.

6. He will bring forth: or 'He will make (your vindication) shine forth . . .'. This usage of the verb *y-ṣ-ʾ* ('to shine') is attested in some of the cognate languages (e.g. Arabic, Assyrian, Ugaritic; cf. *VT*, IV (1954), pp. 305ff.).

your vindication: lit. 'your righteousness' (see on 33:5). Temporarily the true values of life may have been obscured, for some reasons or other, but Yahweh *will* fulfil his part of the Covenant relationship, and this will be experienced either as a blessing or as a curse, according to the promises of God known to all his people (cf. Isa. 62:1).

as the light: i.e. the intervention of God will be as obvious as the appearance of light in darkness (cf. Job 11:17; Isa. 58:10; Jer. 51:10). Dahood (*PAB*, I, p. 228) takes the word 'light' (*ʾôr*) in the sense of 'sun' (cf. Hab. 3:4; also Job 31:26, 37:11,21).

as the noonday: i.e. when the sun is at its brightest.

7. Be still before the LORD: lit. 'Be silent . . .'. This is no mere resignation but a positive effort to replace fretting and doubting by a trust in Yahweh, because the solution of the problem can come only from him (62:1,5 (M.T. 2, 6); Isa. 7:4, 30:15).

wait . . . for him: i.e. for his vindication.

who prospers in his way: or 'who makes his own way prosperous'. The Psalmist has in mind only the wicked man who is successful in material things (cf. 73:3). Material welfare, far from being an evil in itself, can be a blessing of God (cf. Job 42:10ff.; see on 1:1).

who carries out evil devices: i.e. the man who puts into effect his cunning schemes of dubious nature (cf. Jer. 11:5); *PLE* has 'and thrives by villainy'.

8. Refrain from anger . . .: that is, anger, wrath, and irritation serve no useful purpose, at least in this situation; rather they show that the person who displays such an attitude has misinterpreted the purposes of God. So there is the danger that the angry man, young or old, may easily find himself in the camp of the evildoers, in rebellion against God.

9. the wicked shall be cut off: i.e. they shall share the same fate as the nations of Canaan when Israel entered the Promised Land (cf. Dt. 12:29, 19:1).

shall possess the land: this should, perhaps, be rendered emphatically 'they (and no one else) shall possess . . .'. One may also take the Hebrew *hēmmāh* (*RSV* 'they') as a synonym of the Ugaritic *hm* ('behold'); see on 9:6. This will be the blessing of the righteous for only they will have the right of dwelling in Yahweh's land (cf. Prov. 2:21, 10:30; also Isa. 57:13, 60:21, 65:9; Mt. 5:5; CD i:8, xiii:21); see on 25:13, 140:13.

10. The **wicked** (see on 1:1, 28:3) and all their prosperity will last only for a short time, and after that they will be no more (cf. verse 36; Isa. 29:20).

though you look . . .: or 'and even though I look with great care', following the reading of 4Q171 1–2, ii:6 which has *wʾtbwnnh*, 'and I look . . .', for M.T. *wᵉhiṯbônantā*.

he will not be there: or 'it (i.e. his place) will be no more'.

11. the meek: or 'the humiliated' (so Weiser). These are, apparently, the righteous among the people of Israel. See on 34:2. **abundant prosperity** is more than mere material wealth; rather it is a general well-being that is based upon the harmonious relationship between man and God, and man and his fellow.

12. The wicked plots . . .: cf. verses 7 and 32. He schemes wickedness against the godly because of the latter's righteousness, rather than because the faithful prosper (so Dahood); their welfare seems to be as yet in the future. The ungodly man in his anger resembles a wild animal, gnashing his teeth, thus displaying his bitter enmity (cf. Job 16:9; Ps. 35:16, 112:10; Lam. 2:16).

13. the LORD laughs . . .: see on 2:4. The plotting of the wicked is futile in the long run, for their calculations are based on the assumption that God is ineffective in human affairs. If this supposition is wrong, then the Psalmist's description is very apposite: God cannot but laugh at the arrogant and twisted plans of the wicked.

his day: i.e. the day of reckoning and death (cf. 1 Sam. 26:10; Job 18:20; Ob. 12).

14. This verse is probably to be taken metaphorically, and both the **sword** and **bows** would symbolize violence and oppression. The verse seems to be too long, and it may have been expanded by the addition of **to bring down . . . who walk uprightly.** Some exegetes alter the order of the phrases, reading: 'The wicked draw the sword to slay those who walk uprightly, and bend their bows to bring down the poor . . .' (cf. Kraus, *PBK*, p. 287).

sword . . . bows: see on 44:6.

who walk uprightly: or 'whose manner of life is blameless' (Prov. 29:27; 1QH ii:10). The usual phrase for describing this type of man is 'the upright in heart' (7:10 (M.T. 11), 11:2, 32:11, 36:10 (M.T. 11), etc.).

15. The Psalmist states his firm belief that sin eventually destroys the sinner, and that wickedness recoils on its author (cf. 7:14ff. (M.T. 15ff.); Jer. 2:19, 5:25, 6:21).

16. Riches may indeed contribute towards a happy life, but it is not founded on them; therefore the pious man in his poverty may well be happier than the godless man in all his wealth (cf. Prov. 15:16, 16:8; Tob. 12:8).

the abundance of many wicked: or 'the great abundance of the wicked' (following LXX, S, V, and Jerome), which offers a better parallel to verse 16*a*; this involves, however, a change of *rabbîm* ('many') into *rab̲* ('great'). Dahood (*PAB*, I, p. 229) retains M.T. (which is supported also by 4Q171), but renders it 'the wealth of the wicked rich' (cf. Prov. 28:20,27).

17. the arms of the wicked shall be broken: this provides a picturesque description of the shattering of the power of the wicked to do harm. The Hebrew *z*^{e}*rôa*^{c} ('arm') is often a symbol of strength or might (77:15 (M.T. 16), 89:10 (M.T. 11)) and to break it means to render its 'owner' powerless (cf. Job 38:15; Ps. 10:15; Jer. 48:25; Ezek. 30:21; 1QH viii:33). On the other hand, whatever may be the actual strength or weakness of the righteous, they shall not be moved, because they are upheld by Yahweh whose power cannot be broken or rendered ineffective. Therefore they can be confident in their God. Dahood (*PAB*, I, p. 229) translates 'the arms' as 'the resources' (cf. Job 22:8,9). Sometimes *z*^{e}*rôa*^{c} can denote a person as a whole (Job 26:2); for further details, see Johnson, *VITAI*, pp. 50ff.

18. The LORD knows the days . . .: see on 1:6. God cares not only about the ultimate destiny of the upright but he is also concerned for their day-to-day existence. 'Days' may simply mean 'life' (cf. 31:15 (M.T. 16)), although Dahood (*PAB*, I, pp. 77 and 229) takes the word in the sense of 'possessions', deriving it from the Ugaritic *ymm* ('to create') (cf. the Hebrew *ḳ-n-h*, 'to create' and *miḳneh*, 'property'). This would give a better parallel to 'their heritage' in verse 18*b*, but the linguistic argument of Dahood may not convince everyone.

their heritage: i.e. their share among the people of God will continue to be the possession of their descendants for ever.

19. . . . put to shame: or '. . . shall not wither' (from the verb *y-b-š*; *RSV* derives the verb from *b-w-š*); the former reading is more likely.

in evil times: i.e. in adversity. The righteous are not assured of immunity from all troubles but of deliverance out of the apparent disasters (cf. Job 5:19f.). In view of verse 19*b* the reference may be to drought, although the language is, more likely, metaphorical.

days of famine: this calamity was a common scourge of the ancient Near East, yet the righteous are promised provision enough and to spare. This is rather a statement of faith than the result of common experience.

20. Some scholars read verse 25*c* after verse 20*a* (so Duhm, Gunkel), altering 'his children' into 'their children' (*zar*ᶜ*ām*; cf. Job 5:3f., 20:7f.; Ps. 109:9f.).

the enemies of the LORD: 4Q171 1,3–4, iii:5*a* reads 'and those who love Yahweh' (*w*ʾ*whby yhwh*) but M.T. seems to be preferable.

like the glory of the pastures: or 'like the best (or 'costliest') of the he-lambs' (taking *yāḳār* ('precious') as a singular used collectively). In the second alternative the wicked are likened to the fattest of animals chosen for sacrifice (cf. 1 Sam. 15:9,15), and the point of comparison would be the swift change in their fortunes. One day they were the best of the flock, the next they were gone. Another alternative is to read *kîḳōḏ kûrîm* ('as in a fiery furnace') for M.T. *kîḳar kārîm* (*RSV* 'like the glory of . . .'); cf. *TRP*, p. 13. *NEB* 'like fuel in a furnace'.

they vanish—like smoke . . .: or, better, 'they all vanish in smoke' as suggested by 4Q171 1,3–4, iii:7, which reads *kwlw* ('all of them') for the second verb *kālû* ('they vanish') in M.T. If we adopt the *RSV* rendering, then the godless are compared to the short-lived flowers of the pasture lands, and to smoke, both being fitting descriptions of all that is ephemeral (cf. 68:2 (M.T. 3), 102:3 (M.T. 4); Isa. 51:6).

21. cannot pay back: i.e. when the crisis comes, the wicked will become penniless; he will be forced to borrow but will not be able to pay his debts. This is a picture of extreme poverty rather than of dishonesty (cf. Prov. 24:16). The lot of the defaulting debtor in the Biblical period was rather harsh, as seen from 2 Kg. 4:1; Neh. 5:4ff.; Isa. 50:1; Am. 2:6, 8:6; Mt. 18:25. On the other hand, the righteous will have enough for his own needs and he will be in a position to help others also (cf. Dt. 15:6, 28:12, 44).

22. See verse 9 (cf. Exod. 20:5ff.; Dt. 5:9ff.; Prov. 3:33). The blessings and curses (see on 58:6–9) are reminiscent of those pertaining to the Covenant (cf. Dt. 27:11ff., 28:1ff., 28:15ff.).

23. The reading of 4Q171 1,3–4, iii:14 suggests: 'By Yahweh are the steps of a man established, (and) in all his ways he delights', and it supplies *bkwl* ('(and) in all'); a similar division of the verse is also suggested by the main ancient versions, although the two parallel lines become metrically unbalanced. Perhaps the verb 'established' (*kônānû*) is a corrupt dittograph of *bkwl*.

he delights: less likely, 'he preserves' (cf. Arabic *ḥafiẓa*, 'to keep, preserve'; see Winton Thomas, *TRP*, p. 13).

24. The upright man is not exempt from adversity, but for him trouble does not mean a final ruin (cf. 145:14; Prov. 24:16; Mic. 7:8) because 'the LORD is the stay of his hand'.

25. The old sage is now appealing to his own experience, and he affirms that he has never seen an upright man forsaken by God, or his children reduced to begging. This statement is probably not to be taken in an absolute sense, because more than once he has referred to the troubles of the righteous (see verses 7,12,14, 19,24,32,33,39,40). His point is, apparently, that the godly man will not be *permanently* forsaken by God (cf. Prov. 10:3; 11QPs[a] Zion xi).

26. See verse 21 and Dt. 28:11f. The upright man will prosper, and will also know how to use his affluence (cf. Kirkpatrick, *BPCB*, p. 194). 'Lending' in his case is not a business proposition but a means of helping those in need; no interest would be charged on the loans (cf. Exod. 22:25 (M.T. 24); *ANET*, pp. 217b, 221a).

his children become a blessing: either the source of blessing or its mediators (cf. Prov. 10:7; Zech. 8:13). The word 'his children', *zarᶜô*, could also be read as 'his arm', *zᵉrōᶜô* (so Dahood, *PAB*, I, p. 231).

27. Depart from evil . . .: as in 34:14 (M.T. 15) (cf. Prov. 3:7; 1QS vi:15). This is the condition on which the promise in verse 27*b* rests.

abide for ever: LXX adds 'and for ever' (*wāᶜeḏ*), while some commentators suggest the addition of 'in the land' (*bāʾāreṣ*) (cf. verse 29) which may well give the right sense. The Psalmist is thinking of the descendants of the righteous as being in possession of the ancestral inheritance rather than of eternal life (cf. 102:28 (M.T. 29)).

28. the LORD loves justice: (cf. 33:5), i.e. Yahweh acts justly and demands the same behaviour from his servants. Perhaps we should render 'the just' for 'justice', as in Prov. 2:8 (see R. B. Y. Scott, *Proverbs and Ecclesiastes* (*AB* 18, 1965), p. 41).

his saints: or 'his loyal servants' (see on 30:4, 86:2). Verses 28*cd* and 29 form another strophe.

the righteous: this is an interpretative addition to M.T., but some commentators follow LXX^A, in reading: 'the ungodly will perish for ever' (*ᶜawwālîm leᶜôlām nišmedû*); the same idea is also found in verse 38. This proposed reading seems likely, and it is possible that the noun was omitted due to haplography, while the verb was subsequently altered. This variant is also supported by 4Q171 3–10, iv:1 although the text is rather fragmentary; it also gives a line beginning with the required letter *ᶜayin*.

29. See verse 9.

30. . . . utters wisdom: see on 111:10; cf. 49:3 (M.T. 4); Prov. 10:31f. The righteous man speaks words of experience, and since he lives in a right relationship with God, his wisdom is grounded in the fear of the LORD (cf. Prov. 1:7).

speaks justice: i.e. what the LORD loves (cf. verse 28). For *mišpaṭ* ('justice'), see on 36:6, 119:7.

31. The law . . . is in his heart: this may be an echo of Jeremiah's New Covenant (Jer. 31:33; cf. Ezek. 36:27), although similar ideas appear elsewhere (cf. 40:8 (M.T. 9); Isa. 51:7). It is not enough to have a law engraved on a stone (2 C. 3:7) or recorded on a scroll; it must be written in one's heart, so that the whole life is no longer determined by the stubbornness of one's heart but by the law of God. For 'law', see on 119:1.

his steps do not slip: because he does not try to make his own laws, but is guided by God and his law (cf. 18:36 (M.T. 37); Prov. 4:11f.). It is possible that 'steps' in this verse is equivalent to 'feet'.

32. This verse resumes the theme of verses 12–15 but the actual form of oppression remains uncertain. If we take verse 32*b* literally, the author may have had in mind a judicial murder (cf. 1 Kg. 21:8ff.), perhaps for the purpose of acquiring the property of the just man. This may be implied by the repeated references to the possession of the land (verses 9,11,29,34).

33. . . . brought to trial: for a contrast, see 109:7. The accusation, in this instance, is false, and in spite of all the underhand means used (cf. Jer. 18:18), God will not permit the righteous to be condemned.

34. wait: this usually suggests a hopeful expectancy which is never disappointed as long as one waits for the LORD (cf. 25:3, 27:14, 69:6 (M.T. 7)).

keep to his way: this is probably a command to observe the law (cf. Exod. 18:20, 32:8; Dt. 5:33, 8:6; etc.).

he will exalt you: he will confer upon you a special favour (cf. Ezek. 21 : 26)—namely, that you shall possess the land (see verse 9).

the destruction of the wicked: this suggests, in the first place, that justice will be done on this earth, rather than that the righteous will have the opportunity of gloating over the punishment of the godless.

35. I have seen . . .: the author attests the truth of his previous statement by appealing to his observation of the fortunes of his contemporaries.

overbearing: or 'acting like a tyrant'. Some exegetes (e.g. Oesterley) read 'exultant' (*ᶜallîṣ*) which may be implied by LXX; 4Q171 supports M.T. See also on 54:3.

towering like a cedar of Lebanon: so *RSV*, after LXX and V, reading *miṯᶜalleh kᵉʾerez hallᵉḇānôn*; M.T. is probably corrupt. A somewhat forced translation of it is: 'spreading himself like a leafy tree in its native soil' (cf. Cohen, *PSon*, p. 116), similarly *AV*, *RV*. The cedar is a coniferous tree, and in biblical times it was found mainly on the mountains of Lebanon. It could attain some 100 feet in height, and its wood was esteemed for its hardness. It was often used as a symbol of strength and splendour.

36. Again I passed by: M.T. could be rendered: 'and yet he passed away'. The *RSV* rendering is also supported by the ancient versions as well as by 4Q171, and it provides a fitting parallel to verse 36*b*.

37. the blameless man: or 'the man of integrity'. Some commentators read: 'Keep (your) godliness (i.e. *tōm* for M.T. *tām*) and pay attention to uprightness (*yōšer* for M.T. *yāšār*)'; similarly the ancient versions. Dahood (*PAB*, I, p. 232) argues that the reference is to 'two divine messengers who lead the way to virtue' (cf. 25:21); yet *RSV* seems preferable.

posterity for the man of peace: or 'the end of (such) a man is peace' (cf. Kraus, *PBK*, p. 286), but in view of verse 38*b* the *RSV* rendering is more likely. For 'peace', see on 119:165.

38. transgressors: i.e. rebels against the rule of God (see on 51:1).

the posterity of the wicked: or 'the future of . . .' (so Weiser). *RSV* may be right, although 'posterity' is not a common meaning of *ʾaḥᵃrîṯ* (cf. verse 28*d*; 109:13). The total loss of descendants would be a great disaster for the Israelite because, in a way, one continued to 'exist' in one's children.

39. salvation: or 'deliverance from trouble' (see on 35:3).
refuge: or 'their stronghold' (*RV*); cf. 27:1.
time of trouble: Dahood suggests 'in time of siege' (*PAB*, I, p. 232), but this seems less likely.

40. The Psalm concludes with the affirmation that Yahweh is the helper and deliverer of those who have taken refuge in him (cf. 18:30 (M.T. 31); Prov. 30:5; CD 20:34; 1QH ix:28f.).

Psalm 38 The Lament and Confession of a Sick Man

This Psalm is a Lament of the Individual (see Introduction, pp. 37ff.) and the early Church took it as one of the seven Penitential Psalms (the others were 6, 32, 51, 102, 130, 143). This Psalm is said to have 'an alphabetic structure' in that it consists of twenty-two verses, which is the number of the letters in the Hebrew alphabet; but it is not an acrostic Psalm.

The lament is dominated by three main themes: illness, guilt, and the hostility of enemies and former friends. In many ways the sufferer is reminiscent of Job, except that the former is conscious of his sins. It would be pointless to speculate about the nature of the illness; it could have been leprosy, but this is no more than a guess. It is possible that what appear as the details of the misfortune are simply part and parcel of the established pattern. It is plausible that the stereotyped language could be modified in the light of actual circumstances, but it would be impossible to say whether a particular detail belonged to the conventional word-pictures of trouble, or whether it was an actual description of a particular experience (cf. Ringgren, *FP*, pp. 61ff.; *ANET*, pp. 383ff.). The main point of this lament is that the Psalmist regarded his illness and suffering as a punishment inflicted upon him by God; consequently he was led to confess his sins. The situation was aggravated by the aloofness of his friends and kinsfolk, while others (who may have included the former) sought his hurt and planned his destruction. This is not an unknown method of manifesting one's (perverted) piety on the cheap. The Psalm is a testimony to the author's faith in God and in his unfailing goodness. The author may despair of himself but not of God (so Delitzsch).

The date of the Psalm is uncertain, but few would accept the Davidic authorship. Since the Psalm exhibits certain similarities with the Book of Jeremiah, the prophet has occasionally been regarded as the composer of this lament (see Davison, *Cent. BP*, I, p. 200). Rashi and some more recent commentators (e.g. Briggs) interpreted the poem as an expression of the experiences of the nation, but the individual interpretation seems more likely.

The Psalm opens and concludes with a brief petition (verses 1 and 21–22) while the main part of the Psalm consists of the lament itself. Verses 2–10 show a close connexion between sin and suffering, while in verses 11–12 we find a reaction of the friends, relatives, and other members of the community, to the illness of the unfortunate man. The following verses (13–20) continue the description of his plight and express his trust in God who alone can help him. See also R. Martin-Achard, *Approche des Psaumes* (1969), pp. 41–8.

The metre of the Psalm is, with a few exceptions, 3 + 3.

A Psalm of David: see Introduction, pp. 43ff. and 46.
for the memorial offering: see Introduction, p. 48.

THE INTRODUCTORY PRAYER **1**

For the exegesis of this verse, see 6:1, which is practically identical with this verse. This is a further pointer to the stereotyped language of this lament.

THE LAMENTATION **2–20**

2. thy arrows: in verse 2*a* God is depicted as an archer (cf. Dt. 32:23; Job 6:4; Ps. 7:12 (M.T. 13); Lam. 3:12). J. Horst (*Hiob* (*BK* 16, 1960), p. 101) reminds us that in antiquity severe skin diseases were often regarded as due to divine and demonic arrows (cf. 91:5). He also mentions the Phoenician deity 'Resheph of the arrow', whom he compares to Apollo of the Greek myths. In the Ugaritic texts Resheph is the god of plague. The arrows of God can signify divine judgment in general (7:12f. (M.T. 13f.)). For 'arrows', see on 11:2.
thy hand: the Hebrew *yāḏ* ('hand') is often used as a symbol of power. In this verse it forms part of the metaphor of the divine punishment or hostility (cf. 1 Sam. 6:3,5; Job 19:21; Ps. 32:4, 39:10 (M.T. 11)).
has come down: the verb *n-ḥ-t* occurs also in the preceding line ('have sunk') but this is not sufficient reason for emending it (cf. *BH*).

3. no soundness in my flesh: i.e. I am desperately ill (cf.

verse 7). In Isa. 1:6 this phrase is used to describe the critical situation of the whole national existence. In the present verse 'flesh' may be another way of saying 'I'. The Hebrew *bāśār* ('flesh') can denote the physical substance of which men and animals are made (Gen. 40:19), and therefore it is a suitable term for the body as a whole (cf. 79:2, 109:24), or as a metonym for man or mankind (i.e. 'all flesh', Gen. 6:12; Ps. 136:25, 145:21; Isa. 40:5). It can be employed with other anthropological terms to signify the whole man (84:2), but occasionally it could be used to describe man as weak and subject to various limitations, in contrast to God (78:39; Isa. 31:3). In the *OT* there is no indication that flesh in itself is ethically evil; it may be feeble, but not necessarily sinful. Sometimes *bāśār* serves as a periphrasis for the personal pronoun (63:1 (M.T. 2)), or it denotes kinship (Gen. 2:23; Isa. 58:7). For a more detailed discussion on *bāśār*, see F. Baumgärtel, '*Sarx*', *TDNT*, VII, pp. 105ff.; N. W. Porteous, 'Flesh in the OT', *IDB*, II, p. 276; D. Lys, *La chair dans l'Ancien Testament 'Bâsâr'* (1967).

indignation: the Hebrew *zaʿam* is usually used of God; Ringgren (*IR*, p. 76) argues that it was applied *only* to God, and so also *ḥ^a^rôn ʾap̱* ('burning anger'), but it is not certain that the *OT* writers always observed this distinction. God's wrath is generally provoked by human sin, as in 38:3 (M.T. 4), and it is lifted either by the death of the guilty person (Num. 25:1–5; Jos. 7. 22–6; 2 Sam. 6:7) or by repentance and the miracle of forgiveness (32:5, 103:3).

no health: lit. 'no peace' (*šālôm*; see on 119:165).

in my bones: this may be a circumlocution for 'in me' (see on 102:3).

sin: (*ḥaṭṭāʾṯ*) see on 32:1, 51:2. The Psalmist is certain that his suffering is due to his sin although he does not describe it in detail. It is occasionally said that on meeting a misfortune the Israelite would simply assume that he must have sinned, and, rightly or wrongly, this gave a meaning to his suffering, making it more bearable (cf. H. McKeating, 'Divine Forgiveness in the Psalms', *SJT*, XVIII (1965), p. 80).

4. my iniquities: or 'my guilt (and its consequences)'; see on 32:1. The sin or guilt is thought of as a mighty flood about to engulf the sinful sufferer. For a similar word-picture, see 69:2,15 (M.T. 3,16), 124:4f.

like a burden: this is another fitting description of sin and guilt.

Cain (Gen. 4:13) complained in a similar fashion: 'My punishment is greater than I can bear'.

5. wounds: lit. 'blows, stripes'; it is often thought that the allusion is to leprosy, but this is far from certain.

foolishness: the Hebrew *ʾiwwelet* ('folly') is often mentioned in the Book of Proverbs (some 22 times out of a total of 24). In this context at least, 'folly' is not a ridiculous behaviour, but it is equivalent to 'sin' (see verse 3*a*). Similarly in Prov. 24:9: 'The devising of folly is sin . . .'; in Ps. 69:5 (M.T. 6) 'folly' is parallel to 'wrong' (*ʾašmāh*), although the reference here may be to inadvertent sins.

6. This verse depicts the Psalmist as bowed down by this pain and his feeling of guilt. The emphasis may well be on the latter, and that explains why he goes about looking like a mourner. See on 35:14; also 42:9 (M.T. 10); Isa. 58:5.

7. The author continues the description of his illness, and he refers to his loins as 'filled with burning'. 'Loins' are usually regarded as 'the source of man's strength and procreative power' (Johnson, *VITAI*, p. 74). The word-picture is meant to show that the calamity has robbed the afflicted man of all his strength and vitality. For verse 8*b*, see verse 3*a* (cf. Isa. 21:3).

with burning: the word is derived from *ḳ-l-h* I ('to burn'), and the reference may be to fever. *AV* reads 'with a loathsome (disease)', taking the Hebrew *niḳlāh* as from *ḳ-l-h* II ('to be dishonoured').

8. I am utterly spent: i.e. 'I am like a paralysed man'. The same verb is used in Gen. 45:26 of Jacob stating that 'his heart fainted'.

crushed: see on 51:17, where the same verb refers to the crushed or contrite heart; in 51:8 (M.T. 10) the Psalmist speaks about the bones which God has broken or crushed.

I groan: or paraphrasing: 'I roar like a lion' (cf. Job 3:24; Ps. 22:1 (M.T. 2), 32:3). The verb *š-ʾ-g* usually denotes the roaring of lions, but metaphorically it can depict the invaders *roaring* in the sanctuary (74:4) or in the land (Jer. 2:15). Similarly, both the rapacious officials (Zeph. 3:3) and the personal enemies (22:13 (M.T. 14)) can be likened to *roaring* lions. The same verb can even describe Yahweh's voice (Jer. 25:30; Am. 1:2; Jl 3:16) and the anguished cries of a sufferer, as in this verse.

my heart: see on 27:3.

9. my longing: the Hebrew *taʾ^a^wāh* can be used in a good sense, as in 10:17; Prov. 11:23, 19:22; Isa. 26:8, or with a bad connotation, as in 10:3, 106:14, 112:3; Prov. 21:25. G. R. Driver (*JTS*, XLIII (1942), p. 153) suggests 'my lament' (from ʾ-*w-h**, 'to lament', as in Arabic); so also *NEB*.

my sighing: see on 6:6, 31:10.

is not hidden: Dahood (*PAB*, I, p. 233) regards the verb as belonging to the infixed -*t*- conjugation, from *s-w-r* ('to turn aside'), and he renders 'never leaves your presence'. Most commentators derive the verb from *s-t-r* ('to hide').

10. My heart throbs: the Hebrew verb may mean: 'to go to and fro', hence 'my heart beats furiously' (so Boylan, *PSVP*, I, p. 135). Winton Thomas (*TRP*, p. 14) suggests: '. . . is bewitched' (cf. the Arabic *saḥara*, 'to be enchanted').

my strength fails me: (cf. 40:12 (M.T. 13)); for a contrast, see Dt. 34:7, where Moses is described as one whose 'eye was not dim, nor his natural force abated'.

the light of my eyes may refer to actual sight or to one's vitality (cf. 88:9*a* (M.T. 10a)); the phrase itself is a *hapax legomenon* in the *OT*. For a similar idea, see 1 Sam. 14:29: 'my eyes have become bright', i.e. 'my strength has revived'. See on 13:3.

it also: or 'even they'. This phrase is sometimes transposed to verse 11, reading 'Even my friends . . .' (see *BH*). Dahood (*PAB*, I, p. 236) regards the Hebrew *hēm* as a particle of exclamation, rendering: 'Alas, even this . . .' (see on 9:6).

11. plague: Jerome 'leprosy'. The Hebrew *negaʿ* is either 'illness' or 'affliction' in general (39:10 (M.T. 11), 89:32 (M.T. 33), 91:10); occasionally it may denote leprosy (Lev. 13:2; Dt. 24:8) or some similar skin disease. The friends and companions keep aloof not only because of the plague but also, if not more so, on account of the underlying cause. The first part of the verse is overloaded, and the repetition of 'stand afar off' (verse 11*b*) is not stylistically elegant; but the suggested emendations do not offer any great improvement (cf. Gunkel, *PGHAT*, p. 162).

12. Those who seek my life are probably his kinsmen and his former friends; Kraus (*PBK*, p. 296) is probably right in suggesting that they are anxious to find out what is the sin he had committed, and which deserves such a severe punishment. This is not merely a matter of interest, but it is likely that had they found any real or imaginary failure on the part of the afflicted man, they would, no doubt, have acted accordingly in punishing him. For *nep̱eš* ('life'), see on 33:19.

lay their snares: cf. *KBL*, p. 634. Gunkel, Kraus, *et al.* think that 'those who seek my life' and 'those who seek my hurt' may be later additions, overloading the verse.

. . . speak of ruin: Dahood (*PAB*, I, p. 236) derives the verb not from *d-b-r*, 'to speak', but from *d-b-r**, 'to pursue' (cf. also Dahood, *PNWSP*, p. 45), and following him, we could render: 'those who seek my hurt, pursue (me)'. 'Ruin' (see on 52:1) would belong, in such a case, to the following phrase.

meditate: perhaps 'all day long they speak of (my) ruin and of (my supposed) treachery' (cf. 37:30), or 'they plan ruin and treachery without ceasing'. For the verb *h-g-h*, see on 1:2.

13. I do not hear: this is probably a relative clause, 'who does not hear' (see verse 14*a*), i.e. he refuses to listen to the provocations. Being conscious of sin, he does not offer any excuses or arguments, but he leaves his cause to God. In this respect he differs from Job, who insisted on his integrity, and rightly so. The Psalmist keeps silence, because he believes that it is God who is punishing him, even though he may not have been sure of his particular offence(s) (cf. Isa. 53:7; 1 Pet. 2:23); therefore the right course is a humble trust in God.

14. This verse is an echo of the preceding verse and adds a further emphasis; some regard it as an explanatory variant on verse 13 (so Gunkel, Leslie).

no rebukes: or 'arguments, defence' (cf. Job 23:4).

15. . . . I wait: see on 31:24. God is the Psalmist's only hope (cf. 39:7 (M.T. 8), 130:5; Mic. 7:7).

who wilt answer: either by an oracle (so Kraus) or by giving actual help, in healing the smitten man.

16. For I pray: lit. 'For I say (or 'think')'. *AV* offers a paraphrase 'For I said, *Hear me*, lest *otherwise* they should rejoice over me', or it could be rendered: 'For I have uttered (my lament) lest they go on rejoicing over me'.

who boast against me: or 'who triumphed against me', referring to the author's past and present experience. A commentary is provided by Job 19:5: '. . . indeed you magnify yourselves against me, and make my humiliation an argument against me'.

when my foot slips: or 'when my foot stumbled'. This is a figure of misfortune; see on 15:5.

17. I am ready to fall: cf. Job 18:12; Ps. 35:15; Jer. 20:10.

Briggs renders '. . . ready for limping' but the situation envisaged seems far more critical than that. The 'fall' or 'stumbling' mentioned may even lead to the death of the sufferer.

18. I confess: lit. 'For I will declare' (so *AV*). The Hebrew *kî* (*RSV*, *NEB* omit; *AV* 'for') may be an emphatic particle (see on 118:10) meaning 'Indeed', 'Surely'. The Psalmist feels that in his serious situation there is only one way out—namely, to confess his sin or iniquity (see on 32:1) which is the cause of all his misery. Such a confession would have to be more than a mere disappointment at being found out; it must be the beginning of seeing things in the way God sees them.

I am sorry for my sin: or 'I am afraid (anxious) because of my sin' (cf. Jer. 42:16).

19. . . . my foes without cause: lit. 'my enemies (are) lively' (so *AV*, *RV*), but the Hebrew *ḥayyîm* ('lively' or 'living') does not give a very satisfactory sense in this phrase. Therefore some exegetes emend it into *ḥinnām* ('without cause'). Dahood (*PAB*, I, p. 237) suggests that the phrase forms a genitive construction with an intervening pronominal suffix, and reads: 'my mortal enemies', i.e. the enemies of (my) life'. This would give a good parallel to the following line.

who hate me wrongfully: i.e. although the Psalmist is aware that he is not sinless, he is equally certain that his enemies are *wrong* in the things they attribute to him. He is rightly concerned because these foes are both powerful and many, and therefore he has no chance on his own.

20. The irony of the situation is that his adversaries are not strangers but people who had been treated fairly by him. A similar situation is described in 35:12ff., 109:3ff.

are my adversaries: better 'they accuse me (unjustly)', as in 109:4.

because I follow after good: or, more likely, 'in return for my seeking after (their) good'. Cf. 37:12ff.

THE CONCLUDING PRAYER **21–2**

21. Do not forsake me: or 'Do not leave me for ever', since the present distress is due to the fact that God has 'turned away' from the afflicted man (cf. 22:1 (M.T. 2), 27:9, 71:9,18).

be not far: i.e. help me in my calamity (cf. 22:11 (M.T. 12), 35:22).

22. Make haste: as in 22:19 (M.T. 20), 40:13 (M.T. 14),

70:1,5 (M.T. 2, 6), 71:12, 141:1. This is not an expression of irreverence, but of the urgency of the situation.
O Lord, my salvation: see on 27:1; this could be paraphrased 'O Lord, save me!' (cf. 40:13 (M.T. 14)).

Psalm 39 My Hope is in God

Ewald described this Psalm as the most beautiful of all elegies in the Psalter, and it is difficult to be more specific. Gunkel, Kraus, *et al.* class it as a Lament of the Individual (see Introduction, pp. 37ff.), while Briggs, for example, defines it (with less justification) as a National Lament. This Psalm contains elements both of lamentation and of confession, hence Oesterley argues that it is penitential in character although not included among the Penitential Psalms. Eissfeldt (*OTI*, p. 120) thinks that Ps. 39 as well as Ps. 51 and 130 are 'couched in such personal terms . . . that the assumption that they were composed as texts to accompany cultic actions is very artificial . . .'. He would regard them as 'private poetry not tied to the cult'. We do not know when *private* poetry began in Israelite or Jewish literature, but this Psalm may have some claim to be one of the earliest examples of this kind. It has also some kinship with the Wisdom literature.

The date of the Psalm is uncertain. Briggs has argued for a date after the Exile but before the reforms of Nehemiah (in the fifth century B.C.) but any date in the Persian period might be a reasonable possibility.

The Psalm consists of two main parts. The introduction (verses 1–3) provides the setting, while the main part of the poem contains a number of different elements. There is an assertion of the transitoriness of human life (verses 4–6) followed by an expression of hope (verse 7) and further supplications (verses 8–13).

The metre of the lament is irregular, but a good half of the verses are in the 3 + 3 metre.
To the choirmaster: see Introduction, p. 48.
Jeduthun: see Introduction, p. 46.
A Psalm of David: see Introduction, pp. 43ff. and 46.

A REFLECTIVE INTRODUCTION 1–3

1. I will guard my ways: many exegetes emend *d^e^rāḵay* ('my ways') into *d^e^ḇāray* ('my words') because the next line refers to the sins of the tongue; this alteration seems, however, rather pedantic. 'My ways' may denote conduct in general, but the parallel line may suggest that the Psalmist is referring to unworthy thoughts and words in particular. It is usually assumed that the author was afraid that he might sin by murmuring against God (cf. Job 1:22, 2:10), but it is equally possible that he restrained himself from cursing the wicked who prospered, and who scorned him in his affliction. For a parallel, see Job 31:29f.

I will bridle my mouth: lit. 'I will keep my mouth with a bridle' (*AV*, *RV*). M.T. repeats the same verb *ʾešmᵉrāh* ('I will keep'), as in verse 1*a*, for which LXX may have read *ʾāśîmāh* ('I will put').

so long as the wicked are in my presence: probably the Psalmist was reluctant to utter his complaint against God, in the hearing of the wicked (a collective noun?), or it may allude to the unwillingness of the author to criticize God for the apparently inadequate working of his retribution, i.e. its distribution.

2. The Psalmist goes on to describe his mental struggle: although he kept absolutely silent, it was to no purpose. His troubles grew from bad to worse, while the wicked, apparently, went from strength to strength.

I held my peace to no avail: Dahood (*PAB*, I, p. 240) reads: 'I refrained from speaking', deriving *miṭṭōḇ* (lit. 'from good', *RSV* 'to no avail') from *n-ṭ-b** (a by-form of *n-ṭ-p*), 'to drop, drip' and figuratively 'to discourse'. This suggestion has its problems but it is not impossible. Calès takes *miṭṭôḇ* as an exclamation 'No use!', while Kissane (*BP*, p. 174) proposes *miṭṭôḇô*, rendering: 'Because of his prosperity (my pain was stirred up)'.

my distress grew worse: some commentators (e.g. Gunkel, Oesterley) read: 'my feelings' (*kᵉḇēḏî* ('my liver') for M.T. *kᵉʾēḇî* ('my pain')) 'were stirred'; this would balance verse 3*a*, yet the change is not really necessary.

3. my heart became hot: i.e. 'I became exasperated' (cf. Dt. 19:6; Jer. 20:9). For 'heart', see on 27:3.

As I mused: or 'in my thinking' (similarly V: '*in meditatione mea*').

the fire burned: i.e. my feelings got the better of me. 'Fire' (*ʾēš*) can be used figuratively of Yahweh's anger (89:46 (M.T. 47)), his jealousy (Ezek. 36:5), or it can describe the word of God (Jer. 23:29). In this verse it refers to one's emotional outburst.

A MEDITATION ON HUMAN TRANSITORINESS **4–6**

4. let me know my end: Oesterley (*TP*, p. 231) considers this request as unseemly and revealing a wrong spirit; in fact this is not an expression of unseemliness but a stylistic device, a rhetorical question which is answered by the Psalmist himself. The author is not concerned about the brevity of life as such, but he wishes to enjoy the few years that are the lot of mankind. Since life is short and God is just, the Psalmist feels that this provides a suitable foundation for his prayer (cf. Job 6:11).
the measure of my days: this phrase is a *hapax legomenon* in the *OT* (cf. 1QH f. xi:2). LXX has 'the number of days . . .'; similarly *NEB*. In Ec. 2:3 the brief span of human existence is described as 'the few days of their life' (lit. 'the number of the days of their life').
how fleeting my life is: the Psalmist is fully aware of the shortness of human life, but instead of complaining about it, he wishes to be instructed by God on this subject (cf. 89:48 (M.T. 49); *TRP*, p. 14).

5. handbreadths: the Hebrew *ṭepaḥ* is a linear measure being the breadth of the hand at the base of the fingers—roughly 2.9 inches. The same measure is also called 'four fingers' (Jer. 52:21). The shortest measure is 'the finger' (i.e. its width) which forms a fourth of a handbreadth. Since the length of man's life is but a few handbreadths, it is, relatively speaking, as nothing in God's sight (verse 5*b*), because he is from everlasting to everlasting (90:2).
as a mere breath: this is an ambiguous phrase. Weiser (*POTL*, p. 327) has: 'A mere breath is every man who stands (self-assured)', but the explanatory addition 'self-assured' seems less fitting, because *all* human life is 'as nothing'. The most likely suggestion is that the above phrase states that even the life of the man who appears to be firmly established (119:89) is but 'a mere breath'. This seems to be brought out by the following verse (cf. Job 7:7; Ps. 60:9 (M.T. 11), 94:11, 144:4; Ec. 1:2). It is also possible that verse 5*c* belongs to verse 6, and if so, the 'Selah' (see Introduction, pp. 48f.) should come after verse 5*b*.

6. as a shadow: this expresses the unsubstantial nature of life (cf. 73:20, 102:11 (M.T. 12), 144:4; 1 Chr. 29:15). Oesterley (*TP*, p. 232) feels that to depreciate human life by speaking of it as a breath or shadow is 'an insult to God who made man "in his own image" (Gen. 1:27)'. On the other hand, it looks as if the Psalmist was more realistic than some of his expositors. However great may be man's achievements, or however important he may be in the scale of human values, his life is not prolonged thereby. In any case, he is made in the '*image* of God' and not a god. Man may overcome the threat of untimely death, but the end of the earthly life comes to all alike. There is an interesting Egyptian parallel from the tomb of Neferhotep, 'As for the duration of what is done on earth, it is a kind of dream' (quoted from J. M. Myers, *I Chronicles* (*AB* 12, 1965), p. 196).

they are in turmoil: the plural verb is rather odd, and so some exegetes read *hāmôn* (or *hônîm*), 'riches', for M.T. *yeh^{e}māyûn*, rendering 'a mere breath are riches he heaps up' (so Gunkel, Nötscher); cf. Job 27:16f. Dahood (*PAB*, I, p. 241) retains M.T., but he understands the verb as meaning: '. . . is he in turmoil'.

man heaps up: the verb has no object, unless we adopt the emendation mentioned above; the accusative may be implicit.

. . . knows not who will gather: (reading *ʾōs^{e}p̱îm*), lit. '. . . who will gather them' (i.e. the riches, although the antecedent of the pronoun is not expressed in M.T.). The rich man cannot be sure that he will be able to enjoy his own wealth (cf. Ec. 2:26; Sir. 14:15; Lk. 12:20).

A PRAYER FOR DELIVERANCE **7–13**

7. for what do I wait: the answer is found in verse 7*b*; in the light of the previous argument, the Psalmist's only hope is God.

8. my transgressions: (*p^{e}šā^{c}ay*), see on 32:1, 51:1. To deliver a man from his transgression means to forgive his sin and to deal with its consequences (as far as that is possible in the circumstances). In this case pardon would result in healing, since the source of the disease would have been removed. In 79:9 the writer prays: 'Help us, O God . . . deliver us, and forgive our sins'. Kraus (*PBK*, p. 299) renders verse 8*a*: 'Deliver me from all those who rise up against me' (reading *pōš^{ec}ay* for M.T. *p^{e}šā^{c}āy*); similarly *NEB*, cf. also Isa. 66:24. This would provide a good parallel to verse 8*b*, yet the emendation is not absolutely necessary.

Make me not . . .: LXX has 'You have made me . . .' (so also V), but M.T. is more likely.

the scorn of the fool: i.e. the object of the scorn of the godless (see on 119:22). For *nāḇāl* ('fool'), see on 14:1. The substance of the taunts of the fool (a collective noun? so *NEB*) may have been the assertion that the *Psalmist* is a simpleton for trusting in God who does not care for the affairs of men and their world (cf. 10:4, 14:1, 73:11, 109:25).

9. I am dumb: see verse 2 (cf. 38:13 (M.T. 14)). J. R. P. Sclater (*PIB*, p. 207) quotes Ḳimḥi's remark on this verse: 'I could not complain of *man*, for it was *God's* doing; I could not complain of *God*, for I was conscious of *my own sin*'.

thou . . . hast done it: whatever was the plight of the Psalmist, Yahweh had brought it about, although the ultimate cause must have been some sin of the poet (see 30:2 (M.T. 3), 32:1). Because the distress is Yahweh's doing, and because Yahweh is righteous (this must be the author's presupposition), it is better not to argue with him, lest one's sin is increased by foolish accusations. The misfortune was both punitive and disciplinary, consequently the right reaction would be confession and penitence.

10. thy stroke: see on 38:11. Here it denotes the distress which God has brought upon the Psalmist (cf. Job 9:34).

I am spent: or 'I am at the end of my tether'.

the blows of thy hand: lit. 'the hostility of . . .'. LXX has *ischus* which suggests the Hebrew *migg^{e}ḇûraṯ* ('by the strength of . . .'; so also T). The Hebrew *tiḡrāh* ('hostility') is a *hapax legomenon* in the *OT*, but its meaning in this verse may be 'stroke, blow' (so S; cf. *VT*, IX (1959), pp. 251ff.).

11. . . . for sin: or 'for his sin', the pronoun is implied by the context. For *ᶜāwōn* ('sin'), see on 32:1.

like a moth: the Hebrew *ᶜāš* can mean 'moth' (Job 12:28; Isa. 50:9), 'inflamed wound' (Hos. 5:12), or 'bird's nest' (Job 4:19, 27:18); in the present context the first meaning is most likely (cf. *KBL*, p. 743). The simile of a moth may symbolize the destructive power of God (cf. Job 13:28), or it may refer to the life of the Psalmist which is of short duration like that of a moth (so Kissane, *BP*, p. 175).

what is dear to him: this is a translation of the Hebrew *ḥ^{a}mûḏô* while some MSS. read *ḥemdô* ('his desire, splendour'; so Kraus). LXX has *tēn psuchēn autou* ('his life'), which may represent the Hebrew *ḥeldô* ('his duration'). *NEB* reads for 11*b*: 'all his charm festers and drains away'.

Selah: see Introduction, pp. 48f.

12. Hear my prayer: i.e. both hear and answer my supplication. This is a common expression in the Psalter (cf. 4:1 (M.T.

2), 54:2 (M.T. 4), 84:8 (M.T. 9), etc.). For 'prayer', see on 65:2.
give ear: or 'attend'.
hold not thy peace . . .: lit. 'be not deaf'; see on 28:1.
at my tears: i.e. my tearful prayer.
thy passing guest: *gēr* denotes a resident alien who is more or less permanently living in the land of his choice, and who is accorded a protected position. In Lev. 19:33 the Israelites are reminded that 'the stranger who sojourns with you shall be to you as the native among you, and you shall love him as yourself; for you were strangers in the land of Egypt . . .'. The *gērîm* were, as a rule, poor, and dependent upon the goodwill and generosity of the native inhabitants of the land (Lev. 19:10, 23:22: Dt. 24:19ff.). They were subject to the same laws as the Israelites (Exod. 20:10; Lev. 16:29; Num. 19:10), and they could share in the religious life of the people of God (Dt. 16:11,14), provided certain conditions were observed (Exod. 12:48f.). In a way, the Israelites themselves were aliens and sojourners in the Promised land, for it belonged to Yahweh (Lev. 25:23; 1 Chr. 29:15; Ps. 119:19). When the Psalmist, as a *gēr*, appeals to Yahweh, he does not *demand* God's protection, but he humbly entrusts himself to God. For further details, see T. M. Maunch, 'Sojourner', *IDB*, IV, pp. 397ff.
sojourner (*tôšāḇ*) is more or less a synonym of *gēr*, the protected alien, but strictly speaking he is one who resides in the particular country less permanently (cf. Snaith, *LN*, p. 158).

13. Look away from me: this is rather an unusual expression (see Job 7:19, 10:20f., 14:6). Generally the afflicted man asks God to look upon him and not to turn away his face from him (see on 27:9). The meaning of this phrase is that the writer desires to be spared further punishment, not to be relieved of Yahweh's presence or help. Therefore this prayer does not contradict the preceding supplication.
before I depart: i.e. before I die and descend to the land of no return, Sheol.
and be no more: death is not the cessation of existence but rather the end of life. In Sheol one is cut off from Yahweh and his saving help, and therefore, in a real sense, one is no more (cf. Job 7:9, 10:21f.; Ps. 6:5 (M.T. 6), 30:9 (M.T. 10), 88:5 (M.T. 6), 115:17; Isa. 38:11,18).

Psalm 40 A Thanksgiving and a Lament

This Psalm consists of two distinct parts: verses 1–10 form a Thanksgiving of the Individual (see Introduction, pp. 35f.) which praises God for the deliverance from a grave illness, and verses 11–17 make up a Lament of the Individual (see Introduction, pp. 37ff.) in which the writer appeals for help against his enemies and other unspecified evils. Most scholars regard this Psalm as composed of two originally independent poems. This view is partly supported by the unusual sequence, thanks-prayer, and, above all, by the fact that verses 13–17 are found, with minor variations, as Ps. 70. On the other hand, some commentators maintain that the Psalm is a literary unity. Weiser (*POTL*, pp. 333f.) suggests that the first part describes the past experiences of the Psalmist, and forms the basis on which the prayer in the second half of the poem rests. He goes on to say that the author (in verses 13–17) has made use of 'a current liturgical text which appeared to him appropriate to his personal circumstances . . .' (p. 340). Yet whatever was the 'history' of this Psalm, in its present form it is a liturgical composition which begins with thanks for previous succour, and then proceeds with a prayer for deliverance from the present distress (cf. Mowinckel, *PIW*, II, p. 76). The first part with its pattern of *trouble-cry for help-deliverance* gives a welcome assurance to the man in need; what God has done once, he can do again (cf. W. Beyerlin, *ZAW*, LXXIX (1967), pp. 208–24).

This Psalm probably belongs to the post-Exilic period, and the mixed psalm-type and the attitude towards the Law (verses 7–8) are further pointers in that direction.

The prevailing metre is 3+2.

To the choirmaster: see Introduction, p. 48.

A Psalm of David: see Introduction, pp. 43ff. and 46.

HE SET MY FEET UPON A ROCK **1–10**

The thanksgiving begins rather abruptly with an account of the past troubles, and it omits the usual introduction.

1. I waited patiently like a watchman for the morning (130:6). In this religious usage, one usually waits for Yahweh's word (cf. 38:15 (M.T. 16)), or for his salvation, as in Isa. 25:9: 'we have waited for him, that he might save us' (cf. Ps. 39:7 (M.T. 8)). In such a waiting, there is often a tension between the experiences of the present disaster and the hope in God's faithfulness. This is a waiting in the Covenant context, as in Hos. 12:6: 'hold fast to love and justice, and wait continually for your God'.

heard my cry: i.e. he answered my appeal for help.

2. the desolate pit: lit. 'the pit of tumult' which probably refers to the waters of the netherworld. Some exegetes render this phrase by 'miry pit' (*NEB* 'muddy pit'), and find a connection between the Hebrew *šā'ōn* ('roar, tumult') and the Aramaic *s^eyān* ('mud'); cf. Winton Thomas, *TRP*, p. 15.

'To die' means to go down to Sheol or to the Pit (see on 30:3), and even one who is ill is already in the process of being overwhelmed by the deep waters of the underworld (2 Sam. 22:5f.; Ps. 69:14f. (M.T. 15f.)); this is, of course, to be understood metaphorically. Disease is a form of death, and he who suffers from it, or he who is engulfed by *any* disaster, is actually in the sphere of death (cf. Job 33:30; Ps. 30:3 (M.T. 4); Jon. 2:2,7 (M.T. 3, 8)). Consequently, healing or restoration can be described as a deliverance from Sheol, and the saved man is 'brought up' from the netherworld (1 Sam. 2:6; Ps. 30:3; Jon. 2:7 (M.T. 8)). (For many other relevant parallels and references, see Chr. Barth, *ETKD*, pp. 91–122.) On 'pit', see on 28:1.

the miry bog is another picturesque term for the underworld (cf. 69:2,14 (M.T. 3, 15)). It is possible that this and similar descriptions of Sheol were derived from the ancient Near Eastern stories about the realm of the dead, such as the 'Descent of Ishtar to the Nether World' (*ANET*, pp. 107ff.). Cf. Tromp, *PCD*, p. 56.

a rock: this is a symbol of security and safety, in contrast to the miry bog of the underworld. See on 42:9.

my steps: i.e. he made my life (or 'me') secure (cf. 17:5, 44:18 (M.T. 19), 73:2). In 1QS xi:4f we read 'for the truth of God is the rock of my steps . . .' (Leaney, *RQM*, p. 235).

3. a new song: see on 30:3. The newness probably alludes to the events just celebrated, rather than to the recent date of the composition. The successive generations could use the same old poem as an ever new song, praising God for his ever new help.

Many will see and fear: the praise of Yahweh is a public act even when it celebrates the help rendered to the individual. Consequently those who witness this further proof of God's might and love are strengthened in their obedience and loyalty. See on 34:7,9. This phrase may be an example of a word-play on the Hebrew verbs *yirʾû* ('they will see') and *yîrāʾû* ('they will fear'); cf. 52:6 (M.T. 8); Isa. 41:5.

trust in the LORD: see on 26:1, 28:7.

4. Blessed is the man: see on 1:1; cf. Jer. 17:7. The Hebrew *geḇer* ('man') is simply a synonym of *ʾîš* ('man'), without any special stress on his power (cf. the cognate *gibbôr*, 'mighty man'), as suggested by Jacob (*TOTe*, pp. 156f.).

his trust is Yahweh. Others may put their confidence in gold (Job 31:24), idols (Jer. 48:13), chariots and horsemen (2 Kg. 18:24), but the pious man's object of confidence is God. See on 71:5.

the proud: Gunkel, Dahood, *et al.* link the Hebrew *reh̄āḇîm* with *rahaḇ*, the mythical sea monster Rahab, the arrogant one. Hence Dahood (*PAB*, I, p. 243) renders: 'pagan idols', which provides a good parallel to 'false gods' in verse 4*c*. This is also supported by LXX (similarly S and V) which has *mataiotētas* ('vanities, idols').

after false gods: lit. '. . . after a lie'. The Hebrew *kāzāḇ* ('lie') is an expression of a distorted relationship, either between man and God or between man and man. See M. A. Klopfenstein, *LAT*, pp. 211–53.

5. In this verse the Psalmist turns to the mighty deeds of Yahweh on behalf of Israel. These acts of salvation are too many to be recounted (92:5 (M.T. 6), 104:24, 106:2, 139:18) and there is none that can be compared to Yahweh (89:6 (M.T. 7); Isa. 40:18). Perhaps we should read *ʾên ʿōrēḵ*, 'none can oppose (you)' for M.T. *ʾên ʿarōḵ*, 'none can compare . . .' (for details, see Labuschagne, *IYOT*, p. 57). For Yahweh's 'wondrous deeds', see on 9:1; this is also a frequent term in the Dead Sea Scrolls to denote the glorious works of God (1QS xi:3,19; 1QH i:30,33,34, iii:23, vi:11, etc.).

6. sacrifice: *zeḇaḥ* is a communion sacrifice or shared-offering. Its main characteristic was that only a part of it (i.e. the fat) was burnt upon the altar, while the rest was eaten by the worshippers (apart from the portions given to the priest(s)). The sacrificial victim was taken from the cattle, sheep, or goats, and it could be either a male or female. For further information, see R. de Vaux, *Studies in Old Testament Sacrifice* (1961), pp. 31–51; for a more popular account, see H. Ringgren, *Sacrifice in the Bible* (*WCB*, 1962), pp. 23–7.

offering: the Hebrew *minḥāh* can be used both of a present (Gen. 43:11) and a tribute (2 Sam. 8:2; 1 Kg. 4:21), or it can denote sacrifices of any kind, whether grain or animal (Gen. 4:4ff.; 1 Sam. 2:17,29; Isa. 1:13). In the post-Exilic period it came to be restricted to cereal-offerings and oil. See Snaith, *LN*, p. 16.

burnt offering: *ʿôlāh* is that which is made to go up on to the altar, or that which ascends (as smoke) to God. The English rendering of *ʿôlāh* rightly indicates the essential feature of this sacrifice, namely the whole of it was burnt upon the altar, except the hide. The victim was a male animal without blemish; in some cases it was a bird (Lev. 1:14). See R. de Vaux, op. cit., pp. 27–51.

sin offering: (*ḥaṭāʾāh*) is an expiatory sacrifice similar to, and often indistinguishable from, the 'guilt-offering' (*ʾāšām*). Snaith (*LN*, p. 41) regards both sacrifices as quite distinct (see 'The Sin-offering and the Guilt-offering', *VT*, xv (1965), pp. 73–80). The animal used for the sacrifice depended on the rank of the guilty person(s). The flesh of the sacrifice was not eaten by the sacrificer, but it could be consumed by the priests, except in cases where the sin-offering was intended for the priests themselves or for the whole people.

Verse 6 is of great interest because it is often regarded as a repudiation of sacrifice *per se*. Other similar *OT* passages are 1 Sam. 15:22; Ps. 50:8–14, 51:16f. (M.T. 18f.), 69:30f. (M.T. 31f.); Isa. 1:11ff.; Jer. 7:21f.; Hos. 6:6; Am. 5:21f.; Mic. 6:6ff. For a typological interpretation of 40:6ff. (M.T. 7ff.), see Heb. 10:5–10. Some commentators have seen in this verse a denial of the sacrificial system, as such; thus Weiser (*POTL*, p. 338) states that the Psalmist 'categorically pushes aside the whole sacrificial cult'; but it is more likely that the writer offers a re-interpretation of sacrifices, and not necessarily their condemnation (cf. Mowinckel, *PIW*, II, p. 23). As in 1 Sam. 15:22, obedience is regarded as more important than sacrifice. Those obedient to Yahweh will always offer right sacrifices, but not *all* who bring their offerings to God are faithful to him. In other words, the cultic institutions are ineffective when they are used by those who flagrantly break the Covenant of God. What is said of sacrifices is equally true of prayers, cultic songs, etc.; it is not the mere repetition of them that is acceptable to God, but rather the humble and obedient attitude which finds expression, among other things, through prayers and Psalms, and even sacrifices. The cult in all its forms serves as a vehicle, and therefore the contents conveyed are of primary importance. Consequently obedience is indispensable, and the Babylonian exile is a good illustration of the respective values of sacrifice and obedience. See further, H. H. Rowley, 'The Meaning of Sacrifice in the Old Testament', *From Moses to Qumran* (1963), pp. 67–107; E. Würthwein, 'Kultpolemik oder Kultbescheid?', *Tradition und Situation*, ed. by E. Würthwein and O. Kaiser (1963), pp. 115–31.

. . . an open ear: lit. 'ears you have dug for me' which is rather a unique expression, and it is often taken to mean: 'you have made me obedient'. Dahood (*PAB*, I, p. 246) reads *kārattā* (from *k-r-t*, 'to cut, circumcise') for M.T. *kārîṯā* ('you have dug'), and he renders 'you made my ear receptive'. Cf. Jer. 6:10: 'their ears are closed (lit. 'uncircumcised'), they cannot listen', i.e. they are neither attentive nor obedient.

7. Lo, I come: Kraus *et al.* suggest 'I myself am the sacrificial victim', while Cohen (*PSon*, p. 124) takes the phrase as meaning 'behold, here I am' (cf. Isa. 6:8: 'Here I am! Send me').

the roll of the book: cf. Jer. 36:2,4; Ezek. 2:9. It can denote a scroll of book length, or simply a scroll in general. What is meant by it is not clear. Cohen suggests 'the Torah of Moses', while Kirkpatrick, Briggs, *et al.* see here a reference to the Book of Deuteronomy or to a similar document. Perhaps we should regard it as an expression of Yahweh's will without specifying its exact nature. Another possible suggestion is that it refers to the heavenly book in which men's deeds are fully recorded (so Taylor, Rodd; see on 51:1; cf. 56:8 (M.T. 9), 87:6, 139:16). *NEB* omits verse 7*b*.

8. I delight to do thy will: see on 1:2. This service of God is done for its own sake, and not out of fear, or out of a desire for a reward. For *rāṣôn* ('will'), see on 143:10.

thy law: see on 1:2, 119:1.

within my heart: lit. 'in the midst of my inward parts', which is a circumlocution for 'within me' (cf. 22:14 (M.T. 15)). The author stresses that the law of God is the main factor which determines his behaviour and attitudes (cf. Dt. 6:6; Ps. 37:31; Jer. 31:33).

9. deliverance: lit. 'righteousness' (see on 33:5).

the great congregation is probably the worshipping community (see on 89:5; cf. 22:25 (M.T. 26), 35:18). Like a herald of Yahweh, the delivered man declares God's faithfulness and his salvation (cf. *Verbum Domini*, XLII (1964), pp. 26–33). The deliverance of one member of the community is good news to all the people of

God, and this cannot but help to foster a feeling of unity and communion. This is a phenomenon that is rather rare in most modern communities.

10. thy saving help: lit. 'your righteousness'. In this setting it may mean 'healing' which may include forgiveness. See on 33:5.
faithfulness: (*ʾemûnāh*), see on 36:5.
salvation: i.e. deliverance from the present distress; see on 35:3.
. . . thy steadfast love: this is the account of God's Covenant loyalty (see on 26:3), just as faithfulness (*ʾemeṯ*) in verse 10*c* is both the fidelity of Yahweh and its declaration (cf. 89:14 (M.T. 15)).
from the great congregation: (*leḳāhāl*) see verse 9. The preposition *le* is used in the sense of 'from', as in Ugaritic.

THE PRAYER FOR HELP 11–17

11. Do not . . . withhold: Kirkpatrick *et al.* take this verse as an expression of confidence in God's response, i.e. 'God will not (or 'did not') withhold his compassion'. This is plausible, but the *RSV* rendering seems preferable.
thy mercy: see on 51:1. It can be defined as 'a loving act of Yahweh by which he faithfully maintains his covenant relationship with his chosen people' (E. R. Achtemeier, 'Mercy', *IDB*, III, p. 352b), and so it can manifest itself in various ways, e.g. in deliverance (40:11 (M.T. 12), 103:4), forgiveness (51:1 (M.T. 3), 79:8), restoration (Isa. 14:1; Jer. 12:15, 33:26).
thy steadfast love and thy faithfulness: or perhaps 'your abiding Covenant loyalty' (see on 26:3 and 25:5, respectively). Delitzsch (*BCP*, II, p. 41) calls them 'the Alpha and Omega of God's self-attestation in the course of the redemptive history'. Dahood (*PAB*, I, p. 247) sees here two divine characteristics 'personified as two attendants' whose task it is to protect the Psalmist.

12. evils have encompassed me: i.e. the consequences of my sins have come upon me. In verses 14–15 the Psalmist appears to be troubled by enemies, and therefore it is possible that his distress may have been caused by more than one factor. The 'evils' are depicted as the waters of a flood threatening to destroy the afflicted (cf. 2 Sam. 22:5; Jon. 2:5 (M.T. 6); 1QH iii:28, v:39).
my iniquities: see on 32:1, 51:2. The author ackowledges that his misfortune is essentially a chastisement for his sin (see on 30:2).
till I cannot see: or 'I am unable to escape' (so Dahood, *PAB*,

I, p. 247), reading *liḏʾôṯ* (from *d-ʾ-h*, 'to fly, escape') for M.T. *lirʾôṯ* ('to see'), and assuming a confusion between the letters *dāleṯ* and *rêš*. A similar thought is found in 1QH iii:28: 'And pangs of death surrounded (me) without any escape'. On the other hand, M.T. might be understood in the same way as 69:3: 'My eyes grow dim' because of trouble (cf. 6:7 (M.T. 8), 38:10 (M.T. 11)); *NEB* has 'and my sight fails'.

more than the hairs on my head: a similar hyperbolic comparison is found in 69:4 (M.T. 5) (cf. Mt. 10:30).

my heart fails me: or 'my courage deserts me'. For the various uses of *lēḇ* ('heart'), see on 27:3.

13. Be pleased: this is lacking in 70:1 (M.T. 2) but it is required, at least, for metrical reasons. Dahood (*PAB*, I, p. 247) reads *rūṣāh* ('run!') for M.T. *reṣēh* ('be pleased'), thus providing a good parallel to 'make haste' (verse 13*b*), both being emphatic imperatives. He argues that the change was intended to avoid the strong anthropomorphism but it might have been too bold for even the original writer!

make haste: this need not imply any disrespect for God, but it emphasizes the gravity of the situation (cf. 22:19 (M.T. 20), 38:22 (M.T. 23), 70:1, 5 (M.T. 2,6), 71:12, 141:1).

14. For the interpretation of this verse, see 35:4,26 of which it may well be a variant. 'Altogether' and 'to snatch away' are omitted in 70:2 (M.T. 3).

15. Let them be appalled: or 'Let them be stunned' (as in Lam. 1:13) by the sudden reversal of the respective fortunes. Ps. 70: 3 (M.T. 4) has 'Let them be turned back' (cf. 6:10 (MT. 11)).

who say to me: 70:3 (M.T. 4) omits 'to me', probably rightly so.

Aha: this is an onomatopoeic interjection expressing a malicious joy and satisfaction over the misfortune of an enemy (cf. 35:21,25; Ezek. 25:3, 26:2, 36:2).

16. This verse is reminiscent of 35:27.

who seek thee: *b-ḳ-š* ('to seek') is often used as a cultic term denoting worship in general (see on 27:8; cf. 24:3, 69:6 (M.T. 7), 105:4; Hos. 3:5; Mal. 3:1, etc.), as in Jer. 50:4f.: '. . . they shall seek the LORD their God. They shall ask the way to Zion . . .'. Sometimes it may imply a return to Yahweh, as in Hos. 5:15–6:1: '. . . in their distress they seek me, saying, "Come, let us return to the LORD . . ." '. It may also mean 'to care for', as in Neh. 2:10; Ps. 122:9 ('to intercede'?).

who love thy salvation: i.e. who delight in God's saving acts wherever they are manifested or wherever they are proclaimed. Eichrodt (*TOT*, II, p. 311), however, sees here an example of the tendency in which '*the directness of the relationship with God is becoming less important* than obedience to the records of his revelation'.

Great is the LORD: as in 35:27. *RP* renders: 'The Lord be praised', following V. This may well be the response of the worshippers, in contrast to the mocking cries of the enemies: 'Aha, Aha' (verse 15).

17. poor and needy frequently denote the righteous. For 'poor' (*ʿānî*), see on 34:2, and for 'needy' (*ʾeḇyôn*), see on 35:10. **takes thought for me:** a similar expression is found in Jon. 1:6. In 70:5 (M.T. 6) we have 'hasten to me' (i.e. *ḥûšāh* for *yaḥašōḇ* in the present verse); this offers a slightly better parallel to 'do not tarry' (verse 17*d*).

my help: see on 27:9. LXX suggests 'my helper' (*ʿōzerî*) which pairs the concrete term 'my deliverer'.

tarry not: see verse 13. The same phrase occurs also in Dan. 9:19 (cf. Isa. 46:13).

Psalm 41 Blessed are the Merciful

The characteristic feature of this Psalm is the lament which occupies the greater part of the poem (verses 4–10). In it the Psalmist, who apparently suffers from some undefined illness, appeals to God for healing, and complains of his false friends and malicious enemies. The Psalm opens with a didactic introduction praising the enviable happiness of the merciful man who is cared for by Yahweh and protected by him in all circumstances. Verses 11–12 conclude the Psalm with an expression of confidence and certainty, which is based on verses 1–3. If *all* merciful men (i.e. all the righteous) are delivered from their troubles, then also the Psalmist, in so far as he belongs to that category, will certainly be restored to his good fortunes. The final verse (13) does not belong to the Psalm but it is the doxology concluding the First Book of the Psalter (see Introduction, p. 27).

Commentators are not agreed as to the *Gattung* of this Psalm, which depends upon the interpretation given to the separate elements. The majority of exegetes tend to think that Ps. 41 is a Thanksgiving of the Individual, in which the lamentation takes the place of the customary description of the author's past troubles. The poet may be quoting the lamentation which he used when he was in distress (cf. Weiser, *POTL*, p. 343). On the other hand, some exegetes regard the Psalm as an Individual Lamentation (so Nötscher) or as a Psalm of Illness (cf. Mowinckel, *PIW*, II, p. 9). In such a case, verses 11–12 would not be an expression of thanks but rather a statement of confidence in Yahweh's saving help. Since, numerically at least, the larger part of the Psalm is taken by the prayer and the description of the misfortune, the whole Psalm may be regarded as a Lament. The Psalm was recited in the Temple (see verse 12) either at the thanksgiving sacrifice or, more likely, on behalf of (or by) the afflicted man. It belongs probably to the post-Exilic period.

Except for a few variations, the metre is 4+4.

To the choirmaster: see Introduction, p. 48.

A Psalm of David: see Introduction, pp. 43ff. and 46.

THE RIGHTEOUS MAN IS SUSTAINED BY YAHWEH **1–3**

1. Blessed is he . . .: see on 1:1. This expression (*ʾašᵉrê*) is never used of God, and it should not be confused with the similar phrase: 'Blessed be . . .' (*bārûḵ*), in verse 13.

who considers the poor: this is rather an unusual statement although the thought finds some parallels in 35:13f.; Prov. 14: 21,31; Jas. 1:27. LXX and V add: 'and the needy' (*wᵉʾeḇyôn*), which restores the prevailing 4+4 metre. Dahood (*PAB*, I, p. 249) regards 'the poor' (*dal*) as short for 'the door (*dal*) of my lips' (as in 141:3), and he renders the whole phrase 'the man prudent in speech'. Weiser (*POTL*, p. 343) understands this beatitude as an address to the congregation in order to arouse their sympathy, but it could also be taken as a statement of faith which provides the foundation on which the lament is based. The Psalmist does not class himself with the poor (so Weiser) but with the merciful, and therefore he has a good reason to hope that Yahweh will rescue him also (cf. 18:25f. (M.T. 26f.) (=2 Sam. 22:26f.); Prov. 29:7; Mt. 5:7).

2. keeps him alive: Yahweh will protect the righteous man in that he will deliver him from any adversity, and will restore him (cf. Johnson, *VITAI*, pp. 99f.).

he is called blessed: or, following Dahood, 'he (i.e. Yahweh) will bless (him) in the land' (similarly LXX, T, S, and V) taking the verb (*yʾšr*) as an active intensive form (i.e. *piʿēl*; cf. Prov.

31:28; Ca. 6:9, where this verb is used as a parallel to praising someone).

thou dost not give: LXX, S, and V suggest the third person singular which may be right.

the will of his enemies: lit. 'the greed (*nep̱eš*) of...' (so *NEB*); a similar phrase is found in 27:12; for *nep̱eš*, see on 33:19. Dahood (*PAB*, I, p. 248) takes the 'enemies' as a plural of majesty referring to the 'Foe' (i.e. Death); although this mythological imagery is found in the *OT* (cf. Job 18:13; Hab. 2:5), the *RSV* rendering seems more natural.

3. sustains him: i.e. although the righteous is not immune from adversity and illness, Yahweh will uphold him (cf. 18:35 (M.T. 36), 20:2 (M.T. 3), 94:18).

all his infirmities: lit. 'all his bed' (*RSVm*). Dahood (*PAB*, I, p. 250) suggests that M.T. *kol* ('all') should be read as a verb *kūl* (from *k-w-l*, 'to sustain'), hence 'Sustain his confinement, overthrow his very illness itself' (the preposition *b*^{e} is taken as an emphatic particle). This gives a good sense but it weakens the parallelism of the verse; the *RSV* may be nearer the mark, even though it is a free translation.

THE PRAYER IN ADVERSITY 4–10

4. Having outlined the relationship between Yahweh and the righteous, the Psalmist has enough trust in God to appeal for help in his case also. His confession of sin does not contradict his implicit claim to belong to the faithful. Like most of his contemporaries, he believed that sin was the cause of suffering, but the fact that he acknowledged his sin was a proof that he did not side with the godless and the wicked (cf. v. Rad, *OTT*, I, p. 274). There were also such sins as unwitting offences which required cleansing (Lev. 4:27ff.; also Lev. 5–6), and which could have serious consequences if they were not dealt with. Therefore his enemies may have been wide of the mark if they accused him of some *particular* moral offence.

heal me: lit. 'heal my soul' (see on 33:19).

I have sinned: see on 51:2. As all sin is essentially against God, even when it concerns one's fellow men (cf. 2 Sam. 12:13), so also all healing comes from God (Hos. 6:1); see on 30:2.

5. say of me in malice: or 'speak maliciously against me' (so Dahood, *PAB*, I, p. 248).

when will he die ...: this describes the degree of enmity, but it is not clear what was the motive of the enemies. It could have been pure malice coupled with the hope of a material gain, however small (cf. 22:17f. (M.T. 18f.)), or it could have been simply a morbid curiosity.

his name perish: this may refer to the extinction of the person concerned and of his descendants (cf. Dt. 7:24, 9:14, 25:5; 2 Sam. 18:18; Ps. 109:13) or merely to the death of the unfortunate man (see on 9:5), as in this instance. Cf. *VT*, IV (1954), pp. 164f.

6. when one comes to see me: lit. 'if he come . . .'. A similar phrase is used in 2 Sam. 13:5 and 2 Kg. 8:29 for the visitation of sick friends or kinsmen. The classic example of such sick-visiting is Job 2:11, and the purpose was to express one's condolences and to comfort the afflicted person. According to tradition, the comforters were not permitted to say anything until the sufferer himself opened the conversation (see Pope, *JAB*, p. 25).

he utters empty words: or 'his heart (i.e. he himself) speaks hypocrisy (or 'emptiness')', taking 'his heart' with the first part of the verse (so also LXX). For 'heart', see on 27:3.

gathers mischief: i.e. he collects 'material' for making gossip and trouble. Probably by observing the symptoms of the illness, the malicious 'friend' was able to speculate, with some authority, about the causes of the disease and so about the sins committed (cf. Mowinckel, *PIW*, II, p. 6).

7. whisper together: (cf. 2 Sam. 12:19). They were discussing and elaborating the latest information (garnished with morbid and malicious imagination) concerning the supposed evildoer. This seems to be a timeless occupation of certain types of people. The words of Jesus in Mt. 7:1–5 would have been highly relevant to this situation. It is also possible that the verb *l-ḥ-š*, 'to whisper', could be used of casting magic spells (cf. H. Wildberger, *Jesaja* (*BK* 10_2, 1966), pp. 122f.), and it is indeed possible that the enemies resorted to certain dubious practices, just to make sure that the afflicted man did not escape death. Their activity need not have been identical with what was called witchcraft in the Middle Ages.

they imagine the worst for me: or, better with Weiser (*POTL*, p. 342): 'they devise against me what is evil for me'; this is a reasonable literal rendering. For a parallel, see 4Q174 1–2,i:9: 'to devise against them wicked imaginations' (cf. 1QH iv:14).

8. They say: this is not in M.T. but it is rightly supplied from the context.

A deadly thing: lit. 'a thing of Belial' (see on 18:4). This phrase must mean something more sinister than 'a base thing' (so Weiser), and it may allude to the imagined sin of the Psalmist and its consequences, seen as a unity. It is not impossible that the speakers had in mind a curse which, they believed, had been infused into the unfortunate man, operating like a fatal poison. This need not mean that they would have regarded the stricken man as innocent; on the contrary, they would assume that in his case the curse, etc., had been fully deserved.

where he lies: cf. Jg. 5:27. Kraus (*PBK*, p. 314) thinks that verse 8*b* sounds like a magical formula.

9. my bosom friend: lit. 'the man of my peace' (cf. Jer. 20:10, 38:22). Friendship probably involved, at least in some cases, a Covenant (1 Sam. 18:3) which may well have been sealed by a Covenant meal (cf. Gen. 26:29f., 31:53f.; Pedersen, *ILC*, I–II, pp. 304f.). It is equally possible that the phrase 'who ate of my bread' alludes to the privileges and duties of the guest. See also the use of this verse in Jn 13:18, where it is applied to Judas Iscariot.

has lifted his heel . . .: lit. 'he has made great the heel . . .'. Verse 9*b* is also quoted in 1QH v:23f., but its exact meaning is far from clear. Dahood (*PAB*, I, p. 251) proposes: 'Spun slanderous tales about me', taking the verb *g-d-l* ('to become great') in the sense of 'to weave', and *ʿāḳēḇ* ('heel') as 'slander' (cf. also the root *r-g-l* from which is derived the noun 'foot' and the verb 'to slander, go about as a slanderer'). Cohen (*PSon*, p. 129) thinks that the metaphor means to bring about one's fall, while Delitzsch takes it in the sense of giving a great kick (literally). It may suggest, perhaps, a trampling on someone, or an act of violence in general (cf. Gen. 3:15).

10. be gracious to me: this supplication forms both the beginning (verse 4) and the end of the lamentation section. For the phrase, see on 6:2.

that I may requite them: this is not a very fitting motive for one's restoration, but it is understandable in the situation. The famous Jewish scholar Saadya, who was active in the tenth century A.D., interpreted this phrase as: 'I will requite them good for evil' (cf. Cohen, *PSon*, p. 129). Similarly, Rodd (*PEPC*, I, p. 83) thinks that the Psalmist may only mean: 'that his recovery will disprove the evil prophecies of his enemies' (see verses 11–12).

AN EXPRESSION OF CONFIDENCE **11–12**

11. By this I know: or 'Then shall I know', referring to the hoped-for deliverance.
thou art pleased with me: i.e. 'you have regarded me with favour'. For a similar idea, see 18:19 (M.T. 20), 22:8 (M.T. 9), 35:27.
not triumphed over me: the enemy (hardly Death, as suggested by Dahood) is not given the opportunity to raise a shout of victory (cf. Jer. 50:15).

12. thou hast upheld me: Dahood (*PAB*, I, p. 252) regards the verb *t-m-k* ('to support, uphold') as synonymous with *l-ḳ-ḥ* which he defines as a 'technical term for "assume"' (i.e. translation from one form of existence to another). He thinks that the Psalmist is asking for the same privilege of being 'assumed' by God, which was the experience both of Enoch and Elijah (cf. 49:15 (M.T. 16)). This seems rather unlikely; the meaning of the expression is that Yahweh will help the sufferer in his trouble (cf. Isa. 41:13, 42:1).
my integrity: this may seem to contradict verse 4*a* where the author confesses: '. . . I have sinned against thee'. Kirkpatrick (*BPCB*, p. 219) is probably right when he points out that integrity is not synonymous with sinlessness.
in thy presence for ever: i.e. he will be restored to God's favour, and will enjoy his blessings as long as he lives (see on 9:5; cf. 16:11).

13. This verse is generally considered as the doxology concluding the First Book of Psalms; therefore it is not part of the original Psalm.
Blessed be the Lord: see verse 1, and the note on 28:6.
the God of Israel: see on 68:8.
Amen and Amen: this is the response of the congregation. The word 'Amen' is a transliteration of the Hebrew *ʾāmēn*, which could be described as an exclamation or a responsive formula, meaning 'Truly', 'Surely', and it is derived from *ʾ-m-n*, 'to be firm, reliable'. 'Amen' is not a pious 'punctuation mark', but with this affirmation or response the worshipper could join in the blessing, oath, prayer, or doxology, etc., signifying that he is prepared to bear the full responsibilities and possible consequences of his affirmation, or that he is in agreement with what has been said or done. Sometimes it may have a legal significance

as an endorsement of a declaration (cf. Dt. 27:15–26; 1 Kg. 1:36). The double 'Amen' may be used for the sake of emphasis, or it may stress the solemnity of the situation. It was only natural that this expression should find a place in the liturgy of the synagogue and the Church.

BOOK II

Psalms 42–3 The Longing for the Presence of God

Although Ps. 42 and 43 are treated as independent units in M.T. and in the versions, there is a good case for regarding them as a literary unity. The main reasons for this suggestion are: (i) Both Psalms have a common refrain which appears after 42:5,11 (M.T. 6, 12) and 43:5. (ii) Psalm 43 has no title or superscription, and, together with Ps. 71, they are the only exceptions in this respect in the Second Book of the Psalter. (iii) Both Psalms seem to be written in the same Qinah, or elegiac metre (3+2). (iv) There is also a similarity in thought and language. Consequently it would appear that Ps. 42–3 form one poem which may have been broken up for liturgical or other purposes.

Ps. 42–3 resemble a lament, but the problem is whether it should be classed as an Individual Lament (as implied by the use of the first person pronouns), or whether it is a National Psalm of Lamentation intended for the King as the representative of the people (cf. Mowinckel, *PIW*, I, p. 219). If the latter alternative is preferred, then it could be thought of as a cultic composition for situations taking place far from the Holy City, e.g. in time of war. It seems more likely, however, that Ps. 42–3 form a Lament of the Individual (see Introduction, pp. 37ff.). The language is too general to enable us to describe the situation of the Psalmist with any certainty. It has been suggested that he was a refugee forced to dwell far from his native land (cf. Weiser, *POTL*, p. 348), or that he was one of the Babylonian exiles (cf. Kissane, *BP*, p. 185). One could interpret verse 6 as suggesting that the poet dwelt in Northern Palestine, near Mount Hermon, and thus N. H. Snaith (*Hymns of the Temple* (1951), p. 43) regards the author as a cultic official ejected by Nehemiah during his reforms in the fifth century B.C., and who was therefore unable to participate in the Temple worship (cf. Isa. 63:16). Any of these suggestions may be right but the identification is simply an informed guess. There are some doubts about the geographical terms in verse 6, and it is possible that they are metaphors rather than actual locations.

Ps. 42 can be divided into two strophes: verses 1–5 and 6–11, while Ps. 43 forms the third strophe. The last verse in each section is the refrain.

Verses 1–5 describe briefly the author's situation: he finds himself in some unspecified adversity, and is mocked by his fellows. He yearns for the presence of God, and recalls the joyous festivals in the Temple. His only ray of light is his hope in God. Verses 6–11 re-emphasize the seriousness of the plight. The Psalmist has experienced the nearness of death, and the agony of the feeling that he has been forgotten by God. In the end he returns, once more, to his hope in God. Ps. 43:1–5 opens with an appeal to God and a prayer for deliverance, and it concludes with the certainty, born of faith, that he shall yet praise God.

To the choirmaster: see Introduction, p. 48.
A Maskil: see Introduction, p. 47.
the Sons of Korah: see Introduction, p. 45.

THE DESPAIR AND HOPE **1–5**

1. As a hart: or 'hind' (so *NEB*), since the Hebrew verb is feminine in form, while the noun (masculine in form) could be used for both genders (cf. 2 Kg. 2:24).

flowing streams: i.e. perennial watercourses which do not dry out during the summer's drought. Such streams could also be described as 'living waters' which might have suggested to the hearers the thought that Yahweh is 'the fountain of living waters' (Jer. 17:13; cf. Jer. 2:13).

so longs my soul: i.e. a prolonged drought drives the wild animals to search for water (cf. Jl 1:20), and similarly, the misfortunes of the Psalmist have intensified his yearning for God.

2. My soul thirsts for God who is not an optional extra, at least for the Psalmist, but who is as indispensable as food and drink, if not more so (cf. 63:1 (M.T. 2)).

the living God: this phrase brings to mind the parallel with the flowing streams of living waters in verse 1. It is feasible that the expression offered an implicit contrast with the lifeless idols of the Psalmist's opponents (if this is the right interpretation of the evidence); cf. 84:2 (M.T. 3).

behold the face of God: M.T. reads 'I shall appear (before) the presence of God'. The difference is only in the vowel signs of the Hebrew verb, and it is possible that M.T. has preserved an ancient scribal emendation for theological (?) reasons, such as to avoid a certain type of anthropomorphism (cf. Dt. 16:16; Isa. 1:12). 'To see the face of God' was a technical term for the visiting of the sanctuary, and the idiom may well be older than the Hebrew language itself. Its origin may have been a situation where the god was actually seen, being represented by an image (cf. H. Wildberger, *Jesaja*, *BK* 10_{1}, 1965, p. 41). 'To see someone's face' means to be admitted to that person's presence and favour; cf. Gen. 43:3; Ps. 84:7 (M.T. 8).

3. We are not told the specific cause of the distress, but some of the suggestions are 'mortal illness', 'enforced exile among unsympathetic people' (Weiser, *POTL*, p. 348), or 'imprisonment' (Schmidt, *PHAT*, p. 80). **Tears** as one's food is a hyperbolic way of describing the very depths of grief and trouble (cf. 80:5 (M.T. 6)). A similar word-picture is also found in the Ugaritic myth of Baal, where Anat is said to have 'sated herself with weeping, drank tears like wine' (cf. Driver, *CML*, p. 109b).

day and night: i.e. continually.

while men say: M.T. 'while one says'. *RSV* follows some Hebrew MSS and S, which have the same form here as in verse 11.

Where is your God?: this sarcastic question is frequently found on the lips of the enemies of God's people (cf. 79:10, 115:2; Jl 2:17; Mic. 7:10). In view of the Psalmist's distress, the answer expected was that his God was to be found nowhere, i.e. either he was powerless or not concerned with the sufferings of his servant.

4. **These things** may suggest the memories recounted in the following lines; they would be a source of inspiration to one experiencing the 'dark night of the soul'.

I remember: this is not an accidental recollection but a deliberate attempt to call to mind certain past events. The author must have thought not simply of the processions and the gladness as such, but also of the salvation events commemorated by the particular festival(s). Although separated from the Temple and all the ritual, he can participate in the salvation-history through memory of the mighty works of God (cf. Childs, *MTI*, pp. 60ff.).

as I pour out my soul: or '. . . give expression to my pent-up feelings' (cf. 1 Sam. 1:15; Ps. 62:8 (M.T. 9); Lam. 2:19).

how I went: or 'used to go' (a frequentative imperfect?).

with the throng: the Hebrew *sāḵ* ('throng') is found only here in the *OT*, and the traditional rendering is a guess. It might be more reasonable to read *sōḵ* ('booth', probably 'tabernacle'; so Gunkel, *et al.*), which is suggested by most ancient versions.

and led them . . .: this phrase is rather problematic, and the *RSV* rendering is dubious. It has been proposed that we should read *ʾaddīrīm* ('the Majestic One'; a plural of majesty) for M.T. *ʾeddaddēm* ('I led them'?), and render verse 5*b*: 'how I used to go to the tabernacle of the Majestic One, even (to) the house of God'. Dahood (*PAB*, I, p. 257) derives *ʾeddaddēm* from *n-d-d*, 'to bow down' (which is attested in Ugaritic), and renders 'prostrate myself near the temple of God' (the *m* in *ʾeddaddēm* is regarded as an enclitic *mêm*).

a multitude keeping festival: or 'a sound (befitting) a pilgrim' (similarly *NEB*), i.e. in apposition to 'shouts and songs of thanksgiving'; this involves the reading of *hamôn* ('sound, multitude of . . .') for M.T. *hāmôn* ('multitude').

5. **Why are you cast down . . .:** this is not a conversation between one's true self and the weaker 'soul' (so Kirkpatrick), but the Psalmist rebukes himself for his despondency, 'Why on earth am I despairing!', i.e. bowed down like a mourner (cf. 35:14). For *nepeš* ('soul'), see on 33:19.

why are you disquieted: following the reading of verse 11 and 43:5. The verb *h-m-h* is from the same root as the noun 'multitude' (*hāmôn*), and there may be an implicit contrast between the joyful sounds made at the festival, and the writer's present complaint. Perhaps the point is that the mighty acts of God are not like our feelings and moods that come and go, but God has *already*, once for all, claimed his people and so every member of that community, as his own. This is the one certain foundation on which a man can build.

Hope in God: or 'wait for God' (cf. 38:15 (M.T. 16), 39:7 (M.T. 8), 130:5; Mic. 7:7). See on 71:14.

praise him: i.e. as in the days past. For the verb *y-d-h*, see on 18:49.

my help and my God: this rendering follows the reading of verse 11 and 43:5. M.T. could be rendered: 'the acts of salvation (which are the result of) his presence', while 'my God' belongs to the following verse. The M.T. reading may have originated from a wrong division of verses 5 and 6.

MORE TROUBLE AND MORE HOPE **6–11**

6. My soul is cast down: see verse 5*a*.

therefore I remember thee: this is the Psalmist's antidote to despair and depression, even though it may increase the sharpness of his agony. Dahood (*PAB*, I, p. 258) suggests the opposite interpretation by rendering: 'because I remember . . .'; the memories are the cause of the despondency. The former alternative seems, however, more likely.

from the land of Jordan and of Hermon: this reference is usually taken as indicating either the place from which the Psalmist is speaking (i.e. in N. Palestine), or that the author is *away* from the land of Jordan . . . (i.e. Canaan; cf. Kissane, *BP*, p. 189). *NEB* associates these terms with the 'deep' in verse 7. The 'land of Jordan' is often regarded as the region of Jordan's sources; it is less likely that it is used of Canaan as a whole. 'Hermon' or 'Mount Hermon' is situated on the southern spur of the Anti-Lebanon range, and it reaches the height of some 9,100 feet. M.T. has the plural 'Hermons', which may refer either to the three summits of this mountain, or to the whole mountain range.

The location of **Mount Mizar** is unknown, but it may have been a definite point on the Hermon range. It has been suggested that Mount Mizar (lit. 'the little mountain') is simply another name for Mount Zion, in comparison with the high mountains of the Hermon range (cf. 68:16 (M.T. 17)). On the other hand, these geographical references in verse 6 seem slightly odd, while the mythological allusions in verse 7 may suggest that also the so-called geographical terms ought to be understood in a symbolic way. Dahood (*PAB*, I, p. 258) argues that 'the land of Jordan' should be rendered 'the land of descents', i.e. a poetical name for the netherworld, while 'Hermon' could be translated 'nets' (taking *ḥermônîm* as a by-form of *ḥērem* ('net'); cf. 18:5 (M.T. 6)). For 'Mount Mizar' he reads *mēhārīm* *ṣ*ᶜ*r* ('from the mountains at the rim'); according to the Ugaritic myth, *Baal* II, viii:4 (cf. Driver, *CML*, p. 103a), there were two hills at the boundary of the earth, associated with the netherworld. Whether we accept Dahood's interpretation or not, it may well be that verse 6 describes the Psalmist as being near to death (cf. Jon. 2).

7. Deep calls to deep: this has been taken to refer to the torrents of Jordan waters descending from the rocks. It is more likely, however, that the word-picture goes back to the ancient mythology which speaks about the source of the rivers at the two oceans (cf. *Aqhat* II, vi:47; *Baal* II, iv:22; Driver, *CML*, pp. 55, 97). The same word *t^e^hôm* (in Ugaritic *thmt*) occurs both in this Psalm and in the Ugaritic texts mentioned above. This metaphor seems to be a description of trouble and misfortune, as suggested by verse 7*b*. The deep and the waters were always thought to be potentially destructive, and therefore this figure of speech is rather appropriate. Cf. 71:20, 104:6.
thy cataracts are probably the channels of the two oceans near the divine abode (cf. *Baal* III, i:6; Driver, *CML*, pp. 108, 109). Kissane (*BP*, p. 190) thinks that the 'cataracts' denote the flood-gates or the windows of heaven, which let down the rain; this may be part of the previous suggestion. The whole verse implies that God is the ultimate source of his troubles, although the motive may well be punishment (cf. 88:7 (M.T. 8)).
all thy waves and thy billows: the writer feels engulfed by his misfortunes, as by rushing torrents; he finds himself already in the grip of these threatening forces (cf. 18:4f. (M.T. 5f.)) and wellnigh overwhelmed by the waters of the dark underworld.

8. This verse is exegetically problematic, and it may no longer be in its original context or it may be textually corrupt. It is possible that **the Lord** (*yhwh*) is a dittograph of the preceding verb *y^e^ṣawweh* (*RSV* 'commands'), especially because this Psalm belongs to the *Elohistic* psalter. If so, we could render: 'By day he used to command his Covenant loyalty (cf. 111:9), and by night his song; with me was a prayer (or 'praise', as in V) to the God of my life'. Gunkel (*PGHAT*, p. 182) suggests: 'By day I will watch for Yahweh, and for his mercy by night'; this would involve a change from *y^e^ṣawweh* to *ʾ^a^ṣappeh* ('I will watch'), and the transposition of 'mercy' and 'night'. He also prefers the alteration of 'his song' (*šîrōh*) into 'I will sing' (*ʾāšîrāh*), rendering: 'I will sing within me a prayer to the God of my life'. This verse probably contains a reminiscence of the past days of happiness (as in verse 4), and in that case verse 7 may well precede verse 6. The event recalled could have been the Feast of Tabernacles; the allusion to 'his song' reminds us of Isa. 30:29: 'You shall have a song as in the night when a holy feast is kept . . .'.

9. I say to God . . .: or 'I will say . . .'. It is possible that 'to God' should be taken as a vocative 'O God', and the preposition *l*e ('to') could be regarded as *lāmeḏ vocativum* (see on 75:9).
my rock: this may be in apposition to 'God' (as in *RSV*) or it may be a vocative beginning the direct speech, 'My Rock, why . . .' (cf. LXX and V). The word *sela*c ('rock') is used of Yahweh only in the Psalter (cf. 18:2 (M.T. 3) (=2 Sam. 22:2), 31:3 (M.T. 4)). The usual word is *ṣûr* ('rock'); see on 42:9. Both nouns are used as symbols of security and defence. It is not improbable that the present usage contained an implicit contrast to the mire and waters of the underworld (cf. Driver, *CML*, p. 103a). See on 28:1; cf. 69:2 (M.T. 3).
Why: this is not so much a demand for explanation as an expression of perplexity (cf. 13:2, 22:1 (M.T. 2), 77:9 (M.T. 10)).
forgotten me: Two MSS. read 'cast me off' (*z*e*naḥtānî* for M.T. *š*e*ḵaḥtānî*) as in 43:2, but this is probably an unnecessary assimilation. This forgetfulness is not an inability to remember but rather a decision to disregard someone, for a particular reason. Such a condition is very similar to that of the dwellers in Sheol (cf. 6:5 (M.T. 6), 88:5 (M.T. 6)).
Why go I mourning: the reference is primarily to the squalid garments and appearance, rather than to the mental attitude of the person concerned (see on 35:14).
because of the oppression: or 'amidst the . . .'. The noun *laḥaṣ* can be used of the oppression of Israel by foreign invaders (cf. 2 Kg. 13:4; Ps. 44:24 (M.T. 25)), but in this context it refers to the taunts of the opponents (see verses 3 and 10).

10. As with a deadly wound . . .: or, perhaps, 'while one (i.e. the enemy) slays (*birṣōaḥ*) (me) in my bones (or 'body')'; this could be paraphrased: 'while I feel death in my very bones'. Although the detailed interpretation is not certain, the general idea seems to be clear; while the Psalmist is enduring his undefined sufferings, his enemies make fun of him.
Where is your God?: as in verse 3.

11. This verse concludes the second strophe, and it is the refrain (see verse 5).

Psalm 43

(See introduction to Ps. 42–3).

THE PSALMIST'S PRAYER **1–5**

1. The logic of the Psalmist's enemies was that his misfortunes must have been the result of his own sins, unless we regard Ps. 43 as a prayer of an accused man (cf. Schmidt, *PHAT*, p. 80), or of a man pursued by his enemies (cf. 7:1ff. (M.T. 2ff.), 26:1ff.).
Vindicate me: here the writer appeals to Yahweh, the righteous judge, but it is not stated how the vindication was envisaged.
O God: some scholars transfer this vocative to the end of verse 1, thus obtaining a 3 + 2 metre, and a better balance between the two lines.
against: lit. 'from' or '(so as to deliver) from'. It is not clear whether the **ungodly people** are Jews or Gentiles. Both alternatives have found their supporters, but the former seems more likely. The word used is *lō' ḥāsîḏ*, which may denote a *disloyal* man or people, such as do not practise Covenant loyalty; consequently the reference is more likely to the Jews who were in a Covenant relationship with God.
deceitful and unjust men: the Hebrew equivalent for 'men' is the singular *'îš*, which may be taken either collectively or as referring to the leader of the enemies. The former alternative is more plausible, in that it provides a better parallel to 'an ungodly people'.

2. the God in whom I take refuge: lit. 'the God of my refuge (or 'stronghold')'. With a slight alternation in the vocalization (reading *'ᵉlōhay* for *'ᵉlōhê*), we could translate 'For you (and no one else), O my God, are my stronghold' (cf. *NEB*).
why hast thou cast me off?: this vital question is forced upon the Psalmist by the present circumstances (cf. 60:1 (M.T. 3), 74:1, 88:14 (M.T. 15), 108:11; see on 89:38).
Why go I mourning: see on 42:9.

3. thy light and truth appear to be personified, and the Psalmist regards them as if they were two of God's messengers or angels (cf. 91:11).
let them lead me: the author may have had in mind the Exodus experience, when (according to the tradition) the people of Israel were led by a pillar of cloud and a pillar of smoke (cf. Exod. 13:21, 15:13). Some commentators see here a parallel

with the myth of Baal, where Athirat (or Asherah) is guided by Kadesh-and-Amurr to the dwelling place of El (*Baal* II, iv: 3ff.; Driver, *CML.* p. 95).

thy holy hill is Mt. Zion (cf. 2:6, 3:4 (M.T. 5), 15:1, 48:2 (M.T. 3)).

thy dwelling: the Hebrew *miškenôṯeḵā* is plural in form, hence it could be interpreted either as a plural of amplification (for the purpose of intensifying the meaning of the word) or as referring to the various courts and buildings of the Temple. The former alternative seems more feasible.

4. the altar of God: some MSS. read 'your altar' and delete 'God' (*ᵓelōhîm*); this gives a slight improvement in the metre.

to God my exceeding joy: lit. 'to the God of the joy of my rejoicing'. Most exegetes read *śimḥāṯî* ('my joy') for M.T. *śimḥaṯ* ('joy of . . .'), and *ᵓāgîlāh* ('I will exalt') for M.T. *gîlî* ('my rejoicing'), rendering: 'to the God of my joy. I will exalt and I will praise . . .'. This would give us, in verse 4, two lines with a 3+2 metre; metrically this is preferable to the M.T. reading.

I will praise thee: this praise of God may accompany the thanksgiving sacrifice acknowledging the goodness of God.

the lyre was a stringed instrument (see on 98:5), and it could have a varying number of strings (from three to twelve). In Solomon's time it was made of 'almug wood' (a kind of sandalwood?) (cf. 1 Kg. 10:12).

O God, my God: this is obviously the Elohistic editor's equivalent of 'Yahweh, my God' (so LXX), which occurs in many Psalms (cf. 7:1,3 (M.T. 2,4), 13:3 (M.T. 4), 18:28 (M.T. 29), 30:2 (M.T. 3), 35:23, 40:5 (M.T. 6), etc.).

5. For this refrain, see 42:5.

Psalm 44 The Lament of the Defeated Nation

The Psalm is a Communal Lament (see Introduction, p. 39) in a time of great distress. Its life-situation must have been a day of fasting instituted by the nation or by its leaders, for the purpose of appealing to God for help. An event of this type is described in 2 Chr. 20:4ff., belonging to the reign of Jehoshaphat (870–48 B.C.), and it may well be typical of similar occasions.

The early Church fathers, such as Theodore of Mopsuestia, Theodoret and Chrysostom, and some later exegetes, assigned this Psalm to the Maccabean period, but it is more likely that it is pre-Maccabean for various reasons: (i) It belongs to the *Elohistic* psalter, and consequently it may be comparatively early; it could have been adapted to other occasions of a later date. (ii) If indeed the Psalm originated during the Maccabean period, it is strange that it does not allude to the desecration of the Temple and to the enforcement of heathen practices, which were such burning issues at that time. (iii) The Psalm implies that the nation as a whole, as well as its leaders, were faithful to God, but this would not have been true of the Maccabean times. (iv) Too much has been read into verse 22 which need not suggest a religious persecution such as took place during the reign of Antiochus IV. In view of all this, it is not impossible that the Psalm belongs to the late pre-Exilic period, and two probable dates are the time after the death of Josiah in 609 B.C. or, less likely, during Sennacherib's invasion of Judah, in the reign of Hezekiah (715–687/6 B.C.).

The speaker in the Psalm is the nation represented by its King, commander of the armed forces, or its religious leader. It consists of three main sections. Verses 1–3 contain a hymn-like description of the mighty deeds of God in times past, while verses 4–8 are an expression of confidence in God based upon the *Heilsgeschichte*, or the salvation-history. Verses 9–26 form the actual lament in which verses 9–16 depict the present distress, verses 17–22 express a protest and the perplexity of the nation, and, finally, verses 23–6 present a desperate petition to God.

The dominant metre of the Psalm is 3 + 3.

To the choirmaster: see Introduction, p. 48.
A Maskil: see Introduction, p. 47.
Sons of Korah: see Introduction, p. 45.

THE SAVING ACTS OF GOD **1–3**

1. We have heard with our ears: i.e. we have heard it ourselves. Weiser (*POTL*, p. 355) argues that the reference must be to a cultic proclamation of the *Heilsgeschichte* which had just preceded the Psalm. It is equally possible that the writer had in mind the transmission of the salvation-history, in all its forms (cf. Kraus, *PBK*, p. 326); see Exod. 12:26ff., 13:14ff.; Dt. 6:20ff.; Jos. 4:6ff.; Ps. 78:3.

our fathers could be taken as denoting both those who took part in the actual events, and the older contemporaries of the Psalmist who were a link in the chain of tradition.

deeds: lit. 'work' (cf. 64:9 (M.T. 10), 77:12 (M.T. 13), 90:16, 92:4 (M.T. 5), 95:9, 111:3, 143:5).
in the days of old: (cf. Isa. 37:20; Jer. 46:26; Mic. 7:20). The period in question may have been the conquest of Canaan and the Settlement, and the reason for this selection may have been the fact that it was the *possession* of the land that was now threatened by the enemies.

Some scholars transfer 'thou with thy own hand' (verse 2*a*) to the end of verse 1, thus securing a 3 + 3 metre and reading: '. . . in the days of old, with thy own hand', i.e. God had performed his mighty deeds by his own power. Dahood (*PAB*, I, p. 265) proposes 'your hand worked wonders' (*ʾāṯāh yāḏeḵā* for M.T. *ʾattāh yāḏᵉḵā*); he regards the verb as a denominative from *ʾôṯ* ('sign, wonder'). This suggestion would supply the missing verb in verse 1*d*.

2. . . . didst drive out: lit. 'disinherit'. Some commentators (e.g. Duhm, Schmidt) emend this to 'root out' (*šēraštā* for M.T. *hôraštā*), which would correspond to 'didst plant' (verse 2*b*). Yet there is no real reason for this or similar changes.
the nations: the *gôyim* (see on 59:5) were the pre-Israelite inhabitants of Canaan.
but them thou didst plant: i.e. the dispossessed peoples of Canaan are contrasted with Israel, whom God had planted in the land, probably as a tree or vine (cf. 80:8ff. (M.T. 9ff.); Isa. 5:1ff.). The metaphor of planting is used on a number of occasions as a description of Israel's Settlement in Canaan (cf. Exod. 15:17; 2 Sam. 7:10; Jer. 11:7, 12:2).
thou didst afflict: some exegetes (e.g. Weiser) read with T: 'you did crush' (*tārōaᶜ*); but the essential meaning remains unaltered.
but them thou didst set free: M.T. could be paraphrased 'but them (i.e. the Israelites) you let spread out (like the branches of a fruitful vine)'. This picture is fully developed in 80:8ff. (M.T. 9ff.). The figure of a vine is a well-known biblical metaphor for Israel (cf. Isa. 5:1ff.; Jer. 2:21, 12:10; Ezek. 17:1ff.; Jl 1:7). The Herodian Temple had a golden vine (symbolic of Israel) placed over the porch before the Holy of Holies.

3. not by their own sword . . .: this could hardly mean that the Psalmist thought that the Israelites played *no* part in the conquest. In retrospect all the heroic exploits of the ancestors were entirely overshadowed by Yahweh's deeds of salvation;

when a man of God reviews the history of his own people, from the point of view of his faith, then the details of human effort simply merge into the total work of God. Sometimes the relative values must be deliberately over-emphasized to avoid the temptation to become arrogant and proud (cf. Dt. 8:17; Jos. 24:17f.).

their own arm is a metaphor for 'their own strength' (here contrasted with the might of God in verse 3*c*; cf. 33:16f.).

give them victory: lit. '. . . save them' (see on 54:1).

right hand is usually the more active of the two, and therefore it could be regarded as the more important. Consequently it provides a suitable symbol for 'power' or 'strength' (cf. Exod. 15:6,12; Lam. 2:3). In this verse the emphasis is on the possessive pronoun 'thy'.

the light of thy countenance: i.e. God's favour and help (cf. 4:6 (M.T. 7), 89:15 (M.T. 16); Prov. 16:15).

MY GOD AND MY KING **4–8**

4. Thou art my King: this thought that God is the king of Israel, and so the real leader of the people, is frequent in the Psalter, particularly in the so-called Enthronement Psalms (see on 24:7, 68:24, 93:1). See also J. Gray, 'The Hebrew Conception of the Kingship of God: Its Origin and Development', *VT*, VI (1956), pp. 268–85.

and my God: so *RSV* and *NEB* following LXX, S, for M.T. 'O God'.

who ordainest: *RSV* reads *mᵉṣawweh* for M.T. *ṣawwēh* ('ordain', i.e. an imperative), and it is supported by LXX, S, and V.

victories: either separate deeds of deliverance or 'complete victory' (a plural of amplification).

Jacob: this is a poetic name for 'Israel'. Originally it was probably a theophorous name like 'Ishmael' ('May God hear'), and its full form may have been 'Jacob-el' which is found in the lists of Thutmosis III (1490–35 B.C.). See on 20:1, 85:1.

5. Through thee: i.e. by means of your intervention.

we push down our foes: the metaphor is that of a wild ox goring its opponent, and thrusting it about. This is reminiscent of Dt. 33:17, although such word-pictures are well-known metaphors in the *OT* (cf. 1 Kg. 22:11; Ezek. 34:21). It also occurs in the Ugaritic texts (cf. *Baal* III, vi:18; *CML*, p. 115) where, in one instance, Baal and Mot butt each other like wild bulls.

through thy name: the 'name' of God may be here a synonym

for God himself (cf. 20:1 (M.T. 2); see also 1 Sam. 17:45; 2 Chr. 14:11). The phrase could mean: 'through calling upon your name—so that you come to our aid'. See on 124:8.
we tread down: this is probably a continuation of the metaphor of the wild ox trampling upon its victims. Similarly, Shalmaneser III refers to his military exploits, saying: 'His land I trod down like a wild ox' (cf. S. R. Driver, *Deuteronomy* (*ICC*, 1896), p. 407).

6. It was only through the might of God that the people of Israel gained victory (cf. 20:7 (M.T. 8), 33:16, 60:11f. (M.T. 12f.); 1 Mac. 3:18f.).
bow was usually made of seasoned wood or horn, while the so-called bronze bow probably existed only in poetic imagery (cf. 2 Sam. 22:35; Job. 20:24; Ps. 18:34 (M.T. 35)). Bow and sword were regarded as the usual weapons (cf. Gen. 48:22) although the bow came into general use only during the period of the monarchy (cf. de Vaux, *AI*, p. 243).
sword was the most common of the Israelite weapons, and in Hebrew idiom it was often used as a symbol of war (cf. Jer. 14:15, 24:10; Ezek. 7:15, 33:6; etc.). Swords were usually made of bronze or iron, and they could be of different sizes and forms. The most common Israelite type was, probably, the short, straight-bladed sword (cf. also Yadin, *SWSLSD*, pp. 124–31).

7. put to confusion . . .: i.e. by defeating the enemies.
who hate us: these are people whose hatred is expressed not only in their mental attitude but also by their hostile actions.

8. In God we have boasted: that is, we have not praised ourselves or our achievements, but the object of our praise has been none other than God (see on 34:2).
we will give thanks to thy name: i.e. to God himself. The worshipping community is bound to her God not only by faith and hope, but also by her thankfulness for God's acts of deliverance in the past (cf. 34:1f. (M.T. 2f.)).
Selah: see Introduction, pp. 48f.

THE PRESENT DISASTER **9–16**

The contemporary situation seems to deny a faith based upon the past acts of God.

9. Yet: this introduces a stark contrast between the triumphant past and the tragic present.
thou hast cast us off: the hand of God is seen even in the recent defeat, which is not regarded merely as a military reverse, but as a

test case for the nation's faith (cf. Jg. 6:13; Ps. 89:38ff. (M.T. 39ff.)). A war has been fought and lost, but the fight for the meaning of history goes on. The existent view had failed to relate faith to the realities of life, and the actual events had shown that history was more complex than a scheme where rewards and punishments fit neatly the respective deeds down to the last detail. For the verb *z-n-ḥ* ('to reject'), see on 89:38; cf. R. Yaron, *VT*, XIII (1963), pp. 237ff.

our armies: God was the Lord of Hosts who accompanied the armies of Israel (cf. 2 Sam. 5:24; also Jg. 6:16) and on such occasions the Ark was the symbol of God's presence (cf. Num. 10:35; 1 Sam. 4:3–11). Yet God was not 'bound' to the Ark, even though some such view may have existed among certain sections of Israelites (cf. H. W. Hertzberg, *I & II Samuel*, Eng. tr. by J. S. Bowden, 1964, p. 51).

10. our enemies have gotten spoil: or 'our enemies plunder (us)', reading *lānû* for *lāmô* ('for themselves'), with T and S, or paraphrasing 'those who spoil (us) to their heart's content' (cf. Jg. 2:14; 2 Kg. 17:20).

11. sheep for slaughter: the reference may be to such sheep as were regarded inferior to those kept for wool, etc.; or it may be a picture of doom (cf. Jer. 12:3; Zech. 11:4,7). It is possible that the 'devourer' was thought to be Sheol or death; cf. *Baal* II, viii:15ff.: 'Come you not near to Mot son of El lest he make you like sheep in his mouth . . .' (Driver, *CML*, p. 103); see also Hab. 2:5.

hast scattered us: i.e. as refugees, deportees, or prisoners-of-war (i.e. slaves); cf. 2 Kg. 24:14ff.; Jer. 29:1ff.

12. Thou hast sold thy people: this is a frequent figure of speech in the *OT* (cf. Dt. 32:30; Jg. 2:14, 3:8, 4:2,9, 10:7; 1 Sam. 12:9; 1Q27 1, ii:6), and its purpose is to describe the people as completely at the disposal of their enemies, as if they were slaves, the property of their foes. The reason for this turn of events was usually the disobedience of the people.

for a trifle: perhaps 'for nothing' (i.e. God has given them away for nothing).

demanding no high price for them: or 'you have made no gain by their price'. The point seems to be that for some reason the people of Israel were regarded as if of no value in the sight of God, and consequently he had sold them for a song (cf. Isa. 52:3; Jer. 15:13f.).

13. Thou hast made us: Duhm *et al.* read *hāyînû* ('we have become') for M.T. *t^e^śîmēnû* ('you have made us'); this would avoid repeating the same phrase in verse 14, and the reading is also suggested by 79:4 which differs from our verse only on this point (cf. 31:11 (M.T. 12), 89:41 (M.T. 42)).

the taunt of our neighbours: i.e. the Israelites have become an object of derision to their neighbours who may have included Ammonites, Edomites, Moabites, Philistines, etc. Cf. 1QH ii:9,34.

14. a byword among the nations: i.e. the disaster of God's people had assumed such proportions that it had become proverbial, and could serve both as an example, or as an admonition to others (cf. Dt. 28:37; 1 Kg. 9:7; Jer. 24:9). For *māšāl* ('proverb, parable'), see on 49:4.

a laughingstock: lit. 'a shaking of the head'. This must have been a gesture of scorn and mockery, and it is found in a number of *OT* passages (cf. 22:7 (M.T. 8), 64:8 (M.T. 9), 109:25; Jer. 18:16; Lam. 2:15). For this verse, see also 79:4.

15. Humiliation had become an integral part of the Psalmist's daily experience, and its cause was the national disaster as well as its interpretation by other peoples.

shame has covered my face: M.T. is ambiguous, and it could be rendered: 'the shame of my face has covered me' (so LXX, T, S and V). 'Shame of my face' may be a more emphatic expression than simply 'my shame' (see on 69:7). Taylor (*PIB*, p. 231) suggests that 'if to God belongs the glory of victory, to him also belongs the *shame* of defeat'. This is only true in so far as God is thought of as the giver both of victory and defeat.

16. at the words: or 'because of the voice (or 'words')'. The enemies make sure that the defeat of God's people is not forgotten.

the taunters and revilers: the respective verbs (in this instance participles) are found in a similar combination in Isa. 37:23 (=2 Kg. 19:22), where the prophet applied them to Sennacherib, the king of Assyria (705–681 B.C.) who, although he himself may not have been conscious of the fact, had blasphemed against God (cf. J. Skinner, *Isaiah I–XXXIX* (*Camb. B*, 1909), p. 271).

at the sight of: or 'because of the presence of'.

the enemy and the avenger: (cf. 8:2 (M.T. 3)). According to Dt. 32:35 both vengeance and recompense belong to God, while in this passage these functions have been usurped by the enemy or given to them.

THE PROTESTATION OF NATIONAL INNOCENCE **17–22**
The people of Israel had been warned that a breach of the Covenant would result in a punishment (cf. Dt. 4:25ff., 6:14ff., 8:19), but in this particular situation the nation is unaware of any faithlessness. Although the service of God is never perfect, it is possible to speak about loyalty and disloyalty to God, and therefore the claim of the nation need not be taken as an example of gross arrogance.

17. though we have not forgotten thee: the reference is probably both to the past and present; in spite of all the misfortunes they are still loyal to God (cf. 119:16).

. . . false to thy covenant: that is, they have not neglected the Covenant responsibilities as defined by the Covenant text. See on 55:20.

18. Our heart has not turned back: in *OT* thought man's behaviour is often determined by the instrumentality of his heart, the supposed centre of his will and intellect (see on 27:3, 51:10). In this verse the Psalmist points out that the nation has not turned away from God (cf. Jer. 38:22).

nor have our steps departed . . .: many MSS. read 'our step' (*ʾaššūrēnû*) which agrees with the singular verb. Verse 18*b* has no negative itself, but *lōʾ* ('not') in the preceding line serves both parts of the parallelism. The writer affirms that the people have not forsaken the right way of life which has been made plain through the commandments of God (cf. 17:5).

19. in the place of jackals: this phrase may be a proverbial expression denoting ruin and devastation (cf. Isa. 34:13, 35:7; Jer. 9:11, 10:22, 49:33, 51:37). This may mean either that God has crushed the Israelites in the desert places where they had sought refuge (cf. Jer. 4:29; 1 Mac. 2:29ff.), or that he has inflicted upon them a crushing defeat with the result that the country has become a desolation, the haunt of the wild animals. Some commentators (Olshausen, Gunkel, *et al.*) follow some MSS. which read *tannîn* ('dragon') or *tannînîm* ('dragons') for M.T. *tannîm* ('jackals'). Thus Leslie (*PAP*, p. 230) renders 'Thou hast crushed *us* instead of the dragon' (cf. Job 7:12; see on Ps. 74:13). This is possible but hardly an improvement; the 'dragon' (or 'dragons') may be an allusion to the forces of Chaos.

deep darkness: *RSV* reads *ṣalmûṯ*, while M.T. (also LXX *et al.*) has *ṣalmāweṯ* which is usually translated as 'the shadow of death'

(*AV*); *NEB* 'the darkness of death'. The former reading may be more likely, because compound nouns are not very frequent in Hebrew, although there are many compounds among the proper nouns. See on 23:4; cf. D. Winton Thomas, *JSS*, VII (1962), pp. 191–9. To be covered with deep darkness is, more or less, equivalent to dwelling in great darkness (Isa. 9:2 (M.T. 1)), which is a metaphor of trouble and distress (cf. 107:10,14); consequently those who experience such trials are near to the 'land of no return' (cf. Job 10:21), or they are already in the power of death.

20. If we had forgotten . . .: this would have been no simple lapse of memory, but it would have amounted to a rejection of the worship of God, as suggested by verse 20*b*. The opposite of this is to call upon the name of God (cf. Gen. 4:26; Ps. 63:4 (M.T. 5), 79:6), which forms an essential part of worship.

spread forth our hands: the open hand of the worshipper is spread forth towards the deity (cf. Exod. 9:29,33; Ezr. 9:5; Ps. 88:9 (M.T. 10), 141:2, 143:6; Isa. 1:15), towards the Temple (1 Kg. 8:38; Ps. 28:2), or towards heaven (1 Kg. 8:22,54), and it was a well-known gesture in prayer.

a strange god: any deity other than the God of Israel (cf. 81:9 (M.T. 10)).

21. God is the one who searches out all secrets (cf. 139:1, 23ff.; Jer. 17:10), and consequently he would have known of Israel's apostasy, had this been the case.

For he knows the secrets . . .: Dahood (*PAB*, I, p. 267) suggests: '. . . the dark corners of the heart', deriving *ta*^{c}^{a}*lūmôṯ* ('secrets') from ^{c}*-l-m*, 'to be dark'.

22. Not only has the nation been loyal to God, but they are also suffering for this their fidelity. If so, it is God's own honour that is at stake (cf. 79:10). This verse is also quoted in Rom. 8:36. The reference is not necessarily to a religious persecution, but the same plight could apply to any defeated nation. Probably Yahweh is regarded as the author of the troubles; cf. verses 9–14.

all the day long: this suggests that the disaster did not consist of a single blow but that it was of a prolonged nature, and that its end was not, as yet, in sight.

as sheep . . .: see verse 11. Usually this would be a picture of a judgment upon the wicked (cf. Jer. 12:13).

THE CRY FOR HELP **23–6**

23. Why sleepest thou: it is unlikely that the Psalmist meant by this expression a *real* possibility of this sort. At least some Psalmists regarded God as the one who neither slumbers nor sleeps (121:4). The writer probably intended to show that, from the human point of view, God appeared to be inactive, *as if* asleep (cf. 78:65). It is not impossible, however, that some may have been more literal in their understanding of this phrase, as suggested by the Talmudic story (*B.Sota* 48a) about the Levites who, before the reign of Hyrcanus (134–104 B.C.), used to cry daily: 'Awake, why sleepest thou, O Lord'. It is not likely that this phrase was an ironic expression, intended as a taunt to God (cf. 1 Kg. 18:27); rather it was a cry of bewilderment in a puzzling crisis.

do not cast us off: cf. verse 9.

24. Why dost thou hide thy face: or '. . . do you turn your face away' (so Dahood, *PAB*, I, p. 268, who derives the verb from *s-w-r* ('to turn away'), belonging to the infixed *-t-* conjugation). To hide one's face from another person means to disregard him (cf. 13:1 (M.T. 2), 22:24 (M.T. 25), 88:14 (M.T. 15)), or it can indicate displeasure (Isa. 54:8), and even punishment (cf. Dt. 31:17,18, 32:20; Job 13:24; Isa. 57:17), at least in the sense that one is left to oneself.

Why dost thou forget our affliction . . .: i.e. by ceasing to care for thy people in their plight. N. H. Snaith (*Hymns of the Temple* (1951), p. 65) calls this a figure of speech to express the 'delayed action' of God.

25. This verse must be connected with the present trials of the nation, but the meaning of the details is not clear. Possibly it describes the worshippers prostrate upon the dusty ground, in an attitude of deep humiliation before God (cf. Dt. 9:18; 2 Chr. 20:18; Jdt. 4:11); or it is simply a general expression of sorrow (cf. 119:25) unrelated to any possible liturgy of a day of fasting (cf. Jos. 7:6; Ps. 137:1; Isa. 47:1; Jer. 6:26, 14:2). For 'our soul' Dahood (*PAB*, I, p. 268) reads 'our neck', which is a possible meaning of *nep̄eš* (see on 33:19).

26. Rise up: this expression may be associated with the idea of the Ark and Holy War (cf. G. Henton Davies, 'The Ark in the Psalms', *Promise and Fulfilment*, ed. by F. F. Bruce, 1963, p. 60).

come to our help: perhaps the noun in M.T. should be taken as a precative perfect (*ʿāzartāh*) meaning 'help (us)' (so Dahood, *PAB*, I, p. 268).

for the sake of thy steadfast love: i.e. the prayer for help is not based upon any self-righteousness, but it appeals to God's Covenant promises and to his self-imposed loyalty towards the people of his choice.

Psalm 45 The Royal Wedding

This poem is usually regarded as a marriage song belonging to the Royal Psalms. Although marriage was primarily a private and legal affair, a royal wedding must have had a great national significance, because the King was not only the most important political figure of the realm, but also the religious head of the people. Consequently all important events in the life of the King, such as his enthronement, wedding, going to war, etc., were both national and religious events.

It is pointless to identify the royal couple for whom this Psalm was originally composed, but the possible allusion to the oracle of Nathan (2 Sam. 7) may suggest that the King in question must have been a Davidic monarch. Therefore the date of the Psalm may well be pre-Exilic, and the poem may have been used by successive Kings on the day of the royal wedding.

There are also other views. A. Bentzen has argued that the wedding described by the Psalm is the *hieros gamos* of the divine King, and that the event belongs to the annual royal cult. Eaton (*PTBC*, p. 123) thinks that it is possible that 'the marriage was celebrated as a sequel to an annual re-enthronement of the King in the autumnal festival', but he does not interpret it as an *exact* parallel to the 'sacred marriage' found in the neighbouring monarchies. T. H. Gaster (*JBL*, LXXIV (1955), p. 239) has suggested that Ps. 45 is a description of 'conventional wedding ceremonies such as actually survive at the present day'. In it the bridal couple are treated as royalty: 'His Majesty' is none other than the ordinary bridegroom, and the princess is simply his bride. It is doubtful, however, whether such a convention was known to the people of Israel in *OT* times. Occasionally the King and his bride are regarded as the ideal King (the Messiah) and Israel, respectively (so Barnes, Deissler, *et al.*); this interpretation is found in T as well as in the early Church (cf. Heb. 1:8). The Psalm probably owes its place in the Psalter to the Messianic interpretation which was placed upon it. Cf. also C. Schedl, *VT*, XIV (1964), pp. 310–18; Sabourin, *POM*, II, pp. 230ff.

The dominant metre is 4+4+4.

To the choirmaster: see Introduction, p. 48.
according to Lilies: see Introduction, p. 50.
A Maskil: see Introduction, p. 47.
the Sons of Korah: see Introduction, p. 45.
a love song: see Introduction, p. 47.

THE INTRODUCTORY NOTE **1**

My heart overflows: or 'my mind is astir (or 'bubbles over')', perhaps 'I am overwhelmed'.
with a goodly theme: or 'with an auspicious message' (cf. Jos. 23:14,15; 1 Kg. 8:56; Jer. 29:10, 33:14). The author of this Psalm may have been a cultic prophet, and thus his message was, in a sense, a promise of Yahweh, uttered through him (cf. Kraus, *PBK*, p. 333).
I address: *RP* 'I will sing'; M.T. 'I am about to speak'.
my verses: lit. 'my works' or, as most scholars suggest, 'my work' (reading *ma^{ca}śî* for M.T. *ma^{ca}śay*); Kissane 'my poem'.
my tongue is like the pen: *AV et al.* 'my tongue is the pen'.
a ready scribe probably does not denote a quick writer but a learned scribe. The same phrase occurs also in Ezr. 7:6 where it describes Ezra's qualifications, i.e. a scribe *expert* in the law of Moses.

THE DESCRIPTION OF THE ROYAL BRIDEGROOM **2–9**

2. You are the fairest . . .: it is unlikely that the King was of superhuman (i.e. divine) beauty (so Oesterley); rather the author follows the Oriental court style, or his expression may be regarded primarily as a subjective judgment (cf. Ca. 5:10) and not an objective description (cf. also *Genesis Apocryphon*, col. xx). In the ancient world a king was expected to be especially handsome and abounding in other outstanding attributes (cf. 1 Sam. 9:2, 10:23, 16:12; 2 Sam. 14:25; 1 Kg. 1:6, etc.). In the Ugaritic poem about Baal (cf. *ANET*, p. 140) Ashtar sits on Baal's throne but his feet do not reach down to the footstool nor does his head reach its top; in other words, he is not fit to be king. It is possible that 'beauty' in our Psalm did not consist of what might be called 'sex-appeal', but rather of a general perfection. So also in 2 Sam. 14:25: '. . . no one was so much praised for his beauty as Absalom; from the sole of his foot to the crown of his head there was no blemish in him', i.e. he was worthy to be King. In Absalom's case the account may well have been right, but it is doubtful whether *all* dynastic Kings qualified as paragons of perfection.

grace is poured upon your lips: perhaps 'graciousness is established (or 'poured out') by your lips' or '. . . flows *from* your lips' (taking the preposition *b*[e] ('on') in the sense of 'from', as in Ugaritic). The King displays his favour towards all (cf. Lk. 4:22).

therefore God has blessed you: the King is recognized by his outward appearance and by his manner (cf. Jg. 8:18), and as such he is fit to receive God's blessings.

for ever: (see on 9:5, 117:2). This does not suggest a personal immortality but the enduring quality of the royal house (cf. 2 Sam. 7:16), or it simply means 'as long as you live'.

3. Gird your sword . . .: the sword was usually worn in a sheath (1 Sam. 17:51; 2 Sam. 20:8; 1 Chr. 21:27) attached to a girdle and fastened upon one's loins (2 Sam. 20:8; cf. Jg. 3:16).

in your glory and majesty: these words (see on 96:6) may also describe the *sword* of the King, which is seen as his (i.e. the King's) splendour and honour (cf. H. H. Gowen, *The Psalms* (1930), p. 181). It is more likely, however, that the allusion is to the King himself (cf. Pedersen, *ILC*, I–II, pp. 237f.). Some exegetes take 'In your majesty ride forth victoriously' (verse 4*a*) as belonging to verse 3, but they delete 'In your majesty' (verse 4*a*) as a dittograph of the preceding word. In this case we could translate: 'In your glory and majesty ride forth victoriously'. This is not a command to go to war on his wedding day, but it is a wish or assurance that the King will be victorious in all his future wars. When both God and the King are on the same side, success is inevitable, at least from the Psalmist's point of view.

4. In your majesty . . .: see above.

for the cause of truth: the King is not an oppressor, but the champion of truth and of all those things that contribute towards the right ordering of the community.

and defend the right: lit. 'and humility, right' LXX, T, and V suggest 'and humility and righteousness', while Gunkel *et al.* emend the first word *w*[e]*ᶜanwāh*, reading *w*[e]*yaᶜan* ('and for the sake of (righteousness)'). Dahood (*PAB*, I, p. 272) proposes 'and defend the poor' (*w*[e]*ᶜānāw haṣdēḳ*); perhaps we should render: 'for the sake

of truth defend the afflicted' (regarding the conjunction 'and' (*wᵉ*) as an emphatic *wāw*).
your right hand: this is personified, and it refers to the King's strength; see on 20:6.
teach you: Dahood (*PAB*, I, p. 272) suggests '(your mighty deeds) will point you out' (i.e. as the King).
dread deeds: the Hebrew *nôrāʾôṯ* usually refers to the awe-inspiring mighty acts of God (see on 65:5). Here the allusion may be to the royal victories in the fight for truth and righteousness, and thus they are the awe-inspiring deeds of God, in miniature, and performed by the grace of God.

5. **in the heart of the king's enemies:** in M.T. this phrase comes at the end of the verse which could be rendered: 'Your arrows are sharp (i.e. your military strength is great), (consequently) peoples are under you (or 'subject to you'); they (i.e. the arrows) fall in the heart of the enemies of the King'. The second part in the verse could be read (with a slight alteration): 'the heart (i.e. the courage) of the King's enemies shall fail' (changing *yippᵉlû bᵉlēḇ* ('they shall fall in the heart of. . .') into *yippōl lēḇ* ('the heart of. . . shall fall')). The essential meaning of the verse seems to be the same, whatever reading we follow: the King will be triumphant. This expresses the conviction that success must follow the anointed of God.

6. **Your divine throne endures for ever and ever:** this phrase is the main interpretative crux of this Psalm. The ancient versions suggest: 'Your throne, O God, is for ever and ever' (cf. also *AV*, *RV*) but they may have had in mind a messianic interpretation of this Psalm; cf. Heb. 1:8. Originally, however, the Psalm must have referred to the reigning Davidic king, and the question may be asked whether the Israelite king was regarded as divine (in the same manner as the kings of Egypt and some other countries), or whether the right rendering of the verse is to be found in some such translation as that of *RSV*. The former alternative seems less likely, for although the Davidic king was thought to be on very intimate terms with the deity (see on 2:7), he remained a man (cf. Johnson, *SKAI*, p. 27). It is possible that the King is addressed in a hyperbolic language as God (cf. Weiser, *POTL*, p. 361) but it is not very likely because such a usage would be open to misinterpretation. Johnson (op. cit., p. 27, n.1) proposes: 'Thy throne is like that of God (*or* a god)—for ever' (similarly *NEB*), and he points to an analogous

construction in Ca. 1:15, 4:1 (but cf. Ca. 5:12). *RSVm* suggests: 'your throne is a throne of God', which makes good sense, since the throne of David could be described as a throne of Yahweh (1 Chr. 29:23; cf. 1 Chr. 28:5). Wellhausen has recommended an ingenious conjecture, reading 'shall stand' for 'God' (i.e. he assumes that *yihyeh* ('he shall stand') has been corrupted to *yhwh* ('Yahweh') which in turn was altered by the Elohistic editor to *ʾelōhîm* ('God'); cf. *PBP*, p. 183). Dahood (*PAB*, I, p. 269) renders: 'The eternal and everlasting God has enthroned you', and he regards the Hebrew *ksʾ* (*RSV* 'throne') as a verb; this is feasible but the verb is not attested in the *OT*.

Your royal sceptre: or 'the sceptre of your kingdom'. 'Sceptre' was a symbol of kingship and its shape may have varied from time to time. Thus Rameses II is depicted holding a short sceptre reminiscent of a bishop's staff (cf. *GAB*, pl. 130), while the Persian king Darius I is pictured with a long straight sceptre in his hand (*ANEP*, pl. 463). The sceptre (*šēḇeṭ*) was probably a stylized military weapon symbolizing the power of the King. Some have argued that originally it had a magical significance (cf. Kraus, *PBK*, p. 335) but this would have little if any bearing upon the verse.

a sceptre of equity: i.e. the King will exercise his rule justly and not tyrannically (cf. Isa. 9:7 (M.T. 6), 11:4).

7. you love righteousness: that is, the King both acts justly and sees justice done (cf. 11:7, 33:5, 37:28, 99:4; Isa. 61:8). Dahood (*PAB*, I, p. 273) takes the Hebrew verb as a precative perfect, rendering 'You must love . . .'.

and hate wickedness: this means that the wicked are treated according to their deserts (cf. 5:6 (M.T. 7), 11:5f.).

God, your God: originally this must have been 'Yahweh, your God'; see on 43:4.

has anointed you with the oil . . .: the interpretation of this phrase is not clear; it may refer to the consecration of the King during his coronation, or it may be a figurative expression meaning that God has granted to the King blessings that exceed those of other people. It is a well-known fact that the kings of Israel were anointed in the name of Yahweh (i.e. ultimately they were consecrated by Yahweh himself; cf. 1 Sam. 10:1, 15:17; 2 Sam. 12:7; 2 Kg. 9:6). A similar practice is attested among the Canaanites and the Hittites but it is not found in Egypt and Mesopotamia (cf. Kraus, *PBK*, p. 335). Most commentators take verse 7 as a figurative expression but it may well be that the Psalm points back to the enthronement of the King. Because he is Yahweh's anointed, he receives further blessings (i.e. the anointing mentioned here); cf. 23:5; Isa. 61:3; Heb. 1:9.

your fellows: they are either other kings or, more likely, the King's fellow men in general.

8. your robes are all fragrant with . . .: rather than 'your robes are all made of . . .' (Weiser, *POTL*, p. 360). One could, however, think of the King's garments so perfumed that they could be described as myrrh and aloes (cf. Dt. 33:28*b*). This perfuming of the robes may be the result of the King's anointing (cf. 133:2), and the fragrant substances enumerated may be the ingredients of the anointing oil.

myrrh was a fragrant resin of a thorny shrub (*Commiphora myrrha*), and it could be used either in its solid form (as resinous gum), or as oil. It formed part of various perfumes as well as of the sacred anointing oil (cf. Exod. 30:23). It was always a precious commodity, and as such it would make a valuable present (cf. Mt. 2:11).

aloes were an aromatic substance derived from some such tree as the sandalwood, and often used for making perfumes, for embalming, or as incense.

cassia: this word is often regarded as a later addition, since it mars the metre, and it may have been a gloss on 'aloes'. Cassia was the aromatic bark of a tree similar to the cinnamon tree, and it, too, was an ingredient of various perfumes.

From ivory palaces: that is, the buildings themselves were the normal structures, but some of the rooms and the furniture must have been decorated with ivory inlay or ivory plaques (cf. 1 Kg. 22:39; Am. 3:15, 6:4), similar to those found at Megiddo and Samaria (see *ANEP*, pll. 128–30). Although the *OT* mentions specifically the ivory palace of Ahab (1 Kg. 22:39), it does not follow that there were no ivory ornaments in the palace in Jerusalem. Solomon's throne is reported to have been made of ivory (1 Kg. 10:18). The plural 'palaces' may refer to the various halls of the one palace.

stringed instruments: this translation takes the Hebrew *minnî* as an abbreviated plural noun *minnîm* (see on 150:4), and it gives a more intelligible rendering than other suggestions or emendations (cf. *AV*).

9. daughters of kings: Gunkel *et al.* read 'the daughter of kings' (i.e. *baṯ* ('daughter') for M.T. *b^e^nôṯ*; cf. S) because the verb 'stands' (*niṣṣ^e^ḇāh*) is singular, and probably should be taken with verse 10*a*. If so, the reference is to the bride whose ancestry includes many kings, and this would provide a good parallel to verse 10*b*. If we adopt the reading of *RSV* (=M.T.), then the writer may have had in mind the ladies of the King's harem (cf. 1 Kg. 11:3; 1 Chr. 3:1ff.). *NEB* has 'a princess'.
among your ladies of honour: or, perhaps, 'in your precious things (or 'jewels')', referring to the gifts given by the King; a possible paraphrase might be '(Adorned) with your jewels, the daughter of kings takes her place', and it would provide a good parallel to the next line.
at your right hand: i.e. in the place of honour and dignity (cf. 1 Kg. 2:19; Jer. 13:18). She is at the right hand of the King just as he, in the language of the cult, is said to be seated at God's right hand (cf. 110:1).
the queen: the reference seems to be to the royal bride rather than to the Queen Mother (cf. Neh. 2:6; Dan. 5:2,23).
gold of Ophir was probably the choicest gold (see Isa. 13:12; cf. also Job 28:16). The location of Ophir is unknown but among the many suggestions the most likely candidates are India, South Arabia, and Somaliland.

THE DESCRIPTION OF THE BRIDE **10–15**

10. Hear, O daughter: the Psalmist proceeds to address the new queen, and from the manner of expression, the speaker seems to be a man of some authority, perhaps a court prophet.
consider: Gunkel, Oesterley, *et al.* delete this verb because it overloads the line.
forget your people: lit. 'and forget . . .' but the conjunction is usually deleted since this phrase is the beginning of the advice; the conjunction could be, perhaps, an emphatic *wāw*. The fact that the bride is told to forget her own people (i.e. to change her loyalties) may imply that she was a foreigner (cf. Dt. 21:13). Kissane (*BP*, p. 201) argues that 'people' may simply mean 'kinsfolk', and not necessarily an alien people. In the former case, her rule of conduct should be the same as the sentiment expressed by Ruth (Ru. 1:16): 'Your people shall be my people, and your God my God . . .'.

11. and the king will desire your beauty: or 'let the King

desire . . .' which may mean 'let your marriage be consummated' (cf. Prov. 6:25). For the verb ᵓ-*w-h*, 'to desire', see on 106:14.
Since he is your lord: this may well give the reason for the exhortation given in verse 11*a*, i.e. he is your husband. For this use of *ᵓādôn* ('lord, husband'), see Gen. 18:12; Jg. 19:26,27. V reads 'since he is the Lord, thy God' but this is obviously due to the later messianic interpretation of the Psalm.
bow to him: according to the M.T. reading, this phrase is addressed to the bride, and belongs to verse 11. Many commentators, however, add these words to verse 12, and translate: 'The people of Tyre shall prostrate themselves in homage before him, with gifts; the richest of the people shall seek your favour.' This requires a slight emendation: *wᵉhištaḥᵃwû* ('and they shall prostrate themselves') for M.T. *wᵉhištaḥᵃwî* ('and bow'), and *baṯ* ('daughter, people, of') for M.T. *ûḇaṯ* ('and the daughter, people, of'); the conjunction 'and' (*wᵉ*) may represent the emphatic *wāw* (see on 18:41; Brockelmann, *HS*, 123f.).

12. the people of Tyre: lit. 'and the daughter of Tyre'. The reference may be either to a princess from Tyre or, more likely, to the people of this great trading centre. For this use of 'daughter', see such phrases as 'the daughter of Zion' (9:14 (M.T. 15)) or 'daughter of Babylon' (137:8). The meaning of verse 12 may be that envoys will come from the various neighbouring countries bringing their gifts for the royal bride.
the richest of people may suggest the nations (as in T), while Dahood (*PAB*, I, p. 275) proposes 'guests', deriving the Hebrew *ᶜᵃšîrê* ('the richest of . . .' so *RSV*) from *ᶜ-š-r*, 'to invite to a banquet', which is attested in Ugaritic (cf. Driver, *CML*, p. 140, n.18).

13. with all kinds of wealth: *RSV* adds this phrase to the preceding verse, but it may describe the garments of the royal bride (as in *AV*, *RV*, *RSVm*): 'all glorious is the princess within (the palace), her robes are made of gold-embroidered material'. Many exegetes emend *pᵉnîmâh* ('within') to *pᵉnînîm* ('corals'), but this would lead to further alterations (cf. Kraus, *PBK*, p. 330).

14. in many-coloured robes . . .: in verse 9 the bride was already at the King's side but the poem apparently provides us with a number of scenes which are not necessarily in a 'chronological' order, unless the 'queen' mentioned in verse 9 was the Queen Mother.
with her virgin companions: the bride is accompanied by her maids-of-honour (cf. Gen. 24:59ff.; Est. 2:9; Mt. 25:1).

her escort: this may be in apposition to the previous phrase, or the reference is to two groups: the maid-servants and the friends. Perhaps verse 14 could be translated: 'In coloured robes *the* maiden (i.e. *bᵉtûlôṯ* is taken as singular in meaning) is led to the King, her companions are brought in after her, to you' (similarly Dahood).

15. The reference may be to the relatives and friends of the bride, or to her companions, described in the preceding verse.

THE ADDRESS TO THE KING **16–17**

The author expresses the wish that the King's dynasty might be permanent, and that its rule might be universal (cf. Ps. 2).

16. Instead of your fathers . . .: Kirkpatrick (*BPCB*, p. 252) suggests that if the King cannot boast of a long ancestry, at least he will have a distinguished posterity. Cf. also the Ugaritic legend of Keret (cf. *ANET*, p. 146), in which El promises to Keret that the wife he takes into his house shall bear him many sons (cf. Gen. 24:60; Ru. 4:11).

you will make them princes: i.e. high officials (cf. 2 Sam. 8:18; 2 Chr. 11:22ff.).

in all the earth: either 'in all the world' (cf. the court style of Ps. 2) or 'in all the kingdom'.

17. I will cause your name to be celebrated: some commentators prefer to read with LXX 'They (i.e. his sons) will cause . . .' (*yazkîrû* for M.T. *ʾazkîrāh*). The speaker in M.T. is the Psalmist (or God?) who through this song will make the King 'immortal', in that his *name* will live for ever (see on 20:1).

Psalm 46 God is With Us

This Psalm is better known in Luther's splendid paraphrase, 'Ein' feste Burg ist unser Gott', translated into English by Thomas Carlyle as 'A safe stronghold our God is still'. Its *Gattung* or psalm-type is difficult to define; since the subject of its praise is God, it is reminiscent of Hymns, although its structure is different. Verse 10 resembles a prophetic oracle, hence Kittel has described the Psalm as a 'prophetic lyric', while Gunkel referred to it as an 'eschatological hymn'. The emphasis upon the city of God (verses 4ff.) may qualify it as a Hymn of Zion (cf. Kraus, *PBK*, p. 340).

The older commentators saw the origin of this Psalm in some great historical event, and most of them associated it with the deliverance of Jerusalem from the Assyrian threat (2 Kg. 18:13–19:36; Isa. 36:1–37:38). Yet the Psalm offers little concrete help for any such identification, and, even allowing for a poetic exaggeration, the language of the Psalm transcends any known historical occasion. Consequently the origin of the poem may not have been a royal victory but the Jerusalem cult and its ancient traditions. It was probably associated with the great Autumnal Festival at which the kingship of Yahweh was celebrated; Kraus thinks of the Zion Festival, but this may have been one aspect of the Feast of Tabernacles. The main point is that the Psalm belongs to the cult (cf. v. Rad, *OTT*, II, p. 157).

The Psalm consists of three strophes: verses 1–3, 4–7 and 8–11. There seems to be a refrain at the end of the second and third strophes (i.e. verses 7 and 11), and it is probable that there was also a similar refrain at the end of the first strophe. The Psalm may have been sung antiphonally by the congregation or the Temple choirs. The main theme of this hymn is the reality of God's presence with his people.

The metre of the Psalm is irregular.

To the choirmaster: see Introduction, p. 48.
A Psalm: see Introduction, p. 46.
the Sons of Korah: see Introduction, p. 45.
Alamoth: see Introduction, p. 50.
A Song: see Introduction, p. 47.

GOD IS WITH US **1–3**

1. By means of different word-pictures the author shows that if God is with his people, then nothing can disturb their calm.

God is our refuge: i.e. he alone is his people's true safety (cf. 61:3 (M.T. 4), 62:7,8 (M.T. 8,9), 71:7, 73:28, 91:2,9, 142:5 (M.T. 6); Jl 3:16); all else is, in comparison, a self-deception (cf. Isa. 28:15,17, 30:2ff.).

strength: that is, God is the source of his nation's might. The Hebrew *ᶜōz* ('strength') could be also derived from *ᶜ-w-z*, 'to seek refuge', hence it could mean 'shelter, place of safety' (cf. Gunkel, *PGHAT*, p. 200).

a very present help in trouble: lit. 'a help in troubles he is found to be abundantly' (cf. 2 Chr. 15:4,15; Jer. 29:4), i.e. he has fully proved himself to be a reliable help in times of trouble. This is a favourite theme of the Psalmists (cf. 22:19 (M.T. 20), 27:9, 40:13 (M.T. 14), 44:26 (M.T. 27), 63:7 (M.T. 8), etc.), and it expresses both past experience and hope for the future. Dahood (*PAB*, I, p. 278) has proposed 'found from of old to be help in trouble', reading *mēʾāḏ* ('from of old') for M.T. *meʾōḏ* ('abundantly'), and regarding the former as a Canaanite form of *mēʾāz*.

2. The confidence expressed need not have been inspired by some recent deliverance (cf. Davison, *Cent. BP*, I, p. 241) but it rests, most likely, upon the cultic participation in the mighty works of God.

though the earth should change: or should it show a change from its present ordered existence to a repetition of the terrifying primeval conditions. Yet Israel has nothing to fear because Yahweh is mightier than all the elements of the mythological Chaos put together (cf. Job 9:13, 26:12; Ps. 74:12ff., 89:8ff. (M.T. 9ff.), 93:3f.; Isa. 51:9). It is just possible that the author had in mind the world catastrophe which would (so it was believed) precede the messianic age (so Oesterley, Weiser). Dahood (*PAB*, I, p. 278) suggests 'the jaws of the nether world', regarding the Hebrew infinitive *hāmîr* as a noun, associated with the Ugaritic *hmr*, and the Arabic *hamara* ('to pour down') (cf. *Biblica*, XL, 1959, pp. 167f.; *JBL*, LXXXIII, 1964, p. 277). The same root may underlie the Ugaritic *hmry* which was the city of Mot, the god of the underworld. For the use of *ʾereṣ* (*RSV* 'earth') in the sense of 'netherworld', see on 7:5.

though the mountains shake: (cf. Isa. 24:19). The mountains are symbolic of all that is stable and enduring, and consequently this description heightens the intensity of the frightening picture.

in the heart of the sea: i.e. in the midst of the sea (cf. Exod. 15:8; Ezek. 27:26,27; Jon. 2:3 (M.T. 4)). It is possible that 'sea' contains an allusion to its one-time mythological significance (see on 74:13). The 'Sea' (*Yam*) often figures in the Ugaritic myths, as an opponent of Baal (cf. N. C. Habel, *Yahweh Versus Baal* (1964), pp. 62–7). In this Psalm these mythological allusions may serve to emphasize the point that Yahweh is the unquestioned ruler of all the cosmic forces whatever they might be.

3. its waters may refer to those of the sea although the latter (in verse 2) is plural in form (an amplificative plural?).

though the mountains tremble: cf. Jer. 4:24; Nah. 1:5. These and similar expressions were probably derived either from the stories of creation, or from the eschatological expectations, or both.

with its tumult: i.e. the mountains quake at the proud might of the waters (cf. Job 38:11; Ps. 89:9 (M.T. 10)).

Selah: see Introduction, pp. 48f. It is possible that 'Selah' was preceded by a refrain (see verses 7 and 11) and that its omission was due to an unintentional scribal error.

THE FOUNDATION OF ISRAEL'S CONFIDENCE **4-7**

Eaton (*PTBC*, p. 128) is of the opinion that behind these verses may lie the reconsecration of the sanctuary of Zion.

4. river: the Hebrew *nāhār* (see on 72:8) is a perennial stream (cf. 74:15, 107:33) but there was no such river in Jerusalem, unless the writer had in mind the tunnel of Hezekiah, or the spring of Gihon (cf. Guthrie, *ISS*, p. 93); the latter played an important role in the cult of Jerusalem and it may have had some mythical significance (cf. Clements, *GT*, p. 72). It is possible that the 'river' was used as a symbol of God's presence (cf. Isa. 8:6f., 33:21). The word-picture itself may have been borrowed from the 'Garden of Paradise' concept. It is likely that the presence of Yahweh was associated with this primeval garden (cf. Kraus, *WI*, p. 202) just as it was also linked with Zion, and consequently the descriptions of the one place could be applied to the other. As a river flowed out of Eden (Gen. 2:10), so a similar river would give joy and blessing to the city of God, and from here to the whole world (cf. 65:9 (M.T. 10), 87:7; Isa. 33:21; Ezek. 47:1ff.; Jl 3:18; Zech. 14:8). Also in the Ugaritic texts the dwelling of El is situated at the springs of the rivers (*nhrm*) (cf. *Baal* II, iv:21f., III, i:5f.; Driver, *CML*, pp. 97, 109).

streams are reminiscent of the four 'arms' into which the river from Eden divided itself (Gen. 2:10ff.). The **city of God** which is refreshed by these waters is Jerusalem (cf. 48:1 (M.T. 2); Isa. 60:14).

the holy habitation of the Most High: some exegetes follow the reading suggested by LXX and V: 'the Most High has sanctified his habitation' (*ḳiddēš miškānô ᶜelyôn*). 'Sanctify' here would mean 'to set apart' and to make the city impregnable as long as it remains in this relationship to Yahweh (cf. also Exod. 19:23). If we follow the *RSV* translation, then the phrase would be in apposition to **the city of God** (see on 87:3); cf. Sperber, *HGBH*, p. 660. The divine name 'Most High' (*ᶜelyôn*) is probably of Canaanite origin; El-ᶜElyon was the chief god of the Jerusalem Jebusites (cf. Gen. 14:18-24). There is considerable uncertainty as to whether El-ᶜElyon is a fusion of two originally separate gods, El and ᶜElyon, or whether he is simply a manifestation of the principal Canaanite deity, El (for references, see Clements, *GT*, pp. 43ff.). The latter alternative seems more likely, especially if we assume that the cult of El-ᶜElyon may have borrowed certain features which were originally characteristic of the Baal mythology.

5. God is in the midst of her: i.e. the strength of the holy city is not to be found in her massive walls or fortifications but in the fact that her defence is the ever-present God (cf. Jl 3:17; Mic. 3:11; Zeph. 3:15). In the presence of God is security and abundant blessing. Although this belief can be misused (cf. Jer. 7:3ff.), it is not thereby discredited.

right early: lit. 'at the turn of the morning' (cf. Exod. 14:27; Jg. 19:26; 1QH XII:6). That God's help comes in the morning is a frequent thought in *OT* (cf. 1 Sam. 11:9; 2 Chr. 20:17; Ps. 5:3 (M.T. 4), 17:15, 90:14, 143:8, etc.). According to J. Ziegler ('Die Hilfe Gottes "am Morgen" ', *Alttestamentliche Studien: Festschrift für F. Nötscher* (1950), pp. 281–8) the expectation of the divine help in the *morning* has been influenced by certain suggestive parallels, such as the daily rising of the sun, the 'change' of darkness into light, the administration of justice in the morning (cf. 2 Sam. 15:2), and the experience of certain great salvation events at the break of day (cf. Exod. 14:30; Isa. 37:36). Thus it would be natural to speak also of divine help as coming in the morning.

6. The nations rage . . .: many commentators see in this and similar descriptions a historicization of mythology. The primeval enemies (cf. 89:9f. (M.T. 10f.)) now appear as historical foes (cf. 2:2; Isa. 17:12ff.; Jer. 6:23), and historical events can be described in mythical categories. Both myth and history represent different aspects of the drama of salvation, and, in both, the principal character is Yahweh who is engaged in a struggle against his enemies and those of his people. Consequently the metaphors from the creation myths, etc. (in their technical sense) can be applied to historical situations and persons.

he utters his voice: this may be equivalent to 'he thunders' (cf. Job 37:4f.; Ps. 18:13 (M.T. 14), 29:3–9; Jn 12:29).

the earth melts: i.e. not in a literal sense, but 'in fear'; it is terrified at the voice of God (cf. Exod. 15:15; Isa. 14:31, etc.; see also 1QM XIV:6).

7. The LORD of hosts is with us: this brings to mind the symbolic name 'Immanuel' ('God with us'; Isa. 7:14, 8:8,10). The idea of the presence of God with his people is one of the basic elements of the Israelite religion (Gen. 21:20, 26:3,24; Exod. 3:12; Dt. 31:6; Jos. 1:5, 3:7; Jg. 6:12; Ps. 23:4; Am. 5:14; etc.). For 'the LORD of hosts', see on 24:10, 59:5.

The God of Jacob: i.e. the God of Israel, the Covenant people. This phrase is found in a number of Psalms (see on 20:1; cf. 75:9 (M.T. 10), 76:6 (M.T. 7), 81:1,4 (M.T. 2,5), 94:7, 146:5).

our refuge: rather 'our stronghold', and as such also a place of protection. Cf. 9:9 (M.T. 10), 18:2 (M.T. 3), 48:3 (M.T. 4), 59:9,16,17 (M.T. 10,17,18).

Selah: see Introduction, pp. 48f.

COME AND BEHOLD **8–11**

8. It may well be that the worshippers are invited to witness the saving acts of Yahweh in the cultic drama (cf. Weiser, *POTL*, pp. 42ff.), or to participate in the recital of the salvation-history, accompanied by certain symbolic ritual acts (cf. 66:3ff.). It is unlikely that the reference is to some recent historical event or that the 'desolations' (verse 8*b*) are the devastation of Israel by the Assyrian armies (cf. Kissane, *BP*, p. 204). Equally doubtful is the view which regards this and the following verses as an eschatological picture describing the end of war and the beginning of lasting peace. Dahood (*PAB*, I, p. 281) sees in *šammôṯ* ('desolations') an antonym of 'wars', rendering it by 'fertility'; he links the Hebrew word with the Ugaritic *šmt* ('oil, fat') (cf. the Hebrew *šᵉmēnāh*, 'fatness').

9. He makes wars to cease: i.e. he makes peace which is his final purpose, and in the cult one has a foretaste of the happiness to come (cf. 76:3 (M.T. 4); Isa. 2:4; Ezek. 39:9; Zech. 9:10).

the end of the earth: or 'the most extreme part(s) of the world'. The Psalmist wants to stress that God's peace will be universal (cf. Isa. 48:20, 49:6, 62:11).

he breaks the bow: see on 44:6. The bow was a symbol of power (Gen. 49:24; Job 29:20; Jer. 49:35), and to break it meant to deprive one of might or military power (cf. 1 Sam. 2:4; Hos. 1:5).

the spear: see on 35:3.

he burns the chariots . . .: the Hebrew *ᶜᵃgālôṯ* usually means 'wagons', and nowhere in *OT* is it used of war-chariots. Hence many commentators follow LXX, T and V in reading *ᶜᵃgēlôṯ* ('shields') which is also attested in 1QM vi:14 (cf. Yadin, *SWSLSD*, p. 121). In *OT* times captured chariots were burnt (Jos. 11:6,9), as was the case with other weapons (Ezek. 39:9f.). This was possible because chariots, shields, arrows, bows, etc. were largely made of destructible materials: wood and leather. All this may reflect the ancient traditions concerning the Holy War (see on 147:10).

10. Be still: this may be addressed to the nations who are exhorted to abandon their futile hostilities against God (2:10), or, more likely, it is a command directed to the people of God who are counselled to reject all foreign alliances and to depend entirely upon Yahweh (cf. Isa. 30:15).

know that I am God: i.e. acknowledge only my authority and claims. For this use of *y-d-*ᶜ ('to know'), see H. B. Huffmon, 'The Treaty Background of Hebrew *YĀDA*ᶜ', *BASOR*, 181 (1966), p. 37. See also 1 Kg. 18:37; Ps. 59:13 (M.T. 14), 100:3; Jer. 16:21; Ezek. 6:7,13, 7:27, 11:10.

I am exalted: i.e. Yahweh is 'the high and lofty one' (Isa. 57:15; cf. also Isa. 6:1, 52:13), and he will be experienced as such by all the peoples of the earth.

11. This is, apparently, the refrain; see verse 7.

Psalm 47 Our God is The King of All Nations

According to its structure, this Psalm is a double hymn consisting of two introductions (verses 1 and 6) and two main sections (verses 2–5 and 7–10). Its contents link it with such Psalms as 93, 96–99, and therefore it has been described as an Enthronement Psalm (see Introduction, pp. 33ff.), or a Psalm celebrating the Kingship of Yahweh. In the Jewish tradition it was regarded as a hymn for the New Year (cf. Mowinckel, *PIW*, I, 121), and it is possible that this late liturgical usage reflects its original application. If so, its *Sitz im Leben* would be the great Autumn Festival with its varied aspects. Verse 5 may suggest a procession in which the Ark was carried to the Temple of Jerusalem, which was followed by an act of homage before the Ark (cf. verse 8) in the sanctuary. Whether this ceremony should be regarded as an annual enthronement of Yahweh or a yearly celebration of his kingship is not certain, but the latter alternative seems more likely; it probably included a re-presentation of the major events of the salvation-history.

The historical interpretation of this Psalm regards it as a victory song in honour of a recent triumph (e.g. the defeat of Sennacherib; cf. 2 Kg. 19:35ff.), while some exegetes (e.g. Oesterley, *TP*, p.

258) have seen in this hymn a picture of the future establishment of the kingdom of God upon earth. The cultic understanding of this Psalm is the most likely view (for an excellent summary on this subject, see E. Lipiński, 'Les psaumes de la royauté de Yahwé dans l'exégèse moderne', *LPOBL*, pp. 133–272).

In the Christian Church, Ps. 47 has been used for Ascension Day, not as a prophecy of this event, but as a realization that the life and work of Christ are both a continuation and a focal point of the *Heilsgeschichte*, or salvation-history.

The Psalm may be of pre-Exilic origin although some scholars (e.g. Deissler) think that this poem is post-Exilic, and that it was influenced by Deutero-Isaiah and other post-Exilic prophetic writings (*PWdB*, II, p. 26); similarly also Westermann (*PGP*, pp. 145–51).

The metre of the Psalm is irregular but the predominant rhythm is 3+3.

To the choirmaster: see Introduction, p. 48.
A Psalm: see Introduction, p. 46.
the Sons of Korah: see Introduction, p. 45.

LET ALL PEOPLES ACCLAIM THE MOST HIGH **1–5**

1. Clap your hands: this reminds us of a similar expression of joy at the acclamation of the new King (cf. 2 Kg. 11:12; see on Ps. 98:8), and it may suggest that the situations also were analogous, at least in some ways.

all peoples may be either a rhetorical expression (not to be taken literally) or mean the people of Israel, who were thought of as representing all the nations. Oesterley *et al.* stress the eschatological character of the Psalm, and therefore they see the reference as a call to all the nations of the world, which will be subdued by Yahweh at the end-time. Dahood (*PAB*, I, p. 112) has contended that the Hebrew *ᶜammîm* (*RSV* 'peoples') should be derived from *ᶜ-m-m**, 'to be strong, wise', and that therefore the noun means 'the strong ones', alluding to the heathen gods. The evidence for the suggestion is comparatively weak, yet it deserves some consideration. Ps. 29:1 may offer a parallel: 'Ascribe to the LORD, O heavenly beings . . . glory and strength'.

shout to God: the reason for shouting is not only a feeling of joy but also the intention to acclaim the divine king (cf. 98:4) with some such exclamation as 'Yahweh is (or 'has become') king'. It is possible to take *lē'lōhîm* ('to God') as a vocative preceded by a *lāmed vocativum*, which could be translated '(Shout) O gods . . .' (cf. Dahood, *PAB*, I, p. 284; *VT*, XVI (1966), p. 309). This would offer a parallel to the vocative in verse 1*a*, and it would not anticipate 'the LORD, the Most High' in verse 2. On the other hand, the *RSV* rendering is clearly supported by 66:1, 88:1 (M.T. 2), 98:4, 100:1, and one expects in the Introduction to the hymn a mention of him who is to be praised.

2. For: this is the customary hymnic particle introducing the main section of the Psalm (see on 89:2).

the Most High: the Hebrew *ʿelyôn* may originally have been an adjective expressing quality, but it also came to be used independently as a divine name (cf. Dt. 32:8). This usage may belong already to the pre-Israelite period, and it probably designated the king of the gods, or the highest god in the pantheon. This title, when used of Yahweh, had lost its polytheistic character, except that Yahweh could be regarded as the lord of the sons of gods or the divine beings (*bᵉnê ʾᵉlōhîm*); cf. 29:1, 82:1, 89:6 (M.T. 7); Johnson, *SKAI*, pp. 43ff.

is terrible: or 'fear-inspiring, awesome' (see on 65:5).

a great king: 'the great king' was a well-known self-designation of the Assyrian kings in particular (cf. 2 Kg. 18:19), but Yahweh was thought of as the great king *par excellence*, because he alone is the ruler over *all* the earth (cf. 24:1; Mal. 1:14).

3. He subdued: the Hebrew *yaḏbēr* is a rare verbal form found elsewhere only in 18:47 (M.T. 48) (cf. G. R. Driver, *JTS*, XXXI (1929–30), pp. 283f.). The reference seems to be to the conquest of Canaan, and possibly also to the victories of David.

peoples: i.e. the nations of Canaan and their neighbours, unless we follow the less likely eschatological or historical interpretation. This triumph of Yahweh would be seen as an example of his universal might.

nations under our feet: this is a description of a complete conquest; the origin of the idiom may be found in the ancient practice in which the victor placed his foot on the neck of the conquered enemy (cf. Jos. 10:24; Ps. 8:6 (M.T. 7), 110:1).

4. He chose . . .: there is no need to emend this verb to 'he enlarged' (*yarḥēḇ*; so Gunkel, Oesterley, *et al.*). The Most High is the one who gave to all nations their respective inheritance (cf. Dt. 32:8ff.), and this included Israel in particular (cf. Gen. 12:1). For the verb *b-ḥ-r*, 'to choose', see on 65:4.

our heritage: this is obviously the Promised Land, the possession of Israel; see on 28:9, 105:11.

for us: (=*NEB*) or 'for himself' (reading *lannû* (from *lanhû*) for M.T. *lānû*) because the verb *b-ḥ-r* ('to choose') is usually used with a reflexive pronoun (i.e. with its Hebrew equivalent); see Dahood, *PAB*, I, p. 285.

the pride of Jacob is parallel to 'our heritage', and therefore the reference must be to the land of Canaan which is the object of Jacob's pride or 'his proud possession' (so Johnson, *SKAI*, p. 67; cf. Dan. 8:9, 11:16,41). Clements (*GT*, p. 55, n.1) suggests that the term 'probably refers to the Jerusalem Temple, thus connecting Yahweh's inheritance with Mount Zion and its temple'; cf. also A. Caquot, 'Le psaume 47 et la royauté de Yahwé', *RHPR*, XXXIX (1959), p. 318.

whom he loves: the subject is God who loves Jacob (see on 20:1). For the verb 'to love', see on 26:8, 52:4.

Selah: see Introduction, pp. 48f.

5. God has gone up: the verb *ᶜ-l-h* can mean to ascend into heaven (cf. Gen. 17:22, 35:13; Jg. 13:20; etc.) but in this verse the primary meaning seems to be that of going up to the Temple (see on 24:3). Yahweh's person or presence was, most likely, symbolized by the Ark (see G. Henton Davies, 'The Ark of the Covenant', *ASTI*, V (1967), pp. 30–47; cf. 2 Sam 6:5,16,17) which was carried in procession up to the sanctuary (cf. 132:8ff.; but see also D. R. Hillers, *CBQ*, XXX (1968), pp. 48–55). But in as far as the Temple was the earthly counterpart of the heavenly dwelling of God—the place where heaven and earth meet one another—the former meaning of *ᶜ-l-h* ('to go up') may also be implied. The verb may provide a word play on *ᶜelyôn*, 'the Most High'.

with a shout: i.e. accompanied by acclamations; see on 33:3.

the sound of a trumpet: the blowing of trumpets is linked with certain occasions, such as the New Year (Lev. 23:24; Num. 29:1) and the coronation of the King (cf. 1 Kg. 1:39; 2 Kg. 9:13, 11:12). It is possible that in this verse also the purpose of the trumpet signals, or blowing, was similar; it may have been the sign for the acclamation of the heavenly king (cf. 150:3).

SING TO THE KING OF ALL THE NATIONS **6–19**

6. Sing praises: this imperative call is repeated five times in verses 6–7, probably for the sake of special emphasis. The people addressed are, most likely, the Temple singers and musicians (cf. Kraus, *PBK*, p. 352). The Hebrew verb *z-m-r* ('to sing praises') is connected with *mizmôr* ('psalm') (see on 30:4, 66:4). **to God:** some interpreters read with LXX 'to our God' (*lē'lōhênû*) although this variant may be simply an assimilation to 'our king' (verse 6*b*). *NEBm* 'you gods'.

7. For God is the king . . .: the *RSV* rendering makes verse 7*a* too long; therefore some exegetes read *mālak̲* ('he is king') for M.T. *melek̲* ('king'), and add the preposition *ʿal* ('over'), with some Hebrew MSS., translating: 'For he is (or 'has become') king over all the earth'. The word 'God' would then belong to verse 7*b*. The acclamation of Yahweh as king may have had a polemical tone when we recall similar expressions attributed to Baal by the Canaanites; e.g. 'The victor Baal is our king, our judge, and one over whom there is none' (Driver, *CML*, p. 97a; *Baal* II, iv:43f.).

sing praises with a psalm: or, if we adopt the above proposal: 'praise God with a psalm'. The term 'psalm' (*maśkîl*; see Introduction, p. 47) may be the designation of a particular type of psalm, unless it is a description of God as 'one who deals wisely' (cf. Jer. 23:5 where the same term refers to the King). Most commentators prefer some such meaning as 'choice-song' (Oesterley), 'efficacious song' (Mowinckel), 'skilful song' (McFadyen), etc. *NEB* takes *maśkîl* as an adverbial accusative 'with all your art'.

8. God reigns: or, as some exegetes suggest, 'Yahweh reigns' for it seems very likely that in many places in the Elohistic Psalter the original name 'Yahweh' has been replaced by 'God' (*'elōhîm*). This phrase is reminiscent of the so-called 'enthronement formula' (*yhwh mālak̲*), which is usually rendered 'the LORD reigns' (*RSV*) or 'Yahweh has become king' (so Mowinckel). Both translations seem to be equally possible from the grammatical point of view, and therefore the final decision on the alternatives must be determined by the understanding of the Enthronement Psalms (see on 93:1). The main problem is whether this phrase expresses an existing and enduring state, or whether it describes something new and important which has just taken place. Mowinckel obviously prefers the latter alternative, and he draws attention to certain *OT* parallels (cf. 2 Sam. 15:10; 2 Kg. 9:13) where we find a similar formula; the parallels are not, however, identical. Thus Absalom and Jehu had never been kings before, while Yahweh was believed to be a king from everlasting; cf. 93:2: 'thy throne is established from of old; thou art from everlasting'. Consequently it seems less likely that Yahweh was enthroned anew from year to year, as if he had been temporarily defeated and dethroned. We can only speak of an 'enthronement festival of Yahweh' in the sense that his kingship is celebrated in the cult, and that he receives anew the homage of his people. The choice of the formula of acclamation (or proclamation) may have served a particular purpose. The unusual word order (i.e. the subject before the verb) may stress that *Yahweh* is king and no other deity. At the same time this formula is also a declaration of allegiance, for anyone who joins in this joyful cry acknowledges the kingship of the God of Israel; it could well be an annual renewal of allegiance.

over the nations: i.e. Yahweh's rule extends not only over Israel but over all peoples. His victories over the nations (see verse 3) are a sign of it.

God sits on his holy throne: some exegetes (e.g. Oesterley, Leslie, *et al.*) omit 'God', thus obtaining a 3 + 3 metre which is the dominant one in this Psalm. The phrase 'his holy throne' is a *hapax legomenon* in the *OT*. Murray L. Newman, jr. (*The People of the Covenant* (1965), p. 58) expresses the view of several scholars, in saying that from 'the time of Moses the ark seems to have been regarded as the throne of Yahweh . . . an *empty* throne upon which Yahweh was invisibly present'. It is not certain, however, that the idea of the Ark as Yahweh's throne must date from the Mosaic period (cf. Clements, *GT*, pp. 28–39). In 99:1 Yahweh sits enthroned upon the cherubim, and it is possible that Yahweh's throne was originally associated with these mythological figures (see 18:10), and only later with the Ark. In Jeremiah 3:16f. Jerusalem is called the throne of Yahweh, while some other *OT* writers speak of his throne as being in the heavens (cf. 1 Kg. 22:19; 2 Chr. 18:18; Ps. 103:19; Isa. 66:1).

9. This is a highly problematic verse: do the leaders of the nations come willingly to worship Yahweh, or are they captives in the train of the triumphant king (see on 68:18)? It is possible that some representatives of foreign nations were at least occasionally present at the pilgrimage festivals, and this fact could have been viewed as symbolic of Yahweh's universal reign (cf. Kraus, *PBK*, p. 353). There were also times when foreigners were incorporated in Israel, e.g. the Canaanites, and especially the proselytes of later times (cf. Wellhausen, *PBP*, p. 184). It is plausible that since verses 2–4 refer to the salvation-history, so also do verses 9–10, and that in the cultic drama, or in some other symbolic representation, these princes of the peoples were subdued by Yahweh (cf. 107:40), as he had done once or repeatedly during the salvation-history; and so they followed their victor on his return to the holy city (cf. Isa. 60:11). Whatever might be the actual situation of the people of God at that particular time, the above illustration, i.e. the symbolic representation, was a proof of Yahweh's might, and could be relived in the cult. Dahood (*PAB*, I, p. 286) reads: 'O nobles of the peoples, gather round!'; he takes the verb as a precative perfect, and he assigns the rest of verse 9 to the final verse. He also argues that *ᶜam* (*RSV* 'people') ought to be regarded as a divine epithet 'the Strong One', hence: 'The God of Abraham is the Strong One'. The *RSV* rendering: 'as the people of . . .' supplies 'as' which is not in M.T. Another possibility is to follow LXX and V (cf. S) by taking *ᶜam* as *ᶜim* ('with'); Johnson (*SKAI*, p. 68) translates: 'With Him who is the God of Abraham'. It is possible that the preposition *ᶜim* had fallen out due to haplography, and if so, we could render 'with the people of . . .'; *NEB* 'with the families of Abraham's line'. The reference to Abraham may suggest 'the father of all the faithful' (cf. Gen. 18:17f., also Gen. 17:4), but this universalistic aspect ought not to be overemphasized in the light of the rest of the Psalm; cf. 102:22; Isa. 2:2ff.

the shields of the earth seems to be another expression for 'the princes of the peoples'. In 84:9 (M.T. 10) 'our shield' is parallel to 'thine anointed', and in 89:18 (M.T. 19) the same word is synonymous with 'our king'; therefore it is not unreasonable to render this phrase by 'the rulers of the earth' (so LXX); cf. also G. R. Driver, *JTS*, XXXIII (1932), p. 44. Dahood (*PAB*, I, p. 283) suggests 'truly God is Suzerain of the earth'; he takes the preposition *lᵉ* (*RSV* 'to') as an *emphatic lāmeḏ* (see on 89:18), and regards the plural construct *mag̃nê* [*sic*] (M.T. has *māg̃innê*, 'shields' or 'rulers') as a plural of majesty (see on 3:3).

belong to God: *RP* may well provide the right interpretation in paraphrasing 'are become the servants of the Lord' (cf. verse 3).

he is highly exalted: (*naᶜᵃlāh*) may be a word play on 'the Most High' (*ᶜelyôn*) (verse 2) and 'has gone up' (*ᶜālāh*) (verse 5). *NEB* offers an interpretative rendering: 'and he is raised above them all'.

Psalm 48 The City of Our God

Psalms 46–8 have often been regarded as forming a trilogy which celebrated the miraculous deliverance of Jerusalem from the Assyrian threat, during the reign of Hezekiah (715–687/6 B.C.). More recently Ps. 47 has been linked with the Enthronement Psalms, while Ps. 46 and 48 have been described as Hymns of Zion (see Introduction, p. 35). They differ, however, from the usual type of hymn, because they lack the introductory formula which contains an invitation to praise and to bless Yahweh. Since their main theme is the glorification of Zion, the city of God, it is not inappropriate to classify them as Hymns of Zion. Ultimately such hymns are praises of God, because Zion owes her glorious status to him alone. Ps. 48 contains other themes also, some of which appear in literature of an eschatological nature, e.g. the attack of the nations and their defeat, and the thought of Zion as the joy of the whole world, but it is unlikely that therefore this Psalm must have been interpreted eschatologically from the very beginning.

This song belongs, most likely, to the ritual of the many-sided autumnal festival, the Feast of Tabernacles, and it may have been used during, or before, the procession round Jerusalem. Yahweh's power to save is not simply an eschatological expectation, but rather a present reality experienced through the participation in the cultus.

Some commentators have assigned this Psalm to the post-Exilic period, but Weiser (*POTL*, p. 381) may be right in pointing out that there are no cogent reasons why it could not have been composed during the pre-Exilic period.

Verses 1–3 emphasize the significance of Jerusalem, but behind it all is the greatness of Yahweh. This is followed by a description of the gathering of the hostile kings, and their subsequent flight (verses 4–7). In verses 8–11 we find a praise of Yahweh, and in verses 12–14 the Psalmist bids the hearers join the procession round the walls of Zion, so that seeing the unscathed strength of the city, they may become more aware of the might of God who is the protector of this city.

The prevailing metre is 3 + 2.

A Song: see Introduction, p. 47.

A Psalm: see Introduction, p. 46.

the Sons of Korah: see Introduction, p. 45.

THE CITY OF THE GREAT KING **1–3**

1. The city's importance is solely due to the presence of God. Therefore her greatness is but a reflection of the majesty of her king.

Great is the LORD: cf. 1 Chr. 16:25; Ps. 96:4, 145:3. Yahweh is great because he is the great king (47:2 (M.T. 3), 48:2 (M.T. 3)), the ruler of the whole world. Some scholars restore the 3 + 2 metre by deleting the name 'Yahweh', but this is hardly necessary.

greatly to be praised: i.e. Yahweh alone is worthy to receive praise, which is the right response to his intervention in history.

the city of our God is Jerusalem (cf. 46:4 (M.T. 5), 48:8 (M.T. 9), 87:3; Isa. 60:14), which God has chosen as his own. The phrase could also be rendered: 'our divine city' (so Johnson).

His holy mountain: *RSV* links this expression with verse 2; in M.T. it belongs to verse 1 (so also *NEB*), the latter part of which could be rendered: 'in our divine city on his holy mountain', or: '. . . is his holy mountain'; metrically *RSV* is preferable. 'The holy mountain' is Mount Zion, and its holiness is entirely due to its association with Yahweh (cf. 2:6, 3:4 (M.T. 5), 15:1, 43:3, 99:9).

2. beautiful in elevation may be regarded as a phrase expressing a superlative 'the most beautiful height' or 'beautiful by reason of (its) height' (cf. Ca. 2:5: 'I am sick by reason of love'). In the latter case the reference is not so much to the actual height of Mount Zion (which does not exceed that of other peaks), but rather to its mythological or theological significance. It is here that, in a sense, heaven and earth meet.

the joy of all the earth: i.e. Zion is the source of joy of the entire world, and not only of the Jews scattered in different lands. This phrase is quoted in Lam. 2:15; N. K. Gottwald (*Studies in the Book of Lamentations* (*SBT* 14, 1954), p. 57) suggests that phrases of such nature are simply 'proverbial for choice cities' (cf. 50:2; Ezek. 16:14, 27:3,4,11, 28:12).

Mount Zion, in the far north: perhaps: 'Mount Zion is the (true) "Far North" ' (i.e. the dwelling-place of the true God), or '. . . Zion, the heights of Zaphon' (so Johnson, *SKAI*, p. 77). It is very likely that 'North' or 'Zaphon' (*ṣāpôn*) was originally Jebel-el-Aqra some 25–30 miles NNE. of Ugarit. From the Ugaritic myths we know that this mountain, i.e. Mount Zaphon, was the dwelling-place of Baal-Hadad (cf. *Baal* I*, i:11, II, iv:19, v:23,55, III, i:29,34, v, i:21–3). Later *ṣāp̱ôn* came to mean 'north' in Hebrew. Possibly during the Jebusite period Mount Zion, the dwelling-place of *ʾēl ʿelyôn* ('the God Most High'), was identified with Mount Zaphon. During the Israelite period, this and other expressions of the cult of *ʾēl ʿelyôn* may have been adapted to that of Yahweh (cf. Clements, *GT*, pp. 3ff.); see on 89:12.

the city of the great King: cf. verse 1; Mt. 5:35. It was Mount Zion that gave a special importance to Jerusalem; according to Near Eastern beliefs the sacred mountains were regarded as divine abodes, or as fitting symbols of the heavenly habitation of the deity. 'The great king' is a well-known title of the Assyrian kings, e.g. '. . . Esarhaddon, great king, legitimate king, king of the world . . .' (*ANET*, p. 289). From the Israelite point of view Yahweh was what the Assyrian king claimed to be.

3. **Within her citadels:** rather than '. . . her palaces' (so *NEB*, Weiser, *et al.*) (cf. 122:7; Lam. 2:5,7; Hos. 8:14; Am. 6:8). The effectual defence of Jerusalem is not her fortifications but God. Dahood (*PAB*, I, p. 288) renders 'God is her citadel . . .' but, in view of verses 12–13, the *RSV* translation is more likely.

God has shown himself . . .: i.e. in the cultic representation of the saving acts of Yahweh. It is unlikely that the reference is simply to some recent deliverance, such as that in 701 B.C. (cf. Oesterley, *TP*, p. 263).

GOD AND HIS ENEMIES 4–7

Calvin once pointed out that the following description of the kings is reminiscent of Caesar's proud words: 'Veni, vidi, vici', except that *their* final achievement was an inglorious defeat.

4. **the kings assembled:** or, with LXX and V, 'the kings of the earth', as in 2:2. Ringgren (*FP*, p. 106) defines this description as a typical, traditional, half-mythological expression which is 'meant to assert that no enemies, be they ever so strong, will be able to do any serious harm to those who are on the Lord's side'; see on 46:6. (For a historical interpretation, see Kirkpatrick, *BPCB*, p. 264, or, more recently, L. Krinetzki, *BZ*, IV (1960), pp. 70–97.)

they came on together: lit. 'they passed by together' (=*AV*). It is more appropriate to derive the verb from *ʿ-b-r* II ('to rage') (cf. *ʿeḇrāh*, 'fury'), hence 'they stormed furiously' (following Dahood).

5. **they saw it, they were astounded:** the Psalmist does not tell us what the kings saw; some scholars (e.g. Briggs) suggest that

the kings panicked when they saw Zion (so *NEB*) and her defences, but it is far more likely that they were put to flight by some theophany of Yahweh himself. Similarly in 77:16: 'When the waters saw thee, O God . . . they were afraid'; cf. Isa. 29:5–8, 66:18. Dahood may be right in regarding the pronoun 'they' (*hēmmāh*) as an interjection 'behold' (as in Ugaritic) (cf. *HAL*, p. 240a); thus we could render: 'Behold, they saw (it), so (as a result) they were dumbfounded'.

they were in panic . . .: this brings to mind the accounts of the Holy Wars where the decisive action came from Yahweh, while the human 'contribution' was trust and faith (cf. 1 Sam. 7:10). See G. v. Rad, *Studies in Deuteronomy* (*SBT* 9, 1953), pp. 45ff.

6. trembling took hold of them: cf. Exod. 15:14; Isa. 33:14; 1QH x:33.

there may be the place where they perceived Yahweh's greatness. Dahood (*PAB*, I, p. 291) takes it as 'alas', linking it with *šumma* ('behold') in the El Amarna letters.

a woman in travail is a familiar picture to describe panic and agony (cf. Isa. 13:8, 21:3; Jer. 4:31, 6:24; etc.); it is found in an expanded form in 1QH iii:7–12; Rev. 12:2,4ff.

7. By the east wind: or 'as the east wind' (*kᵉrûaḥ*; cf. Jer. 18:17), following some Hebrew MSS. The 'east wind' may be a synonym of any destructive wind (cf. Kraus, *PBK*, p. 359), or it may be taken literally (cf. Job 27:21; Isa. 27:8).

the ships of Tarshish may be the large sea-going vessels or ships built in Tarshish, which was probably the Phoenician colony of Tartessus in Spain. J. Bright (*PCB* 424h) suggests that *taršîš* means 'refinery', and that therefore 'the ships of Tarshish' must be vessels for carrying cargo from the copper-refineries in Sardinia and Spain to Phoenicia (cf. also 1 Kg. 10:22). J. Morgenstern (*HUCA*, XVI (1941), pp. 7ff.) argues that this verse describes the partial destruction of the fleet of Xerxes, just before the Battle of Artemisium in 480 B.C., and that this achievement was attributed to Yahweh. Such a view is as unlikely as the other historical interpretations. Ringgren (*FP*, p. 16) may be right in suggesting that the ships of Tarshish also represent the enemies of God (cf. 72:10), and so their destruction points to the limitless power and extent of the divine intervention. See also M. Palmer, *Biblica*, XLVI (1965), pp. 357ff.

THE PRAISE OF GOD 8–11

8. As we have heard . . .: this may refer to the detailed account of the saving works of God, which were, apparently, accompanied by certain symbolic actions (cf. Jonhson, *SKAI*, p. 79). This seems to be supported by the next phrase 'in the city of the LORD . . .'. In a sense the very existence of Jerusalem is a proof that the claims made for her are true. The positive affirmation involves, however, certain conditions without which the people could easily lapse into a false security (cf. Jer. 7:3f.).

the LORD of hosts: see on 24:10, 59:5.

the city of our God: see on verse 1.

establishes for ever: or 'maintaineth for ever' (so Johnson). Cf. 87:5; Isa. 62:7.

Selah: see Introduction, pp. 48f.

9. We have thought on thy steadfast love is a reasonable rendering of M.T., but it is better to follow Johnson's translation (*CPAI*, pp. 42f.) '. . . we have pictured Thy devotion' which suggests a ritual drama similar, in some ways, to what is known as prophetic symbolism (cf. J. Lindblom, *Prophecy in Ancient Israel* (1962), pp. 165ff.). *NEB* 'we re-enact the story . . .'. Thus the cultic presentation would be not only concerned with the past but also with the forward-looking aspect. For 'steadfast love', see on 26:3, 51:1.

in the midst of thy temple: if the above interpretation is right, then the symbolic representation of Yahweh's victories took place in the Jerusalem Temple, i.e. in its courts.

10. As thy name . . .: the Hebrew *šēm* ('name') in the *OT* can also mean 'reputation, one's record' (see on 20:1), and therefore the author of Ecclesiastes can say: 'A good name is better than precious ointment' (7:1). In our verse 'thy name' is roughly equivalent to 'thy record' or 'fame', and therefore it is unnecessary to emend it to 'the report of you' (*kešîmᶜaḵā*), or 'your heavens' (*kešāmêḵā*; cf. Dahood, *PAB*, I, p. 292). Corresponding to God's mighty deeds is his praise throughout the whole world or **to the ends of the earth.** Praise is not only the expression of an awe-filled amazement at God's works but also a realization that they are relevant to the person concerned.

Thy right hand . . .: i.e. God's power has wrought an absolute victory (*ṣeḏeḳ*; see on 33:5), and there is nothing more one could desire (cf. Isa. 41:10). Dahood proposes 'generosity' as a possible rendering of *ṣeḏeḳ*. For metrical reasons verse 10*c* should be taken with verse 11*a*.

11. let Mount Zion be glad: i.e. let God's people rejoice at the triumphs of their King.

daughters of Judah are the towns and villages of Judah, or their inhabitants. See on 97:8.

because of thy judgments: cf. 97:8. These are the acts of God whereby he had been victorious over his enemies; from Israel's point of view they are deeds of deliverance.

THE PROCESSION **12–14**

12. Walk about Zion: those who interpret the Psalm historically see here an invitation to inspect the city in order that the people may assure themselves that the city is indeed unharmed (cf. Kissane, *BP*, p. 211), in spite of all the recent attacks. It is more likely, however, that this circumambulation had a cultic significance, although the former alternative cannot be excluded. The actual meaning of this rite is unknown, but Gunkel suggests a thanksgiving procession (cf. Neh. 12:27ff.; *EP*, pp. 17f.). This procession brings to mind the cultic act described in Jos. 6:3ff., although the underlying purposes are quite different. The cultic act may have been a continuation of the sacred drama enacted on the Temple courts.

number her towers: i.e. either the separate structures or the various parts of the walls (cf. de Vaux, *AI*, p. 235). In Isa. 33:18 there is an account of the enemy counting the towers of Jerusalem for the purpose of estimating the strength of the city.

13. her ramparts: see de Vaux, *AI*, p. 232. The Psalmist probably had in mind the outer wall or the glacis (i.e. the sloping bank) which protected the foot of the wall (cf. 2 Sam. 20:15).

her citadels are the more heavily fortified parts of the palace (cf. 122:7).

that you may tell: cf. 44:1 (M.T. 2). Whether they have experienced this deliverance in history or in the cult, it is their duty to tell of it to the future generations (cf. 22:30 (M.T. 31), 78:3ff., 79:13, 102:18 (M.T. 19)).

14. that this is God: or 'For such is God' (so Kirkpatrick); lit. 'for this is God'. Dahood's rendering (*PAB*, I, p. 293) 'This is God's' (referring to Mount Zion in verse 2) seems less likely than *RSV*. The Psalmist probably wanted to sum up his main theme that God alone, and not the strength of the city or the ingenuity of her people, is the source of all success. All the glory of Zion points to the majesty of God.

He will be our guide: this picture may well be that of a shepherd going before his flock (cf. 77:20 (M.T. 21), 78:52, 80:1 (M.T. 2); Isa. 49:10, 63:14). *PLE* has '. . . our Shepherd eternally'.

for ever: (*NEB* 'eternally') this involves a slight emendation, reading *ᶜōlāmôṯ* for M.T. *ᶜal mûṯ* which some scholars have considered as a musical direction (see Introduction, p. 50), belonging to Ps. 49. Mowinckel, Johnson, *et al.* translate 'he shall be our guide against death' (*ᶜal māweṯ*). This interpretation, if correct, would be reminiscent of the fight of Baal against his enemy, Mot, or Death, known from the Ugaritic texts (cf. *ANET*, pp. 138ff.). It is possible that in our context 'death' may symbolize all the forces threatening the existence of God's people (cf. Mt. 16:18).

Psalm 49 MAN'S DESTINY DEPENDS UPON GOD NOT RICHES

Most scholars are in general agreement that this Psalm is a Wisdom poem, the purpose of which is to instruct men about the inequalities of life. It appears, at least on the surface, that the oppressive rich are neither suddenly cut off, nor are they afflicted with misfortune, while the righteous poor continue to be poor and their only reward seems to be misfortune. The Psalmist provides his explanation of the perplexing problems; he believes that life with God is far superior to the existence where God occupies a place of secondary importance, and where the foundation of one's confidence is only wealth. Death comes to all, and no man can ever redeem his life from the grasp of the underworld, nor can he prolong his years by 'paying a ransom to God'. It is only God himself who can redeem the upright man from Sheol, for the sake of his own righteousness. Whether this deliverance implies only a reprieve (i.e. an escape from untimely death), or whether it suggests a *lasting* fellowship with God, is difficult to say (see verse 15); perhaps the latter view is more likely.

Kirkpatrick (*BPCB*, p. 268) thought that the eighth century B.C. would provide a suitable setting for this Psalm, but most recent exegetes would assign it either to the early or late post-Exilic period. It may well be one of the latest poems in the whole Psalter; Deissler (*PWdB*, II, p. 33) suggests a date *c.* 200 B.C. The author seems to have belonged to the Wisdom circles, and there are a number of parallels between this Psalm and the Books of Job, Proverbs, and Ecclesiastes.

Verses 1–4 provide an introductory call, while verses 5–12 and 13–20 form the two main sections. The first one deals with the limitations of wealth, while the second outlines the respective destinies of the rich and the poor; verses 12 and 20 could be regarded as a refrain, rounding off the two main parts.

The prevailing metre is 3 + 3.

To the choirmaster: see Introduction, p. 48.
A Psalm: see Introduction, p. 46.
Sons of Korah: see Introduction, p. 45.

THE INTRODUCTION **1–4**

1. Hear . . . give ear forms a common beginning of poems and speeches (cf. Gen. 4:23; Num. 23:18; Jg. 5:3, 9:7; etc.).
all peoples: since this Psalm belongs to Wisdom literature, it is addressed not only to Israel but to all peoples.
inhabitants of the world: the Hebrew *ḥeleḏ* ('world') occurs in this sense elsewhere only in 17:14 and Isa. 38:11. The particular shade of meaning implied may be 'the dwellers of the world where all existence is transitory' (cf. S. R. Driver and G. B. Gray, *The Book of Job* (*ICC*, 1921), II, p. 73).

2. both low and high: i.e. both simple folk and men of influence. 'The low' (*bᵉnê ʾāḏām*) are probably the ordinary men (cf. Jacob, *TOTe*, p. 156), while 'the high' (*bᵉnê ʾîš*) are the persons of influence (see on 4:2; cf. 62:9 (M.T. 10); Lam. 3:33). This distinction need not have been observed in all contexts (cf. 107:8, 140:1).
rich and poor: the Psalmist addresses his teaching to men of all classes. The affluent members of the community must learn that wealth has its limitations, while the destitute should realize that God is greater than their problems. T regards the rich and the poor as the unjust and the righteous respectively. At a later time the term 'poor' (*ʾeḇyôn*; see on 35:10) became practically identical with the 'pious' or the 'oppressed' (cf. H. Ringgren, *The Faith of Qumran* (1963), pp. 141ff.; Menahem Mansoor, *The Thanksgiving Hymns* (1961), pp. 49, 110).

3. wisdom: the Hebrew *ḥoḵmôṯ* (see on 111:10) is plural in form, probably for the sake of emphasis; hence it could be rendered 'profound wisdom'.
understanding: (plural in form) might be translated 'deep

insight'. Both 'wisdom' and 'understanding' may refer to practical wisdom rather than to a speculative knowledge.

the meditation of my heart: Weiser (*POTL*, p. 384) renders it by 'my heart schemes to create understanding' (cf. 19:14 (M.T. 15); 1QH xi:2).

4. proverb: the Hebrew *māšāl* has various possible meanings, e.g. 'taunt' (44:14 (M.T. 15); Mic. 2:4), 'allegory' (Ezek. 17:2, 20:49), 'poem' (Num. 21:27; Ps. 78:2), 'instruction' (Prov. 10:1), 'oracle' (Num. 23:7). In the present passage it may well mean 'instruction (given by God)' (cf. Nötscher, *PEB*, p. 110). For further details on *māšāl*, see A. R. Johnson, *SVT*, 3 (1955), pp. 162–9.

I will solve: lit. 'I will open', hence 'I will explain' (cf. Shekalim 5:1).

my riddle: (*ḥîḏāh*) may mean a 'parable' or 'allegory' (Ezek. 17:2), 'riddle' (Jg. 14:12ff.), 'perplexing question' (1 Kg. 10:1), etc. In this verse its meaning is probably 'a perplexing problem'.

to the music of the lyre: for 'lyre', see on 98:5. Music was occasionally used to induce ecstasy (cf. 1 Sam. 10:5; 2 Kg. 3:5), but nowhere else in the *OT* is there any other reference to instruction being accompanied by musical instruments.

THE LIMITATIONS OF WEALTH **5–12**

5. Why should I fear . . .: this is not a mere rhetorical question but an expression of confidence which has come to maturity in evil times (cf. 27:5, 41:1 (M.T. 2), 94:13).

the iniquity of my persecutors is the rendering of an ambiguous Hebrew phrase. *AV* translates 'the iniquity of my heels' (similarly LXX), but this would be tantamount to a confession of sin, and it would hardly make sense of verse 5*a*. *RV* suggests '. . . at my heels', i.e. the wickedness of the rich pursues me. The *RSV* rendering may be preferable; this is also implied by Origen's transcription *ᶜaḳubbay* ('my deceitful enemies') (cf. Jer. 17:6).

6. men who trust in their wealth: this is a further description of the enemies of the Psalmist. They seem to rely upon their riches instead of depending upon God (cf. 52:7 (M.T. 9)). See on 78:22.

boast of the abundance . . .: their boast should have been God (cf. 34:2 (M.T. 3), 44:8 (M.T. 9)) and not their possessions. The Psalmist does not argue that wealth is wrong in itself, but he points out that its importance can be misunderstood. The two lines of verse 6 provide a good example of a chiastic arrangement, in that the order of the respective terms in the second line is reversed.

7. Truly: so *RSV*, reading with some Hebrew MSS. *ʾaḵ*, for M.T. *ʾāḥ* ('brother') (cf. *RSVm*). Dahood (*PAB*, I, p. 298) suggests that 'brother' is used as an interjection, meaning 'Alas' (see also *HAL*, p. 28).

no man can ransom himself: this presupposes a repointing of *yip̄deh* ('will ransom') into *yippāḏeh*. This expression seems to be an emphatic denial of the possibility to escape death, at least by means of man's own powers or possessions. In certain legal cases a person could avoid capital punishment by paying a ransom (see Exod. 21:29ff.; Num. 35:31; Prov. 6:35, 13:8), but when God claims man's life—there is no other alternative.

the price of his life: lit. 'his ransom'. God cannot be bought off, and no wealth, however great, can alter the purposes of God.

8. the ransom of his life is costly: (following LXX). M.T. has '. . . of *their* life', probably referring to men in general, or to the rich in particular. Some exegetes wrongly regard verse 8 as a secondary addition to emphasize the thought expressed in the previous verse. The ransom of a man's life is not only costly but also beyond all price and human powers. Dahood (*PAB*, I, p. 299) proposes a different solution; he takes the Hebrew *yḳr* (*RSV* 'costly') as a synonym for 'Sheol' (cf. *Syria*, XIX (1938), pp. 99–102), and renders: 'But the Mansion shall be the redemption of his soul'. The improvement, if any, seems to be rather small.

can never suffice: or '. . . he shall cease for ever'. Kirkpatrick (*BPCB*, p. 271) renders 'And he must let it alone for ever', i.e. any idea of paying a ransom to God is too futile to be attempted. Some scholars transpose the letters of *ḥāḏal*, obtaining *ḥālaḏ* ('(that) he should live (for ever)'); for *ḥ-l-d*, see *HAL*, p. 303b. For *leʿôlām* ('for ever'), see on 9:5, 117:2.

9. This verse is often regarded as the sequel of verse 7, while verse 8 is viewed either as a later gloss, or as the continuation of verses 7 and 9.

to live on for ever: i.e. enjoying his wealth rather than the service of God. For *lāneṣaḥ* ('for ever'), see on 74:1.

and never see the Pit: 'to see the Pit' means to experience death (cf. 16:10). 'Pit' (*šaḥaṯ*) (see on 7:15) is a synonym of 'Sheol' (cf. 16:10, 30:9 (M.T. 10), 55:23 (M.T. 24); Isa. 38:17, 51:14). LXX and V derive it from the verb *š-ḥ-t* ('to go to ruin') rather than from *š-w-ḥ* ('to sink down'), and translate it by 'corruption' (cf. E. F. Sutcliffe, *The Old Testament and the Future Life* (1946), p. 78). Sometimes *šaḥaṭ* is used figuratively of retribution or destruction (cf. 94:13).

10. This verse is difficult. If we accept it as it stands, then verses 10–12 describe a levelling-down process, and death is seen as the ultimate equalizer. Yet this would be at odds with verses 13–15, which envisage different destinies for different people. Consequently some exegetes regard verse 10*a* as a later addition. The point may be, however, the *limited* value of wealth.

Yea, he shall see: perhaps, 'surely, one sees (by simple observation) that all men die, be they ever so wise'. Dahood (*PAB*, I, p. 298) translates: 'If he looks', and he considers God as the subject. One look from God—and the wise as well as the fools perish.

the wise and **the fool** are favourite terms of the Wisdom writers. It is possible that in our verse they are equivalent to the good and the wicked respectively (so Kissane *et al.*).

the fool (*keŝîl*) is not a half-wit, but he deliberately rejects the wisdom whose beginning is the fear of the Lord (Prov. 1:7).

the stupid (*baʿar*) is described in Prov. 12:1 as a man who hates reproof, and who regards himself above criticism; see on 92:6.

leave their wealth to others: men leave this world without being able to take their possessions with them (cf. Lk. 12:20). In *Aboth* vi:9 the writer observes that man can take with him neither silver nor gold nor anything else, save '(his knowledge of) the Law and good works'.

11. Their graves: reading *ḳiḇrām*, while M.T. has *ḳirbām* ('their inward (thought)'?), lit. 'their inward part', which does not make much sense in this context; this reading may be due to a scribal error, and therefore the *RSV* reading seems preferable; it is also supported by the principal ancient versions.

their homes for ever: this brings out the implicit irony. The splendid houses and the wealth of the rich were theirs but for a few years, while the grave will be their '*eternal* home' (cf. Ec. 12:5).

though they named lands their own: i.e. however large may be a man's estate, his ultimate inheritance is the narrow grave and the darkness of the underworld. This phrase does not refer to the giving of their names to their property (cf. places such as Alexandria, Antioch, Herodium), but rather to the legal transaction whereby a deal was concluded (cf. K. Galling, 'Die Ausrufung des Namens als Rechtsakt in Israel', *ThLZ*, LXXXI (1956), col. 67). Dahood (*PAB*, I, p. 299) sees here an allusion to the heirs 'who invoke their names' (i.e. those of the dead testators), but the former alternative seems more likely.

12. This verse recurs at the end of the Psalm, and it may be a sort of refrain.

Man cannot abide in his pomp: *ʾāḏām* ('man') may be a general term for mankind, but the phrase 'in his pomp' seems to point to the rich. The life of the poor man is often cut short by adverse circumstances, but even the wealthy man cannot continue in his riches for ever. In verse 20 instead of '. . . abide' M.T. has *w^e lōʾ yāḇîn* ('and does not understand'). This variation may well be original, unless one of the readings has been changed accidentally or intentionally.

he is like the beasts . . .: for his end is no different from that of the beasts (cf. Ec. 3:19), but for the God-fearing man there is, apparently, another destiny (cf. verse 15).

THE TWO DESTINIES **13–20**

13. This is the fate: or 'This is the experience'.

foolish confidence: the opposite attitude is described in Job 31:24 where Job denies that he has made gold his confidence. At death the rich will be parted from the object of their trust, and therefore before them there is only the abyss of darkness (cf. Prov. 3:25f.).

the end of those: reading *ʾaḥ^a rîṯām* (similarly also T). M.T. has *ʾaḥ^a rêhem* ('after them') which makes little sense, although Dahood (*PAB*, I, p. 300) suggests that it equals the Ugaritic *uhrit* ('final end') (cf. *Aqhat* II,vi:34); perhaps we could render 'their latter end' (cf. *HAL*, p. 34b).

who are pleased with their portion: lit. '. . . with their mouth' which may mean '. . . with their words (or 'sayings')' (so Cohen, *PSon*, p. 154). Dahood (*PAB*, I, p, 300) thinks that they are accused of gluttony.

14. The text of this verse is rather corrupt, especially the second half.

Like sheep . . . for Sheol: in this context 'Sheol' is a synonym of 'death', and the godless are like sheep appointed for slaughter (see on 44:11). This may suggest the inescapability of death, and, perhaps, the idea that they will perish *before* their time (cf. Kissane, *BP*, p. 217).

Death shall be their shepherd: this presents a sharp contrast with the experience described in Ps. 23. Of some interest is the personification of death, which reminds us of Mot, the god of the Underworld, in the Ugaritic texts (cf. also Job 18:14).

straight to the grave they descend: this rendering follows one of the suggested textual emendations (*wᵉyērᵉḏû bᵉmêšārîm lakkeḇer*). M.T. could be translated: 'the upright shall have dominion over them in the morning', but it is difficult to imagine that the Psalmist intended to portray the righteous as ruling over the wicked in Sheol. Dahood (*PAB*, I, p. 296) suggests: 'When they descended into his gullet like a calf' (i.e. into Sheol), reading *wᵉyārᵉḏû bᵉmêšārîm lᵉḇāḳār*.

and their form shall waste away: or (with Dahood) 'their limbs will be devoured by Sheol' (*wᵉṣîrām lᵉḇallôṯ šᵉʾôl*). For the idea, see Job 18:13 which speaks of the first-born of death consuming the limbs of the wicked.

Sheol shall be their home: Dahood (*PAB*, I, p. 301) takes 'Sheol' with the preceding verse, and translates the rest as 'consumed by the Destroyer' (cf. Dt. 32:24), reading *mᵉzê ḇōleh lô*. Yet M.T. may be corrupt beyond recovery, and the various renderings are little more than guesses.

15. Here we find the climax of the whole Psalm but the exact meaning of the verse is far from clear, probably it forms a contrast to verse 7; there is no real reason to regard it as a later addition.

But God will ransom my soul . . .: no man, however rich he may be, can ransom himself or anybody else (cf. verses 7f.), but God can redeem the life of his servant. The reference may be to a deliverance from the present suffering or untimely death (cf. 18:4ff. (M.T. 5ff.), 30:2f. (M.T. 3f.), 86:13, 88:6ff. (M.T. 7ff.), 103:3f., 116:3,8), but in view of the whole Psalm the allusion may be to the redemption from death (cf. H. H. Rowley, *FI*, pp. 171ff.). If Sheol were the ultimate goal for both the righteous and the wicked, then the latter would be better off than the former, and the whole argument of the Psalm would be very feeble (cf. Lk. 16:25). Therefore it seems that either the Psalmist believed that he would not see Sheol (or death) at all (cf. Enoch and Elijah, in Gen. 5:24 and 2 Kg. 2:11 respectively), or he hoped that, having died, he would be raised to life again to enjoy the fellowship with God (cf. Isa. 26:19; Dan. 12:2).

for he will receive me: it seems better to regard the Hebrew *kî* (*RSV* 'for') as an emphasizing particle (see J. Muilenburg,

HUCA, XXXII (1961), p. 143), rendering: 'But God will ransom me (i.e. my soul), from the power of Sheol he will certainly take me'. The verb *l-ḳ-ḥ* ('to take') is the same verb used in the Enoch story (Gen. 5:24) and it is possible that the Psalmist meant to allude to the story of Enoch's translation. Yet neither the author of the Genesis story nor the Psalmist explains in what manner this life with God would be continued; therefore it may be more appropriate to speak of a daring hope than of an established doctrine of afterlife.

Selah: see Introduction, pp. 48f.

16. Be not afraid . . .: this is addressed either to the Psalmist himself (so Kirkpatrick) or to his hearers (collectively). In the light of the previous argument, there is no reason to fear that the rich might become even richer or more influential; all their wealth and pomp are, at the most, a fleeting advantage. Dahood (*PAB*, I, p. 302) reads *ʾal tērēʾ* ('be not envious'), deriving the verb from *r-ʾ-h* ('to see'), which may occasionally mean 'to look with envy' (so perhaps in 73:3; Isa. 53:2).

the glory: *RSVm* 'wealth' which seems more appropriate. For a similar meaning of 'glory' (*kāḇôḏ*) cf. Gen. 31:1; Isa. 10:3, 66:12; Nah. 2:9. See on 19:1. Verse 16*b* could be rendered as 'when he increases the wealth of his house'.

17. he will carry nothing away: this is the tragedy of the rich, as depicted in verse 6, for *they* must lose the very thing that was of the utmost importance to them (cf. Job 1:21; Ec. 5:15; 1 Tim. 6:7). For the pious the opposite is the case: they trusted in God, and he will receive them.

his glory: or 'his wealth' (see on verse 16).

18. he counts himself happy: lit. 'he blesses his soul (or 'himself')'. This indicates once more his attitude to God. Instead of praising God, the giver of all blessings, the recipient has praise only for himself (cf. Dt. 29:19; 1QS iii:13f.; Lk. 12:16ff.).

and though a man gets praise . . .: lit. 'and (though) they (i.e. other people) praise you.' He may praise himself on his attainments, and others may flatter him, yet this will change nothing.

19. he will go to the generation of his fathers: in M.T. the verb is third person feminine (referring to his soul), or second person masculine (so Dahood). *RSV* follows LXX and V. The 'generation of his fathers' may refer to the ancestral tomb (cf. Gen. 49:29) or, more likely, to the realm of the dead in general.

who will never more see the light: Sheol is the land of continual darkness (cf. Job 17:13; Ps. 88:12 (M.T. 13)) and consequently its inhabitants are doomed to dwell in gloom for ever.

20. See verse 12.

Psalm 50 The Meaning of True Worship

The larger part of this Psalm is in the form of a divine utterance (in the first person), and its contents are reminiscent of the oracles of the classical prophets, with their admonitions and conditional promises. Consequently the Psalm has been described as a prophetic liturgy. Its *Sitz im Leben* or life-setting, is to be found in the Jerusalem cult (cf. verse 2) and the particular occasion may have been associated with the renewal of the Covenant. Weiser (*POTL*, p. 393) assigns it to the cult of the Covenant Festival, while Mowinckel, as can be expected, links it with Yahweh's Enthronement Festival. See also J. Jeremias, *Kultprophetie und Gerichtsverkündigung in der späten Königszeit Israels* (*WMANT*, 35, 1970), pp. 125ff.

The Psalm could have originated in the circles of cultic prophets, and Kraus (*PBK*, p. 374) would place it either in the time of the great religious reforms of Hezekiah or Josiah, or possibly in the early part of the post-Exilic period. If the poem is an imitation of earlier forms of literature, then its date may well be the Persian period; an earlier date seems, however, more likely.

Verses 1–6 form a hymnic introduction to the Psalm, and contain a description of Yahweh's theophany. Verses 7–15 and 16–21 are the two main sections; the former is dealing with the significance of sacrifice, while the latter with the neglect of the Covenant Law. Verses 22–3 are the conclusion; and they resemble, to some extent, the curses and blessings of the Covenant.

The prevailing metre is 3 + 3.

A Psalm: see Introduction, p. 46.

Asaph: see Introduction, pp. 45f.

GOD COMES TO JUDGE **1–6**

1. The Mighty One, God the Lord: lit. 'El, Elohim, Yahweh' (cf. Jos. 22:22). Many exegetes have suggested that this combination of divine names was used for the sake of emphasis; LXX, S, and V have: 'the God of gods, the Lord' (cf. 84:7 (M.T. 8)). It is unlikely that each divine name in this verse denoted a different aspect of God's character, e.g. 'the Mighty One, the Judge, the Gracious One' (Cohen, *PSon*, p. 156). It is possible that the phrase 'El Elohim' is to be understood as 'God of gods', i.e. as a superlative (so Dahood, *PAB*, I, p. 306).

and summons the earth: certain elements of this Psalm are reminiscent of the so-called divine lawsuit of which we find good examples in Isa. 1:2ff.; Mic. 6:1ff. (cf. H. B. Huffmon, 'The Covenant Lawsuit in the Prophets', *JBL*, LXXVIII (1959), pp. 285–95). 'The earth' or 'its inhabitants' are called to witness the charge against God's people (cf. verse 4).

from the rising of the sun . . .: i.e. from one end of the earth to the other, meaning 'the whole earth' (or 'all the nations'); cf. 113:3; Mal. 1:11.

2. Out of Zion: Yahweh appears out of his holy city (cf. Am. 1:2), as once he came from Sinai (cf. Dt. 33:2; Jg. 5:4f.; Hab. 3:3).

the perfection of beauty refers to Zion (as in Lam. 2:15; cf. Ps. 48:2 (M.T. 3)); the metaphor probably belongs to the traditions dealing with the glorification of Jerusalem as the city of God (cf. Kraus, *PBK*, p. 375). The city may have been regarded as exceptionally beautiful, because it was the object of Yahweh's choice (cf. v. Rad. *OTT*, I, p. 367).

God shines forth: sometimes the biblical writers think of God as clothed in light (104:2; for the opposite view, see 18:11 (M.T. 12)), or as dwelling in it (1 Tim. 6:16; cf. Exod. 13:21; Dan. 2:22). It can also be a symbol of God's presence: where God is, there is light in more than one sense (cf. 4:6 (M.T. 7), 18:28 (M.T. 29), 27:1, 36:9 (M.T. 10), 43:3; Mic. 7:8); see on 80:1.

3. Our God . . . does not keep silence: this line is regarded by some scholars (e.g. Wellhausen, Duhm, Snaith) as a later addition; on the other hand, it may well be original because it is presupposed by verse 21*a*. God had been silent and this inactivity had been misinterpreted by the wicked as his approval of their actions. In view of these circumstances he must speak; he cannot keep silence any longer.

before him is a devouring fire: we need not assume that the divine appearance on Mt. Sinai has been transferred to Mt. Zion (cf. Taylor, *PIB*, p. 262); rather the Sinai story may have coloured all subsequent descriptions of other theophanies. Sometimes God himself can be described as a devouring fire (Dt. 4:24, 9:3) consuming all his enemies. In our verse the 'consuming fire' may well be the lightning (cf. 11:6; Isa. 29:6, 30:30)

a mighty tempest: this is frequently part of the description of a theophany (cf. Job 38:1, 40:6, also 1 Kg. 19:11f.); the origin of the symbolism may be traced to Canaanite sources, although it was not unknown in other parts of the ancient Near East (cf. Kraus, *PBK*, p. 235).

4. It is possible that Near Eastern treaties have influenced, to greater or lesser extent, the *OT* language concerning the Covenant and related themes. Consequently relevant comparisons may illumine our understanding of the Covenant relationship (see *ANET*, pp. 199–206). In the Hittite treaties heaven and earth, mountains and rivers, are included among the witnesses to the treaty (cf. also K. A. Kitchen, *Ancient Orient and Old Testament* (1966), pp. 92–102). G. E. Wright ('The Lawsuit of God: A Form-Critical Study of Deuteronomy 32', *IPH*, p. 46) suggests that these natural elements listed as witnesses in the Hittite treaties, are not additional deities but rather 'summarizing categories into which all gods, known and unknown, would have fallen in polytheistic thought'. Dahood (*PAB*, I, p. 306) cites a Ugaritic tablet which mentions offerings to different gods, and among them we find also 'earth and heaven'. This need not imply that in our Psalm also 'heaven and earth' were regarded as members of the divine assembly (cf. H. W. Robinson, *JTS*, XLV (1944), pp. 151ff.; F. M. Cross, jr., *JNES*, XII (1953), pp. 274–77), rather they are witnesses who confront the people of God with their broken oath (cf. Jos. 24:26f.). The Psalm is closely linked with the so-called Covenant lawsuit in which Yahweh, as the suzerain, both accuses and sentences his disobedient people (for other examples, see Isa. 1:2; Jer. 2:4ff.; Mic. 6:1ff.).

that he may judge his people: lit. 'to judge his people'. Since the subject of the verb is not explicitly expressed, some scholars (e.g. Gunkel, Kissane, Nötscher) have argued that **the heavens** and **the earth** are called to act as judges. Yet verse 6 clearly states that God himself is the judge. Mowinckel (*PIW*, II, p. 71) has pointed out that 'to judge' here means 'to rebuke and admonish' (cf. verse 21).

5. Gather to me: this may be addressed to the angels (cf. Dt. 33:2), but since they are not mentioned in this Psalm, the command may be directed to the heavens and the earth, especially if they are not 'elements of the natural world, but are called upon as population areas—the heavenly hosts and the people of earth respectively (so R. B. Y. Scott; quoted from G. E. Wright's article, *IPH*, p. 48).

my faithful ones: this may suggest a touch of irony, unless we should understand the phrase as 'my Covenant people', i.e. those whose main characteristic is not so much any special virtue or obedience, as their responsibility to God and his laws.

who made a covenant with me . . .: this may refer to the ratification of the Covenant described in Exod. 24:5ff. (so Kissane, *BP*, p. 222), or it may be linked with the cultic ceremony of the Covenant renewal which probably took place during the Feast of Tabernacles (cf. W. Beyerlin, *Origins and History of the Oldest Sinaitic Traditions* (1965), pp. 38ff.).

by sacrifice: or 'in the presence of sacrifice' (so Dahood, *PAB*, I, p. 307). The reference seems to be to the Covenant sacrifice which may have been, among other things, a symbolic action denoting the oath. Thus we read in Jer. 34:18: 'And the men who transgressed my covenant and did not keep the terms of the covenant which they made before me, I will make like the calf which they cut in two and passed between its parts'. For another parallel see *JCS*, XII (1958), p. 129, where in a treaty of the eighteenth century B.C. a man swears to his partner, as he cuts the throat of a sheep: '(Let me so die) if I take back that which I gave thee'.

6. his righteousness: or 'his rightful claim', as the witnesses can testify. For *ṣeḏeḳ*, see on 33:5.

for God himself is judge: Kraus *et al.* would read *ʾelōhê mišpāṭ* ('(for he is) a God of justice'); for a similar phrase, see Isa. 30:18; Mal. 2:17.

THE TRUE MEANING OF SACRIFICE 7–15

7. Hear, O my people is reminiscent of the stereotyped formula in Dt. 5:1, 6:4, 9:1, 20:3, 27:9, which may have been the traditional address in the assembly of the people (cf. Dt. 20:2f.). Perhaps we should read: 'Hear, O my people, and let me speak, O Israel'.

I will testify against you: (cf. 81:8 (M.T. 9); Jer. 42:19; Am. 3:13), i.e. 'I will provide evidence against you.'

I am God, your God: perhaps, 'I am Yahweh, your God', or 'Yahweh, your God, am I', since it is very likely that in this Elohistic Psalm the name 'Yahweh' has been replaced by 'God' (*ʾelōhîm*). This phrase recalls the formula of self-identification of the Covenant-God, found in the introduction to the Decalogue (Exod. 20:2; Dt. 5:6). As the giver of the Covenant, God is fully justified in admonishing and in punishing his people who have broken this Covenant.

8. your sacrifices: i.e. communion sacrifices (*zᵉḇāḥîm*). The purpose of Yahweh's theophany is to rebuke his people (cf. verse 21), and, at this point, the condemnation is not directed against sacrifices as such but rather against the wrong interpretation of the *meaning* of sacrifice. N. H. Snaith (*Hymns of the Temple* (1951), pp. 96ff.) suggests that although God approves of sacrifices (*zᵉḇāḥîm*), yet he rejects burnt offerings. He arrives at this conclusion by taking the copula 'and' (*wᵉ*) as an adversative 'but'. It seems more likely, however, that the force of 'I do not reprove you' extends also over the second line. Cf. H.-J. Hermisson, *Sprache und Ritus im Altisraelitischen Kult* (*WMANT*, 19, 1965), pp. 35f.

burnt offerings: see on 40:6.

9. I will accept no bull from your house because the motives underlying the sacrifices are wrong. A man's house includes not only his dwelling place but also all that belongs to him, e.g. in 1 Kg. 13:8: 'If you give me half your house, I will not go in with you.'

he-goat from your folds: i.e. from your flock; wild animals were not regarded as a legitimate sacrifice.

10. every beast of the forest: or 'every wild animal'. For similar expressions, see Gen. 1:24; Ps. 79:2, 104:11,20; Isa. 56:9.

the cattle on a thousand hills is an ambiguous phrase, and its construction is strange. Kissane (*BP*, p. 220) may be right in reading '. . . on my mountains (*bahᵃrāray*) in their thousands' (similarly *NEB*); some other exegetes suggest '. . .on the mountains of God' (changing *ʾelep̱* into *ʾēl*) which may be another way of saying 'on the highest mountains'.

11. I know: i.e. I have both knowledge of and mastery over . . .

the birds of the air: so *RSV*, reading *šāmayim* ('heavens') for M.T. *hārîm* ('mountains'). Most ancient versions suggest either 'air' or 'heavens'.

all that moves in the field: this expression occurs elsewhere only in 80:13 (M.T. 14), where it is used of the enemies of Israel. In the present verse it probably denotes *all* kinds of animal.

is mine: lit. 'with me', probably 'in my care or possession' (cf. Job. 28:14).

12. If I were hungry: the context suggests that the conditional clause is unlikely to be fulfilled (cf. *GK* 159m). In this and the following verse the writer alludes to the primitive idea that gods require both food and drink, which are supplied by the offerings of the worshippers. See Dt. 32:38: 'Where are their gods . . . who ate the fat of their sacrifices, and drank the wine of their drink offering?' In antiquity it was believed that one of the main tasks of mankind was to provide the gods with sustenance, and a parody of this view is found in Bel and the Dragon (*Apoc.*). In the case of Yahweh, none can give him anything that is not already his property, because he is the lord of the *whole* world and all that is in it (cf. Dt. 10:14; Ps. 24:1).

13. Do I eat the flesh of bulls: this reflects a naïve concept common in the ancient world, and which must have been shared by some Israelites also. Lev. 3:11 refers to certain portions of the sacrificial animals, burnt on the altar, as 'food offered by fire to the LORD'. In Lev. 21:6 the offerings by fire are called 'the bread of their God' (cf. also Lev. 21:8,17,21; Num. 28:2; Ezek. 44:7). It is unlikely that this kind of language was taken literally by the *OT* writers, but it is probable that some worshippers had a more literal understanding of this ancient sacrificial terminology. **the blood of goats:** the blood of the sacrificial animals was not consumed by the worshippers (cf. Gen. 9:4; Dt. 12:23), and one reason for this was the belief that blood somehow represented life, or was linked with life (Lev. 17:11). In sacrifices, blood was usually poured out upon the altar (Lev. 1:5,11, 3:5; Dt. 12:27), at the base of the altar (Exod. 29:12), or sprinkled on the people and various objects (Exod. 12:22; Lev. 4:6,17).

14. The interpretation of this verse is difficult. 'Sacrifice of thanksgiving' (*tôḏāh*) can mean both a thank-offering (a kind of communion or shared sacrifice; cf. Lev. 7:12, 22:29; Am. 4:5), or a hymn of thanksgiving (cf. 26:7, 42:4 (M.T. 5), 69:30 (M.T. 31), etc.). Both alternatives are possible but the former may be more likely. The verb *z-b-ḥ* (*RSV* 'offer') means, literally, 'to slaughter', and this may well point to a material sacrifice rather than to hymns and prayers (cf. Kraus, *PBK*, p. 378). The point of this verse seems to be that sacrifice is not *food* for Yahweh, but that it can become a vehicle for expressing the right attitude to him, and a means of blessing for the worshipper.

pay your vows: if we follow the previous suggestion, then *nēḏer* ('vow') must be a votive sacrifice which the worshipper has bound himself to perform (cf. R. de Vaux, *Studies in Old Testament Sacrifice*, p. 33). Like the thank-offering, the 'vow' belongs to the communion sacrifices (cf. 22:25f. (M.T. 26f.); see on 56:12).

15. and call upon me: probably by means of a Psalm of lamentation (so Gunkel) or prayer (so Weiser). All that man needs to do is to trust in God's faithfulness; there is no necessity, and indeed it is impossible, to bribe God by various gifts or sacrifices.

I will deliver you: i.e. from your troubles; see on 116:8.

and you shall glorify me: some exegetes read: 'and I will glorify you' (*waʾᵃḳabbᵉḏeḵā*), as in 91:15. Yet M.T. gives a reasonable sense, and therefore there is no need to emend it.

REBUKE TO THE COVENANT-BREAKERS **16–21**

They profess allegiance to God's commands, but in real life they disregard him.

16. But to the wicked God says: this phrase appears to stand outside the metre, and therefore many scholars regard it as a later addition by someone who found it difficult to understand how the faithful ones (see verse 5) could be accused of such things.

In this verse **statutes** (see on 119:5) and **covenant** (see on 55:20) are parallel terms, and it is not impossible that the reference is to the Covenant text (cf. verses 18–20).

take my covenant on your lips: or 'utter my Covenant (conditions or law) with your mouth'. For this use of *n-ś-ʾ* ('to take'), see Exod. 20:7; Dt. 5:11; Ps. 16:4.

17. For you hate discipline: i.e. *mûsār* which may also mean 'instruction'. In Prov. 12:1 he who loves 'instruction' is said to love knowledge, but he who hates reproof is stupid (cf. Prov. 10:17, 13:18, 15:5,32); in 1QH ii:14 the 'men of truth' are called 'lovers of instruction'.

you cast my words behind you: the content of the instruction is the words of God, which remind us of the Ten Words, or the Decalogue (Exod. 34:28; cf. also Dt. 4:13, 10:4). 'To cast something behind one' means to reject it (1 Kg. 14:9), or to disregard (Isa. 38:17).

18. If you see a thief . . .: LXX, T, and S read '. . . you ran with him' (*wattārāṣ* for M.T. *wattīreṣ* ('you are a friend . . .')),

i.e. you threw in your lot with him' (cf. Prov. 1:14ff.). M.T. could be rendered '. . . you comply with him' (cf. Job 34:9), or '. . . and yet you are pleased with him'.
you keep company with adulterers: lit. 'with adulterers is your portion'; the full significance of this can be seen by recalling its opposite: 'The LORD is my portion' (119:57; cf. 73:26, 142:5 (M.T. 6); Lam. 3:24). They have their share with those to whom infidelity has become a part of their life, and, as such, they have no share in God (cf. CD xx:10,13; 1 C. 6:9f.; Gal. 5:21; Eph. 5:5). It is possible that these 'pious humbugs' were not thieves and adulterers themselves, but that they condoned such acts.

19. You give your mouth free rein . . .: i.e. you utter your words in mischief (cf. 15:3, 34:4 (M.T. 5)).
your tongue frames deceit: i.e. you do not hesitate to make use of (lit. 'to harness') deceit to achieve your purpose.

20. You sit among your type of friends (cf. 1:1). Some scholars (e.g. Gunkel, Kraus) suggest *bōšeṯ* ('shame') for M.T. *tēšēḇ* ('you sit'), rendering '(you speak) shamefully' (or 'shameful things'). Perhaps we should render the M.T. reading 'You continue to speak . . .' (cf. Winton Thomas, *TRP*, p. 19).
your brother could be a fellow countryman or, in view of verse 20*b*, it might be taken literally. Such a situation was not uncommon (cf. Jer. 9:4; Mic. 7:6).
you slander your own mother's son: evil talk was, and still is, a common weapon to damage or to destroy one's neighbour or his reputation (some typical examples are provided by 2 Sam. 16:1–4; 1 Kg. 21:8–14).

21. . . . I have been silent: this probably suggests that, although they had disregarded the Covenant Law, God had been patient with them, and he had not brought upon them an immediate punishment. Consequently they came to the conclusion that God had given his approval to their way of life. Some exegetes (e.g. Nötscher, Dahood; similarly *NEB*) take the phrase interrogatively: 'and shall I remain silent?'; this would agree with verse 3.
you thought . . .: or, following LXX, Theod, and S, 'you scheme destructive plans (*hawwôṯ* for M.T. *hᵉyôṯ*), shall I be like you?' (similarly Dahood). The answer is provided by verse 21*c*: God will rebuke them and will charge them with breaking his Covenant (for similar instances of setting forth a legal case, see Job 13:18, 23:4, 33:5).

WARNING AND PROMISE **22–3**

22. you who forget God: i.e. by neglecting his commands (cf. Jg. 3:7; Dt. 8:19; Job 8:13).

lest I rend: (like a lion). LXX and S read 'lest he rend you' (*yiṯrōp̄*), but the alteration is not necessary to the meaning of the verse. For the expression, see Hos. 5:14.

and there be none to deliver: this expresses the conviction that God is the *only* deliverer (cf. Isa. 43:3,11; 49:26) and therefore he who is condemned by God is hopelessly lost.

23. He who brings thanksgiving: or 'he who sacrifices a thank-offering' (see on verse 14).

honours me by obedience (as in Mal. 1:6). Dahood (*PAB*, I, p. 310) reads 'will be feasted by me' (i.e. *t^{e}kubb^{e}ḏēnî*), regarding the verbal suffix as having a datival force, expressing agency.

to him who orders his way aright: lit. 'to him who prepares a way' of which *RSV* may be a correct paraphrase. Some exegetes render 'he that walks uprightly' (*w^{e}ṯam* for M.T. *w^{e}śām*); *NEB* '. . . who follows my way'.

the salvation of God: or, perhaps, 'my salvation' (*b^{e}yišʿî*). M.T. could be explained as a misreading of the suggested Hebrew word, by regarding the suffix as an abbreviation for 'Yahweh' which in turn would be changed into 'God' (*ʾ^{e}lōhîm*) by the Elohistic editor.

Psalm 51 THE GREAT PENITENTIAL PRAYER

This Psalm is one of the most moving prayers in the *OT*; it belongs to the seven so-called Penitential Psalms (which include also Ps. 6, 32, 38, 102, 130, and 143) which form a subdivision of the Lamentations.

The historical note in the heading of the Psalm ascribes it to David. Although there are certain similarities between this Psalm and the Davidic history in 2 Sam. 11–12, as well as verbal parallels (cf. E. R. Dalglish, *Psalm Fifty-One* (1962), p. 211) its Davidic origin is doubtful. The religious ideas of the Psalm are, on the whole, more related to the concepts of the seventh and sixth centuries B.C. than to the thought of any earlier period. We may note in particular the apparent rejection of sacrifice (verses 16–17), as well as the idea of a new beginning (verse 10), and the phrase 'thy holy spirit' (verse 11). The composition of the

Psalm may belong to the latter half of the seventh century; Dalglish (op. cit., p. 223) suggests the time of Josiah. We may be on a safer ground, however, in placing its date of origin sometime between the period of Jeremiah and Ezekiel on the one hand, and that of Nehemiah on the other hand (cf. Kraus, *PBK*, p. 384). If we adopt this view, we have to explain the historical note, and there are several possibilities: (i) the Psalm could be regarded as an old Davidic composition modified in the course of time; (ii) a later editor may have misunderstood the phrase 'of David', taking it to imply authorship, and consequently he provided the Psalm with what in his opinion was its appropriate historical setting; (iii) the most likely explanation is the view that 'the Psalmist may have composed it with David in mind, to be used by others who were conscious of heinous sins' (H. H. Rowley, 'The Meaning of Sacrifice', *From Moses to Qumran*, (1963) p. 96). The poem may well be the writer's expression of his own consciousness of sin and the need for forgiveness. It is possible that the immediate cause was some serious illness which the Psalmist, as well as others, regarded as God's punishment for sin; the function of the Psalm would be found in the religious ceremonies performed by the afflicted man, or on his behalf, in the sanctuary.

Alongside this individualistic approach to the Psalm, there is also the collective interpretation. Theodore of Mopsuestia (who died in A.D. 428) thought that the Psalm referred to Israel in Babylon confessing its sins and praying for forgiveness and restoration from Exile. This view received a further stimulus in 1888 when Rudolf Smend (cf. *ZAW*, VIII (1888), pp. 49ff.) argued for a collective interpretation of the 'I' in the Psalms. A middle of the road position was taken by H. W. Robinson (*TPst*, p. 47) who pointed out that although the Psalms gave us the viewpoint of the individual writer, the latter was often so conscious of his identity with the group that he could also speak in the name of the group without any sense of inconsistency and without any explicit indication of the transition. Dalglish (op. cit., p. 226) thinks that the Psalm should be understood as 'a royal penitential psalm spoken by or for the king', and similarly also Bentzen who argued that the poem was patterned after the penitential ritual of the Babylonian New Year Festival.

The Psalm opens with an invocation (verses 1–2) followed by the author's confession of sins (verses 3–5). Verses 6–12 could be regarded as a prayer for cleansing and renewal. The poem ends with verses 13–17, which can be described as the Psalmist's vow and thanksgiving, while verses 18–19 are usually taken as a later liturgical addition.

To the choirmaster: see Introduction, p. 48.

A Psalm of David: see Introduction, pp. 46 and 43ff.

Nathan was apparently a court prophet, and a contemporary of David and Solomon.

came (from *b-w-*ʾ) occurs twice in the superscription; once it is used in its literal sense, and once in a euphemistic sense (of sexual intercourse). It is less likely that it was employed both times with the meaning 'to go', and with Nathan as the subject.

Bathsheba was the former wife of Uriah, the Hittite, and later the consort of David, and mother of Solomon (see 2 Sam. 11–12; 1 Kg. 1–2).

THE INVOCATION **1–2**

1. Have mercy on me: or 'be gracious to me' (similarly in 2 Sam. 12:22). The verb *ḥ-n-n* usually expresses the attitude of a superior to an inferior, and carries with it the idea of unmerited favour (cf. N. H. Snaith, *The Distinctive Ideas of the Old Testament* (1944), p. 128); see on 6:2, 57:1.

steadfast love: (*ḥesed̲*) is essentially a Covenant word which is easier to paraphrase than to translate. When it is used of God, it usually refers to his gracious and reliable Covenant promises, and hence it could be rendered as 'Covenant loyalty' (see on 26:3; cf. Nelson Glueck, *HB*, pp. 56–101).

abundant mercy: its Hebrew equivalent, *raḥ*ᵃ*mîm*, is always used in the plural, while the singular form (*reḥem* or *raḥam*) means 'womb'. From this we might venture the guess that 'mercy' is a feeling similar to that which a mother normally has towards her baby (cf. Isa. 49:15), or it could be described as a brotherly feeling; *raḥ*ᵃ*mîm* may also mean 'bowels', which were regarded as the seat of the emotions (cf. J. Gray, *I & II Kings* (*OTL*, 1964), p. 212), and so 'mercy' could also be described as one's deepest feelings for another person.

blot out . . .: this is the first of three word-pictures which the Psalmist uses to describe his separation from God, and his deep desire for restoration. The threefold picture does not necessarily suggest three different kinds of sin committed by the author, rather its purpose is to emphasize the completeness of the separation, and the firm conviction that only God can restore the impaired or broken relationship. For the writer sin is not a passing shadow but a deeply ingrained stain.

transgressions: the Hebrew *peša*ᶜ primarily means a rebellion against an authority (cf. Jacob, *TOTe*, p. 281). The cognate verb is often used to describe an act of revolt, e.g. when Israel rebelled against the house of David (1 Kg. 12:19), or when Moab revolted against Israel (2 Kg. 1:1). Consequently *peša*ᶜ denotes sin as a deliberate defiance of God, and as a rebellion against his will. Therefore 'transgression' is not an adequate term because it may merely suggest a violation of some law or rule.

blot out: this calls to mind the idea of the divine books in which the sins of men were recorded against the time of judgment. Thus Weiser (*POTL*, p. 402) simply adds after 'blot out' the phrase 'from the book of guilt'. Probably it was believed that both good and evil deeds were written in a book or on a tablet. Nehemiah besought God not to wipe out the good deeds which he had done (Neh. 13:13), while in Dan. 7:10 the seer envisaged the divine court in session and 'the books were opened'. In the Mishnah (*Aboth* ii:1) man is reminded that all his deeds are written in a book. Also in Babylonian literature we find a mention of the 'tablet of one's sins' (cf. Dalglish, p. 87). Thus the first figure of speech portrays God as if he were a presiding judge whom the penitent is beseeching to blot out 'the incriminating record with which he is charged' (ibid., p. 89).

2. The second word-picture speaks of sin as an ingrained stain which could not be removed by any ordinary washing, i.e. human means.

wash: lit. 'tread' or 'wash by treading'. The Hebrew *k-b-s* is a verb of some vigour, and it is usually used of washing clothes (cf. Exod. 19:10,14; 2 Sam. 19:24). It is employed metaphorically in Jer. 2:22: 'Though you wash yourself with lye and use much soap, the stain of your guilt is still before me . . .'.

iniquity: the Hebrew ᶜ*āwōn* probably represents two nouns of different etymological origins. ᶜ*ayin*, the initial letter of ᶜ*āwōn*, may stand for two different sounds, and this distinction still existed at the time of the Greek translation of the *OT*, and it appears in the transcription of various Hebrew proper names. Thus although 'Gaza' and 'Amalek' begin in Hebrew with the same letter (ᶜ*ayin*), the transcription shows that the different sounds were still distinguished in pronunciation, and this distinction was reproduced, as far as possible, in the transliteration. Consequently *ʿāwōn* may be derived either from the root meaning 'to bend, twist', or from the verb 'to err, go astray' (cf. S. R. Driver, *NHTS*, pp. 170f.). Thus the cognate nouns may mean either 'crookedness, perverseness' or 'error, deviation from the right path'; the latter alternative seems more likely. But whether we think of iniquity (*ʿāwōn*) as a perverse action or as a going astray, it is a *deliberate* act, and not an accidental wrongdoing. 'It is not a question of slipping, but of deliberately going in for a long slide' (N. H. Snaith, *The Seven Psalms* (1964), p. 50).

The third word-picture is taken from cultic life, and here the Psalmist describes his sin as a defiling uncleanness which might even be compared with leprosy, and which has placed him outside the fellowship of God and that of his people.

cleanse: the Hebrew *ṭ-h-r* occurs frequently in cultic terminology although it can also be used of such activities as the removing of dross from metals (Mal. 3:3). Leslie (*PAP*, p. 399) renders 'declare me clean of my sin' (for such a usage, see Lev. 13:6,13,17, etc.), but in view of the other metaphors the *RSV* rendering is preferable.

sin: (*ḥaṭṭāʾṯ*) in its original sense suggests 'missing the mark' or 'mistake' (cf. Job 5:24; Prov. 8:36, 19:2), but in its religious application it implies that a person has missed the mark or lost his way because he chose to do so (cf. C. Ryder Smith, *The Bible Doctrine of Sin* (1953), p. 17). One could, however, sin unwittingly (cf. Lev. 4:2).

THE CONFESSION OF SIN 3–5

In verses 1–2 the Psalmist expresses his knowledge of God's grace, while in verses 3–5 he confesses the knowledge of his sin; both are equally indispensable for a true repentance.

3. For I know: this is an emphatic statement that the writer himself has become fully aware of his rebellious actions and disloyalty, which had been known to God all along (cf. Isa. 59:12). A striking contrast to this attitude is provided by a Sumerian prayer:

'The transgression I have committed—I know not;
The sin I have sinned—I know not . . .' (*DOTT*, p. 113).

On the other hand, there are also some Babylonian parallels that express a sentiment similar to that found in Ps. 51:3 (cf. Widengren, *AHPL*, pp. 262f.).

my sin is ever before me: this may suggest not only a continual awareness of sin but also an ever present tension which is the source of fear and shame, hope and despair. The preposition 'before' (*neḡeḏ*) may carry with it a sense of hostility, and so V renders it *contra me* ('against me') (cf. Job 10:17).

4. Against thee, thee only . . .: although the Psalmist confesses his sin against God, this does not mean that he has never committed any sins against his fellow men. Either the writer is thinking of one particularly grievous sin against God (idol worship?) or, more likely, he regards all human relationships as established and upheld by God, and therefore he who disrupts their proper functioning has sinned against Yahweh. H. H. Rowley (*The Rediscovery of the Old Testament* (1945), p. 154) has pointed out that 'sin against man is not the infringement of rights which are man's by nature, but the infringement of rights which are his because God willed that they should be his'. This view finds a good illustration in 2 Sam. 12, where David is charged with the murder of Uriah the Hittite, and with adultery; yet in his confession he exclaims: 'I have sinned against the LORD' (verse 13; cf. also Gen. 39:9). A similar thought is found in Proverbs, 'He who oppresses a poor man insults his Maker . . .' (14:13; cf. Prov. 17:5).

that which is evil in thy sight: cf. 2 Sam. 12:9: 'Why have you despised the word of the LORD, to do what is evil in his sight?' This phrase is the opposite of 'to do what is right and good in the sight of the LORD' (Dt. 6:18, 12:25,28, etc.).

so that thou art justified . . .: this phrase has created many problems, and one of the difficulties is the interpretation of 'so that' (*l^ema^can*). The most natural interpretation would be to take *l^ema^can* as expressing a purpose, but then we would have the extraordinary statement that 'I sinned . . . that thou mightest be justified' (G. Quell, '*Hamartanō*,' *TDNT*, I, p. 277). One could conceive that a special emphasis on the sovereignty of God might lead to the idea of sinning to the glory of God, but the rest of this Psalm (and the *OT* as a whole) would scarcely support such an interpretation. On the other hand, verse 4*cd* may express the result or consequences (so Dahood, *PAB*, II, p. 4) of the action in verse 4*ab*, but such a use of *l^ema^can* would be unusual (cf. *BDB*, p. 775; M. Buttenwieser, *The Psalms* (1938), p. 193). Perhaps the best solution is to take verse 4*cd* as a final clause, and to assume that either a phrase (such as 'I confess this so that . . .') has been omitted for poetical reasons, or verse 4*cd* resumes the thought of verse 3. The point of verse 4 is that, whatever punishment the Psalmist may have received (see verse 8), and whatever further judgment Yahweh may pronounce upon him, Yahweh has been both right and just. This is reminiscent of the so-called *doxology of judgment* (cf. v. Rad, *OTT*, I, pp. 357f.), which is an acknowledgment of the justice of one's punishment; it also glorifies God's acts in judgment. A good example is Joshua's advice to Achan, 'My son, give glory to the LORD God of Israel, and render praise to him; and tell me now what you have done . . .' (Jos. 7:19); this is followed by Achan's confession.

in thy sentence: lit. 'when you speak'. LXX adds the phrase 'in your words', but M.T. forms a better parallel to verse 4*d*.

blameless: lit. 'pure' or 'clear'. LXX, followed by other versions and Rom. 3:4, took the verb *z-k-h* (*RSV* '(to be) blameless') in a sense similar to its Aramaic cognate, 'to be victorious, prevail' (cf. Kirkpatrick, *BPCB*, p. 290) but the rendering of *RSV* is more natural.

in thy judgment: or 'when you judge'. LXX took the Hebrew verb as a passive, rendering: 'when you are judged', or 'when you come into judgment'.

5. This controversial verse does not advocate celibacy, nor does it assert that marital relationships are sinful in themselves. If sons are a heritage from the Lord (127:3) and children a blessing of God (Gen. 1:28, 9:1, 12:2, etc.), then family life in all its aspects could hardly be regarded as immoral or wrong. See J. Scharbert, *Prolegomena eines Alttestamentlers zur Erbsündenlehre*, (1968), pp. 10–14; also J. K. Zink, *VT*, XVII, (1967), pp. 354–61.

It is doubtful whether this verse actually teaches a doctrine of original sin, although it may have prepared the way for such a doctrine. It alludes, more likely, to the universality of sin. The Psalmist confesses his total involvement in human sinfulness, from the very beginning of his existence. While God desires faithfulness in man, man resides in sinfulness. The Psalmist does not offer any excuse, but he affirms emphatically that any ground for mercy must be found in God alone, and not in man. The expressions 'in iniquity' and 'in sin' do not qualify human birth and conception respectively, nor do they suggest that the birth of the poet was the result of an illegitimate attachment (cf. Mowinckel, *PIW*, II, p. 14); rather they describe the status of mankind in general. Due to the solidarity of the community, the individual is involved in the sin of his social group, and the society as a whole

implicates each single individual (cf. Jos. 7:1; 1 Sam. 14:36–46). It is true that sexual intercourse and childbirth rendered the parties concerned ceremonially unclean (cf. Lev. 12:2,5; 15:18), but it does not follow that they were therefore regarded as sinful acts; ceremonial uncleanness is not identical with sinfulness.
conceive: the verb *yiḥam* is usually used with reference to animals but it is doubtful whether it is justifiable to overstress this point (cf. Delitzsch, *BCP*, II, p. 137) in order to argue that marital relationships are impure.

THE PRAYER FOR CLEANSING AND SPIRITUAL RENEWAL **6–12**

6. The interpretation of this verse is difficult, and grammatically it seems to be linked with verse 5; the *RSV* rendering may, however, be right. Leslie (*PAP*, p. 400; so also Mowinckel) thinks that at this point in the rendition of the Psalm, a revelation was given to the suppliant, and that **the inward being,** lit. 'what is covered over (?)' (verse 6*a*) and **my secret heart,** lit. 'what is closed up' (verse 6*b*) are two technical terms indicating the means of revelation. Dalglish (p. 123f.) suggests that 'the inward being' (*ṭuḥôṯ*) and 'my secret heart' (*sāṯūm*) may refer to the womb, and that there the Psalmist had been taught wisdom by God (cf. also Winton Thomas, *TRP*, p. 19), so that he has sinned knowingly and has no excuse. The Talmud (*Niddah* 30b) states that already the embryo is taught the whole Torah, although at birth he forgets completely.

The *RSV* rendering is, however, preferable. Verse 6 offers a contrast to verse 5; the latter describes what man is, while the former shows what God desires from man.
truth (*ʾᵉmeṯ*; see on 25:5) is probably 'faithfulness, fidelity', while **wisdom** (verse 6*b*) may well be 'the fear of the Lord' (see on 111:10).

7. The language of this Psalm is derived from cultic life, but it is doubtful whether corresponding ritual acts accompanied the recitation of the Psalm.
purge me: this is a comparatively late term. The *qal* form of the Hebrew verb *ḥ-ṭ-ʾ* means 'to miss the way (or 'goal')' or 'to sin' (cf. verse 2) but in its intensive form it signifies 'to purify from sin' (lit. 'to de-sin' or 'to un-sin').
hyssop: this was a small bushy plant (cf. 1 Kg. 4:33 where it is said to grow out of the wall), probably the Syrian marjoram (*Origanum maru*, L.; cf. J. C. Trever, 'Hyssop', *IDB*, II, pp. 669f.).

A bunch of hyssop was used at the first Passover (Exod. 12:22) for the sprinkling of the lintels and door-posts of the Hebrew homes; in later times it was used in the cleansing of a leper (Lev. 14) as well as in the purification of one defiled by contact with a corpse (Num. 19), and in the rite of the Red Heifer (Num. 19:6). It is probable that one of these ritual acts may have formed the background of the Psalmist's word-picture, and was employed as a symbol of that inward cleansing which only God could effect. Dahood ('Congruity of Metaphors', *Hebräische Wortforschung*, (*SVT*, 16 (1967), pp. 48f.) suggests that *ʾēzôḇ* (*RSV* 'hyssop') should be rendered '(Unsin me that I may be purer than) gushing water', deriving it from *z-w-b* ('to gush, flow').

wash me: see verse 2.

whiter than snow: cf. Isa. 1:18 where snow is contrasted with the scarlet of sin. Snow is relatively rare in Palestine, but it was proverbial for whiteness (cf. Exod. 4:6; Num. 11:10; 2 Kg. 5:27; Lam. 4:7; Dan. 7:9). When a man, however sinful, is cleansed by God, he is pure indeed; in fact he is a new creature (see verse 10).

8. Fill me: lit. 'satisfy me' (*taśbîʿēnî* for M.T. *tašmîʿēnî*); this is the reading of S, and it presupposes a confusion between two Hebrew letters (*mêm* and *bêṯ*). M.T. reads 'make me hear' (*RSVm*), and has the support of many ancient versions; it appears to be the better reading. In this case the reference would be to a divine oracle which the Psalmist expected to receive through the mediation of a priest or cultic prophet (cf. Gunkel, *EP*, p. 137; see also 38:15 (M.T. 16), 130:5; Jl 2:17f.). Consequently 'joy and gladness' would denote the oracle promising forgiveness, or in other words, the effect of that revelation is used for the revelation itself.

Verse 8*b* may be a continuation of verse 8*a*, being an additional petition (so *RSV*), but it may also be understood as the consequence of the action described in the preceding line (cf. *RP* 'that the bones . . . may rejoice').

the bones which thou hast broken: this may refer either to the distress of the Psalmist caused by his consciousness of sin and guilt, or to his illness which had made him aware of his transgressions (cf. Gunkel, *PGHAT*, p. 224). The term **bones** (see on 102:3) may denote one's personality or self (cf. 6:2 (M.T. 3), 35:9f.), so that the writer may simply mean: 'let me whom you have afflicted (and rightly so), rejoice'.

9. This verse describes in two different but picturesque ways the same basic thought: forgiveness. 'To hide one's face' usually means to 'withdraw one's favour, show displeasure' (cf. Johnson, *VITAI*, p. 44; see on 27:9), but in the present context it is applied to the plea that God would disregard the Psalmist's sins so that they would no longer separate him from his God.

sin: (*ḥēṭ*ᵓ), see on verse 2.

blot out: this re-echoes verse 1, and suggests the obliterating of the record of one's iniquities.

10. The thought of a renewal is not peculiar to Israel; it is found also among other peoples (cf. *ERE*, x, pp. 664ff.). The more important *OT* parallels are 1 Sam. 10:6,9; Jer. 32:39; Ezek. 11:29, 36:26. The main consequence of a new heart and spirit is that the renewed people are enabled to walk in God's statutes, and to do his will (cf. also 1QH iv:30ff., xi:10–14). The Psalmist realizes that God's pardon, wonderful as it is, does not provide the full answer to all his problems. Unless a radical change is wrought by God, the future will be but a repetition of the past; therefore the writer appeals to God for a clean heart and a new spirit.

Create: the verb *b-r-*ᵓ is a characteristic term of the Priestly source and Deutero-Isaiah. The subject of the verb is always God, while its accusative is the product of the action, and not the material. The main idea of the verb was probably to express the extraordinariness and the newness of the result rather than the thought of *creatio ex nihilo*. The Psalmist is not asking for a transformation (so Briggs, *CECBP*, II, pp. 8, 11) but for a new creation (cf. 2 C. 5:17). Also the parallel accounts in Ezek. 11:19, 36:26 speak about God *giving* a new heart and spirit, and not about transformation.

heart: (*lēḇ*) was regarded as the mainspring of man's inner life, and what affected the heart, concerned the whole man. Sometimes the stress may be, however, on the intellectual and volitional aspects of his personality (see on 27:3). 'A clean heart' may be described as an undivided will or single-mindedness which seeks only one thing: to do the will of God (cf. S. Kierkegaard, *Purify your Hearts* (1937), pp. 41ff.).

spirit: (*rûaḥ*; see on 76:12); here it is probably a synonym of 'heart' (cf. verse 17), or it is the inner power which is behind all action. 'A right spirit' is one which manifests itself in deeds pleasing to God.

11. from thy presence: lit. 'from before your face'. To dwell in God's presence means to enjoy the fullness of life (cf. 140:13 (M.T. 14)), while to be cast away from his presence is to be separated from him who is not only the source of joy but also of life itself (2 Kg. 13:23). The phrase may also suggest the exclusion from worship (so Briggs, *CECBP*, II, p. 8).

thy holy Spirit is an unusual expression in the *OT*, and it is found elsewhere only in Isa. 63:10,11. It is often argued that since the Psalmist was in permanent possession of the spirit of Yahweh, he must have been the King who was the only official in Israel who enjoyed this privilege (so Dalglish, pp. 157f.). This is possible, but, on the other hand, 'thy holy Spirit' may be simply another term for the personal presence of Yahweh, as in Isa. 63:10–14 (cf. G. W. H. Lampe, 'Holy Spirit', *IDB*, II, p. 629).

12. salvation may suggest a deliverance from sin and its consequences (as far as that is possible), and it may also include subsequent blessings, both material and spiritual (so Kraus, *PBK*, p. 389). Some exegetes take it to mean 'help' or 'the helpful nearness of God' (Weiser, *POTL*, p. 407), which is a good paraphrase.

joy: this is one of the characteristic elements of the Israelite religious life; 'the joy of thy salvation' is the subjective measure of God's deliverance (cf. 13:5f. (M.T. 6f.), 35:9).

a willing spirit: this is not a reference to the 'holy Spirit' (verse 11) but rather to the new and right spirit mentioned in verse 10. The Psalmist appeals to God to support him by *providing* him with a willing spirit (for the construction, see Gen. 27:37) which is an inclination to render a spontaneous obedience and not a grudging service (cf. Exod. 35:5,21).

THE VOW AND THANKSGIVING 13–17

13. The Psalmist knows nothing of an egoistic piety (?) or of a solitary religion, but he thinks of the service of God within the community of his people. An indispensable part of this service is one's testimony to the saving acts of God (cf. 9:1f. (M.T. 2f.), 22:22 (M.T. 23), 40:9f. (M.T. 10f.)), and therefore the singer promises to 'teach transgressors thy ways'—i.e. both what men should do and what God can do for them.

sinners: see 1:1.

will return: or 'shall be converted' (so Snaith, p. 60). The verb *š-w-b* ('to return') is a characteristic term of the prophetic proclamations; it is also a word of grace because it already presupposes the turning of God to the sinner (cf. Jer. 31:18; Lam. 5:21).

14. bloodguiltiness: lit. 'blood(s)' (plural). The exact meaning of this word is the crux of this verse. The older commentators saw here an allusion to the murder of Uriah (i.e. they assumed that the author was David). Dalglish (p. 227) relates the Psalm to the time of Josiah, and sees here a reference to the unrequited blood which threatened the life of the nation. Others take it to mean 'bloodshed' (*NEB*) or 'death' as the result of some sickness, persecution, etc. The word *dāmîm* (*RSV* 'bloodguiltiness') probably means 'impending death' as the result of his previous misdeeds which may have included bloodshed and so also bloodguiltiness. A parallel is found in 30:9 (M.T. 10): 'What profit is there in my death (lit. 'my blood') . . . Will the dust praise thee?'
thou God of my salvation is probably a later (although a fitting) addition to the original poem because it repeats the term 'God' and breaks the regularity of the metre. Perhaps 'my God, my deliverer' (i.e. *ᵓᵉlōhay* for *ᵓᵉlōhēy*).
my tongue: or simply 'I' (a part representing the whole).
deliverance: lit. 'righteousness' (*ṣᵉḏāḳāh*), which is primarily a term belonging to the vocabulary of salvation (cf. 22:31 (M.T. 32), 31:1 (M.T. 2)). Yahweh is 'a righteous God and a saviour' (Isa. 45:21) and his righteousness is most clearly manifested in his acts of deliverance.

15. This verse is well known through its liturgical use. It may be linked with the thought expressed in verse 13.
open my lips: i.e. remove the impediment which renders me speechless (cf. Ezek. 3:26f.). In the Psalmist's case this hindrance may have been his broken relationship with God, and it was not a question of eloquence but of inability to speak; cf. Ezek. 16:23: '. . . that you may remember and be confounded, and never open your mouth again because of your shame . . .'.
praise: the Psalmist suggests that true praise requires the authorization of God in the form of a deliverance and restoration, or blessing in general, otherwise it would lack the very substance which makes it what it is.

16–17. These two verses deal with the value of sacrifice and its nature. There is no need, however, to consider them as a later addition to the original composition because they reflect the same spiritual depth as the preceding verses. The real problem is the interpretation of this passage: does it express an absolute rejection of the sacrificial system (cf. Leslie, *PAP*, p. 401), or is it a denial of the value of sacrifice in particular circumstances? The so-called anti-sacrificial passages (1 Sam. 15:22; Ps. 40:6 (M.T. 7), 69:30f. (M.T. 31f.); Prov. 21:3; Isa. 1:11–17; Jer. 7:21ff.; Hos. 6:6; Am. 5:21f.; Mic. 6:6ff.), when seen in their respective contexts, rather suggest a relative repudiation of sacrifice (see also H. H. Rowley, 'The Meaning of Sacrifice in the Old Testament', *From Moses to Qumran* (1963), pp. 67–107). The circumstances which occasioned such a radical reconsideration of the meaning of the sacrificial system may have differed from case to case; in some instances the objection may have been a magical concept of sacrifice, or a misunderstanding of the true function of sacrifice. Our Psalm is not dealing with the God-man relationship in general but rather with a particular situation. In verse 16 the underlying thought is, so it seems, that the Law simply does not prescribe any atoning sacrifices for such things as murder and adultery, and since these or similar grave offences may have been the cause of the Psalmist's downfall, it is clear that the only alternative was penitence (see verse 17; 2 Sam. 12:13f.). Even so, the cleansing is not the inevitable end-product of man's contrition, but it depends upon the faithfulness of God. Sacrifice, as a God-given means, functions only within the setting of the Covenant; if the Covenant relationship is broken by man, then also sacrifice and any other cultic means have lost their significance (cf. Eichrodt, *TOT*, I, p. 168).

For: (*kî*), better 'Indeed' because verse 16 is hardly an explanation of verse 15 (see on 118:10).

sacrifice: lit. 'what is slaughtered' (*zeḇaḥ*), see on 40:6, 106:28.

were I to give: or 'else would I give it' (*AV*), in which case the phrase belongs to verse 16*a*. *RSV* follows T, and adds this phrase to verse 16*b*; this is preferable for metrical reasons.

burnt offering: see on 40:6.

17. The sacrifice acceptable to God: lit. 'the sacrifices of God'. Some exegetes read 'my sacrifice, O God' (so *NEB*); this involves a change from *ziḇeḥê* ('sacrifices of . . .') into *ziḇḥî* ('my sacrifice').

broken spirit and **contrite heart** are probably synonymous, denoting a way of life characterized by humility and openness to God. In 1QS xi:1 we have a parallel, '. . . to respond with humility to those who are haughty in spirit, and with a broken spirit to men of authority . . .' (Leaney, *RQM*, p. 235).

a broken and contrite heart: S omits 'broken and'; this would avoid the repetition of 'broken', as well as the overloading of the second line of the verse. The reading of M.T. may be due to dittography. 'Contrite heart', lit. 'crushed heart', is perhaps the opposite of 'stony heart' (cf. Ezek. 11:19, 36:26).

A LITURGICAL ADDITION **18–19**

These verses are often regarded as a later gloss of Exilic or post-Exilic origin because their general character, setting and attitude to sacrifice are different from the rest of the Psalm. The reason for this addition may have been the desire to adapt this individual Psalm for the use of the community, or to correct the false impression that God required only spiritual sacrifices. For a different view, see Eaton, *PTBC*, p. 142.

18. Zion: see on 65:1.

the walls of Jerusalem: this may imply that the date of this addition must be between 586 and 444 B.C. when the walls were once more restored during Nehemiah's governorship. The term 'walls' could refer not only to the defences of the city, but also to the walls of the Temple.

19. Then wilt thou delight: or, in a jussive sense, 'then may you be pleased'.

right sacrifices: lit. 'sacrifices of righteousness', i.e. legitimate sacrifices, or those offered in the right spirit; cf. Dt. 33:19; Ps. 4:5 (M.T. 6). Winton Thomas renders 'sacrifices in their appointed seasons' (*TRP*, p. 1).

burnt offerings and whole burnt offerings: most scholars omit this phrase (so also *NEB*) as an explanatory gloss, while a few exegetes prefer to delete 'right sacrifices'. 'Whole burnt offering' (*kālîl*) is a descriptive synonym of 'burnt offering' (*ᶜôlāh*), probably emphasizing the fact that the whole sacrifice was consumed on the altar. It is no longer clear what was the original difference between these two types of sacrifice.

bulls: i.e. costly sacrifices.

Psalm 52 True and False Security

The historical note ascribes this Psalm to David, and places its composition during David's flight from Saul. On closer examination of the Psalm it becomes apparent that the superscription is a secondary addition, because the character of Doeg and his deeds does not fit the Psalm. Doeg was no liar but, at the most, an informer, and his chief crime (?) was the execution of the priests of Nob (1 Sam. 22:17f.), but this is not even alluded to in the Psalm.

Verses 1–7 remind us of a lamentation, while the conclusion of the Psalm has the characteristics of a thanksgiving song. The definition of the psalm-type depends upon the emphasis placed upon either the first or second part of the Psalm. Gunkel (*PGHAT*, pp. 228f.) links this Psalm with the Laments of the Individual (see Introduction, pp. 37ff.), while Schmidt (*PHAT*, p. 103) sees the Psalm as a thanksgiving where, in the place of an account of past troubles, we have a 'curse' against the evil man. It is not impossible that the poem is an imitation of the prophetic 'judgment speech to the individual' (cf. C. Westermann, *Basic Forms of Prophetic Speech*, Eng. tr. by H. C. White (1967), p. 137), an example of which is found in Isa. 22:15–19. The Psalm opens with the direct speech of the Psalmist in the form of a prophetic reproach (*Scheltrede*), which is followed by an announcement of the judgement (verse 5) and a mocking saying (verse 7). Weiser (*POTL*, p. 412) thinks that this Psalm may refer to 'an act of the covenant community based on ritual law (verses 6f.), the purpose of which was the cursing of the evildoer and his expulsion from the community'.

On the whole it seems likely that the Psalm should be classed as a Lamentation of the Individual, or as a Psalm of Trust. It may belong to the late pre-Exilic period; Deissler (*PWdB*, II, p. 45) places it in the post-Exilic period.

The metre of the poem is mainly 3 + 2.

To the choirmaster: see Introduction, p. 48.

A Maskil: see Introduction, p. 47.

of David: see Introduction, pp. 43ff.

Doeg, the Edomite, was according to 1 Sam. 21:7 the chief of Saul's herdsmen, who informed the King of the help which David had obtained from the priests of Nob. He was also the executioner of the eighty-five priests who were accused of high treason.

Ahimelech was one of the priests of Nob, 'the city of the priests' (1 Sam. 22:19).

THE ACCUSATION **1–4**

1. Why do you boast: i.e. why do you brag about your mischief-making (cf. 10:3). The Hebrew verb *h-l-l*, in its *hiṯpaʿēl* form, often denotes the self-glorifying or boasting which is incompatible with trusting in God. There is what might be called a legitimate boasting when a man takes pride that he knows God (Jer. 9:23f.), or according to Sir. 9:16: '. . . let your glorying be in the fear of the Lord' (cf. *TDNT*, III, pp. 646f.).

O mighty man: or 'O you tyrant' (Moffatt); some scholars (Graetz, Gunkel, Kraus, *et al.*) read 'O man' (*haggeḇer* for M.T. *haggibbôr*), as in verse 7.

against the godly: so *RSV* following S and reading *'el ḥāsîḏ*; M.T. has 'the mercy of God' (*RV*). If M.T. has preserved the original text, we could render: 'Why do you brag about evil, O man of (ruthless) might? (Don't you see that) the Covenant loyalty of God (lasts) continually?' C. Schedl (*BZ*, N.F., v (1961), pp. 259f.) links the Hebrew *ḥsd* with its Syriac cognate which comes from 'to revile, scorn', and M.T. could be rendered '(why do you) revile God all day long?', regarding *ḥsd* as a *piʿēl* infinitive absolute used instead of a finite verb (cf. *GK* 113y).

you are plotting destruction: in M.T. this phrase belongs to the next verse. 'Destruction' (*hawwāh*) is in the first place a 'yawning gulf', and hence an 'engulfing destruction, ruin'. Mansoor (*TH*, p. 105) renders *hawwôṯ* in 1QH ii:6 by 'threats' (cf. 1QH v:26) which he links with the Ugaritic *hwt* II ('word').

2. a sharp razor may be a knife or sometimes a more elaborate tool, used for shaving or cutting the hair. In this verse it serves as a simile of the deadly power of the tongue: 'Death and life are in the power of the tongue' (Prov. 18:21).

you worker of treachery: this phrase occurs elsewhere in the *OT* only in 101:7 which warns that none who practises deceit shall be permitted to dwell in God's house (cf. 1QS iv:23, vii:5; 1QH i:27).

3. The deceitful man has a perverted sense of values; he loves evil more than good (cf. Mic. 3:2), and he does evil instead of good (cf. Klopfenstein, *LAT*, p. 71). Thus his life is a contradiction of the divine will which is summed up in 'Depart from evil, and do good' (34:14 (M.T. 15)).

lying (*šeḳer*; see on 119:29) refers, most likely, to slander or to the false accusation which the influential man (see verse 1) must have brought against the righteous man (cf. Exod. 23:1–9).

more than speaking the truth: or 'instead of speaking righteousness'. Here *ṣeḏeḳ* ('righteousness') is contrasted with 'lying' and therefore it may approximate to what we might call 'truth' in the context of human relationships (cf. Prov. 12:17).

Selah: see Introduction, pp. 48f.

4. You love: i.e. you take pleasure in . . .; similarly one can love or take pleasure in 'wisdom' (Prov. 29:3), 'wine' (Prov. 21:17), 'violence' (11:5), 'cursing' (109:17), 'sleeping' (Prov. 20:13), etc. For the verb 'to love', see on 26:8.

words that devour: or 'destructive accusation'; lit. 'words of swallowing'. The expression suggests that the lies of the 'mighty man' were aggressive in nature (35:25).

deceitful tongue: this stands as *pars pro toto* for the whole man (cf. 120:2). 'Deceit' (*mirmāh*) can also be used in connection with 'deceitful weights' (Mic. 6:11), 'false balances' (Am. 8:5), 'ill-gotten gains' (Jer. 5:27), 'deceitful action' (Gen. 27:35, 34:13), 'false testimony' (Prov. 12:17), etc. (cf. Klopfenstein, *LAT*, p. 312).

THE JUDGMENT ON THE WICKED 5

5. God: the etymology of the Hebrew *ʾēl* is uncertain. Two likely possibilities are the derivation from *ʾ-w-l* ('to be strong'), hence 'the strong one', and the one from a similar root (?) meaning 'to be in front', hence 'leader, lord' (for a more detailed discussion, see *HAL*, pp. 47f.). *ʾĒl* is the generic Semitic name for 'god', and in the *OT* it is usually used as an appellative noun, or as the designation of the God of Israel. In the Ugaritic texts *ʾĒl* is the name of the chief god of the pantheon (see M. H. Pope, *El in the Ugaritic Texts* (*SVT*, 2, 1955), pp. 25–54).

. . . will break you down: this and the other three word-pictures in this verse, are probably poetic variations on the doom of the treacherous man. LXX takes this verse as a wish or prayer 'may (God) destroy you', but *RSV* is preferable (cf. Isa. 22:17ff.). The Hebrew verb *n-t-ṣ* usually means 'to demolish', but here it is used figuratively of an individual who is depicted as if he were a building to be destroyed for ever.

he will snatch: the verb *ḥ-t-h* can denote, e.g., the snatching of fire from the hearth (Isa. 30:14; cf. *DTTM*, p. 512a). This metaphor may emphasize the suddenness of the change in the fortunes of the wicked. It is unlikely that the verb (plus the verbal suffix) should be derived from the Ugaritic *ḥtk*, 'father', and used in a privative sense 'he will unfather you' (cf. A. F. Scharf, *Verbum Domini*, XXXVIII (1960), pp. 217f.; Dahood, *PNWSP*, p. 19).

from your tent: i.e. from your dwelling-place, or from your comfortable home (Job 18:14; Ps. 132:3) rather than a reference to the Temple, suggesting the expulsion of the offender from the worshipping community (cf. Weiser, *POTL*, p. 413).

he will uproot you: the intensive form of the verb *š-r-š* is used in a privative sense 'to uproot, destroy' (cf. Jer. 11:19). The righteous man, on the other hand, will be like a tree planted by the streams of water (1:3).

the land of the living: see on 27:13. It is the opposite of the netherworld, and it denotes the present existence, or the world of life. In Job 28:13 LXX renders this phrase by *en anthrōpois* ('among men') (cf. also 116:9, 142:5; Isa. 38:11, 53:8; Jer. 11:19; Ezek. 26:20, 32:23,24, etc.).

Selah: see Introduction, pp. 48f.

THE LESSON OF GOD'S JUDGMENT **6–7**

6. The righteous: see on 1:5.

shall see, and fear: the Hebrew *weyirʾû* and *weyîrāʾû* respectively (cf. 40:3 (M.T. 4)) provide a word play which cannot be reproduced in English. The faithful servants of God, seeing his retributive intervention, will be filled with awe (see on 34:9).

shall laugh at him: this is not to be taken as an expression of malicious joy, for such an attitude is explicitly condemned: 'Do not rejoice when your enemy falls . . .' (Prov. 24:17; cf. Job 31:29). In form, verses 6f. are reminiscent of the mocking song or saying (cf. Eissfeldt, *OTI*, pp. 92f.). A. Bentzen (*Introduction to the Old Testament* (1959), p. 127) regards the mocking song as 'a sort of *curse*, *incantation*, *imprecation*' to create misfortune for the enemy. It seems that the Psalmist has used a similar literary form to anticipate the divine retribution which, at the same time, will be an occasion of joy for the godly, for their God will have acted and manifested his righteousness.

7. See the man: Weiser (*POTL*, p. 413) thinks that originally the cult community sanctioned the curses and passed its judgment while the accused man was still present; therefore the expression 'Behold the man' would be quite appropriate. This is a plausible conjecture.

his refuge: or 'his stronghold' (*māʿuzzô*), so *PNT*, Cohen, but the former alternative seems slightly more likely (see on 27:1).

trusted: i.e. he hoped that the present state would continue, and the basis for his confidence was the fact that he possessed wealth. The Hebrew *b-ṭ-ḥ* may suggest not a relationship but a condition

of 'feeling oneself safe because of something'; thus it can describe both a false security and a genuine one (see Barr, *SBL*, pp. 180f.). He who chooses the wrong alternative will perish, or 'He who trusts in his riches will wither' (Prov. 11:28). See on 78:2.
sought refuge: (from ᶜ-*w*-*z*), or 'grew strong' (from ᶜ-*z*-*z*); similarly *AV*, *RV*, *PNT*.
in his wealth: (*bᵉhônô*) following T and S. M.T. reads 'in his lust' (cf. Prov. 11:6); LXX has 'in his vanity' (supporting T and S?), *NEB* 'in wild lies'.

THE BLESSING OF THE RIGHTEOUS MAN **8–9**

8. a green olive tree: i.e. a luxuriant one; for the use of this metaphor, see Jer. 11:16; cf. Ps. 1:3. The olive tree was an evergreen, and one of the most valuable trees in Canaan. It could reach the height of some 30–40 feet, and it could produce its olives for hundreds of years (usually in alternate years). The berries could be used for eating, or they could be pounded and crushed in the oil press, to extract their oil which had many applications. The cultivation of olive trees was a slow process, but in the long run a profitable undertaking. On the average, an established tree could give some twenty stone of olives, which would yield some six gallons of oil.
in the house of God: i.e. in the Temple area, although some exegetes have doubted whether trees actually grew in the sacred precincts of the Temple (cf. Cheyne, *BPPI*, p. 151). Sometimes it has been suggested that the phrase was intended to denote the whole land of Canaan (cf. Hos. 9:15).
steadfast love: see on 26:3.
for ever and ever: i.e. as long as his life will last. For the expression, see on 9:5.

9. I will thank thee: see on 18:49. This is the difference between the treacherous man and the godly Israelite. The former arrogantly uses his blessings, while the latter humbly acknowledges God as the giver of all good things.
for ever: i.e. his life will be one long praise of God.
because thou hast done it: or 'because you have acted (on my behalf)'. The verb ᶜ-*ś*-*h* is used absolutely, without an object (cf. Isa. 38:15).
I will proclaim: the Hebrew *ḳ*-*w*-*h* I usually means 'to wait for' (*BDB*, p. 875b), while *ḳ*-*w*-*h* II is rendered 'to collect'. Dahood (*PAB*, ii, p. 17) derives ʾ*aḳawweh* from the second root to which he

assigns the meaning 'to call'; some other exegetes read *wa'ᵃḥawweh*, 'and I shall proclaim' (Gunkel, Nötscher, *et al.*).

thy name: see on 20:1.

in the presence of the godly: i.e. before the worshipping community. For *ḥᵃsîḏîm* ('godly'), see on 30:4.

Psalm 53 Is God Irrelevant?

Since this Psalm is a variant, or a parallel version, of Ps. 14, they have been dealt with together (above, pp. 130–35).

Psalm 54 God is My Helper

This poem, like Ps. 52, is ascribed to David during his flight from Saul (1 Sam. 23:19, 26:1) but the contents of the Psalm lend little support to this alleged Davidic authorship.

It can be classed as a Lament of the Individual, and it reflects the usual structure of this *Gattung* (see Introduction, p. 37). It opens with an invocation of the deity (verses 1–2), which is followed by a brief description of the Psalmist's plight (verse 3) and an expression of his trust in God (verses 4–5). The lament concludes with a promise to thank God for his salvation (verses 6–7). Mowinckel (*PIW*, I, p. 220) describes this poem as a Protective Psalm in which the prominent feature is the confidence of the Psalmist and the assurance of obtaining help.

The Psalmist was hard pressed by his enemies (verse 3), but it is not clear what means they used to further their schemes. It is possible that they resorted to false accusations (see verse 1), and that the setting of the Psalm is to be found in some such situation as that in 1 Kg. 8:31f. Although the Psalm alludes to 'strangers' (*RSV* 'insolent men'), there is no real need to regard the Psalmist as a king (so Bentzen), or the Psalm as a royal prayer (so Eaton, *PTBC*, p. 145; Dahood, *PAB*, II, p. 23).

It is impossible to say much concerning the date of this composition. Oesterley assigned it to the Greek period, while Kraus (*PBK*, p. 397) concludes from the 'theology of the name' that the Psalm must be post-Deuteronomic.

The dominant metre is 3 + 3.

To the choirmaster: see Introduction, p. 48.

stringed instruments: see Introduction, p. 48.

Maskil: see Introduction, p. 47.

Ziphites were the inhabitants of Ziph, a town in the Judaean hill country, some 3 miles SE. of Hebron (cf. Baly, *GB*, p. 158). They informed Saul of David's hiding place (1 Sam. 23:19, 26:1), and put the King on David's track. This historical note seems to be of a late origin, and S has preserved a different account.

THE PETITION **1–2**

1. Save me: the Hebrew *y-š-*^{c} is usually linked with the Arabic *waši*^{c}*a* ('to be wide, broad'), and thus its basic meaning may be 'to be wide', and in a causative form it would suggest 'to give room', hence 'to deliver' (i.e. from the imprisoning circumstances which choke the vitality of the person involved; cf. S. R. Driver, *NHTS*, p. 118). This verb has a wide application, denoting actions which bring deliverance or help. Very often the implication is that if the help were not forthcoming, the afflicted person would perish (cf. Barth, *ETKD*, p. 127). The subject of the verb can be either God or man, but more often the former. The appeal to save usually assumes that the person implored has the power and authority to intervene. So in 2 Kg. 16:7 Ahaz, the King of Judah, sends messengers to the king of Assyria, saying: 'I am your servant and your son. Come and rescue me . . .'. The human ability to save is, of course, greatly limited, and theologically it is desirable only in so far as it operates within the purposes of God, as in Jg. 3:9: 'But when the people of Israel cried to the LORD, the LORD raised up a deliverer for the people of Israel, who delivered them . . .' (cf. Jg. 2:16; Neh. 9:27).

by thy name: see on 20:1. The name of God and his might are the manifestations of God in saving the oppressed. The name of a person or thing generally expresses one's character or the essence of a thing. Therefore Abigail could say concerning her husband: '. . . as his name is, so is he; Nabal (i.e. 'fool') is his name, and folly is with him' (1 Sam. 25:75). Conversely, if the person is important and powerful, so also is his name, as is the case with the *divine* name. Eichrodt (*TOT*, ii, p. 43) regards the name of Yahweh '*as the medium of his operation*' and he sees here 'a transition from the Name as an interchangeable term for the divine person to its use as a designation for the divine power . . .'. Similarly, Jacob (*TOTe*, p. 84) takes the 'name' as 'a means which Yahweh has available for action and not simply a formula of invocation'.

vindicate me: the Psalmist turns to Yahweh as the Judge *par excellence*. The vindication expected was, probably, by means of the divine judgment in the court of justice (Prov. 31:9).

2. Hear my prayer: this is parallel to 'give ear . . .'. These two expressions mean both to hear and to answer the supplication (cf. 4:1 (M.T. 2), 84:8 (M.T. 9), 102:1 (M.T. 2), 143:1; cf. also 11QPsª Plea, ll. 5f.). In Ugaritic, too, the verb *šm*ᶜ is sometimes tantamount to 'to obey' (cf. Gordon, *UT*, p. 492).

THE COMPLAINT **3**

This verse is practically identical with 86:14.

3. insolent men: this is the reading of some Hebrew MSS. and T (i.e. *zēḏîm*; see on 119:21,51). M.T. has *zārîm* ('strangers') which often denotes 'aliens, foreigners'. It can also be used of Israelites who have become outsiders, having placed themselves outside the Covenant relationship. Thus in Isa. 1:4 the prophet speaks of his contemporaries, 'They have forsaken the LORD, they have despised the Holy One of Israel, they are utterly estranged' (cf. L. A. Snijders, 'The Meaning of *zr* in the *OT*', *OTS*, x (1954), pp. 1–154).

ruthless men: the Hebrew *ᶜārîṣîm* can describe any powerful and dreaded persons, especially such as have no scruples about the use of force or treachery to obtain their wish (cf. Patton, *CPBP*, p. 43). The same term is also found in 1QH i:39, ii:11,21 where Mansoor (*TH*, pp. 104, 106f.) renders it by 'tyrants'.

seek my life: lit. 'seek my soul' (see on 33:19).

they do not set God before them: this is the characteristic of ruthless and insolent men, and it means that they disobey the commands of God (cf. 16:8, 119:30).

Selah: see Introduction, pp. 48f.

THE EXPRESSION OF TRUST **4–5**

4. God is my helper: LXX 'God succours me' (cf. 30:10 (M.T. 11), 72:12, 118:7).

the upholder of my life: *RV* renders it rather literally 'of them that uphold my life', as if God were one among many helpers. *GK* 119i suggests that this expression does not mean that God belongs to the class of 'upholders', but that it ascribes to him a similar character. Kissane (*BP*, p. 234) takes it as an idiomatic way of expressing the superlative, 'the upholder *par excellence*' or 'the great Upholder' (so Rodd).

5. He will requite: so *RSV* following *Ḳᵉrê*, LXX, Sym, while *Kᵉṯîḇ* and T read '(The evil) shall return . . .'; Kissane (*BP*, p. 234) suggests 'The evil shall recoil upon my foes'.

my enemies: the Hebrew *šôrᵉrāy* is derived from *š-w-r* ('to behold, regard') which is a common verb in the Book of Job. The Hebrew term could be rendered '(insidious) watchers' (*BDB*). The same word is also found in 5:8 (M.T. 9), 27:11, 59:10 (M.T. 11), 92:11 (M.T. 12).

thy faithfulness: for the Hebrew *ʾᵉmeṯ*, see on 25:5. God, being true to himself and to his Covenant, cannot but put an end to the wicked who have rejected his authority (verse 3*c*). Oesterley (*TP*, p. 282) regards verse 5 as a wish which he finds distasteful; yet the Psalmist should be judged in the light of his own time and by the theological structure of *his* world. For him, divine justice had to be worked out within the span of this brief life, for there was, as yet, no worthwhile belief in an existence to come where the present injustice could be redressed. Therefore the deliverance of the oppressed man is co-terminous with the punishment of the oppressors. Thus mischief had to return upon the head of the mischief-maker. The ideas of the Psalmist may be deficient from our point of view but the essence of his argument, i.e. that divine justice also functions in this world, still retains its validity for faith.

THE VOW AND THANKSGIVING **6–7**

6. free-will offering: the Hebrew equivalent *nᵉḏāḇāh* can signify either voluntariness (which could be used here as an adverbial accusative 'freely'), or a sacrifice which is offered as a voluntary gratitude, apart from any specific promise. The free-will offering can be a kind of communion sacrifice (see on 40:5) of which only a part was offered to God, while the rest was eaten by the worshippers; or it can be a whole burnt offering (cf. Lev. 22:18–30; Num. 15:1–10).

I will give thanks: see on 18:49.

to thy name: perhaps, 'to you' (see verse 1).

for it is good: this is a common formula in the Thanksgiving Psalms (cf. 52:9 (M.T. 11), 100:5, 106:1, 135:3).

7. For thou hast delivered me: lit. 'For he has . . .' (so Gunkel, Kraus, *et al.*) and the subject of the verb may be either Yahweh or his name (see verse 6).

from every trouble: Dahood (*UHP*, p. 44) sees here an example

of balancing a concrete noun (**my enemies**) with one that is abstract (**every trouble**), and the result is that both can be rendered concretely, hence: 'from my adversary'.
has looked in triumph: lit. 'has seen' (cf. *GK* 119k), or one could say that the discomfiture of the enemies has provided 'a sight for sore eyes' (cf. 58:10 (M.T. 11), 59:10 (M.T. 11), 92:11 (M.T. 12)).

Psalm 55 Cast Your Burden upon The Lord

This Psalm is generally considered as a Lament of the Individual (see Introduction, pp. 37ff.), although some exegetes (e.g. Mowinckel, Eaton) assign it to the National Laments. There is also the suggestion that this poem is composite in origin, and that it consists of two originally independent units (verses 1–18 and 19–23). It seems more likely that it is a literary unity, and that the changes in mood and style may be accounted for by the emotional strain of the author. He was oppressed not only by wicked men but also deceived by his closest friend. He was tempted to escape his trials by fleeing from his native land or place, yet, finally, he decided to seek refuge in God alone.

There is little to indicate any definite date but Deissler (*PWdB*, II, p. 52) suggests the early post-Exilic period which may be right.

The metre of the Psalm is mainly 3 + 2.
To the choirmaster: see Introduction, p. 48.
stringed instruments: see Introduction, p. 48.
A Maskil of David: see Introduction, pp. 43ff. and 47.

THE APPEAL TO GOD **1–2**

1. Give ear to my prayer: see on 54:2. For 'prayer', see on 65:2.
hide not thyself: it seemed to the Psalmist that God had not taken any notice of his serious situation, and that he was unwilling to help. The same verb is used in Dt. 22:4: 'You shall not see your brother's ass or his ox fallen down by the way, and withhold your help (i.e. hide yourself)' (cf. Isa. 58:7). For this supposed aloofness of God, see on 10:1.
supplication: i.e. my prayer for your favour (see on 86:6; cf. 1QH ix:11).

2. Attend to me: cf. 5:2 (M.T. 3), 17:1, 61:1 (M.T. 2), 142:6 (M.T. 7).

answer me: i.e. by granting my request and by helping me in my troubles (cf. 27:7).

I am overcome: lit. 'I am restless'. LXX reads *elupēthēn* ('I was grieved') which may suggest the Hebrew *ʾēraʿ* (from *r-ʿ-ʿ*, 'to break', 'be in a sad state' (?), so Wutz (*DP*, p. 138)); Jerome has *humiliatus sum*. Winton Thomas (*TRP*, p. 20) reads *ʾûraḏ* (from *r-d-d*), 'I am beaten down', for M.T. *ʾārîḏ*. Dahood (*PAB*, II, p. 31) takes the verb as an *ʾap̄ʿēl* imperative 'descend' (from *y-r-d*, 'to go down').

my trouble: or 'my complaint' (*RV*) concerning the desperate situation. For *śîaḥ* ('complaint'), see on 142:2.

THE DESCRIPTION OF THE AFFLICTION 3–5

3. I am distraught: in M.T. this phrase belongs to the preceding verse, but the metre and the general sense of the passage supports *RSV* (so also Gunkel, Kraus, *et al.*).

the noise of the enemy: i.e. the threatening voice of the foes.

oppression: the Hebrew *ʿāḳāh* is a *hapax legomenon* in the *OT*, and it may be an Aramaism from *ʿ-w-ḳ* ('to press'). Perhaps we should render verse 3*b* 'because of the *shouts* of the wicked' (cf. G. R. Driver, *JBL*, LV (1936), p. 111); this would provide a good parallel with verse 3*a*.

the wicked: see on 1:1, 28:3.

they bring: or 'they cause to fall' (cf. 140:10).

trouble: for *ʾāwen*, see on 36:4. Some exegetes find here an allusion to the magic power of the curse (cf. Kraus, *PBK*, 403).

they cherish enmity: Dhorme (*CJ*, p. 234) suggests that the verb *ś-ṭ-m* means not only 'to hate' but also 'to pursue, persecute', hence 'in anger they persecute me' (cf. also N. H. Tur-Sinai, *The Book of Job* (1957), p. 265).

4. My heart: see on 27:3.

the terrors of death: or 'deadly terrors' (a superlative?). Some commentators (e.g. Gunkel, Briggs) delete *māweṯ* ('death'), which overloads the metre, as a dittograph of *ʾêmôṯ*. The phrase refers to the terror inspired by the threat of death; cf. Exod. 15:16; 1QS i:17, x:15.

5. Fear: i.e. a fright or a state of anxiety, and not an 'awareness of the holy God' (see on 25:12). 'Fear and trembling' probably means 'great fear'.

horror overwhelms me: i.e. the physical effects of fear, such as shuddering, have taken control of me; lit. 'shuddering covers me (completely)' (cf. Job 21:6; Ezek. 7:18).

THE PSALMIST'S DAY-DREAMS **6–8**

6. a dove: it is not clear why the poet chose 'dove' for his particular word-picture. Perhaps he had in mind the rock doves which would nest in the clefts of inaccessible precipices (cf. Jer. 48:28: '. . . like a dove that nests in the sides of the mouth of a gorge') and this would provide a fitting symbol of safety and remoteness. In 74:19 'dove' is used to denote Israel, and in Mt. 10:16 it is a symbol of innocence.

7. The Psalmist wishes to flee far away, and to escape his oppressors (cf. 11:1). The other alternative was to take refuge in the sanctuary; but even this asylum was not always a safe place, as proved by Joab (1 Kg. 2:28–34), although he could be regarded as a guilty man.

the wilderness: (*miḏbār*) may sometimes denote a barren, uncultivated region (cf. Gen. 21:14), 'a land not sown' (Jer. 2:2) 'in which there is no man' (Job 38:26). In other instances it may be a place of pastures (1 Sam. 17:28; Ps. 65:12 (M.T. 13); Jer. 23:10; Jl 2:22). In the rainy season it would be well covered with grass and flowers but rather barren during the dry season (see Baly, *GB*, p. 90).

Selah: see Introduction, pp. 48f.

8. As a traveller surprised by a tempest flees for a place of shelter, so the Psalmist longs to steal away from the hostilities of his opponents.

THE FURTHER COMPLAINT **9–11**

9. Destroy their plans: *RSV* follows T in adding 'their plans' (*ᶜaṣāṯām*). In M.T. the verb has no object, but the two verbs in verse 9*a* may be co-ordinated (cf. *GK* 120d) and we could render: 'Confuse completely, O Lord, their speech'. This may be an allusion to the parable of the Tower of Babel and the confusion of languages (Gen. 11:5–9). The result of God's intervention was not only a loss of the common language, but also the dispersion all over the earth, as a punishment (Gen. 11:9). Did the Psalmist expect the repetition of the same 'pattern' in his home town? It is possible that he expected the silencing of the malicious tongues (i.e. the people themselves), as in 12:3f. (M.T. 4f.). The Hebrew *b-l-ᶜ* (*RSV* **Destroy**) can also denote 'to confuse' (cf. *HAL*, p. 129; see also 1QpHab xi:15; 1QH iii:14). The other verb *p-l-g* means 'to divide' (cf. 4Q169 3–4, iv:1).

violence and strife are rife in the city. The expression 'I see' may mean 'I have experienced' (cf. Hab. 1:3). This perverted city could be Jerusalem itself, but this is, obviously, a guess.

10. they go around it: the subject of the verb is not explicitly stated but it could be the evildoers who were always on the alert (like watchmen) to do some mischief, or the reference might be to the 'violence and strife' (verse 9) which have taken complete control of the city, and have become its 'guardians' (cf. Dahood, *PAB*, ii, p. 33).

mischief: (*ʾāwen*), see on 36:4.

trouble: (*ʿāmāl*) means basically 'labour, toil', as in Ec. 1:3: 'What does man gain by all the toil at which he toils . . .'. It can also be used to denote suffering or trouble, so in Isa. 53:11: 'he shall see the fruit of the *travail* of his soul . . .'. If the *ʿāmāl* is done to others, it is usually rendered by 'mischief, trouble' (cf. 7:16: 'His mischief returns upon his own head'; see also 140:9 (M.T. 10)).

11. ruin: see on 52:1. It probably means 'acts that bring about ruin'.

oppression: the same word (*tōḵ*) occurs also in 10:6, 72:14. The root *t-k-k* has to do with oppression, perhaps with various sorts of injustice.

market place: the Psalmist may have thought of it as the meeting place of the legal assembly (see L. Köhler, *Hebrew Man*, Eng. tr. by P. R. Ackroyd (1956), pp. 152–65), which was no longer governed by justice and righteousness, but by oppression and fraud.

THE TREACHERY OF A FRIEND **12–14**

12. It is not an enemy . . .: LXX suggests: 'For if (only my) enemy had reviled me' (i.e. *lû* instead of M.T. *lōʾ* ('not'); so also Gunkel, Kissane, Kraus, *et al.*). The greatest disappointment of the Psalmist was that one of his trusted friends had thrown in his lot with his enemies.

then I could bear it: M.T. lacks the object of the verb, and the line is metrically short; consequently a word, such as *kᵉlimmāh* ('reproach') (cf. Ezek. 16:52), or something similar, may have dropped out.

it is not an adversary: or, following LXX and paraphrasing: 'had it been a man who hated me that had magnified himself at my expense' (35:26, 41:9 (M.T. 10)).

then I could hide from him: i.e. I would have been prepared for such an attack.

13. But it is you: this is an 'anticipation' of the famous phrase: 'Et tu, Brute!'

my equal: lit. 'a man according to my valuation'. The Hebrew *ʿēreḵ* may denote valuation for the purposes of taxation (2 Kg. 12:5), sin-offering (Lev. 5:15), or for other ends (Lev. 27:2f.). Cf. 4Q159 1 ii:6: '. . . money of Valuations that a man gives as a ransom for his soul . . .'.

my companion: or 'my close friend'. The repetition of the various synonyms for 'friend' expresses the severity of the accusation of the treacherous companion.

14. . . . sweet converse: the Hebrew *sôḏ* (see on 25:14) may also mean 'council, intimate circle', as in 89:7: 'God is feared in the council of the holy ones'. Perhaps we could paraphrase verse 14*a*: 'we used to enjoy fellowship together' (cf. Job 19:19).

we walked in fellowship: M.T. has 'we used to walk with the throng', which attended the Temple during the pilgrimage festivals. LXX reads *en homonoia*, 'in unity' (similarly S). The community and fellowship were two important aspects of the life of Israel during *OT* times. It has been said that where these two factors are lacking, there can hardly be life in the full sense of the word (cf. Barth, *ETKD*, p. 26; cf. Gen. 2:18).

THE INVECTIVE 15

15. Let death come upon them: this is the reading of *Ḳᵉrê*, LXX, Sym, *et al.*; it involves a splitting up of *yaššîmāweṯ* ('desolations') into *yaššî*(ʾ) *māweṯ*. Briggs derives the verb from *n-š-*ʾ ('to beguile') which seems better than the derivation from *š-w-*ʾ ('to ruin (?)'), so Gunkel (cf. Klopfenstein, *LAT*, p. 315); Dahood (*PAB*, II, p. 34) suggests *wāšāh* * ('to overcome').

. . . to Sheol alive: (see on 6:5). This was the fate of Korah and his family (Num. 16:31ff.). The word-picture probably denotes the suddenness of the destruction: they perished as quickly as if the earth had opened its mouth and swallowed them up (cf. Prov. 1:12; Isa. 5:14).

let them go away . . .: M.T. has 'for evils are in their dwelling, (even) in their midst (or 'even in their very selves')'. *RSV* follows the common emendation *yaᶜaḇᵉrû bimᵉḡûrām bᵉḳiḇrām*, but M.T. gives a satisfactory sense. One could, however, accept the suggestion that *bᵉḳirbām* ('in their midst') is an explanatory gloss, and should be deleted for metrical reasons.

AN EXPRESSION OF TRUST IN GOD **16–19**

16. But I call . . .: this introduces a contrast with the oppressors who do not set God before them (verse 3). The true solution of the Psalmist's problem is not escapism (verses 6ff.), but a turning to God.

and the LORD will save me: the divine name 'Yahweh' is slightly odd in the Elohistic psalter (see Introduction, p. 25), and some exegetes have emended *yhwh* into *wᵉhûᵓ* ('and he'). For the verb 'to save', see on 54:1.

17. Evening and morning . . .: this order may suggest that, in the Psalmist's time, day began with the sunset and not with the dawn. Daniel is said to have prayed three times a day (Dan. 6:10), but it is not certain that our Psalm refers to any *set* times for prayer, although this is possible (see on 141:2). The writer probably means that *whenever* he prays to God, the Almighty hears and answers him.

18. he will deliver: for *p-d-h*, see on 119:134.

my soul: i.e. 'me' (see on 33:19).

in safety: or 'in peace' (see on 119:165). This is the result of God's deliverance.

from the battle that I wage: or 'from the hostilities against me'; LXX has 'from them that draw near to me' (similarly T and V). Gunkel, Kraus, *et al.* resort to emendations, and they find in verse 19 an allusion to certain Arab tribes (the Ishmaelites and the Jaalamites, and the inhabitant(s) of the East) (cf. *NEB*). It is doubtful, however, whether this interpretative conjecture is really necessary because it is not certain that the Psalm is of a composite nature. Dahood (*PAB*, II, p. 29): 'He drew near to me when . . .' (*ḳāraḇ lî*).

many: the preposition *bᵉ* in *bᵉrabbîm* can be explained as an emphasizing particle (cf. Dahood, *PAB*, I, p. 177), rendering 'many indeed'.

19. God will give ear: or 'God will hear' (see on 54:2).

he who is enthroned from of old: Gunkel, Kraus read: 'the inhabitant(s) of the East' which is a possible interpretation but the context seems to favour *RSV* (similarly also LXX, T, S, and V). For the idea, see Dt. 33:27; Ps. 9:7 (M.T. 8), 29:10, 74:12.

because they keep no law: the Hebrew *ḥªlîpôṯ* usually means a 'change of garment' (Gen. 45:22) or 'relays' (1 Kg. 5:14 (M.T. 28)), and it comes from the same root as the word 'Caliph' (Arabic *ḥalīfa*) which was used of the *successors* of Muhammad. In 1QM xvi:10 (cf. Yadin, *SWSLSD*, p. 337) the word is employed in a military sense as 'reserve', while in Job 14:14 it may denote 'relief' or 'reward' (cf. Tur-Sinai, op. cit., pp. 236–9). We could render verse 19*c*: 'because (?) there are no changes to them', i.e. they show no change or turning away from their godlessness (similarly Nötscher); there is, however, no parallel for such a usage. A possible paraphrase might be: 'Because they have not received a retribution (for their evil deeds)—they do not fear God'.

Selah: in M.T. occurs after '. . . from of old', i.e. in the middle of a verse; it may well have been misplaced.

A FURTHER DESCRIPTION OF THE UNFAITHFUL FRIEND **20–1**

20. My companion: this is supplied from the context; M.T. simply has 'he stretched out . . .' (so Dahood) which could allude to each of the enemies mentioned in verse 19, but the *RSV* rendering is preferable.

against his friends: *RV* (similarly *RP*) 'against such as were at peace with him' which is a more literal translation than that of *RSV*. Dahood (*PAB*, 1, p. 42) suggests 'against his allies' (*šᵉlūmāyw* from *š-l-m* ('to make a covenant'); cf. Job 22:21).

his covenant: *NEB* 'their promised word'. The Hebrew *bᵉrîṯ* is of uncertain etymology (cf. *HAL*, p. 150), but, essentially, it is a solemn promise which is made binding by an oath (and sacrifices). The *OT bᵉrîṯ* appears in different types, and the two main groups are secular covenants which do not involve the deity as one of the parties concerned, and the religious covenants in which God is the giver of the Covenant. It is doubtful whether there were purely unconditional religious covenants, even though the Abrahamic and Davidic Covenants may appear to be of this type. (For further information, see R. E. Clements, *Abraham and David*, (*SBT*, 2nd ser., 5, 1967).) Our Psalm refers to the so-called secular covenant which also has a religious significance because God is the witness to the Covenant and its guardian; for a detailed discussion, see G. E. Mendenhall, 'Covenant', *IDB*, 1, pp. 714–23; J. Gray,

JJR, pp. 32–5; cf. also G. Quell, '*Diathēkē*', *TDNT*, II, pp. 106–24; K. A. Kitchen, *Ancient Orient and Old Testament* (1966), pp. 90–102.

21. His speech . . .: M.T. has 'Smooth were the buttery (words?) of his mouth'. *RSV* follows some Hebrew MSS. and T, reading *mēḥᵃmāʾōṯ* ('. . . than butter').

yet war was in his heart: Dahood (*PAB*, II, p. 29) renders: 'but his intention was war'. For 'heart', see on 27:3.

softer than oil: this is parallel to 'smoother than butter', and both expressions describe flattering and hypocritical words.

drawn swords: for a similar idea, see 52:2: 'Your tongue is like a sharp razor . . .' (cf. Mic. 5:6 (M.T. 5)).

THE TRUST AND CONFIDENCE IN GOD **22–23**

22. This verse is regarded by some as an oracle of salvation (cf. Kraus, *PBK*, p. 405) uttered by a cultic prophet (?). Verse 23 would be a final expression of trust on the part of the suppliant.

your burden: lit. 'what he has given you' (*RSVm*). LXX (also 1 Pet. 5:7) reads *tēn merimnan* ('(your) care'). The later Greek versions (Aq, Sym, *et al.*) suggest '(Cast (your cause) upon Yahweh for) he loves you' (*yeʾᵉhāḇeḵā*).

the righteous: see on 1:5. God will protect him so that he will not be moved, i.e. he will not meet with a final disaster, although he may be experiencing trouble for the time being. See on 15:5.

23. the lowest pit: LXX suggests 'the pit of destruction' (so also *NEB*) (see on 49:9), but in either case the reference is to Sheol or to the abode of the departed. 'The lowest pit' need not necessarily imply that there were divisions in the netherworld, such as were thought of by the Apocalyptic writers (see D. S. Russell, *MMJA*, pp. 364–6).

shall not live out half their days: i.e. bloodthirsty men (cf. 26:9, 59:2 (M.T. 3), 139:19) and the like shall die before their time. On the other hand, the sign of God's favour is length of days (21:4 (M.T. 5), 91:16).

I will trust in thee: see on 26:1, 37:5.

Psalm 56 In God I Trust

Most scholars regard this Psalm as an Individual Lament (see Introduction, pp. 37ff.), although some commentators (e.g. Briggs, Mowinckel) class it as a National Lamentation (a royal prayer?). The variations in the title, which appear in LXX and T, suggest that the poem came to be interpreted as a communal lament.

Schmidt (*PHAT*, p. 109) has argued that the background of the poem is formed by the false accusations against the Psalmist, and that the lament is a prayer of an accused man. Weiser (*POTL*, p. 422) is of the opinion that the Psalm may have been recited 'in public worship after the prayer had been answered and before the thank-offering'. If so, we must assume that the complaints and appeals to God for help belonged to the original lament which is now quoted or referred to, instead of the traditional account of the adversity. It is equally possible that verses 12–13 express the conviction of the author that he will soon be delivered and that he will yet give thanks to God.

Occasionally the Psalm is divided into two strophes consisting of verses 1–3 and 5–9. Both contain a brief lamentation and an expression of confidence in God, and both end with a refrain (verses 4 and 10–11). To this is added the promise to thank God (verses 12–13).

The date of this composition may be early post-Exilic. The metre is, with a few exceptions, 3 + 3.

To the choirmaster: see Introduction, p. 48.

The Dove . . .: see Introduction, p. 50.

A Miktam of David: see Introduction, pp. 43ff. and 47.

Gath was one of the five principal cities of the Philistines (for its location, see Y. Aharoni, *The Land of the Bible* (1967), pp. 250f.). According to the Biblical tradition, the Philistines originated from Caphtor, i.e. from Crete (Jer. 47:4; Am. 9:7). This may be true of some Philistine elements but it is doubtful whether they *all* came from (or via) Crete. The Philistines were the Pulusatu mentioned in Egyptian sources (from the fifteenth to the twelfth centuries B.C.) and they were part of the so-called 'sea-peoples', who brought down the Hittite empire in Asia Minor and North Syria *c.* 1200 B.C., and who attacked Egypt during the reigns of Merneptah and Rameses III. Later they settled along the coastal plains of Palestine or Canaan, and their main centres were Ashdod, Ashkelon, Ekron, Gath, and Gaza.

The historical note concerning David seems to refer to his flight to Gath mentioned in 1 Sam. 21:10–15. Most scholars rightly regard it as a later gloss.

THE PSALMIST'S COMPLAINT 1–2

1. Be gracious to me: this is a common cry for help in the lamentations, see on 6:2.

God: in the Elohistic psalter (see Introduction, p. 25) this term, *ʾelōhîm*, has in most places supplanted the divine name Yahweh.

for men trample upon me: this introduces the reason for the author's petition. The Hebrew verb *š-ʾ-p* I means 'to crush, trample upon', while the root II denotes 'to gasp, pant'. LXX, S and V follow the former alternative (so also *RP*, *PNT*, Nötscher, *et al.*), while the latter alternative is chosen by Kittel, Gunkel, Kraus, *et al.* The ancient versions and their modern followers may be right.

foemen: (lit. 'warrior'). *RSV* takes the Hebrew word collectively (like *ʾenôš*, 'man', in the preceding sentence; see on 8:4).

2. my enemies: see on 54:4. Weiser suggests 'who lie in wait for me' (*POTL*, p. 421).

all day long: i.e. without ceasing.

proudly: The Hebrew *mārôm* (see on 68:18) is taken by *RSV*, *PNT*, and some exegetes, as an adverbial accusative. Another possibility is to regard it as a designation of Yahweh, i.e. 'O thou most High' (*AV*) or 'O Exalted One' (so Dahood, *PAB*, I, p. 45). The latter alternative may be more likely; as the petition began with the vocative 'O God', so also it concludes with a vocative 'O Exalted One'. Dahood (*PAB*, II, p. 40) transfers it to verse 3.

THE AFFIRMATION OF TRUST 3–4

3. When I am afraid: lit. '(In) the day (that) I am afraid'; a similar construction is found in verse 9*a*. The Psalmist is not overcome by fear, for he overcomes his fear by trust in God (see on 37:5). Weiser (*POTL*, p. 423) makes the apposite comment: 'Trust in God robs fear of its quality of terror'. LXX suggests: 'They (i.e. the enemies) will be afraid, but I shall trust in you', but this seems inferior to M.T. See also 11QPs[a] Plea, ll. 12–13.

4. This verse may have suffered some textual corruption, as can be seen from its counterpart, verses 10–11. McCullough (*PIB*, p. 292) treats verse 4 as a variant of verses 10–11, and as a marginal gloss, while Kirkpatrick, Briggs, *et al.* argue that we are dealing with a genuine refrain.

whose word I praise: *dāḇār* ('word') probably denotes the promises of God to his people, or it may refer to an oracle of salvation which the Psalmist expects to receive shortly (cf. 130:5). For 'praise', see on 119:164.

without a fear: i.e. the fear of God is the true antidote for the fear of men (see on 102:15).

flesh: (*NEB* 'mortal men') see on 38:3. Jacob (*TOTe*, p. 158) suggests that in the *OT* 'flesh is always what distinguishes man qualitatively from God, not in the sense of a matter-spirit dualism, but of a contrast between strength and weakness'. Similarly, in this verse the Psalmist contrasts the essential weakness of the strongest of his oppressors with the all-powerfulness of God. In 2 Chr. 32:8 Hezekiah, the King of Judah, says concerning the mighty Sennacherib, the monarch of Assyria: 'With him is an arm of flesh (i.e. human power); but with us is the LORD our God . . .'.

THE ENEMIES OF THE PSALMIST 5–6

5. they seek to injure my cause: lit. '. . . my words' (see on 119:9); *AV*, *RV* have 'they wrest my words'. Kraus *et al.* emend, since the verb *ᶜ-ṣ-b* usually means to 'grieve, pain'; yet there is another verb *ᶜ-ṣ-b* (cf. *KBL*, p. 725b), 'to shape, twist', hence 'they twist (or 'manipulate') my words' (cf. N. H. Tur-Sinai, *The Book of Job* (1957), p. 177).

all their thoughts: i.e. all their plans are designed to hurt me.

6. They band themselves together: (*yāḡôddû*), this follows the rendition of T and Jerome. Delitzsch considers the M.T. *g-w-r* as synonymous with *ʾ-g-r* ('to gather'). The more common meaning of M.T. *yāḡûrû* would be: 'they stir up strife' (cf. *BDB*, 158b; 140:2 (M.T. 3)).

they lurk: so *Ḳᵉrê* (cf. 10:8); *Kᵉṯîḇ* reads 'they set an ambush (?)'.

they watch my steps: the pronoun 'they' is emphatic since it is represented not only by the verbal form itself but also by *hēmmāh*. Perhaps *hēmmāh* should be taken as an equivalent of the Ugaritic *hm* ('look, behold') (for more details, see Dahood, *PAB*, I, p. 56), and so we could render 'behold, they (even) watch my every step'.

. . . waited for my life: i.e. '. . . my soul' (see on 33:19). The enemies were probably seeking to destroy the Psalmist by means of a legal murder (cf. 1 Kg. 21:8–14).

THE APPEAL TO GOD 7

7. recompense them: i.e. weigh out to them (your justice). *RSV* accepts the common alteration of M.T. *palleṭ* ('deliverance' (?)) to *pallēs* ('weigh') (i.e. recompense). A possible rendering of

M.T. is 'on account of (their) iniquity, can there be any escape for them?' (similarly LXX; cf. *NEB*).
their crime: for *ʾāwen* ('mischief'), see on 36:4.
cast down the peoples: Kirkpatrick (*BPCB*, p. 318) sees here a 'desire for a general judgment of the world' but it need not necessarily indicate that the author lived in the Diaspora, or that he must have been a representative of his people (i.e. the King). The reference to the nations may be part of the cultic language employed by the Psalmist.

THE CERTAINTY OF GOD'S HELP **8–11**

8. . . . count of my tossings: or 'you have taken account of my homelessness' (*nōḏî*; or 'lamentation' (from *n-w-d*, 'to show grief'; cf. *TRP*, p. 21)). In Gen. 4:10 Cain settled in the land of Nod (i.e. in the land of wanderings (?)). Eaton (*PTBC*, p. 149) sees here a reference to certain gestures in the penitential rites.
. . . my tears in thy bottle: in this imaginative metaphor God is pictured as collecting the tears of the afflicted in a bottle, i.e. in a wineskin or waterskin. The point of this word-picture is to emphasize that God is *concerned* with the fortunes of the individual, and that sooner or later full justice will be done.
Are they not in thy book?: this is probably an explanatory gloss (*NEB* omits it) on 'in thy bottle', and it could be rendered: 'Does it not mean "In your book"?' (cf. G. R. Driver, 'Glosses in the Hebrew Text of the Old Testament', *L'Ancien Testament et L'Orient* (Orientalia et Biblica Lovaniensia 1, 1957), p. 130). The book in question is probably similar to the book of remembrance mentioned in Mal. 3:16, or to those in Dan. 7:10 (see on 51:1).

9. will be turned back: i.e. they will be defeated or suffer a reverse in their fortunes; so in 44:10: 'Thou hast made us turn back from the foe', and in 1QM xv:9: 'be not turned back' (i.e. do not flee) (cf. Yadin, *SWSLSD*, p. 332).

10–11. See its variant (?), or the similar refrain, in verse 4. For verse 11, see on 118:6.

THE THANKSGIVING **12–13**

12. The author may mean that he is about to thank God and bring sacrifices, or that he is confident that he will have ample cause to thank God for his deliverance in the near future.
My vows: lit. 'Your vows, (O God, are upon me)', i.e. I am under a moral obligation to perform the vows I made to you

(during the time of my affliction). The Hebrew *nēḏer* may denote both a 'vow' and a 'votive sacrifice' (see on 50:14) as the fulfilment of a promise. See also R. de Vaux, *Studies in Old Testament Sacrifice*, p. 33.

thank offerings: (=*NEB*) or 'praises' (so Dahood), since the Hebrew *tôḏāh* can have either meaning. Both praise and thank-offering were expressions of gratitude for help and favour received (see on 69:30; H.-J. Hermisson, *Sprache und Ritus im Altisraelitischen Kult* (*WMANT*, 19, 1965), pp. 29–41).

13. This verse occurs also in 116:8f.

For thou hast delivered: this is the reason for the Psalmist's thankfulness. There is, however, the question of the tense of this Hebrew verb: some treat it as a prophetic perfect which describes an imminent action (cf. *GK* 106n), or it may refer to something which has already taken place (cf. Kraus, *PBK*, p. 410), so *NEB*. Dahood regards it as a precative perfect (*PAB*, II, p. 48).

from death: i.e. from the danger of death. Any form of trouble can be regarded as a condition of being in the very grasp of death or Sheol. Therefore the deliverance from such dangers can be depicted as salvation from death. See on 40:2, 49:15.

yea, my feet from falling: this seems to be an explanatory gloss meaning (omitted by *NEB*), perhaps: '(Have you) not (delivered) my feet from stumbling?', referring back to verse 6 where the enemies watch his every step. Cf. G. R. Driver, op. cit., p. 130; see on 116:8.

walk before God: i.e. according to his will and in obedience to his law.

in the light of life: or 'in the light of the living'. 'Light' (*ʾôr*) is frequently used as a symbol of life (Job 3:20), happiness (Isa. 9:2), salvation (Isa. 58:8), etc.; in the present context the expression denotes earthly existence as God intended it to be. It brings to mind (by the implicit contrast) also the other possibility: the Sheol existence in 'the land of gloom and deep darkness' (Job 10:21). The expression 'the light of life' is found in 1QS iii:7, where Leaney (*RQM*, p. 143) takes it to mean 'life-giving enlightenment' (cf. also 1QIsa[a] 53:11: 'he shall see light'). Dahood (*PAB*, II, p. 48) has argued that we should read *ʾûr* ('field') instead of M.T. *ʾôr* ('light'), rendering 'in the land of the living', as in 116:9*b*.

Psalm 57 Be Exalted, O God

This Psalm consists of two main parts: a prayer for help (verses 1–4) and a hymnic thanksgiving (verses 7–10). Verses 5 and 11 appear to be the refrain, while verse 6 forms the link between the two principal sections. Some scholars (e.g. Duhm, Briggs) think that this Psalm is a composite work, but the refrain (if such it is) and the reference to 'steadfast love' and 'faithfulness' in both parts may suggest that there is little reason to question the unity of the Psalm. It is true that 57:7–11 (M.T. 8–12) = 108:1–5 (M.T. 2–6), and verse 10 is similar to 36:5 (M.T. 6), but Ps. 108 is obviously a sort of mosaic, and therefore Ps. 57 may be the original source of the common material.

This Psalm is ascribed to David, yet it reflects later cultic traditions of Jerusalem, e.g. the mention of 'Most High' (*ᶜelyôn*), the phrase 'the shadow of thy wings', etc. and therefore a late pre-Exilic date is reasonable (cf. Kraus, *PBK*, p. 412).

The life-setting of this poem may be similar to that of Ps. 56 (see the Introduction to it). Dahood (*PAB*, II, p. 50) calls it 'the lament of a king'. The metre of verses 1–5 and 11–12 is mainly 3 + 3, while verses 6–9 exhibit a 3 + 2 metre.

To the choirmaster: see Introduction, p. 48.

Do Not Destroy: see Introduction, p. 50.

A Miktam of David: see Introduction, pp. 43ff. and 47.

when he fled from Saul: the reference is probably to some incident recorded in 1 Sam. 22–4 (perhaps 22:1), but this historical note seems to be an editorial interpretation of the Psalm.

THE LAMENTATION **1–6**

1. Be merciful: (see on 6:2), i.e. grant (me) your unmerited favour (by saving me). Cf. 1QH xvi:9: 'You have granted me your favour through your spirit of mercy'. See also K. W. Neubauer, *Der Stamm CHNN im Sprachgebrauch des Alten Testaments* (1964), pp. 73–105. Neubauer takes *ḥ-n-n* as the intervention of God to save and to help his faithful servant or nation, so that the *emphasis* is on loyalty rather than on grace and love (p. 104).

my soul: or 'I'. For *nep̱eš*, see on 33:19.

in the shadow of thy wings: i.e. in your protective care; see on 17:8, 36:7. Weiser (*POTL*, p. 427) understands this expression as suggesting that the suppliant is seeking refuge in the Temple.

The Aramaic translator must have found the Psalmist's expression too 'strong', and he rendered it: 'in the shadow of your presence' (*škyn*ᵓ).

the storms of destruction: perhaps, 'the threatening destruction' (see on 52:1).

2. God Most High: the Hebrew *ᵓᵉlōhîm ᶜelyôn* occurs also in 78:56; it is a variation of *yhwh ᶜelyôn* (7:17 (M.T. 18)) and *ᵓēl ᶜelyôn* (78:35). On 'Most High' (*ᶜelyôn*), see on 46:4, 47:2; this term is not found, so far, in the Ugaritic texts (cf. M. H. Pope, *El in the Ugaritic Texts* (*SVT*, 2, 1955), pp. 55–8; see also G. Wanke, *Die Zionstheologie der Korachiten* (*BZAW*, 97, 1966, pp. 46–54).

who fulfils his purpose for me: or 'who avenges me' (for this use of the verb *g-m-r*, see Dahood, *PAB*, I, p. 45). The latter suggestion is more likely because the object of the verb ('his purpose') is not expressed in M.T. LXX must have read a different verb, probably *g-m-l* ('to deal bountifully, repay'), but M.T. is more plausible (cf. 135:8).

3. He will send from heaven: once again the object is not expressed, but it must be the same as that of the parallel phrase at the end of this verse. God will send forth his steadfast love (see on 26:3) and his faithfulness (see on 25:5). This pair, God's Covenant loyalty and his dependableness, are portrayed as if they were actual messengers of God; see on 43:3.

save me: see on 54:1.

. . . put to shame: lit. 'he will say harsh things against . . .'; and what God says is already in the process of being done. The word of God is creative, and this is well illustrated by the Priestly creation story in Gen. 1. The same thought is also reflected in the Psalter, e.g. 'he spoke, and it came to be; he commanded, and it stood forth' (33:9; cf. 107:20, 145:15,18).

4. I lie in the midst of lions: the Hebrew *napšî* ('my soul') is used as a periphrasis for the personal pronoun (see on 33:19) Schmidt (*PHAT*, p. 110) has suggested that the Psalmist must have been accused of some crime, and that one way to find the guilt or innocence of the indicted man was to make him spend the night in the sanctuary. During the night God would test the accused (see on 17:3) and the verdict would be given in the morning (cf. 17:15, 59:16 (M.T. 17); 11QPs[a] 154:18f.). Schmidt thinks that the accusers, too, may have stayed overnight at the sanctuary, and therefore verse 4*a* would appropriately express the feelings of the 'Daniel' of the Psalter (cf. Dan. 6:16–24). This reconstruction is ingenious, but the metaphor may simply denote that the poet in his day-to-day life was surrounded by vicious enemies.

The verse is, however, rather obscure, and another possible rendering may be: 'My soul (i.e. I) is among lions, I lie among them that are greedy to devour' (M.T. 'that are on fire'). Some scholars emend M.T. *lōh^{a}ṭîm* ('(that) are aflame') into *lō^{ca}ṭîm* ('(that) greedily devour'), but the same meaning could be obtained without emendation (cf. *KBL*, p. 474).

their teeth . . .: this continues the lion-metaphor which is a common picture of dangerous and savage enemies (cf. 7:2 (M.T. 3), 10:9, 17:12). Their teeth are like spears (see on 35:3) and arrows (see on 11:2), and their tongues are like sharp swords (see on 44:6). The metaphor alludes to the destructive activities of the enemies who use their tongue (i.e. their false accusations and slanders) to bring about the ruin of the oppressed man.

5. Be exalted, O God: Weiser, Kraus, *et al.*, see here an allusion to a theophany (cf. *POTL*, p. 427) but it is equally possible that, in his prayer, the Psalmist has used the *language* of a theophany to refer to the manifestation of God's justice in saving him from his enemies (cf. 7:6 (M.T. 7), 18:46 (M.T. 47), 21:13 (M.T. 14)). Dahood (*PAB*, II, p. 52) suggests '(your) stature is . . .'.

thy glory: see on 26:8. 'Glory' gives a man importance and standing in the community, and it may express itself in such things as riches (Gen. 13:2), status (Gen. 45:13), prestige (Isa. 21:16), etc. In respect of God, one could say that glory is 'that which makes God impressive to man, the force of his self-manifestation' (G. v. Rad, '*Doxa*', *TDNT*, II, p. 238). Thus God 'gets glory' by means of a victory over the Pharaoh and his forces (Exod. 14:4,17,18), or his glory can be seen in the meteorological phenomena (97:2–5); the exercising of his glory before Israel may involve the punishment of certain offenders (Lev. 10:1ff.). It is possible that in our verse the Psalmist is longing for the manifestation of God's just rule which, at the same time, would bring deliverance to him (cf. 138:5).

6. This verse can be regarded as forming the transition from the lamentation in verses 1–4 to the thanksgiving in verses 7–10, while verses 5 and 11 may be the refrain. Some exegetes transpose verses 5 and 6.

They set a net: usually it is said that the enemies *hide* a net (cf. 9:15 (M.T. 16), 31:4 (M.T. 5), 35:7,8). In this verse the opponents are described as hunters (a frequent metaphor in the Psalter) who use their nets (see on 9:15) and pits (see on 7:15) to 'catch' their human prey.
my soul was bowed down: LXX has 'they have bowed down my soul' (i.e. me; Dahood 'my neck'), suggesting *kāp^{e}pû* for *kāp̄ap̄*, which may be right (so Nötscher, Kraus, *et al.*). For the verb *k-p-p*, see on 145:14.
they have fallen into it themselves: i.e. wickedness is self-destructive. This is not seen as an impersonal law but as the result of the personal intervention of God because evil and wickedness are opposed to the divine will. See also 7:15 (M.T. 16), 9:15 (M.T. 16). The thought that evil recoils upon the head of its doer was a favourite theme in the Wisdom circles; cf. the Words of Ahikar (*DOTT*, p. 274 (XXXVIII)): '. . . he that diggeth a pit for his neighbour filleth it with his own body'.
Selah: see Introduction, pp. 48f.

THE THANKSGIVING **7–11**
These verses are found in 108:1–5 (M.T. 2–6) with minor variations.

7. My heart is steadfast: i.e. 'I am true and loyal to you, and no circumstances can disturb my trust in you' (cf. 112:7f.), hence 'I am calm (because of what God is)'. For a contrast, see 78:37: 'Their heart was not steadfast toward him; they were not true to his covenant' (cf. 1QH vii:13,25). The repetition of 'my heart is steadfast' is omitted in 108:1 (M.T. 2) but is retained by LXX and S.
I will sing . . .: i.e. I will praise you in song (cf. 9:11 (M.T. 12); see on 68:4).
make melody: see on 30:4, 66:4.

8. Awake my soul: lit. 'Awake my glory (*k^{e}ḇôḏî*)'. 'My glory' is usually taken as a poetic expression for 'my soul' (see on 7:5, 16:9, 30:12).
harp and lyre: see on 33:2 and 98:5 respectively. The Psalmist wishes to offer his thanksgiving to the accompaniment of music which sometimes may not have been much more than an 'organized noisemaking' (cf. Jg. 7:18), and one of its functions may have been to inspire the participants to greater efforts; thus Elisha found prophetic inspiration during the playing of a minstrel (2 Kg. 3:13).

I will awake the dawn: this may be taken to mean that the Psalmist will rise *before* the dawn, instead of letting the dawn wake him. Kraus (*PBK*, p. 414) suggests that originally the expression may have been understood mythologically (see on 110:3). *NEB* has '. . . at dawn of day'.

9. I will give thanks: see on 18:49.

among the peoples . . . the nations: McCullough regards this as 'the hyperbole of a joyful heart' (*PIB*, p. 301); this expression may have been derived from the language appropriate to the Royal Psalms (cf. 9:11 (M.T. 12), 18:50 (M.T. 51)).

10. This verse (practically identical with 36:5 (M.T. 6)) gives the reason for praising God, and is hymnic in nature. The poet extols the *magnitude* of God's Covenant loyalty (see on 26:3, 51:1) and his constancy (see on 25:5).

11. This concluding verse is a repetition of verse 5.

Psalm 58 SURELY THERE IS A GOD WHO JUDGES ON EARTH

Most exegetes class this Psalm as a lament and, in the absence of any personal allusions, the poem may well be a National Lamentation (see Introduction, p. 39). In some ways it is reminiscent of Ps. 14; there are also points of contact with the prophetic and sapiential literature.

The title ascribes this lament to David, and Briggs (*CECBP*, II, p. 42) is sure that it is 'doubtless one of the oldest in the Psalter' written in the early period of the Hebrew monarchy. Yet there is little evidence on which to base our judgment concerning the date of this Psalm; many scholars assign it to the post-Exilic period and the general tenor of the Psalm may point in the same direction.

In verses 1–2 the Psalmist adopts the role of a prosecutor in a court, and he charges the divine beings (or human dignitaries?) with the neglect and perversion of justice on earth. In verses 3–5 we find a brief description of the evil-doers, which emphasizes their practically innate wickedness. The next section (verses 6–9) contains seven curses (a *complete* malediction?) on the depraved, while in verses 10–11 the righteous man looks forward to the day of God's vengeance. This characterizes the poem as an imprecatory Psalm (cf. H. H. Rowley, *WAI*, pp. 267ff.).

The prevailing metre is 4+4 (and 4+3).

To the choirmaster: see Introduction, p. 48.

Do Not Destroy: see Introduction, p. 50.
A Miktam of David: see Introduction, pp. 43ff. and 47.

THE UNJUST JUDGES **1–2**

1. you gods: M.T. has *ʾēlem* which may mean 'silence' (so *RV*), as in the title of Ps. 56, but this does not give a satisfactory sense in the present context. *AV*, following Ḳimḥi, has 'O congregation' (from *ʾ-l-m*, 'to bind') but the usual explanation is that M.T. originally had *ʾēlîm* ('gods') which was later modified because of its possible mythological implications. Yet from various *OT* passages it is clear that the Israelites believed that God was surrounded by various divine beings who did his bidding (cf. Exod. 15:11; Dt. 32:8; Job 1:6, 38:7; Ps. 82:1,6, 138:1). The *ʾēlîm* in 58:1 may be the angels of the nations who, it is suggested, were originally national deities, but in the course of time they were reduced to the ranks of angels. This situation was not regarded as inconsistent with Yahweh's supremacy. For a more detailed account of the guardian angels of the nations, see Russell, *MMJA*, pp. 244–9; Mansoor, *TH*, pp. 77–84. It was the duty of the divine beings or angels both to judge rightly and to see that justice was done and respected by the 'sons of men' (see Ps. 82). Some scholars have interpreted these 'gods' in the present verse as 'mighty lords' (*RSVm*) or 'mighty (ones)' (cf. Kissane, *BP*, p. 250), i.e. princes (*NEB* 'rulers'), judges, etc. In the light of Ps. 82 it seems that the *ʾēlîm* must be understood as divine beings who had a certain delegated authority and great responsibility for the wrongs on earth.

2. This verse continues the accusation in verse 1.
in your hearts: (see on 27:3); at the very centre of your decisions. S suggests *kullᵉkem* ('all of you') for *bᵉlēḇ* ('in your heart'), which gives a reasonable sense: 'Nay, all of you work unjust deeds'.
deal out violence: the Hebrew *p-l-s* means 'to weigh out', and in this context it suggests 'to mete out justice'. This expression may involve an oxymoron (i.e. the combination of two contradictory terms) which could be rendered 'with injustice (you pretend) to mete out justice'. For weighing as a metaphor of judgment, see Job 31:6; Ps. 62:9 (M.T. 10); Prov. 16:2, 21:2, 24:12; Dan. 5:27; Mt. 7:2. Similar metaphors are also found in Egypt (cf. *ANEP*, pl. 639).

Although evil is traced back to the divine beings, this does not absolve the human agents.

THE CONDUCT OF THE WICKED **3–5**

3. The wicked: see on 1:1, 28:3. Kissane (*BP*, p. 251) assumes that the wicked are the same as the 'mighty ones' addressed in verses 1–2, but this is less likely.

go astray: or 'are estranged', i.e. they have placed themselves outside the Covenant relationship (as far as the positive aspects of the Covenant are concerned). Cf. Eph. 4:18: 'they are strangers to the life that is in God' (*NEB*).

they err from their birth: Gunkel, Kraus, *et al.* take the verb with what precedes: '. . . they err from the womb, they speak lies from their birth'. In any case the expression is a poetic exaggeration: if taken literally, it would come near to what is known, theologically, as 'original sin' (cf. H. W. Robinson, *The Christian Doctrine of Man* (1911), pp. 56f.). See on 51:5.

. . . speaking lies: M.T. could be rendered: 'the speakers of lies', i.e. liars who err from their very birth (cf. Klopfenstein, *LAT*, p. 227). LXX has 'they speak lies' (i.e. *dibbᵉrû* for M.T. *dōḇᵉrê*).

4. They have venom: the reference is probably to their venomous words (slander, false accusation, curses, and the like). Cf. 1QH v:27: 'a lying tongue like the venom of serpents . . .'.

serpent: *nāḥāš* is a general name for the various species of snakes. It is very likely that the popular belief was that all snakes were poisonous (cf. 140:3 (M.T. 4)).

the deaf adder: the Hebrew *peṯen* may denote the Egyptian cobra (so Nötscher), but the exact identification remains uncertain. The word *peṯen* is also found in the Ugaritic texts as *bṯn* meaning 'serpent, dragon' (cf. Gordon, *UT*, p. 378). Rabbi Solomon 'explained' the stopping of the ears by saying that the snake put one ear to the ground and stopped the other with its tail (cf. *HDB*, IV, p. 460b).

5. The wicked are incorrigible and therefore they are like the 'deaf adder' which cannot be charmed or influenced, and which therefore remains dangerous. Snake-charming is also mentioned in Ec. 10:11; Isa. 3:3; Jer. 8:17; Sir. 12:13, and it may have been more than a mere entertainment. The obtaining of 'oracles' from snakes was not an unknown phenomenon in the ancient world (cf. W. McKane, *Prophets and Wise Men* (*SBT* 44, 1965), p. 96, n.3).

the cunning enchanter: probably 'he who cunningly binds by magic spells' (cf. S. R. Driver, *Deuteronomy* (*ICC*, 1896), p. 225).

THE PETITION TO GOD **6–9**

Occasionally this passage is referred to as the 'sevenfold curse' (so Rhodes), while Weiser (*POTL*, p. 432) describes it as a 'prayer of vengeance'. The maledictions mentioned in verses 6–9 belong to what is called the East Semitic type of curse where the reliance for the execution of the curse is placed upon the deity. The imprecations are not effective in their own right, as if by some power inherent in the words themselves (as in the so-called West Semitic type of curse), but their performance is left to God. On the other hand, evil words and curses (irrespective of the "theology" behind them) were always potentially dangerous. For more details, see J. Gray, 'Blessing and Curse', *DB*, pp. 109f.; H. C. Brichto, *The Problem of 'Curse' in the Hebrew Bible* (1963); D. R. Hillers, *Treaty Curses and the Old Testament Prophets* (1964).

Since the wicked are obstinate in their wickedness, they must be rendered powerless or destroyed. The malediction is often the last line of defence, and it is employed when other measures have proved inadequate, or when any other protection is lacking.

6. break the teeth . . .: (=*NEB*) LXX reads 'God has broken . . .' which would point to a Hebrew perfect of certainty (cf. *GK* 106n). The poet uses the lion-metaphor (cf. 57:4 (M.T. 5)), and the point of the petition is that the enemies should be rendered harmless (see on 3:7). It is less likely that the author was thinking of the poisonous snakes. The 'young lions' in verse 6*b* is understood by *RP* as 'the ungodly' (*NEB* 'the unbelievers'), associating the M.T. *kᵉpîrîm* with the Arabic *kafara* ('to become an unbeliever'), and reading *kōpᵉrîm* (cf. 34:10 (M.T. 11), 35:17; R. Gordis, *Louis Ginzberg Jubilee Volume* (1945), pp. 180f.).

7. The imprecations seem to increase in their intensity but this may be a stylistic feature rather than a blue-print for God's retribution.

Let them vanish like water: the writer may have had in mind the wadi that appears like a torrential stream during the rainy season but dries up in the summer (cf. Job. 6:15ff.). 'Water' often has a rich symbolic meaning; sometimes it may be a sign of cleansing (Ezek. 36:25), or a 'water of bitterness', bringing a curse (Num. 5:18). It may also denote what is essential to life (Isa. 3:1), or it may represent a threat to life (104:9; Isa. 43:2). Sometimes 'water' is used to suggest instability and weakness, as in 2 Sam. 14:14: '. . . we are like water spilt on the ground, which cannot be gathered up again'. See on 69:1.

like grass . . .: verse *7b* is rather obscure in M.T., and it may be textually corrupt. A possible literal rendering would be: 'he shall tread (aim?) his arrow (so *Keṯîḇ* and LXX; *Ḳerê*, T, and S have 'arrows') like the ones (that) are cut off (wither?)'. Perhaps we should emend it to read 'they shall be trodden down like grass, they shall wither' (*yiddāreḵû ḵemô ḥāṣîr yiṯmōlālû*); cf. Winton Thomas, *TRP*, p. 22.

8. like the snail: G. R. Driver seems right in suggesting that the Hebrew *šabbelûl* is a 'miscarriage'; this would be parallel to 'the untimely birth' in the next line (for details, see 'Studies in the Vocabulary of the Old Testament. V', *JTS*, XXXIV (1933), pp. 41–4). Verse 8 could be rendered: '(Let them be) like a miscarriage (which) melts away, (let them be like) the untimely birth (that) never sees the sun'. From Job 3:16 and Ec. 6:3 it appears that the comparison of stillbirth suggests something that is as if it had not been (cf. Job 10:18f.). So the Psalmist's wish is that the wicked might become as if they had never existed, their name and their influence gone for ever.

9. This verse, too, is in some textual disorder; Driver's suggestion (op. cit., p. 44) provides a satisfactory solution of the difficulties, with comparatively little emendation. The verse could be translated: 'Before they perceive (their impending doom) he will tear them up, like weed(s) he will sweep them away in (his) burning anger'; the only changes are *yisterēm kāʾāṭāḏ* for M.T. *sîrōṯêḵem ʾāṭāḏ*, and *bemô* for the second *kemô*. For another reasonable alternative, see Winton Thomas, *TRP*, p. 22.

THE VINDICATION OF THE RIGHTEOUS **10–11**

10. The righteous: see on 1:5. Gunkel takes it as a collective noun (like 'the wicked' in the following line; see on 28:3). The righteous rejoice primarily because God is justified, rather than because the wicked are punished. H. A. Brongers ('Die Rache- und Fluchpsalmen im Alten Testament', *OTS*, XIII (1963), pp. 41f.) mentions three points which are essential for the understanding of the imprecatory Psalms, namely, what concerns Israel concerns also Yahweh, and vice versa; furthermore, for the Israelites, God's justice had to be vindicated here and now, and, finally, Yahweh had called every Israelite to be an upholder of righteousness, consequently those who destroy the peace (*šālôm*) of the community must be either changed or destroyed. We may also add a fourth point; curses or maledictions have a wide application in the ancient Near East. They could serve as protective devices in various private agreements or national treaties, or they could be used to ensure the reliability of certain statements and actions. Sometimes curses were uttered as part of the religious ritual (cf. Dt. 27:11–26); therefore maledictions would cause no surprise to the Israelite worshippers. We need not whitewash sentiments which are obviously pre-Christian in more than one sense, but it would be equally wrong to misunderstand these Psalms. The wicked could well be described as breakers of the Covenant oath, and therefore the Psalmist simply asks God to take the evil-doers at their word; this is hardly different from taking action against a perjurer in modern courts.

in the blood of the wicked: this is clearly a hyperbolic expression which affirms, in its own way, that the righteous will see the total defeat of wrong and evil (see on 68:24). Similarly, when Job experienced his great prosperity, it could be said that his 'steps were washed with milk' (Job 29:6). In the Ugaritic texts (*Baal* v, ii:13f., 26f.) it is Anat, the sister and consort of Baal, who wades through the blood of the fallen warriors.

11. a reward for the righteous: or, in other words, 'a man reaps what he sows' (Gal. 6:7 (*NEB*)). Cf. Job 4:8; Ps. 128:2; Isa. 3:10f.

there is a God . . .: LXX reads '. . . who judges them (i.e. *šōpᵉṭām*) in the land'. Cf. 94:2.

Psalm 59 PROTECT ME, O MY STRENGTH

This is a lament, but scholarly opinion differs as to whether it should be described as an Individual or National Lamentation. It exhibits the characteristics of both types and therefore its classification depends upon the particular aspects emphasized. Mowinckel, Birkeland, *et al.* see the poem as an expression of collective experience, while Gunkel, Kraus, *et al.* regard it as an Individual Lament. Some other exegetes follow Schmidt (*PHAT*, pp. 113f.) in interpreting this Psalm as a prayer of an accused man (so also Deissler) who has sought God's help in the sanctuary (see on 57:4), and who is awaiting his vindication. At the same time Schmidt suggests that it was later adapted for the needs of the whole nation, and that verses 5, 8–11, and 13*b* are secondary. It is possible, however, that the national features of the Psalm were derived from the cultic language; since Yahweh is the ruler of the whole world, his intervention even in the affairs of the individual has also a universalistic aspect (cf. Klopfenstein, *LAT*, pp. 299f.).

The structure of the Psalm has been described as 'curious' (cf. Oesterley, *TP*, p. 294). There are what appear to be two sets of refrains (or variants?): verses 6–7 and 14–15, and verses 9–10 and 17. Weiser (*POTL*, p. 435) may be right in dividing the Psalm into two main parts (verses 1–10 and 11–17), in which the lamentation elements are separated from those of the thanksgiving, by verses 6–7 and 14–15.

The Psalm offers little clue as to its date; Kraus thinks that the poem may be of pre-Exilic origin, but equally well it may be assigned to the early post-Exilic period.

The prevailing metre of the Psalm is 3 + 3.

To the choirmaster: see Introduction, p. 48.

Do Not Destroy: see Introduction, p. 50.

A Miktam of David: see Introduction, pp. 43ff. and 47.

when Saul sent men . . .: the incident alluded to is described in 1 Sam. 19:11–17, but most commentators regard this note about the historical situation as an interpretative addition.

THE FOURFOLD PETITION FOR HELP **1–2**

1. Deliver me: this is a frequent call for help, especially in the Lamentations (cf. 7:1 (M.T. 2), 25:20, 31:2,15 (M.T. 3,16), 39:8 (M.T. 9), 51:14 (M.T. 16), etc.); see on 107:6.

O my God: LXX, S, and V have 'O God', which points to an original reading 'Yahweh'.

protect me: lit. 'set me on high' (i.e. beyond the reach of the adversary). God himself is this inaccessible place or stronghold (*miśgāḇ*), as in verses 9 and 17 (cf. 9:9 (M.T. 10), 18:2 (M.T. 3), 46:7 (M.T. 8), etc.).

2. who work evil: for *pōᶜalê ᵓāwen*, see on 28:3. It is very likely that the four different terms for the evil-doers in verses 1–2 are synonymous, and refer to the oppressors in general without specifying particular types (cf. H. H. Rowley, *WAI*, pp. 182f.). On the other hand, Kraus (*PBK*, p. 422) sees in these terms a clear movement towards the climax, 'the men of blood'; yet the former alternative seems more likely.

bloodthirsty men: lit. 'men of blood' (= *NEB*). They need not have been actual murderers (i.e. men guilty of bloodshed); rather they were unscrupulous persons for whom the end justified all possible means (cf. 5:6 (M.T. 7)).

THE LAMENT AND PROTESTATION OF INNOCENCE **3–4a**

3. they lie in wait . . .: i.e. they set an ambush for the Psalmist (cf. Prov. 1:11; Mic. 7:2); the description is probably metaphorical.

my life: lit. 'my soul' (see on 33:19).

fierce men: or 'mighty men' (cf. 18:17*a* (M.T. 18*a*)).

for no transgression . . .: i.e. for no wrong on my part. Dahood (*PAB*, I, p. 94) takes the pronominal suffix in a local sense, '(there is) no transgression in me'. For *pešaᶜ* ('transgression'), see on 32:1.

sin: see on 51:2.

4a. no fault of mine: or 'there is no crookedness in me' (see on 32:1). The point of the three synonyms for sin is to emphasize that the Psalmist has neither committed a wrong against his enemies, nor offended God; therefore he is suffering innocently from an unprovoked attack.

they run: probably 'they attack', so in Job 16:14: 'he runs upon me like a warrior' (cf. Job 15:26). Probably this and the following verb ('make ready') are co-ordinated (cf. *GK* 120d): 'they rush to make ready (to attack)'.

THE APPEAL TO GOD **4b–5**

4b. Rouse thyself: see on 7:6, 44:23. Since God is the one who 'will neither slumber nor sleep' (121:4), the expression must be taken metaphorically, i.e. it *appears* that God has been inattentive to the prayers of the needy.

5. LORD God of hosts: Kraus *et al.* delete *ᵓᵉlôhîm* ('God') as a variant of 'Yahweh', and so also the following phrase 'art God of Israel' (*ᵓᵉlōhê yiśrāᵓēl*). The term 'Yahweh of hosts', or one of its variants, occurs some 279 times in the *OT* (so *KBL*, p. 791a), while in the Psalter it is found only 15 times. Therefore it seems that most of the Psalmists (as also Hosea, Deuteronomy, and Ezekiel) avoided the use of this epithet for reasons which we can hardly guess (cf. Ringgren, *IR*, pp. 68ff.; G. Wanke, *Die Zionstheologie der Korachiten*, *BZAW*, 97, 1966, pp. 40–6).

Awake: see verse 4*b* and 7:6 (M.T. 7).

all the nations: *gôy* (plural *gôyîm*) can be used also of Israel, as in 33:12: 'Blessed is the nation (*haggôy*) whose God is the LORD' (cf. Exod. 19:6; Ps. 83:4 (M.T. 5), 106:5, etc.), but more often it came to denote the non-Israelite nations. In rabbinical Hebrew *gôy* is the usual term for 'Gentile'. This reference to the nations is problematic. Either the Psalm was a national lamentation, or the references to the 'nations' are later additions to adapt an individual lament for the use of the community. Perhaps the right answer is found along the lines suggested by Weiser (*POTL*, p. 434) that 'the personal request of the worshipper is incorporated in the larger context of the cult community' and that this accounts for the nationalistic traits in the Psalm.

spare none: i.e. do not show favour. For *ḥ-n-n* ('to favour'), see on 6:2, 57:1.

who treacherously plot evil: this phrase is a *hapax legomenon* in the *OT* (cf. 25:3). LXX renders it by the same expression as 'those who work evil' in verse 2, and probably rightly so. For *ʾāwen* ('evil'), see on 36:4.

Selah: see Introduction, pp. 48f.

THE ENEMIES **6–7**

6. they come back: or 'they go to and fro' (*RP*) taking the verb *š-w-b* in the sense of the Arabic *sāba* ('to run about, wander'), which is more fitting in the present context. Dahood (*PAB*, II, p. 69): 'they wait' (*š-w-b* as a by-form of *y-š-b*).

like dogs: i.e. the enemies are compared to wild dogs (see on 22:16) which haunted the refuse dumps, and which were regarded as unclean and savage. Their activities would be thought offensive and disgusting. This simile is further elaborated in verses 7 and 15. The term 'dog' may also be used to signify 'male temple-prostitutes', although the term need not necessarily be derogatory (cf. D. Winton Thomas, 'Kelebh, "Dog": its Origin and Some Usages of it in the Old Testament', *VT*, x (1960), pp. 424ff.).

7. bellowing with their mouths: Weiser, Kraus, *et al.* suggest 'they slaver with . . .', which is a possible rendering of the Hebrew verb *n-b-ᶜ*. It is just possible that the simile of the dog has been changed for a metaphorical description of the wicked (so Kirkpatrick, Briggs). Yet the elaboration of verse 14 in verse 15 suggests that verse 7 also may be an expansion of verse 6 (=verse 14). See *NEB*.

snarling with their lips: M.T. has 'swords are in their lips'.

Some exegetes suggest 'taunts (*ḥᵃrāp̱ôṯ* for M.T. *ḥᵃrāḇôṯ*) from their lips, (taking the preposition *bᵉ* in the sense of 'from', as in Ugaritic). The alteration is not really necessary, because the tongue is often described as a sharp weapon (cf. 52:2 (M.T. 4), 55:21 (M.T. 22), 57:4 (M.T. 5), 64:3 (M.T. 4), etc.).
for 'Who' . . .: this is a rhetorical question which may well be outside the metre, as a later addition. It probably reflects the thinking of the enemies who scorn at the possibility of a divine retribution (cf. 10:4,11, 64:6 (M.T. 7), 73:11, 94:7).

THE EXPRESSION OF CONFIDENCE **8–10**

8. But thou: this brings out the contrast between the imaginary world of the evil-doers and the reality of God.
laugh at them: this may be a traditional description of God's reaction against the schemes of the wicked (see 2:4, 37:13; cf. 2 Kg. 19:21). For the question of the anthropomorphism, see on 35:23. When the godless are arrogant and blasphemous, it is natural for the Psalmist to assert that it is God who will have the laugh of the wicked.
nations: see verse 5.

9. O my Strength: so many Hebrew MSS., LXX, T, and V; M.T. has 'His strength' (so also *AV*), but the former reading seems to be right in view of the parallel in verse 17. This description of God is intended to bring to mind the 'fierce men' or 'mighty men' (*ᶜazzîm*) in verse 3. Although these evildoers may be strong, God is the 'Strong One' *par excellence.*
I will sing praises . . .: so S, following verse 17. M.T. has: 'I will watch for you, O my Strength' (see above); this may point back to the title of the Psalm: 'when Saul sent to *watch* his house'. Therefore it is possible that the M.T. variant is a later modification of the original (see verse 17).
my fortress: alluding to verse 1*b*.

10. . . . steadfast love: see on 26:3. M.T. could be rendered 'My gracious God' (so Kraus, Nötscher).
will meet me: i.e. as a friend, or 'will come to help' (cf. Rowley, *FI*, p. 26, n.6). Cf. Isa. 21:14; for the opposite idea cf. Dt. 23:4.
look in triumph: lit. 'he made me see . . .'; cf. 54:7 (M.T. 9). This same idiom is also found on the Moabite Stone (cf. *DOTT*, pp. 196, 197).

THE PRAYER FOR THE PUNISHMENT OF THE ENEMIES **11–13**

11. Slay them not . . .: i.e. the enemy should not be destroyed suddenly, for in such a case the value of the punishment as a warning to others might soon be forgotten. For a parallel, see Exod. 9:16: '. . . but for this purpose have I let you live, to show you my power . . .' (cf. 1 Sam. 17:46). The prayer need not necessarily suggest that the wicked should linger on in some terrible suffering; rather it asks for a reversal in their fortunes which would concern primarily their wealth and status. The former alternative, however, is not impossible. Verse 11 does not contradict verse 13, which may suggest that the end of the divine punishment will be a final destruction of the evil-doers. Another probable suggestion is that the negative *ᵓal* ('not') should be taken as an asseverative particle, hence 'Do indeed slay them' (cf. Dahood, *UHP*, p. 22; *Biblica*, XLIV (1963), p. 294, but see *PAB*, II, p. 71).

make them totter: or 'scatter them, cause them to wander about with no settled home' (cf. Num. 32:13; 2 Sam. 15:20; Am. 8:12). Thus they would be living witnesses to the reality of God's retribution.

by thy power: or 'by your army' (so Cheyne, Briggs), but this seems less likely.

and bring them down: i.e. overthrow them, or bring them down to Sheol (cf. 55:23 (M.T. 24)).

our shield: see on 3:3.

12. For the sin . . .: the literal rendering is rather tautologous: 'The sin of their mouth is the word of their lips' (so Weiser). Cheyne (*BPPI*, p. 164) offers a good paraphrase 'Their mouth sins by each word of their lips'.

let them be trapped . . .: or '. . . caught in their own pride'. The Hebrew *gāᵓôn* ('exaltation, pride') can be used both in a good sense (cf. 47:4 (M.T. 5); Isa. 60:15), and in a bad connotation, as here (cf. Prov. 16:18: 'Pride goes before destruction'). The only truly exalted being is God, and therefore man's pride or his self-exaltation practically always brings him into rebellion against God (Isa. 2:11). The wicked in their pride have no regard for God, and their dominant thought is: 'There is no God' (10:4). If this 'hope' of theirs is false, then they are indeed caught by their own words and ensnared by their own pride.

cursing and lies: this may suggest false accusations (cf. verses

3*b* and 4*a*; see also 10:7f.) by means of which the enemies seek the life of the Psalmist. The cursing may refer to the utterance of certain words supposed to have a magical power; this could well be the case if the Psalm were a national lament.

13. consume them: the object 'them' is correctly supplied from the context. The repetition of 'consume' serves the purpose of emphasis.

that men may know . . .: this suggests that God is the judge of the whole world (see verse 5); cf. 1 Sam. 17:46.

God rules over Jacob: (see on 20:1), or '. . . is the ruler over . . .'.

to the ends of the earth: i.e. in all the inhabited world, or in all the earth (cf. 2:8, 22:27 (M.T. 28), 67:7 (M.T. 8), 72:8, 98:3).

Selah: see Introduction, pp. 48f.

THE REFRAIN (?) **14–15**

See verse 6. It is possible that these verses form a refrain, although some exegetes regard verses 6–7 and 14–15 as two variants. *NEB* omits verse 14, and transfers verse 15 to follow verse 6.

they growl: M.T. has 'they tarry all night' (*AVm*, *RV*). *RSV* follows LXX and V, deriving the verb from *l-w-n* ('to murmur').

THE EXPRESSION OF THANKS **16–17**

16. But I, in contrast to the arrogant wickedness of the godless, will sing praises to God.

of thy might: *ʿuzzeḵā* is a reference to 'my Strength' (*ʿuzzî*) in verse 9 (cf. verse 17).

in the morning: see on 57:4. The Psalmist is probably not thinking of the morning prayers or the morning worship as such, but perhaps of his response to God's judgment which may have been given in the morning (cf. 30:5 (M.T. 6)).

fortress: see verse 1*b*. In the time of distress (cf. 102:2) God has been the Psalmist's place of refuge.

17. See the parallel verse 9.

the God who shows me steadfast love: perhaps 'for God, my gracious God, has been my fortress'. Comparing verses 9–10 with verse 17, it seems that the latter may have been incompletely preserved. *NEB* omits verse 17*c*.

Psalm 60 WITH GOD WE SHALL YET TRIUMPH

This Psalm is clearly a Communal Lament, uttered in a time of great national distress on some day of fasting (see Introduction, p. 39). The nation had lost a war against an unspecified enemy (Edom?), and the Psalm offers a prayer to God for help and deliverance. The superscription ascribes it to David, and sets it against the background of David's wars. Most scholars, however, treat this information as secondary, because the context of the Psalm itself has little in common with the historical note. Verses 6–7 may actually imply that Northern Israel was already in the hands of foreign peoples, and so the date would be after 722 B.C. but hardly as late as the Maccabean period (as suggested by Hitzig, Duhm).

Verses 1–5 form a lament describing the calamity of the nation, ending with a prayer for salvation (verse 5). This is followed by an encouraging oracle (verses 6–8) which emphasizes God's lordship over Canaan as well as over Edom, Moab, and Philistia. The last part of the Psalm (verses 9–12) contains elements of lamentation (verses 9–11), and concludes with an assertion of confidence in God (verse 12). It has been suggested that the oracle may be 'a quotation of a poem, otherwise lost, which described the triumphs of Yahweh' (Oesterley, *TP*, p. 297), or an older oracle which belonged to the sacred traditions of the sanctuary. The metre of the lamentation part of the Psalm is 3 + 3, while that of the oracle is 3 + 3 + 3; this fact may point to different origins. The content of the oracle is not very appropriate to the lamentation, but this would be understandable if the divine utterance came from an older source (cf. H. H. Rowley, *WAI*, pp. 166f.). The repetition of 60:5–12 (M.T. 7–14) in 108:6–13 (M.T. 7–14) is a good example of how existing material could be re-applied in a new context.

To the choirmaster: see Introduction, p. 48.

Shushan Eduth: see Introduction, p. 50.

A Miktam of David: see Introduction, pp. 43ff. and 47.

for instruction: see Introduction, p. 48.

Aram-naharaim: or 'Aram of the Two Rivers'; this is not Central Mesopotamia but N. Mesopotamia, the ancient home of the patriarchs (Gen. 24:10).

Aram-zobah was an Aramaean kingdom N. of Damascus,

probably in the valley between Lebanon and Anti-Lebanon. The wars of David against the Aramaean kingdoms are described in 2 Sam. 8:3–8, 10:6–18; 1 Chr. 18:3–11, 19:6–19.

twelve thousand of Edom: the figure given in 2 Sam. 8:13 and 1 Chr. 18:12 is 'eighteen thousand'. The variation may be due to a textual error. If the passages quoted allude to the same event, the victory is ascribed to different persons. 1 Chr. 18:12 attributes it to Abishai, the son of Zeruiah, and the brother of Joab, while in 2 Sam. 8:13 it was David who achieved the triumph over the Edomites. The differences need not be regarded as contradictions, but they may be different ways of reporting the same event.

the Valley of Salt is probably the region immediately S. of the Dead Sea, and not the wadi of that name E. of Beersheba.

THE PLIGHT OF GOD'S PEOPLE **1–5**

1. thou hast rejected us: i.e. the nation is fully aware of having been cast off by God (see on 44:9), and at least some of its members are primarily concerned not with the defeat as such but with its theological implications (cf. 74:1, 77:7 (M.T. 8), 89:38 (M.T. 39)). This divine abandonment was not regarded as a final break in the relationships, but rather as a temporary condition.

broken our defences: lit. 'you have broken us' or '. . . made a breach (in our ranks)' (cf. 2 Sam. 5:20). The expression suggests that God has brought a great disaster upon the people (cf. Jg. 21:15).

thou hast been angry: the verb *ʾ-n-p* ('to be angry') is a denominative verb from *ʾap̱* ('nose, anger'), and strictly speaking it would refer to snorting in anger or 'to the dilation of the nostril in (*ʾap̱*) anger' (J. Gray, *I & II Kings* (1964), p. 211). The same verb is also used on the Moabite Stone (line 5) to express the wrath of Chemosh, the god of Moab, towards his people (cf. *DOTT*, p. 196).

oh, restore us: Dahood (*UHP*, p. 29) suggests 'you turned from us', taking the preposition *l*ᵉ in the sense of 'from', as in Ugaritic (cf. Gordon, *UT*, p. 425). This gives a reasonable sense but it is uncertain whether the intensive form of *š-w-b* can have this meaning.

2. This verse is a metaphorical description of the disaster: the world of the nation has collapsed as if by some terrifying earthquake.

the land: T has 'the land of Israel', which is a correct interpretation.

thou hast rent it open: the verb *p-ṣ-m* ('to split open') is a *hapax legomenon* in the *OT*, but it probably refers to the cracks in the ground which could be seen after a severe earthquake. One such event is described by Josephus in *Antiquities of the Jews* (xv, v:2). LXX renders the above phrase: 'you have thrown it into utter confusion'.

repair its breaches: literally it might refer to the rifts in the ground, but here it is used metaphorically of the calamity brought about by God; the people are asking God for a healing, or a reversal of their fortunes.

3. **Thou hast made thy people suffer . . .:** the Psalmist does not say that the distress has been undeserved, unlike the author of Ps. 44 (verses 17–22). M.T. could be rendered literally: 'You have made your people see hard things' (similarly *AV*, *RV*); but the parallel line (verse 3*b*) suggests that *r-ʾ-h* ('to see') should be understood as *r-w-h* ('to drink one's fill'); cf. G. R. Driver, *JTS*, xxxvi (1935), pp. 152ff.; D. Winton Thomas, *VT*, xii (1962), pp. 499f. *RP* has: 'Thou hast made thy people to drink a cup of bitterness' (cf. *TRP*, p. 23).

wine to drink . . .: or 'to drink the wine of staggering' (for a similar phrase, see Isa. 51:17,22). The Psalmist uses the well-known image of the cup of God's wrath, to depict the punishment of his people. The origin of this figure is not known, but it could have been derived from the practice of ordeal by drinking the water of bitterness (see Num. 5:11–31; cf. J. Bright, *Jeremiah* (*AB* 21, 1965), p. 161). The opposite of the cup of wrath is the cup of salvation (116:13).

4. **set up a banner:** lit. 'To those who fear you (see on 34:7,9), you have given a banner'. Kraus thinks of it as a signal for flight, as in Jer. 4:6: 'Raise a standard (*nēs*) toward Zion, flee for safety . . .'. Other exegetes have suggested the emendation *mānôs* ('refuge') instead of M.T. *nēs* ('banner'), but no change seems to be required.

to rally to it: or 'to flee (from the bow)'.

from the bow: the Hebrew *ḳōšeṭ* is a *hapax legomenon* in the *OT*; it may be the Aramaic form of the Hebrew *ḳešeṯ* ('bow'). This interpretation is also suggested by most of the ancient versions. For the idiom, see Isa. 31:8. *AV*, *RV* render: 'because of the truth', which gives little sense in the present context.

Selah: see Introduction, pp. 48f.

5. thy beloved: (cf. Dt. 33:12; Isa. 5:1; Jer. 11:15), i.e. the people of God. This expression conveys something of the faith of the Psalmist who, in spite of all the distress and disgrace, can still think of his people as the beloved of God.

give victory: or 'save' (*AV*, *RV*); see on 54:1.

by thy right hand: (see on 20:6), i.e. by your might.

answer us: so *K^e^ṯîḇ*; *Ḳ^e^rê* and the versions read 'answer me', thinking perhaps of David as the author of the Psalm. The divine answer expected would be deliverance and victory over the enemies. Dahood 'grant us triumph' (*PAB*, II, p. 79).

THE ORACLE OF HOPE **6–8**

6. God has spoken in his sanctuary: or '. . . by his holiness' which might suggest that God has sworn by his holiness, as in 89:35 (M.T. 36); Am. 4:2 (cf. van Imschoot, *ThOT*, I, p. 40). This phrase forms the introductory formula to the oracle which was uttered either by a priest or a cultic prophet. *NEB*, Dahood render: '. . . from his sanctuary'.

with exultation: lit. 'I will exult' (*RV*). In 108:7 (M.T. 8) one MS. reads *w^e^ʾa^c^aleh* ('and I will go up'), which is followed by *RP*, *NEB*.

I will divide up: this is a declaration of Yahweh's ownership of the land. Weiser (*POTL*, p. 440) thinks that the figure of speech is derived 'from the sacred tradition of the distribution of the land . . . settled afresh every seven years at the autumnal feast'.

Shechem was an ancient city which the Hebrews took over from the Canaanites. It was situated some forty miles N. of Jerusalem, near the pass between Mount Gerizim and Mount Ebal. It is usually identified with *Tell Balāṭa*.

Vale of Succoth: the town of Succoth was located on the east side of Jordan, N. of the river Jabbok where it enters the plain of the Ghor (cf. Baly, *GB*, p. 229a). The reason for linking Shechem and Succoth is not apparent. Some see here an allusion to the Jacob tradition in Gen. 33:17f., claiming ancient territorial rights. The two locations may be used to denote the whole land, as *pars pro toto*.

7. Gilead: its borders may have changed from time to time, but it could be roughly defined as being confined by the river Arnon on the south, the Jordan valley on the west, the river Yarmuk on the north, and the desert on the east. Gilead was a

mountainous region, rising up to some 3,000 feet. The southern part of this territory was occupied by Reuben and Gad, while the northern part was the possession of Manasseh (cf. Y. Aharoni, *The Land of the Bible* (1967), pp. 35f.).
Manasseh was one of the Israelite tribes, and also the territory occupied by this tribe. In Palestine Manasseh inhabited the northern part of the hill country of Ephraim, as well as part of Gilead (cf. Aharoni, op. cit., pp. 26f.).
Ephraim may denote the hill country of Ephraim, or the whole of Northern Israel, as in this verse (so Kraus).
my helmet: lit. 'the protection of my head'. The helmet was usually made of leather, but kings and other important persons may have used bronze helmets (1 Sam. 17:5,38; *ANEP*, pll. 160, 174–5). The word-picture presents Yahweh as a warrior whose helmet is Northern Israel, and whose commander's staff is Judah (cf. Gen. 49:10; Zech. 9:13).
my sceptre: this is a symbol of military or royal authority.

8. Moab is my washbasin: Gunkel, Kraus, *et al.* read 'The sea of Moab' (or 'the waters of . . .'); this involves a change of *yām mô'āḇ* or *mê mô'āḇ* for the M.T. *mô'āḇ*, and the reference might be to the Dead Sea. This metaphor is usually taken to signify the disgrace and vassalage of Moab (and Edom).
I cast my shoe: this is, most likely, a symbolic action denoting ownership (cf. Ru. 4:7; see also Dt. 11:24).
over Philistia I shout in triumph: so *RSV*, following S and 108:9 (M.T. 10). M.T. has 'Philistia, shout because of me!' (similarly *AV*, *RV*); Weiser (*POTL*, p. 437) renders it 'acclaim me with shouts of joy . . .'.

THE PRAYER FOR HELP **9–12**

9. Who will bring me . . .: the speaker may be the King or some other representative of the people. The verse may suggest either that the survivors of the disaster are intending to flee to Edom and its fortified capital (?), or, more likely, that they are planning or contemplating an attack (a punitive expedition?) against Edom, even though the nation has been heavily defeated quite recently. This latter alternative receives some support from the following verses. In either case it is impossible to identify the actual situation; it is very likely that we do not possess an account of *all* the major military events in Israel's history.

10. Hast thou not rejected us . . .: Weiser, following LXX and V, renders: 'Wilt thou not do it, O God', which is a possible translation; but *RSV* is more likely (cf. verse 1*a*).

Thou dost not go forth . . .: see on 44:9.

11. help against the foe: or 'help from trouble' (LXX and V); the former alternative is supported by verse 12*b*.

for vain is the help of man: this statement provides the motive for God's intervention. For 'help', see on 35:3. The phrase '. . . help of man' is found only here, but the idea itself is more frequent (cf. 33:16f., 146:3).

12. The Psalm ends on a note of confidence and certainty.

we shall do valiantly: i.e. we shall triumph or perform deeds of valour (cf. 1 Sam. 14:48; Ps. 118:15,16).

tread down our foes: see on 44:5.

Psalm 61 God is My Refuge

This Psalm seems to be an Individual Lament, although some commentators (e.g. Mowinckel, Eaton) would class it as a Royal Psalm. It is also possible to regard this poem as a Thanksgiving (so Weiser), but this seems less likely.

A problem is posed by verses 6–7 which express a prayer for the King. Gunkel regarded this section as a later interpolation, but it has been pointed out (see Kraus, *PBK*, p. 434) that such intercessions for the King are not unknown in Babylonian prayers, and therefore verses 6–7 may be an integral part of the original Psalm. Furthermore, in view of the great significance of the Davidic monarch, such a supplication would seem to be quite natural. The King was, after all, Yahweh's representative on earth, and upon him rested the responsibility for the administration of justice in his kingdom (cf. Ps. 72). Thus the Psalm may be a Lament of the Individual (see Introduction, pp. 37ff.) which also includes an intercession for the King. Kraus (*PBK*, p. 433) suggests that it was uttered by the suppliant far from the Temple, but, on the other hand, it is possible that the worshipper had already sought refuge in the sanctuary. Mowinckel (*PIW*, I, p. 220) interprets the poem as a Royal Psalm, and he sees in it a prayer which accompanied the sacrifices made by the King, before the forthcoming battle and far away from the Temple. This suggestion seems, however, less suitable.

The Psalm is hardly of Davidic origin, although it belongs to the Jerusalem traditions, and is pre-Exilic in its date. It begins with a call for help (verses 1–2), and gives a passing glimpse at the distress of the Psalmist. Verses 3–4 utter a firm trust in God and a fervent wish for a better future. This is followed by an expression of confidence that God has heard the prayer (verse 5); or it could be taken as a continuation of the supplication. In verses 6–7 we find a brief prayer on behalf of the King, and the Psalm concludes on a note of trust and certitude (verse 8).

To the choirmaster: see Introduction, p. 48.
stringed instruments: see Introduction, p. 48.
A Psalm of David: see Introduction, pp. 43ff. and 46.

THE INVOCATION OF GOD 1–2

1. Hear my cry . . .: this is a customary opening of the Psalms of Lamentation. The Israelite Psalmists do not begin their laments with a lengthy list of honorific divine names, as is often the case in the Babylonian prayers (cf. Gunkel, *EP*, p. 213).
listen to my prayer: i.e. 'attend to my cry, and answer me by helping me'.

2. from the end of the earth: this may mean 'from a distant place' (cf. Dt. 28:49; Ps. 46:9 (M.T. 10)), and consequently some scholars have argued that the Psalmist was in Exile (so Baethgen, Calès), or far away from the Temple (so Gunkel, Mowinckel). Dahood (*PAB*, I, pp. 118, 260) sees here a reference to the edge of the netherworld (cf. Barth, *ETKD*, p. 113). Eichrodt also (*TOT*, II, p. 95) regards *ʾereṣ* ('earth') as another name for the underworld. For other possible examples, see Dahood (*PAB*, I, p. 106). For disease, etc., as a form of death, see on 40:2.
when my heart is faint: a similar expression occurs in 1QH viii:29: 'For (my life) has come near to the pit (i.e. Sheol) . . . and my soul faints day and night' (cf. 77:3 (M.T. 4), 142:3 (M.T. 4), 143:4; Jon. 2:7 (M.T. 8)). The phrase probably suggests that not only has the Psalmist's courage failed (so Dahood), but also his very vitality is ebbing away, and the nearness of Sheol is becoming more and more manifested. For 'heart', see on 27:3.
the rock that is higher than I: or '. . . that is too high for me'. Dahood (*PAB*, I, p. 260) renders 'Onto a lofty rock you lead me from it' (i.e. from the edge of the underworld). This gives a good sense, but it is not certain that the translation itself can be justified. LXX has 'You lifted me up on a rock . . ' (i.e. *t^erômemēnî* for M.T. *yārûm mimmennî*). The verse suggests that when a man finds

himself in extreme trouble, it is only God who can bring him to safety.

THE TRUST IN GOD 3–4

This confidence in the divine help forms the very basis of this prayer (see Gunkel, *EP*, p. 232). At the same time it also shows something of the relevance of God to the Psalmist.

3. my refuge: LXX has 'my hope'. The Hebrew *maḥseh* is a frequent term in the Psalter to describe God as the refuge *par excellence* (46:1 (M.T. 2), 62:8 (M.T. 9), 71:7, 73:28, 91:2,9, etc.). Kraus, Weiser, *et al.* see here a reference to the protection offered by the sanctuary and the presence of God.

a strong tower: or 'a tower of protection' (see on 21:1). In Prov. 18:10 it is the name of Yahweh that is 'a strong tower' and 'the righteous man runs into it and is safe' (cf. 1QSb v:23; 1 QH vii:8).

against the enemy: this may suggest that the distress of the Psalmist was caused by a particular enemy, or enemies (taking the singular noun collectively). Dahood (*PAB*, I, p. 105) regards *ʾôyēḇ* as *the* Enemy, i.e. Death.

4. thy tent: *ʾōhel* is the usual term for the dwelling of the nomad; it could also denote the 'tent of meeting' (cf. Exod. 33:7–11; Num. 11:16f.; Clements, *GT*, pp. 28–39). The same word is used in the Ugaritic texts to signify the dwelling of a deity (cf. *Keret* III, iii:18). The 'tent' may be an archaic term applied to the Temple (see on 15:1, 27:5; cf. Isa. 33:20). It is less likely that it is a metaphorical description of divine hospitality and protection (so Cohen), or that it suggests that the author 'wants to be a priest in God's tent for ever' (Rhodes, *LBCP*, p. 96), or that it refers to God's celestial abode (so Dahood).

for ever: see on 9:5. Verse 4*a* is reminiscent of 23:6: 'and I shall dwell in the house of the LORD for ever'.

Oh to be safe: or 'Let me find refuge'.

the shelter of thy wings: see on 36:7. T has 'in the shadow of your presence (*škyntk*)' which is an obvious Targumic alteration.

Selah: see Introduction, pp. 48f.

THE CERTAINTY OF BEING HEARD 5

This verse may describe the certainty that God will answer the prayer, or it may refer to the received prayer in retrospect; the former alternative seems more likely.

For thou . . . hast heard: Dahood (*PAB*, I, p. 19) regards the Hebrew *kî* (*RSV* 'for') as an emphatic particle followed by an optative perfect ('Oh that you would hear . . .'). If this or a similar interpretation is right, then the Psalm must be a lament and not a thanksgiving.

my vows: (*nēḏer*), see on 50:14, 56:12. The vow is a promise, usually made in time of trouble. Occasionally it refers to a 'bargain' between God and the worshipper (cf. Gen. 28:20ff.; Jg. 11:30f.), but in the Psalter the vows may be on a higher plane: not a conditional promise of a gift, but an expression of certainty that God has already accepted the prayer. Eichrodt (*TOT*, I, p. 145) suggests that 'a real element in the vow is the spontaneous conviction that God's gifts require from men not merely words, but deeds of gratitude . . .' (cf. Gunkel, *EP*, p. 247–50).

thou hast given me: or 'Oh that you would give me . . .' (see above).

the heritage: *RP* 'the desire' (similarly Gunkel, Kraus, *et al.*), i.e. the Hebrew *yršt* is taken as a by-form of *ʾršt* ('desire') (cf. 21:2 (M.T. 3); Winton Thomas, *TRP*, p. 23; Gordon, *UT*, p. 367). Perhaps we should render 'you have granted (or 'Oh that you would grant') the desire of. . . .'. Weiser (*POTL*, p. 444) retains the usual rendering 'heritage', and he links it with the redistribution of the land which, in his opinion, was carried out 'every seven years in the autumn within the framework of the Covenant Festival . . .' (ibid, p. 44).

who fear thy name: see on 34:7,9. See also J. Becker, *Gottesfurcht im Alten Testament* (*Analecta Biblica* 25, 1965).

THE INTERCESSION FOR THE KING **6–7**

6. Prolong the life of . . .: lit. 'Add days to the days of . . .', i.e. grant a long life to the King, and stability to his dynasty. T sees here a reference to the Messiah, and renders '. . . the King, Messiah'. For the above idiom, cf. 2 Kg. 20:6.

. . . to all generations: *RV* 'His years shall be as many generations'; the writer had in mind not only the reigning King but also his house (cf. 1 Kg. 1:31; Neh. 2:3).

7. enthroned for ever before God: this is another reference to the royal house, as in 89:36: 'His line shall endure for ever, his throne as long as the sun before me'. 'Before God' means to enjoy his favour and blessings (cf. 56:13 (M.T. 14)). *NEB:* 'may he dwell in God's presence for ever'.

steadfast love: see on 26:3.
faithfulness: see on 25:5; here it means 'reliability' as opposed to fickleness (cf. Prov. 20:28).
watch over him: M.T. reads: 'Prepare . . . (that) they may keep him', but the verb *man* ('prepare') is omitted by some Hebrew MSS., Sym, and Jerome.

THE CONFIDENCE OF THE PSALMIST **8**

8. sing praises: see on 30:4, 66:4. The author is certain that he will have ample cause to sing God's praises for ever (i.e. as long as he lives). This is not primarily a duty to be performed but a privilege, for it 'is good to give thanks to the LORD' (92:1).
to thy name: see on 20:1.
vows: see verse 5.

Psalm 62 God Only is My Rock

This Psalm is characterized by a serene trust in God, and therefore it could be classed as an Individual Psalm of Confidence (see Introduction, p. 39). It is difficult to outline the actual situation which might have given rise to this Psalm, and the author does not elaborate the description of his distress. We can deduce, however, that he had been harassed by certain treacherous and unscrupulous enemies, and that he had taken refuge in the sanctuary (verses 2, 6, 7). There he received divine oracle(s), or he learned from the cult the relevance of God to his problems. Although the practical solution of his difficulties may have been as yet in the future, he had gained a new trust in God, and he was able to share with others his faith in the God of his salvation.

The title ascribes the Psalm to David, but there is nothing in the composition itself to demand a Davidic authorship. The date of the Psalm is uncertain; Kraus suggests that it may be either late pre-Exilic or early post-Exilic; the latter alternative seems the more likely.

The Psalm can be divided into three main parts. Verses 1–7 express the author's confidence in God, in spite of the circumstances which were anything but favourable. In verses 8–10 the writer addresses the worshipping community, and he exhorts his fellow-worshippers (in the style of a Wisdom teacher) to trust God above everything else. Finally, verses 11–12 briefly summarize the lesson learnt from the divine revelation.

The metre of the Psalm is irregular.
To the choirmaster: see Introduction, p. 48.
Jeduthun: see Introduction, p. 46.
A Psalm of David: see Introduction, pp. 43ff. and 46.

THE FAITH FOR TIMES OF TROUBLE **1–7**

1. It is possible that verses 1–2 and 5–6 form a sort of refrain, or they are variants on the same theme. Another possibility is that they represent the so-called 'correspondence of beginning and end' (cf. N. H. Ridderbos, *OTS*, XIII (1963), p. 46). This need not imply that verses 1–6 (or 7) form an independent Psalm; rather they comprise a distinct part of the poem.
alone translates the Hebrew *ʾaḵ*, which can be used either with an asseverative ('surely, truly') or with a restrictive force ('but, only'). In this Psalm *ʾaḵ* is found six times at the beginnings of verses 1, 2, 4, 5, 6, and 9; its purpose may be to set the tone for the whole Psalm: none but God will prevail; while a man, in *opposition* to God, is nothing.
my soul waits in silence: lit. 'silence (is) my soul', which seems rather odd. In the parallel verse 5 we have the imperative 'be silent' (*dômmî*) instead of 'silence' (*dûmiyyāh*), which may be the right reading. Dahood (*PAB*, I, p. 24) has suggested that the Hebrew *d-m-m* may be associated with the Ugaritic *dmm* I, 'to cry' (cf. Gordon, *UT*, p. 385), hence we could render the verse: 'My soul, cry only unto God . . .' (cf. *HAL*, p. 217b). See, however, *PAB*, II, pp. 90f.
from him comes my salvation: or we might add, with verse 5, the conjunction *kî* ('for'; so LXX, S, and V) and translate 'for from him . . .'. For 'my salvation' (see on 35:3) verse 5 has 'my hope' which is an expectation of good, hence a synonym of 'my salvation (-to-come)'.

2. my rock: see on 42:9. This is an appellation of Yahweh, and it probably portrays the divine strength and constancy. The impressive descriptive titles of Yahweh must be seen in contrast with the essential nothingness of man when he is estranged from God, the ground of his being (see verses 9–10).
. . . my salvation: i.e. only God can deliver the needy person (see on 27:1, 119:81).
my fortress: (see on 59:1), this suggests that God both gives refuge to the oppressed and protects him.
. . . greatly moved: i.e. although he is troubled by adversity,

this state of affairs will not last for ever; he may be shaken but not broken. Kraus, *NEB*, *et al.* delete *rabbāh* ('greatly') which is not found in the corresponding verse 6.

3. . . . set upon: the Hebrew *t^ehôṯ^eṯû* is of uncertain origin. According to *BDB* (p. 223b) it is to be derived from *h-w-t* ('to shout') (cf. *HAL*, p. 233a; see also the Ugaritic *hwt* ('word'), hence 'to rush upon one with shouts'). *KBL* (p. 243) links it with *h-t-t* ('to speak continually') of which the intensive form of the verb might mean 'to overwhelm with reproaches'. LXX has *epitithesthe* ('. . . attack'). *NEB* has '. . . assail'.

to shatter him: lit. 'you (plural) shall be slain' or '(that) you may slay (him)', reading *t^eraṣṣ^eḥû* (so also the text of Ben Naphtali, LXX, and V). According to J. J. Stamm (*The Ten Commandments in Recent Research* (*SBT*, 2nd ser. 2, 1967), p. 99) the verb *r-ṣ-ḥ* 'only occurs when it is a matter of killing or murdering a personal enemy' (the one exception being Num. 35:30). It denotes primarily an illegal killing, whether it is a murder or manslaughter (cf. Dt. 4:41f.), both of which are harmful to the community.

a leaning wall: this may be a description of the persecuted man rather than of the enemies (so Dahood). The simile depicts utter weakness, and Kirkpatrick (*BPCB*, p. 349) states that it can be said of a man at the point of death: 'The wall is bowing'. For a contrast, see Jer. 15:20: 'And I will make you to this people a fortified wall of bronze'.

a tottering fence: better 'a broken-down parapet' (cf. 18:29 (M.T. 30); CD iv:12).

4. from his eminence: LXX 'my honour'. This may suggest that the troubled man was a person of importance. On the other hand, Weiser thinks that the eminence of the Psalmist was nothing more than the respect which might have been given to any God-fearing man. Some exegetes suggest *maššû'ôṯ* ('deceptions') for M.T. *miśś^e'ēṯô* ('from his exaltation'), and they render 'They only plan deceptions, they delight in thrusting (him) down'.

they take pleasure in falsehood: perhaps 'falsehood' belongs to the next sentence, 'Falsely they bless . . .' (so Gunkel, Kraus), in which case the last two phrases of verse 4 are parallel.

inwardly they curse: the behaviour of the enemies is that of hypocrites (see 12:2 (M.T. 3), 28:3, 55:21 (M.T. 22)). Outwardly they bless their victim (or they praise him) but their real intention is to do him harm by resorting to what might be called a magical use of the curse (cf. Mowinckel, *PIW*, ii, p. 3).

5–6. For the exegesis, see verses 1–2.

7. my honour: the Hebrew *kāḇôḏ* ('honour, glory') is not simply a personal reputation, but it includes everything that makes a man important and gives him a standing in the community.

my mighty rock: this is similar to 'a strong tower' (cf. 61:3 (M.T. 4); 1QH ix:28). LXX and V have 'the God of my help'.

my refuge: see on 61:3. LXX reads 'my hope' which is probably an interpretation of M.T.

THE EXHORTATION OF THE PEOPLE **8–10**

8. Trust in him and not in material things, human power, or anything else. See on 26:1, 28:7.

at all times: LXX has 'all the congregation of . . .' which suggests the Hebrew *kol* *ᶜᵃḏaṯ*; this may well be right (so also V).

pour out your heart: i.e. give utterance to all your wishes and hopes (cf. 42:4 (M.T. 5)), or appeal to God with your prayers (cf. 102:1 (M.T. 2), 142:2 (M.T. 3)).

refuge for us: see verse 7. For a similar idea cf. 46:7,11 (M.T. 8, 12).

Selah: see Introduction, pp. 48f.

9. Men of low estate: *bᵉnê ʾāḏām* (see on 49:2) (*NEB* 'men') may simply be a general term for mankind. The same may be true of *bᵉnê ʾîš* ('men of high estate'; see on 4:2). Men as such are a mere breath (i.e. ephemeral) and they present a deceptive picture (cf. 1QH vii:32). This may be intended as a contrast to God who is like a mighty rock (verse 7) and a fortress (verses 2 and 6). Yet even the mortal man can share in what God is, when the latter becomes *his* 'mighty rock' and *his* 'fortress'.

in the balances they go up: (see on 58:2). The idiom of weighing a man or his heart (cf. Prov. 16:2, 21:2, 24:12) may be derived from Egyptian sources (cf. *ANEP*, pl. 639). The allusion in our verse is to the divine judgment in this life (cf. Job. 31:6; 1QS ix:12) and not to a reckoning in the underworld, as in Egyptian thought.

lighter than a breath: or 'they are altogether nothing', i.e. they have no weight at all (cf. Isa. 41:24), and therefore they are the unrighteous (cf. 1 Enoch 41:1, 61:8). LXX reads 'they (are made) of vanity altogether'.

10. Put no confidence in extortion: this is the negative aspect of the exhortation given in verse 8: 'Trust in *him* at all times'; the same verb is used in both phrases. 'Extortion' (*ᶜōšeḳ*) can be the actual oppression (73:8; Jer. 6:6, 22:17), or the gain derived from it, as here (cf. Ec. 7:7).
set no vain hopes . . .: i.e. do not become nothing by trying to gain something by means of robbery (cf. Ezek. 22:29).
if riches increase: material prosperity is not regarded as evil in itself, but it is wrong to set one's heart on it, or to let wealth be the *decisive* factor in one's life. Riches are the gift of God to be enjoyed and shared, but God alone can provide true security. See 1 Tim. 6:17, which probably alludes to this verse.

GOD HAS SPOKEN **11–12**
This section begins with the so-called formula of the graded numerical sayings (cf. W. M. W. Roth, *Numerical Sayings in the Old Testament* (*SVT*, 13, 1965), p. 55). The 'numerical values' of these sayings are often parallel to each other, and the greater numeral is the one intended.

11. Once God has spoken: in view of the parallelism and due to the literary form, the Psalmist seems to have in mind *two* divine utterances (i.e. 'twice have I heard this'). God has spoken and the Psalmist has learned (i.e. heard). It is less certain whether the reference is to oracles of salvation granted to the Psalmist, or to the cultic recital of Yahweh's mighty deeds (cf. Ps. 136), from which he has learned two things in particular: the power of God and his perfect Covenant loyalty.
twice have I heard this: T has a characteristic expansion: 'Twice I have heard this from the mouth of Moses, the great Teacher'.
power belongs to God: i.e. Yahweh is not only loyal to his people, but he is also able to fulfil his promises and to take action against any Covenant-breakers.

12. steadfast love: see on 26:3.
thou dost requite a man: i.e. God is true to his Covenant in that he punishes the iniquity of the rebellious and blesses those who love him and keep his commandments (Exod. 20:5f.; Dt. 5:9f.; cf. Prov. 24:12).

Psalm 63 God has been My Help

This Psalm is traditionally ascribed to David, who is said to have composed it while he was in the Wilderness of Judah, probably fleeing from Absalom and his army. The contents of the Psalm itself show that this must be a later interpretation of the poem, which may have originally been a Prayer of an accused man. It could be classed as an Individual Lament (see Introduction, pp. 37ff.).

The composition includes various elements: verses 1–2 (or at least verse 1) are characteristic of a lamentation, while verses 3–7 could well belong to a thanksgiving; in verses 8–10 we find expressions of confidence, similar to those of a Psalm of trust. The final verse contains a 'dart prayer' for the King (verse 11*a*), and the last two phrases compare the final prospects for the righteous and the liars respectively.

Some commentators have rearranged the verses, e.g. Taylor (*PIB*, p. 327) suggests that the sequence should be 1–2; 6–8; 4, 5, 3; 9–10; 11*c*; 11*ab*. This proposal is slightly superior to the M.T. order, but this is no proof of its originality.

The Psalm is pre-Exilic; Oesterley associates it with Jehoiachin in the Babylonian exile, but the exegesis of the Psalm seems to refute any such suggestion.

The metre of the composition is mainly 3 + 3.

A Psalm of David: see Introduction, pp. 43ff. and 46.

the Wilderness of Judah was not a strictly defined region. G. A. Smith (*The Historical Geography of the Holy Land*, 5th edn (1897), p. 263) locates it between the central plateau and the Dead Sea (cf. Jos. 15:61), while Jg. 1:16 links it with the Negeb in southern Judah; Baly (*GB*, p. 297) identifies it with Jeshimon, the Dead Sea desert. For 'wilderness', see on 55:7.

It is not clear what particular incident is suggested by this historical note. Kraus (*PBK*, p. 441) thinks of 1 Sam. 23:14 or 1 Sam. 24:2, while Kirkpatrick associates it with David's flight from Absalom.

The Psalmist's Thirst for God 1–2

1. O God: this was originally 'O Yahweh', because in the Elohistic psalter (Ps. 42–83) the divine name 'Yahweh' has been changed, in most cases, into 'God' (*ʾelōhîm*); hence the name 'Elohistic psalter'.

thou art my God: Gunkel, Kraus, *et al.* regard 'thou' as belonging to the next phrase, emphasizing the verbal suffix; if so, we could render 'O God, my God, you (alone) I seek' (similarly LXX and V).

I seek: the verb used is not the cultic *b-ḳ-š* (see on 27:8), but the verb *š-ḥ-r* which seems to belong to Wisdom literature (Job 7:21, 8:5, 24:5; Prov. 1:28, 7:15, 8:17); it describes one's turning to Yahweh in times of trouble. This verb is often regarded as a denominative from *šaḥar* ('dawn'); hence 'to look for dawn' and 'to seek early' (cf. *BDB*, p. 1007).

my soul thirsts for thee: for a similar idea, see on 42:2, 143:6 (cf. 84:2 (M.T. 3)). Thirst is a metaphor of one's most imperative need, and therefore a good description of the righteous man's longing for God. For 'soul', see on 33:10.

my flesh faints for thee: the verb *k-m-h* is a *hapax legomenon* in the *OT*, but its Arabic cognate can mean 'to be pale (of face)' while the corresponding Syriac verb suggests 'to be blind, dark'. 'Flesh' (see on 38:3) and 'soul' (see on 33:19) simply denote the *whole* man.

weary land: (cf. 143:6; Isa. 32:2), i.e. a land that is 'weary' for the lack of water. This waterless desert is *not* the place where the Psalmist has fled for refuge, but it is part of the metaphor. The poet is as thirsty for God as an exhausted wanderer is for water in a parched desert.

2. I have looked upon thee: this is usually understood as a reference to a theophany in the Temple (cf. Isa. 6:1ff.). The verb *ḥ-z-h* is often used as a technical term for receiving prophetic visions (cf. Johnson, *CPAI*, pp. 12ff.); the participle *ḥōzeh* is one of the names for a 'seer'. Yet the allusion in verse 2 need not be to a theophany or a vision, but it may suggest that the Psalmist is seeking help and protection, or that he has experienced the presence of God through the cultic acts, symbols, and institutions (e.g. the right of asylum). The expression can also imply that the author is looking for God's deliverance (cf. 5:3 (M.T. 4), 27:4; Hab. 2:1; van Imschoot, *ThOT*, I, p. 209).

thy power and glory: Kissane (*BP*, p. 269) thinks of 'the manifestation of God's omnipotence in the psalmist's favour . . .', while Weiser (*POTL*, p. 455) suggests that 'God revealed his "power and glory" to the congregation in the theophany'. One could regard the Ark of the Covenant, as a symbol of God's presence and his 'power and glory' (cf. 1 Sam. 4:21; Ps. 24:7,

78:61, 132:8), or the 'glory and power' could be perceived in the protection afforded by the sanctuary.

GOD AS THE PSALMIST'S HELPER **3–8**

3. thy steadfast love: (see on 26:3). This is the author's supreme good, and to him it is more precious than life itself. In the *OT* in general, life is 'the greatest good of all' (v. Rad, *PHOE*, p. 259) but the Psalmist has become convinced that the *only* priceless possession is communion with God (cf. Eichrodt, *TOT*, II, p. 489). Life without the divine *ḥesed* ('Covenant loyalty') is worse than death itself. God's Covenant loyalty cannot be experienced (so it was believed) in the grave (cf. 88:11 (M.T. 12)), but it is far more terrifying to be alive and yet miss the love of God.

my lips will praise thee: here 'lips' are mentioned as active in praise, but the *whole* person is meant (cf. Johnson, *VITAI*, p. 46). The verb *š-b-ḥ* is probably an Aramaism; it is found in the Psalter (5 times) as well as in 1 Chr. 16:35; Ec. 4:2, 8:15. In 117:1 it is parallel to *h-l-l*, which is the usual word for praising God (see on 119:164).

4. I will bless thee: see on 104:1. This blessing or praising God will be his life-long privilege (cf. 104:33, 146:2), not merely an occasional duty.

I will lift up my hands: for this customary attitude of the worshipper in prayer, see on 28:2 (cf. 1 Tim. 2:8). It is not so much a symbol of an uplifted heart (so Kirkpatrick) as a sign of an expectant trust that one's empty hands will be 'filled' with divine blessings. It is questionable, however, to what extent the worshippers were aware of the original significance of various cultic symbols and actions.

call on thy name: lit. 'I will lift up my hands in thy name' (*AV*, *RV*), i.e. I will utter my prayer as I call Yahweh by pronouncing his name. For 'name', see on 20:1; cf. also van Imschoot, *ThOT*, I, pp. 195–9.

5. My soul is feasted: or 'My soul shall be satisfied . . .', i.e. I shall be spiritually refreshed (so v. Rad, *PHOE*, p. 259, who sees here a spiritualization of the sacrificial meal). Strictly speaking, no fat of any animal was to be eaten by the Israelites (Lev. 7:23), for it was *taboo* to men; 'all fat is the LORD's' (Lev. 3:16), just like all blood. The 'marrow' (*ḥēleḇ*) and 'fat' (*dešen*; see on 36:8) are more or less synonymous, and some exegetes delete the latter as a gloss. It is more likely, however, that both terms denote the choicest food in general, and should not be taken literally (cf. Gen. 45:18).

my mouth: may simply be a roundabout expression for the first person pronoun, 'I'. LXX omits 'my mouth', and makes 'lips of great joy' the subject of the verb 'to praise'.

praises thee: or 'shall praise . . .'. For the verb *h-l-l*, see on 119:164. The object 'thee' is supplied from the context, while LXX adds *to onoma sou*, 'your name'.

6. when I think of thee: lit. 'when I remember . . .' (see on 119:52). The hours of night were often regarded as a dangerous time when demons and evil spirits were particularly active. On the other hand, night was considered a suitable time to seek God's presence in prayer and meditation (see on 119:62; cf. 4:4 (M.T. 5), 16:7, 77:6 (M.T. 7); *TDNT*, IV, pp. 1123f.).

meditate: (*h-g-h*), see on 1:2.

the watches of the night: see on 119:148.

7. my help: the Psalmist has already experienced the divine succour in finding refuge in the Temple. The function of the sanctuary as a place of asylum is well illustrated in cases of manslaughter. The involuntary killer would flee for safety to the sanctuary, or to one of the cities of refuge (Exod. 21:13; Num. 35:9–34; Dt. 4:41ff., 19:4–13). This provision gave time to make the necessary inquiries, and if it actually was a case of homicide, then the refugee could go on enjoying the safety of the sanctuary, while the *wilful* murderer would be handed over to the 'avenger of blood'.

in the shadow of thy wings: i.e. in your protection. For the metaphor, see on 17:8, 36:7.

I sing for joy: some commentators emend the Hebrew *ʾarannēn* into *ʾeṯlōnān* ('I will lodge', i.e. I shall find refuge). See also Dahood, *PAB*, II, p. 99.

8. My soul clings to thee: or 'I follow hard after you' (for the construction, see Jer. 42:16). The verb *d-b-ḳ* ('to cling') can be used of a tongue cleaving 'to the roof of its mouth for thirst' (Lam. 4:4), or it can denote keeping close to someone (Ru. 2:8; Ps. 101:3), etc. Figuratively it may signify loyalty or clinging to God by keeping his commandments; this usage is frequent in the Book of Deuteronomy to express the devotion of the people to their God (4:4, 10:20, 11:22, 13:5, 30:20). The verb has a similar meaning in our verse.

thy right hand may denote Yahweh himself (as *pars pro toto*), who, in his might, has intervened on behalf of the needy man (cf. 18:35 (M.T. 36), 41:12 (M.T. 13)).

THE SOLUTION OF THE PROBLEM **9–11**

9. to destroy: lit. 'for destruction'. LXX suggests: 'vainly, without reason', which may be a translation of the Hebrew *l^ešāwʾ* instead of M.T. *l^ešôʾāh* (so also Kraus, Nötscher, *et al.*).
my life: lit. 'my soul', see on 33:19.
the depths of the earth: i.e. the depths of Sheol, as in 86:13 (cf. Isa. 44:23; Ezek. 26:20; Eph. 4:9). This does not suggest divisions in Sheol itself but rather refers to the netherworld as the place far below the surface. The word *ʾereṣ* seems to be a synonym of underworld; for this use of 'earth', see on 61:2. It is not necessary to assume that the enemies would be swallowed up like Korah and his house (so Kirkpatrick).

10. the power of the sword: lit. 'pour them out to the power of (or 'upon the hands of') the sword', i.e. they shall most certainly receive their due punishment. For similar expressions, see Jer. 18:21; Ezek. 35:5.
prey for jackals: their dead bodies will be desecrated by jackals (or any other wild animals). It is possible that this thought presupposes the belief that the welfare of the dead is somehow linked with the corpse. According to Assyrian and Babylonian ideas on this subject, 'to be left unburied or unprovided for was . . . a grievous misfortune or a terrible punishment' (A. Heidel, *The Gilgamesh Epic and Old Testament Parallels* (1963), p. 155; cf. S. G. F. Brandon, *Man and his Destiny in the Great Religions* (1962), pp. 110–22). Thus it is possible that the punishment of the wicked will have some effectiveness even after death, at least as far as their name and reputation is concerned. The same kind of punishment is also envisaged by the writers in Isa. 18:6 and Jer. 7:33.

11. This brief prayer for the King at the beginning of the verse may be part of the original Psalm and not a later interpolation. It does not follow, however, that the King *must* be identified with the Psalmist (so Kirkpatrick) or that the composition is a Royal Psalm (so Mowinckel).
the king shall rejoice . . .: this is probably a variation on the more common intercession for the King, which asks God to grant him a long and prosperous reign (cf. 61:6 (M.T. 7)).

all who swear by him: i.e. by the King, although it is possible that the Psalmist had in mind the oaths taken in the name of God (so *NEB*; cf. 1 Kg. 8:31). Yet there are a number of instances where Israelites swear by Yahweh and the King (cf. 1 Sam. 17:55, 25:26; 2 Sam. 11:11, 15:21; for non-Israelite parallels, see Klopfenstein, *LAT*, p. 368, n. 157).
liars: this additional description of the enemies implies that the Psalmist was accused unjustly, and that the false charges were serious enough to carry a capital punishment (verse 9). If so, the legal 'victory' of the accused would inevitably bring an identical retribution upon the accusers (see on 27:12).
the mouths . . . will be stopped: i.e. the enemies will be proved wrong (cf. 107:42; also Job 5:16).

Psalm 64 Even A Hidden Enemy is No Match for God

The text of this Psalm must have suffered in the course of transmission, and therefore its translation and interpretation is rather problematic in several places.

This Psalm is often described as a Lament of the Individual (see Introduction, pp. 37ff.), but it could well be a Protective Psalm (cf. Mowinckel, *PIW*, 1, p. 219) which is concerned with an *imminent* danger and is not the result of a disaster which has *already* overtaken the righteous. If so, the Psalmist is anxious about the threats of the enemies (verse 1*b*) and their plots (verses 2, 5, and 6), and he is seeking divine protection. Weiser (*POTL*, pp. 457ff.) takes verses 7–9 as an account of the retribution that had been meted out to the wicked, and he regards the Psalm as a testimony to the retaliatory judgment of God.

Like most laments, this Psalm starts with a brief petition to God (verses 1–2), which is followed by a description of the scheming of the enemies (verses 3–6). Verses 7–9 give an account either of what God has already done for the righteous, or what he will most certainly do (in which case the verbs would be perfects of certainty; cf. *GK* 106n). The Psalm ends with a call to rejoice in Yahweh (verse 10).

There are no indications as to the date of this composition. The metre is irregular.
To the choirmaster: see Introduction, p. 48.
A Psalm of David: see Introduction, pp. 43ff. and 46.

THE INVOCATION AND PETITION 1–2

1. Hear my voice: this lament opens with the usual call for help, and with the invocation of God (or 'Yahweh', see on 63:1); see on 61:1.
in my complaint: or 'as I complain' of the oppression (or its threat) of the enemies, and not of the providence of God (cf. 1 Sam. 1:16; Ps. 55:17 (M.T. 18)).
preserve my life: LXX and V have '. . . my soul' (reading *napšî* for M.T. *ḥayyāy*), but the meaning remains the same.
dread of the enemy: i.e. the fear inspired by the adversary or adversaries; *ʾôyēḇ* ('enemy') could be taken in a collective sense. The Hebrew *paḥaḏ* denotes great fear and anxiety; it may also suggest an experience which is terrifying to a man, so that he may become practically paralysed with fear (cf. 2 Chr. 17:10, 20:29; Job 13:11).

2. hide me: i.e. shelter me. This idea may be associated with the belief that the sanctuary offered the right of asylum (see on 63:7; cf. 1QH v:11).
the secret plots: or 'the company' (similarly *RP*, *PNT*). The Hebrew *sôḏ* (see on 25:14) can denote either a council or its deliberations. In view of the secrecy of the enemies, the reference may be to their planning. Cf. 1QH vi:5.
the wicked: *meréʿîm* suggests people who act wickedly and whose deeds are designed to harm others and to work mischief. It is one of the usual words employed to denote the enemies of the righteous (see on 28:3).
scheming: or 'the raging mob, gathering' (cf. Dan. 6:6,11). The interpretation of this word is linked with the meaning given to *sôḏ* in verse 2*b*.

THE ACTIVITIES OF THE ENEMIES 3–6

This brief account is expressed in a stereotyped language, and therefore we should exercise some caution in the reconstruction of the circumstances which gave rise to this poem.

3. The hostile words of the enemies are likened to the sharp sword (cf. 55:21 (M.T. 22), 57:4 (M.T. 5); 1QH v:13) and arrows, but the exact nature of these hostile utterances is not clear. The writer may have thought of slanders or false accusations—perhaps, even, of magic spells or curses, which, but for the intervention of God, could have proved disastrous (so Mowinckel,

Schmidt). The opponents use 'bitter words' (*dāḇār mār*) which is an expression found only here, and it could be taken in any of the three connotations mentioned above. Dahood (*PAB*, I, p. 251) renders verse 3*b* 'They tipped their arrows with poisonous substance', but *RSV* seems more likely. The force of the preposition *k*ᵉ ('like') in verse 3*a* extends also to the parallel line. A difficulty is caused by the verb *dārᵉḵû*, which is usually translated 'they aim'; the verb is, however, more appropriate to the bow which *can* be trodden (i.e. bent or strung) (see on 37:14); yet the *RSV* rendering is not impossible.

4. from ambush: lit. 'in secret places' but the preposition *b*ᵉ ('in') has here, apparently, the meaning 'from', like the Ugaritic *b* (cf. Gordon, *UT*, p. 370).

the blameless: (see on 119:1), i.e. a man of irreproachable character and integrity. The same verb *tām* is used to describe Job as 'blameless (*tām*) and upright' (Job 1:1,8, 2:3), or one who does right for the sake of right.

shooting at him suddenly: this metaphor suggests that the enemies strike unexpectedly with their slanderous attacks, or that they resort to what might be called 'sorcery'; therefore the writer emphasizes the secretiveness of their activities.

without fear: lit. 'and they do not fear (God?)' (cf. Dt. 25:18; Ps. 55:19 (M.T. 20)), i.e. they do not worry about their motives nor about the means used to attain their desires. Many exegetes follow S in reading 'and they are not seen' (*yērā'û* for M.T. *yîrā'û*) (similarly *NEB*), or '(from a place where) they are not seen' which provides a parallel to 'from ambush' (verse 4a).

5. They hold fast . . .: i.e. they have hardened themselves to pursue their evil course.

they talk of laying snares . . .: the hunting metaphor is frequently used to describe the machinations of the enemies (cf. 7:15 (M.T. 16), 9:15 (M.T. 16), 35:7, 140:5 (M.T. 6), 142:3 (M.T. 4), etc.). Some scholars emend *y*ᵉ*sapp*ᵉ*rû* ('they talk') to *yaḥp*ᵉ*rû* ('they dig (pits)'), to lay snares for the righteous.

snares: the Hebrew *môqēš* may denote the bait or lure for the trap, and probably the trap itself. Figuratively it suggests something which attracts and then destroys the unsuspecting victim (Dt. 7:16; 1 Sam. 18:21; Prov. 22:24f.).

Who can see us?: so S and Jerome. The evildoers think that not even God will interfere with their twisted plans, because he is not actively interested, or involved, in the rights and wrongs of this world (as in 11:4,11,13). M.T. has 'Who can see them?', i.e. their plots (?) (cf. Isa. 29:15).

6. This verse seems to be textually corrupt, and none of the suggested emendations is really convincing.

Who can search out . . .: lit. 'They search for injustice', which probably means that they are looking for opportunities to do evil.

We have thought out . . .: lit. 'We are complete . . . (?)', but many MSS. read: 'They have concealed' (*ṭām^enû* for *tamnû*). The object of the verb is not certain but the 'cunningly conceived plot' (*RSV*) is as good as any suggestion.

the inward mind . . .: this may be a quotation of a well-known proverb (cf. Jer. 7:9), the purpose of which is to stress the supposed impossibility of frustrating the well thought-out schemes. Yet however deep may be man's thoughts and plans, they are not deep enough to be hidden from God.

THE INTERVENTION OF GOD 7–10

7. God will shoot his arrows: God will mete out his just retribution. This recompense is described in terms reminiscent of the actions of the enemies; what they have planned and done will rebound on them.

8. he will bring them to ruin: reading *yak̲šîlēmô* for M.T. *wayyak̲šîlûhû* ('they have made him stumble') which hardly fits the context. Kirkpatrick (*BPSB*, p. 359) thinks of some mysterious divine agents which bring about the downfall of the enemy. Eaton (*PTBC*, p. 163) suggests: 'by their tongue they bring him down upon themselves', i.e. they provoke God.

wag their heads in triumph (see on 22:7), deriving the verb from *n-w-d*, 'to wag (one's head)'. Some exegetes link the verb *yiṯnōḏ^aḏû* with *n-d-d*, 'to flee, depart' (so *RP*); the idea is paralleled by 31:11 (M.T. 12).

9. all men will fear: i.e. those who witness the retribution will realize that it is God's doing, and that he is the Lord and Judge of all men. Weiser (*POTL*, p. 459) identifies 'all men' with the cult community, while some commentators (e.g. Cohen, Kraus) take the expression in a universal sense.

10. Let the righteous rejoice because God rules the world of men, and because the faithful will be the heirs of the divine blessings (cf. 5:12 (M.T. 13), 32:10, 58:11 (M.T. 12). For *ṣaddîḳ* ('righteous'), see on 1:5; here it is parallel to 'the upright in heart' (see on 7:10). The verb *ḥ-s-h* ('to seek refuge') is discussed on 7:1, 16:1; the phrase 'and take refuge in him' may be a later gloss (cf. *BH*).

Psalm 65 Praise is Due to Thee, O God

This Psalm exhibits certain hymnic characteristics: verse 1 actually describes it as a praise (*tᵉhillāh*), and in verses 6–7 we find the distinctive hymnic participles (usually rendered by a relative clause). Also the main themes of the Psalm suggest a hymn which might have been sung at the beginning of the barley harvest, i.e. at the Feast of Unleavened Bread. Another reasonable view is to consider the composition as a National Psalm of thanksgiving which was offered when a threatening drought and famine had been averted, the crops were showing a promise of a fine harvest, and the flocks were greatly increased. Also the allusion to the prayers (verse 2) and the vows (verse 1) tends to support this view which implies a situation similar to that mentioned in 1 Kg. 8:35f., and which was by no means unique. This account in 1 Kings shows that a drought, or a delay of the rains, could be interpreted as a punishment for sin, and that forgiveness and the giving of rain go together. Mowinckel classes this Psalm as a 'harvest festival thanksgiving psalm' (*PIW*, 1, p. 185) used at the Feast of Tabernacles. The previous suggestion seems, however, more likely.

Another problem is the unity of the Psalm. Gunkel, Kraus, *et al.* think that it is composed of two originally independent parts: verses 1–8 and 9–13. The argument could be supported by the metre; the first part is dominated by a 3+2 metre, while the second part by 3+3. On the other hand, although the composite nature of the Psalm is a possibility, there is no really convincing reason why the Psalm could not be a unity.

In the present form, this Psalm consists of three main sections. Verses 1–4 praise God as one who answers the prayers of his people, and who grants forgiveness and blessings. The second part (verses 5–8) exalts God as Saviour and as the Creator who subdued the raging waters of Chaos. The last section (verses 9–13) lauds God as the Giver of rain, and it may have an implicit polemical tendency. It shows that Israel's God does what Baal was thought to do for his people; yet, although Yahweh gives fruitfulness, he is not a fertility god, as Baal was.

The date of the Psalm is uncertain but it may be late pre-Exilic.
To the choirmaster: see Introduction, p. 48.
A Psalm of David: see Introduction, pp. 43ff. and 46.
A Song: see Introduction, p. 47.

PRAISE TO ZION'S GOD **1–4**

1. Praise: *tᵉhillāh* refers to a descriptive praise or a hymn. It can be a synonym of 'thanksgiving' (*tôḏāh*) (100:4) and it may also denote the glorious deeds of Yahweh (78:4). It is addressed to God, and its purpose is to praise and glorify him. It does not deal so much with one particular aspect or act of God, as with the works of God as a whole and with his full glory. Such songs generally open with a call to praise and to adore God, but our Psalm offers a variation to this introductory call. See on 119:171; Westermann, *PGP*, pp. 15–25, 122–42.
is due to thee: this follows the reading of LXX, S, and V which suggest *dōmiyyāh*, a participle from *d-m-h* I, 'to be like', which in the Talmud can denote 'to be right, fitting' (cf. Jastrow, *DTTM*, p. 313a). M.T. has *dūmiyyāh* ('silence') from *d-m-h* II, 'to be silent', hence *RVm* renders '(There shall be) silence before thee (and) praise', but the construction is rather forced. The *RSV* rendering is preferable; *NEB:* 'We owe thee praise'.
Zion: its etymology is uncertain (see *TDNT*, VII, p. 294) and it is, most likely, of pre-Israelite origin. It could have been the name of the Canaanite fortress on the SE. hill, or of the hill itself. In 2 Sam. 5:7 David is said to have taken 'the stronghold of Zion, that is, the city of David', i.e. the fortified area on the Zion hill. Later the name 'Zion' was used to denote the Temple hill (e.g. 132:13; Isa. 8:18; Mic. 4:2), and even the whole city of Jerusalem (Isa. 10:24); thus Zion is the city of Yahweh (Isa. 60:14), or the city of the great king (48:2 (M.T. 3)). Zion can also be employed as a synonym of 'Israel' (149:2; Isa. 46:13), 'Judah' (Jer. 14:19), and 'the people of Jerusalem' (and Judah) (48:11 (M.T. 12); Lam. 2:13). See also G. A. Barrois, 'Zion', *IDB*, IV, 959f.
vows: the Hebrew *nēḏer* (see on 61:5) is used collectively. For the collocation of 'praise' and 'vows' cf. 22:25 (M.T. 26), 61:8 (M.T. 9). The vows may presuppose a time of trouble (drought?), or they may allude to the promises made by the Israelite farmers at the time of sowing (so Leslie). Some Greek MSS. add at the end of this verse: 'in Jerusalem', which is a correct interpretative addition.

2. prayer: the Hebrew *tᵉpillāh* (cf. D. R. Ap-Thomas, 'Notes on Some Terms Relating to Prayer', *VT*, VI (1956), pp. 230–41) can suggest spoken (cf. 2 Sam. 7:27; Dan. 9:21) or sung prayers. A number of Psalms are actually designated as prayers by their titles (Ps. 17, 86, 90, 102, 142; cf. also 72:20). These prayers are addressed to God, and their substance may vary considerably according to the circumstances of the worshipper(s). He can ask God for a blessing or deliverance; he can also offer an intercession for others (109:4). *Tᵉpillāh* denotes both cultic and non-cultic prayers, the former being far more common; consequently the Temple can be called a 'house of prayer' (Isa. 56:7; Mt. 21:13; Mk 11:17; Lk. 19:46), and it is towards Jerusalem (i.e. towards the Temple, and ultimately towards God) that the worshipper stretches out his hands (1 Kg. 8:28; Ps. 28:2, 134:2), or turns himself (Dan. 6:10). Prayers would often accompany sacrifices, and at times the former might even serve as a substitute for the latter (cf. 141:2), or they could be regarded as superior to the animal sacrifices (51:15ff. (M.T. 17ff.), 69:30f. (M.T. 31f.)). The latter possibility would apply in cases where sacrifice had become a mere external observance, and no longer an expression of man's true attitude to God. Yet prayer itself could suffer a similar fate, as in Isa. 1:15, 29:13. In the *OT*, prayers are means of communication between man and God, and not a technique for imposing one's will or wishes on the deity (cf. Rowley, *WAI*, p. 250). God always remains a free agent, and he cannot be reduced to the status of a servant of man's selfish desires. The expression 'O thou who hearest prayer' may well belong to verse 1*b*, and it may form a parallel to 'O God, in Zion', thus improving the metre.

all flesh: see on 56:4. This may refer to the whole of mankind, or simply to all Israel. The latter would be more likely if the Psalm was uttered after the fructifying rains had removed the threat of a drought which would have been regarded as a punishment for the sins of the nation (cf. Lev. 26:3f.; 1 Kg. 8:35).

3. on account of sins: *ᶜāwōn* ('iniquity') (see on 51:2) can also denote the results of sin, i.e. punishment. M.T. could be rendered '(with) words of iniquities', i.e. with tales of iniquity (see Winton Thomas, *TRP*, p. 25) or 'confessing sins' (similarly *RP*).

our transgressions: for *pešaᶜ* ('transgression, rebellion'), see on 51:1.

prevail over us: so LXX, V reading *mennû* for M.T. *mennî* ('over me'). For the idea, see 38:4 (M.T. 5), 40:12 (M.T. 13).
thou dost forgive them: the verb used is *k-p-r*, which is of uncertain origin. The two most common explanations are 'to cover over', i.e. to appease (cf. Gen. 32:20; Job 9:24) and 'to wash away', 'to wipe off' (cf. Isa. 6:7). G. R. Driver (*JTS*, XXXIV (1933), p. 38) argues that the latter meaning rather than the former 'underlies the ritual significance of the Hebrew *kipper*'. Yet, whatever the etymology might be, the verb came to denote the removal of the effects of sin. This removal or atonement could be achieved in several ways; it could be made by offering a sacrifice (cf. Exod. 29:36; Lev. 4:20), or by giving the atonement money (Exod. 30:16). The sin could also be laid on the scapegoat, that it might be carried away (Lev. 16:10), or one could seek atonement through prayers, as e.g. Moses in Exod. 32:30. Usually it is man who makes atonement by making some amends, but at times it is God himself who, being merciful, atones or forgives the iniquity, as in this verse (cf. also Dt. 21:8; Ps. 78:30). On the whole, atonement is not so much, if at all, the propitiation of an angry God, as the removal of the barrier between God and man. Therefore *k-p-r* may signify 'to forgive', i.e. to restore the previous relationship. Man does not, however, *earn* forgiveness or atonement, but God does it for his own sake (cf. Isa. 43:25). The value of the various acts of man is that they help him to express his changed attitude to God, and they enable him to offer the loyalty of a contrite heart and a broken spirit (51:17 (M.T. 19)). For further details, see J. Herrmann, '*Hilaskomai*', *TDNT*, III, pp. 302–10.

4. **Blessed is he:** or 'How enviable is the man' (see on 1:1).
whom thou dost choose: the Hebrew *b-ḥ-r* denotes the making of a decision in favour of one of the possibilities open; e.g. Lot chose the Jordan valley, and not the land on the west (Gen. 13:11). Of more interest is the theological use of *b-ḥ-r*; it can be used both of man's choice of God or gods (cf. Jos. 24:15; Jg. 10:14), or of the divine election, the object of which may be an individual (78:70, 89:3 (M.T. 4), 106:23), a city (132:13), or the nation as a whole (Dt. 7:6ff., 14:2). For a detailed discussion and further references, see *TDNT*, IV, pp. 145–68.
bring near: this language of choosing and bringing near to God is used of the priests (Num. 16:5), and consequently some scholars (e.g. v. Rad, *OTT*, I, p. 405, n.49) see here an allusion to a group

of Levitical priests. Yet it is more likely that the reference is to the worshipping community – those who are judged worthy to enter the holy place and to 'sojourn' there (cf. 15:1ff., 24:3ff.). It is not only the priests who could be said to dwell in God's courts (cf. 96:8), but also every Israelite who is faithful to the divine Covenant (see on 15:1, 23:6, 84:2 (M.T. 3)).

satisfied with the goodness of thy house: Cohen (*PSon*, p. 201) thinks that the reference is to the spiritual refreshment found in the sanctuary, but it is more likely that the Psalmist had in mind the sacrificial meal (so Ringgren, Kraus; cf. 22:26 (M.T. 27), 23:5, 36:8 (M.T. 9)). This does not exclude the divine blessings which were remembered by the thank-offering and the following banquet. In that case the gifts of God could include the abundant rain, the promise of good crops and fine herds, as well as forgiveness (cf. 90:14), the presence of God, and the privilege of dwelling in Yahweh's land.

thy holy temple: lit. 'the holy place of thy temple' (*RV*; cf. 46:4*b* (M.T. 5*b*)). LXX has 'your temple is holy' (so also Kraus).

GOD AS THE CREATOR **5–8**

5. By dread deeds . . .: lit. '(By) awe-inspiring deeds you answer us in righteousness'. The Hebrew *nôrā'* is often used to denote that quality of God which inspires fear and terror in his enemies (cf. 47:2 (M.T. 3), 76:7 (M.T. 8), 89:7 (M.T. 8)), but worshipful awe and a spirit of praise in the righteous (68:35 (M.T. 36), 96:4, 99:2f.). Both the singular and the plural (*nôrā'ôṯ*) can signify the mighty deeds of God in saving his people (Exod. 34:10; 2 Sam. 7:23; Ps. 66:3, 106:21f., 145:6). For further information, see S. Plath, *Furcht Gottes* (1962), pp. 109–13. Cf. also J. Becker, *Gottesfurcht im Alten Testament* (1965).

thou dost answer: the immediate reference must be to the present help but it may also include, by way of reminiscence, the dread deeds performed at the time of the Exodus and the Conquest (Exod. 34:10; Dt. 10:21; Ps. 106:21f.).

O God of our salvation: i.e. he is the God who gives us deliverance (see on 35:3). The same phrase is found in 1 Chr. 16:35; Ps. 79:9, 85:4 (M.T. 5).

the hope of: or '(you are) the object of the confidence of . . .' (cf. 40:4 (M.T. 5), 71:5; for gold as one's object of trust, see Job 31:24).

the ends of the earth: i.e. the whole world (see on 72:8).

the farthest seas: lit. 'the sea of the distant ones (or 'distant people')'. An old conjecture is to read *ʾiyyîm* ('isles') for *yām* ('sea'); *RP* has 'the isles that are far away' (cf. Isa. 66:19; similarly Weiser, Leslie, Kraus, *et al.*). S reads 'the distant peoples (*ʿammîm*)'.

6. who . . . established the mountains: the verse begins with a participle which is characteristic of the hymnic style. Yahweh founded the mountains, which in themselves are a symbol of all that is permanent and mighty. It is possible that in this verse the mountains represent the whole earth, the creator of which is God. In Weiser's opinion (*POTL*, p. 60) the idea of creation was originally borrowed from the Near Eastern religions and therefore it was a comparatively late element in the Yahwistic traditions. Yahwism in ancient Israel was primarily a religion of salvation (cf. v. Rad, *OTT*, I, pp. 136ff.), but it does not prove that the belief in Yahweh as the creator of the world was not known at an earlier date, even though it did not receive the same prominence as in later times. See also Eichrodt, *TOT*, II, pp. 93–117; W. Foerster, '*Ktizō*', *TDNT*, III, pp. 1005–28.

by thy strength: (*b*ᵉ*ḵōḥ*ᵃ*ḵā*) so LXX^B, Jerome, and V. M.T. has 'by his strength'.

girded with might: (cf. 93:1; Isa. 51:9f.) the poetic picture portrays God as a warrior preparing for action, his girdle being might which had no equal in the whole universe.

7. This verse describes one aspect of Yahweh's creative work which consisted of his victory over the waters of Chaos (see on 93:3). It is questionable how far this description is a poetic figure of speech, and how far it represents a broken myth which was originally derived from Babylonian or Canaanite sources, or both. The Israelites believed that the world was continually threatened by the powers of Chaos, and only by the might of Yahweh the destructive waters were held in check (89:9 (M.T. 10f.), 93:3) and made to serve his purposes (cf. 104:9ff.).

the tumult: this represents the same Hebrew word (*šāʾôn*) as 'the roaring' in verse 7*b*. Therefore it is possible that verse 7*c* is a later addition (so Mowinckel, Kraus) (cf. Isa. 17:12f.).

8. who dwell at earth's farthest bounds: this phrase occurs only here in the *OT*, and it means 'all the inhabitants of the world' (cf. 67:7: 'let all the ends of the earth fear him'). Yahweh's might and power know no national boundaries, and therefore the whole world stands in awe of him. Mowinckel (*PIW*, I, p. 162) regards these 'dwellers at the ends of the earth' as the demonic powers whom Yahweh defeated when he gained victory over the primordial ocean.

thy signs: the Hebrew *ʾôṯ* is a sign which usually represents something else. In the Lachish Ostraca (iv:11), the same word (in the plural) is used of fire-signals which conveyed a particular message. Similarly, in Num. 2:2 *ʾôṯ* is used of the tribal banners (as in 1QM; cf. Yadin, *SWSLSD*, p. 38). In Gen. 1:14 the heavenly luminaries serve as signs, i.e. as indicators of seasons and cultic occasions. The word *ʾôṯ* can also denote various astrological portents which are the source of fear (Jer. 10:2). The prophet can offer a sign as guarantee that his message is authentic and reliable (cf. 1 Sam. 2:34; 2 Kg. 19:29). The same word can also signify the works of God, and it is frequently associated with *môp̄ēṯ* ('wonder'; cf. Exod. 7:3; Dt. 4:34, 26:8; Ps. 78:43). In this verse the meaning of *ʾôṯ* is not very clear. Nötscher (*PEB*, p. 139) thinks of the wonders of creation or national disasters, while Kissane (*BP*, p. 278) takes them as 'the signs in the heavens'. Possibly 'signs' in this context are all those things through which Yahweh makes known his majesty and power (cf. Kraus, *PBK*, p. 452), or his deliverance (cf. 86:17). For a more detailed discussion on *ʾôt*, see K. H. Rengstorf, '*Sēmeion*', *TDNT*, VII, pp. 208–21.

the outgoings of . . .: this probably denotes the places from which the morning and the evening come forth (cf. Job 38:19; similarly Calès, Kraus). The phrase may be another way of saying 'the ends of the earth'.

GOD AS THE GIVER OF RAIN AND PROSPERITY **9–13**

9. Thou visitest: i.e. you have cared for (as in Gen. 21:1; Exod. 13:19; Ps. 8:4 (M.T. 5)), or the poet may be thinking of God as coming in the rain-storm (cf. 29:3–9). Weiser renders: 'Thou didst bless the land' (*POTL*, p. 460). Dahood (*PAB*, II, p. 109) takes the Hebrew perfects as precative perfects (i.e. imperative in sense).

the earth: probably not the whole world but the land of Israel.

waterest it: so most of the ancient versions, deriving the verb from *š-ḳ-h* which, in its causative form, may denote 'to water'. The verb in M.T. comes from *š-w-ḳ*, 'to be abundant', hence 'give it abundance' (so *NEB*).

the river of God: Kirkpatrick (*BPCB*, p. 364) thinks that God's 'stream' is the rain (similarly Cohen, Kissane), but it is more likely that the reference is to the channel cleft for the torrents of rain (Job 38:25), which is probably an alternative expression for the 'windows of the heavens' (Gen. 7:11, 8:2). It is possible, although less likely, that this 'river of God' should be linked with the river that makes 'glad the city of God' (see on 46:4; cf. Isa. 33:21; Ezek. 47:1–12; Jl 3:18; Zech. 14:8). See also Kraus, *WI*, p. 202.

their grain: (*NEB* 'rain') probably 'its grain' (*d^e^gānāh*; so also S) which, as one of the chief products of the land, represents all its produce.

for thou hast prepared it: the allusion is to the preparation of the soil, and not to the grain. Verse 10 gives a more detailed account of this process.

10. Thou waterest its furrows: this refers to the early rains which softened the ground for ploughing. The rainy season lasts from October to May, and the rainy days alternate with bright periods. On the average there were only a few days of rain during October–November and April–May but a much more frequent rainfall during the rest of the period. The early or autumn rain and the latter or spring rain were really the first and last showers of the rainy season, but they were specially named because of their importance for the preparation of the soil and for the maturing of the crops. The main rainfall was during the months of January and February.

settling its ridges: probably the rain softened and broke up the clods of earth. The word *g^e^ḏûḏ* ('clods') occurs only here in the *OT*; another word *g^e^ḏûḏ* ('band, troop') is much more common.

showers: the Hebrew *r^e^ḇîḇîm* may be the spring rain, or it suggests the copious showers during the middle of the winter (see on 72:6).

11. . . . the year with thy bounty: lit. '. . . the year of your goodness', i.e. the year characterized by your providential care, is further crowned and adorned with additional blessings.

the tracks of thy chariot: lit. 'your tracks' (Dahood (*PAB*, I, p. 146) has 'your pastures'). The Psalmist may have had in mind the poetic picture of Yahweh riding on the storm-clouds as in a chariot (cf. 18:10 (M.T. 11), 68:4,33 (M.T. 5,34); Baal, too, is sometimes called 'the Rider of the Clouds' (see on 18:10)). So wherever Yahweh went with his storm-clouds, there was blessing or, in other words, his tracks dripped with fatness or goodness (see on 36:8). *NEB* has 'the palm-trees drip with sweet juice'.

12. the pastures of the wilderness drip: this does not give a satisfactory sense. Either we should read 'They (i.e. the tracks of God) drip (on) the pastures . . .' (so Kirkpatrick, *PNT*), or we should emend (so Gunkel, Kraus, *et al.*) the M.T. *yir*^{ca}*pû* ('they drip') to *yārî*^{c}*û* ('they shout for joy') which would provide a reasonable parallel to the hills girding themselves with joy (verse 12*b*). The pastures and the hills are personified as rejoicing in their richness (cf. 96:12, 98:8; Isa. 55:12).

13. This is a further elaboration of the picture in verse 12. The flocks (for a different meaning, see Dahood, *PAB*, I, p. 230) in the meadows are seen as the festive robes of the pastures, and the growing corn is pictured as the covering of the valleys.

Psalm 66 Hymn to God and Thanksgiving

This Psalm is composed of two or three more or less distinct parts. The first section (verses 1–7)is reminiscent of a hymn in praise of God, while the second section (verses 8–12) deals with the trials of the people and their thankfulness for the subsequent deliverance. The third part (verses 13–20) is obviously a thanksgiving of an individual. The problem is how to relate the separate parts. It is often suggested that a private individual wrote verses 13–20 and that he borrowed verses 1–12 as a hymnic introduction to his own prayer of thanks. A variation of this view is Weiser's explanation (*POTL*, p. 468) that the first part was taken from the liturgy of the annual festival of Yahweh, and that it formed the framework within which the individual worshipper's thanksgiving was recited. Another possibility is to regard the speaker in verses 13–20 as the King (or some other national figure), and the whole Psalm as a National Thanksgiving after a victory or some deliverance from a political distress (so Mowinckel, *PIW*, II, p. 28). One can also assume that the two (or three) parts originally formed independent songs, or that they were parts of such poems, which were at a later time combined by an editor.

The life-setting of the whole Psalm and its separate parts depends upon the interpretation adopted. Perhaps some such theory as that of Weiser's may best account for the Psalm and its present form. Since the individual thanksgiving was the affair of the whole worshipping community (cf. verse 16), it is reasonable to think that the individual's experience of the saving power of God would be set in the wider context of the nation's salvation-history.

The date of the Psalm is uncertain, but many exegetes place it in the post-Exilic period. There is a certain similarity between this Psalm and Deutero-Isaiah (cf. verses 10,12), and this fact, as well as the mixed psalm-type, may add some support to the argument for the post-Exilic date.

The metre of the Psalm is uneven.

To the choirmaster: see Introduction, p. 48.
A Song: see Introduction, p. 47.
A Psalm: see Introduction, p. 46.

THE HYMN IN PRAISE OF GOD'S MAJESTIC POWER **1–7**

Verses 1–4 form the hymnic introduction to the Psalm, followed by the main section (verses 5–7) which describes the mighty works of God.

1. Make a joyful noise: this is the first of a series of imperative calls to praise God. The same expression occurs also in 98:4, 100:1, except that instead of 'to God' (see on 63:1) we find 'to Yahweh'.

all the earth: all the world and all that dwell in it.

2. the glory of his name: *šēm* ('name') (see on 20:1) probably denotes Yahweh himself, while *kāḇôḏ* ('glory') (see on 26:8) may suggest the marvellous works of God, as in 96:3.

give to him glorious praise: this represents a difficult Hebrew expression which might be rendered literally: 'make his praise glorious' (*RV*), or 'make glory his praise'. *RSV* adds 'to him' (*lô*) (cf. Jos. 7:19; Isa. 42:12), and takes 'glory' as a noun in the construct state (*k^e^ḇôḏ*), following T and S. For 'praise' (*t^e^hillāh*), see on 65:1.

3. How terrible are thy deeds: i.e. the works of God strike fear into his enemies but they inspire praise and joy in his people. For *nôrā'* ('terrible') see on 65:5. The awe-inspiring deeds of God are described in more detail in verse 6.

enemies cringe before thee: the Hebrew verb *kiḥēš* is often used of 'to deceive' or 'to act deceptively' but in a few instances, as here and in 18:44 (M.T. 45) (=2 Sam. 22:45), 81:15 (M.T. 16), it denotes an unwilling homage (i.e. it is feigned). See Dt. 33:29; cf. Klopfenstein, *LAT*, pp. 284ff. LXX renders 'your enemies shall lie to you'.

4. . . . worships thee: see on 29:2. The whole world does obeisance to God, or at least should do.

they sing praises: *zimmēr* is a verb characteristic of the Psalter, and it can mean either to make music or to sing to the accompaniment of stringed instrument(s) (cf. 33:2, 71:22, 92:1,3 (M.T. 2,4), 98:5, 146:2, 147:7, 149:3).

to thy name: i.e. to Yahweh himself (see on 20:1).

Selah: see Introduction, pp. 48f.

5\. . . . **what God has done:** lit. '. . . the works of God'. Practically the same expression is found in 46:8*a* (M.T. 9*a*); in both places the reference may be to certain symbolic acts accompanied by the recital of the salvation-history.

he is terrible: better 'he is awe-inspiring' (see on 65:5); cf. Exod. 15:11; Jer. 32:19.

deeds: so some MSS. and the ancient versions. M.T. has the singular (*ᶜalîlāh*) which may well have a collective meaning.

6. Out of the many works of Yahweh, the writer mentions only two (or one?): the passing through the Sea of Reeds during the time of the Exodus from Egypt (Exod. 14:21f., 15:19) and the crossing of the river Jordan at the beginning of the Conquest of Canaan (Jos. 3:14–17; for the different views on the Conquest, see J. Bright, *Early Israel in Recent History Writing* (*SBT* 19, 1956)). These two basic events represent the whole *Heilsgeschichte*, and they were most likely re-presented by word and action, in the cult. Consequently the worshipping community saw these events not as past history but as possessing a present reality. Similarly the Israelites could say: 'Not with our fathers did the LORD make this covenant, but with us, who are all of us here alive this day' (Dt. 5:3).

the river: the Hebrew *nāhār* (see on 72:8) can denote the river Jordan (cf. 114:3,5), but it could also be a parallel to 'the sea' (*yām*) in verse 6*a*, so that in both halves of the verse the reference would be to the crossing of the Reed Sea. The 'Sea' (*ym*) and the 'River' (*nhr*) are well-known parallel terms in Ugaritic (cf. Jirku, *MK*, pp. 54f.; W. Schmidt, *Königtum Gottes in Ugarit und Israel* (*BZAW*, 80, 2nd edn, 1966), pp. 37f.).

There did we rejoice in him: Kraus (*PBK*, p. 457) raises the question 'Where?', and he suggests Gilgal as a possible place where these events could have been re-enacted and celebrated (cf. *VT* 1 (1951), pp. 181ff.). This seems a reasonable suggestion, but equally well the events could have been re-actualized anywhere. Some exegetes emend *šām* ('there') into *śāmôaḥ*, rendering: 'Let us then indeed rejoice in him' (similarly *RP*, *PNT*, Nötscher, *et al.*), yet there is no justification for this conjecture (cf. 14:5,

36:12 (M.T. 13)). Dahood (*PAB*, I, p. 81) takes *šām* as an exclamation 'Behold'.

7. who rules: the Hebrew *mōšēl* is a hymnic participle (see on 65:6). God's power was clearly manifested in the Exodus events, and by the same might he rules for ever. This is the factor that gives relevance to the re-actualization of the *Heilsgeschichte*.

whose eyes keep watch . . .: the eyes, of course, represent Yahweh himself who effectively governs the world (cf. 11:4, 33:13). 'He oversees all and overlooks none' (C. H. Spurgeon). For 'nations' (*gôyīm*), see on 59:5.

the rebellious: *sôrēr* (see on 68:6) denotes one who is both stubborn and rebellious (cf. Jer. 5:23, 6:28; Hos. 4:16, 9:15; 1QS x:21; 1QH v:24). The Psalmist offers a warning to the disobedient: they should not exalt themselves, because God has not surrendered his dominion to anyone and his unparalleled might has not decreased.

Selah: see Introduction, pp. 48f.

THE COMMUNAL THANKSGIVING TO GOD **8–12**

8. Bless our God: see on 104:1. This call is addressed to the peoples (*ᶜammîm*). According to E. A. Speiser (cf. *JBL*, LXXIX (1960), pp. 157–60) the word *ᶜam* ('people') properly denotes 'a religious group with a common god, with whom they stand in a kin-relation, at least ethically'.

his praise: see on 65:1.

9. who has kept us: lit. . '. . . our soul', while some MSS. read: '. . . our souls' (LXX has '. . . my soul'). For *nep̱eš* as a substitute for the personal pronoun, see on 33:19.

among the living: probably '(who has set us) in life' (or 'in good fortune'); see Eichrodt, *TOT*, II, p. 361; cf. 21:5 (M.T. 6). This is parallel to 'has not let our feet slip', i.e. he has preserved us from misfortune (10:6, 55:22 (M.T. 23), 121:3).

10. tested us: the Hebrew *b-ḥ-n* means 'to examine, test', but here it may have a more specific significance. The parallel line refers to silver that is tried, and consequently *b-ḥ-n* may well have a similar connotation; so in Job 23:10: 'when he has tried me, I shall come forth (or 'shine forth') as gold'. Silver was one of the precious metals in the ancient Near East, and at times its value was higher than that of gold. The process of refining silver or gold is sometimes used figuratively of trying a man's heart (26:2) or of purifying the nation of its 'baser' elements by means of affliction, as if in a furnace; so in Isa. 48:10: 'I have tried you in the furnace of affliction' (cf. Isa. 1:25; Jer. 6:29; Zech. 13:9; Mal. 3:3).

11. The Psalmist does not give a definite account of the misfortunes, but he acknowledges that God has brought them upon the people. The purpose of this testing may have been to remove the godless from among the righteous of the nation (cf. Jer. 6:29f.).

into the net: God is depicted as a hunter who takes the wicked in his snares (Ezek. 12:13, 17:20). The word *meṣûḏāh* ('net') can also mean 'stronghold' ('dungeon'?), and it is so understood by Delitzsch, Cohen, *et al.*, but the *RSV* rendering may be more likely. Dahood takes it to mean 'wilderness' (see *Gregorianum* XLIII, 1962, pp. 71f., and *UHP*, p. 29).

affliction: the Hebrew *mûʿāḳāh* is a *hapax legomenon* in the *OT*, and *KBL* (p. 504) simply remarks on it 'unexplained'. T has *šwšltʾ* ('chains'), which may suggest Hebrew *ziḳḳîm*; this gives a reasonable parallel to verse 11*a*, but it may only be a good guess. Gunkel regards *mûʿāḳāh* as an Aramaism from *ʿ-w-ḳ* ('to be narrow, in distress', hence 'affliction') (cf. also *PAB*, II, p. 123).

12. men ride over our heads: this may depict the defeated survivors trodden down by the enemy horses (so Kirkpatrick). A similar situation is described in Isa. 51:23, and possibly in Am. 1:3 (cf. Yadin, *AWBL*, pp. 243, 334f., 384f.).

fire . . . water: these are symbolic of extreme danger. For a similar metaphor, see Isa. 43:2. Gunkel finds the origin of this word-picture in a fairy-tale motif, while Schmidt traces it to the practice of ordeal by fire and water; such an ordeal is not actually mentioned in the *OT*, but it was known in the Near East.

. . . brought us forth to a spacious place: (*NEB* '. . . into liberty') this follows the reading of the ancient versions (*lārewāḥāh*); M.T. has *lārewāyāh* ('to saturation') which is taken to mean 'abundance' (Cohen), 'wealthy place' (*AV*, *RV*). Kraus sees here an allusion to the deliverance from the Egyptian slavery. Dahood (*UHP*, p. 29) translates verse 12*c*: 'after you have led us out of abundance' (cf. Num. 11:4f.), making this phrase parallel with the thoughts expressed in verses 10–12*b*.

THE THANKSGIVING FOR DELIVERANCE **13–20**

13. burnt offerings: see on 40:6.

my vows: the content of these vows is briefly described in verse 15. For *nēḏer* ('vow'), see on 61:5.

14. In Jg. 11:30ff., 35–40 we find an interesting parallel to the vows made in times of trouble.

when I was in trouble: this is all the Psalmist says about the nature of his misfortunes; we can only speculate about the details.

15. Certain problems are raised by the apparently great quantity of sacrifices offered; either the man was exceptionally wealthy, or the poetic language should not be taken literally.

burnt offerings of fatlings: according to Lev. 22:18f. an offering in payment of a vow may be 'a male without blemish, of bulls or of the sheep or of the goats'. The 'fatlings' may include any young animal—bull, sheep, or goat—but the emphasis is placed upon their quality.

with the smoke: the Hebrew *ḳᵉṭōreṯ* means 'that which ascends as smoke', and may be a synonym for burnt offerings. In the post-Exilic period *ḳᵉṭōreṯ* was used to signify incense (cf. *VT*, x (1960), pp. 123f.).

. . . bulls and goats: this does not introduce different kinds of sacrifice but the three lines of verse 15 are parallel, and therefore the same type of offering is described in three different ways. This may account for the seemingly large quantity of animals offered by one person. He could be, of course, thought of as a representative of the nation.

Selah: see Introduction, pp. 48f.

16. Come and hear: in a sense every worshipper has his own *Heilsgeschichte* (Weiser, *POTL*, p. 471), but it concerns not only the individual himself but also the whole congregation. Therefore the experience of Yahweh's saving work is shared by all (cf. 22:22 (M.T. 23), 34:11 (M.T. 12)).

who fear God: i.e. his fellow worshippers (see on 34:7,9).

17. I cried aloud: lit. 'with my mouth I cried'.

he was extolled with my tongue: lit. 'and praise was under my tongue', i.e. it was kept in readiness. For the idiom, see 10:7; it is reminiscent of our expression: 'on the tip of one's tongue'. For 'praise' (*rômām*), see on 149:6.

18. If I had cherished: lit. 'If I had seen'. There is no need for the emendation 'I said in my heart, "The Lord will not hear"' (so Gunkel, Leslie, *et al.*). For 'iniquity' (*ʾāwen*), see on 36:4. The Psalmist points out that hypocrisy or downright wickedness is an insurmountable barrier between the suppliant and God. As long as one clings to them, it is impossible to cling to God (Isa. 59:2f.), and one does not need self-righteousness to realize that (cf. 17:1f., 18:20f. (M.T. 21f.); Isa. 1:15).

19. God has listened: and he has answered my supplication. For 'prayer', see on 65:2.

20. Blessed be God: see on 28:6. Both blessings and curses were of great importance in the ancient world, and it was believed that they could be transferred from one person to another by means of actions or words, or both. In blessings and curses, it was thought, a power was released or transmitted which went on operating unless it was neutralized by a more powerful force (cf. Dt. 23:5; Neh. 13:2). In the case of divine blessings in *OT*, God remained the master of his word and deed (cf. 24:4). In a sense God's blessing was not an independent force, but rather the active help of God himself, so that one could not have the blessing without its giver. It is possible that in primitive thought the power of the deity could be increased by human blessings, but of this there is no trace in the Psalter. Here to bless God means to praise him or his gracious help and mighty works by which he is known. See H. W. Beyer, '*Eulogeō*', *TDNT*, II, pp. 755–61.

he has not rejected my prayer: the word 'prayer' may be a gloss from verse 19, since there is only one verb (not two, as it appears from the *RSV* rendering), *hēsîr*, which cannot very well describe God's attitude to the Psalmist's Prayer and his own 'steadfast love', at the same time.

Psalm 67 May God be Gracious to Us

This poem is often described as a harvest thanksgiving Psalm sung by the whole community, or for the people (so Gunkel, Schmidt, Kissane, etc.). Its life-setting could be the Harvest Festival at the end of the agricultural year (so Oesterley), but this explanation is far from satisfactory. The Psalm begins and ends with the words 'May God bless us' (cf. verses 1 and 7) which is slightly odd in a Psalm of thanks for blessings *already* received. A partial answer is the suggestion that the Feast of Tabernacles does not only look back to the past but also forward to the future. The lack of emphasis upon the harvest blessings could be seen as a deliberate reaction against the Canaanite fertility religion; the Israelites stressed the nature of God rather than the processes of nature and its produce. So in Dt. 26:1–11 the presentation of the firstfruits of the harvest is an occasion for the recital of the *Credo* as a shortened version of the salvation-history.

Nevertheless, the above interpretation of the Psalm is based almost entirely upon verse 6*a*; if indeed *nāṯenāh* cannot be anything but a verb describing a past event (i.e. 'the earth *has yielded* its increase'), then the Psalm must be a harvest thanksgiving. It is more likely, however, that the verb is a precative perfect (see below): 'May the earth yield . . .', which fits in with the rest of the Psalm. If this is so, then the composition is a national lament or a prayer for God's blessing. Dahood (*PAB*, I, p. 27) would define it as 'a prayer for rain'.

This Psalm is usually regarded as post-Exilic; its metre is 3 + 3; the two exceptions being verses 4 (3 + 3 + 3) and 7 (2 + 2 + 2).

Verses 3 and 5 may form the refrain; Gunkel *et al.* suggest that we should also have a refrain at the end of the Psalm.

To the choirmaster: see Introduction, p. 48.
stringed instruments: see Introduction, p. 48.
A Psalm: see Introduction, p. 46.
A Song: see Introduction, p. 47.

THE PRAYER FOR GOD'S BLESSINGS **1–7**

1. May God be gracious to us: this expression, and indeed the whole verse, seems to be derived from the priestly blessing in Num. 6:24ff., or from a similar cultic formula (cf. 4:6 (M.T. 7), 31:16 (M.T. 17)). For the verb *ḥ-n-n*, see on 6:2.
and bless us: (see on 66:20) by granting us increase in fields and flocks (cf. Dt. 28:2–14) and success in all our undertakings (cf. 115:12–15).
his face to shine upon us: lit. '. . . to shine forth (so as to be) with us'. A 'shining' face is an expression of pleasure and delight. G. B. Gray (*Numbers* (*ICC*, 1903), p. 73) quotes a story about two men reporting that Rabbi Abbahu had found a treasure. When they were asked how did they know, they replied: 'Because his face shines'. To make one's face shine forth towards another person means to show him favour, as in Prov. 16:15: 'In the light of a king's face there is life, and his favour is like the clouds that bring spring rain'. The same idea would be even more appropriate to the grace of God (cf. A. M. Gierlich, *Der Lichtgedanke in den Psalmen* (1940), pp. 1, 60). Eichrodt (*TOT*, II, p. 37) comments that 'God's lifting up the light of his countenance' is an expression 'for the restoration of a relationship of favour between God and Man'. If this is true of our Psalm, then it may suggest that the composition is a lament of the community, or a prayer for God's gracious help.

Selah: see Introduction, pp. 48f.

2. thy way: perhaps 'your power' or 'your dominion', taking *dereḵ* (*RSV* 'way') as an equivalent of the Ugaritic *drkt* (see Dahood, *PAB*, I, p. 2; Aistleitner, *WUS*, p. 82; *HAL*, p. 223a). This would provide a good parallel to 'thy saving power' in verse 2*b*. The nation asks for God's blessings, not simply for their own selfish reasons, or for the sole purpose of self-preservation, but they also desire to see God's power and authority acknowledged by the whole world.

thy saving power: lit. 'your salvation' (see on 35:3), i.e. your power to help and to sustain. S reads 'his salvation' (*yᵉšûᶜāṯô*; as well as *dᵉrāḵāyw* ('his ways') in verse 2*a*, while some Hebrew MSS. read *darkô* ('his way')).

3. This verse, together with verse 5, forms the refrain of the Psalm.

Let the peoples . . .: i.e. all the nations that inhabit the world. For *ᶜam* ('people'), see on 66:8. The verb used for praising God is the causative form of *y-d-h* which can mean both to give thanks and to praise (see on 18:49).

let all the peoples . . .: this partial repetition of verse 3*a* is for the sake of emphasis.

4. Let the nations be glad because God judges or rules all the peoples with equity or judicial fairness, and with justice and mercy (cf. 96:10*c*). For the verb *š-p-ṭ* ('to judge'), see on 72:2.

guide the nations: the verb *n-ḥ-h* means 'to guide, lead' or 'to treat kindly, care for' (as in Job 31:18*b*). Usually God is the subject of the verb (cf. Gen. 24:48; Dt. 32:12; Ps. 78:14, 107:30; Isa. 57:18, etc.) and he is often depicted as guiding his people like a shepherd (23:3, 78:52f.), or leading them by a pillar of cloud and a pillar of fire (Exod. 13:21; Neh. 9:12,19). Those who are insolent enough to rebel against him, he leads to destruction (Job 12:23).

Selah: see Introduction, pp. 48f.

5. For the exegesis of this refrain, see verse 3.

6. The earth has yielded its increase: Dahood (*PAB*, II, p. 126) takes the verb *nāṯᵉnāh* as a precative perfect, hence 'May the earth yield . . .'. This interpretation is also supported by the verb in the parallel line, which may well be jussive in form (i.e. '*may* God . . . *bless* us'). Thus the poem may well be a lament. The word *yᵉḇûl* ('increase') usually refers to the produce of the land (so also in Ugaritic; cf. Gordon, *UT*, p. 408). For a spiritualized interpretation of it, see Cohen (*PSon*, p. 208), but the literal meaning is clearly the one intended by the Psalmist.

God, our God: originally, no doubt: 'Yahweh, our God'.

7. God has blessed us: probably 'May God bless us' since the same verbal form is used in verse 1*a* where it has a jussive meaning.

ends of the earth: i.e. the whole earth (see on 72:8).

fear him: see on 34:7,9.

Psalm 68 A Song of Procession

The interpretation of this Psalm is a difficult task because its structure is very complex, and the text is clearly corrupt in more than one place.

This Psalm does not fit into any of the major psalm-types, although it comes nearer to the Hymns than to any other *Gattung*. Dahood (*PAB*, II, p. 133) calls it 'a triumphal hymn'. It also contains elements which do not belong, strictly speaking, to the Hymns, e.g. oracles (verses 11f., 22f.), an expression of thanks (verses 19f.), a description of various cultic acts (verses 24f.), etc.

There are two main ways of interpreting this Psalm: it can be regarded either as a unity or as a collection of more or less independent units. A good representative of the latter view is W. F. Albright (*HUCA*, XXIII (1950–1), pp. 1–39). He points to the ancient Hebrew practice of identifying poetic compositions by citing their first line or strophe (following Sumerian, Akkadian, and Canaanite models), and he comes to the conclusion that Ps. 68 is a catalogue of poems, containing some thirty *incipits* (i.e. the beginnings of poems); the Elohistic editor, apparently, failed to recognize that he was dealing with a *list* of songs. This suggestion, although not impossible, seems rather unlikely. A slightly similar position is held by Schmidt (*PHAT*, pp. 127ff.), who believes that the Psalm is made up of some sixteen short, independent songs strung together for liturgical purposes. The alternative is to place the emphasis either upon the literary unity of the Psalm (cf. R. Kittel), or upon its unity of purpose (cf. Kraus, *PBK*, pp. 469ff.). Perhaps the best explanation is that the Psalm in its present form is a song of procession, which provided an explanation or the libretto of the various stages of the solemn festival procession. The composer of the poem may have drawn upon older cultic materials from various sources. This need not imply a lack of a poetical ability, but it may point to a time when the salvation-history was yet in the making, and when different aspects of the *Heilsgeschichte* may have been stressed at different localities, especially if the event concerned had taken place near the particular sanctuary (see verse 27).

The *Sitz im Leben* of our Psalm may have been the Autumnal Festival which included the celebration of Yahweh's kingship and his mighty deeds, as well as a praise of his providential care. A purely eschatological interpretation of the poem is unlikely, nor is it simply a song of victory after a battle.

The date of the composition may be early pre-Exilic. Albright places the compilation of his 'catalogue' in the Solomonic period, or a little later, while the composition of the original Israelite poems or adaptations from Canaanite poetry, he dates between the thirteenth and the twelfth centuries B.C. It is probable that some of the traditions drawn upon by the Psalmist may go back to the pre-Davidic period, but the Psalm itself must be a post-Davidic work, because of the references to the Jerusalem Temple. It seems less likely that it should be assigned to the post-Exilic period (so Podechard, Taylor, Deissler).

The metre of the Psalm is varied.

To the choirmaster: see Introduction, p. 48.
A Psalm of David: see Introduction, pp. 43ff. and 46.
A Song: see Introduction, p. 47.

THE MIGHT OF GOD **1–3**

1. This verse reproduces, with slight variations, Num. 10:35 which is classed by A. Bentzen (*Introduction to the Old Testament*, I, (1948), p. 140) as belonging to the so-called ' "Words of Signal", by which the Ark of the Covenant was greeted on its going out and return'. The present form of these 'Words of Signal' may derive from their cultic usage (see S. Mowinckel, *Der Achtundsechzigste Psalm* (1953), p. 24).

Let God arise: according to Num. 10:35, this signal was given whenever the Ark set out (on a march or in a battle), and similarly in this verse this utterance may mark the beginning of the festal procession at the head of which there may have been the Ark, the symbol of God's presence. One of the purposes of this procession may have been the representation and reliving of the salvation-history.

let his enemies be scattered: or 'his adversaries are scattered'. The connexion between the Ark and the overthrow of the enemies is illustrated by 1 Sam. 4:1–11, which tells the story of Israel's defeat at the hands of the Philistines. In order to reverse the fortunes, the elders of Israel suggested, 'Let us bring the ark of the covenant of the LORD here from Shiloh, that he may come among us and save us from the power of our enemies' (1 Sam. 4:3). Whatever may have been the specific interpretation of the Ark at that point, it was bound up with the presence of Yahweh (cf. also 1 Sam. 7:2; 2 Sam. 6:16). It is possible that in some Israelite circles it was regarded as the throne of Yahweh (cf. v. Rad, *OTT*, I, p. 237), or associated with it, while for the Deuteronomist it was primarily a container for the tablets of the law (see Clements, *GT*, p. 28, n.1).
those who hate him: cf. Exod. 20:5; Dt. 5:9. This expression is parallel to 'his enemies' (verse 1*a*) and to 'the wicked' (verse 2*b*). The verb *ś-n-ʾ* is used both of hatred or dislike among men (Gen. 29:31; Jg. 11:7; 2 Sam. 5:8; 1 Kg. 22:8) and of God's hostility towards the disobedient (cf. Mal. 1:3), or certain types of conduct (Prov. 6:16–19; Isa. 1:14, 61:8). Men may also hate God and all that is his (Dt. 7:10; Ps. 83:2 (M.T. 3), 139:21), either by deliberately disobeying his commandments and ignoring him, or by trying to take possession of what belongs to him (see also O. Michel, '*Miseō*', *TDNT*, IV, pp. 685–8).

2. As smoke is driven away: reading *k^{e}hinnāḏēp̱* for M.T. *k^{e}hindōp̱*, which may be an error or a mixed form (cf. *GK* 51k). 'Smoke' can sometimes accompany the theophany of God (Exod. 19:18, 20:18; Isa. 6:4), or it can be associated with God's wrath (18:8 (M.T. 9); Isa. 30:27). Frequently 'smoke' serves as a metaphor of that which is unsubstantial and ephemeral (37:20, 102:3 (M.T. 4); Isa. 51:6).
so drive them away: LXX '(so) let them come to an end' (similarly T, S, and V). M.T. has '(so) you shall drive (them)'.
as wax melts before fire: this is another word-picture which suggests instability, or the process of vanishing away. For other examples, see 22:15 (M.T. 16), 97:5; Mic. 1:4.
the wicked: (*r^{e}šāʿîm*), see on 28:3. Mowinckel (op cit., p. 25) suggests that the wicked are not simply the godless in the modern sense of the word, but they are all Yahweh's enemies both cosmic (mythological) and historical.

3. the righteous are the people of Yahweh, or the worshipping

community (see on 1:5) who may well be joyful. To them the destruction of the enemies of God means deliverance and peace.
let them exult: (cf. 5:11 (M.T. 12), 9:2 (M.T. 3)), i.e. let them extol the help and salvation given by God.

THE PRAISE TO THE PROTECTOR OF THE WEAK **4–6**
Verse 4 reminds us of a hymnic introduction which is followed by the main part of the 'hymn' (verses 5–6) giving the grounds for praising God.

4. Sing to God: the worshippers are called upon to praise Yahweh in their song. This imperative call to praise God (usually 'Yahweh') is a frequent hymnic introduction (cf. Exod. 15:21; Ps. 33:3, 96:1, 105:2, 149:1; Isa. 42:10; Jer. 20:13; etc.).
sing praises to his name: for *zimmēr* ('to sing'), see on 66:4. 'To his name' may be a circumlocution for 'to him' (see on 20:1). At a later time the 'name' became one of the main roundabout expressions for God.
lift up a song: the verb *s-l-l* usually means 'to lift up, cast up', as in Isa. 62:10: '. . . build up (i.e. cast up), build up the highway' (cf. Isa. 57:14), and consequently Oesterley (*TP*, p. 321) renders our verse: '. . . build a highway for him . . .', yet the immediate context demands that we should take the verb in the sense of 'lift up (one's voice)' (cf. *nāśā' ḳôl*, 'to lift up voice', in 93:3; cf. 84:5 (M.T. 6)).
who rides upon the clouds: in Ugaritic literature *rkb ᶜrpt* ('the Rider of the Clouds'; cf. Gordon, *UT*, p. 461) was one of the stock epithets of Baal, the fertility-god of Canaan; many scholars regard our phrase *rōḵēḇ bāᶜᵃrāḇôṯ* as identical with the Ugaritic expression. The Hebrew *bᵉ* instead of the Ugaritic *p* is explained as a normal mutation of consonants, and therefore no emendation is necessary. It is possible that the appropriation of Baal's distinctive title reflects a deliberate religious polemic against the Canaanite beliefs. The Psalmist stresses that the giver of rain and prosperity is not Baal, but the one whose **name is the LORD**. The clouds are Yahweh's chariot which may have been represented by the '*kappōreṯ* (lid) of the Ark with its winged cherubim' (so W. Beyerlin, *Origins and History of the Oldest Sinaitic Traditions*, Eng. tr. by S. Rudman (1965), pp. 108f.). Another possible explanation of *rōḵēḇ bāᶜᵃrāḇôṯ* is that of Johnson (*SKAI*, p. 70), who takes *ᶜᵃrāḇôṯ* as the plural of *ᶜᵃrāḇāh* ('steppe, desert'); consequently Yahweh is depicted as riding through the deserts, and the allusion

is to the desert wanderings of Israel. This view receives some support from verses 7–8. Perhaps the choice of *ᶜarāḇôṯ* was meant to suggest both the title of Baal, the giver of rain (cf. verse 9) and the Wilderness tradition (cf. verse 7).

his name is the LORD: M.T. has *yāh*, the shorter form of *yhwh* ('Yahweh'). Some scholars believe that the longer form is the original one, while the others, such as *yāh*, *yô*, *yāhû*, etc., are abbreviations. Cf. G. R. Driver, *ZAW*, XLVI (1928), pp. 7–25; *JBL*, LXXIII (1954), pp. 125–31; R. Mayer, *BZ*, N.F., II (1958), pp. 26–53. The other alternative is to assume that one of the shorter forms is the more ancient one. *Yāh* is thought to have been originally a cultic exclamation which was used in worship. It is not, however, the etymology of the word that is all important, but rather the understanding of God associated with his name. *Yāh* is found in *OT* theophoric names (e.g. Elijah (*ʾēliyyāh*)), in various poetic texts (cf. Exod. 15:2), and in cultic expressions, such as 'Praise the Lord' (i.e. *Yāh*) or 'Hallelujah' (cf. 104:35, 106:1, etc.). The preposition *bᵉ* before *yāh* may be an emphasizing particle (see Dahood, *PAB*, I, p. 177); hence 'his name is none other than Yāh'.

5. **Father of the fatherless:** God overthrows the wicked as the wind scatters smoke, but he helps and protects the weak and the oppressed. In the Ugaritic texts (cf. 'The Legend of Keret', *ANET*, p. 149a; 'The Tale of Aqhat', *ANET*, p. 151a) the protection of widows and orphans was one of the specific tasks of the ideal king. In Israel the same function was performed by Yahweh (and it was also entrusted to his regent, the King), and this Psalm praises the divine king by mentioning certain aspects of his work.

protector: the Hebrew *dayyān* is a 'judge' (as in 1 Sam. 24:15), but it can also denote one who delivers or defends the oppressed (see on 72:2).

in his holy habitation: this could refer to Yahweh's heavenly dwelling, as in Dt. 26:15: 'Look down from thy holy habitation, from heaven . . .', or the Temple which was, in a sense, the meeting point between heaven and earth (so Mowinckel, Nötscher, Kraus, *et al.*). LXX takes the preposition *bᵉ* (*RSV* 'in') as meaning 'from' (like the Ugaritic *b*); also some Hebrew MSS. read *m*(*in*) ('from').

6. **the desolate:** (*NEB*: 'the friendless') Albright (op. cit., p. 19) thinks that the reference is to an unmarried man who has

no means to purchase a bride; but it is more likely that the writer had in mind the lonely, those who for some reason or other did not have a family or a clan to protect their rights (cf. Mowinckel, op. cit., p. 30). In a manner of speaking they would be like the alien who was dependent upon the good-will of the local community, and who is often mentioned in the *OT* as in need of special protection. Such people are given a home and protection, similar to that enjoyed by others having a family.
he leads out the prisoners: better '. . . the captives'. The word *ʾāsîr* could be used of a real prisoner (e.g. of Joseph in the Egyptian prison (Gen. 39:20; cf. Ps. 107:10)), but more often it was applied to captives in a foreign land (69:33 (M.T. 34); Isa. 14:17; Lam. 3:34; Zech. 9:11). They would be employed at various heavy tasks, such as mining, metal working, building, etc. It is possible that this verse refers to the Egyptian slavery, while the rebellious (verse 6*c*) may allude to the generation of the Wilderness period, which perished.
to prosperity: the Hebrew *kôšārôṯ* is a *hapax legomenon* in the *OT*, but it has been explained on the basis of the Ugaritic *kṯrt* ('woman singer') and *kṯr* (or *kṯr-w-ḫss*) which is the name of the Canaanite god of music and merry-making (cf. Gordon, *UT*, pp. 424f.). Hence Albright (op. cit., p. 37) translates *bakkôšārôṯ* as 'with music' (similarly Mowinckel and Dahood); Johnson suggests 'skilfully' (*SKAI*, p. 70); *NEB* 'safe and sound'.
the rebellious: represent the Hebrew *sôrēr* which in this case denotes the stubborn among the Israelites (cf. 78:8; Isa. 30:1, 65:2; Jer. 5:23; Hos. 4:16), and not the foreign nations. The same word is also used of the stubborn and rebellious son in Dt. 21:18.
in a parched land: or 'wasteland', i.e. a land which is dazzling in its barrenness.

GOD COMES IN POWER AND BLESSING **7–10**

7. God is addressed in the second person, and this feature is more appropriate to a thanksgiving than to a hymn. The language of verses 7–8 is an adaptation of Jg. 5:4f. God comes to the help of Israel against the Canaanite oppressors. Verses 7–8 probably allude to the Exodus, the Wilderness Period, and the Entry into the Promised Land. Yet Yahweh is not simply a God who gives only deliverance and victory in war; he is also the giver of rain and fertility.
when thou didst go forth: i.e. from Egypt, leading his people

(cf. Exod. 13:21f.) as if he were the commander-in-chief of the Israelite army (Num. 27:17).
the wilderness: *yᵉšîmôn*, without the article, may refer to any desert place (cf. Dt. 32:10). With the article it denotes the Wilderness of Judah (cf. 1 Sam. 23:19,24, 26:1,3). See Introduction to Ps. 63.
Selah: see Introduction, pp. 48f.
8. Earthquake and rain (i.e. storm) are often used to describe the coming of God as well as his presence (cf. Exod. 19:16ff.; Ps. 18:7–13 (M.T. 8–14)).
yon Sinai: lit. 'who is Sinai' (so Johnson, *SKAI*, p. 71, n.1) which implies that 'Sinai' is both the name of the mountain and the name of the deity worshipped there. (For a brief bibliography on this subject, see Johnson, *SKAI*, p. 71, n.1.) Albright (op. cit., p. 20) renders this phrase by 'The One of Sinai' (cf. Gray *JJR*, p. 278) which could be paraphrased as 'the lord of Sinai' (so *NEB*). The other point about this expression is the question whether it is a gloss. Mowinckel, Kraus, *et al.* regard it as an explanatory note, while the opposite view is held by Albright, Johnson, *et al.* The association of Yahweh with Sinai, belongs to a very ancient tradition, but even in Mosaic times Yahweh was not confined, metaphorically speaking, to the holy mountain. He was able to manifest his power in Egypt and in the Wilderness, and he came to the rescue of his people in Canaan (see Beyerlin, op. cit., p. 102).
at the presence of God: or 'before God'; this is repeated twice, and it is possible that one of the occurrences is a gloss. The Hebrew *pānîm* ('face, presence'), when used with the suffix (i.e. our possessive pronoun), may serve as a periphrasis for the personal pronoun. Occasionally it may have a reflexive force (cf. Ezek. 6:9: 'in their own sight', i.e. to themselves). For a more detailed discussion on *pānîm*, see Johnson, *VITAI*, pp. 40–5.
the God of Israel: Yahweh is the God of Israel (cf. Jg. 5:5), i.e. the God who is worshipped by Israel, rather than the God who belongs to the tribes of Jacob (cf. 41:13 (M.T. 14)). An older form of this same term is 'El-Elohe-Israel' (Gen. 33:20), i.e. El, the God of Israel.
9. Rain in abundance: or 'generous rain'. The Hebrew *gešem* ('rain') probably signifies the heavy showers in the late autumn, which soften the soil and make cultivation possible (see on 65:10). Some exegetes see here an allusion to the miraculous

provision of the manna and the quails during the sojourn in the Wilderness (cf. Exod. 16:4; Ps. 78:24,27; so Cohen, Nötscher). See also E. Vogt, *Biblica*, XLVI (1965), pp. 359–61.

thou didst restore thy heritage: Kissane, Nötscher, *et al.* take the 'heritage' as denoting Israel or the Israelites, but it is far more likely that the writer had in mind the land of Canaan which is often described as Yahweh's inheritance or possession (see v. Rad, *PHOE*, pp. 79–93).

as it languished: lit. 'and it languished'. The conjunction 'and' (*wᵉ*) may represent an emphatic *wāw*, hence '. . . your languishing possession' (see on 28:9).

10. thy flock: the Hebrew *ḥayyāh* can mean either 'a living thing, animal', or 'a camp, community' (cf. 2 Sam. 23:13). LXX has 'your creatures', and similarly Kissane ('thy wild beasts'). From the context it seems that the reference must be to the Israelites; Johnson (*SKAI*, p. 71) renders 'Thy family'; *AV*, *RV* have 'Thy congregation'; *NEB* 'thy own people'.

in it: i.e. in Yahweh's possession or inheritance.

the needy: for *ᶜānî*, see on 34:2.

THE VICTORY OF GOD OVER THE KINGS **11–14**

11. The Lord gives the command: or '. . . utters a word'. This probably refers to Yahweh's voice in the thunder (cf. verse 33*b*, also 29:3–9) which puts the enemies to flight. Once he has spoken, the enemies are defeated, and the good news (quoted in verse 12*a*) is spread all over the land. Other commentators see here a reference to some particular oracle or command (cf. Jg. 4:6). Kraus (*PBK*, p. 473) suggests that the Psalmist is drawing upon the cultic traditions preserved at the sanctuary on Mount Tabor.

who bore the tidings: i.e. the women of Israel who spread the triumphant news in their songs (cf. Exod. 15:20f.; 1 Sam. 18:6f.), or by means of informative gossip. Albright (op. cit., p. 37) reads: 'Rejoicing (*mᵉḇaśśereṯ*) a mighty host'; this is the result of Yahweh's oracle. Yet the *RSV* rendering seems preferable.

12. This verse gives the substance of the good news: the enemy is in flight, and the spoils are already being divided.

The kings of the armies are probably the kings of Canaan who were with Sisera at the battle of Taanach (Jg. 5:19). This expression brings to mind 'Yahweh of Hosts', in whose sight the 'kings of the hosts' are as nothing.

they flee: the repetition of this phrase is for the purpose of emphasis, to draw a special attention to the complete rout of the enemy, unless the repetition is a scribal error; it is lacking in some Hebrew MSS. and S.

the women at home: lit. 'the one dwelling at home'. Albright suggests 'In the meadows they divide the spoil' (reading *ûḇᵉnāwōṯ* for M.T. *ûnᵉwaṯ bayiṯ*); Mowinckel, Kraus, *et al.* suggest *ûḇinᵉwaṯ bayiṯ* ('on the floor of the house').

13. There is some textual disorder in this verse, and it is impossible to know what the original reading might have been.

though they stay among the sheepfolds: some exegetes regard this phrase as a gloss from Jg. 5:16. According to the *RSV* rendering it refers to the women dividing the spoils. The main problem is the Hebrew *šᵉpattāyim*. *KBL* (p. 580b) reads *mišpᵉṯayim* ('saddle-bags' of a donkey), while Johnson (*SKAI*, p. 71) thinks that verse 13*a* may be an idiomatic expression for behaving 'like a lazy donkey'. Albright takes this obscure Hebrew word as meaning 'hearth' (but cf. Aistleitner, *WUS*, p. 341; Driver, *CML*, p. 161, *sub mṯpd*). The meaning of the whole verse may be that, although some tribes stayed away from the battle, the loyal Israelites returned laden with spoils.

the wings of a dove . . .: the translation of this phrase (verse 13*bc*) does not provide any real difficulties, but its interpretation is anything but clear. Doves and pigeons covered with gold and silver would hardly be used to carry news of military victories (as suggested by Eerdmans). Possibly the allusion is to the rich booty represented by the gold and silver figure of a dove (a symbol of Astarte, the goddess of love (?); cf. Ca. 2:12,14,5:2, 6:9). Mowinckel suggests that the dove may be either a description of the oppressed Israel, now rewarded with a rich spoil (similarly Calès), or a designation for Yahweh's beloved (i.e. the people of Israel). Weiser (*POTL*, p. 487) thinks that the dove may be 'a simile alluding to the cloud in which . . . Yahweh appeared on the battlefield . . .'. In this connection, see Exod. 25:18 (also Ezek. 1:4), which speaks about the gold cherubim who probably represent Yahweh's chariot of clouds (cf. 18:10 (M.T.11)).

green gold: this is a late expression or, more likely, a poetical phrase (cf. *HAL*, p. 338b). The reference seems to be to 'yellow gold' (*NEB*) (cf. Driver, *CML*, p. 166, n.9).

14. This verse may contain a reminiscence of an ancient victory. Apart from the military success, the outstanding feature of the day was the snow-fall on Mount Zalmon. Jg. 9:48 mentions a Mount Zalmon near Shechem, but it is unlikely that the reference is to this particular hill. Most commentators identify Zalmon with 'the modern *Ǧebel Ḥaurân*' (cf. Johnson, *SKAI*, p. 72, n.3).

the Almighty: the Hebrew *šadday*, according to Exod. 6:3, was the name by which God made himself known to the Patriarchs. It is found in the *OT* some 48 times, mainly in the Book of Job (as an archaism?). The etymology of *šadday* is uncertain, although many scholars associate it with the Akkadian *šadû* ('mountain') (cf. also the Hebrew *śāḏeh* ('field')), hence the divine name might indicate 'the one of the mountain(s)'. The English rendering 'Almighty' is based on LXX *pantokratōr*, and V *omnipotens*. The rabbinic explanation of *šadday* is 'the one who is self-sufficient' (i.e. *šedday*). Kraus (*PBK*, p. 473) regards the name to be of Canaanite origin, possibly the name of the deity who dwelt on Mount Tabor. For further references, see Rowley, *WAI*, p. 9, n.4.

THE HOLY MOUNTAIN **15–18**

15. O mighty mountain: lit. 'O mountain of God' (or 'gods') (cf. D. Winton Thomas, 'A Consideration of some Unusual Ways of Expressing the Superlative in Hebrew', *VT*, III (1953), pp. 209–24). Mowinckel (op. cit. p. 41) suggests 'the (true) mountain of God is the mountain of Bashan', and he assumes that at one time Yahweh was worshipped on this sacred mountain. Its location is not certain but it may be linked with the region of Bashan (see on 22:12), or the name 'Bashan' may have an appellative force like 'Zaphon' (see on 48:2). In verse 22 'Bashan' probably means the 'highest mountain' or 'highest height' in contrast to the 'depths of the sea' (cf. Kraus, *PBK*, p. 470). It seems more likely, however, that the Mount (or 'mountain-range') of Bashan is rebuked for its jealousy of Mount Zion, which Yahweh had chosen as his dwelling place instead of his old abode, Sinai.

many-peaked: the Hebrew *gaḇnunnîm* is found only in this Psalm, and its exact meaning is not clear. It is probably associated with *gibbēn* which occurs in Lev. 21:20 with the possible meaning of 'hump-backed'. Johnson (*SKAI*, p. 72) takes it in the sense of 'lofty' (cf. *HAL*, p. 167).

16. look . . . with envy: the verb *r-ṣ-d* is a *hapax legomenon* in the *OT*, and the ancient versions vary considerably in their interpretation of it. Albright follows the meaning of the Arabic cognate, *raṣada* ('to watch') but *RSV* may better represent the author's intention. It is possible that the Psalmist is rejecting the rival claims of a sanctuary in the North (so Weiser), but equally well he may have been aware of the fact that Mount Zion was not the highest mountain in Canaan, and therefore its claim to be the mountain of God *par excellence*, and thus the 'highest' mountain, rested upon Yahweh's choice and not on its actual elevation.

17. With mighty chariotry: lit. 'The chariot (or 'chariots') of God'. The Hebrew *reḵeḇ* ('chariot') may be used collectively. The ancient chariot was a two-wheeled vehicle, normally made of wood and leather or wickerwork, and the chariot box itself was open at the back. It was usually drawn by two horses, and manned by two, three, or even four men. See de Vaux, *AI*, pp. 222–5; Yadin, *AWBL*, pp. 129, 190f. The 'chariots of God' may refer to the heavenly armies which accompany Yahweh (cf. 2 Kg. 6:17; Isa. 66:15; Hab. 3:8; Zech. 14:5).

twice ten thousand: the M.T. *ribbōṯayim* is probably to be taken in a multiplicative sense (*GK* 97h), 'thousands upon thousands'. It is, apparently, an explanatory note on the next phrase *ʾalᵉpê šinʾān*. The word *šinʾān* is rendered by *BDB* as 'repetition', hence 'thousands upon thousands'. LXX probably took it as *šaʿᵃnān*, rendering '(thousands of) those who rejoice'; S has '(thousands of) hosts', and similarly *AV*, *RP* 'even thousands of angels'.

the Lord came from Sinai: this follows the usual emendation of *bām sînay* ('. . . among them, Sinai . . .') into *bāʾ missînay*. M.T. is well rendered by Johnson (*SKAI*, p. 73): 'The Lord is amid them, the God of Sinai is in the sanctuary' (see verse 8).

into the holy place: Johnson's translation above seems preferable. Mowinckel takes *baḳḳōḏeš* in the sense of 'in power' which gives a possible rendering; *ḳōḏeš* ('holiness') is etymologically of uncertain derivation (cf. N. H. Snaith, *The Distinctive Ideas of the Old Testament*, pp. 24–39; O. Procksch, '*Hagios*', *TDNT*, I, pp. 89–97). The two main suggestions are that the root-meaning is either the idea of setting apart or that of brilliance, perhaps the latter. In biblical language 'holy' means 'the wholly other', i.e. the divine: that which is holy belongs to God (Dt. 7:6); or it describes God himself (Lev. 11:44; Ps. 99:5; Isa. 6:3), and it is charged, in a way, with awesome power (Jer. 2:3). God's holiness may have either a destructive (cf. 2 Sam. 6:7) or a saving aspect (cf. 'your Redeemer, the Holy One of Israel', Isa. 48:17; cf. also Isa. 41:14, 43:3,14, 49:7, 54:5). *Ḳōḏeš* can also denote the Temple

(74:3, 150:1) as the place that belongs to God. See van Imschoot, *ThOT*, I, pp. 40–9; Vriezen, *OOTT*, pp. 150f.

18. Thou didst ascend the high mount: or '. . . on high'. The Hebrew *mārôm* means 'height' (i.e. an elevated place, mountain top; cf. 2 Kg. 19:23; Jer. 31:12) or 'heaven' (71:19, 93:4, 102:19 (M.T. 20), 148:1). Albright (op. cit., p. 25) points out that the Ugaritic *mrym* (=Hebrew *mārôm*) always appears together with *ṣpn* (i.e. Zaphon) which was the holy mountain (see on 48:2), and that it carries the corollary that *mārôm* in geographical extension means 'north'. But Mowinckel (op. cit., p. 47) has remarked that, just as *ṣpn* is a dwelling-place of gods, so also *mārôm* may be in this verse the abode of God, i.e. the sacred mountain.

leading captives . . .: (cf. Jg. 5:12), i.e. the Canaanite kings who threatened the existence of Yahweh's people, or, perhaps in a wider sense, all the forces that have opposed the rule of God (cf. Isa. 24:21f.; also 2 C. 2:14).

receiving gifts among men: or '. . . from men' (taking the preposition *b* (*RSV* 'among') to mean 'from', as in Ugaritic; cf. R. T. O'Callaghan, *VT*, IV (1954), pp. 171f.). The gifts may refer to the tribute received from the conquered nations (cf. 2 Sam. 8:11; 1 Kg. 4:21), or to the gifts offered to God in homage. The expression may be a metaphor of allegiance. Verse 18 is quoted in Eph. 4:8 with some modifications, and for our phrase it has 'he gave gifts to men' (so also T and S).

even among the rebellious . . .: Johnson thinks that the rebellion is a disapproval of Yahweh's choice of his home, lit. 'at the settling down of *Yāh*, God'. The word 'God' may be a gloss on *Yāh* (see on verse 4) while some commentators regard the whole phrase as a later addition (so Mowinckel *et al.*). Albright (op. cit., p. 26) comments: 'I have no idea what to do with them (the words of the above phrase)', and the expression seems to be out of its proper context. Perhaps we might paraphrase: 'Even the rebellious (did homage) in establishing (i.e. in accepting) *Yāh* as God' (for the verb, see Gordon, *UT*, p. 490, *sub škn*; cf. also Dt. 12:11, 14:23), or 'Even the stubborn rebels are (prepared) to submit to *Yāh* as God' (cf. *KBL*, p. 971a).

THE GOD OF OUR SALVATION **19–23**

19. Blessed . . .: i.e. God is worthy to be worshipped and adored. This is a characteristic expression of the Thanksgiving Psalms; see on 104:1.

who daily bears us up is a metaphor of divine care. The word 'daily' (*yôm yôm*) should be added to the previous line, reading: 'Blessed be the Lord, day by day' (so M.T.). The rest of the verse could be rendered 'He carries us (cf. Exod. 19:4; Dt. 1:31; Ps. 28:9); God is our salvation'.

Selah: see Introduction, pp. 48f.

20. Our God . . .: lit. 'God (*ʾēl*, see on 52:5) is to us (a God of saving acts)'. The Hebrew *môšāʿāh* is a *hapax legomenon* in the *OT*, but it is obviously a synonym of *t*ᵉ*šûʿāh* and its cognates (for 'salvation', see on 35:3).

belongs escape from death: Yahweh is the Lord also over the sphere of death. This is slightly reminiscent of Baal's victory over Mot, the god of the netherworld, except that Yahweh did not die and rise like Baal, for he, undefeated, has subdued all his enemies whatever their sphere of action (cf. 1 Sam. 2:6).

21. But: the Hebrew *ʾaḵ* may also mean 'surely, yea' (see on 62:1).

shatter the heads of his enemies: i.e. he will utterly defeat them (cf. 110:6; Hab. 3:13). The enemies may include in their ranks also the so-called 'mythological foes', as in 74:13: 'Thou didst break the heads of the dragons on the waters'.

the hairy crown: Albright (op. cit., p. 38) suggests: 'The skull of the goat-demon (?)', reading *śāʿîr* for M.T. *śēʿār* ('hair'); but the *RSV* rendition seems more fitting, because verses 21–3 seem to describe God's unlimited might over the human enemies. The 'hairy crown' may be an allusion to the ancient practice of wearing one's hair long during the Holy Wars or other special periods. Thus the Nazirites remained unshaven and unshorn during the time of their vow (cf. Num. 6:1–5). Another possibility is to read *rāšāʿ* ('wicked') for M.T. *śēʿār*, hence '(God will shatter . . .) the pate of the wicked who walks . . .' (cf. R. T. O'Callaghan, op. cit., pp. 171ff.). For the parallelism of 'head' and 'pate', see *Keret* II, vi:56–7 (cf. Driver, *CML*, p. 47). *NEB* has 'their flowing locks'.

who walks in his guilty ways: or 'who continues in his guilt'. The Hebrew *ʾāšām* can denote both the offence or guilt (cf. Gen. 26:10; Jer. 51:5), and the compensation, substitute, or the so-called guilt-offering (cf. Lev. 5:19, 7:5, 14:22; 1 Sam. 6:3,8; Isa. 53:10). In this verse *ʾāšām* is not to be understood in a strictly ethical sense but it may suggest those nations which covet the land of Israel (cf. R. de Vaux, *Studies in OT Sacrifice*, pp. 98–106).

22. The Lord said: this can be taken as an introduction to the oracle (verses 22–3).

I will bring them back from Bashan: the object of the verb is not expressed in M.T., and it is not clear whether the author thought that God would bring back all the enemies that they might be punished, or whether he expected that all the Israelites would be restored to their land (cf. Isa. 43:5f., 49:12). The former alternative may be more likely, showing that none of Israel's enemies (mentioned in verse 21) shall escape the divine retribution, whereever they might flee (cf. Am. 9:2f.). 'From Bashan' seems to suggest 'from the highest heights' in antithesis to 'the depths of the sea'. Some exegetes regard Bashan as the region in Trans-Jordan, while other commentators emend *mibbāšān* ('from Bashan') into *mikkiḇšan ʾēš*, ('from the fiery furnace'; so *RP*), yet this seems less likely. *NEB* renders 'from the Dragon'.

23. . . . bathe your feet in blood: this reminds us of the exploits of Anath in the Ugaritic myths. She, too, wades through blood and washes her hands in it (cf. *Baal* v,ii:11–35; *ANET*, p. 136a), yet it is unlikely that the Psalmist had in mind this Canaanite story. The language of both may belong to the traditional hyperbolic descriptions of battles (see on 58:10). The *RSV* rendering follows the ancient versions; M.T. has *timḥaṣ* ('you will shatter') which seems to be an error for *tirḥaṣ* ('you will bathe'; so LXX, T, and S).

the tongues of your dogs . . .: i.e. the dogs shall lick the blood of the fallen enemies. This, too, may have been a proverbial expression for a rightful retribution (cf. 1 Kg. 21:19, 22:38; 2 Kg. 9:36).

THE SOLEMN PROCESSION **24–7**

24. Thy solemn processions: i.e. the procession led by Yahweh who was represented by the Ark.

are seen: reading *nirʾû* (so LXX); M.T. has 'they have seen' but since the subject is indefinite, it may be, perhaps, translated by a passive construction (see Johnson, *SKAI*, p. 74, n.3).

my King: *meleḵ* was a well-known title of certain deities in the ancient world, and this is well attested by the numerous theophoric names which include *mlk* ('king') as one of their constituent parts, e.g. Melchizedek, Abdi-milki, Melkart, etc. (cf. M. H. Pope, *El in the Ugaritic Texts* (1955), p. 26). Kraus regards the Israelite divine title 'king' as originally of Canaanite origin, which designated the highest deity in the pantheon (cf. J. Gray, *VT*, XI (1961), pp. 1–29). In the Ugaritic texts both El and Baal are called kings (cf. W. H. Schmidt, *Königtum Gottes in Ugarit und Israel* (*BZAW*, 80, 2nd edn, 1966), pp. 64–8). Eichrodt (*TOT*, I, p. 195) suggests that although Yahweh could have been spoken of as King before the institution of the monarchy, it was with the introduction of political kingship that *meleḵ* came into favour as a title of Yahweh. In his view, the pre-Exilic prophets, and in particular the Deuteronomists, were critical of this divine title, but it was Deutero-Isaiah who re-instated the title in the usage of the prophetic circles. When the prophets speak of the kingship of God, their emphasis is on the *Heilsgeschichte* which, originally, had little connection with the divine kingship; see also on 24:7. In the Psalms *meleḵ* is a frequent title of Yahweh and it does not follow that these Psalms *must* be late (cf. 5:2 (M.T. 3), 10:16, 24:7,8,10, 29:10, 44:4 (M.T. 5), 47:2,6 (M.T. 3,7), etc.).

into the sanctuary: (=*NEB*) or 'in holiness' (so Albright) which seems less likely (cf. verse 17*b*).

25. Here the Psalmist gives a more detailed description of the procession. The singers (LXX wrongly 'princes') went before the main body of the participants, and the players of stringed instruments followed. It is less clear whether the maidens surrounded (reading *b*e*ṯôḵ*, so M.T.), or whether they were between, the singers and the minstrels (reading *battāweḵ*).

timbrels: see on 81:2.

26. Bless God: originally, perhaps, 'Bless Yahweh' (see on 28:6). Some exegetes suggest 'they blessed (i.e. they greeted) . . .' (reading the perfect *bērᵉḵû*) in which case the subject would be the singers and minstrels, as representatives of all the worshippers, or the description might include the whole worshipping community.

in the great congregation: or 'in companies' (so Nötscher, Johnson). The Hebrew *maḵhēlôṯ* is plural in form used either for the sake of emphasis (as in *RSV*), or it may allude to the different sections of the procession (cf. also 1QH ii:30).

. . . of Israel's fountain: i.e. all true Israelites. Johnson sees here a reference to the starting point of the procession, namely 'the Spring of Israel' which he takes to be the 'Spring of Gihon' (see on 110:7; *SKAI*, p. 74). Another possibility is to read *mᵉḳôr* ('the fountain of (Israel)') instead of M.T. *mimmᵉḳôr*, making it into a title of Yahweh (so *RP*). Dahood (*PAB*, II, p. 148) renders

'Yahweh in the convocation of Israel', deriving *māḳôr* from *ḳ-w-r* ('to call').

27. The festival must have been an amphictyonic feast, and the four tribes mentioned probably represented all twelve. It is not clear why these four tribes have been chosen, but it is possible that Benjamin and Judah stood for the southern tribes, while Zebulun and Naphtali were mentioned on behalf of the northern tribes. If the Psalmist was using old traditions, then the reference to Zebulun and Naphtali might suggest that *one* of the author's sources must have been the cultic traditions of Mt. Tabor, the sanctuary of Zebulun, Issachar, and Naphtali (cf. Dt. 33:18f.; Jos. 19:33f.). Our Psalm contains several allusions to the Song of Deborah (Jg. 5) which celebrates the victory over Sisera, near Mt. Tabor; in this battle Zebulun and Naphtali played an important role (rather than Ephraim and Manasseh who became important at a later time; cf. Jg. 4:6,10, 5:18). All these links may be not purely accidental, and therefore it is a reasonable conclusion that Ps. 68 may have adapted material derived from the sanctuary at Mt. Tabor (see Kraus, *PBK*, p. 471). If this is so, the mention of Judah does not belong to the original material.
Benjamin . . . in the lead: (cf. Jg. 5:14). M.T. has '. . . rules over them'. Mowinckel (op. cit., p. 53) thinks that this implies a time when Benjamin actually dominated the other tribes, i.e. during the reign of Saul. Another less likely possibility is that Benjamin represents Jerusalem, for the latter was theoretically in Benjamin's territory.
princes are not the members of the royal house, but they are the leaders of the various groups. See on 119:23.
in their throng: the Hebrew *rigmāṯām* is a problematic word, possibly associated with the Ugaritic *rgm* ('to speak'). Johnson (*SKAI*, p. 75) reads *rōgēm tām* ('honest-spoken') as describing Judah (cf. Gen. 38:26, 44:18–34). One Hebrew MS. (and similarly Jerome) read *b^erikmāṯām* ('in their coloured garments').

THE PRAYER TO GOD **28–31**

28. The text of this verse may be textually corrupt.
Summon thy might . . .: M.T. has 'Your God has commanded strength' (similarly *AV*), but *RSV* follows many Hebrew MSS., LXX, T, S, and V.
show thy strength: perhaps read *ᶜōz hā'^elōhîm* ('(even) the awe-inspiring strength (which you have manifested for us in the past)'),

taking *ʾelōhîm* as a means of expressing a superlative (see verse 15).

29. The rendering of this verse is rather uncertain. From the various emendations suggested, that of Johnson (*SKAI*, p. 75) seems the most satisfactory. He reads *mah yekolekā* (for M.T. *mēhêkālekā* ('Because of thy temple')) 'How potent Thou art on behalf of . . .', or, perhaps, 'How you have prevailed on behalf of Jerusalem'. Dahood (*PAB*, II, p. 132): 'Your temple, Most High, is Jerusalem'.
kings bear gifts . . . : as an expression of their homage to Yahweh (cf. 76:11 (M.T. 12); Isa. 18:7, 60:3–7).

30. Rebuke the beasts . . .: or '. . . the wild beast'. What particular animal was intended by this general term is not apparent. Among the suggested possibilities, the more likely candidates are the hippopotamus and the crocodile. This 'beast' (or 'beasts') may symbolize a historical enemy, such as Egypt (so Briggs, Kraus, Dahood, *et al.*), or it may denote the powers of Chaos (so Mowinckel). Verse 31 may favour the former suggestion although historical and mythical allusions are often found together in cultic songs (cf. 87:4; Isa. 30:7).
the herd of bulls: this may refer to the kings or leaders of the foreign enemies. For a similar usage, see also *Keret* III, iv:6,7; Driver, *CML*, p. 39, n.4.
with the calves of the peoples: Johnson renders: 'the bull-like people' (cf. the expression 'a brute of a man'). Kraus *et al.* follow the common emendation *baʿalê* ('the lords of . . .') for M.T. *beʿegelê* ('with the calves of . . .'). This emended phrase 'the lords of the peoples' would be in apposition to 'the herd of bulls'.
Trample under foot . . .: (lit. 'Trampling . . .') which would continue the imperative 'Rebuke' at the beginning of the verse. *RP* has 'who trample . . .' referring to the peoples. Cf. *ANEP*, pl. 309 Yadin, *AWBL*, p. 150.
who lust after tribute: reading *berōṣê* for *beraṣṣê* which might mean '(Trampling) on pieces of (silver)'. Some commentators render 'those (whom you have) tried as silver' (i.e. *ṣerūpê kesep*) (cf. Winton Thomas, *TRP*, p. 27), but the *RSV* translation may be slightly more suitable in view of verse 30*d*.

31. bronze: *ḥašmannîm* is a *hapax legomenon* in the *OT*, and it is often associated with the Egyptian *ḥsmn*, which may mean either 'natron' or 'bronze'. Albright (op. cit., p. 34) prefers the former alternative since, he argues, bronze was usually brought into Egypt, not exported from it. Yet this verse deals not with exports but tribute, and so 'bronze' may be the more likely meaning.

The plural form of the noun may suggest things made of bronze rather than the raw material itself. Dahood (*PAB*, II, p. 150) suggests 'blue cloth'.

to stretch out her hands: Dahood (*PAB*, I, p. 229) asserts that 'hands' in this expression connotes 'possessions' or 'resources', hence: 'Let Ethiopia bring her possessions to God'; this would give a reasonable parallel to verse 31*a*, if the suggestion can be further substantiated.

EXTOL THE MIGHT OF GOD **32–5**

The Psalm concludes with a miniature hymn containing a summons to adore God, and giving the motivation for it.

32. Sing to God: see on verse 4. Dahood (*PAB*, I, p. 284) takes *lēʾlōhîm* (*RSV* 'to God') as a vocative 'O gods', yet the *RSV* rendering seems preferable.

kingdoms of the earth are exhorted to sing praises to Israel's God.

sing praises: see on 66:4. For **Selah,** see Introduction, pp. 48f.

33. who rides in the heavens: this is a synonym of 'who rides upon the clouds' (see verse 4). Dahood (*PAB*, I, p. 115) suggests 'who rides forth from his heavens', taking the preposition b^e (*RSV* 'in') in the sense of 'from', and the *y* (in *bšmy*) as a third person suffix (but cf. *PAB*, II, p. 132). *RSV* may well be right.

. . . the ancient heavens: lit. 'in the heavens of heavens of ancient time', or 'the ancient and lofty heavens' (so Johnson), since 'heavens of heavens' could mean 'the highest heavens' (cf. Dt. 10:14; 1 Kg. 8:27).

his mighty voice: i.e. the thunder (see on 29:3).

34. Ascribe power to God: lit. 'give might to God'. It is possible that in primitive thought the cultic words and actions were attributed a mysterious power which could increase the honour and might of the deity, but it is doubtful whether the Psalmists shared a similar 'dynamic' view (see Mowinckel, op. cit., pp. 66f.).

whose majesty: or 'dignity'. The Hebrew *gaʾawāh* is often used in a bad sense meaning 'pride, haughtiness' (cf. 10:2, 31:18,23 (M.T. 19, 24), 73:6); only in Dt. 33:26 is it used of God.

. . . over Israel: Dahood (*PAB*, I, p. 46) points to the possibility that the Hebrew *ʿal* ('over') may be an abbreviation of *ʿelyôn* ('the Most High').

35. Terrible is God: better 'Awe-inspiring is God'; see on 65:5.
in his sanctuary: following Jerome; *AV* has 'out of thy holy places' which is a literal rendering of M.T. Albright suggests 'thy shrines', but the plural *miḳdāšêḵā* may be a plural of amplification (cf. *GK* 124e). The reference is to the Jerusalem Temple, although some exegetes take it as the heavenly sanctuary (so N. C. Habel, *Yahweh Versus Baal* (1964), p. 85).
Blessed be God: (so also *NEB*) Johnson (*SKAI*, p. 76) takes this phrase with the preceding word 'peoples', and translates 'To a people divinely blessed', but *RSV* may be right, and the phrase would form a short concluding doxology (cf. 89:52 (M.T. 53); see also 1 Chr. 16:36).

Psalm 69 My Prayer is to Thee, O Lord

This Psalm is a Lament of the Individual who has been afflicted by some illness, and by the unsympathetic attitude of his family and unjust accusations of his enemies. The information is not, however, explicit enough to form a more detailed picture of the plight envisaged. If the concluding verses (35–6) are authentic, then the setting of the Psalm may be the period of reconstruction, soon after 537 B.C., and the author may have been one of the Jews anxious for the rebuilding of the Temple (so Kraus). On the other hand, the Psalmist may have advocated certain changes in the Temple ritual, or he may have been critical of certain aspects of the worship of his day. This is implied by his attitude to sacrifice (verses 30f.). For a different interpretation, see Eaton (*PTBC*, p. 175). The Psalm may well belong to the early part of the post-Exilic period.

Another problem is created by the latter part of the Psalm (verses 30–36), which is very like a thanksgiving. Such a transition from lamentation to praise also occurs in other Psalms (see Introduction to Ps. 22), and the most likely explanation is that this change in mood is due to an oracle which promised deliverance to the Psalmist (so Kraus, *PBK*, p. 480), or we could assume that the concluding part of the Psalm is a vow to praise God when the situation has altered.

The metre of the Psalm is mainly 3 + 3.
To the choirmaster: see Introduction, p. 48.
according to Lilies: see Introduction, p. 50.
A Psalm of David: see Introduction, pp. 43ff. and 46.

THE APPEAL TO GOD AND LAMENTATION 1–4

1. Save me: this is a frequent cry for help in the Psalms of lamentation (cf. 3:7 (M.T. 8), 6:4 (M.T. 5), 7:1 (M.T. 2), 22:21 (M.T. 22), 31:16 (M.T. 17), 54:1 (M.T. 3), 59:2 (M.T. 3), etc.). For the verb *y-š-*ᶜ ('to save'), see on 54:1.

up to my neck: lit. 'unto my soul' (see on 33:19). The expression is to be taken figuratively: the waters (i.e. extreme danger) threaten his very existence (cf. 144:7; Jer. 4:10). 'Waters' (see on 58:7) in this verse may be a synonym for the realm of the dead and its sphere of influence (cf. Barth, *ETKD*, p. 112), and the same may be true of the mire and flood (verse 2).

2. I sink in deep mire: it is not impossible that the author was accused of stealing (verse 4) and that he was thrown into a miry pit, like Jeremiah (Jer. 38:6); more likely, however, the reference is to the netherworld (see on 40:2).

I have come into deep waters: the metaphor itself may be derived from the sudden floods that follow heavy rains, and it is used to describe the afflicted man's experience of the power of the underworld. It is not only the floods of calamity that sweep over his head, but the very realm of the dead is clutching him in its grasp (cf. verse 15). See on 130:1.

3. The Psalmist is distressed by the activities of his enemies, as well as by the apparent inactivity of God and his aloofness. In spite of the intensity of his prayers and the severity of his trouble, he is still waiting for the divine answer and help (cf. 6:6 (M.T. 7); Isa. 57:10).

My eyes grow dim is a picturesque way of describing one's exhaustion, both mental and physical (cf. 119:82; Jer. 14:6; 1QH ix:5); see on 13:3.

with waiting: so LXX and T, reading *miyyaḥēl* for M.T. *mᵉyaḥēl* ('while I wait') (so also *AV*). For the verb, see on 71:14.

for my God: Dahood (*UHP*, p. 36) reads: 'O my God', taking the preposition *lᵉ* (*RSV* 'for') as a *lāmeḏ vocativum.*

4. More in number than . . .: for a similar hyperbolic expression, see on 40:12 (cf. Mt. 10:30).

who hate me . . .: on *ś-n-*ᵓ, 'to hate', see on 68:1. The phrase is quoted in Jn 15:25 where it is applied to the enemies of Jesus.

mighty are those: better 'numerous are those' (cf. Isa. 31:1; Jer. 5:6) which gives a good parallel to 'More in number than . . .' (verse 4*a*).

who would destroy me: S has 'than my bones' (*mēʿaṣᵉmôṭay* for M.T. *maṣmîṭay*). Formally this would provide a satisfactory parallelism, but it is unlikely that the bones of one's body could be described as numerous.
who attack me with lies: falsehood is the characteristic mark of their dealings with the Psalmist (cf. 35:19, 38:19 (M.T. 20)). It is possible that *šeḳer* ('lie') denotes the false accusations of the enemies (cf. Klopfenstein, *LAT*, p. 70). For 'lie', see on 119:29.
What I did not steal . . .: some scholars regard this as a proverbial expression of 'injured innocence' (so Kirkpatrick; cf. 35:11; Jer. 15:10). The thief had to restore what he had stolen, or he had to make restitution; according to Lev. 6:5 he had to add a fifth of the value of the stolen object, and he was expected to bring a guilt offering. In the Code of Hammurabi (cf. *DOTT*, p. 30) the person who commits robbery is put to death (*CH* 22), while in the case of ordinary stealing the restitution can be as high as thirty-fold. If the thief had nothing with which to pay, he was put to death (*CH* 8; cf. *DOTT*, p. 30).

THE CONFESSION TO GOD **5**
The Psalmist is suffering from some unspecified illness (verses 1–2, 36), as well as from his adversaries. Since any illness would be regarded as a divine punishment (see on 30:2), the afflicted man rightly makes a confession of his sins—folly (see on 38:5) and wrongs, which may well be sins of inadvertence and ignorance. This confession does not suggest that the charge of the enemies is true, and the Psalm as a whole shows that this is not the case.

THE PRAYER TO THE LORD OF HOSTS **6**
6. who hope in thee: see on 25:3.
put to shame through me: i.e. not through his sins (whatever they might be), but because of what is happening to him. If God would not answer the humble prayers of his servant, then others, too, might be in danger of losing their faith.
O Lord GOD of hosts: lit. 'O Lord, Yahweh of hosts' (or '. . . whose are the hosts'); see on 24:10, 59:5.
who seek thee: see on 40:16.

THE CONTINUATION OF THE LAMENT 7–12

7. For it is for thy sake . . .: or '. . . in your place . . .'. The reason why the Psalmist is persecuted may well be his zeal for God's house, or his desire to uphold the honour of God (see verse 9).

shame has covered my face: a similar expression occurs in 44:15 (M.T. 16); cf. 83:16 (M.T. 17), and it simply means: 'I have been put to shame'.

8. I have become a stranger . . .: even his closest relatives treat him as a complete stranger (cf. Job 19:13f.; Ps. 38:11 (M.T. 12); Jer. 12:6). In a world where one's existence depends to a very large extent upon the family or the larger group, such an ostracism was a very serious matter.

to my mother's sons: this phrase may denote a closer family tie than 'my brethren' (see on 50:20) which in many cases signifies not actual brothers (cf. Gen. 47:1) but kinship in a wider sense, e.g. the membership of the same people (cf. Exod. 4:18; Dt. 15:12). In this verse the expressions are synonymous, and they may refer to the Psalmist's own family.

9. zeal for thy house . . .: how this zeal was actually expressed is not stated. The writer may have been eager to see certain reforms introduced in the Temple; verse 9*a* is quoted in Jn 2:17 in connection with the cleansing of the Temple by Jesus. Some commentators have contended that the Psalmist belonged to that group of Jews who were anxious to restore the Temple after the return from Babylon sometime after 537 B.C. (cf. Schmidt, *PHAT*, p. 133; Klopfenstein, *LAT*, p. 69). 'Thy house' is usually taken to mean the Jerusalem Temple, but Kissane suggests 'thy honour', while Cheyne has: 'the ordering of thy household', but the *RSV* interpretation is more likely. *NEB:* 'bitter enemies of thy temple'.

has consumed me: i.e. the unswerving devotion to God's house (or 'household') has been the cause of his ruin (so Gunkel, Calès). For 'zeal', *ḳinʾāh*, see on 119:139; A. Stumpff, '*Zēlos*', *TDNT*, II, pp. 878ff.

those who insult thee: either by mocking the faithful servants of God, or by actually blaspheming against Yahweh, which the righteous would feel as keenly as if it had been directed against them. Verse 9*b* is applied to Jesus in Rom. 15:3.

10. . . . I humbled my soul . . .: the exact translation of verse 10*a* is uncertain. *RSV* follows LXX and S in reading *wāʾekkōp̱* (or *wāʾadakkeh*); M.T. could be rendered: 'I wept with fasting, (even) my soul'. Dahood (*PAB*, I, p. 213) suggests 'And I poured out my soul with fasting', deriving the verb *ʾbkh* from *n-b-k/n-p-k*, 'to pour out' (cf. *UHP*, p. 66). Verse 10*a* is not to be taken as referring to the Psalmist's repentance (so Kissane); rather he fasted on account of the house of God, and afflicted himself on behalf of his people who refused to humble themselves before God (cf. 35:13; Jer. 6:26). For 'fasting', see on 35:13.

11. sackcloth: see on 30:11. It is possible that the enemies interpreted his fasting and garb of penitence as an acknowledgment of his personal guilt, or as an expression of a hardened hypocrite. The result was that he became a byword or an object of scorn (cf. Job 30:9).

12. who sit in the gate: the gate of the settlement (town or village) was the place where the ancient Israelites conducted their business transactions (cf. Gen. 23:10ff.; Ru. 4:1ff.) and dispensed justice (Dt. 21:19; Jos. 20:4). It was also the 'civic centre' of the community, where people could discuss news (1 Sam 4:12–18) and exchange gossip. See Köhler, *Hebrew Man*, pp. 149–75.

. . . songs about me . . .: i.e. I have become the object of ridicule and the subject of the drunkard's songs (cf. Job 30:9; Lam. 3:14; 1QH ii:11). The versions suggest: 'they make (ribald) songs about me' (*niggenû ḇî*).

THE PRAYER FOR DELIVERANCE **13–18**

13. my prayer: see on 65:1, 119:171.

At an acceptable time: Kraus suggests that it might be the hour of morning which was often considered as the time of divine answer and help (see on 46:5). A more general interpretation of the phrase seems more likely: the time (known only to Yahweh) when he will hear and answer the Psalmist's prayer; cf. Isa. 49:8: 'In a time of favour I have answered you'. Kissane (*BP*, p. 302) reads 'let this be a time of favour', and he adds *yehî zeh* ('let this be . . .') after *yhwh* ('Yahweh'), assuming an omission due to haplography.

thy steadfast love: see on 26:3. This is the foundation on which the sufferer bases his hopes.

14. With thy faithful help: according to M.T. this belongs to the previous verse but it may have been wrongly separated from verse 14. *AV*, *RV* take this phrase with verse 13, rendering 'in the truth of thy salvation'. *PNT* offers a fine paraphrase 'with your help that never fails'. For 'truth' (*ʾemeṯ*), see on 25:5, and for 'salvation' (*yēšaʿ*), see on 35:3.

from sinking in the mire: this is a slightly varied repetition of verse 2*a* but the allusion is the same. Sheol is often regarded as characterized by mire and filth (cf. T. H. Gaster, *Thespis* (1961), pp. 203f.) and this is not necessarily contradicted by the other word-picture which speaks of the netherworld as a place of dust; Dahood (*PAB*, I, p. 140) argues that *ʿāp̄ār* (usually rendered as 'dust') means 'mud', and that it is another name 'for the infernal regions' (op. cit., p. 43). See also Job 7:21, 21:26; Ps. 22:29 (M.T. 30); Isa. 26:19.

from my enemies: it has been suggested (cf. G. R. Driver, *HTR*, XXIX (1936), pp. 184f.) that since 'enemies' (*śōneʾay*) is not a suitable synonym of 'mire' and 'deep waters', we should read *śeyān* ('mud'), hence 'let me be delivered from the mud (of the netherworld)'.

from the deep waters: see verse 2.

15. In verse 2 the Psalmist depicts how Sheol is gradually overwhelming him but in verse 15 he begs God not to allow the underworld to overpower his servant permanently.

the pit: the Hebrew *beʾēr* may denote a well that has been made by digging (cf. Gen. 21:25,30), or a pit (cf. the 'bitumen pits' in Gen. 14:10); it may be also used as a synonym of the grave or Sheol (cf. 55:23 (M.T. 24)). For *bôr* ('pit'), see on 28:1. The pit or Sheol could be personified as a monster with an insatiable appetite (Prov. 30:15f.; Isa. 5:14), so that 'its mouth' may belong to the metaphor; literally it would signify the opening of the pit.

16. Answer me: see on 27:7.

for thy steadfast love is good: or, to improve the parallelism, 'according to the goodness (*keṭûḇ* for M.T. *kî ṭôḇ*) of your Covenant loyalty' (see on 26:3).

abundant mercy: see on 40:11, 51:1.

turn to me: i.e. look favourably upon me. Cf. 25:16: 'Turn thou to me, and be gracious to me', consequently it is the opposite of hiding one's face from someone, or rejecting that person (see verse 17).

17. Hide not thy face . . .: or 'Do not withdraw your favour'. The metaphor is a graphic picture of indifference (cf. 44:24 (M.T. 25), 104:29), displeasure (Dt. 31:17), anger (27:9; Isa. 54:8), or even hostility (Job 13:24; Ps. 88:14 (M.T. 15); Isa. 57:17). For the verb *s-t-r* ('to hide'), see on 13:1.

thy servant: see on 36:1. This is probably a humble self-designation which, at the same time, points to the existing Covenant relationship.
I am in distress: or 'trouble is my present lot in life' (as in 31:9 (M.T. 10)).
make haste to answer me: i.e. answer me quickly for I am in grave danger. For the construction, see *GK* 120g; cf. 102:2 (M.T. 3), 143:7.

18. Draw near to me: i.e. in order to help me (cf. Lam. 3:57); lit. '. . . to my soul (see on 33:19)'.
redeem me: lit. 'redeem her' (i.e. my soul). For the verb *g-ʾ-l* ('to redeem'), see on 119:154. 'Set me free' (in verse 18*b*) is a synonym of 'to redeem', and is discussed in 119:134.
because of my enemies: (so also in 5:8 (M.T. 9), 27:11). God's own honour would be called in question if his faithful servant were abandoned to the godless.

THE ENEMIES OF THE PSALMIST **19–21**

19. This verse seems to be overloaded but it is not clear which phrase is out of place (or what is missing). Kraus, for example, transfers 'my shame and my dishonour' to follow verse 20*a*, but it is equally possible that 'all my foes' should follow after 'I am in despair' (because of all my foes; i.e. *mikkol ṣôrᵉrāy*). In this case verse 19*b* could be rendered 'and my shame and my dishonour are before you' (i.e. they are known to you); this would provide a good parallel to verse 19*a*. Cf. Jer. 12:3, 15:15.

20. Insults have broken my heart: i.e. the writer is not brokenhearted but he is extremely upset (cf. Jer. 23:9). For 'heart', see on 27:3.
I am in despair: perhaps we should add 'because of my enemies' (see verse 19). The verb *n-w-š* is a *hapax legomenon* in the *OT*, but it may be cognate with *ʾ-n-š* ('to be weak, sick').
I looked for pity: or 'I waited eagerly (for someone) to show sympathy'. The verb *n-w-d* means primarily 'to move to and fro', and it can also be used of shaking one's head, as a gesture of grief and sympathy (cf. Job 2:11, 42:11; Jer. 22:10). Some versions presuppose the participle *lannāḏ* ('for someone to have pity' (cf. *TRP*, p. 28)).

21. They gave me poison for food: at a later time at least, it was a custom for the friends to offer the bereaved person a 'funeral meal' (cf. Sanhedrin ii:1,3), and it is possible that a similar practice also existed at an earlier date (see 2 Sam. 3:35, 12:17) and that it included not only those bereaved but also others severely tried by various tribulations (cf. Kraus, *PBK*, p. 483). The Psalmist experienced the very opposite; instead of receiving any kindness he received scorn, or, metaphorically, he was given poison for food and vinegar to quench his thirst. By **vinegar** is probably meant some sour, undrinkable wine (cf. 1QH iv:11; Mt. 27:48; Lk. 23:36; Jn 19:29).

THE PRAYER FOR GOD'S RETRIBUTION **22–8**

These verses contain a series of maledictions or curses, and it is impossible to explain them away by assuming that these lines represent the utterances of the enemies, or by interpreting the adversaries as the spiritual foes of the soul. There is no reason to doubt that the writer actually wished that the evils mentioned would overwhelm his foes (see also 58:6–9). The only right approach to these maledictions is to understand the Psalmist and his times. We need to bear in mind that there was little distinction between the sinner and his sin, and that justice and vindication could only be found (so it was believed by most people) in *this* world. Therefore a tolerance of wrong and wrongdoers would be an implicit admission that God is not greatly interested in the affairs of this world. The very Covenant of God sets before the people both blessings and curses (cf. Jos. 8:34), and the Psalmist simply uses the conventional terminology for depicting the inescapable fate of the godless (cf. Dt. 27:15–26; 28:15–68; see also Lev. 26:14–39).

22. Let their own table . . .: the reference is probably not to ordinary fare or feasting, but to the sacrificial meals in the Temple, which were supposedly in honour of Yahweh (cf. Kraus, *PBK*, p. 484). What was deceitfully meant to demonstrate their fellowship with God would become a snare to them, for there can be no fellowship or common interests between determined wrongdoers and God. For *paḥ* ('snare'), see on 119:110. The table might be a mat of straw, or a skin; it could even be made of wood or metal in the form of a flat-topped stand, some twelve inches high. This verse is quoted, with certain variations, in Rom. 11:9. **their sacrificial feasts . . .:** following the reading of T (which suggests *wᵉšalᵉmêhem*, 'their peace-offerings'). M.T. could be rendered 'and (their table will become) to those who are at prosperity, a trap' (see on 64:5). LXX and V must have read or understood *šillûmîm*, 'recompense', which is less likely. Dahood (*PAB*, I, p. 43) takes *šlwm* as an ordinary passive participle, meaning 'ally', yet the *RSV* translation seems more fitting. For 'trap', see on 64:5.

23. Let their eyes be darkened . . .: perhaps 'Let them become blind' (cf. Dt. 28:28f.). Blindness may represent all the ills that are likely to come upon those who disobey the commands of God (see Dt. 28:27f.). This phrase is quoted in Rom. 11:10. It is possible that the Psalmist is using certain formulae derived from the broken oaths of the enemies. For a parallel, see 'The Soldiers' Oath', *ANET*, pp. 343f.

make their loins tremble . . .: the Hebrew *moṯnayim* ('loins') often denotes the source of man's strength and vigour (cf. Dt. 33:11; Job 40:16). 'Loins' can also experience anguish (Isa. 21:3; Nah. 2:10), or shake in fear (Ezek. 29:7). Our phrase probably means 'deprive them of all their strength' (by means of some illness or disaster; cf. Dt. 28:22,35).

24. Pour out thy indignation . . .: similarly in 79:6; Ezek. 21:31, 22:31; Zeph. 3:8. For *zaᶜam* ('indignation'), see on 38:3.

. . . overtake them: i.e. the anger of God (see on 38:3) will catch up with the evil-doers, like the curses of the Covenant (Dt. 28:15,45) which pursue and overtake the disobedient. For the opposite view, see 23:6.

25. their camp: this is strictly the nomad's encampment (Num. 31:10), but here it is used, perhaps, of the ordinary dwelling place, just like 'their tents' in the next verse.

let no one dwell . . .: i.e. may they and their families perish. This is the worst punishment one can receive, and this was the fate traditionally reserved for the wicked (see Job 18:17ff.; Prov. 14:11). See also the quotation of this verse in Ac. 1:20.

26. For they persecute him . . .: so *RSV* following LXX, S, and Jerome, in reading *ʾēṯ* (the accusative sign) for *ʾattāh* ('you'). The Psalmist accepts God's chastisement but he also knows that his enemies persecute him for things he has not done, or what he has done in God's name and for his sake.

they afflict . . . still more: reading (with LXX, S, and V) *yôsîpû* ('they add') for M.T. *yesappērû* ('they recount'). *AV* has 'and they talk to the grief of those whom thou hast wounded' which is a reasonable rendering of M.T., but the parallelism favours the variant in the ancient versions.

27. punishment upon punishment: i.e. punish them severely but not necessarily more than they deserve, as Kissane would suggest. C. S. Lewis (*Reflections on the Psalms* (1961), p. 26) regards expressions of this nature as made by 'ferocious, self-pitying, barbaric men'; yet the Psalmist reflects, more or less, the thought of the whole *OT*, and the same 'ferocious' words are quoted by *NT* writers. It seems that although we can no longer use the maledictions of the Psalmists as a right expression of our feelings, however hurt, they nevertheless represent the belief that justice must triumph over wrong, and truth over lie. *How* this victory is envisaged or achieved, can be described only in terms of one's own times, and it is very likely that also our present terminology of right and wrong may one day be called ferocious and barbaric. On the other hand, since value judgments have to be made, one can only follow the Psalmist's example in being true to what is known of God's will.
may they have no acquittal: or 'may they not experience your salvation' (lit. 'righteousness', see on 33:5). This, of course, presumes that the wicked remain happily unrepentant in their wrongdoing.

28. the book of the living: the idea of the heavenly books is not unknown in Biblical literature, and it is possible that the nature of these heavenly records was not always exactly the same. Probably there were books which recorded the good and bad deeds of all men (Neh. 13:14; Ps. 109:13ff.; cf. also *Aboth* ii:1), and other books which contained the names of all the righteous (Exod. 32:32f.; Isa. 4:3; Dan. 12:1; Enoch 47:3, 108:3; Rev. 3:5, 13:8, etc.). Later this idea was expanded into separate registers for the righteous and the wicked, as in Jubilees 30:20,22, 36:10. See also note on 51:1. Our Psalm may refer to the register of the righteous; he whose name was written in it kept on receiving the gift of life and other blessings, but he whose name was blotted out of this book of life perished. It is less likely that this concept of the heavenly books involved, at this stage, a predestinarian teaching. The metaphor of the book of life may have been derived from, or influenced by, the idea of having registers of citizens (cf. Neh. 7:64; R. H. Charles, *The Revelation of St. John* (*ICC*, 1920), I, p. 84; *TDNT*, I, pp. 619f.).

THE PRAYER FOR DELIVERANCE **29**

29. But I am afflicted: this provides a word play on the Hebrew *ᵓanî* ('I') and *ᶜānî* ('afflicted') for which see on 34:3; cf. also 40:17.
thy salvation: see on 35:3.

THE THANKSGIVING TO GOD **30–6**

30. the name of God: T has '. . . of my God' (i.e. *ᵓelōhay*) but originally it may have been 'the name of Yahweh' (see on 145:2).
a song: the Hebrew *šîr* is the usual word for 'song', and it could be a cultic or a secular composition. It was probably accompanied by musical instruments (cf. Am. 6:5).
I will magnify him by glorifying and praising him (cf. 34:3 (M.T. 4)) with songs of thanksgiving. The Hebrew *tôḏāh* ('thanksgiving') may be either a thank-offering (cf. Lev. 7:12, 22:29), or a hymn of thanks to God, as here (cf. 26:7, 42:4 (M.T. 5)); see also Westermann, *PGP*, p. 32.

31. more than an ox: this is probably another word play, and it refers back to 'song' in verse 30*a*. Yahweh is more pleased with a *šîr* ('song') which does express true gratitude, than with a *šôr* ('ox'), a valuable sacrifice in itself but which does not represent an obedient spirit or a humble attitude to God (see on 40:6). In other words the material of the offering is subordinated to the meaning of sacrifice, or the significance of the 'vehicle' lies in the content (i.e. attitude) conveyed. If so, the misuse of 'spiritual sacrifices' may be even worse than the abuse of material sacrifices, for the latter involved at least some expenses.
a bull with horns . . .: this is a fully grown animal, and therefore a more costly offering than a young bullock. The mention of hoofs suggests that the sacrificial victim was a ritually clean animal, fit for sacrifice (cf. Lev. 11:3–8).

32. the oppressed: for *ᶜanāwîm*, see on 34:2. The intervention of God in the life of one man gives joy to all the faithful servants of God, for it gives an encouragement to their faith (cf. 52:6 (M.T. 8), 107:42).
who seek God: see on 24:6.
let your hearts revive: or 'let your courage be restored'; lit. 'and let . . .'. The conjunction *wᵉ* ('and') is usually deleted but it may also be regarded as an emphatic *wāw* (see Dahood, *PAB*, I, p. 24).

33. the LORD hears and takes notice of the plight of the needy man (for *ʾeḇyôn*, see on 35:10) by delivering him from his troubles. **his own that are in bonds:** this may suggest those who are punished by Yahweh but who are delivered when they turn to him (so Kirkpatrick, Cohen); see on 22:24. *NEB* 'those bound to his service' (similarly Dahood).

34. The whole world is exhorted to praise God for his acts of salvation by which he has manifested himself as the judge and ruler of all (see on 96:11).

35. This and the following verse are sometimes regarded as a later liturgical addition to adapt this lament of the individual to communal worship (so Nötscher). On the other hand, the Psalm may be of post-Exilic origin, and the verses in question authentic.

God will save Zion: i.e. he will help the Holy City. For 'Zion', see on 65:1.

rebuild the cities of Judah: this may allude to the aftermath of the rebellion against the Babylonian rule in 589 B.C. (cf. J. Bright, *HI*, p. 308). See also Isa. 44:26, 61:4; Ezek. 36:10.

and his servants shall dwell there: following S in adding *ʿaḇāḏāyw* ('his servants'). M.T. reads 'and they shall dwell . . .'. Verse 35*c* may be out of place because it anticipates the following verse; perhaps it belongs after verse 36.

36. the children: lit. 'the seed of . . .'.

who love his name: i.e. who love him; see on 26:8, 119:47. For 'name', see on 20:1.

Psalm 70 AN INDIVIDUAL LAMENT

This Psalm is a doublet of 40:13–17 (q.v.).

To the choirmaster: see Introduction, p. 48.

A Psalm of David: see Introduction, pp. 43ff. and 46.

memorial offering: see Introduction, p. 48.

Psalm 71 GOD IS ALSO THE HOPE OF THE AGED

In this poem elements from various psalm-types follow one another without any real logical sequence; the thread that holds them together is the author's unshakable trust in God. Kraus (*PBK*, p. 490) classes this Psalm as a Lament of the Individual, and he may be right.

The Psalmist seems to be an old man (see verses 9 and 18) suffering from some illness which has brought him near to the gates of death. As if his troubles were not enough, his enemies plotted against him. Some of them used his illness as an opportune moment to humiliate him and to persecute him. The adversaries may have been misled by their oversimplification of life and 'theology', arguing that all suffering is caused by sin and that the sufferer must be a sinner.

This poem has affinities with a number of other Psalms, especially Ps. 22 and 31. The writer may be quoting, intentionally or otherwise, from 31:1–3, while other similarities may be accounted for by the author's acquaintance with the language common to particular literary types. It would not be true to describe Ps. 71, without any reservations, as 'little more than a mosaic of fragments and reminiscences of other Psalms' (Kirkpatrick, *BPCB*, p. 409), although there is some truth in this statement.

The date of the Psalm is post-Exilic, as suggested by the disregard (?) for the traditional psalm-types. It also lacks a title, although LXX attributes it to David, and regards it as a song sung by the sons of Jonadab (the Rechabite?) in the Babylonian captivity. This seems to be a later interpretation of the Psalm.

THE PETITION AND CONFIDENCE IN GOD **1–8**

1. Verses 1–3 are practically the same as 31:1–3*a*. For the interpretation of verse 1, see 31:1. Dahood (*UHP*, p. 36) takes *l*ᵉ*ᶜôlām* ('for ever') as a vocative, reading 'O Eternal'. This would balance 'O LORD' in verse 1*a*.

2. . . . deliver me and rescue me: see on 31:1*c*. 'Deliver me' (*t*ᵉ*pall*ᵉ*ṭēnî*) is not in 31:1*c*. The Hebrew *p-l-ṭ* means 'to escape', while in the intensive form (as here) it signifies 'to deliver' (cf. Barth, *ETKD*, pp. 128f.). Most of the occurrences of this verb are in the Psalter. It is found also in the Ugaritic texts, with a similar meaning (cf. Gordon, *UT*, p. 468).

incline thy ear: see on 31:2*a*.

3. a rock of refuge: reading with many Hebrew MSS., LXX, T, S, and V *ṣûr māᶜôz* (so in 31:2) which could be rendered 'a rock of strength' (see on 27:1). M.T. has 'a rock of habitation' (cf. 90:1).

a strong fortress: so *RSV* following LXX and 31:2, in reading *l*ᵉ*ḇêṯ m*ᵉ*ṣûḏôṯ* for M.T. *lāḇôᵓ tāmîḏ ṣiwwîṯā* ('you have commanded to come continually'); *AV* renders: 'whereunto I may continually resort: thou hast given commandment to save me'. It is possible that M.T. of this verse is a corruption of the reading preserved in 31:2 (M.T. 3).

my rock: this represents the Hebrew *sela*ᶜ, which may be a synonym of *ṣûr* used in verse 3*a*; see on 42:9.

my fortress: see the parallel expression in 31:3 (M.T. 4).

4. Rescue me: for the Hebrew *p-l-ṭ*, see verse 2.

from the hand of the wicked: from the power of men who are wicked, and who are proud of this fact (see on 28:3). 'The wicked', as well as 'the unjust and cruel man', may be used in a collective sense.

cruel man: the Hebrew *ḥômēṣ* is a *hapax legomenon* in the *OT*, but it probably denotes an 'oppressor' (cf. *KBL*, p. 312a; P. Wernberg-Møller, *ZAW* (LXXI), 1959, p. 58).

5. my hope: the Hebrew *tiḳwāh* is parallel to *mibṭāḥ* ('trust, confidence'), and it suggests that the writer believes that he still has a future in God. *OT* hope is not wishful thinking, but could be described as a God-inspired certainty that he will help and deliver the sufferer. So in Jer. 29:11: 'For I know the plans I have for you, says the LORD . . . to give you a future and a hope' (cf. Jer. 31:17). God is the only reliable object of trust and confidence, for everything else provides a merely illusory security. Not even idols (Jer. 48:13), gold (Job 31:24), or chariots and horsemen (2 Kg. 18:24) can give us a hope that would not let us down. See *TDNT*, II, pp. 522f.; C. Westermann, 'Das Hoffen im Alten Testament', *Forschungen am Alten Testament* (1964), pp. 226–32.

from my youth: i.e. from his early days the Psalmist has been faithful to God, because God's Covenant loyalty was there first.

6. This verse is reminiscent of 22:10 (M.T. 11); cf. 1QH ix:30.

Upon thee I have leaned . . .: God had cared for him from his birth. The Psalmist's hope and confidence is not based on what he had done for God but on what God had done for him.

who took me from my mother's womb: Kraus (*PBK*, p. 488) suggests 'from my mother's womb you have been my strength' (reading ᶜ*ôzî* for M.T. *gôzî*). The Hebrew *gôzî* is probably a *ḳal* participle from *g-z-h*, 'to cut off' (cf. *HAL*, p. 178b); cf. 22:10 (M.T. 11) where we find *gôḥî* ('my bringer forth'?).

My praise: see on 65:1, 119:171; for parallels cf. 109:1; Jer. 17:14.

7. a portent to many: *NEB* 'To many I seem a solemn warning'. The Hebrew *môpēṯ* may be a special display of divine power which may strike fear and terror into the enemies of God (Exod. 7:3, 11:9; Dt. 6:22), or at other times it may inspire an attitude of worship (cf. 105:5). It can also be a token of a future event (1 Kg. 13:3,5; Isa. 20:3), but it is always God who is ultimately the source of the portent (cf. *ThWB*, VIII, pp. 117ff.). Etymologically *môpēṯ* is sometimes linked with the idea of suffering harm (cf. H. W. Robinson, *Inspiration and Revelation in the Old Testament*, p. 36), and in many a case *môpēṯ* contains within it a suggestion of calamity for some; nearly half its occurrences in *OT* refer to the plagues in Egypt. *Môpeṯ* is often found together with *ʾôṯ* ('sign') and the difference between the two is defined by S. R. Driver (*Deuteronomy* (*ICC*, 1896), p. 75) as: '*Môpēṯ* is a *portent*, an occurrence regarded merely as something extraordinary: *ʾôṯ* is a *sign*, i.e. something ordinary (Exod. 12:13, 31:13; Isa. 20:3, etc.) or extraordinary, as the case may be, regarded as significant of a truth beyond itself, or impressed with a Divine purpose'. In 71:7 it is not clear whether the Psalmist had been regarded as a sign of God's providential care (so Weiser) or a typical example of divine punishment (so Kirkpatrick, Gunkel, Kraus *et al.*); cf. 31:11 (M.T. 12) and Dt. 28:46. The latter alternative seems more likely, in view of verse 7*b*.

my strong refuge: this expression is found only here in the *OT* but a similar thought is expressed in 46:1 (M.T. 2). Dahood (*PAB*, I, p. xl) renders 'my refuge of strength', regarding the *y* in *mḥsy* ('my refuge') as an intervening pronominal suffix between the genitive and the construct state (cf. *GK* 89). On *maḥ*ᵃ*seh* ('refuge'), see on 61:3.

8. This verse is probably an expression of confidence in God's help, or it may be a vow to praise God.

thy praise: see on 119:171.

with thy glory . . .: LXX and V add after verse 8*a* *lᵉmaʿan ʾᵃhallēl kᵉḇôḏeḵā* ('that I may praise your glory') (cf. Wutz, *DP*, p. 182) which is regarded as the original reading by some scholars, but M.T. gives a more satisfactory sense.

glory: *tipʾereṯ* can be used to denote festive garments (Isa. 52:1), women's finery (Isa. 3:18), etc., or glory (Jg. 4:9; Ps. 89:17 (M.T. 18)), renown (Dt. 26:19). In our verse it means the glory of God, or the telling forth of it (cf. Prov. 28:12). In 1QS x:12, xi:15 it denotes 'majesty' (which belongs to God).

THE LAMENT AND PETITION 9–16

9. Do not cast me off: i.e. do not drive me away from your presence (as in 51:11 (M.T. 13)), and do not exclude me from the fellowship with you. For a man to be alone is a great curse but to be without God is, ultimately, the worst fate that any man can choose. The whole verse (also verse 18) is an antithesis to verses 5f.; God had been the Psalmist's helper from his early days but now, when he has grown old, God seems to be far away. Yet through faith or trust in God even this apparent contrast can become a stepping stone instead of a stumbling block, for the God of the Psalmist's youth is still the God of his old age. Cf. Isa. 46:3f.: '. . . who have been borne by me from your birth . . . even to your old age I am He (i.e. I remain constant), and to grey hairs I will carry you'.

10. speak concerning me: some commentators (e.g. Lagarde, Gunkel, McCullough) read *ʾārᵉḇû* ('they lie in wait') for M.T. *ʾāmᵉrû* ('they say'), but the latter reading is preferable, for the enemies are *still forging* their plans to destroy the aged saint of God. Dahood (*PAB*, II, p. 174) takes the verb *ʾ-m-r* in the sense of 'to see' (i.e. they eye me with hostility); see on 3:2, yet *RSV* gives the more likely parallel to verse 10*b*.

watch for my life: '. . . for my soul' (see on 33:19). For the idea, see 56:6 (M.T. 7); Jer. 20:10.

11. and say: this is usually taken to be a gloss to indicate the direct speech of the adversaries.

God has forsaken him: the Psalmist must have been afflicted by some illness (which is not described), or by some other calamity which was interpreted by the opponents as a divine punishment upon the 'sinner'. The severity of the affliction would be taken as an indication of the gravity of the offence. A similar attitude is described at length in Job 19:13–21.

pursue and seize him: possibly this was not so much an act of kicking a man when he is down, as a way of dissociating oneself from the stricken man and from his supposed (or sometimes real) crimes.

12. be not far from me: as in 22:11*a* (M.T. 12*a*) (cf. 35:22, 38:21 (M.T. 22)).

make haste to help me: lit. 'make haste for my help' (*AV*); this is identical with 40:13*b* (M.T. 14*b*), and similar to 38:22*a* (M.T. 23*a*). The expression suggests no disrespect to God, but it stresses the urgency of the situation.

13. my accusers: lit. 'the accusers of my soul' (see on 33:19). The Hebrew word for 'accusers' is the *ḳal* participle of *ś-ṭ-n*, from which is also derived *śāṭān* ('adversary at law, accuser') (cf. Job 1:6; Ps. 109:6; Zech. 3:1,2). At a later time this common noun become a proper noun, Satan, as in 1 Chr. 21:1; cf. also T. H. Gaster, 'Satan', *IDB*, IV, pp. 224–8.
put to shame: i.e. let their charges be refuted and let them be disgraced (cf. 35:4*a*, 26*a*, 40:14 (M.T. 15)).
and consumed: some exegetes (similarly *NEB*) follow S in reading *wᵉyikkālᵉmû* ('and let them be humiliated') for M.T. *yiḵlû* ('let them be consumed'), as in 35:4, 40:14 (M.T. 15).
may they be covered with disgrace as with a garment; see on 109:29.
who seek my hurt: or 'who seek to harm me'. It is repeated in verse 24 but this is not sufficient reason for its deletion. For the same thought in different words, cf. 35:4, 40:14 (M.T. 15), 70:2 (M.T. 3).

14. But I will hope . . .: the verb *y-ḥ-l* means 'to wait, hope for', and it usually suggests a waiting characterized by expectant hope. It is not used to denote the expectation of something evil or unpleasant. So in 130:7: 'O Israel, hope in the LORD . . . with him is plenteous redemption'. Such a hope or waiting for God's help is only reasonable when it is exercised within the context of one's loyalty to God (33:18, 147:11). What is required of man is not perfection but honest determination to serve God.
praise thee: i.e. he shall yet have occasion to praise God for his deliverance and other deeds of kindness. See on 65:1.

15. thy righteous acts: lit. 'your righteousness' or '. . . deliverance' (see on 33:5) which is parallel to 'thy deeds of salvation' (see on 36:6).
their number: the Hebrew *sᵉpōrôṯ* occurs only here in the *OT*; LXX understood it as 'books' (V has *litteraturam*) but some Greek MSS. have *pragmatias* ('business'). T and Sym support the *RSV* rendering which is uncertain but possible (cf. G. R. Driver, *HTR*, XXIX (1936), p. 185). By this expression the author suggests either that God's acts of grace are more than he can number, or that they are too wonderful to be fully recounted or described. *NEB* 'although I have not the skill of a poet'.

16. . . . I will come: perhaps 'I will enter upon' (cf. *TRP*, p. 29). *RSV* suggests that the Psalmist will come to the Temple with the testimony of God's gracious deeds on his behalf (cf. 106:2), which he will declare before his fellow worshippers. Kissane (*BP*, p. 312) renders 'I will consider', i.e. 'I will "enter" into the subject of God's deeds of salvation'.

I will praise: the verb used is *z-k-r* ('to remember') which in the causative form may mean 'to mention' (1 Sam. 4:18) or 'to pronounce' (45:17 (M.T. 18)); in a judicial sense it may suggest 'to accuse' (Isa. 43:26). In this verse, the mention of the righteousness of Yahweh is tantamount to praising his saving deeds (cf. 33:5), or giving him thanks.

thine alone: this emphasizes the preceding pronoun 'thy'.

THE CONFIDENCE IN GOD AND THE VOW **17–24**

17. thou hast taught me: the following line may suggest that he had learned the *Heilsgeschichte* of his people (so Weiser), or the more detailed description of what he has been taught is found in verse 20, i.e. he has learned to praise God.

thy wondrous deeds: see on 9:1.

18. thy might: lit. 'your arm'. The Hebrew *z^e^rôa^c^* ('arm') can be taken as a symbol of strength which is used either for aggressive or defensive purposes; see on 37:17. Here Yahweh's arm denotes his mighty help, and the writer seems to have in mind not so much the nation's salvation-history, as the saving acts of God in his own life. This then becomes yet another living testimony to the unchangeable power of God.

to all the generations to come: this is the reading of LXX which suggests *l^e^ḵol dôr yāḇô^ɔ^*; M.T. has 'to a generation, to all that come' (*RSVm*). Perhaps we should read with S 'to the coming generation' (*l^e^ḏôr yāḇô^ɔ^*; see on 22:30 (M.T. 31)).

19. Thy power: according to M.T. this phrase belongs to the preceding verse (so also *RP*) of which a possible rendering might be: '. . . till I proclaim your might to (the next) generation, your power to every one that is to come' (cf. Cohen, *PSon*, p. 225).

and thy righteousness: (see on 33:5) this may refer to God's acts of deliverance, the 'great things' (see on 106:21) which he has wrought in the life of the nation and of the individual.

. . . reach the high heavens: that is, God's works are beyond our comprehension (cf. 36:5 (M.T. 6), 57:10 (M.T. 11)).

who is like thee: i.e. Yahweh is incomparable in his might and righteousness (cf. 35:10, 86:8, 89:6,8 (M.T. 7,9); Mic. 7:18; 1QM x:8; Labuschagne, *IYOT*, p. 100).

20. who hast made me see . . .: following the reading of

Ḳᵉrê and most of the ancient versions. *Kᵉṯîḇ* has '. . . made us see. . .' which may be a later attempt to adapt the Psalm to communal worship. This may also account for the overloading of the verse (cf. *BH*).
wilt revive me again: lit. 'you will return, you will quicken me'; for this construction, see *GK* 120d,g.
the depths of the earth refers, most likely, to the waters under the earth, and not to the lower parts of the earth. *Tᵉhôm* ('deep') (see on 104:6) is probably the primordial sea which may be the Hebrew equivalent of the Babylonian Tiamat (for the opposite view, see K. A. Kitchen, *Ancient Orient and Old Testament* (1966), pp. 89f.). It is related to the Ugaritic *thm* ('deep') or *thmtm* ('the two deeps': cf. Gordon, *UT*, p. 497; *JBL*, LXXIV (1955), pp. 9–21). In this verse the depths or the subterranean waters denote the sphere of Sheol. The sufferer believes that he is, in a real sense, surrounded by these waters, and therefore his deliverance can be depicted as a rescue from the depths of the underworld.
thou wilt bring me up again: for the construction, see on 85:6. For a more detailed exegesis, see Barth, *ETKD*, pp. 112f.

21. Thou wilt increase my honour: or 'Thou shalt increase my greatness' (*AV*, LXX has *tēn dikaiosunēn sou* ('your righteousness') but the M.T. reading provides a slightly better parallel to verse 21*b*. 'Greatness' (*gᵉḏullāh*) is usually used of God (cf. 145:3,6), but here it may be a synonym of man's 'honour' (*kāḇôḏ*), which is not so much a public regard for a person, as the possession of the gifts of God, which make one's life both secure and enjoyable, if used responsibly. *RP* has 'Set thou me free from all my troubles' and assumes *gᵉʾullāṯi* ('my redemption') for M.T. *gᵉḏullāṯî* ('my greatness').
comfort me again: the root meaning of the Hebrew *n-ḥ-m* is given as 'breathe deeply' (cf. D. Winton Thomas, *ET*, XLIV (1932–3), pp. 191f.; LI (1939–40), p. 252). In the *nip̄ʿal* form it means 'to be sorry, have pity, repent' (cf. 90:13), while in the *piʿēl* it denotes 'to comfort, console' (cf. Isa. 12:1; 1QH ix:13, xi:32).

22. I will also: this is emphatic: 'So even I'. For 'praise' (*hôḏāh*), see on 18:49; it can also mean 'to give thanks'.
the harp: see on 33:2.
thy faithfulness: lit. 'your truth' (see on 25:5) or 'your fidelity' (to your Covenant promises).
I will sing praises: for *z-m-r* ('to sing'), see on 66:4. 'Lyre' (*kinnôr*) is briefly discussed in 98:5.

Holy One of Israel: this is a divine title frequent in the Book of Isaiah, while it seldom occurs elsewhere. Procksch (*TDNT*, I, p. 93) suggests that the expression was coined by Isaiah; this is possible if Ps. 78 and 89 do not precede Isaiah's time. In any case, the 'Holy One of Israel' seems to belong to the Jerusalem tradition, or to a particular section of it, since this term is used very rarely in the Psalter. Cf. *ZAW*, LXXIV (1962), pp. 62–6; for 'holy' (*ḳāḏôš*), see on 16:3, 34:9. 'Yahweh is the holy one of Israel not because he is consecrated to Israel but because he has consecrated Israel to himself . . .' (Jacob, *TOTe*, p. 89).

23. In this verse **my lips** (see on 63:3) and **my soul** (see on 33:19) are roundabout expressions for the author himself. H. W. Robinson (p. 263) regards them as 'instruments of praise'.

24. . . . will talk: for the verb *h-g-h*, see on 1:2.
thy righteous help: lit. 'your righteousness' (see on 33:5) which has manifested itself as a help to the needy person, and as a strict justice to the enemies of the afflicted man.
put to shame . . .: this is a variation on 35:26.

Psalm 72 The Righteous King

This poem is usually described as a Royal Psalm (see Introduction, pp. 39f.), and it is more or less 'a matter of personal judgment whether it is to be called an intercession or a blessing wish' (Mowinckel, *PIW*, II, p. 51). The setting of the Psalm or its *Sitz im Leben* was, most likely, the enthronement of the King or the yearly celebration of his kingship which may have formed a part of the New Year Festival. It seems to have been composed for the use of successive Kings on the appropriate cultic event. The title of the Psalm ascribes it to Solomon, but it could hardly have been written by him, although T expands the title in saying 'By Solomon, spoken in prophecy'. LXX, followed by *AV*, thought of Solomon as the subject of this Psalm, but the only support for this interpretation is the possible allusion to his reign in verse 10. Equally unlikely is the view that the poem is a prayer of David (see verse 20) on behalf of Solomon (so Calvin).

From the Psalm itself we can deduce that it must be pre-Exilic in its origin, and that it is concerned with the Davidic kings (cf. 2 Sam. 7). The early Jewish exegetes, as well as the early Church, understood the Psalm messianically. The language of the Psalm and the actual reigns of the successive Davidic kings, are such as to suggest that the Psalm must have looked not only to the present but also to the future (cf. Rowley, *WAI*, p. 200), when the ideals and hopes expressed by this poem would be realized. Therefore it is understandable why this and similar Psalms were eventually taken in a messianic sense.

The metre of the Psalm is irregular.

A Psalm of Solomon: see Introduction, pp. 43 and 46.

THE PRAYER FOR THE JUST KING **1–7**

1. Give the king thy justice: so *RSV* following the ancient versions, while M.T. has the plural *mišpāṭeḵā* which could be rendered 'judgments, statutes, divine ordinances' (see on 36:6, 119:7). If the Psalm is part of the enthronement liturgy, the allusion may be to the handing over of the written law to the King (cf. Dt. 17:18ff.; 1 Sam. 10:25). For a parallel, see the picture of Hammurabi receiving his laws from the Babylonian sun-god, Shamash, the deity concerned with justice (*DOTT*, p. 28, pl. 2); for references to other Near Eastern parallels, see Kraus, *PBK*, p. 497. If we accept the *RSV* rendering then it is possible to interpret 'justice' (*mišpāṭ*) as a spirit of justice (cf. Isa. 28:6) which would characterize all the dealings of the King, and would by a synonym of 'righteousness', i.e. a scrupulous faithfulness to one's obligations as they are defined in each particular situation (see on 33:5). It is a gift of God to be able to judge rightly (1 Kg. 3:9,28) but it is by deliberate arrogance that men misuse justice.

the royal son is the same person as the King in verse 1*a*, being the parallel terms in the respective lines. The 'royal son' indicates that the King is no usurper but a legitimate successor of the previous King. If the Psalm was used at the accession of the King then the 'King's son' would be the crown-prince who was now enthroned.

2. May he judge: the Hebrew *dîn* is a synonym of the more frequent verb *šāp̄aṭ* which occurs some 185 times as against some 25 times of the verb *dîn*. Although both verbs can be found in parallel passages, e.g. in 7:8 (M.T. 9), 9:8 (M.T. 9), they are by no means identical. Roughly speaking *dîn* means 'to judge', while *šāp̄aṭ* can signify 'to judge' as well as 'to rule', and the same observation is, more or less, true of the Ugaritic counterparts *dyn* and *ṯpṭ*. When these two verbs refer to the functions of the judge, they can suggest either 'to defend, deliver', or 'to avenge, punish', and they are concerned with the restoration of the right legal relationship. In our verse 'to judge' means to see that justice is done whenever the need arises (see verse 2*b*), rather than 'to rule' (so Briggs), although in the case of the King 'to rule' is inclusive of 'to judge rightly'.

thy people: the King is God's viceroy, and the subjects of the King are God's people. So the King is both dependent upon God and resposible to him for the use of his royal power.

thy poor: see on 34:3. The parallelism does not suggest that *all* the people were afflicted but rather that the poor were that part of the nation which required a special protection.

with justice: this is the same word as in verse 1*a* (see on 119:7) but singular in form.

3. prosperity: (*šālôm*, see on 119:165) the allusion is rather to the harmonious relationship between the nation and nature, the result of which is prosperity. The mountains and the hills are the characteristic features of Canaan, and they represent the whole land which brings forth plenty because the nation and its leaders practise righteousness. In other words, the counterpart of moral stability of the nation is stability in the realm of nature (cf. Johnson, *SKAI*, p. 7).

in righteousness: some scholars (e.g. Gunkel, Kraus) delete the preposition *b*ᵉ ('in'), taking 'righteousness' as the second object of the verb 'bear' (so also some Greek MSS.). The other alternative is to retain M.T. and to regard 'in righteousness' as the means (i.e. 'through . . .'), or the preposition may be an emphatic particle (cf. Dahood, *PAB*, I, p. 74), in which case the second line could be translated '(and may) the hills (bring) true righteousness (to your people)'.

4. May he defend: or '. . . . grant justice' (so Johnson); the verb used is *š-p-ṭ* ('to judge'), see verse 2.

give deliverance: or 'help'. For the verb *y-š-*ᶜ, see on 54:1.

to the needy: the preposition *l*ᵉ (*RSV* 'to') may be an emphatic *lāmeḏ* (see Dahood, *PNWSP*, p. 8). Perhaps we should read 'may he help (above all) the needy'. *B*ᵉ*nê* ᵓ*eḇyôn* is a *hapax legomenon* in the *OT*, and it may denote either those who belong to the class of the poor, or those who are literally the children of the poor, which might include orphans who are often mentioned as exposed to oppression (cf. 94:6; Isa. 1:23, 10:2; Jer. 22:3; Mic. 2:9; Zech. 7:10). Sir. 4:10 exhorts: 'Be like a father to orphans . . . you will then be like a son of the Most High'.

and crush the oppressor: either this is a later addition providing a contrast, or the parallel to this line is missing. A similar thought is found in Prov. 22:23: 'for the LORD will plead their cause and despoil those who will despoil them (i.e. the poor)'.

5. May he live: *RSV* follows LXX and V, reading *w^{e}yaʾ^{a}rîḵ* or *w^{e}yaʾ^{a}rēḵ* ('and he shall prolong (his days)'; cf. Dt. 17:20; Isa. 53:10) for M.T. *yîrāʾûḵā* ('may they fear you'). The *RSV* rendering may be interpreted as a poetical variation of the royal acclamation formula 'Long live the king' (cf. 1 Sam. 10:24; 2 Sam. 16:16; 2 Kg. 11:12). M.T., if correct, would suggest that a righteous rule inspires the worship of God.

while the sun endures: lit. 'with the sun' (so only here in *OT*). The poet ascribes 'eternal' reign to the King, which follows the language of the oriental court style. On the other hand, the perpetuity really concerns the dynasty rather than the individual King, except in as far as he lives on in his descendants. Similarly Yahweh is made to say concerning David: 'His line shall endure for ever, his throne as long as the sun before me' (89:36 (M.T. 37)); see on 21:4.

as long as the moon: lit. 'in the presence of the moon' (cf. 89:37 (M.T. 38)), i.e. 'for ever' (not in an absolute sense).

throughout all generations: this and similar expressions are frequent in *OT* to describe a long duration in the past (Isa. 51:9), or in the future, usually the latter. It is less likely that they ever denoted 'eternity' in our sense of the word (cf. Dahood, *PAB*, 1, p. 144).

6. May he be like rain that falls . . .: lit. 'He shall come down like rain . . .' of which the *RSV* rendering is a correct interpretation. It is very unlikely that in this verse there is a suggestion of the King's heavenly origin or pre-existence (for references see R. E. Murphy, *A Study of Psalm 72 (71)* (1948), p. 25). The verse is intended to describe the beneficent reign of the King, which is likened to the 'life-giving' rain.

on the mown grass: this can hardly be right, for the effect of the rain upon cut grass would be anything but beneficial. The Hebrew *gēz* ('shearing, mowing') seems to indicate also what is ready for mowing (or cutting), or what is intended for that purpose. Johnson (*SKAI*, p. 8, n.2) draws attention to the English words 'fleece' and 'crop' which may denote 'growth either before or after being cut'. *NEB* has 'on early crops'. For a parallel, see 2 Sam. 23:4 where the just reign of the King is likened to 'rain that makes grass to sprout from the earth' (cf. Isa. 32:2; Hos. 6:3).

showers: the Hebrew *r^e^b̲îb̲îm* may be the spring showers (see on 65:10; cf. Jer. 3:3), but at other times it may be used in a less specific sense (Jer. 14:22). The usual word for 'rain' is *māṭār* (verse 6); see on 65:10; cf. 1QM xii:9.

. . . that water: reading *yazrîp̲û* for M.T. *zarzîp̲* ('irrigation'?); cf. *HAL*, pp. 269, 272.

7. may righteousness flourish: so some Hebrew MSS., LXX, S, and V, while M.T. has 'may the righteous man . . .' (cf. 92:12 (M.T. 13)). The parallel term 'peace' supports the former variant.

and peace abound: lit. 'and abundance of peace'; it is possible to assume that the force of 'flourish' (verse 7*a*) extends also to the second line. *RSV* reads *w^e^rab̲* (or *yireb̲*) for M.T. *w^e^rōb̲* ('and abundance of . . .').

till the moon be no more: this phrase is found only here in *OT*, and there is no corresponding term in the parallel line. This may not, however, provide sufficient justification for an emendation because similar idioms occur more than once; cf. Job 14:12; Isa. 5:14; Mal. 3:10.

THE PRAYER FOR WORLD DOMINATION 8–11

8. The Psalmist asks from God a world-wide kingdom for the Davidic king. If this request were thought of merely in political terms, the wish might be absurd, yet the writer links the rule of the earthly King with the universal rule of God. It is only as Yahweh's representative that the King has a claim to dominion over the world; in a way the King sits upon *Yahweh's* throne (1 Chr. 28:5, 29:23; 2 Chr. 9:8). At the same time it is possible that the language of the Psalm has been influenced by the court style of the ancient Near East (cf. v. Rad, *OTT*, I, p. 321).

from sea to sea: this is sometimes interpreted in the light of Exod. 23:31: 'from the Red Sea to the Sea of the Philistines', or as extending from the Mediterranean Sea to the Red Sea or to the Persian Gulf. More likely is the view that sees here an allusion to the cosmic sea (cf. Johnson, *SKAI*, p. 9). According to Hebrew cosmology (or what was one of the Israelite views on this subject) the earth was suspended above the cosmic waters and surrounded by them (24:2, 88:6 (M.T. 7), 136:6; cf. also Job 26:10; Prov.

8:27), and so 'from sea to sea' may mean 'the whole earth' (cf. Mic. 7:12; Zech. 9:10; Sir. 44:21).

from the River: *nāhār* can denote the Euphrates (Gen. 15:18, 31:21; Num. 22:5; 2 Sam. 10:16, etc.) but it can also suggest any river (see Job 14:11, 40:23; Ps. 105:41). It is very likely that some *OT* passages assign to it a mythological and cosmological significance; it may be linked with the current or currents of the cosmic ocean (see on 46:4; cf. 66:6).

ends of the earth: see on 59:13. Mowinckel (*He That Cometh* (1956), p. 178) thinks that the phraseology is derived from Babylonian sources, and that the River (i.e. Euphrates) denotes the centre of the earth (i.e. from the Babylonian point of view), while the ends of the earth suggest its farthest borders. Therefore both phrases verse 8*a* and *b*) are synonymous expressions.

9. his foes: reading *ṣārāyw* for M.T. *ṣiyyîm* which has been variously translated as 'They that dwell in the wilderness' (*AV, RV*), 'Ethiopians' (so LXX, V, *NEB*, *et al.*), etc. The emendation is supported by the parallel term 'his enemies' in verse 9*b*.

lick the dust: this is a hyperbole of self-humiliation, and it is found several times in *OT* (cf. Isa. 49:23; Mic. 7:17).

10. Verses 10f. speak of the universal homage which will be rendered to the viceroy of Yahweh. The various geographical locations mentioned are representative of all the world, near and far. This may be a deliberate allusion to Solomon's glory (cf. Murphy, op. cit., p. 31). Tarshish (see on 48:7) and the isles (of the Mediterranean) represent the furthest west. The word *ʾiyyîm* ('isles') may denote also the coastlands (of the western sea).

Sheba is often identified with Arabia Felix, i.e. the present Yemen. The reference is, apparently, to the Sabaean kingdom which flourished in Arabia at that time.

Seba is not identified, but it has been suggested that it might have been a Sabaean colony in Africa. Josephus placed it in Ethiopia (cf. Murphy, op. cit., p. 31), but Dahood in S. Arabia.

11. This is a more general expression of the thought of verse 10, and it re-emphasizes the world-rule of the Davidic king.

fall down before him: see on 29:2; cf. *ANEP*, pl. 355.

THE KING AS THE DELIVERER OF THE NEEDY **12–14**

12. For he delivers the needy: the Hebrew *kî* ('for') may imply that the King's universal rule is based upon his just government (so Kirkpatrick). It is possible, however, that *kî* in this verse serves as an emphatic particle (cf. Dahood, *UHP*, p. 22), hence 'He will certainly deliver . . .'. For the 'needy' (*ʾeḇyôn*), see on 35:10.

when he calls for help. LXX (similarly also S) reads *ek dunastou* ('from the (harsh) master'). Yet there is no real need to alter M.T.; but cf. *NEB*.

the poor: this is simply a synonym of 'the needy', see on 34:2.

and him who has no helper: this may be a relative clause defining 'the poor' as persons who are helpless. Johnson (*SKAI*, p. 10) takes it as a temporal clause 'when he hath no helper' (cf. 107:12; 1QM i:6).

13. He has pity on the weak: this may suggest a contrast with those kings who had little sympathy with the needy ones of their communities. Because of this characteristic of Yahweh's viceroy, his throne will stand for ever (cf. Prov. 29:14).

the needy: *ʾeḇyôn* was also used in the preceding verse, and the plural form occurs in verse 13*b*. This may not be a good style but it does not follow that verse 13 must be a later addition (so Gunkel).

saves the lives of . . .: lit. '. . . the souls of . . .' (see on 33:19). For *y-š-ʿ* ('to save'), see on 54:1.

14. From oppression and violence: some scholars (e.g. Gunkel, Briggs) suggest that 'violence' is a gloss on 'oppression', and this may be implied by the metre, although metrical irregularities are not infrequent in the Psalter.

he redeems their life: for the verb *g-ʾ-l*, see on 119:154. The verb may imply that the King has a *responsibility* towards the needy; indeed, it is his sacred privilege to restore the oppressed to a life of freedom (cf. Barth, *ETKD*, pp. 133ff.).

precious is their blood: i.e. the King will preserve them and look after their true welfare (cf. 1 Sam. 26:21; 2 Kg. 1:13,14; Ps. 116:15).

LONG LIVE THE KING 15–17

15. Long may he live: *RV et al.* add this phrase to verse 14, reading 'And they shall live'. It is, however, far more natural to see here a reference to the King, which takes up the thought already expressed in verse 5. The *RSV* rendering is reminiscent of the acclamation formula or the salutation 'Long live the king'. (1 Sam. 10:24; 2 Sam. 16:16, etc.).

gold of Sheba: this resumes verse 10, and it represents *all* the various kinds of tribute brought to the King from all over the world.

be given to him: i.e. to the King. It is less likely that the gold will be given by the King to the poor (cf. Murphy, op. cit., pp. 36f.).

May prayer be made . . .: i.e. by the people on behalf of the King. LXX has 'and (men) shall pray for him . . .'.

blessings may refer to God's blessings which are implored for the King, or, more likely, they denote the grateful people's response to the King's righteousness (cf. 16:7). Blessing, like curse, was thought to have at least some inherent power, so that its utterance could either increase or lessen the vitality of the person blessed or cursed (cf. Eichrodt, *TOT*, I, pp. 173f.). Their influence, either for better or for worse, was, however, dependent upon many factors but on the whole blessings and curses would be regarded as *potentially* effective.

16. This verse, and the Psalm as a whole, shows that what we call the 'moral realm' and the 'realm of nature' form one indivisible whole for the Israelites. A community which lives according to righteousness, enjoys not only internal harmony, but also prosperity in field and flock (so it was believed). This resumes verses 3 and 7.

abundance of grain: the Hebrew *pissāh*, a *hapax legomenon* in the *OT* is probably an Aramaism, meaning 'lot, plenty' (cf. G. R. Driver, *HTR*, XXIX (1936), p. 185; *VT*, I (1951), p. 249).

on the tops of the mountains: Johnson 'to the top . . .' (*SKAI*, p. 11), or perhaps '(even) on the mountain tops'. Corn would normally grow in the valleys but sometimes also the hill-side would bear a small plot of corn. The above expression is parallel to 'in the land' and both are meant to depict the extraordinary fertility of the land.

may it wave: *RP* 'growing thick', associating the Hebrew *r-ᶜ-š*, not with the usual verb ('to quake, shake'), but with the Arabic *raǵasa* ('to give abundantly'; cf. G. R. Driver, *JTS*, XXXIII (1932), p. 43), hence: 'May it grow thick (even) on the tops of the mountains' where the soil is usually very thin.

its fruit probably refers to the crops of the fields, which are likened to Lebanon (see on 29:5), or to its magnificent cedars. The word-picture is intended to describe the excellent crops in Yahweh's land.

may men blossom forth . . .: this may be textually corrupt.

The word 'men' is not in M.T. which could be rendered 'may they blossom forth from the city . . .' but this gives little sense. Some exegetes emend the M.T. *mēʿîr* ('from the city') to *waʿamîrô* ('and its grain (or 'sheaves')'; cf. Winton Thomas, *TRP*, p. 29).

like the grass is a simile of abundance. Cf. Job 5:25: '. . . your descendants shall be many, and your offspring as the grass of the earth'.

17. his name: see on 20:1. This term is also used in the following line, with a slightly different connotation. Some scholars omit the second *šᵉmô* ('his name') or replace it with *zarʿô* ('his seed, descendants'); so Gunkel, Oesterley, *et al.* LXX reads: 'May his name be blessed for ever, may his name endure . . .'.

continue: Johnson (*SKAI*, p. 11) has suggested that the underlying idea of the verb *n-w-n* (or *n-y-n*) is 'the continuation of the male line'. The noun *nîn* means 'offspring' (see Gen. 21:23; Job 18:19; Isa. 14:22).

May men bless themselves . . .: LXX and V suggest 'and all the tribes of the earth shall be blessed in him'; this rendering is followed, more or less, by Kissane, Johnson, *RP*, *et al.* This verse seems to be an allusion to Yahweh's promise to Abraham (Gen. 12:2f., 22:18), and the intention may have been to stress the fact that the divine promise to the patriarch has been fulfilled in the house of David (cf. R. E. Clements, *Abraham and David SBT*, (2nd ser., 5, 1967), p. 59).

call him blessed: or 'call him happy' (see on 1:1).

THE CLOSING DOXOLOGY **18–19**

These two verses are often considered as a later addition which marks the close of the Second Book of the Psalter. In view of verse 20, Weiser (*POTL*, p. 504) wonders whether verses 18–19 are not an integral part of the original Psalm.

18. Blessed be the LORD: see on 28:6.

wondrous things are the special works of God in nature and in history. See on 9:1, 40:5; cf. 77:14 (M.T. 15).

19. his glorious name: lit. 'the name of his glory' (Neh. 9:5; Isa. 63:14); see on 20:1. Kirkpatrick (*BPCB*, p. 424) defines it as 'the Majesty of His Being, as it is revealed to men'.

Amen and Amen: this double 'Amen' seems to be used for the sake of emphasis (see on 41:13).

20. The prayers of David . . .: this is the note of the compiler, reminiscent of a similar note in Job 31:40. The annotation (lacking in some Hebrew MSS.) probably dates from a time when *this* collection of Davidic Psalms was not followed by other Psalms of David, probably when it existed as the Elohistic psalter. Then it would separate the prayer of David from the Asaphite psalms. The Hebrew *t^epillôṯ* ('prayers') is rendered by LXX as *hymnoi* which points to the Hebrew *t^ehillôṯ* ('praises'), see on 119:171.